THE AGE OF

TO THE AMERICAN CENTURY

ENCOUNTERS

A WORLD HISTORY READER

DIANE O'BRIEN

THOMAS O'BRIEN

Pearson
Custom
Publishing

Copyright Acknowledgments

Contents

Introduction

This world history reader is designed to meet the needs of students in three different courses, World History, World Revolutions and the CIA in the Third World. As distinct as the three courses may appear at first glance, they in fact deal with many closely related themes. The World History course which focuses on the past five centuries of global events places particular emphasis on the encounters between Western and non-Western cultures. More specifically it examines the phenomena of Westernization or Modernization as it emerged in the West and the effects of that phenomenon both in Western and non-Western societies.

The largely interchangeable terms Westernization and Modernization refer to a series of interrelated cultural, social and economic developments. Those developments include the scientific and industrial revolutions stressing rational thought and capitalist development, liberal political and social philosophies focusing on representative government and individualism, and the emergence of a culture that emphasized secular and materialistic interpretations of the world as well as a firm belief in the idea of progress. These values, ideas and social relations had profound, even revolutionary, effects upon both the Western nations where they emerged, and on societies throughout the world which Westerners have tried to reshape in their own image. It is the revolutionary responses to the sweeping changes of Modernization that provide the focal point of the course on World Revolutions.

In the process of modernization and revolutionary responses, the United States has played a pivotal role, especially during the twentieth, or what is often termed the American century. The United States, the first society to emerge as a fully modern capitalist society, has been the principal global engine of modernization during the past century. And as the dominant world power in the second half of the twentieth century it has devoted vast resources to promoting Westernization and confronting the often-revolutionary consequences of that process around the world. The interactions between the United States and societies around the world provide the central theme for the course on the CIA in the Third World.

The seven parts of this reader explore the interrelated themes of the three courses through a series of primary documents and secondary sources. The primary materials, most of them generated by actual participants in the historical dramas of the past five centuries, allow students to experience first hand many of the events that have forever changed the course of human history. At the same time a select number of secondary works by humanists and social scientists offer the reader some thoughtful perspectives on the significance of many of these same events. Part I offers students a few highly selective glimpses at world cultures about 1500 C.E. (Christian Era), on the eve of intensifying encounters and interactions between these distinct human communities. The documents in this section give examples of the very different values and world views of people in Asia, Europe, Africa, the Middle East and the Western Hemisphere on the eve of the Age of Encounters. Part II consists primarily of documents from the Age of Encounters. These materials present both Western and non-Western perspectives on the encounters and also explore some of the types of interactions, which range from visits of solitary travelers and organized commercial interchanges to conquest and enslavement. The third segment of the reader examines the process of Modernization as it emerged in the West with the development of rationalism, secularism, capitalism, as well as political and social liberalism. This section also offers some examples of criticisms of Westernization in the work of Karl Marx and an attempt to adopt aspects of Modernization outside of Western Europe in Czarist Russia. Part IV explores the process of colonialism in which European nations attempted to impose their political and economic control upon much of the world as well as attempts to resist that process. In part V the selections illustrate some of the doubts which arose even in the West in regard to the process of Modernization. From the horrors of the First World War and the Holocaust to the troubling implications of Freudian analysis and the theory of relativity, these documents reveal some of the serious concerns which have arisen concerning the process of Modernization. The sixth section offers readers insight into modern radical responses to Westernization from the Mexican and Russian Revolutions to the rise of Iran's Islamic Republic. The seventh and final collection of readings explores the role of the United States as the foremost promoter of Modernization, its attempts to curtail radical reactions to that process and some of the consequences of Westernization or Globalization as the world enters the twenty-first century.

PART I
THE WORLD IN 1500

The documents in this segment offer examples of the varied cultures of the world about 1500 C.E. Most of the perspectives and views presented here had evolved a thousand years or more before the beginning of the early modern era, but they continued to resonate with great power through human societies. You will note that the overwhelming majority of these documents deal with religious themes. How important and how predominant were religious values in human societies at this time? Did people of this period view the physical world around them in different ways than we do today?

While religious ideas offer a common theme for most of these documents, there are also substantial differences in the way humans viewed their societies and the values which they held most dear. In reading the work of Confucius what can you say about the importance of social hierarchy in Chinese culture? Reading the selections from the Koran, what can you conclude about the appeal that the precepts and rules of Islam would have for people in a world marked by uncertainty about morals and ethics? What role did nature play in religions such as those practiced by the Incas? How would you compare these perspectives on society and the material world with those offered by Machiavelli and Copernicus?

THE ANALECTS, BOOK ONE, NUMBERS 1–16

Confucius

BOOK I

1. The Master said, To learn and at due times to repeat what one has learnt, is that not after all[1] a pleasure? That friends should come to one from afar,[2] is this not after all delightful? To remain unsoured even though one's merits are unrecognized by others, is that not after all what is expected of a gentleman?

2. Master Yu[3] said, Those who in private life behave well towards their parents and elder brothers, in public life seldom show a disposition to resist the authority of their superiors. And as for such men starting a revolution, no instance of it has ever occurred. It is upon the trunk[4] that a gentleman works. When that is firmly set up, the Way grows. And surely proper behaviour towards parents and elder brothers is the trunk of Goodness?

3. The Master said, 'Clever talk and a pretentious manner'[5] are seldom found in the Good.

---

[1] The 'after all' implies 'even though one does not hold office.'

[2] Several of the disciples belonged to other States (e.g. Wei and Ch'i); but there is no evidence that they came to Lu on account of Confucius. Unless, however, there is here some allusion that escapes us, the phrase must refer to the visits of admirers from abroad, perhaps friends made during the Master's journeys in Honan.

[3] See p. 20.

[4] i.e. upon what is fundamental, as opposed to 'the twigs,' i.e. small arts and accomplishments, which the gentleman leaves to his inferiors.

[5] Traditional phrase. Cf. *Shu Ching,* Kao Yao Mo.

4. Master Tsêng said, Every day I examine myself on these three points: in acting on behalf of others, have I always been loyal to their interests? In intercourse with my friends, have I always been true to my word? Have I failed to repeat[6] the precepts that have been handed down to me?

5. The Master said, A country of a thousand war-chariots cannot be administered unless the ruler attends strictly to business, punctually observes his promises, is economical in expenditure, shows affection towards his subjects in general, and uses the labour of the peasantry only at the proper times of year.[7]

6. The Master said, A young man's duty is to behave well to his parents at home and to his elders abroad, to be cautious in giving promises and punctual in keeping them, to have kindly feelings towards everyone, but seek the intimacy of the Good. If, when all that is done, he has any energy to spare, then let him study the polite arts.[8]

7. Tzu-hsia said, A man who

> Treats his betters as betters,
> Wears an air of respect,
> Who into serving father and mother
> Knows how to put his whole strength,
> Who in the service of his prince will lay down his life,
> Who in intercourse with friends is true to his word—

others may say of him that he still lacks education, but I for my part should certainly call him an educated man.

8. The Master said, If a gentleman is frivolous,[9] he will lose the respect of his inferiors and lack firm ground[10] upon which to build up his education. First and foremost he must learn to be faithful to his superiors, to keep promises, to refuse the friendship of all who are not like him.[11] And if he finds he has made a mistake, then he must not be afraid of admitting the fact and amending his ways.

---

[6] And so keep in memory.

[7] i.e. not when they ought to be working in the fields. Bad rulers, on the contrary, listen to music or go hunting when they ought to be attending to business, continually employ labour on ostentatious building-schemes, etc.

[8] i.e. learn to recite the *Songs,* practise archery, deportment, and the like.

[9] i.e. irresponsible and unreliable in his dealings with others.

[10] The sentence runs awkwardly and is probably corrupt.

[11] i.e. of those who still reckon in terms of 'profit and loss,' and have not taken *jên* (Goodness) as their standard.

9. Master Tsêng said, When proper respect towards the dead is shown at the End and continued after they are far away the moral force (*tê*) of a people has reached its highest point.

10. Tzu-Ch'in[12] said to Tzu-kung, When our Master arrives in a fresh country he always manages to find out about its policy.[13] Does he do this by asking questions or do people tell him of their own accord? Tzu-kung said, Our Master gets things by being cordial, frank, courteous, temperate, deferential. That is our Master's way of enquiring—a very different matter[14] certainly, from the way in which enquiries are generally made.

11. The Master said, While a man's father is alive, you can only see his intentions; it is when his father dies that you discover whether or not he is capable of carrying them out. If for the whole three years of mourning he manages to carry on the household exactly as in his father's day, then he is a good son indeed.

12. Master Yu said, In the usages of ritual it is harmony[15] that is prized; the Way of the Former Kings from this[16] got its beauty. Both small matters and great depend upon it. If things go amiss, he who knows the harmony[17] will be able to attune them. But if harmony itself is not modulated by ritual, things will still go amiss.

13. Master Yu said,

In your promises cleave to what is right,
And you will be able to fulfil your word.
In your obeisances cleave to ritual,
And you will keep dishonour at bay.

---

[12] Disciple of Confucius. See XVI, 13 and XIX, 25.

[13] Not, of course, about the details of administration, but about the secret, general maxims which inspire the ruler.

[14] The double particle *ch'i-chu,* peculiar to the *Analects* and *Kungyang Chuan,* does not seem to differ in meaning from the ordinary modal *ch'i.*

[15] Harmony between man and nature; playing the musical mode that harmonizes with the season, wearing seasonable clothes, eating seasonable food, and the like.

[16] i.e. from harmony.

[17] i.e. the act that harmonizes with the moment.

> Marry one who has not betrayed her own kin,
> And you may safely present her to your Ancestors.[18]

14. The Master said, A gentleman who never goes on eating till he is sated, who does not demand comfort in his home, who is diligent in business and cautious in speech, who associates with those that possess the Way and thereby corrects his own faults—such a one may indeed be said to have a taste for learning.

15. Tzu-kung said, 'Poor without cadging, rich without swagger.' What of that?[19] The Master said, Not bad. But better still, 'Poor, yet delighting in the Way; rich, yet a student of ritual.' Tzu-kung said, The saying of the *Songs*,[20]

> As thing cut, as thing filed,
> As thing chiselled, as thing polished

refers, I suppose, to what you have just said? The Master said, Ssu, now I can really begin to talk to you about the *Songs*, for when I allude to sayings of the past, you see what bearing they have on what was to come after.

16. The Master said, (the good man) does not grieve that other people do not recognize his merits. His only anxiety is lest he should fail to recognize theirs.

---

[18] Lines 2, 4, and 6 rhyme. For the last rhyme, which belongs to a well-established type, see Karlgren, *The Rimes in the Sung section of the Shi King*. For the presentation of the bride to the husband's ancestors, see *The Book of Songs*, p. 90.

[19] i.e. what of it as a motto?

[20] *The Book of Songs* p. 46, which describes the elegance of a lover. Tzu-kung interprets it as describing the pains the gentleman has taken to improve his character, and suggests that Confucius prefers the second maxim ('Poor, yet delighting . . . ') because it implies a greater effort of self-improvement.

AN INTRODUCTION TO HINDUISM

Prakash Arumugam

It has been pointed out by Dr. Arnold J. Toynbee, in *A Study of History*, that the principal civilisations of the world lay different degrees of emphasis on specific lines of activity. Hellenic civilisation, for instance, displays a manifest tendency towards a prominently aesthetic outlook on life as a whole. Indian civilisation, on the other hand, shows an equally manifest tendency towards a predominantly religious outlook. Dr. Toynbee's remark sums up what has been observed by many other scholars. Indeed, the study of Hinduism has to be, in a large measure, a study of the general Hindu outlook on life.

Receptivity and all-comprehensiveness, it has been aptly stated, are the main characteristics of Hinduism. Since it has had no difficulty in bringing diverse faiths within its ever-widening fold, it has something to offer to almost all minds. Monier-Williams in his notable work *Brahmanism and Hinduism* dwelt on this aspect about a hundred years ago. The strength of Hinduism, he emphasized, lies in its infinite adaptability to the infinite diversity of human character and human tendencies. It has its highly spiritual and abstract side suited to the philosopher; its practical and concrete side congenial to the man of the world; its aesthetic and ceremonial side attuned to the man of the poetic feeling and imagination; and its quiescent contemplative aspect that has its appeal for the man of peace and the lover of seclusion. The Hindus, according to him, were Spinozists more than 2,000 years before the advent of Spinoza, Darwinians many centuries before Darwin, and Evolutionists many centuries before the doctrine of Evolution was accepted by scientists of the present age.

No civilisation anywhere in the world, with the probable exception of China, has been as continuous as that of India. While the civilisations of Egypt, Babylon and Assyria have disappeared, in India the ideas emanating from the Vedic times continue to be a living force.

European scholars of Sanskrit like Sir William Jones noted similarities in the languages, terminology and substances of Indian scriptures with those of Greece and Rome. Even a superficial study convinced them that, while the language of the Vedas is a great critical instrument in the construction of the science of philology, the Vedic hymns constitute a compilation of most Indo-European myths in their primitive form. Max Muller went so far as to say that the Vedas are the real theogony of the Aryan races, Homer and Hesiod having given a distorted picture of the original image.

The excavations at Harappa and Mohenjo-daro and those in Saurashtra have disclosed the existence of a highly evolved culture long before the Aryan immigration, perhaps dating back to 3000 B.C. or later. Among the remains discovered are a three-faced prototype of Siva seated in a yogic posture, representations of the Linga, and a horned goddess associated with the pipal tree. These symbols, evolved by a very ancient civilisation, were assimilated by the Aryan immigrants in slow stages—their earliest literary work, the Rg-Veda, almost overlooks these aspects. The Vedic Aryans, it has been suggested, partly assimilated and partly destroyed the earlier culture.

VEDIC ARYANS AND ZOROASTRIANISM

It seems clear from the hymns of the Rg-Veda and the Persian Gathas and Avesta that the Vedic Aryans and the Zoroastrians had a common origin. The languages in which Zoroaster preached and the Rsis sang their hymns are almost identical, and Vedic meters are re-produced in the Avesta. Evidently, the two groups of Aryans separated after a violent quarrel, so that several deities of one group—Indra or Jindra, Sarva and Nasatya—were transformed in the other into evil spirits. It is, however, to be noticed that Mitra, Aryama, Vayu and Vrtraghna are divine in both the systems. A period of unity was probably followed by civil war, as envisaged in the fight between Asuras and Devas.

The Vedic Aryans were warlike, while the Avesta reflects an abhorrence of war. In the period when the ancestors of the Iranians and the Hindus had lived together, Asura had been a term of honour; and the Zoroastrian Ahura Mazda was Asura Mahat, the great Asura. The Rg-Veda (III-55-11 & 15) cites several Asura qualities of the Divinities. Varuna, Mitra and several other gods were called Asuras. Later, when differences were accentuated between the two communities, Asura became equivalent to a spirit of evil and Sura came to signify a good spirit.

The undivided Indo-Iranians must have passed a long time in their Central Asian home. The Indo-Iranian culture and religion have been reconstructed, at least in part, by comparing the Vedas with the Avesta. Before the occupation of Iranian high lands by tribes from the Indo-Iranian original home, the plateau was the seat of a culture that was probably matriarchal, and the people worshipped snake-gods in the manner of India's primitive non-Aryans. It is likely that the pre-Aryan cultures of Northwestern India and Iran were alike in origin and spirit.

This ancient cultural link between pre-Aryan Iran and pre-Aryan India, instead of getting strengthened by Aryan migration into the two countries, as could be normally expected, was to all appearances completely severed. Also, there is nothing to show that the Vedic Aryans of India maintained an active cultural relation with their brethren in Iran.

In the earliest days, while the Aryans of India must have been connected with the Aryans of Iran as friends or as foes, actual historical contact cannot be asserted with any degree of probability. The two peoples turned their backs upon each other, as it were, and developed their distinctive civilisations apparently without the least mutual influence, although in language, culture and religion their similarity in the earliest period had been little short of identity. When, later in history, under the Achaemenids, Greeks, Bactrians and Sakas, the Iranians and the Indians were forced to meet as citizens of the same empire, they met as complete strangers, not as cousins or as scions from the same stock. The earliest literary productions of the Aryan settlers in India were the Rg-Veda, Sama Veda (consisting of chants), Yajur Veda and the Atharva Veda (a composite religious and magical compilation). The Vedas comprise Mantras (hymns), Brahmanas (ritual and ceremonies), Aranyakas (forest speculations) and the philosophical Upanisads. In the context of this commonly accepted interpretation of the Vedas, it may be recalled that European Orientalists have too often considered them mainly from the theological, anthropological and sociological points of view. A study of the material in its religious aspect is difficult, since even the great commentary of Sayana is in terms of the ideas of his own age. On the presumption that the Vedas originated in primitive times, the Rg-Veda hymns were regarded as the outpourings of a child-like nature worship. John Dowson in his Hindu Classical Dictionary observed: "The Aryan settlers were a pastoral and agricultural people, and they were keenly alive to those influences which affected their prosperity and comfort. They knew the effects of heat and cold, rain and drought, upon their crops and herds, and they marked the influence of warmth and cold, sunshine and rain, wind and storm, upon their own personal comfort. They invested these benign and evil influences with a personality; and behind the fire, the sun, the cloud, and the other powers of nature, they saw beings who directed them in their beneficent and evil operations. To these imaginary beings they addressed their praises, and to them they put up their prayers for temporal blessings. They observed also the movements of the sun and moon, the constant succession of day and night, the intervening periods of morn and eve, and to these also they gave personalities, which they invested with poetical clothing and attributes. Thus observant of nature in its various changes and operations, alive to its influences upon themselves, and perceptive of its beauties, they formed for themselves deities in whose glory and honour they exerted their poetic faculty." But on a careful analysis of the Vedas it would be apparent that the Vedic view is more subtle and deeper in concept. The One Being whom the sages call by many names (Ekam-sat) is referred to in the neuter gender, signifying divine existence and not a divine individual. The monotheistic God stands in relation to

9

man as a father and a patriarch, while in a Rg-Veda hymn to Agni he is called "my father, my kinsman, my brother and my friend." Monotheism, it has been aptly stated, "contemplates the Divine in heaven and polytheism contemplates the Divine in the universe. Polytheism believes in the assembly of gods, each possessing a character of his own. Max Muller coined the word henotheism for indicating the tendency of the Vedic seers to magnify the importance of the particular deity they are praising in a hymn at the expense of the other gods. This has been described as "opportunist monotheism." One deity is identified with another or different deities are identified with one divine entity, indifferently described as Ekam (one) and Tat Sat (the reality).

VEDIC CONCEPTS

Apart from these concepts, there are two basic ideas underlying the Vedas—Satya (truth) and Rta (eternal order); and every god or goddess exemplifies and represents these two ideas. As Abinash Chandra Bose says in his *Call of the Vedas,* Vedic theism is based on moral values which (also in the case of Buddhism) may be upheld in a non-theistic way. In India it is not the atheist who is denounced but the person who repudiates Dharma, moral law. The Rg-Veda (X-85-1) states that the earth is sustained not by the will of God but by truth, and of this truth God is the supreme exponent, revealing Himself through Rta or eternal order. Examining the Vedic hymns as a whole, one discovers a doctrine, not of oneness, but of one divine substance pervading all. It is stated that the One Being is contemplated by the sages in many forms: Ekam santam bahudha kalpayanti (Rg-Veda, X-114-5). It may also be observed that the Vedic ritual or Yajna is a uniform ceremonial; whatever deity is worshipped, the ritual is the same.

The universality of the Vedas is not often realised. The Rg Veda asserts that God is the God of Dasa as well as of Arya—"Lord God is he to whom both Arya and Dasa belong." (Rg-Veda, VIII-51-9). There is a special prayer for the forgiveness of sins against the foreigner (Rg-Veda, V-35-7). According to the Atharva Veda, God is of the foreigner (Videsya) no less than of our own land (Samdesya). There are mantras which extend this principle to all living beings (sarvani bhutani) (Yajur Veda, 36-18) so that we come to a grand conception of universal peace and serenity—the harmony with Nature (sarvam santhi) (Yajur Veda, 36-17).

MANY SCHOOLS OF THOUGHT

Panini is one of the world's earliest as well as the greatest of scientific grammarians. The consensus of opinion fixed his date not later than the 5th century B.C. At that period Yajna, or sacrifice, and the worship of various deities were current and popular, and theistic devotion to particular divinities, generally expressed by the term Bhakti, had become prevalent. Panini refers to Vasudev as the object of devotion, and Paramatma Devata Visesa, a form of the One Supreme Divinity. The doctrine which assumed great importance later—that custom has the force of law—is also exemplified by the twofold meaning, in Panini's *Astadhyayi*, attached to Dharma. Dharma is not only equivalent to Rta, primordial law, but also denotes custom (acara) as in the later Dharma Sutras.

Already in Panini's days different schools of thought had arisen, both theistic and non-theistic. A non-theistic doctrine, which is described in Buddhist philosophy as the doctrine of non-causation and also as the doctrine of Yadrccha—(fortuitous accident), was current in Panini's time. That all existence was the result of chance was the doctrine of the Ahetuvadins. The Svetasvatara Upanisad which advocates the doctrine of the supreme spirit refers to other varieties of thought like those of the advocates of Svabhava or materialistic philosophy. Orthodox thought was later developed in the Samkhya philosophy and attained its climax in the Vedanta Sutras. Panini refers to Parasara Sutra, one of the earliest of the Vedanta treatises, and also to the atheistic school, known later as the Lokayata. There is mention also of Nihsreyasa which, in the Upanisads, denoted supreme bliss as also of Nirvana, possibly associated with Buddhism. From all these examples it is clear that, in the times of the Buddha and Panini, practically all the varieties of speculation which have flourished in India had already evolved.

Philosophical discourses and pursuits were at first specially developed by the Ksatriyas, but they soon became the prerogatives of the Brahmins. The Chandogya and Kausitaki Upanisads illustrate these successive stages. A solution of the ultimate problems of life is outlined in the early Upanisads, and it takes the form of Monism, absolute (according to Sankaracarya) or modified (according to Ramanuja). Filled with zeal for this doctrine of the Unity or Interdependence of all life, a social order was founded. Dr. Ananda Coomaraswamy in his Dance of Siva says that the great Epics represented the desired social order as having actually existed in the golden past; they put into the mouths of their heroes not only the philosophy but the theory of its application in practice. This is evident, above all, in the long discourse of the dying Bhisma in the Santiparva of the Mahabharata. "The heroes themselves they made ideal types of character for the guidance of all subsequent generations; for the education of India has been accomplished deliberately through hero-worship. In the Dharmashastra of Manu and the Arthashastra of Chanakya—perhaps the most remarkable sociological documents the world possesses—they set forth the picture of the ideal society, defined from the stand point of law. By these and other means they accomplished what has not yet been effected in any other country, in making religious philosophy the essential and intelligible basis of popular culture and national polity."

What, then, is this view of life? The inseparable unity of the material and spiritual world is made the foundation of Indian culture and that determines the whole character of Indian social ideals. Later Hindu thought is founded on the rhythmic nature of the world process, including evolution and involution, birth, death and rebirth, srsti and samhara. Every individual life—mineral, vegetable, animal, human—has a beginning and an end; this creation and destruction, appearance and disappearance, are of the essence of the world process and equally originate in the past, present and future. According to this view, then, every individual ego (jivatman) or separate expression of the general will to life (icchatrsna), must be regarded as having reached a certain stage of its own cycle. This is also true of the collective life of a nation, a planet or a cosmic system. It is further considered that the turning-point of this curve is reached in man, and hence the immeasurable value which Hindus (and Buddhists) attach to birth in human form. Before the turning-point is reached—to use the language of Christian theology—the natural man prevails; after it, the regener man. To sum up, Indian philosophic thought developed in several stages. The Vedic period is generally placed between 2500 B.C. and 600 B.C. As already indicated, the four Vedas, the Bramanas, Aranyakas, and Upanisads are creations of the early sages.

BUDDHIST INFLUENCE

We now come to the greatest contribution made by the Buddha to Indian thought and world culture. Dr. Radhakrishnan, in his edition of "Dhammapada" (which embodies Buddhist teachings), has stated that, judged by intellectual integrity, moral earnestness and spiritual insight, the Buddha is undoubtedly one of the greatest figures in history. The same scholar pointed out that, although there were different streams of thought operating on men's minds in the 6th century B.C. philosophic thought was agreed at that time on certain fundamentals. Life does not begin at birth or end at death; it is a link in an infinite series of lives, each of which is conditioned and determined by acts done in previous existences. Relief from the round of births, resulting in life in eternity is the goal, indicated by such terms as Moksa (deliverance) and Nirvana (union with the Brahman). The means of attainment are prayer and worship; ritual and sacrifice; and Vidya (realization by knowledge).

Even though the Buddha accepted the doctrines of Karma and rebirth and the non-reality of the empirical universe, he declined to speculate on Moksa and on the doctrine of the Atman and Paramatman. He laid stress on the supremacy of the ethical aspect, and his outlook was definitely practical and empirical. In fact, the Buddha did not tolerate any doctrines which, he thought, diverted the mind from the central problem of suffering, the cause of suffering and its removal, and the urgency of the moral task.

He rejected the doctrine of the Vedanta that the ego is permanent and unchanging. At the same time, he did not countenance the view that, at death, it is destroyed. As Dr. Radhakrishnan says, the Buddha came to the conclusion that interest in the super-natural diverts attention and energy from the ethical values and the exploration of actual conditions: Karma builds the world and Dharma is an organic part of all existence.

THE BHAGAVAD-GITA

Every variety of Hindu philosophy has its source in the Upanisads, the Brahma Sutras of Badarayana of Vyasa and the Bhagavad-Gita which forms a part of the Mahabharata. It was as a reaction to the tendencies exhibited by Buddhism and Jainism that the orthodox schools of Indian philosophy had their origin and the Bhagavad-Gita is their epitome.

This work contains the essence of Indian teaching about the duties of life as well as spiritual obligations. Everyone has his allotted duties of various kinds. Sin arises not from the nature of the work itself but from the disposition with which the work is performed. When it is performed without attachment to the result, it cannot tarnish the soul and impede its quest. True Yoga consists in the acquisition of experience and the passage through life in harmony with the ultimate laws of equanimity, non-attachment to the fruits of action, and faith in the pervasiveness of the Supreme Spirit. Absorption in that Spirit can be attained along several paths; and no path is to be preferred exclusively and none to be disdained. These doctrines have been interpreted as marking a Protestant movement which lays stress on the personality of God and His accessibility to devotion. While following the Hindu ideal of the Asramas, the Gita emphasizes the importance of knowledge, charity, penance and worship, and does not decry life as evil:

"Nor indeed can embodied beings completely relinquish action; verily, he who relinquisheth the fruit of action, he is said to be a true relinquisher."

FUSION WITH NON-ARYANS

The Aryans marched en masse, guided by a leader who was often a poet, and came into contact with the Dasas and the Dasyus. The point to be noted is the speedy fusion of the Aryans with the non-Aryans. The process had three phases:
(1) The elevation of non-Aryans and aboriginals by intermarriages with Aryans.
(2) The incorporation of non-Aryans into Aryan society in various other ways.
(3) Social reactions by which forms of life and modes of thought of the two groups underwent a kind of osmosis, intensified by the Buddhist protestant reformation.

The Aitareya Brahmana gives an example of the manner in which progressive leaders of the Aryans facilitated the assimilation of other communities. A Rsi was performing a sacrifice on the banks of the Sarasvati; and to this sacrifice was admitted one Kesava Ailusa, a Sudra, whose learning is stated to have put all the Brahmins to shame. The Vajasaneyi Samhita condemned intercommunal marriage, but it is narrated in that work (ch. 23, 30 and 31) that a Sudra was the lover of an Arya woman. By the time of the Mahabharata such great personages as Vyas and Vidura were described as the offspring of the connection of the Aryans with other groups. The story of Santanu and Satyavati, the vow of Bhisma as well as the story of Ambika and Ambalika and the birth of Vidura, also illustrate the above process.

Again, in the Mahabharata, it is narrated that Bhima married Hidimbi, a non-Aryan woman, and Arjuna married a Naga girl, Ulupi. A new class of Aryans called Utkrsta came into existence, and was admitted to the privileges of sacrifice. By the time of the Satapathabrahmaa Sudras became incorporated in the polity—a notable instance being the Nisadas. It is a curious fact (Panini's Grammar, ch. VI, 62, 58) that there were non-Aryan Brahmins as well.

Parasara, one of the great sages of India, married Satyavati, a fisher girl, who became the mother of Vyasa, the compiler of the Mahabharata and the Puranas. Such intermarriages or unions were frequent all through Indian history. Emperor Candragupta Maurya, who belonged to a lower caste, married Kumara Devi of the Licchavi clan, who was either a Brahmin or a Ksatriya, and she was the grandmother of Asoka.

It should be remembered that the groups which crystallized later into the Indian castes were initially not based on any gradation of superiority, the difference being functional rather than racial or communal. These groups, moreover, had their analogues in the Avesta, and the Iranian names do not suggest the idea of colour or superiority. Co-operation of all the classes was needed for administration, and a passage in the Mahbharata indicates that the King's Council included representatives of all classes of the people.

The current rigidity of the rules relating to intermarriage as also interdining among the Indian castes is a comparatively recent innovation. These lines found in several Puranas are significant: "The great sage Vasistha was born of a divine courtesan, but by austerity and penance he made himself recognized as a Brahmin. The transforming process was attained by self-improvement." Another passage says, "Vyas was by birth a fisherman, Parasar was born in a dog-eating tribe. Many non-Dvijas have in the past attained Brahmanhood by their merit." The Bhagavad-Gita affirms: "Castes developed according to the differentiation of Guna and Karma", i.e., disposition or temperament and inherited instincts or aptitudes.

Both among the Old Iranians and the Aryans of India the original caste system of three classes based on the practical distribution of functions was in existence. The Iranians, however, did not develop another class as the Hindus did—the Sudra. Clearly, the three Hindu caste divisions were not unalterably rigid. The definition of the word Dvija, twice-born, makes the position clear. Dvija is a person who has certain basic qualities: "If a man's activities be derived from his jati or birth, from his occupation, from study and knowledge, and if all these are found combined, then he is to be called a Dvija, and not otherwise."

CULTURAL SYNTHESIS

In their great trek to India the colonizing groups of Aryans encountered races who professed a firm belief in the doctrine of transmigration. It has indeed been suggested that this doctrine of metempsychosis itself, the cult of serpent worship, the worship of Ganesa, of Uma or Durga, of Skanda or Subrahmanya (the hunter-god) were all adopted by the Aryans from earlier settlers in India. Even the incarnation of Krsna, it has been said, was an adaptation from an aboriginal deity; his life is an instance of the mingling of the Aryans and the Yadavas. In any case, it seems clear that there was a good measure of synthesis of the thoughts and beliefs of the Aryan and pre-Aryan races.

There are widespread traditions of the southern migration of the Vedic sage, Agastya, the reputed author of several hymns of the Rg-Veda. His asrama was located south of the Vindhyas; and he is said to have introduced the Vedic religion and literature in the South in his capacity as a unifying factor between the Sanskritic and Dravidian tongues and ideals. When the Aryan colonisers in the wake of Agastya penetrated to the South, they found an advanced civilisation. The Ramayana describes Madurai as adorned with golden jewels. The grammarian Katyayana mentions the Pandyas and the Colas. Asoka's Buddhist missions were sent to the Pandya and Cola countries as far as Tamrapani river in the Tirunelveli District. An extensive commercial and cultural intercourse grew up between the Aryans and the Dravidians, as also between the Dravidians and countries to the east and west of India.

The close contact between the Aryan and Dravidian elements continued all through history and manifested itself in every aspect of life. There is strong ground for the supposition that the importance of Siva, Sakti and Skanda was due largely to Dravidian influence, since the cult of An (Siva), Amma (Sakti) and Anil (Muruga or Skanda) was a cardinal belief from the beginning of Dravidian history.

These facts illustrate the composite character of Hindu civilisation. The Sama Veda spoke at length of the Vratyastoma (a particular sacrifice or ritual) by which non-Aryan Vratyas were admitted into Aryan society. The equalization of castes and communities was, of course, brought to a head by Gautama Buddha, though he was no opponent of the Brahminical civilisation. Both he and Mahavira, the expounder of Jainism, while admitting that the Brahmin ideal is the right one, led a crusade against certain aspects of Brahmin culture. Hindu civilisation itself adapted for its use many ideals and precepts of Buddhism and Jainism. For instance, among many communities, offerings of rice and ghee took the place of animal sacrifice—a compromise with the Vedic ritualism. The early Aryans had, of course, been meat-eaters, but probably under the influence of Buddhist and Jain ideas many groups of Brahmins as well as non-Brahmins became vegetarian.

THE ORIGINS OF BUDDHISM

Robert Allen Mitchell

THE FOUR SIGNS

Then eight brahmins (Rama, Dhadya, Laksana, Manti, Kaundinya, Bhodya, Svayama, and Sudatta) who were well versed in the art of prophesying fortunes from a consideration of bodily marks and characteristics stepped forward and examined the Bodhisattva [the prince] carefully. Seven of the eight each raised two fingers and gave a double interpretation, saying:

"If a man possessing such marvelous marks and characteristics continue in the household life, he becomes a universal monarch; but if he retire from the world, he becomes a Buddha, a Supremely Awakened One."

The youngest of the eight brahmins, a mere youth whose family name was Kaundinya, raised only one finger and gave but a single interpretation.

"I see nothing to make him stay in the household life," said Kaundinya. "He will undoubtedly become a Buddha and save the world from ignorance and pain."

"Now, King Suddhodana became increasingly disturbed by predictions of Buddhahood for his son. The Sakyas were a race of warriors; and Suddhodana, as their chieftain, was determined that Prince Siddhartha should one day become a ruler of men, even a king of all earth. The very thought that his own son might enter religious life, calling nothing his own and begging his daily bread, filled the proud sovereign with dismay.

"What makes you so sure that there is nothing here to detain my son from embarking upon the life of a religious mendicant?" demanded Suddhodana of the young brahmin.

"Several characteristics, O king; thirty-two in all, and four in particular," replied Kaundinya. "Do you see the tiny circlet of white hairs on his forehead between the eyebrows? And the protuberance of the top of his head? And his black body hairs curling to the right? And the fine golden color of his skin?

17

Without any doubt at all, the Four Signs will induce the prince to renounce the worldly life."

"The Four Signs?" asked the king with dread in his voice. "Pray, brahmin, name the four!"

"An old man, a sick man, a dead man, and a monk."

Suddhodana rose to his feet, eyes flashing anger.

"From this time forth," he commanded, "let no such persons approach the prince! It will never do for my son to become a Buddha! Prince Siddhartha is destined to exercise sovereign rule and authority over all great continents with their thousands of attendant isles!"

When the Bodhisattva was twenty-nine years old, [his wife] Princess Yasodhara was far gone with child. And on the morning of a beautiful day when winter had been vanquished by summer, Yasodhara addressed the prince, saying, "Go, beloved husband, to the park of the summer palace and enjoy the trees and flowering plants which are now coming into bloom. I shall remain here in Kapilavastu, for the time of my delivery draws near."

Prince Siddhartha accordingly summoned Chandaka, his charioteer, and proceeded to the park in an elegant chariot drawn by four white horses of royal breed.

As the Bodhisattva passed through a village of gardeners not far from Kapilavastu, a decrepit old man, bent of body, leaning on a staff, toothless and gray-haired, stumbled out into the road.

The horses neighed with fright as Chandaka tightened the reins to avoid running down the tottering old man.

"Chandaka!" cried the prince in astonishment. "What kind of man is that? Never before have I seen a man in such a deplorable condition!"

"It is an old man, master," replied Chandaka, "a man who has seen many years come and go."

"But his face—see how wrinkled it is! Was he born in that unfortunate state?"

"No, master, he was once young and blooming as you are now."

"Are there many more such old persons in the world?"

"Yes, master. It is the course of nature that all who are born must grow old and feeble if they do not die young."

"I, also, Chandaka?"

Chandaka lowered his head out of deference to the Bodhisattva. "You also, master."

The ardor of youth fled at once from the prince. "Shame on birth, since to everyone born old age must come! Return to the palace, Chandaka!"

And so the prince returned to his father's palace in Kapilavastu.

King Suddhodana, astonished by his son's hasty return, summoned the charioteer.

"What happened on the way? Why has my son returned so quickly?"

"He has seen an old man, O king," answered Chandaka, "and because he has seen old age he desires to seek out the nature of Birth and Death."

"Do you want to kill me, man, that you say such things? We must not let the prince enter the religious life. We must not allow the prophecies of the brahmin soothsayers to come true."

The next day the Bodisattva again desired to go to the park; and the king, learning of this, stationed guards all along the road. But despite these preparations, Siddhartha's eyes fell upon a sick man, suffering and very ill, fallen in his own excrements by the roadside.

"Chandaka!" cried the Bodhisattva. "Stop the chariot at once!"

When Chandaka failed to stop, Siddhartha took the reins from the charioteer's hands. And after the chariot had been turned around, the prince drew to the side of the road where the sick man was.

"What, Chandaka, has that man done that his eyes are not like the others' eyes? nor his voice like the voice of other men?"

"He is what is called sick, master."

"Sick? Are all people liable to sickness?"

"Yes, master."

"Then, I, too, could become like this, I, the glory of the Sakyas! Let us return to the palace: enough of going to the park!"

Notwithstanding his discovery of human misery, the Bodisattva set out for the third time on the following morning.

The trip was uneventful until the chariot had reached the outskirts of the gardener's village. There a corpse was being carried to a funeral pyre by weeping relatives.

Prince Siddhartha looked upon the scene with impatience, not knowing what to make of it. But perspiration broke out on Chandaka's forehead as he silently prayed to the gods to withhold the sight of death from the prince.

The gods, however, were of a different mind. Like an invisible hand, a sudden gust of wind swooped down upon the bier and ripped away the pall in fluttering tatters.

Prince Siddhartha's mouth opened in horror when his gaze fell upon the dead body. Could *that* once have been human? Could *that* even have been alive?

"And to think," gasped the prince, "that that vile body was once a thing of delight to its owner, a source of fleeting pleasures! Is the man dead, Chandaka, hopelessly and irretrievably dead?"

"His relatives and friends will not see him any more," replied Chandaka, "nor will he see them."

"It has become clear to me, Chandaka, that death is universal. I, too, am subject to death, not beyond the sphere of death. Now what if I, being subject to old age, sickness, and death, were to investigate the nature of birth, likewise the nature of old age, sickness, and death? What if I, having seen the wretchedness of mundane existence, were to seek out the Unborn, the Undying, the supreme peace of Nirvana?". . . .

Early in the morning of the fourth day, the Bodhisattva set out again for the pleasure park of the summer palace. And as the chariot approached the park, the prince caught sight of a religious recluse walking by the side of the road.

"Who, Chandaka, is that man clad in a simple yellow robe, his head shaved, his face radiant with peace and joy?"

"That man," replied the charioteer, "is a monk, one who has gone forth from the household life and lives on food he has begged. He is one who is thorough in the religious life, thorough in the peaceful life, thorough in good actions, thorough in meritorious conduct, thorough in harmlessness, thorough in kindness to all living beings."

"A monk!" exclaimed the Bodhisattva. "Never before have I seen such happiness and inner peace shining forth from the face of a man! Is it possible, friend Chandaka, that I, too, might find rapture and peace of mind by leaving the world, by becoming such as he and living on food I have begged?"

"We are approaching the summer palace, master."

"Friend, I beg you to tell me! Why, pray, do men leave the world?"

"For the sake of subduing and calming themselves," replied Chandaka, "and for attaining Nirvana."

NIRVANA! "Happiness" or "Extinction" as one looks at the world! On hearing the word *Nirvana,* the Great Being was delighted; and taking pleasure in the thought of abandoning the world, he bade Chandaka to drive into the park.

THE SUPREME ENLIGHTENMENT

Night had fallen, and the full moon peeped over the trees of the forest as if from a desire to behold the Great Being. And while the Bodhi tree sprinkled coral-red sprigs of bloom upon his robes as though doing homage to him, the Bodhisattva attained and abode in the Four Absorptions of the fine-material sphere:

1. Detached from sensual desires and unwholesome thoughts, he entered the First Absorption, which is accompanied by reasoning and discursive thought, born of detachment, and filled with rapture and happiness.

2. After the fading away of reasoning and discursive thought, and by the gaining of inward tranquility and one-pointedness of mind, he entered into a state free from reasoning and discursive thought, the Second Absorption, which is born of concentration and filled with rapture and happiness.

3. After the fading out of rapture, he abode in equanimity—clearly conscious, mindful, and experiencing that feeling of which the Arya[n]s

say, "happy lives the man of equanimity and attentive mind,"—and thus entered the Third Absorption.

4. After the rejection of pleasure and pain, and through the cessation of previous joy and grief, he entered into a state beyond pleasure and pain, the Fourth Absorption, which is purified by equanimity and attentiveness.

    a. Then beginning in the first watch of the night, with mind purified and concentrated, the Great Being directed his mind to the remembrance of his former existences up to hundreds of thousands of births, up to many cycles of dissolution and evolution of the universe.

    "There I was of such and such a name, family, station of life, and livelihood," Gautama realized. "Such pleasure and pain did I experience; and passing away from there I was reborn elsewhere. Thus do I remember all of my former existences with their special modes and details."

    b. Then in the middle watch of the night the Great Being directed his mind to the passing away and rebirth of beings. With superhuman vision he saw them dying and being reborn, low and high, in happy or wretched existences according to their karma.

    "Those beings who lead evil lives in deed, word, or thought," he realized, "who hold to false views and acquire unfavorable karma thereby, are reborn in a state of misery and suffering in hell. But those beings who lead good lives in deed, word, or thought, who hold to right views and acquire favorable karma thereby, are reborn in a state of joy and bliss in heaven."

    c. Then in the last watch of the night the Great Being directed his mind to the complete destruction of the "Poisons," thereby acquiring a Wisdom in conformity with the reality of the Four Aryan Truths, namely, Suffering, its Cause, its Cessation, and the Path which leads to its cessation.

And as he thus knew and thus perceived, his mind was completely emancipated from the Poison of lust (sensual desire), from the Poison of existence-infatuation (the desire for continued separate existence or for annihilation at death), from the Poison of false view (delusion and superstition), and from the Poison of ignorance (of the Four Aryan Truths).

And as the Great Being reflected on the Four Aryan Truths, his Fully Awakened Mind fathomed the Twelve Causes in the chain of Dependent Origination.

"This being present as a cause, that arises. This not being present as a cause, that does not arise."

In the past life (he realized):

1. There is ignorance.
2. Ignorance conditions the predisposing mental formations.

In the present life:

3. The predisposing mental formations condition discriminative consciousness.
4. Discriminative consciousness conditions mind-and-body.
5. Mind-and-body conditions the six senses.
6. The six senses condition contact.
7. Contact conditions feeling.
8. Feeling conditions craving.
9. Craving conditions attachment.
10. Attachment conditions the process of becoming.

In the future life:

11. The process of becoming conditions rebirth.
12. Rebirth conditions decay and death, likewise sorrow, lamentation, pain, grief, and despair.

"Thus does the entire mass of suffering arise. But on the complete fading out and cessation of ignorance, this entire mass of suffering comes to an end."

THE FOUR NOBLE TRUTHS

1. What, monks, is the Aryan Truth about Suffering? Birth is suffering, old age is suffering, sickness is suffering, death is suffering, likewise sorrow, lamentation, pain, grief, and despair. Contact with the unpleasant is suffering, separation from the pleasant is suffering, unsatisfied desire is suffering. . . .

2. What, monks, is the Aryan Truth about the Cause of Suffering? Verily, suffering originates in that rebirth-causing craving which is accompanied by sensual pleasure and which seeks satisfaction now here, now there—craving for sensual pleasures, craving to be born again, craving to be annihilated.

3. What, monks, is the Aryan Truth about the Cessation of Suffering? Verily, it is passionlessness, the complete destruction of this craving for sensual pleasures, for becoming, and for annihilation; the forsaking and relinquishing of this craving, the harboring no longer of this craving.

4. What, monks, is the Aryan Truth about the Path that leads to the Cessation of Suffering? Verily, it is this Aryan Eightfold Path of Right View, Right Thought, Right Speech, Right Action, Right Livelihood, Right Effort, Right Attentiveness, and Right Concentration.

EXCERPTS FROM THE QURAN

Elijah Muhammad

The Quran is a collection of the teachings of the prophet Muhammad, compiled by his disciples after his death.

BELIEVERS AND NON-BELIEVERS

But he who performs good deeds, whether man or a woman, and is a believer, will surely enter Paradise, and shall not be deprived even of an iota of his reward. . . . [W]hosoever kills a human being, except as punishment for murder, or for spreading corruption in the land, it shall be like killing all humanity; and whosoever saves a life, saves the entire human race. Our apostles brought clear proofs to them; but even after that most of them committed excesses in the land. The punishment for those who wage war against God and His Prophet, and perpetrate disorders in the land, is to kill or crucify them, or have a hand on one side and a foot on the other amputated, or banish them from the land. Such is their disgrace in the worlds, and in the Hereafter their doom shall be dreadful. But those who repent before they are subdued should know that God is forgiving and kind.

We sent down the Torah which contains guidance and light, in accordance with which the prophets who had submitted (to God) gave instructions to the Jews, as did the rabbis and priests, for they were the custodians and witnesses of God's writ. So therefore, do not fear men, fear me, and barter not My messages away for a paltry gain. Those who do not judge by God's revelations are infidels indeed. And there (in the Torah) We had ordained a life for a life, and an eye for an eye, and a nose for a nose, and an ear for an ear, and a tooth for a tooth, and for wounds retribution, though he who forgets it out of charity, atones for his sins. And those who do not judge by God's revelations are unjust. Later in the train of the prophets, we sent Jesus, son of Mary, confirming the Torah which had been (sent down) before him, and gave him the Gospel containing guidance and light which corroborated the earlier Torah, a guidance and warning, for those who preserve themselves from evil follow the straight path.

O believer, do not hold Jews and Christians as your allies. They are allies of one another; and anyone who makes them his friends is surely one of them; and God does not guide the unjust.

O believers, any one of you who turns back on his faith (should remember) that God could verily bring (in your place) another people whom He would love as they would love Him, gentle with believers, unbending with infidels, who would strive in the way of God, unafraid of blame by any slanderer. . . . Your only friends are God and His Messenger, and those who believe and are steadfast in devotion, who pay the zakat [charitable tax] and bow in homage (before God). And those who take God and His Prophet and the faithful as their friends are indeed men of God, who will surely be victorious.

O Prophet, announce what has reached you from your Lord, for if you do not, you will not have delivered His message. God will preserve you from (the mischief of) men; for God does not guide those who do not believe. Say to them: "O people of the Book, you have no ground (for argument) until you follow the Torah and the Gospel and what has been revealed to you by your Lord." But what has been revealed to you by your Lord will surely increase rebellion and unbelief in many; so do not grieve for those who do not believe. All those who believe, and the Jews and the Sabians and the Christians, in fact any one who believes in God and the Last Day, and performs good deeds, will have nothing to fear or regret. We had taken a solemn pledge from the children of Israel, and sent messengers to them; but whenever an apostle came to them bringing what did not suit their mood, they called one imposter, another they slew, and imagined that no trials would befall them; and they turned deaf and blind (to the truth). But God still turned to them; yet many of them turned blind and deaf again; but God sees every thing they do. They are surely infidels who say: "God is the Christ, son of Mary." But the Christ had only said: "O children of Israel, worship God who is my Lord and your Lord." Whosoever associates a compeer with God, will have Paradise denied to him by God, and his abode shall be Hell; and the sinners will have none to help them. Disbelievers are they surely who say, "God is the third of the trinity; but there is no god other than God the one." And if they do not desist from saying what they say, then indeed those among them who persist in disbelief will suffer painful punishment. Why do they not turn to God and ask His forgiveness? God is forgiving and kind. The Christ, son of Mary, was but an apostle, and many apostles had (come and) gone before him; and his mother was a woman of truth. They both ate the (same) food (as men). Behold, how We show men clear signs, and behold, how they wand[er] astray!

Tell them: "O people of the Book, do not overstep the bounds of truth in your beliefs, and follow not the wishes of a people who had erred before, and led many others astray, and wandered away from the right path."

WOMEN IN ISLAMIC SOCIETY

. . . God has given you instructions about [women]. You also read them in the Book concerning orphaned women [in your charge] to whom you deny their ordained rights and yet wish to take them in marriage, as well as in respect of helpless children, that you should be just in the matter of orphans. The good you do is known to God. If a woman fears ill treatment from her husband, or his tiring of her, there is no harm if they make a peaceful settlement, and peace is an excellent thing. Yet avarice is part of man's nature. If you do good and fear God, God is cognizant of all that you do. Howsoever you may try you will never be able to treat your wives equally. But do not incline (to one) exclusively and leave (the other) suspended (as it were). Yet if you do the right thing and are just, God is verily forgiving and kind. If both (decide to) separate, God in his largess will provide for them, for God is infinite and all-wise.

PRESCRIPTIONS FOR BEHAVIOR

O You who believe, fulfil your obligations. Made lawful (as food) for you are animals except those mentioned (here); but unlawful during Pilgrimage is game. . . . Forbidden you is carrion and blood, and the flesh of the swine, and whatsoever has been killed in the name of some other than God, . . . or killed . . . unless slaughtered while still alive; and that which has been slaughtered at altars is forbidden, . . . all this is sinful.

O believers, when you stand up for prayer, wash your faces and hands up to the elbows, and also wipe your heads and wash your feet up to the ankles. If you are in a state of seminal pollution, then bathe and purify yourself well. But in case you are ill or are travelling, or you have satisfied the call of nature, or have slept with a woman and you cannot find water, then take wholesome dust, and pass it over your face and your hands. . . .

O believers, . . . do not transgress. God does not love transgressors. . . . The expiation (for breaking an oath) is feeding ten persons who are poor, with food that you give your own families, or clothing them, or freeing a slave. But he who cannot do so should fast for three days. . . . O believers, this wine and gambling, these idols, and these arrows you use for divination, are all acts of Satan; so keep away from them . . . [:] Satan only wishes to create among you enmity and hatred through wine and gambling, and to divert you from the remembrance of God and prayer. . . .

THE PILGRIMAGE

Announce the Pilgrimage to the people. They will come to you on foot and riding along distant roads on lean and slender beasts . . . let them then attend to their persons and complete the rites of pilgrimage, fulfil their vows and circuit round the ancient House.

ROYAL COMMENTARIES OF THE INCAS

Ynca Garcilasso de la Vega

THE ORIGIN OF THE YNCAS KINGS OF PERU.

It pleased our Lord God that, while these people were living and dying in the way we have described, the glimmerings of dawn should appear amongst themselves, which, in the midst of that pitch darkness, might give some indications of the natural law, of civilisation, and of the respect which men ought to have for each other. Afterwards, some further progress was made, and these wild creatures were converted into men, and made capable of reason and of comprehending any good doctrine. Thus, when the same God, who is the Sun of Justice, saw fit to extend the light of his divine rays to these idolaters, they were found not to be such savages, but more ready to receive the Catholic faith, and the teaching and doctrine of our holy church, than those who had not had such early advantages; as will be seen in the course of this history. For it has been clearly shown by experience how much more prompt and ready the Indians who had been conquered, governed, and instructed by the Kings Yncas were to receive the gospel than the other neighbouring people, to whom the teaching of the Yncas had not yet extended. Many of the latter are even now as barbarous and brutal as they ever were, after the Spaniards have been seventy-one years in Peru. And now that we are at the entrance of this great labyrinth, it will be well for us to pass onwards, and relate what there is in it.

After having sketched out many plans, and taken many roads for entering upon a narrative of the origin of the Yncas, the former native kings of Peru, it seemed to me that the best and clearest way would be to relate what I have often heard, in my childhood, from my mother, and from her brothers, uncles, and other relations, touching this origin and beginning. For all that is said on the subject from other sources may be reduced to the same as we shall relate, and it is better that it should be made known in the actual words in which the Yncas have told it, than in those of strange authors. My mother resided in Cuzco, her native town, and almost every week some of the few male and female relations, who escaped the cruelty and tyranny of Atahualpa (as we shall relate in the account of his life), came to visit her. On the occasion of these visits their usual conversation was on the subject of the origin of the Yncas, of their majesty, of the grandeur of their empire, of their greatness, of their mode of government in peace and war, and of the laws which they ordained for the good of their subjects. In short, they omitted nothing relating to the flourishing period of their history in the course of these conversations.

From their past greatness and prosperity, they went on to the present state of affairs; they mourned for their dead kings, their lost rule, their fallen state. Such and the like discourses were held by the Yncas and Pallas when they visited my mother, and, at the memory of their lost happiness, they always concluded their conversations with tears and mourning, saying "We are turned from rulers into vassals." During these conversations I, as a boy, came in and out of the place where they were assembled many times, and was entertained at hearing them, just as lads always like to hear stories told. So days, months, and years passed away, until I was sixteen or seventeen years old. At that time it happened that, one day when my relations were engaged in these discourses, talking of their royal ancestors, I said to the most aged of them, who usually related the stories of his family—"Ynca my uncle, you have no writings which preserve the memory of past events; but what accounts have you of the origin of our kings? For the Spaniards, and other people who live on their borders, have divine and human histories, and they know through them when their kings began to reign, when one empire gave place to another, and even how many thousand years it is since God created heaven and earth. But you, who have no books, what memory have you preserved respecting your ancestors? Who was the first of our Yncas? What was his name? What was his origin? In what manner did he begin to reign? With what people and arms did he conquer this great empire? What beginning had our history?"

The Ynca, as soon as he had heard my questions, was delighted to have the opportunity of replying to them; and I, though I had heard his stories many times before, never listened with so much attention as on that occasion. He turned to me and said, "Nephew, I will tell you what you ask with great pleasure, and you should preserve what I have to say in your heart" (which is their phrase, instead of saying in the memory). "Know then that, in ancient times, all this region which you see was covered with forests and thickets, and the people lived like wild beasts without religion, nor government, nor town, nor houses, without cultivating the land, nor clothing their bodies, for they knew not how to weave cotton nor wool to make clothes. They lived two or three together in caves or clefts of the rocks, or in caverns under ground. They ate the herbs of the field and roots or fruit like wild animals, and also human flesh. They covered their bodies with leaves and the bark of trees, or with the skins of animals. In fine they lived like deer or other game, and even in their intercourse with women they were like brutes; for they knew nothing of living with separate wives."

It will be well, in order to avoid tiresome repetition, to say here that the phrase "Our Father the Sun," was a mode of expressing veneration and respect in the language of the Yncas. They always named the Sun, because they were proud of being descended from him, and it was not lawful for any man who was not of Ynca blood to have the word in his mouth; for it was looked upon as blasphemy, and the blasphemer was stoned.

"Our Father the Sun," said my uncle the Ynca, "seeing the human race in the condition I have described, had compassion upon them, and sent down from heaven to the earth a son and daughter to instruct them in the knowledge of our Father the Sun, that they might adore Him, and adopt Him as their God; also to give them precepts and laws by which to live as reasonable and civilised men, and to teach them to live in houses and towns, to cultivate maize and other crops, to breed flocks, and to use the fruits of the earth like rational beings, instead of living like beasts. With these commands and intentions, our Father the Sun placed his two children in the lake of Titicaca, which is eighty leagues from here; and He said to them that they might go where they pleased, and that at every place where they stopped to eat or sleep, they were to thrust a sceptre of gold into the ground, which was half a yard long, and two fingers in thickness. He gave them this staff as a sign and token that in the place where, by one blow on the earth, it should sink down and disappear, there it was the desire of our Father the Sun that they should remain and establish their court. Finally, He said to them:—'When you have reduced these people to our service, you shall maintain them in habits of reason and justice, by the practice of piety, clemency, and meekness, assuming in all things the office of a pious father towards his beloved and tender children. Thus you will form a likeness and reflection of me. I do good to the whole world, giving light that men may see and do their business, making them warm when they are cold, cherishing their pastures and crops, ripening their fruits and increasing their flocks, watering their lands with dew, and bringing fine weather in the proper season. I take care to go round the earth each day, that I may see the necessities that exist in the world, and supply them, as the sustainer and benefactor of the heathens. I desire that you shall imitate this example as my children, sent to the earth solely for the instruction and benefit of these men who live like beasts. And from this time I constitute and name you as kings and lords over all the tribes, that you may instruct them in your rational works and government.' Having declared His will to His children, our Father the Sun dismissed them. These children set out from Titicaca, and travelled northwards, trying at every place where they stopped on the road whether their sceptre of gold would sink into the earth, but it never did. At last they came to an inn or small resting-place, which is seven or eight leagues south of this city, and is called *Paccari-Tampu*" (that is to say, *the resting-place of the dawn*). The Ynca gave it this name because he set out from it in the early morning. It is one of the towns which this prince afterwards ordered to be founded; and the inhabitants are very proud of the name to this day, because it was given by the Ynca. From this place he and his wife, our queen, advanced to the valley of Cuzco, which at that time was entirely covered with wild forests."

WHAT AN AUTHOR SAYS CONCERNING THEIR GODS

In the papers of Father Blas Valera I found what follows, which I have taken the trouble to translate and insert in this place, because it is apposite to the point we have been discussing, and because of the value of the observations made by this authority. Speaking of the sacrifices which the Indians of Mexico offered up, and of those in other countries, and of the gods they worshipped, he says as follows:—

"One cannot explain in words, nor imagine without horror and dismay, how contrary to religion, terrible, cruel, and inhuman were the sacrifices which the Indians were accustomed to offer up in the time of their heathenry, nor the multitude of gods they had, insomuch that in the city of Mexico and its suburbs there were more than two thousand. The general name for their gods and idols was *Teutl*, though each one had a particular name. But that which Pedro Martyr, the Bishop of Chiapas, and others affirm, that the Indians of the island of Cuçumela, subject to the province of Yucatan, had for their God the sign of the cross, and that they worshipped it; and that the natives of Chiapa knew of the most Holy Trinity and of the incarnation of our Lord; these were interpretations which those authors and other Spaniards invented out of their imaginations, and then applied to those mysteries. In the same way, in their histories of Cuzco, they referred the three statues of the sun to a belief in the Trinity, as well as those to thunder, lightning, and thunderbolts. If in this our day, after having received so much instruction from priests and bishops, these barbarians scarcely know yet whether there be any Holy Ghost,—how could they, while in such thick darkness, have so clear an idea of the mysteries of the Incarnation and of the Trinity? The method that our Spaniards adopted in writing their histories was to ask the Indians, in Spanish, touching the things they wanted to find out from them. These, from not having a clear knowledge of ancient things, or from bad memories, told them wrong, or mixed up poetical fables with their replies. And the worst of it was that neither party had more than a very imperfect knowledge of the language of the other, so as to understand the inquiry, and to reply to it. This arose from the great difficulty there is to understand the Indian language, and from the slight knowledge the Indians then had of Spanish. Thus the Indian understood little of what the Spaniard said in his questions, and the Spaniard comprehended still less of the Indian's reply. So that very often the Spaniard and the Indian both understood the opposite of what they had said to each other: still oftener they arrived at some approach to what had been said, but not at the exact meaning. In this great confusion, the priest or layman who asked the questions placed the meaning to them which was nearest to the desired answer, or which was most like what the Indian was understood to have said. Thus they interpreted according to their pleasure or prejudice, and wrote things down as truths which the Indians never dreamt of. For no mystery of our holy Christian religion can really be taken from their true histories. Nevertheless there can be no doubt that the devil, in his great pride, obtained worship for himself as God, not only in the rites and ceremonies of the heathens, but even in some customs of the Christian religion. He has introduced these rites (like an envious monkey) in many regions of the Indies, so that he may be more honoured amongst those miserable men. Thus, in one country, oral confession was practised, to free men from their sins; in another the washing of the heads of children; in another very severe fasts were kept. In other districts they suffered death for their religion's sake: so that, as in the Old World, the faithful Christians offered themselves as martyrs for the Catholic faith, so in the New World the heathens offered themselves to death for the sake of the accursed devil. But the assertion that *Icona* is their word for God the Father, and *Bacab* for God the Son, and *Estruac* for God the Holy Ghost; and that *Chiripia* is the most holy Virgin Mary, and *Ischen* the blessed St. Anne, and that *Bacab* killed by *Eopuco* represents Christ our Lord crucified by Pilate: all these and similar things are inventions and fictions of Spaniards, and the natives are entirely ignorant of them. The truth is that the above were the names of men and women whom the natives of that land worshipped as gods and goddesses. Some of these, which were very filthy, were looked upon as the gods of the vices: such as *Tlasolteutl,* god of lust; *Ometochtli,* god of drunkenness; *Vitsilopuchtli,* god of murder. *Icona* was the father of all these gods. It is said that he begot them on certain concubines; and he was looked upon as the god of the fathers of families. *Bacab* was the god of the sons of families; *Estruac* was god of the air; *Chiripia* was the mother of the gods, and the earth itself. *Ischen* was the nurse of the gods. *Tlaloc* god of the waters. Other gods were worshipped as the authors of moral virtues. Such was *Quesalcoatl,* the aerial god and reformer of manners. Others were venerated as the patrons of human life in its various stages. They had innumerable figures and images of their false gods for various uses and purposes. Many of them were very filthy. Some gods were in common, others special. They had annual rotations, and they were changed each year in accordance with their superstitions. The old gods were forsaken as infamous, or because they had been of no use, and other gods and demons were elected. Other imaginary gods were believed to preside and rule the ages of children, young people, and the aged. Sons when they inherited, either accepted or repudiated the gods of their fathers, for they were not allowed to hold their pre-eminence against the will of the heir. Old men worshipped other greater deities, but they likewise dethroned them, and set up others in their places when the year was over, or the age of the world, as the Indians had it. Such were the gods which all the natives of Mexico, Chiapa, and Guatemala worshipped, as well as those of Vera Paz, and many other Indians. They thought that the gods selected by themselves were the greatest and most powerful of all the gods. All the gods that were worshipped, when the Spaniards first arrived in that land, were made and set up after the renewing of the sun in the last age; and, according to Gomara, each sun of these people contains 860 years, though, according to the account of the Mexicans themselves, it was much less. This method of counting the age of the world by suns was a common usage among the people of Mexico and Peru, and, according to their account, the years of the last sun were reckoned from the year 1403 of our Lord's era. Thus there can be no doubt that the ancient gods, which were worshipped by the natives of the empire of Mexico in the sun before the last, must have perished in the sea, and that they invented many other gods in their place. From this it must be manifest that the interpretation by which *Icona, Barac,* and *Estruac* are made to signify the Father, the Son, and the Holy Ghost is false.

"All the other people inhabiting the northern parts, corresponding to the northern regions of the Old World, such as the provinces of the great Florida, and all the islands, did not have idols nor conjuring gods. They only worshipped what Varro calls natural gods, such as the elements, the sea, lakes, rivers, springs, forests, wild beasts, serpents, corn, and other things of this class. This custom had its beginning and origin amongst the Chaldees, whence it spread over many and divers nations. Those who ate human flesh occupied the whole empire of Mexico, all the islands, and most of the countries bordering on Peru. They kept up the custom in the most bestial way, until they were brought under the rule of the Yncas, or of the Spaniards."

All this is from Blas Valera. In another part he says that "the Yncas did not worship anything but the sun and the planets," and that "in this they imitated the Chaldees."

GOVERNMENT, TAXES, AND WAR IN BENIN

John Barbot

The government of Benin is principally vested in the king, and three chief ministers, call'd great *Veadors;* that is, intendants, or overseers; besides the great marshall of the crown, who is intrusted with the affairs relating to war, as the three others are with the administration of justice, and the management of the revenue; and all four are obliged to take their circuits throughout the several provinces, from time to time, to inspect into the condition of the country, and the administration of the governors and justices in each district, that peace and good order may be kept as much as possible. Those chief ministers of state have under them each his own particular officers and assistants in the discharge of their posts and places. They call the first of the three aforemention'd ministers of state, the *Onegwa,* and second *Ossade,* and the third *Arribon.*

They reside constantly at court, as being the king's privy council, to advise him on all emergencies and affairs of the nation; and any person that wants to apply to the prince, must address himself first to them, and they acquaint the king with the petitioner's business, and return his answer accordingly: but commonly, as in other countries, they will only inform the king with what they please themselves; and so in his name, act very arbitrarily over the subjects. Whence it may well be inferr'd, that the government is entirely in their hands; for it is very seldom they will favour a person so far as to admit him to the king's presence, to represent his own affairs to that prince: and every body knowing their great authority, endeavours on all occasions to gain their favour as much as possible, by large gratifications and presents, in order to succeed in their affairs at court, for which reason their offices and posts are of very great profit to them.

Besides these four chief ministers of state, there are two other inferior ranks about the king: the first is composed of those they call *Reis de Ruas,* signifying in *Portuguese,* kings of streets, some of whom preside over the commonalty, and others over the slaves; some again over military affairs; others over affairs relating to cattle and the fruits of the earth, &c. there being supervisors or intendants over every thing that can be thought of, in order to keep all things in a due regular way.

The king's income is very great, his dominions being so large, and having such a number of governors, and other inferior officers, each of whom is obliged, according to his post, to pay into the king's treasury so many bags of *Boejies*, some more some less, which all together amount to a prodigious sum; and other officers of inferior rank are to pay in their taxes in cattle, chicken, fruits, roots and cloths, or any other things that can be useful to the king's household; which is so great a quantity, that it doth not cost the king a penny throughout the year to maintain and subsist his family; so that there is yearly a considerable increase of money in his treasury. Add to all this, the duties and tolls on imported or exported goods, paid in all trading places, to the respective *Veadors* and other officers, which are also partly convey'd to the treasury; and were the collectors thereof just and honest, so as not to defraud the prince of a considerable part, these would amount to an incredible sum.

This prince is perpetually at war with one nation or other that borders on the northern part of his dominions, and sometimes with another north-west of his kingdom, which are all potent people, but little or not at all known to *Europeans*, over whom he obtains from time to time considerable advantages, subduing large portions of those unknown countries, and raising great contributions, which are partly paid him in jasper, and other valuable goods of the product of those countries. Wherewith, together with his own plentiful revenue, he is able, upon occasion, to maintain an army of an hundred thousand horse and foot; but, for the most part, he doth not keep above thirty thousand men, which renders him more formidable to his neighbours than any other *Guinea* king: nor is there any other throughout all *Guinea*, that has so many vassals and tributary kings under him; as for instance, those of *Istanna, Forcado, Jaboe, Issabo* and *Oedoba*, from whom he receives considerable yearly tributes, except from him of *Issabo*, who, though much more potent than all the others, yet pays the least.

Source: G. M. Theal, ed., *Records of South-East African History*, vol. II (London/Capetown: Government of Capetown, 1898–1903), pp. 384–88.

TRAVELS IN THE INTERIOR DISTRICTS OF AFRICA: URBAN LIFE AND WOMEN IN WEST AFRICA

Mungo Park

Sego, the capital of Bambarra, at which I had now arrived, consists, properly speaking, of four distinct towns; two on the northern bank of the Niger, called Sego Korro and Sego Boo; and two on the southern bank, called Sego Soo Korro and Sego See Korro. They are all surrounded with high mud-walls; the houses are built of clay, of a square form, with flat roofs; some of them have two stories, and many of them are whitewashed. Besides these buildings, Moorish mosques are seen in every quarter; and the streets, though narrow, are broad enough for every useful purpose, in a country where wheel carriages are entirely unknown. From the best inquiries I could make, I have reason to believe that Sego contains altogether about thirty thousand inhabitants. The King of Bambarra constantly resides at Sego See Korro; he employs a great many slaves in conveying people over the river, and the money they receive (though the fare is only ten Kowrie shells for each individual) furnishes a considerable revenue to the king, in the course of a year. . . .

. . . The view of this extensive city; the numerous canoes upon the river; the crowded population, and the cultivated state of the surrounding country, formed altogether a prospect of civilization and magnificence, which I little expected to find in the bosom of Africa.

I waited more than two hours, without having an opportunity of crossing the river; during which time the people who had crossed, carried information to Mansong the King, that a white man was waiting for a passage, and was coming to see him. He immediately sent over one of his chief men, who informed me that the king could not possibly see me, until he knew what had brought me into his country; and that I must not presume to cross the river without the king's permission. He therefore advised me to lodge at a distant village, to which he pointed, for the night; and said that in the morning he would give me further instructions how to conduct myself. This was very discouraging. However, as there was no remedy, I set off for the village; where I found, to my great mortification, that no person would admit me into his house. I was regarded with astonishment and fear, and was obliged to sit all day without victuals, in the shade of a tree; and the night threatened to be very uncomfortable, for the wind rose, and there was great appearance of a heavy rain; and the wild beasts are so very numerous in the neighbourhood, that I should have been under the necessity of climbing up the tree, and resting amongst the branches. About sunset, however, as I was preparing to pass the night in this manner, and had turned my horse loose, that he might graze at liberty, a woman, returning from the labours of the field, stopped to observe me, and perceiving that I was weary and dejected, inquired into my situation, which I briefly explained to her; whereupon, with looks of great compassion, she took up my saddle and bridle, and told me to follow her. Having conducted me into her hut, she lighted up a lamp, spread a mat on the floor, and told me I might remain there for the night. Finding that I was very hungry, she said she would procure me something to eat. She accordingly went out, and returned in a short time with a very fine fish; which, having caused to be half boiled upon some embers, she gave me for supper. The rites of hospitality being thus performed towards a stranger in distress; my worthy benefactress (pointing to the mat, and telling me I might sleep there without apprehension) called to the female part of her family, who had stood gazing on me all the while in fixed astonishment, to resume their task of spinning cotton; in which they continued to employ themselves great part of the night. They lightened their labour by songs, one of which was composed extempore; for I was myself the subject of it. It was sung by one of the young women, the rest joining in a sort of chorus. The air was sweet and plaintive, and the words, literally translated, were these. "The winds roared, and the rains fell. The poor white man, faint and weary, came and sat under our tree. He has no mother to bring him milk; no wife to grind his corn. *Chorus.* Let us pity the white man; no mother has he, &c. &c." Trifling as this recital may appear to the reader, to a person in my situation, the circumstance was affecting in the highest degree. I was oppressed by such unexpected kindness; and sleep fled from my eyes. In the morning I presented my compassionate landlady with two of the four brass buttons which remained on my waistcoat; the only recompence I could make her.

Source: Mungo Park, *Travels in the Interior Districts of Africa* (London, 1799), pp. 195–98.

THE PRINCE

Niccolò Machiavelli

NICCOLÒ MACHIAVELLI TO LORENZO THE MAGNIFICENT SON OF PIERO DI MEDICI

It is customary for those who wish to gain the favour of a prince to endeavour to do so by offering him gifts of those things which they hold most precious, or in which they know him to take especial delight. In this way princes are often presented with horses, arms, cloth of gold, gems, and suchlike ornaments worthy of their grandeur. In my desire, however, to offer to Your Highness some humble testimony of my devotion, I have been unable to find among my possessions anything which I hold so dear or esteem so highly as that knowledge of the deeds of great men which I acquired through a long experience of modern events and a constant study of the past.

With the utmost diligence I have long pondered and scrutinised the actions of the great, and now I offer the results to Your Highness within the compass of a small volume: and although I deem this work unworthy of Your Highness's acceptance, yet my confidence in your humanity assures me that you will receive it with favour, knowing that it is not in my power to offer you a greater gift than that of enabling you to understand in a very short time all those things which I have learnt at the cost of privation and danger in the course of many years. I have not sought to adorn my work with long phrases or high-sounding words or any of those superficial attractions and ornaments with which many writers seek to embellish their material, as I desire no honour for my work but such as the novelty and gravity of its subject may justly deserve. Nor will it, I trust, be deemed presumptuous on the part of a man of humble and obscure condition to attempt to discuss and direct the government of princes; for in the same way that landscape painters station themselves in the valleys in order to draw mountains or high ground, and ascend an eminence in order to get a good view of the plains, so it is necessary to be a prince to know thoroughly the nature of the people, and one of the populace to know the nature of princes.

May I trust, therefore, that Your Highness will accept this little gift in the spirit in which it is offered; and if Your Highness will deign to peruse it, you will recognize in it my ardent desire that you may attain to that grandeur which fortune and your own merits presage for you.

And should Your Highness gaze down from the summit of your lofty position towards this humble spot, you will recognize the great and unmerited sufferings inflicted on me by a cruel fate.

1: The Various Kinds of Government and the Ways by Which They Are Established

All states and dominions which hold or have held sway over mankind are either republics or monarchies. Monarchies are either hereditary in which the rulers have been for many years of the same family, or else they are of recent foundation. The newly founded ones are either entirely new, as was Milan to Francesco Sforza, or else they are, as it were, new members grafted on to the hereditary possessions of the prince that annexes them, as is the kingdom of Naples to the King of Spain. The dominions thus acquired have either been previously accustomed to the rule of another prince, or else have been free states, and they are annexed either by force of arms of the prince himself, or of others, or else fall to him by good fortune or special ability. . . .

5: The Way to Govern Cities or Dominions That, Previous to Being Occupied, Lived under Their Own Laws

When those states which have been acquired are accustomed to live at liberty under their own laws, there are three ways of holding them. The first is to despoil them; the second is to go and live there in person; the third is to allow them to live under their own laws, taking tribute of them, and creating within the country a government composed of a few who will keep it friendly to you. Because this government, being created by the prince, knows that it cannot exist without his friendship and protection, and will do all it can to keep them. What is more, a city used to liberty can be more easily held by means of its citizens than in any other way, if you wish to preserve it.

There is the example of the Spartans and the Romans. The Spartans held Athens and Thebes by creating within them a government of a few; nevertheless they lost them. The Romans, in order to hold Capua, Carthage, and Numantia, ravaged them, but did not lose them. They wanted to hold Greece in almost the same way as the Spartans held it, leaving it free and under its own laws, but they did not succeed; so that they were compelled to lay waste many cities in that province in order to keep it, because in truth there is no sure method of holding them except by despoiling them. And whoever becomes the ruler of a free city and does not destroy it, can expect to be destroyed by it, for it can always find a motive for rebellion in the name of liberty and of its ancient usages, which are forgotten neither by lapse of time nor by benefits received; and whatever one does or provides, so long as the inhabitants are not separated or dispersed, they do not forget that name and those usages, but appeal to them at once in every emergency, as did Pisa after so many years held in servitude by the Florentines. But when cities or provinces have been accustomed to live under a prince, and the family of that prince is extinguished, being on the one hand used to obey, and on the other not having their old prince, they cannot unite in choosing one from among themselves, and they do not know how to live in freedom, so that they are slower to take arms, and a prince can win them over with greater facility and establish himself securely. But in republics there is greater life, greater hatred, and more desire for vengeance; they do not and cannot cast aside the memory of their ancient liberty, so that the surest way is either to lay them waste or reside in them. . . .

8: Of Those Who Have Attained the Position of Prince by Villainy

But as there are still two ways of becoming prince which cannot be attributed entirely either to fortune or to ability, they must not be passed over, although one of them could be more fully discussed if we were treating of republics. These are when one becomes prince by some nefarious or villainous means, or when a private citizen becomes the prince of his country through the favour of his fellow-citizens. And in speaking of the former means, I will give two examples, one ancient, the other modern, without entering further into the merits of this method, and I judge them to be sufficient for any one obliged to imitate them.

Agathocles the Sicilian rose not only from private life but from the lowest and most abject position to be King of Syracuse. The son of a potter, he led a life of the utmost wickedness through all the stages of his fortune. Nevertheless, his wickedness was accompanied by such vigour of mind and body that, having joined the militia, he rose through its ranks to be praetor of Syracuse. Having been appointed to this position, and having decided to become prince, and to hold with violence and without the support of others that which had been constitutionally granted him; and having imparted his design to Hamilcar the Carthaginian, who was fighting with his armies in Sicily, he called together one morning the people and senate of Syracuse, as if he had to deliberate on matters of importance to the republic, and at a given signal had all the senators and the richest men of the people killed by his soldiers. After their death he occupied and held rule over the city without any civil strife. And although he was twice beaten by the Carthaginians and ultimately besieged, he was able not only to defend the city, but leaving a portion of his forces for its defence, with the remainder he invaded Africa, and in a short time liberated Syracuse from the siege and brought the Carthaginians to great extremities, so that they were obliged to come to terms with him, and remain contented with the possession of Africa, leaving Sicily to Agathocles. Whoever considers, therefore, the actions and qualities of this man, will see few if any things which can be attributed to fortune; for, as above stated, it was not by the favour of any person, but through the grades of the militia, in which he had advanced with a thousand hardships and perils, that he arrived at the position of prince, which he afterwards maintained by so many courageous and perilous expedients. It cannot be called virtue to kill one's fellow-citizens, betray one's friends, be without faith, without pity, and without religion; by these methods one may indeed gain power, but not glory. For if the virtues of Agathocles in braving and overcoming perils, and his greatness of soul in supporting and surmounting obstacles be considered, one sees no reason for holding him inferior to any of the most renowned captains. Nevertheless his barbarous cruelty and inhumanity, together with his countless atrocities, do not permit of his being named among the most famous men. We cannot attribute to fortune or virtue that which he achieved without either.

Some may wonder how it came about that Agathocles, and others like him, could, after infinite treachery and cruelty, live secure for many years in their country and defend themselves from external enemies without being conspired against by their subjects; although many others have, owing to their cruelty, been unable to maintain their position in times of peace, not to speak of the uncertain times of war. I believe this arises from the cruelties being exploited well or badly. Well committed may be called those (if it is permissible to use the word well of evil) which are perpetrated once for the need of securing one's self, and which afterwards are not persisted in, but are exchanged for measures as useful to the subjects as possible. Cruelties ill committed are those which, although at first few, increase rather than diminish with time. Those who follow the former method may remedy in some measure their condition, both with God and man; as did Agathocles. As to the others, it is impossible for them to maintain themselves.

Whence it is to be noted, that in taking a state the conqueror must arrange to commit all his cruelties at once, so as not to have to recur to them every day, and so as to be able, by not making fresh changes, to reassure people and win them over by benefiting them. Whoever acts otherwise, either through timidity or bad counsel, is always obliged to stand with knife in hand, and can never depend on his subjects, because they, owing to continually fresh injuries, are unable to depend upon him. For injuries should be done all together, so that being less tasted, they will give less offence. Benefits should be granted little by little, so that they may be better enjoyed. And above all, a prince must live with his subjects in such a way that no accident of good or evil fortune can deflect him from his course; for necessity arising in adverse times, you are not in time with severity, and the good that you do does not profit, as it is judged to be forced upon you, and you will derive no benefit whatever from it.

17: Of Cruelty and Clemency, and Whether It Is Better to Be Loved or Feared

Proceeding to the other qualities before named, I say that every prince must desire to be considered merciful and not cruel. He must, however, take care not to misuse this mercifulness. Cesare Borgia was considered cruel, but his cruelty had brought order to the Romagna, united it, and reduced it to peace and fealty. If this is considered well, it will be seen that he was really much more merciful than the Florentine people, who, to avoid the name of cruelty, allowed Pistoia to be destroyed. A prince, therefore, must not mind incurring the charge of cruelty for the purpose of keeping his subjects united and faithful; for, with a very few examples, he will be more merciful than those who, from excess of tenderness, allow disorders to arise, from whence spring bloodshed and rapine; for these as a rule injure the whole community, while the executions carried out by the prince injure only individuals. And of all princes, it is impossible for a new prince to escape the reputation of cruelty, new states being always full of dangers.

Nevertheless, he must be cautious in believing and acting, and must not be afraid of his own shadow, and must proceed in a temperate manner with prudence and humanity, so that too much confidence does not render him incautious, and too much diffidence does not render him intolerant.

From this arises the question whether it is better to be loved more than feared, or feared more than loved. The reply is, that one ought to be both feared and loved, but as it is difficult for the two to go together, it is much safer to be feared than loved, if one of the two has to be wanting. For it may be said of men in general that they are ungrateful, voluble, dissemblers, anxious to avoid danger, and covetous of gain; as long as you benefit them, they are entirely yours; they offer you their blood, their goods, their life, and their children, as I have before said, when the necessity is remote; but when it approaches, they revolt. And the prince who has relied solely on their words, without making other preparations, is ruined; for the friendship which is gained by purchase and not through grandeur and nobility of spirit is bought but not secured, and at a pinch is not to be expended in your service. And men have less scruple in offending one who makes himself loved than one who makes himself feared; for love is held by a chain of obligation which, men being selfish, is broken whenever it serves their purpose; but fear is maintained by a dread of punishment which never fails.

Still, a prince should make himself feared in such a way that if he does not gain love, he at any rate avoids hatred; for fear and the absence of hatred may well go together, and will be always attained by one who abstains from interfering with the property of his citizens and subjects or with their women. And when he is obliged to take the life of any one, let him do so when there is a proper justification and manifest reason for it; but above all he must abstain from taking the property of others, for men forget more easily the death of their father than the loss of their patrimony. Then also pretexts for seizing property are never wanting, and one who begins to live by rapine will always find some reason for taking the goods of others, whereas causes for taking life are rarer and more fleeting.

26: Exhortation to Liberate Italy from the Barbarians

Having now considered all the things we have spoken of, and thought within myself whether at present the time was not propitious in Italy for a new prince, and if there was not a state of things which offered an opportunity to a prudent and capable man to introduce a new system that would do honour to himself and good to the mass of the people, it seems to me that so many things concur to favour a new ruler that I do not know of any time more fitting for such an enterprise.

FROM THE REVOLUTIONS
OF THE HEAVENLY BODIES

Nicolas Copernicus

That the universe is spherical. FIRST WE must remark that the universe is spherical in form, partly because this form being a perfect whole requiring no joints, is the most complete of all, partly because it makes the most capacious form, which is best suited to contain and preserve everything; or again because all the constituent parts of the universe, that is the sun, moon and the planets appear in this form; or because everything strives to attain this form, as appears in the case of drops of water and other fluid bodies if they attempt to define themselves. So no one will doubt that this form belongs to the heavenly bodies.

That the earth is also spherical. That the earth is also spherical is therefore beyond question, because it presses from all sides upon its center. Although by reason of the elevations of the mountains and the depressions of the valleys a perfect circle cannot be understood, yet this does not affect the general spherical nature of the earth. This appears in the following manner. To those who journey towards the North the North pole of the daily revolution of the heavenly sphere seems gradually to rise, while the opposite seems to sink. Most of the stars in the region of the Bear seem not to set, while some of the Southern stars seem not to rise at all. So Italy does not see Canopus which is visible to the Egyptians. And Italy sees the outermost star of the Stream, which our region of a colder zone does not know. On the other hand to those who go towards the South the others seem to rise and those to sink which are high in our region. Moreover, the inclination of the poles to the diameter of the earth bears always the same relation, which could happen only in the case of a sphere. So it is evident that the earth is included between the two poles, and is therefore spherical in form. Let us add that the inhabitants of the East do not observe the eclipse of the sun or of the moon which occurs in the evening, and the inhabitants of the West those which occur in the morning, while those who dwell between see those later and these earlier. That the water also has the same form can be observed from the ships, in that the land which cannot be seen from the deck, is visible from the mast-tree. And conversely if a light be placed at the masthead it seems to those who remain on the shores gradually to sink and at last still sinking to disappear. It is clear that the water also according to its nature continually presses like the earth downward, and does not rise above its banks higher than its convexity permits. So the land extends above the ocean as much as the land happens to be higher.

Whether the earth has a circular motion, and concerning the location of the earth. As it has been already shown that the earth has the form of a sphere, we must consider whether a movement also coincides with this form, and what place the earth holds in the universe. Without this there will be no secure results to be obtained in regard to the heavenly phenomena. The great majority of authors of course agree that the earth stands still in the center of the universe, and consider it inconceivable and ridiculous to suppose the opposite. But if the matter is carefully weighed it will be seen that the question is not yet settled and therefore by no means to be regarded lightly. Every change of place which is observed is due, namely, to a movement of the observed object or of the observer, or to movements of both, naturally in different directions, for if the observed object and the observer move in the same manner and in the same direction no movement will be seen. Now it is from the earth that the revolution of the heavens is observed and it is produced for our eyes. Therefore if the earth undergoes no movement this movement must take place in everything outside of the earth, but in the opposite direction than if everything on the earth moved, and of this kind is the daily revolution. So this appears to affect the whole universe, that is, everything outside the earth with the single exception of the earth itself. If, however, one should admit that this movement was not peculiar to the heavens, but that the earth revolved from west to east, and if this was carefully considered in regard to the apparent rising and setting of the sun, the moon and the stars, it would be discovered that this was the real situation. Since the sky, which contains and shelters all things, is the common seat of all things, it is not easy to understand why motion should not be ascribed rather to the thing contained than to the containing, to the located rather than to the location. From this supposition follows another question of no less importance, concerning the place of the earth, although it has been accepted and believed by almost all, that the earth occupies the middle of the universe. But if one should suppose that the earth is not at the center of the universe, that, however, the distance between the two is not great enough to be measured on the orbits of the fixed stars, but would be noticeable and perceptible on the orbit of the sun or of the planets: and if one was further of the opinion that the movements of the planets appeared to be irregular as if they were governed by a center other than the earth, then such an one could perhaps have given the true reasons for the apparently irregular movement. For since the planets appear now nearer and now farther from the earth, this shows necessarily that the center of their revolutions is not the center of the earth: although it does not settle whether the earth increases and decreases the distance from them or they their distance from the earth.

Refutation of the arguments of the ancients that the earth remains still in the middle of the universe, as if it were its center. From this and similar reasons it is supposed that the earth rests at the center of the universe and that there is no doubt of the fact. But if one believed that the earth revolved, he would certainly be of the opinion that this movement was natural and not arbitrary. For whatever is in accord with nature produces results which are the opposite of those produced by force. Things upon which force or an outside power has acted, must be injured and cannot long endure: what happens by nature, however, preserves itself well and exists in the best condition. So Ptolemy feared without good reason that the earth and all earthly objects subject to the revolution would be destroyed by the act of nature, since this latter is opposed to artificial acts, or to what is produced by the human spirit. But why did he not fear the same, and in a much higher degree, of the universe, whose motion must be as much more rapid as the heavens are greater than the earth? Or has the heaven become so immense because it has been driven outward from the center by the inconceivable power of the revolution; while if it stood still, on the contrary, it would collapse and fall together? But surely if this is the case the extent of the heavens would increase infinitely. For the more it is driven higher by the outward force of the movement, so much the more rapid will the movement become, because of the ever increasing circle which must be traversed in twenty-four hours; and conversely if the movement grows the immensity of the heavens grows. So the velocity would increase the size and the size would increase the velocity unendingly. According to the physical law that the endless cannot wear away nor in any way move, the heavens must necessarily stand still. But it is said that beyond the sky no body, no place, no vacant space, in fact nothing at all exists; then it is strange that some thing should be enclosed by nothing. But if the heaven is endless and is bounded only by the inner hollow, perhaps this establishes all the more clearly the fact that there is nothing outside the heavens, because everything is within it, but the heaven must then remain unmoved. The highest proof on which one supports the finite character of the universe is its movement. But whether the universe is endless or limited we will leave to the physiologues; this remains sure for us that the earth enclosed between the poles is bounded by a spherical surface. Why therefore should we not take the position of ascribing to a movement conformable to its nature and corresponding to its form, rather than suppose that the whole universe whose limits are not and cannot be known moves? And why will we not recognize that the appearance of a daily revolution belongs to the heavens, but the actuality to the earth; and that the relation is similar to that of which one says: "We run out of the harbor, the lands and cities retreat from us." Because if a ship sails along quietly, everything outside of it appears to those on board as if it moved with the motion of the boat, and the boatman thinks that the boat with all on board is standing still, this same thing may hold without doubt of the motion of the earth, and it may seem as if the whole universe revolved.

What shall we say, however, of the clouds and other things floating, falling or rising in the air—except that not only does the earth move with the watery elements belonging with it, but also a large part of the atmosphere, and whatever else is in any way connected with the earth; whether it is because the air immediately touching the earth has the same nature as the earth, or that the motion has become imparted to the atmosphere. A like astonishment must be felt if that highest region of the air be supposed to follow the heavenly motion, as shown by those suddenly appearing stars which the Greeks call comets or bearded stars, which belong to that region and which rise and set like other stars. We may suppose that part of the atmosphere, because of its great distance from the earth, has become free from the earthly motion. So the atmosphere which lies close to the earth and all things floating in it would appear to remain still, unless driven here and there by the wind or some other outside force, which chance may bring into play; for how is the wind in the air different from the current in the sea? We must admit that the motion of things rising and falling in the air is in relation to the universe a double one, being always made up of a rectilinear and a circular movement. Since that which seeks of its own weight to fall is essentially earthy, so there is no doubt that these follow the same natural law as their whole; and it results from the same principle that those things which pertain to fire are forcibly driven on high. Earthly fire is nourished with earthly stuff, and it is said that the flame is only burning smoke. But the peculiarity of the fire consists in this that it expands whatever it seizes upon, and it carries this out so consistently that it can in no way and by no machinery be prevented from breaking its bonds and completing its work.

The expanding motion, however, is directed from the center outward; therefore if any earthly material is ignited it moves upward. So to each single body belongs a single motion, and this is evinced preferably in a circular direction as long as the single body remains in its natural place and its entirety. In this position the movement is the circular movement which as far as the body itself is concerned is as if it did not occur. The rectilinear motion, however, seizes upon those bodies which have wandered or have been driven from their natural position or have been in any way disturbed. Nothing is so much opposed to the order and form of the world as the displacement of one of its parts. Rectilinear motion takes place only when objects are not properly related, and are not complete according to their nature because they have separated from their whole and have lost their unity. Moreover, objects which have been driven outward or away, leaving out of consideration the circular motion, do not obey a single, simple and regular motion, since they cannot be controlled simply by their lightness or by the force of their weight, and if in falling they have at first a slow movement the rapidity of the motion increases as they fall, while in the case of earthly fire which is forced upwards—and we have no means of knowing any other kind of fire—we will see that its motion is slow as if its earthly origin thereby showed itself.

The circular motion, on the other hand, is always regular, because it is not subject to an intermittent cause. Those other objects, however, would cease to be either light or heavy in respect to their natural movement if they reached their own place, and thus they would fit into that movement. Therefore if the circular movement is to be ascribed to the universe as a whole and the rectilinear to the parts, we might say that the revolution is to the straight line as the natural state is to sickness. That Aristotle divided motion into three sorts, that from the center out, that inward toward center, and that around about the center, appears to be merely a logical convenience, just as we distinguish point, line and surface, although one cannot exist without the others, and none of them are found apart from bodies. This fact is also to be considered, that the condition of immovability is held to be more noble and divine than that of change and inconstancy, which latter therefore should be ascribed rather to the earth than to the universe, and I would add also that it seems inconsistent to attribute motion to the containing and locating clement rather than to the contained and located object, which the earth is. Finally since the planets plainly are at one time nearer and at another time farther from the earth, it would follow, on the theory that the universe revolves, that the movement of the one and same body which is known to take place about a center, that is the center of the earth, must also be directed toward the center from without and from the center outward. The movement about the center must therefore be made more general, and it suffices if that single movement be about its own center. So it appears from all these considerations that the movement of the earth is more probable than its fixity, especially in regard to the daily revolution, which is most peculiar to the earth.

Source: Oliver J. Thatcher, ed., *The Library of Original Sources* (Milwaukee: University Research Extension Co., 1907), *Vol. V: 9th to 16th Centuries,* pp. 95–101.

Scanned by: J. S. Arkenberg, Dept. of History, Cal. State Fullerton. Prof. Arkenberg has modernized the text.

IDENTIFICATIONS PART I

Define each of the following items with a two-sentence identification. Your definition must specifically draw on material in one of the documents in this section.

Quran

_____

_____

Analects of Confucius

_____

_____

Copernicus

_____

_____

Cuzco

_____

_____

Machiavelli's The Prince

_____

_____

PART II
THE AGE OF ENCOUNTERS

The items in this section focus on the Age of Encounters, which refers to encounters between European and non-Western societies as merchants and travelers like Marco Polo as well as explorers and conquerors like Columbus and Cortez began to spread Western influence around the globe. What does Marco Polo's account suggest about the way Europeans viewed other cultures in the early stages of the Age of Encounters? How would you contrast that view with the Spaniards' treatment of the Aztecs? What were the Aztecs' reactions to and views of the Spanish? How would you contrast the encounter of the Spanish and the Aztecs with the interactions between the Portugese and the people of the Kingdom of the Kongo? What problems did the King of the Kongo face in his dealings with the Portuguese? What is the experience of Africans who face life in slavery in Brazil? How would you describe the goals and experiences of the sailors who carried out the missions of the East India Company? What factor or factors eventually gave Europeans a decisive advantage over their commercial competitors around the globe?

THE GLORIES OF KINSAY (HANGCHOW)

Marco Polo

DESCRIPTION OF THE GREAT CITY OF KINSAY,[1] WHICH IS THE CAPITAL OF THE WHOLE COUNTRY OF MANZI[2]

When you have left the city of Changan and have travelled for three days through a splendid country, passing a number of towns and villages, you arrive at the most noble city of Kinsay, a name which is as much as to say in our tongue "The City of Heaven," as I told you before.

And since we have got thither I will enter into particulars about its magnificence; and these are well worth the telling, for the city is beyond dispute the finest and the noblest in the world. In this we shall speak according to the written statement which the Queen of this Realm sent to Bayan the conqueror of the country for transmission to the Great Kaan, in order that he might be aware of the surpassing grandeur of the city and might be moved to save it from destruction or injury. I will tell you all the truth as it was set down in that document. For truth it was, as the said Messer Marco Polo at a later date was able to witness with his own eyes. And now we shall rehearse those particulars.

First and foremost, then, the document stated the city of Kinsay to be so great that it hath an hundred miles of compass. [*note: probably a hundred Chinese* li, *about 4/10ths of a mile*] And there are in it twelve thousand bridges of stone, for the most part so lofty that a great fleet could pass beneath them. And let no man marvel that there are so many bridges, for you see the whole city stands as it were in the water and surrounded by water, so that a great many bridges are required to give free passage about it. And though the bridges be so high the approaches are so well contrived that carts and horses do cross them.

---

1. *Kinsay* is the modern Hangchow

2. *Manzi* comprised the greater part of China, being all the territory south of the Hwang-Ho (the Yellow River) in the East and the province of Shensi in the West.

The document aforesaid also went on to state that there were in this city twelve guilds of the different crafts, and that each guild had 12,000 houses in the occupation of its workmen. Each of these houses contains at least 12 men, whilst some contain 20 and some 40,—not that these are all masters, but inclusive of the journeymen who work under the masters. And yet all these craftsmen had full occupation, for many other cities of the kingdom are supplied from this city with what they require.

The document aforesaid also stated that the number and wealth of the merchants, and the amount of goods that passed through their hands, were so enormous that no man could form a just estimate thereof. And I should have told you with regard to those masters of the different crafts who are at the head of such houses as I have mentioned, that neither they nor their wives ever touch a piece of work with their own hands, but live as nicely and delicately as if they were kings and queens. The wives indeed are most dainty and angelical creatures! Moreover it was an ordinance laid down by the King that every man should follow his father's business and no other, no matter if he possessed 100,000 bezants [*note: a Byzantine coin, often used as a standard coinage*].

Inside the city there is a Lake which has a compass of some 30 miles [*note: probably 30* li] and all round it are erected beautiful palaces and mansions, of the richest and most exquisite structure that you can imagine, belonging to the nobles of the city. There are also on its shores many abbeys and churches of the Idolaters. In the middle of the Lake are two Islands, on each of which stands a rich, beautiful and spacious edifice, furnished in such style as to seem fit for the palace of an Emperor. And when any one of the citizens desired to hold a marriage feast, or to give any other entertainment, it used to be done at one of these palaces. And everything would be found there ready to order, such as silver plate, trenchers, and dishes, napkins and table-cloths, and whatever else was needful. The King made this provision for the gratification of his people, and the place was open to every one who desired to give an entertainment. Sometimes there would be at these palaces an hundred different parties; some holding a banquet, others celebrating a wedding; and yet all would find good accommodation in the different apartments and pavilions, and that in so well ordered a manner that one party was never in the way of another.

The houses of the city are provided with lofty towers of stone in which articles of value are stored for fear of fire; for most of the houses themselves are of timber, and fires are very frequent in the city.

The people are Idolaters; and since they were conquered by the Great Kaan they use paper-money. Both men and women are fair and comely, and for the most part clothe themselves in silk, so vast is the supply of that material, both from the whole district of Kinsay, and from the imports by traders from other provinces. And you must know they eat every kind of flesh, even that of dogs and other unclean beasts, which nothing would induce a Christian to eat.

Since the Great Kaan occupied the city he has ordained that each of the 12,000 bridges should be provided with a guard of ten men, in case of any disturbance, or of any being so rash as to plot treason or insurrection against him. Each guard is provided with a hollow instrument of wood and with a metal basin, and with a time-keeper to enable them to know the hour of the day or night. And so when one hour of the night is past the sentry strikes one on the wooden instrument and on the basin, so that the whole quarter of the city is made aware that one hour of the night is gone. At the second hour he gives two strokes, and so on, keeping always wide awake and on the look out. In the morning again, from the sunrise, they begin to count anew, and strike one hour as they did in the night, and so on hour after hour.

Part of the watch patrols the quarter, to see if any light or fire is burning after the lawful hours; if they find any they mark the door, and in the morning the owner is summoned before the magistrates, and unless he can plead a good excuse he is punished. Also if they find any one going about the streets at unlawful hours they arrest him, and in the morning they bring him before the magistrates. Likewise if in the daytime they find any poor cripple unable to work for his livelihood, they take him to one of the hospitals, of which there are many, founded by the ancient kings, and endowed with great revenues. Or if he be capable of work they oblige him to take up some trade. If they see that any house has caught fire they immediately beat upon that wooden instrument to give the alarm, and this brings together the watchmen from the other bridges to help to extinguish it, and to save the goods of the merchants or others, either by removing them to the towers above mentioned, or by putting them in boats and transporting them to the islands in the lake. For no citizen dares leave his house at night, or to come near the fire; only those who own the property, and those watchmen who flock to help, of whom there shall come one or two thousand at the least.

Moreover, within the city there is an eminence on which stands a Tower, and at the top of the tower is hung a slab of wood. Whenever fire or any other alarm breaks out in the city a man who stands there with a mallet in his hand beats upon the slab, making a noise that is heard to a great distance. So when the blows upon this slab are heard, everybody is aware that fire has broken out, or that there is some other cause of alarm.

The Kaan watches this city with especial diligence because it forms the head of all Manzi, and because he has an immense revenue from the duties levied on the transactions of trade therein, the amount of which is such that no one would credit it on mere hearsay.

All the streets of the city are paved with stone or brick, as indeed are all the highways throughout Manzi, so that you ride and travel in every direction without inconvenience. Were it not for this pavement you could not do so, for the country is very low and flat, and after rain 'tis deep in mire and water. But as the

Great Kaan's couriers could not gallop their horses over the pavement, the side of the road is left unpaved for their convenience. The pavement of the main street of the city also is laid out in two parallel ways of ten paces in width on either side, leaving a space in the middle laid with fine gravel, under which are vaulted drains which convey the rain water into the canals; and thus the road is kept ever dry.

You must know also that the city of Kinsay has some 3000 baths, the water of which is supplied by springs. They are hot baths, and the people take great delight in them, frequenting them several times a month, for they are very cleanly in their persons. They are the finest and largest baths in the world; large enough for 100 persons to bathe together.

And the Ocean Sea comes within 25 miles of the city at a place called Ganfu, where there is a town [*note: since covered by the sea, which is much closer*] and an excellent haven, with a vast amount of shipping which is engaged in the traffic to and from India and other foreign parts, exporting and importing many kinds of wares, by which the city benefits. And a great river [*the Ts'ien T'ang*] flows from the city of Kinsay to that sea-haven, by which vessels can come up to the city itself. This river extends also to other places further inland.

Know also that the Great Kaan hath distributed the territory of Manzi into nine parts, which he hath constituted into nine kingdoms. To each of these kingdoms a king is appointed who is subordinate to the Great Kaan, and every year renders the accounts of his kingdom to the fiscal office at the capital. This city of Kinsay is the seat of one of these kings, who rules over 140 great and wealthy cities. For in the whole of this vast country of Manzi there are more than 1200 great and wealthy cities, without counting the towns and villages, which are in great numbers. And you may receive it for certain that in each of those 1200 cities the Great Kaan has a garrison, and that the smallest of such garrisons musters 1000 men; whilst there are some of 10,000, 20,000, and 30,000; so that the total number of troops is something scarcely calculable. The troops forming these garrisons are not all Tartars. Many are from the province of Cathay, [*note: Cathay means China north of the Hwang-ho*] and good soldiers too. But you must not suppose they are by any means all of them cavalry; a very large proportion of them are foot-soldiers, according to the special requirements of each city. And all of them belong to the army of the Great Kaan.

I repeat that everything appertaining to this city is on so vast a scale, and the Great Kaan's yearly revenues therefrom are so immense, that it is not easy even to put it in writing, and it seems past belief to one who merely hears it told. But I will write it down for you.

First, however, I must mention another thing. The people of this country have a custom, that as soon as a child is born they write down the day and hour and the planet and sign under which its birth has taken place; so that every one among them knows the day of his birth. And when any one intends a journey he goes to the astrologers, and gives the particulars of his nativity in order to learn whether he shall have good luck or no. Sometimes they will say no, and in that case the journey is put off till such day as the astrologer may recommend. These astrologers are very skillful at their business, and often their words come to pass, so the people have great faith in them.

They burn the bodies of the dead. And when any one dies the friends and relations make a great mourning for the deceased, and clothe themselves in hempen garments, and follow the corpse playing on a variety of instruments and singing hymns to their idols. And when they come to the burning place, they take representations of things cut out of parchment, such as caparisoned horses, male and female slaves, camels, armour, suits of cloth of gold (and money), in great quantities, and these things they put on the fire along with the corpse, so that they are all burnt with it. And they tell you that the dead man shall have all these slaves and animals of which the effigies are burnt, alive in flesh and blood, and the money in gold, at his disposal in the next world; and that the instruments which they have caused to be played at his funeral, and the idol hymns that have been chanted, shall also be produced again to welcome him in the next world; and that the idols themselves will come to do him honour.

Furthermore there exists in this city the palace of the king who fled, him who was Emperor of Manzi [*the Emperor Tu-Tsong*], and that is the greatest palace in the world, as I shall tell you more particularly. For you must know its demesne hath a compass of ten miles, all enclosed with lofty battlemented walls; and inside the walls are the finest and most delectable gardens upon earth, and filled too with the finest fruits. There are numerous fountains in it also, and lakes full of fish. In the middle is the palace itself, a great and splendid building. It contains 20 great and handsome halls, one of which is more spacious than the rest, and affords room for a vast multitude to dine. It is all painted in gold, with many histories and representations of beasts and birds, of knights and dames, and many marvellous things. It forms a really magnificent spectacle, for over all the walls and all the ceiling you see nothing but paintings in gold. And besides these halls the palace contains 1000 large and handsome chambers, all painted in gold and divers colours.

Moreover, I must tell you that in this city there are 160 *tomans* of fires, or in other words 160 *tomans* of houses. Now I should tell you that the *toman* is 10,000, so that you can reckon the total as altogether 1,600,000 houses, among which are a great number of rich palaces. There is one church only, belonging to the Nestorian Christians.

There is another thing I must tell you. It is the custom for every burgess of this city, and in fact for every description of person in it, to write over his door his own name, the name of his wife, and those of his children, his slaves, and all the inmates of his house, and also the number of animals that he keeps. And if any one dies in the house then the name of that person is erased, and if any child is born its name is added. So in this way the sovereign is able to know exactly the population of the city. And this is the practice also throughout all Manzi and Cathay.

And I must tell you that every hosteler who keeps an hostel for travellers is bound to register their names and surnames, as well as the day and month of their arrival and departure. And thus the sovereign hath the means of knowing, whenever it pleases him, who come and go throughout his dominions. And certes this is a wise order and a provident.

FURTHER PARTICULARS CONCERNING
THE GREAT CITY OF KINSAY

The position of the city is such that it has on one side a lake of fresh and exquisitely clear water (already spoken of), and on the other a very large river. The waters of the latter fill a number of canals of all sizes which run through the different quarters of the city, carry away all impurities, and then enter the Lake; whence they issue again and flow to the Ocean, thus producing a most excellent atmosphere. By means of these channels, as well as by the streets, you can go all about the city. Both streets and canals are so wide and spacious that carts on the one and boats on the other can readily pass to and fro, conveying necessary supplies to the inhabitants.

At the opposite side the city is shut in by a channel, perhaps 40 miles in length, very wide, and full of water derived from the river aforesaid, which was made by the ancient kings of the country in order to relieve the river when flooding its banks. This serves also as a defence to the city, and the earth dug from it has been thrown inwards, forming a kind of mound enclosing the city.

In this part are the ten principal markets, though besides these there are a vast number of others in the different parts of the town. The former are all squares of half a mile to the side, and along their front passes the main street, which is 40 paces in width, and runs straight from end to end of the city, crossing many bridges of easy and commodious approach. At every four miles of its length comes one of those great squares of 2 Miles (as we have mentioned) in compass. So also parallel to this great street, but at the back of the market places, there runs a very large canal, on the bank of which towards the squares are built great houses of stone, in which the merchants from India and other foreign parts store their wares, to be handy for the markets. In each of the squares is held a market three days in the week, frequented by 40,000 or 50,000 persons, who bring thither for sale every possible necessary of life, so that there is always an ample supply of every kind of meat and game, as of roebuck, red-deer, fallow-deer, hares, rabbits, partridges, pheasants, francolins, quails, fowls, capons, and of duck and geese an infinite quantity; for so many are bred on the Lake that for a Venice groat of silver you can have a couple of geese and two couple of ducks.

Then there are the shambles where the larger animals are slaughtered, such as calves, beeves, kids, and lambs, the flesh of which is eaten by the rich and the great dignitaries.

Those markets make a daily display of every kind of vegetables and fruits; and among the latter there are in particular certain pears of enormous size, weighing as much as ten pounds apiece, and the pulp of which is white and fragrant like a confection; besides peaches in their season both yellow and white, of every delicate Ravour.

Neither grapes nor wine are produced there, but very good raisins are brought from abroad, and wine likewise. The natives, however, do not much care about wine, being used to that kind of their own made from rice and spices. From the Ocean Sea also come daily supplies of fish in great quantity, brought 25 miles up the river, and there is also great store of fish from the lake, which is the constant resort of fishermen, who have no other business. Their fish is of sundry kinds, changing with the season; and, owing to the impurities of the city which pass into the lake, it is remarkably fat and savoury. Any one who should see the supply of fish in the market would suppose it impossible that such a quantity could ever be sold; and yet in a few hours the whole shall be cleared away; so great is the number of inhabitants who are accustomed to delicate living. Indeed they eat fish and flesh at the same meal.

All the ten market places are encompassed by lofty houses, and below these are shops where all sorts of crafts are carried on, and all sorts of wares are on sale, including spices and jewels and pearls.

Some of these shops are entirely devoted to the sale of wine made from rice and spices, which is constantly made fresh, and is sold very cheap.

Certain of the streets are occupied by the women of the town, who are in such a number that I dare not say what it is. They are found not only in the vicinity of the market places, where usually a quarter is assigned to them, but all over the city. They exhibit themselves splendidly attired and abundantly perfumed, in finely garnished houses, with trains of waiting-women. These women are extremely accomplished in all the arts of allurement, and readily adapt their conversation to all sorts of persons, insomuch that strangers who have once tasted their attractions seem to get bewitched, and are so taken with their blandishments and their fascinating ways that they never can get these out of their heads. Hence it comes to pass that when they return home they say they have been to Kinsay or the City of Heaven, and their only desire is to get back thither as soon as possible.

Other streets are occupied by the Physicians, and by the Astrologers, who are also teachers of reading and writing; and an infinity of other professions have their places round about those squares. In each of the squares there are two great palaces facing one another, in which are established the officers appointed by the King to decide differences arising between merchants, or other inhabitants of the quarter. It is the daily duty of these officers to see that the guards are at their posts on the neighbouring bridges, and to punish them at their discretion if they are absent.

All along the main street that we have spoken of, as running from end to end of the city, both sides are lined with houses and great palaces and the gardens pertaining to them, whilst in the intervals are the houses of tradesmen engaged in their different crafts. The crowd of people that you meet here at all hours, passing this way and that on their different errands, is so vast that no one would believe it possible that victuals enough could be provided for their consumption, unless they should see how, on every market-day, all those squares are thronged and crammed with purchasers, and with the traders who have brought in stores of provisions by land or water; and everything they bring in is disposed of.

To give you an example of the vast consumption in this city let us take the article of *pepper;* and that will enable you in some measure to estimate what must be the quantity of victual, such as meat, wine, groceries, which have to be provided for the general consumption. Now Messer Marco heard it stated by one of the Great Kaan's officers of customs that the quantity of pepper introduced daily for consumption into the city of Kinsay amounted to 43 loads, each load being equal to 2–23 lbs.

The houses of the citizens are well built and elaborately finished; and the delight they take in decoration, in painting and in architecture, leads them to spend in this way sums of money that would astonish you.

The natives of the city are men of peaceful character, both from education and from the example of their kings, whose disposition was the same. They know nothing of handling arms, and keep none in their houses. You hear of no feuds or noisy quarrels or dissensions of any kind among them. Both in their commercial dealings and in their manufactures they are thoroughly honest and truthful, and there is such a degree of good will and neighbourly attachment among both men and women that you would take the people who live in the same street to be all one family.

And this familiar intimacy is free from all jealousy or suspicion of the conduct of their women. These they treat with the greatest respect, and a man who should presume to make loose proposals to a married woman would be regarded as an infamous rascal. They also treat the foreigners who visit them for the sake of trade with great cordiality, and entertain them in the most winning manner, affording them every help and advice on their business. But on the other hand they hate to see soldiers, and not least those of the Great Kaan's garrisons, regarding them as the cause of their having lost their native kings and lords.

On the Lake of which we have spoken there are numbers of boats and barges of all sizes for parties of pleasure. These will hold 10, 15, 20, or more persons, and are from 15 to 20 paces in length, with flat bottoms and ample breadth of beam, so that they always keep their trim. Any one who desires to go a-pleasuring with the women, or with a party of his own sex, hires one of these barges, which are always to be found completely furnished with tables and chairs and all the other apparatus for a feast. The roof forms a level deck, on which the crew stand, and pole the boat along whithersoever may he desired, for the Lake is not more than 2 paces in depth. The inside of this roof and the rest of the interior is covered with ornamental painting in gay colours, with windows all round that can be shut or opened, so that the party at table can enjoy all the beauty and variety of the prospects on both sides as they pass along. And truly a trip on this Lake is a much more charming recreation than can be enjoyed on land. For on the one side lies the city in its entire length, so that the spectators in the barges, from the distance at which they stand, take in the whole prospect in its full beauty and grandeur, with its numberless palaces, temples, monasteries, and gardens, full of lofty trees, sloping to the shore. And the Lake is never without a number of other such boats, laden with pleasure parties; for it is the great delight of the citizens here, after they have disposed of the day's business, to pass the afternoon in enjoyment with the ladies of their families, or perhaps with others less reputable, either in these barges or in driving about the city in carriages.

TREATING OF THE GREAT YEARLY REVENUE THAT THE GREAT KAAN HATH FROM KINSAY

Now I will tell you about the great revenue which the Great Kaan draweth every year from the said city of Kinsay and its territory, forming a ninth part of the whole country of Manzi.

First there is the salt, which brings in a great revenue. For it produces every year, in round numbers, fourscore *tomans* of gold; and the *toman* is worth 70,000 *saggi* [*A Venetian saggi was 1/6th of an ounce*] of gold, so that the total value of the fourscore *tomans* will be five millions and six hundred thousand *saggi* of gold, each *saggio* being worth more than a gold florin or ducat; in sooth, a vast sum of money! [This province, you see, adjoins the ocean, on the shores of which are many lagoons or salt marshes, in which the sea-water dries up during the summer time; and thence they extract such a quantity of salt as suffices for the supply of five of the kingdoms of Manzi besides this one.]

Having told you of the revenue from salt, I will now tell you of that which accrues to the Great Kaan from the duties on merchandize and other matters.

You must know that in this city and its dependencies they make great quantities of sugar, as indeed they do in the other eight divisions of this country; so that I believe the whole of the rest of the world together does not produce such a quantity, at least, if that be true which many people have told me; and the sugar alone again produces an enormous revenue. However, I will not repeat the duties on every article separately, but tell you how they go in the lump. Well, all spicery pays three and a third per cent on the value; and all merchandize likewise pays three and a third per cent. But sea-borne goods from India and other distant countries pay ten per cent. The rice-wine also makes a great return, and coals, of which there is a great quantity; and so do the twelve guilds of craftsmen that I told you of, with their 12,000 stations apiece, for every article they make pays duty. And the silk which is produced in such abundance makes an immense return. But why should I make a long story of it? The silk, you must know, pays ten per cent, and many other articles also pay ten per cent.

And you must know that Messer Marco Polo, who relates all this, was several times sent by the Great Kaan to inspect the amount of his customs and revenue from this ninth part of Manzi, and he found it to be, exclusive of the salt revenue which we have mentioned already, 210 *tomans* of gold, equivalent to 14,700,000 *saggi* of gold; one of the most enormous revenues that ever was heard of. And if the sovereign has such a revenue from one ninth part of the country, you may judge what he must have from the whole of it! However, to speak the truth, this part is the greatest and most productive; and because of the great revenue that the Great Kaan derives from it, it is his favourite province, and he takes all the more care to watch it well, and to keep the people contented.

Now we will quit this city and speak of others.

From *The Book of Ser Marco Polo the Venetian concerning the Kingdoms and Marvels of the East,* trans. and ed. by Henry Yule, 3rd ed. revised by Henri Cordier (London: John Murray, 1903), Vol II. Pp. 185–193, 200–205, 215–216.

COLUMBUS' LETTER TO THE KING AND QUEEN OF SPAIN, 1494

(Undated, probably 1494)

Most High and Mighty Sovereigns,

In obedience to your Highnesses' commands, and with submission to superior judgment, I will say whatever occurs to me in reference to the colonization and commerce of the Island of Espanola, and of the other islands, both those already discovered and those that may be discovered hereafter.

In the first place, as regards the Island of Espanola: Inasmuch as the number of colonists who desire to go thither amounts to two thousand, owing to the land being safer and better for farming and trading, and because it will serve as a place to which they can return and from which they can carry on trade with the neighboring islands:

1. That in the said island there shall be founded three or four towns, situated in the most convenient places, and that the settlers who are there be assigned to the aforesaid places and towns.

2. That for the better and more speedy colonization of the said island, no one shall have liberty to collect gold in it except those who have taken out colonists' papers, and have built houses for their abode, in the town in which they are, that they may live united and in greater safety.

3. That each town shall have its alcalde [Mayor] . . . and its notary public, as is the use and custom in Castile.

4. That there shall be a church, and parish priests or friars to administer the sacraments, to perform divine worship, and for the conversion of the Indians.

5. That none of the colonists shall go to seek gold without a license from the governor or alcalde of the town where he lives; and that he must first take oath to return to the place whence he sets out, for the purpose of registering faithfully all the gold he may have found, and to

return once a month, or once a week, as the time may have been set for him, to render account and show the quantity of said gold; and that this shall be written down by the notary before the alcalde, or, if it seems better, that a friar or priest, deputed for the purpose, shall be also present.

6. That all the gold thus brought in shall be smelted immediately, and stamped with some mark that shall distinguish each town; and that the portion which belongs to your Highnesses shall be weighed, and given and consigned to each alcalde in his own town, and registered by the above-mentioned priest or friar, so that it shall not pass through the hands of only one person, and there shall he no opportunity to conceal the truth.

7. That all gold that may be found without the mark of one of the said towns in the possession of any one who has once registered in accordance with the above order shall be taken as forfeited, and that the accuser shall have one portion of it and your Highnesses the other.

8. That one per centum of all the gold that may be found shall be set aside for building churches and adorning the same, and for the support of the priests or friars belonging to them; and, if it should be thought proper to pay any thing to the alcaldes or notaries for their services, or for ensuring the faithful perforce of their duties, that this amount shall be sent to the governor or treasurer who may be appointed there by your Highnesses.

9. As regards the division of the gold, and the share that ought to be reserved for your Highnesses, this, in my opinion, must be left to the aforesaid governor and treasurer, because it will have to be greater or less according to the quantity of gold that may be found. Or, should it seem preferable, your Highnesses might, for the space of one year, take one half, and the collector the other, and a better arrangement for the division be made afterward.

10. That if the said alcaldes or notaries shall commit or be privy to any fraud, punishment shall be provided, and the same for the colonists who shall not have declared all the gold they have.

11. That in the said island there shall be a treasurer, with a clerk to assist him, who shall receive all the gold belonging to your Highnesses, and the alcaldes and notaries of the towns shall each keep a record of what they deliver to the said treasurer.

12. As, in the eagerness to get gold, every one will wish, naturally, to engage in its search in preference to any other employment, it seems to me that the privilege of going to look for gold ought to be withheld

during some portion of each year, that there may be opportunity to have the other business necessary for the island performed.

13. In regard to the discovery of new countries, I think permission should be granted to all that wish to go, and more liberality used in the matter of the fifth, making the tax easier, in some fair way, in order that many may be disposed to go on voyages.

I will now give my opinion about ships going to the said Island of Espanola, and the order that should be maintained; and that is, that the said ships should only be allowed to discharge in one or two ports designated for the purpose, and should register there whatever cargo they bring or unload; and when the time for their departure comes, that they should sail from these same ports, and register all the cargo they take in, that nothing may be concealed.

- In reference to the transportation of gold from the island to Castile, that all of it should be taken on board the ship, both that belonging to your Highnesses and the property of every one else; that it should all be placed in one chest with two locks, with their keys, and that the master of the vessel keep one key and some person selected by the governor and treasurer the other; that there should come with the gold, for a testimony, a list of all that has been put into the said chest, properly marked, so that each owner may receive his own; and that, for the faithful performance of this duty, if any gold whatsoever is found outside of the said chest in any way, be it little or much, it shall be forfeited to your Highnesses.

- That all the ships that come from the said island shall be obliged to make their proper discharge in the port of Cadiz, and that no person shall disembark or other person be permitted to go on board until the ship has been visited by the person or persons deputed for that purpose, in the said city, by your Highnesses, to whom the master shall show all that he carries, and exhibit the manifest of all the cargo, it may be seen and examined if the said ship brings any thing hidden and not known at the time of lading.

- That the chest in which the said gold has been carried shall be opened in the presence of the magistrates of the said city of Cadiz, and of the person deputed for that purpose by your Highnesses, and his own property be given to each owner.

I beg your Highnesses to hold me in your protection; and I remain, praying our Lord God for your Highnesses' lives and the increase of much greater States.

This text is widely available on the Internet, but there is no statement of its printed origins. If you know, please send references to be included here, halsall@murray.fordham.edu.

AZTEC ACCOUNT OF THE CONQUEST, 1519

Miguel Leon Portilla, translated by missionaries in the 1500s and 1600s

SPEECHES OF MOTECUHZOMA AND CORTES

When Motecuhzoma had given necklaces to each one, Cortes asked him: "Are you Motecuhzoma? Are you the king? Is it true that you are the king Motecuhzoma?"

And the king said: "Yes, I am Motecuhzoma." Then he stood up to welcome Cortes; he came forward, bowed his head low and addressed him in these words: "Our lord, you are weary. The journey has tired you, but now you have arrived on the earth. You have come to your city, Mexico. You have come here to sit on your throne, to sit under its canopy.

"The kings who have gone before, your representatives, guarded it and preserved it for your coming. The kings Itzcoatl, Motecuhzoma the Elder, Axayacatl, Tizoc and Ahuitzol ruled for you in the City of Mexico. The people were protected by their swords and sheltered by their shields.

"Do the kings know the destiny of those they left behind, their posterity? If only they are watching! If only they can see what I see!

"No, it is not a dream. I am not walking in my sleep. I am not seeing you in my dreams. . . . I have seen you at last! I have met you face to face! I was in agony for five days, for ten days, with my eyes fixed on the Region of the Mystery. And now you have come out of the clouds and mists to sit on your throne again.

"This was foretold by the kings who governed your city, and now it has taken place. You have come back to us; you have come down from the sky. Rest now, and take possession of your royal houses. Welcome to your land, my lords!"

When Motecuhzoma had finished, La Malinche translated his address into Spanish so that the Captain could understand it. Cortes replied in his strange and savage tongue, speaking first to La Malinche: "Tell Motecuhzoma that we are his friends. There is nothing to fear. We have wanted to see him for a long time, and now we have seen his face and heard his words. Tell him that we love him well and that our hearts are contented."

Then he said to Motecuhzoma: "We have come to your house in Mexico as friends. There is nothing to fear."

La Malinche translated this speech and the Spaniards grasped Motecuhzoma's hands and patted his back to show their affection for him.

ATTITUDES OF THE SPANIARDS AND THE NATIVE LORDS

The Spaniards examined everything they saw. They dismounted from their horses, and mounted them again, and dismounted again, so as not to miss anything of interest.

The chiefs who accompanied Motecuhzoma were: Cacama, king of Tezcoco; Tetlepanquetzaltzin, king of Tlacopan; Itzcuauhtzin the Tlacochcalcatl, lord of Tlatelolco; and Topantemoc, Motecuhzoma's treasurer in Tlatelolco. These four chiefs were standing in a file.

The other princes were: Atlixcatzin [chief who has taken captives][1]; Tepeoatzin, The Tlacochcalcatl; Quetzalaztatzin, the keeper of the chalk; Totomotzin; Hecateupatiltzin; and Cuappiatzin.

When Motecuhzoma was imprisoned, they all went into hiding. They ran away to hide and treacherously abandoned him!

THE SPANIARDS TAKE POSSESSION OF THE CITY

When the Spaniards entered the Royal House, they placed Motecuhzoma under guard and kept him under their vigilance. They also placed a guard over Itzcuauhtzin, but the other lords were permitted to depart.

Then the Spaniards fired one of their cannons, and this caused great confusion in the city. The people scattered in every direction; they fled without rhyme or reason; they ran off as if they were being pursued. It was as if they had eaten the mushrooms that confuse the mind, or had seen some dreadful apparition. They were all overcome by terror, as if their hearts had fainted. And when night fell, the panic spread through the city and their fears would not let them sleep.

In the morning the Spaniards told Motecuhzoma what they needed in the way of supplies: tortillas, fried chickens, hens' eggs, pure water, firewood and charcoal. Also: large, clean cooking pots, water jars, pitchers, dishes and other pottery. Motecuhzoma ordered that it be sent to them. The chiefs who received

---

[1] Military title given to a warrior who had captured four enemies.

this order were angry with the king and no longer revered or respected him. But they furnished the Spaniards with all the provisions they needed—food, beverages and water, and fodder for the horses.

THE SPANIARDS REVEAL THEIR GREED

When the Spaniards were installed in the palace, they asked Motecuhzoma about the city's resources and reserves and about the warriors' ensigns and shields. They questioned him closely and then demanded gold.

Motecuhzoma guided them to it. They surrounded him and crowded close with their weapons. He walked in the center, while they formed a circle around him.

When they arrived at the treasure house called Teucalco, the riches of gold and feathers were brought out to them: ornaments made of quetzal feathers, richly worked shields, disks of gold, the necklaces of the idols, gold nose plugs, gold greaves and bracelets and crowns.

The Spaniards immediately stripped the feathers from the gold shields and ensigns. They gathered all the gold into a great mound and set fire to everything else, regardless of its value. Then they melted down the gold into ingots. As for the precious green stones, they took only the best of them; the rest were snatched up by the Tlaxcaltecas. The Spaniards searched through the whole treasure house, questioning and quarreling, and seized every object they thought was beautiful.

THE SEIZURE OF MOTECUHZOMA'S TREASURES

Next they went to Motecuhzoma's storehouse, in the place called Totocalco [Place of the Palace of the Birds],[2] where his personal treasures were kept. The Spaniards grinned like little beasts and patted each other with delight.

When they entered the hall of treasures, it was as if they had arrived in Paradise. They searched everywhere and coveted everything; they were slaves to their own greed. All of Motecuhzoma's possessions were brought out: fine bracelets, necklaces with large stones, ankle rings with little gold bells, the royal crowns and all the royal finery—everything that belonged to the king and was reserved to him only. They seized these treasures as if they were their own, as if this plunder were merely a stroke of good luck. And when they had taken all the gold, they heaped up everything else in the middle of the patio.

La Malinche called the nobles together. She climbed up to the palace roof and cried: "Mexicanos, come forward! The Spaniards need your help! Bring them

---

[2] The zoological garden attached to the royal palaces.

food and pure water. They are tired and hungry; they are almost fainting from exhaustion! Why do you not come forward? Are you angry with them?"

The Mexicans were too frightened to approach. They were crushed by terror and would not risk coming forward. They shied away as if the Spaniards were wild beasts, as if the hour were midnight on the blackest night of the year. Yet they did not abandon the Spaniards to hunger and thirst. They brought them whatever they needed, but shook with fear as they did so. They delivered the supplies to the Spaniards with trembling hands, then turned and hurried away.

THE PREPARATIONS FOR THE FIESTA

The Aztecs begged permission of their king to hold the fiesta of Huitzilopochtli. The Spaniards wanted to see this fiesta to learn how it was celebrated. A delegation of the celebrants came to the palace where Motecuhzoma was a prisoner, and when their spokesman asked his permission, he granted it to them.

As soon as the delegation returned, the women began to grind seeds of the chicalote.[3] These women had fasted for a whole year. They ground the seeds in the patio of the temple.

The Spaniards came out of the palace together, dressed in armor and carrying their weapons with them. They stalked among the women and looked at them one by one; they stared into the faces of the women who were grinding seeds. After this cold inspection, they went back into the palace. It is said that they planned to kill the celebrants if the men entered the patio.

THE STATUE OF HUITZILOPOCHTLI

On the evening before the fiesta of Toxcatl, the celebrants began to model a statue of Huitzilopochtli. They gave it such a human appearance that it seemed the body of a living man. Yet they made the statue with nothing but a paste made of the ground seeds of the chicalote, which they shaped over an armature of sticks.

When the statue was finished, they dressed it in rich feathers, and they painted crossbars over and under its eyes. They also clipped on its earrings of turquoise mosaic; these were in the shape of serpents, with gold rings hanging from them. Its nose plug, in the shape of an arrow, was made of gold and was inlaid with fine stones.

They placed the magic headdress of hummingbird feathers on its head. They also adorned it with an *anecuyotl*, which was a belt made of feathers, with a cone at the back. Then they hung around its neck an ornament of yellow parrot feathers, fringed like the locks of a young boy. Over this they put its nettle-

---

3 Edible plants also used in medicines.

leaf cape, which was painted black and decorated with five clusters of eagle feathers.

Next they wrapped it in its cloak, which was painted with skull and bones, and over this they fastened its vest. The vest was painted with dismembered human parts: skulls, ears, hearts, intestines, torsos, breasts, hands and feet. They also put on its *maxtlatl*, or loincloth, which was decorated with images of dissevered limbs and fringed with amate paper. This *maxtlatl* was painted with vertical stripes of bright blue.

They fastened a red paper flag at its shoulder and placed on its head what looked like a sacrificial flint knife. This too was made of red paper; it seemed to have been steeped in blood.

The statue carried a *tehuehuelli*, a bamboo shield decorated with four clusters of fine eagle feathers. The pendant of this shield was blood-red, like the knife and the shoulder flag. The statue also carried four arrows.

Finally, they put the wristbands on its arms. These bands, made of coyote skin, were fringed with paper cut into little strips.

THE BEGINNING OF THE FIESTA

Early the next morning, the statue's face was uncovered by those who had been chosen for that ceremony. They gathered in front of the idol in single file and offered it gifts of food, such as round seedcakes or perhaps human flesh. But they did not carry it up to its temple on top of the pyramid.

All the young warriors were eager for the fiesta to begin. They had sworn to dance and sing with all their hearts, so that the Spaniards would marvel at the beauty of the rituals.

The procession began, and the celebrants filed into the temple patio to dance the Dance of the Serpent. When they were all together in the patio, the songs and the dance began. Those who had fasted for twenty days and those who had fasted for a year were in command of the others; they kept the dancers in file with their pine wands. (If anyone wished to urinate, he did not stop dancing, but simply opened his clothing at the hips and separated his clusters of heron feathers.)

If anyone disobeyed the leaders or was not in his proper place they struck him on the hips and shoulders. Then they drove him out of the patio, beating him and shoving him from behind. They pushed him so hard that he sprawled to the ground, and they dragged him outside by the ears. No one dared to say a word about this punishment, for those who had fasted during the year were feared and venerated; they had earned the exclusive title "Brothers of Huitzilopochtli."

The great captains, the bravest warriors, danced at the head of the files to guide the others. The youths followed at a slight distance. Some of the youths wore their hair gathered into large locks, a sign that they had never taken any captives. Others carried their headdresses on their shoulders; they had taken captives, but only with help.

Then came the recruits, who were called "the young warriors." They had each captured an enemy or two. The others called to them: "Come, comrades, show us how brave you are! Dance with all your hearts!"

THE SPANIARDS ATTACK THE CELEBRANTS

At this moment in the fiesta, when the dance was loveliest and when song was linked to song, the Spaniards were siezed with an urge to kill the celebrants. They all ran forward, armed as if for battle. They closed the entrances and passageways, all the gates of the patio: the Eagle Gate in the lesser palace, the Gate of the Canestalk and the Gate of the Serpent of Mirrors. They posted guards so that no one could escape, and then rushed into the Sacred Patio to slaughter the celebrants. They came on foot, carrying their swords and their wooden or metal shields.

They ran in among the dancers, forcing their way to the place where the drums were played. They attacked the man who was drumming and cut off his arms. Then they cut off his head, and it rolled across the floor.

They attacked all the celebrants, stabbing them, spearing them, striking them with their swords. They attacked some of them from behind, and these fell instantly to the ground with their entrails hanging out. Others they beheaded: they cut off their heads, or split their heads to pieces.

They struck others in the shoulders, and their arms were torn from their bodies. They wounded some in the thigh and some in the calf. They slashed others in the abdomen, and their entrails all spilled to the ground. Some attempted to run away, but their intestines dragged as they ran; they seemed to tangle their feet in their own entrails. No matter how they tried to save themselves, they could find no escape.

Some attempted to force their way out, but the Spaniards murdered them at the gates. Others climbed the walls, but they could not save themselves. Those who ran into the communal houses were safe there for a while; so were those who lay down among the victims and pretended to be dead. But if they stood up again, the Spaniards saw them and killed them.

The blood of the warriors flowed like water and gathered into pools. The pools widened, and the stench of blood and entrails filled the air. The Spaniards ran into the communal houses to kill those who were hiding. They ran everywhere and searched everywhere; they invaded every room, hunting and killing.

LETTER[1] FROM DOM AFONSO I, KING OF THE CONGO, TO DOM MANUEL I, KING OF PORTUGAL, 15 OCTOBER 1514

Translation and notes by Bentley Duncan

Most high and most powerful prince, king, and lord.

We, Dom Afonso,[2] by the grace of God, King of the Congo and Lord of the Ambundos,[3] &c.

We commend ourselves to your Highness as a King and Lord whom we love much, and we make it known to you that in the life of our father,[4] we being Christian and believing firmly in the faith of our Lord Jesus Christ, as did also Dom Pedro, my cousin, a nobleman of our country told our lord the king that I and my cousin Dom Pedro were Christians, and that we believed in God and not in the king's idols—whereupon the king our father said that he wanted the

---

[1] This is the longest and most detailed of twenty-two extant letters written by or for Afonso, king of the Congo, to the kings of Portugal, during the years 1512–40. The original manuscript is in Lisbon in the collection "Corpo Cronológico," Pt. I, Maço 16, Doc. 28, in the Arquivo Nacional da Torre do Tombo (Portuguese National Archives). Printed texts can be found in *História do Congo*, Paiva Manso, ed. (Lisbon, 1877), pp. 13–31, and in *Monumenta Missionaria Africana: África Ocidental 1471–1531*, António Duarte Brásio, ed. (Lisbon, 1952), pp. 294–323. The original text, which has virtually no punctuation, is marked by monotonous repetition, a limited vocabulary, strangled syntax, and strange errors (particularly in verb forms)—but these characteristics argue for its authenticity and support Afonso's claim, made at the end of the letter, that he dictated it without help from the Portuguese, whom he had reasons for avoiding. This translation necessarily presents a somewhat tidier apearance than the original.

[2] "Afonso" was the baptismal name given by the Portuguese to Nzinga a Mvemba, the *Mani-Congo* or "lord of the Congo," who ruled certain territories on the south bank of the Congo estuary from 1506 until his death in 1543.

[3] The lords of the Congo claimed sovereignty over their southern neighbors, the "Ambundos" or *Mbundu* of the Ndongo, whom they seldom managed to control.

said Dom Pedro brought to his compound where he would order him to be killed to see whether God would deliver him from there; and the king said that he would take away our incomes and would leave us to wander about like men blown by the wind until we died, or until he ordered us killed, and then he would see whether our Lord God would give us other people [followers?], since we were such great believers in Him.

And when the message reached us that our father wanted to have us killed, my cousin and I gave praises to our Lord God, for as to the flesh we feared greatly and felt much pain and anguish, but on the other hand as to our souls we felt much delight in dying for the love of our Lord, and not from any evil which we had ever done to our father. And while things were in this pass, our father died, and we, with the help of our Lord and of the glorious Virgin His Mother, came to this city[5] to take possession of the kingdom—and all the people and relatives and brothers were against us, and we had no other help save our Lord, and fathers Rodrigues Anes and António Fernandes,[6] who strongly aided us, since both prayed to our Lord to give us the upper hand over our enemies; and so it proved that He, by His mercy, gave us such a victory that we defeated them.[7]

Then there arrived in our kingdom a ship of Gonçalo Rodrigues[8] which had gone to Mina [in Guinea], and had come for these fathers, who had been here a long time—and we therefore sent them away and gave each of them, and also Gonçalo Rodrigues, 1,500 bracelets[9] and 50 slaves. And we wrote a letter to

---

[4] Nzinga a Nkuwu, lord of the Congo, who was baptized as João I (or John I) on 3 May 1491, and who died in 1506.

[5] Mbanza Congo ("Congo Place of Palaver"), seat of the lords of the Congo, and known to the Portuguese as São Salvador do Congo. It was about 130 miles inland from the mouth of the Congo, built on high ground away from the river.

[6] Rodrigues Anes and António Fernandes, missionaries to the Congo, are identified only as "cléricos de missa" (mass priests). According to a later reference in this letter, both died on their journey back to Portugal.

[7] The Congo was an elective monarchy, perhaps matrilineal in principle, with succession often going to the king's nephew (i.e., the king's eldest sister's son), and not to his sons. On the death of his father, Afonso—assisted by his mother, by the Christian lord of the coastal province of Sonyo, and by thirty-seven warriors, with their retainers—marched on the capital, where the heathen heir, Nzinga a Mpunza, was already entrenched. Afonso's forces defeated, captured and beheaded his rival. Afonso attributed the victory to divine intervention, in the form of a great white cross that appeared in the sky. These events probably occurred in 1506.

[8] Gonçalo Rodrigues Ribeiro was a ship captain and slave trader who spent many years in the Congo area. He was later brought to trial by the Portuguese authorities on charges of fraud, theft, and inhuman cruelty.

[9] Brass or copper bangles, which, although intended for the adornment of arms or ankles, were widely used on the West African coast as a kind of currency.

your Highness, which was in the hand of a certain Francisco Fernandes,[10] in which we gave you an account of the great victory and conquest which our Lord granted to us, and of how our kingdom was already that of Christians, and that your Highness should send us some clerics or friars to teach us and help us to increase the faith. So we sent Dom Henrique[11] our son, and our nephew Rodrigo de Santa Maria, to your Highness to have them taught. And also in the same ship we wrote a letter to Fernão de Melo[12] in which we requested him to send some priests to visit us so that we could be taught the things of God. And when the said fathers and Gonçalo Rodrigues reached the island [of São Tomé], and when Fernão de Melo saw how much cargo they were carrying, greed possessed him— and he sent here a ship without anything except one bed blanket, a door curtain, a carpet, a bed canopy, and one glass bottle—and he also sent one clergyman in the said ship. Gonçalo Pires came as captain and pilot, and João Godinho was the notary;[13] and we received the ship with great pleasure, for we understood her to have come in the service of God, but she had come out of great greediness.

Then we asked the said Gonçalo Pires if Fernão de Melo had a few ships in which to send us some cannon and rifles so that we could have the assistance necessary for burning a great house of idols—because if we tried to burn it without the help of the Christians, then soon war would be waged against us to kill us. He then told us that there were no ships, but that if we dispatched some goods with him he would exchange them and send us all the help we needed. And we, Sire, then wished to send whatever there was in our kingdom, and that all should be spent rather than have us lose the faith of our Lord; and this because if we, who were Gentiles a short time ago and had so recently been

---

[10] Francisco Fernandes served Afonso as a scribe for a certain time, but the king, as he explains later in this letter, soon grew to distrust him.

[11] This remarkable person, Dom Henrique, son of the king of the Congo, was sent to Portugal for training in theology. In 1513 he went to Rome for further study. By a brief of Pope Leo X, issued on 8 May 1518 at the request of the king of Portugal, Henrique was created Bishop of Utica (a town in North Africa) *in partibus infidelium*. Henrique returned to the Congo in 1521, and died there in 1535.

[12] Fernão de Melo, captain and governor of the island of São Tomé during the years 1499–1516, was the chief target of Afonso's complaints. The Equatorial island of São Tomé (330 sq. miles in area, 140 miles from the African mainland, and 570 miles northeast of the Congo estuary) had been settled by Portuguese convicts, adventurers, and expelled Jews, who, with the assistance of slave labor, developed large sugar plantations. The various officials in São Tomé controlled the religious, secular, and commercial affairs of the Congo, and they did not welcome any intrusion from Lisbon. For this reason Fernão de Melo, and others, tried to discourage Afonso from sending messages, emissaries, or presents to the king of Portugal.

[13] Large Portuguese ships usually carried four senior officers: captain, master, pilot, and notary—each with independent jurisdiction within his own sphere. The notary or scribe (*escrivão*) dealt with contracts, documents, and all legal matters.

taught the things of God, still grieved at losing the faith, how much more so Fernão de Melo, who was a Christian and the son of a Christian? And thus it seemed to us that he would be concerned for the faith of our Lord, and that with the property we sent him he would buy some ships and send them to us very quickly, so that he would help us to increase the faith of our Lord Jesus Christ and destroy the service of the Devil, and we would burn whatever idols could be found.

Then we asked the said Gonçalo Pires if fathers Rodrigues Anes and António Fernandes had arrived in Portugal, for they carried our letter to your Highness, and he told us that one of them had died at sea, and the other died on the island of Cape Verde. We felt great distress at the news, not only for their deaths but also because your Highness had not seen our letter, nor was there anyone to tell you about the great victory we had won.

Therefore, Sire, we decided to write another letter to your Highness, and we sent it with one of our nephews, called Dom Gonçalo, and one of our servants, called Manuel, and we sent them in the said ship of Fernão de Melo; and we sent 800 bracelets and 50 slaves to the said Fernão de Melo, and to his wife, to buy for us the succour that we need, and 50 bracelets to his son,[14] and 30 to the captain, and 20 to the notary. And crying many tears we have implored Fernão de Melo, for the love of our Lord, that he come and help us to win the faith of our Lord—for there were no other Christians among us except we, our cousin Dom Pedro, and our servants, and all the other people inclined to idols and were against us.

Then the said ship sailed on her way to Portugal and we remained—our cousin Dom Pedro and Francisco Fernandes, with the Christian people from Sonyo who had helped us to win that battle—waiting for a message from the said Fernão de Melo, and we waited one whole year without receiving his reply. Then, Sire, we decided to burn all those idols the most secretly that we could, and we no longer bothered about waiting for Fernão de Melo's help, because the assistance of Heaven is greater than that of earth, and our Lord would help us. And if it should happen that the people of our kingdom rose against us and murdered us, we would have received that death with patience, for our souls would have been saved.

So we started to burn all the idols. When the people saw this, they began to say that we were a wicked man, and they went and told tales to Dom Jorge Moxuebata,[15] who was the head man in our kingdom, inciting him to burn and destroy us. But our Lord worked on him in such a manner that He inspired him to be a Christian, and he answered those who spoke evil of us that he wished to

---

14 João de Melo, who in 1516 succeeded his father as captain of São Tomé.

15 I.e., Dom Jorge the *Mani-Mbata*, lord of Mbata, a large and populous district to the east and south of the capital. Next to the king, the *Mani-Mbata* was the most important personage in the domain, and his voice was evidently essential in the election of a new *Mani-Congo*.

learn about the faith of our Lord Jesus Christ, and that if he destroyed us, who were his uncle, that he who was closest in parentage to him would be king.[16] And in this brotherly manner we maintained our kingdom and Christianity.

A little time afterwards the fathers of Saint Eloy[17] arrived, whom your Highness had sent to us, and we, as soon as we had heard of their arrival in our kingdom, ordered that it be made known that all our nobles should go and receive them on the way. As soon as they had arrived at this city, we went into the compound and preached a sermon to all our people, in the following manner:

> Yea, brethren, ye know that the faith we have believed in up until now is all phantasm and wind, because the true faith is of our Lord God, creator of Heaven and Earth, who made our parents Adam and Eve and placed them in terrestrial paradise and forbade them to eat of a fruit that was there, and, by the deceits of the Devil, our mother Eve went and ate and broke the command of God and sinned, and then made our father Adam sin, by which all of us were condemned. And so we see that they, for breaking only one commandment, were lost, how much more so with us, who have ten commandments? But know ye how merciful is our Lord, who, seeing that our perdition was caused by a woman, wished that by another woman, our Lady the glorious Virgin, we should be saved—and sent his blessed Son to take on human flesh in her precious womb so that we could be redeemed and saved. He received passion and death to save us, and left twelve apostles to preach in all the world and teach His holy faith, and whosoever believed would be saved and gain His holy Kingdom—of which, until now, we have not had the means of knowing. Now, brethren, that He has opened the way to our salvation, let all of you rejoice to be Christians and learn the things of His faith, and follow the example of these men, who are His servants, and who are very chaste and virtuous, and maintain much austerity and fasting, and keep a very holy life. And as for the sticks and stones that you others worship, our Lord gave us the sticks for timber and the stones for the making of houses.

---

[16] Meaning not clear; possibly an allusion to the succession of nephews.

[17] The first Congolese to arrive in Portugal were entrusted to the care of the convent-church of St. Eloy (or St. Eligius) in Lisbon to be trained there in the Portuguese language and in Christian doctrine. The secular canons of St. John the Evangelist, who served in the cloister of St. Eligius—and were therefore loosely known as "Lóios" ("Eloyans" or "Eligians"), or as the fathers of St. Eloy, and often called the "Blue Canons" (from their blue-colored habit)—thus acquired a special interest in African missions. Judging from Afonso's complaints, these Portuguese priests, as mere secular canons, were poorly trained and unsuited for the austerities and temptations of the Congo mission. Their major missionary venture came in 1509, when thirteen canons, with Father João de Santa Maria as head of mission, arrived in the Congo.

And then a multitude of men and women were converted and became Christians. After this we gathered together all our brothers, sons, nephews, and our servants' sons—so that there were a good 400 boys and young men—and we ordered them to build some great walls, with many thorns on top, so that they could not leap over them and run away, and we delivered them to the said fathers to be taught. Also we ordered that other walls be erected adjacent to these walls, with four houses inside, so that the fathers could remain together [in cloister], as their order required. The said fathers did not remain together for more than three or four days, and João de Santa Maria[18] soon disrupted the community—and then two of the fathers asked our permission to return to Portugal, for your Highness had sent them here to serve God and give a good example, but that others were disregarding the rules of the order, and they wished to leave rather than witness so great an evil—and they were António de Santa Cruz and Diogo de Santa Maria—and Father Aleixos died of disgust. And then the other fathers asked us to elect Pero Fernandes as their superior, for they did not wish to remain encloistered and they devised this snare for us, so that each man would be on his own—but we told them that we had not the ecclesiastical power of appointment. And thus they separated, each one to his own house, and each took certain boys he himself taught, and then they came to us every day in the world to importune us and ask for money, which we gave them—so that they all began to deal in buying and selling.

We, seeing their laxity, besought them for the love of our Lord Jesus Christ, that if they were to buy some slaves, that they should not purchase any women, so that they would not give a bad example, nor make a liar out of us before our people, concerning the things we had preached. Yet notwithstanding they began to fill the houses with whores, in such a fashion that Father Pero Fernandes impregnated a woman in his house and she gave birth to a mulatto. Therefore the boys whom they taught and kept in their houses would run away and tell their fathers, mothers, and relatives. And thus all began to mock and ridicule us, saying that what we had told them was all lies, and that the white men had deceived us—at which we were much distressed and knew not what to answer.

Sometime later, Estevão da Rocha[19] arrived at the river in a ship, and he told us that he was your Highness' chamber boy, and that he came with your orders to arrest Gonçalo Rodrigues,[20] so that we were greatly pleased. Since we asked him about your Highness' order to arrest Gonçalo Rodrigues, he told us that the order was for Fernão de Melo to arrest him if he were at the island [of São Tomé], but that since Fernão de Melo did not know his whereabouts, he had come to look for him—and that if we wished to write to your Highness, or send

---

[18] See the preceding note.

[19] Not otherwise identified.

[20] See note 8.

some message, that he would take it. And we, trusting him, since he said he was your servant, sent Dom Pedro with him. Dom Pedro was once our opponent, who had a great host of people to fight against us, but a Cross appeared to them in the sky, and impressed them in such a manner that they had not the heart to fight. And then the said Dom Pedro turned Christian with many people, because of the miracle they had all seen.[21] We sent him to your Highness so that he himself could relate what he had seen. And thus we sent Dom Pedro our cousin, Dom Manuel our brother, and some others (our nephews) and we sent a letter to your Highness and another to Queen Dona Leonor[22]—and with our relatives we sent 700 bracelets, many slaves, parrots, animals, and civet cats.

Estevão da Rocha asked us to send the goods on ahead of him, which we did, and they were placed in the said ship—and afterwards he followed with our relatives. As soon as he arrived at the ship and saw that the goods were already inside, he seized the letters to your Highness and threw them away on to the ground; he also broke the arm of one of our nephews, Dom Pedro de Castro by name, who was there and did not wish to leave the ship, but clung to her. And thus he ejected the said Dom Pedro and all our relatives, and left with everything we were sending to your Highness. This was done on the advice of Francisco Fernandes, who wrote him a letter by one of our school boys, and for this reason we ordered the arrest of the said Francisco Fernandes; and then we ordered the schoolboy to be killed, for he was ours, and then released Francisco Fernandes.[23] And many other things happened that are too long to relate, but when our people and our noblemen saw these things they began to take little heed of our commands, and made fun of us.

At this time we left to go to a forest and have some timber cut to make wooden walls to keep the schoolboys inside. And then a ship of Fernão de Melo's arrived at our kingdom, with his nephew Estevão Jusarte as captain, and Lopo Ferreira as notary, with whom came our nephew Dom Gonçalo[24] and our servant Manuel. And then we asked the said Estevão Jusarte if he brought an answer to the letter which we had sent to your Highness by our nephew, and he told us that, when Dom Gonçalo was leaving [Lisbon], your Highness had him sent for, to give him the reply, but he did not wish to return and for this reason did not bring it—but that your Highness had written to us by way of another ship, com-

[21] See note 7.

[22] She was Leonor the queen dowager (d. 1525), widow of John II (king of Portugal during 1481–1495), and sister of Manuel I (king of Portugal during 1495–1521). She should not be confused with Leonor (d. 1558), sister of the Emperor Charles V, who became Dom Manuel's third wife in 1518.

[23] Francisco Fernandes served Afonso as a scribe for a certain time.

[24] Dom Gonçalo was one of quite a few upper-class Congolese who traveled to Portugal. Gonçalo and his manservant Manuel seem to have left the Congo in the middle of 1508, and both returned about 1510.

ing behind, and was sending us many things, and clergy for the service of God. And then we told him that everything your Highness did, even though we might be hurt by the possible delay, we would receive with patience.

Then we asked him to come to this our city, and he gave us twenty pieces of foreign [European] cloth, which were not for dressing mice in,[25] the which pieces amounted in all to 40 or 50 *covados*.[26] And the said Estevão Jusarte, as soon as he arrived at this city, began to communicate with a certain Cristóvão de Aguiar, a nephew of Gonçalo Rodrigues,[27] who had once been in our kingdom—and the said Cristóvão de Aguiar gave us a blue bed blanket and 15 *covados* [about 33 feet] of foreign cloth. He told us that these things were a gift, and that when he wished to return to Portugal that we should give him some slaves, or some money to buy slaves—and so we gave him so much money,[28] aside from the other things we gave him, that he bought 27 slaves. And the said Estevão Jusarte told us that he was your Highness' nephew, and that Fernão de Melo was your cousin—and when we learned this we rejoiced with him, for we assumed that what he said was true, and we did him many favors, attended to him quickly, and sent 1,000 bracelets and certain slaves to the said Fernão de Melo, and 300 bracelets and 20 slaves to the said Estevão Jusarte, for he told us he was your Highness' nephew[29]—and so we gave him many cloths, certain leopard skins, 20 pots of honey, and four civet cats, for Fernão de Melo—for he told us that if we sent bracelets and slaves to your Highness, that your Highness would remember us. Thus we sent João Fernandes[30] with him, with 400 bracelets and 20 slaves for your Highness, so that in Portugal some clothes could be bought for us, and we would not go about dressed like a savage.

The said Fernão de Melo, as soon as the ship reached the island [of São Tomé], took for himself one-half the bracelets and 9 slaves—leaving us with 11—and he ordered the bracelets exchanged for slaves, commanding that 30 bracelets be given for each slave. Then the said João Fernandes took the few remaining slaves to Portugal, and bought for us what we had asked him to. He was bringing us a chest full of black satin and velvets, but Fernão de Melo seized

---

[25] A colloquial expression meaning cloth of fine quality.

[26] Between 87 and 108 feet of cloth. The Portuguese *covado* equalled about 26 English inches.

[27] See note 8.

[28] In various places Afonso speaks of giving people "money." No metallic currency circulated in the Congo, not even Portuguese coins. The "money" in question consisted of cowrie shells (*nzimbus*), often exchanged in very large numbers.

[29] The stress indicates Afonso's resentment at being told this lie. The cleverness of the falsehood lay in the fact that, among the matrilineal societies of the Congo, the relationship of uncle-(*sister*)-*nephew* was often closer and more important than the relationship of *father-son*.

[30] Not otherwise identified.

and opened the chest—arrested João Fernandes and sent him away to Portugal—and then sent us the empty chest.

We have already written to your Highness of the derangement of Gonçalo Rodrigues[31] and of his wrongheadedness, yet now we wish to give an account of the masons he brought us for building the church, so that your Highness may know how much it pleases Fernão de Melo to disrupt the service of God—but God will give him his just deserts. Your Highness will know that Gonçalo Rodrigues brought us eight artisans and left them in our kingdom and went on his way to the island—and as soon as Fernão de Melo knew of his bad conduct, and of the masons being left here, he sent one of his ships here, with one of his clergymen, called Manuel Gonçalves, and with some of his servants—and in the ship he sent us 4 basins of lead, 12 glass bottles, a cloth belt, a piece of ordinary brocade, and a sword (the sword was in return for a much better sword that we had sent to him, requesting that he send us a scabbard for it—but he kept the sword and sent us instead one of his servants' swords that was not worth two ceitis).[32]

That clergyman, as soon as he reached this city, began to beguile the masons in such a manner that all of them asked us for permission to leave—and each of them already had bought from 15 to 20 slaves with the money we had given him, and had done nothing for us. And when we perceived this we well knew that Fernão de Melo had ordered them to leave so as to dishonor us—but we were ready to suffer for the love of our Lord God. Those masons left, and took as many slaves and goods as they had, and no more than three remained here. We despatched the said ship promptly and sent 200 bracelets and 60 slaves to Fernão de Melo, aside from those we gave to his servants; and we sent our nephew Pedro Afonso on the ship, with a letter to your Highness in which we gave an account of affairs here, and sent your Highness 200 bracelets and certain slaves, so that Pedro Afonso could take them to Portugal and buy us some clothes there—and this was because Fernão de Melo had sent us one of his decrees by which we were to despatch any goods we pleased in his ships.

As soon as the ship reached the island, Fernão de Melo took from us one-half of the bracelets and slaves, after having issued to us the said decree—and he did not want to permit Pedro Afonso to go to Portugal, but kept him on the island one year. He ordered our goods to be sold at the lowest possible price. He bought a Guinea slave, and another we had sent to him on his first ship, and remitted them to us, saying that they were "carpenters." He also sent us one and a half covados [a little more than three feet] of blue cloth, all chewed by rats, and returned to us the letter we had written to your Highness. And in addition to

---

[31] See note 8.

[32] I.e., "not worth two cents." The ceitis were small copper coins, engraved with the towers of the North-African Portuguese garrison town of Ceuta and worth only one-sixth of one real.

stealing what was ours from us, he called us many names, and did us such dishonest injuries that they are not to be told your Highness. And we suffered this for no other reason than because of our love for our Lord Jesus Christ—for even if they inflict deceit and dishonor upon us, we shall not leave the service of our Lord nor cease to believe in Him; for we would rather suffer the dishonor of this world and gain the other world, which is eternal, than live in this world with many pleasures and praises and lose our soul. And for this cause, brother,[33] we have suffered so many martyrdoms and vituperation and importunities, which every day we receive from the world.

So that your Highness may learn of the deceits done to us, your Highness should know that we asked the three masons (who remained) to build us a house, where we could be with our Queen, safe from those who might set it afire (as can be done to our straw houses)—and they began and it took them a whole year to lay the foundations. They would come every day and put one stone in place and then return to their houses—and then they would come and ask for money. For each stone we gave them one *lufuco* of the *lufucos*.[34] When it came time to make the quicklime, we asked many retainers to bring stones and wood. They spent another whole year in kilning the stone,[35] and they beat and spit on our retainers, causing them to flee from the works. And then they would come to us and say that they had no laborers; and we would say to them that we had given them money to buy their slaves and food for them, and why did they not take their slaves there to work? They would answer that the slaves had escaped from them. And then they would come to us and tell us that they had no wine, and we would order money to be given to them. And thus it was that they did not want to do anything for us except on payment of money; and in this way they have

---

[33] In the rest of the letter, Afonso addressed King Manuel as "brother" several times. It is evident that Afonso, as paramount chief in the lower Congo, considered himself to be the equal of the king of Portugal or of any other prince on earth. Indeed the lord of the Congo had more subjects than the king of Portugal, and ruled over a territory that was at least as large, and perhaps much larger, than continental Portugal. Although King Afonso—who consistently used the royal plural—was obedient to the Portuguese in religious matters, was quick to adopt Portuguese manners and customs (such as Portuguese dress) if he wanted to, and was even willing to acquiesce in a symbolic vassalage to the king of Portugal, he was not a puppet. For Afonso often acted against Portuguese interests. He prevented the Portuguese from penetrating into the hinterland, stopped them from prospecting for minerals, refused to enforce Portuguese laws, compelled the Portuguese to trade only with him and only at his capital, and so forth.

[34] One *lufuco* (or *lifuco*) contained 10,000 *nzimbus*, or cowrie shells. The decimal system of *nzimbu* measurements ran as follows: 1 *cofo* (or *bondo*) = 10 *lufucos* (*lifucos*) = 100 *fundas* = 100,000 *nzimbus*.

[35] In spite of Afonso's strictures, the three masons, assuming that the king's house was a large structure, faced a formidable task. They had to prepare ovens, bake the limestone to make quicklime, manufacture their own mortar, make their own bricks, and cut and prepare the timber. It is possible that the king's servants were more a hindrance than a help to them.

been working at this house for five years and have not finished it yet, nor will they finish it in ten years—so that we ask your Highness, for the love of our Lord God, to remedy this matter, for the deceptions and injuries done by these men are done to your Highness. Nor do they content themselves with taking our things from us, but also they give a very bad example in that which concerns the service of God—and our nobles laugh at the mistakes they see us making. When we want to punish them they tell us that they do not live under your Highness nor under us, and that they do not owe us anything. When we heard this we had not the heart to punish them, but kept quiet about our injuries. And thus we give your Highness an account of all the suffering we have been through every day—however, let all of it be for the love of God.

Now we wish to tell your Highness about a certain Rui do Rego whom your Highness sent here to teach us and set an example for us, but as soon as he arrived here he wished to be treated like a nobleman and never wanted to teach a single boy. During the Lenten season he came to us and asked for an ox, and we ordered one to be given to him. Then he said he was dying of hunger, and we ordered two sheep to be given to him, but that he was to eat them secretly, so that our people would not see him. Yet he, disregarding this, went and killed the ox in the middle of Lent, in front of all our nobles, and even tempted us with the meat; so that when our people saw it, those who were young and had only been Christians a short time all fled to their lands, and the older ones who remained with us said things that are not to be repeated, stating that we had forbidden them to eat meat, while the white men had plenty of meat, and that we had deceived them and they wanted to kill us. Then we, with much patience and many gifts, were able to pacify them, telling them that they should save their souls and not look at what that man was doing, and that if he wished to go to Hell then they should let him go.

We were so disgusted with all this that we could not see Rui do Rego again and ordered him to go to Chela,[36] so that he could board the first ship that arrived—for he had not taught as your Highness had ordered him to, but had caused to return to idols those whom we, with much fatigue, had converted. So he went and stayed at Chela—and at this time Simão da Silva[37] arrived with two ships and found the said Rui do Rego, who told him so many evil things and so many lies that there is no reckoning them, and that he had been cheated. And

---

[36] Seems to be another name for Mpinda, the port at the mouth of the Congo.

[37] In 1512 the king of Portugal sent Simão da Silva, with several ships and many men and supplies, as ambassador to the king of the Congo. The king of Portugal instructed Simão da Silva to correct the abuses of which Afonso had complained: he was to send home unworthy priests for punishment, enforce respect for the king of the Congo, and punish all Portuguese delinquents. Unfortunately the sudden death of Simão da Silva, the intrigues of his subordinates, the diversion of supplies and animals to São Tomé, and the resolute opposition of the São Tomé traders, helped to frustrate the aims of the embassy.

then Simão da Silva believed him, through the wrongheadedness of Rui do Rego and what he had said—but Rego did not tell him of the wickedness and heresy that he had practiced here. So that Simão da Silva did not wish to come to where we were (as your Highness had ordered him to) and sent the [ship's] physician with your letters, whom we sheltered as if he had been our brother. A vicar from the island [of São Tomé], who was present here, asked us to let him take the physician to his house to stay with him—but that ecclesiastic spoke so evilly of us to the physician that the physician's mind was changed, and he became persuaded that Simão da Silva should not come [to the capital]. And your Highness will know that it was Fernão de Melo who had ordered all this, since your Highness has no trading station here, and he has tainted goods [to sell?] and always steals from us.

Yet notwithstanding this, Sire, the physician fell ill with fever and could not return to Simão da Silva with an answer, and he wrote him a letter advising him not to come here; that we were a "João Pires" [a "Mr. Nobody," a nonentity], and that we did not deserve any of the things sent by your Highness.[38] The which letter he gave to one of our servants, and it came into our hands and we showed it to all of your Highness' servants who had come in the fleet. When we saw those things we well understood that they had been done at the command of Fernão de Melo—and we gave thanks to our Lord God for having been called a "João Pires" for His love. And all these things, lord and brother, we have suffered with good judgement and prudence, crying many tears—and we have reported nothing to our nobles and people, so that they may not conspire against us.

Then we sent one of our cousins with a young nobleman and wrote to Simão da Silva that, for the love of God, he should come and comfort us, and punish the people who were here, for we would not send him to ask anything of your Highness, except to ask that everyone be treated justly. Because of our entreaties, and those of Dom João our cousin, he left to come, but halfway here the fevers afflicted him with such force that he died. When we heard the news it broke our feet and hands,[39] and we suffered so much vexation that never again, not until this day, have we ever had any pleasure, because of the great disorders and evils later done by the men who came with him. As soon as he died, the men all came to us at a gallop to ask for the captain's post. And the first who reached us was a certain Manuel Cão, who told us that your Highness had appointed both Simão da Silva and himself as captains, and that if either died the other would take his place, and that since God had taken Simão da Silva, that we should make him captain. And we replied that he should let all the people come,

---

[38] The king of Portugal had sent an impressive diversity of supplies, animals, luxuries, plants, and seeds with his ambassador to the Congo.

[39] A peculiar expression—"*nos quebraram os pés e as mãos*—indicating great anguish.

and that the most competent person should be the captain. And two days later Lourenço Vaz and Jorge de Lemos arrived and asked us to make them captains. When we perceived that we were so importuned by them, and that all of them wanted to be captain, we ordered all the white men to be called together, and we asked them who among them was most fit to be captain; and they told us that, aboard the ship *O Gaio* ["The Jay"], there came your Highness' factor, who was more fit than anyone else—and that, in the event of the factor's death, that Jorge de Lemos or Lourenço Vaz should be the man.

Then they all began to talk to a vicar, kept here by Fernão de Melo, and the said vicar began to mislead them, and told them that they should all return, that that was what Fernão de Melo had ordered, so that they would not destroy Fernão de Melo's factory here. The vicar forbade us to look at your Highness' instructions[40]—and we demanded of him that, if we could not see your Highness' instructions, then how could we learn what had been ordered? For three days they refused to show us the papers; but after we had seen them, and learned what your Highness had commanded, we were very glad.

At this time our retainers arrived with certain chests of clothes, which we ordered kept within our walls, thinking that your Highness had sent them to us. Only after three days had passed did all the [Portuguese] men come to us and ask for them, saying that the goods were theirs. Then we ordered them to be given only three chests, those of Simão da Silva, that we had with us—and the things your Highness had sent us were still on the ship. Then, Sire, we quickly despatched Lourenço Vaz to the ships, to remit those things which your Highness had sent us—and we let him know that, if the *Gaio* did not arrive, that we would make him captain, for he had more votes than anyone else. Lourenço Vaz departed and as soon as he reached Chela the ship *Gaio* arrived, bringing Dom Pedro[41] and Álvaro Lopes. The said Alvaro Lopes told Lourenço Vaz not to send us the clothes until he had seen us. Lourenço Vaz left everything as it was, and soon fell ill with a fever, from which he died.

Álvaro Lopes and Dom Pedro left for here in a great hurry, to overtake a certain pilot of Fernão de Melo's who was on his way here, to tell us not to do the pilot any favors—and to give us an account of the injuries and offences Fernão de Melo had meted out to Dom Pedro, and to us, and of how he had ordered the arrest of Dom Pedro and Dona Ana. And they told us that as soon as Dom Pedro had reached the island that Fernão de Melo had dishonored him and called him a dog and said that he was on his way to deceive your Highness—that

---

[40] The troublesome "vicar" seems to have been Friar Diogo Belo.
[41] A Congolese who had been trained in Lisbon.

we waged no war with the Pamzelunguos,[42] that we deserved none of the things your Highness sent us, that we were an infidel dog, and he heaped another thousand insults upon us that it would be shameful to relate to your Highness. (For all of which, nonetheless, we sang a thousand praises to our Lord God—for when we were yet a youth, during my father's lifetime, we received a thousand million threats and injuries for the love of God; we always believed firmly in Him and were Christian. And afterwards, during many wars and troubles, burning many idols, and never amidst all these circumstances have we abandoned His service. And should we now, that we are old and have Christian sons and grandsons, leave Him because of Fernão de Melo's mouth?) And in addition to this he took all the horses your Highness had sent us.

When Dom Pedro and Álvaro Lopes had finished giving us this account, we begged Álvaro Lopes to return quickly and have the clothes despatched to us—for your Highness had sent them to us. But he said that he was tired and would leave the next morning. But then, from morning to morning, he never wished to go—and we, perceiving this, did not give way to anger, for we had asked nothing of your Highness except such as would help us to augment the faith of our Lord God, and that was what we wished. As for the clothes, if they arrived, we would receive them because your Highness had sent them to us, but if they did not arrive, then we would not concern ourselves—for we had not ordered them to be bought; but if we *had* ordered them then we would have worked hard to get them.

Then we soon began to despatch your Highness' ships. And we ordered the sending of twenty-two youths of our family. In the large ship and the caravel we sent two of our nephews, with our son Dom Francisco—and 500 slaves for both ships, with 30 extra slaves, so that if some of the 500 slaves died their number could be made up from the 30. We ordered our son Dom Francisco to kiss your Highness' hands and to present the slaves *as the son of a king,* and not as the thing Fernão de Melo calls us—and so also our nephews [were to conduct themselves in the same dignified manner]. And with Dom Pedro nineteen would go in the *Gaio.* In this manner, lord and brother, we sent our son and gave him our blessing and he left.

Five days later news reached us that Munza, a lord of the Ambundos, was at war with one of our sons, on his border, and wished to kill him. And it was

---

[42] Panzelungos—a neighboring people with whom Afonso was at war. The point is this: Afonso believed that the Portuguese were legally obligated to trade for slaves with him, and were not permitted to trade with heathen enemies of the Christian king of the Congo. Fernão de Melo, who wanted more slaves and at a cheaper rate, maintained that there was not really any war between the king of the Congo and the Panzelungos, and that therefore the Portuguese could trade with the pagan Panzelungos on the same basis as with any other African people.

necessary for us to go to war,[43] and we left in this our city Álvaro Lopes as captain, and left one of our servants with him, so that all the slaves we were sending your Highness would be well guarded. And if any person did anything he was not supposed to do, then the said Álvaro Lopes would punish him justly, as your Highness ordered, whether he was one of ours or a white man. And then we left for the wars—and of the people your Highness sent here [recently] only three came with us, and all the rest stayed with Álvaro Lopes, for none of them wanted to come. But among those who lived here, the following went with us: Manuel Conçalves, António Vieira, João de Estremós, Joao Gomes, Pero Fernandes, and Fernão Vaz; and also a mason called Diogo Alonso, who went with us halfway and then told us that he was dying of hunger—and we ordered meat to be given to him, and as soon as it was given to him he turned back to the Congo and left us in the war.

As soon as we had gone off to war [the vicar] Diogo Belo[44] and Manuel Cão left for Chela, to go in the ship *Gaio,* and they took one hundred or more slaves. But they kept so poor a guard over them that, when they were drinking at a stream, the slaves seized them and killed Manuel Cão, and wounded the vicar very badly. So that the said vicar returned with a few slaves to this our city, and the others, who had killed Manuel Cão, escaped. And as soon as the vicar arrived, his slaves wandered about in all vicinities, stealing and robbing the markets, and destroying our walls and burning our houses—in such a manner that it looked like the great destruction caused by some war. Álvaro Lopes, perceiving the damage done by these slaves and knowing that the vicar did not want to punish them, having bought the slaves with our money, he ordered them apprehended and ordered them whipped. The Queen my wife ordered the slaves who had killed Manuel Cão rounded up, and had them apprehended. And then she commanded Álvaro Lopes to have them killed—for our custom is that those who kill are killed—and Álvaro Lopes carried out the order and had them killed.

At this time, while we were at the wars, the clothes which your Highness had sent arrived, and with them the bachelor notary of the fleet, who brought a book listing all the goods, to give it to us. As soon as he reached the city he turned back again, and left the book here, but gave us no account of anything. So everyone helped himself to the goods, as if the property belonged to orphans—and when we returned here we found all the chests empty; but we have made a list of all that they contained and shall send it to your Highness. And after all this, your Highness will know that we sent 410 slaves, from the wars, to be taken by the ship *Gaio,* and our *belyguyns* [police officers or bailiffs]

---

[43] This expedition against Munza, a lord of the Mbundo, shows how slaves were captured in the Congo.

[44] Friar Diogo Belo was evidently the unnamed vicar (see note 40) who was always undermining Afonso.

brought them, and also the mason João Estremós, who brought 190—and all these slaves were delivered to Álvaro Lopes in our compound, and from them he chose 320 very good ones and took them away—leaving in our compound 90 thin and old ones. Of the said slaves we have seen neither a list nor any books, and we do not know how many he sent to your Highness.

When we arrived here we found the bachelor, Diogo Fernandes,[45] who met us on the way, even before we had reached our houses, giving us no leisure at all—and he began to tell us that Álvaro Lopes was not fit to be captain and we should remove him, and appoint him instead. And we answered him that he already had what pertained to him—for we had been told that it was the custom that, when a captain and a factor came out, the factor would become captain if the captain died—and as Diogo Fernandes was already a *corregedor* [chief magistrate], how could he be a captain as well? That it was better for him to be a *corregedor* and Álvaro Lopes the captain, so that both could jointly judge and oversee judicial affairs. But he did not want to do this; and when we saw that he would not even talk to the said Álvaro Lopes (nor join him in judging cases together), we ordered him to return to the ship, and we quickly sent him away. He left for the ships, but spent so much time on the way that, when he arrived, he found no vessel and did not wish to leave.

And after we had sent him on his way to the ships, we quickly sent Dom Pedro after him. And Dom Pedro took 190 slaves—that is, 100 of ours and 90 for your Highness—to make up for those who had remained here because they were too thin. With him went all our nephews, and he was to convey our obedience to the pope. But Fernão de Melo's ecclesiastics, and Rui do Rego, who went on ahead, as soon as they heard that Dom Pedro was on his way, they made the greatest haste in the world, and made the ship leave without Dom Pedro, and without our messages. And this was at Fernão de Melo's orders, who wanted everything in confusion, so that his lies could appear as truths. In this way the ship left without taking a notary, nor anyone else who could have given your Highness an accounting of the slaves we sent your Highness, nor anyone to look after them. Each sailor helped himself to the slaves he wanted, as if the slaves belonged only to God.[46]

Thus, brother, when Dom Pedro reached the river and saw them sailing away, he took a dugout canoe and went after them, shouting at them to wait. But they did not want to—and then, when Dom Pedro perceived this, he turned back and brought back the slaves with him, both your Highness' ninety as well as our one hundred. And the reason, brother, why they did not wish to take Dom

---

[45] Diogo Fernandes, a bachelor at law and legal expert, was sent to the Congo at Afonso's request, and brought with him the five books of Portuguese law—the *Ordenações Manuelinas*—which were printed in a revised version during the years 1512–14.

[46] A difficult but unimportant clause—"*como que era cousa de por Deus*" (literally, "as if it were a thing of for God")—of doubtful meaning.

Pedro, was because they had all stolen the goods we were sending to your Highness—and they did not wish Dom Pedro to tell you this. And for these reasons we had ordered that ship prepared—chiefly to convey our obedience [to the pope], and so that Dom Pedro could go and give an account to your Highness of what we had sent in your Highness' ships, and also an account of the services performed here by the salaried men [the artisans] your Highness sent here: to wit, first of all, your Highness should know, concerning a shoemaker who arrived here, that we ordered him to be given 50 hides, so he could cut them and make shoes for us—and there were 20 goatskins, 20 sheepskins, and 20 other skins[47] of animals we have here—but he did not know how to cut them, or did not want to. So he damaged them all so that they could not be used, and made us no more than five pairs of leather shoes—even though he had many skins and all the things necessary. That is the extent to which this man has profited us.

The tailor has made us a robe with velvet sleeves, and has mended some things, now and then, against his will. The tile-maker has never wanted to make tiles or bricks for us. Every day we have given him money and sent him to do his job, but he never gets anything done. We, perceiving that they mocked us, did not want to let our blood burn up again.[48] They have never tried to teach any of our servants, but if any one approached them to be taught something, he received so many blows that he would run away and would not dare to return. We are told that the nobles who live far away are more afraid of us than those who live at our court—and it is true, because these men cause it through the ill deeds our nobles witness here, and by the bad examples they set. Because if those who are far off could see what those who are with us see, then they would be much worse [i.e., would rebel]. Thus, my brother sovereign, these are the benefits which they confer on your Highness and us. Let your Highness see whether they deserve their salaries and order what should be given to them—because we are obliged to do no more than to write the whole truth to your Highness, and it does not seem good to us that they should take your Highness' money and salaries and do nothing.

Now we wish to tell your Highness about how, after these events, one of Fernão de Melo's ships arrived at our kindgdom, with Lopo Ferreira as captain, bringing our brother Dom Manuel[49] and our nephews. Dom Manuel brought certain letters from Fernão de Melo to father Friar Nuno,[50] in which he wrote

---

[47] The total then must have come to 60 hides (not to 50 hides, as the letter has it).

[48] Another curious expression—"*não queremos mais queimar nosso sangue*"—meaning that the king did not want to boil over with anger, for it was not worth it.

[49] Dom Manuel, Afonso's brother, had once been in Portugal and had returned to the Congo, and then went to São Tomé and back. He was considered one of the best instructed of the Congolese Christians.

[50] Friar Nuno—another of the worldly, slave-trading missionaries of the Congo, who served the interests of Fernão de Melo and was a sworn enemy of the royal factor, Álvaro Lopes.

imploring him for the love of God to look after his affairs in the Congo—even though he has nothing here, and all of this referred to your Highness' factory.[51] Fernão de Melo promised to send a ship soon, to fetch the friar and all those who helped him, and he requested that one of his slave girls, held by Álvaro Lopes, be taken to the friar's house. He also wrote to Álvaro Lopes that he was soon going to have him arrested. These letters had no sooner arrived than they stirred up great conflict and greed, not only among the salaried men but also among the priests, for they all wanted to kill Álvaro Lopes, and they all began to buy slaves—in spite of the fact that your Highness' instructions forbade it. And then we posted our own decree that no one was to buy slaves except the factor.

These events occurred only after they had seen Fernão de Melo's letters, when enormous avarice possessed them—for all the time previously they had all lived in peace, and the priests lived holy lives—but after they had seen those letters they never lived in peace again. At this time father Friar Nuno came to us and said that it would be good to make the bachelor [at law] a *corregedor*, so that he could adjudicate in matters judicial—and he brought a patent already made out and made us sign it.[52] And after we had signed it, he told us to appoint as notary a certain Tomé Lopes, a salaried man who was staying with him. When we heard this advice it seemed to us that he, being a priest, should not proffer advice except in matters pertaining to God's service—but, nonetheless, we appointed the said Tomé Lopes as notary and signed another patent to that effect.

As soon as they possessed these patents of appointment they began to confer, one with another, and they all ate and drank together, both the laymen and the priests. In this way they all began to take care of the business affairs of Fernão de Melo, just as he had written for them to do, and every day they [in a judicial proceeding] interrogated Álvaro Lopes, your Highness' factor and ours, all wishing to do him injury. Everybody was a witness and a magistrate and a notary.

At this juncture someone stole a goat which we had given to the priests. Because of the goat the priests all gathered in the church and rang the bells and

---

[51] Although the settlers of São Tomé had the right to purchase slaves in Africa for their own use, the king of Portugal was trying to monopolize the slave trade. During these years (1512–14) in the Congo, the royal factor Álvaro Lopes acted as King Manuel's agent. This one-to-one relationship, between the king of the Congo and the Portuguese royal factor, suited Afonso, who tried to prevent his own subjects from dealing directly with the Portuguese. But the trading arrangement between the factor and the king enraged the slave traders of São Tomé, who saw their own ventures withering away. Therefore almost all the Portuguese were eager to get rid of Álvaro Lopes and bypass the king of the Congo, and welcomed Fernão de Melo's invitation to defy the king of Portugal by taking the slave trade into their own hands.

[52] According to a letter Afonso wrote seventeen months later (on 4 March 1516), he signed the patent only under threat of excommunication. This bachelor at law and *corregedor* was the same Diogo Fernandes mentioned previously (see note 45).

published excommunications (sometimes with candles as well).[53] They cut a green branch, uttered many curses, and said that when the branch dried up so would all those dry up who opposed them and spoke ill of them. Beyond all this, Friar Nuno fetched into his house the Negress, whom Álvaro Lopes had kept as a concubine, and kept her within his walls—at which our nobles murmured every day. Many other very disreputable things were done, but we dare not relate them to your Highness, out of concern for the excommunication placed upon us.[54]

Notwithstanding all of this, they were all up in arms against the said Álvaro Lopes. Once, to insult us further, when Álvaro Lopes one day was kneeling in front of us asking for food supplies for the slaves he had in the factory, the *corregedor* came up behind him and, to our very face, seized him by the hair and struck him many blows—which we felt keenly, for it was done to no person if not to we ourselves. The said Alvaro Lopes had a dagger in his belt, but he was so patient that he did not wish to draw it, but reminded his aggressor that they were in our presence, but that he would pay him back in good coin once they were outside.

But this was not enough for the *corregedor*—for, sometime later, one day when we were talking casually, we started to tell him that your Highness had sent him there—along with Jorge Machado, Álvaro Lopes, and all their servants—for no purpose other than that all of them should live with us and teach us the things pertaining to the service of God, and not to live with the tailor or with the mason—and he replied that not for all your Highness' treasure, nor yet for all the riches of Portugal, would he ever live with us, and that it would be an evil hour indeed when he had to live with a Negro. Thus, brother, these are the services they have rendered us and taught us—and another thousand discourtesies and deeds they have done to us, which are very shameful to tell your Highness. All these things we place in your Highness' hands, so that each of them can receive the punishment he deserves—for that is no way to talk to a king, nor should men be assaulted in a king's presence—and justice needs to be served. But let your Highness' wishes be done, for we will suffer patiently for the love of our Lord God, as we have suffered hitherto many other things for His love.

After Fernão de Melo's ship, brother, had placed Dom Manuel and our nephews ashore, she went to the coast of Pamzelungua, where Fernão de Melo sent many silks and textiles to trade for slaves with them, since they were his friends, and knowing that we were at war with them, for they are infidels. We have waged great wars on them, during which they have killed many of our nobles, relatives, and white men. Fernão de Melo did all these things, brother, to

---

[53] I.e., with solemn ceremonies, as with "bell, book, and candle."

[54] The circumstances of this excommunication are not clear; perhaps Afonso meant only the threat of excommunication that had been made.

harm us and to give a bad example to our nobles, so that they would say that the white men wished to be friends with the Pamzelunguos, for the Pamzelunguos had the true faith, and God's faith which they had taught us was a lie, and so they would all rise against us and return to the idols. But our Lord God saw their evil intentions and gave them the reward of those who put themselves in the service of the Devil—so that, as soon as they reached Pamzelungua, they landed to arrange the trade and the infidels who met them killed the said Lopo Ferreira, who was the captain, and another three or four men, and the others fled in a small boat and got away.[55]

Consider, your Highness, the many ways in which Fernão de Melo has tried to destroy us, and has told your Highness bad tales about us, so that you would forget to have us visited. We ask your Highness to demand of Fernão de Melo why he imprisoned our Dom Francisco, and why he did not allow him to proceed on your Highness' ships to the place we sent him, out of love—for your Highness had sent word that we should despatch 20 or 30 youths of our kin. And we sent our son to your Highness, so that he could present all the slaves and goods we were remitting—and Fernão de Melo did not wish to let him go, but kept him there on his island, with a stick in his hand, making him beg for the love of God—and likewise our nephews—for which reason we are keenly sorrowful. And as to the flesh, we feel much pain, because he is the fruit of our loins; but as to the soul, it grieves us not, for we sent our son to search for the things of God and learn them, and thus all the travails of the world that visit him, while he searches for the faith of our Lord Jesus Christ and learns it, we take to be blessings, and suffer them for the love of our Lord God, for He will ever remember us.

And now we beg of your Highness that, for the love of our Lord Jesus Christ, that you will not forsake us, nor allow the loss of the fruits of Christianity growing in our kingdom—for we can do no more, and have but one mouth to preach and instruct. We have already married, and all the nobles near us have been married—but those who are afar off do not want to be married, because of the evil examples they see every day, and they do not wish to obey us. So we ask your Highness to help us, so that we can make them get married. And if your Highness does not wish to help us in the spiritual realm, we will kiss your royal hands and ask that you send us five or six ships to take us and our sons and relatives, so that we will not witness so great a perdition.

---

[55] See note 42.

And now we ask your Highness that in our behalf you will bring Fernão de Melo to justice,[56] because he defames us and has worked hard to destroy us. Make him pay for all the goods he has taken from us, taken by fraud, for he has never bought anything from us. And if he has no property to use in repayment, then order him to give us the island [of São Tomé], for it is his, and if we were to possess it we could rest in peace. And do not suppose, your Highness, that we have any other purpose in requesting the island save that of increasing the number of Christians by means of her; because your Highness will realize that the boys cannot learn as well if they are kept with their fathers and mothers, as they can apart from them. For this purpose we will send a man of our blood, and your Highness can send a good and virtuous priest, so that together they can govern the island, taking care first of spiritual matters, and then of the temporal. And since the said island is so close to our kingdom,[57] we will send many boys and girls there to learn, because here they all run away and one day two hundred students come and the next day only one hundred. There, on the island, they will learn in no time; and, in this manner, the island will furnish us with priests, and with bread and wine for the Holy Sacrament.

We shall not write more to your Highness because we would have need of a whole ream of paper to relate all the imbroglios that occur here, but Dom Pedro will give your Highness a detailed account of everything. And if anything in this letter be badly written, we ask pardon, because we do not know the styles of Portugal. And we write this with one of our schoolboys,[58] for we do not dare to use any of the [Portuguese] men who are here, for those who best know how to write are guilty of one misdeed or another.

We would kiss the royal hands of your Highness if you would write a letter, on your own behalf, to the *Moynebata* Dom Jorge,[59] and another to the *Moinepanguo*,[60] who are the principal lords in our kingdom, in which your

---

[56] In response to Afonso's complaints, and to other complaints from the São Tomé settlers, King Manuel of Portugal suspended Fernão de Melo from all his offices in 1516 and sent out to the island a *corregedor*, Bernardo Segura, with powers to conduct a full inquiry and bring the guilty to justice. Segura arrived at São Tomé on 28 October 1516 and began his investigation. He uncovered evidence of many irregularities, but the proceedings were halted by the news of the death of Fernão de Melo, which probably occurred during the last weeks of 1516. Melo's son, João de Melo, succeeded as captain, donatary, and governor of São Tomé.

[57] São Tomé is about 570 statute miles from the Congo estuary. Fernão de Melo was the donatary, or lord proprietor, of the island, and hence could be described as its owner, although the donation was at the king's pleasure and had to be renewed for every succeeding heir.

[58] A Congolese schoolboy, João Teixeira. It is evident from this, and from other references to Congolese schoolboys, that Afonso had managed to train a number of youths in the reading and writing of Portuguese and in the knowledge of Christian doctrine.

[59] See note 15.

[60] The *Mani-Mpangu*, lord of Mpangu, an island territory to the northeast of the capital.

Highness would thank them for being good Christians, and also send them two priests, in addition to those sent to us, so that in their own churches they can say mass, hear confessions, and teach all the things pertaining to God's service. Your Highness should realize that these two lords live a good 80 or 90 leagues distant from us, and each of them has his own church wherein to see God.[61] In both places we have put two schoolboys to teach them [the lords], and their sons and relatives. In this way we have begun the work there and may reap a great harvest. So now let your Highness see if you can complete it, for our powers are thinly spread out and that is all that we can do—but if they can have priests, to say mass to them and confess them, it will be of great merit and they will be strengthened.

May our Lord increase the life and royal estate of your Highness, so that you will always be able to help us to propagate His holy faith.

Done by João Teixeira,[62] servant of the most patient and much tormented Prince and King of the Kingdom of the Congo, and in the era of one thousand five hundred and xiiij years [1514], on the fifth day of October.

[signed] El Rey + Dom Aº
[The King + Dom Afonso][63]

---

[61] The original is obscure, possibly garbled.

[62] A Congolese schoolboy, João Teixeira, Afonso's scribe.

[63] This precise form of signature, very much in the Portuguese style and designed to make forgery difficult, was recommended to Afonso by Dom Manuel I. The king of the Congo always used it.

PEOPLE: FREE AND SLAVE

Henry Koster

The free population of Brazil at the present time consists of Europeans; Brazilians, that is, white persons born in Brazil; mulattos, that is, the mixed caste between the whites and blacks, and all the varieties into which it can branch; mamalucos, that is, the mixed caste between the whites and Indians, and all its varieties; Indians in a domesticated state, who are called generally caboclos; and those who still remain in a savage state, and are called generally tapuios; Negroes born in Brazil, and manumitted Africans; lastly, mestizos, that is, the mixed caste between the Indians and Negroes.

First we must treat of the whites. The Europeans who are not in office, or who are not military men, are, generally speaking, adventurers who have arrived in that country with little or no capital. They look down upon the Brazilians, or rather they wish to consider themselves superior to them.

I have observed that, generally speaking, Europeans are less indulgent to their slaves than Brazilians. This difference between the two descriptions of owners is easily accounted for; the European has probably purchased part of his slaves on credit, and has during the whole course of his life made the accumulation of riches his chief object. The Brazilian inherits his estate, and as nothing urges him to the necessity of obtaining large profits, he continues the course that has been pointed out to him by the former possessors.

Notwithstanding the relationship of the mulattos on one side to the black race, they consider themselves superior to the mamalucos; they lean to the whites and, from the light in which the Indians are held, pride themselves upon being totally unconnected with them. Still the mulattos are conscious of their connection with men who are in a state of slavery, and that many persons even of their own color are under these degraded circumstances; they have therefore always a feeling of inferiority in the company of white men, if these white men are wealthy and powerful. This inferiority of rank is not so much felt by white persons in the lower walks of life, and these are more easily led to become familiar with individuals of their own color who are in wealthy circumstances. Still the inferiority which the mulatto feels is more that which is produced by poverty than that which his color has caused, for he will be equally respectful to a person of his own caste who may happen to be rich. In Brazil, even the trifling regulations which exist against them remain unattended to. A mulatto enters into holy orders or is appointed a magistrate, his papers stating him to be a white man, but his appearance plainly denoting the contrary. In conversing on one occasion with a man of color who was in my service, I asked him if a certain *capitão-mor* was not a mulatto man; he answered, "he was, but is not now." I begged him to explain, when he added, "Can a *capitão-mor* be a mulatto man?"

The regiments of militia, which are called mulatto regiments, are so named from all the officers and men being of mixed caste; nor can white persons be admitted into them.

Marriages between white men and women of color are by no means rare, though they are sufficiently so to cause the circumstance to be mentioned when speaking of an individual who has connected himself in this manner; but this is not said with the intent of lowering him in the estimation of others. Indeed the remark is only made if the person is a planter of any importance, and the woman is decidedly of dark color, for even a considerable tinge will pass for white. If the white man belongs to the lower orders, the woman is not accounted as being unequal to him in rank, unless she is nearly black. The European adventurers often marry in this manner, which generally occurs when the woman has a dower. Still the Brazilians of high birth and large property do not like to intermarry with persons whose mixture of blood is *very* apparent.

The mamalucos are more frequently to be seen in the sertão than upon the coast. They are handsomer than the mulattos; and the women of this caste particularly surpass in beauty all others of the country; they have the brown tint of mulattos, but their features are less blunt, and their hair is not curled. I do not think that the men can be said to possess more courage than the mulattos; but whether from the knowledge which they have of being of free birth and on both sides, or from residing in the interior of the country where government is more loose, they appear to have more independence of character, and to pay less deference to a white man than the mulattos. When women relate any deed of danger that has been surmounted or undertaken, they generally state that the chief actor in it was a large mamaluco, as if they thought this description of men to be superior to all others. Mamalucos may enter into the mulatto regiments, and are pressed into the regiments of the line as being men of color, without any regard to the sources from which their blood proceeds.

I now proceed to mention that numerous and valuable race of men, the creole Negroes—a tree of African growth which has been transplanted, cultivated and much improved by its removal to the New World. The creole Negroes stand alone and unconnected with every other race of men, and this circumstance alone would be sufficient, and indeed contributes much to the effect of uniting them to each other. The mulattos, and all other persons of mixed blood, wish to lean toward the whites, if they can possibly lay any claim to relationship. Even the mestizo tries to pass for a mulatto, and to persuade himself, and others, that his veins contain some portion of white blood, although that with which they are filled proceeds from Indian and Negro sources. Those only who can have no pretensions to a mixture of blood call themselves Negroes, which renders the individuals who do pass under this denomination much attached to each other, from the impossibility of being mistaken for members of any other caste. They are handsome persons, brave, hardy, obedient to the whites, and willing to please; but they are easily affronted, and the least allusion to their color being made by a person of a lighter tint, enrages them to a great degree. They will sometimes say, "A Negro I am, but always upright." They are again distinct from their brethren in slavery, owing to their superior situation as free men.

The free creole Negroes have their exclusive regiments, as well as the mulattos, of which every officer and soldier must be perfectly black.

The creole Negroes of Recife are, generally speaking, mechanics of all descriptions; but they have not yet reached the higher ranks of life, as gentlemen, as planters, and as merchants. Some of them have accumulated considerable sums of money, and possess many slaves. The Negroes are excluded from the priesthood; and from the offices which the mulattos may obtain through their evasion of the law, but which the decided and unequivocal color of the Negro entirely precludes him from aspiring to. In law all persons who are not white, and are born free, class equally; manumitted slaves are placed upon the same footing as persons born free. However, although the few exclusions which exist against the Negroes are degrading, still in some instances they are befriended by them. They escape the persecutions under which the other castes suffer during the time of recruiting.

The men whose occupation it is to apprehend runaway Negroes are, almost without exception, creole blacks; they are called *capitães-do-campo*, captains of the field; and are subject to a *capitão-mor-do-campo* who resides in Recife, and they receive their commissions either from the governor or from this officer. By these they are authorized to apprehend and take to their owners any slaves who may be found absent from their homes without their master's consent. Several of these men are to be found in every district, employing themselves in such pursuits as they think fit, when their services are not required in that calling which forms their particular duty. They are men of undaunted courage, and are usually followed by two or three dogs.

It is scarcely necessary to name the mestizos, for they usually class with the mulattos; nor are they to be easily distinguished from some of the darker varieties of this caste. A dark-colored man of a disagreeable countenance and badly formed person is commonly called a mestizo, without any reference to his origin.

Indian slavery has been for many years abolished in Brazil, and the individuals who are now in bondage in that country are Africans, and their descendants on both sides, or individuals whose mothers are of African origin; and no line is drawn at which the near approach to the color and blood of the whites entitles the child, whose mother is a slave, to freedom. I have seen several persons who were to all appearance of white origin still doomed to slavery.

Slaves, however, in Brazil have many advantages over their brethren in the British colonies. The numerous holidays of which the Catholic religion enjoins the observance give the slave many days of rest or time to work for his own profit; thirty-five of these, and the Sundays besides, allow him to employ much of his time as he pleases. The slave can oblige his master to manumit him, on tendering to him the sum for which he was first purchased, or the price for which he might be sold, if that price is higher than what the slave was worth at the time he was first bought. This regulation, like every one that is framed in favor of slaves, is liable to be evaded, and the master sometimes does refuse to manumit a valuable slave; and no appeal is made by the sufferer, owing to the state of law in that country, which renders it almost impossible for the slave to gain a hearing. Likewise this acquiescence in the injustice of the master proceeds from the dread that if he was not to succeed he would be punished, and that his life might be rendered more miserable than it was before.

A slave is often permitted by his owner to seek a master more to his liking; for this purpose a note is given, declaring that the bearer has leave to enter into the service of anyone, upon the price which the master demands being paid by the purchaser. With this the slave applies to any individual of property whom he may wish to serve.

A considerable number of slaves are manumitted at the death of their masters, and indeed some persons of large property fail not to set at liberty a few of them during their own lifetime. A deed of manumission, however simply it may be drawn out, cannot be set aside. The price of a new-born child is £5 (20,000 mil-reis), and the master is obliged to manumit the infant at the baptismal font, on the sum being presented. In this manner a considerable number of persons are set at liberty, for the smallness of the price enables many freemen who have had connections with female slaves to manumit their offspring.

All slaves in Brazil follow the religion of their masters; and notwithstanding the impure state in which the Christian church exists in that country, still such are the beneficent effects of the Christian religion that these, its adopted children, are improved by it to an infinite degree; and the slave who attends to the strict observance of religious ceremonies invariably proves to be a good servant. The Africans who are imported from Angola are baptized in lots before they leave their own shores, and on their arrival in Brazil they are to learn the doctrines of the church, and the duties of the religion into which they have entered. The unbaptized Negro feels that he is considered as an inferior being, and therefore he is desirous of being made equal to his companions.

The slaves have their religious brotherhoods as well as the free persons; and the ambition of a slave very generally aims at being admitted into one of these, and at being made one of the officers and directors of the concerns of the brotherhood. The Portuguese language is spoken by all the slaves, and their own dialects are allowed to lay dormant until they are by many of them quite forgotten. No compulsion is resorted to to make them embrace the habits of their masters, but their ideas are insensibly led to imitate and adopt them. The masters at the same time imbibe some of the customs of their slaves, and thus the superior and his dependent are brought nearer to each other.

The slaves of Brazil are regularly married according to the forms of the Catholic church; the banns are published in the same manner as those of free persons; and I have seen many happy couples (as happy at least as slaves can be) with large families of children rising around them. The masters encourage marriages among their slaves, for it is from these lawful connections that they can expect to increase the number of their creoles. A slave cannot marry without the consent of his master, for the vicar will not publish the banns of marriage without this sanction. It is likewise permitted that slaves should marry free persons; if the woman is in bondage, the children remain in the same state; but if the man is a slave, and she is free, their offspring is also free.

The great proportion of men upon many of the estates, produces, of necessity, most mischievous consequences. If an adequate number of females are placed upon the estate, and the slaves are trained and taught in the manner which is practiced upon well-regulated plantations, the Negroes will be as correct in their behavior as any other body of men.

The slaves who are employed in Recife may be divided into two classes, household slaves and those which pay a weekly stipend to their owners proceeding from the earnings of some employment which does not oblige them to be under the immediate eye of the master. The first class have little chance of gaining their freedom by their own exertions. This second class consists of joiners, shoemakers, canoemen, porters, etc. and these men may acquire a sufficient sum of money to purchase their own freedom.

Creole Negroes and mulattos are generally accounted quicker in learning any trade than the Africans. This superior aptitude to profit by instruction is doubtless produced by their acquaintance from infancy with the manners, customs and language of their masters. From the little experience, however, which I have had, and from the general remarks which I have gathered from others, who might be judged better acquainted than myself with slaves, I think that an African who has become cheerful, and seems to have forgotten his former state, is a more valuable slave than a creole Negro or mulatto.

The newly-imported Negroes are usually sent to work too soon after their arrival upon the estates; if proper care is taken of them, they may indeed be employed in almost any description of labor at the end of eight or ten months, but not much before this period.

There are considerable numbers of white persons and of color who possess two or three slaves, and share with them the daily labor, even of the field. These slaves are, generally speaking, creoles, who have been reared in the family, or they are Africans who have been purchased very young for a trifling sum of money. They are frequently considered as part of the family, and share with the master the food for which both are working. These slaves appear on gala days well dressed, and they have a certain air of independence, which shows that they think themselves to be something more in the world than mere drudges. The difference of the feeling of one of these men toward his master, and that of the generality of the slaves which are owned by great proprietors, is very striking.

From the vastness of the country, it might be supposed that if a slave escapes from his master, the chances would be against his return, but this is not the case. The Africans particularly are generally brought back; they are soon distinguished by their manner of speaking the Portuguese language; and if any one of them cannot give a good account of himself, he will not be allowed to remain long unmolested, for the profit arising from the apprehension of a runaway slave is considerable.

Some of the Negroes who escape determine to shun the haunts of man. They conceal themselves in the woods, instead of attempting to be received into some distant village as free persons. They form huts, which are called *mocambos*, in the most unfrequented spots, and live upon the game and fruit which their places of retreat afford. These persons sometimes assemble to the number of ten or twelve, and then their dislodgment is difficult; for their acquaintance with the woods around gives them the advantage over any party which may be sent to attack them.

That the general character of persons who are in a state of slavery should be amiable, and that goodness should predominate, is not to be expected. We ought rather to be surprised at the existence of that degree of virtue which is to be found among those who are reduced to a situation of so much misery. Slaves are much inclined to pilfer, and particularly toward their masters this is very frequent; indeed many of them scarcely think that they are acting improperly in so doing. Drunkenness is common among them. A direct answer is not easily obtained from a slave, but the information which is required is learnt by means of four or five questions put in various ways. The Negroes show much attachment to their wives and children, to their other relations if they should chance to have any, and to their *malungos* or fellow-passengers from Africa. The respect which is paid to old age is extremely pleasing to witness. Superannuated Africans, upon the estates, are never suffered to want any comforts with which it is in the power of their fellow-slaves to supply them. The old Negroes are addressed by the term of *pai* and *mãe*, father and mother. The masters likewise add this term to the name of their older slaves, when speaking to them. That the generality of the slaves should show great attachment to their masters, is not to be expected; why should they? The connection between the two descriptions of persons is not one of love and harmony, of good producing gratitude, of esteem and respect; it is one of hatred and discord, of distrust and of continual suspicion; one of which the evil is so enormous that if any proper feelings exist in those who are supposed to benefit from it, and in those who suffer under it, they proceed from our nature, and not from the system.

JOURNAL OF RALPHE CROSSE

[This is a Journal of the Tenth Voyage, kept by Ralph Crosse, the purser on board the *Hoseander*, which vessel sailed from Gravesend in company with the *Hector, James,* and *Solomon,* on the 3rd of February 1612, the general of the whole fleet being Captain Best. The Journal commences with the following "Articles" issued under Captain Best's own hand, with orders that they were to be read every month in the hearing of the respective crews.]

"To thend that Almightie God may have glorie, the King honor, our merchants profitablie served, and our vaiges[1] soberlie governed, I, Thomas Best, chief captaine and comaunder of the Dragon, James, and Sallomon, and Hosiander, do establish and ordeyne thes lawes and ordinances followinge, straitlie chargeinge and comaundinge both captaines, merchauntes, and mrs., with all other officers and mariners, saillers, or other persons whatsoever imployed in this vaige, to observe and keepe the said lawes and ordinances so far as doth concerne him, or eyther of them upon the penaltie herein comprised, from the daie of the publicacion hereof."

"1. Imprimis, that everie morneinge and eveneing you the chief comander or mr, assemble together your men, or company to heare Devyne Service, and care be taken that your praieres and the Word of God be read in all sobernes, as in the presence of God, that He may have glorie and yourselves comfortt, with increase of knowledge, and that no man absentt himselfe from thes your publick praieres and excersses of Religion, neyther willinglie nor neicligentlie, nor yᵗ no man causse any disturbance nor lewdlie demeane himselfe in this your Devyne Service upon paine of punishment."

"2. Item. That you, the chief comaunder or mr, suffer nott the name of our great and glorious God to be dishonored amongst yow by blaspheming, sweareinge, cursseinge, or by any other idle takeinge of our God in vayne upon dew punishement, videz: for the first oath sworne, or for the first tyme cursseinge or baneinge, to receve thre blowes from yᵉ mr with the bole of his wissle; for the second tyme, either sweereinge or cursseinge, to receve six blowes, as aforesaid;

---

[1] Voyage.

for the third tyme, nyne blowes; and for the fourth tyme, to stand 24 houres in the bilbowes without eyther meatt or drink, and so for everie tyme hearafter."

"3. Item. That muttuall love and concorde be preserved amoungst yow; that no man offer abuse to other in word or deed; that therfore all drunkennes, all mallice, envie, hatred, backbitinge, and slanderinge be avoided, upon paine of severe punishment; that love, kindnesse, humillittie, and humanittie be enter-tyned of all and of each man to other; and that no man darr, or presume from wronges rec: to revenge his owne cause, upon payne of such punishment as to that partie belongeth which first comitted the offence; butt that everie partie so wronged shall repaire to the captayne or m^r for justice; with whom, if yow fynd nott sattisfaction in justice, that then, oportunittie and tyme servinge, that then they repaire to me, the General or Chief Comaunder, from whom he shall have justice, according to the qualitie of the offence."

"4. Item. That no man, of what condicon or place soever shall darre to challenge into the field or upon the shoare dureing the tyme of this our vaige, any of these our men, imploied in thes our shippes; nor any person or persons shall dare to accept any such challenge; nor no man to accompanye any that goes into the field, under paine of 40 strippes upon the bareback, and to stand in the bilbowes att the discretion of the Generall: neyther that no man feight, nor strike any maliciouslie of thes our men upon this vaige, imploied in shipboard or on shore, upon paine of severe punishment."

"5. Item. Whoesoever shall conspire to maik away his Governor by trea-son, mallice, or otherwise in any of the shippes, or shall be a mutineer or factious fellow to taik part with any man against his Comaunder or Governor, or shall have knowledge of such conspiracies or malitiouse purpose, and do not spedily maik known and discover the same, shall suffer death for the same."

"6. Item. Everie officer in thes shippes, both att sea and att land, shall do ther best endevoures to reforme all thes disorderes, and shall maik known and aprehend all mallefacteres, that they may receve dew punishment; and that no man lift upp his hand with weappon violentlie to resist any officeres, upon payne of grevouse punishment, or to suffer death for yt if the cause so require."

"7. Item. Whosoever shall break open or pick any chest or trunke or cabin to taik anything there hence, or shall pick any man's pockett or other place to steall from him, shall be for the first tyme grevouslie punished, and for the sec-ond time suffer death."

"8. Item. That no play att dice, cardes, nor table be suffered in your shippes for money nor otherwisse, upon payne of severe punishment."

"9. Item. That no man lodge out of the shipp wherein he is shipped, or detayne himself aboard any other shipp for the wholle night without leave of his captayne, under payne of punishment."

"10. Item. That no man shoott of any peece, greatt or small, after the setting of the watch, because yt is an alarme to the rest of the shippes, under payne to be punished."

"11. Item. That greatt and especiall care be taiken for the relief and cumfort of all sick men; that they be kept cleane and refreshed and comforted with all good provisions; and that the Chirurgions extend ther best endeav: and labores towardes there care and cumfortes; and if yt should happen, notwithstanding, that any should die, that then good care be taken that a trew inventorie be maid of all the goodes, moneys, apparell, and provission belonging unto the partie deceassed; and for all apparell and provissions not fit to be keept to the end of the vaige, that yt be sould at the maynemast; and that therin such order be taken as is provided in the 11th article of our Comission; and the purser to have for registring it 11 des per £1."

"12. Item. That in all places where we shall staie to relyve, refresh, and cumfort our men or ourselves, eyther by fresh water or vittualles, that everie man carie himselfe wth sobrietie and meeknesse towards the people of the countrey; that justlie of our partes no offence be geven; and that no man presume to wander or stragle from his company without leave, but that he contayne himselfe within his lymites and boundes, upon payne of punishment, for by this indescretion and libertie taken many have lost ther lyves, our force and strength in our shippes therby weakined, and our mayne vaiges often indangered."

"13. Item. For so much as the preservacon, care, and good husbandrie of our vittualles is the conservacon of our vaige and of all our lyves; that therefore you the officeres extend your best cares and endeavoures to ye preservation of all our vittualles; that so all abusses may be prevented and our vittualles prolonged for the relief of our countynuall neecessities; that so accordinge to the larg proporcons from the Wor^{ll} Comp^y receved ther may be no want."

"14. Item. That all barteringes and bargaynes, buyinge and sellinge betweene man and man, be registred and entered in the purseres booke for that purpose provided, therby to avoid all purloyneinge and steallinge; and that all such bargaynes and barteres that shall be maid without such registringe shall be void, aud the offenders to undergoe dew punishm^t, and the purser for his service to receive 11 des per £1."

"15. Item. That especiall care be had by yow the boatson, your towe mates, to see the shipp be keept cleane swept and washed in all corneres, as oft as occasion shall be offered, and to see such portes left open in hot countres as we may convenientlie beare out for the better aireinge of our shipp and health of our men, and that ther be no eating and drinking under the uppermost deck, except upon necessity yow be constrayned therunto eyther by rayne or fowlle wether; and this to be performed by yow all, as yow will answer yt."

"16. Item. That no man presume to go downe into the hould at any time, upon any occasion, without acquaynting of the m^r upon payne of severe punishment."

"17. Item. Whosoever shall be found absent from his watch, eyther at sea or in any roode or herber wher we shall come, or being at watch, bee found asleeppe, shall be severlie punished."

"Item. That yow the cooke with your mate be carefull yow have your vittualles well seasoned, both flesh and fishe, and that yt be provided in dewe tyme, vidz., dynner to be reedie at 10 of the clocke at the furthest, and supper by five o'clock; and likewisse that yow have a speciall care to keep your steeppstubs sweet and cleane, together with the furnace, kettles, pottes, and platters, or any other thinge which shall be used, eyther about the dressinge or servinge out of the companies vittualles, for yt is a principall thing to be regarded for the preservacon of our healthes. Faille not heereof, as yow will answeer yt, by sitting in the bilbowes 24 houres with bread and water."

"Lastlie. The God of all Peace so order and guide us, that we maie continewe in all piettie and love each towardes the other, according to place and callinge; that the end of this our vaige maie be with more glorie to Gode, and better reformacon of our synfull lives then the beginninge thereof, and that by our example other men maie be encouraged and stirred upe to like laudable enterprisses, in which God is the giver of all good successe, graunt us prosperitie in peace to go forth and in saifty to retourne to the great glorie of God, honor to the kinge, comodittie to the Comonwealth, gayne to the merchants, credit and reputacon to us the factors."

[The fleet anchored off the bar of Surat in October 1612, and on November 27th news came that a Portuguese expedition had sailed from Goa to capture the English fleet. Captain Best gave orders to prepare the vessels for action, and next day four galleons and twenty-five frigates were seen off the bar.]

"Twenty-ninth November in the morninge, being Saboath, Mr Aldsworth,[2] Mr Canninge[3] (who had just been released from captivity), and all the rest of the merchauntes were comed to the waterside, where Mr Canninge did take leave of Mr Aldsworth and came aboard, haveing verie importunatlie perswaded Joo. Jooson to repaire abord with others of our yong merchauntes,

---

[2] Thomas Aldsworth was the chief factor at Surat. He died there in 1616.

[3] Paul Canninge, one of the Surat factors. In 1613 he went on a diplomatic mission to Agra, to obtain a reply from the Emperor Jehanghir to a letter sent him from James I, and also to beg for a firman securing to the English an anchorage free from danger of attacks from the Portuguese. After a long and tedious journey, Canninge reached Agra, but died there on May 27th, 1613. His kinsman, Lancelot Canninge, a musician, died a few days after, and another of his followers, named Richard Temple, died on his return to Surat on June 27th, 1613. Mr. Keridge, with Edward Hunt, was sent to take the place of Canninge at Agra. Keridge was afterwards chief factor at Surat, and came home in 1621.

which refused and found many delayes, or elles durst nott. Everie man was reedy with great spirit and courage to encounter the enemie."

"Mr Canninge did first repaire abord the Dragon, where he did relat unto the Genl so much as he knew was pretended by the Portingaille against us. How they meant to taike both our shippes, money, and goodes, which, before they came from Goa, they had vowed and receved the Sacrament upon yt, and then yt must need be performed. How they had in ther shippes some 200, some 150 men; ther frigotes 50 or 60 souldieres, besides sailleres, which number, the Lord knowes, was far unequall with us, they being about 2,000 men, we little more then 200 in both our shippes; but the Lord I hope will feight for us, in whom is our trust in the daie of battaille. Ther ammerall 36 peeces, cullverin and deme canon; the rest 20, some more, some lesse, all brasse ordinance; and, further, the Portingailles did verielie think when wee see ther forces that we would not feight, but yield in hope of favour."

"Our Genl came this morneinge to see our shipp and feightes. All things was to his content. He made a speech unto the company, the effect wherof was this, that although ther forces were more then oures, yet they were both basse and cowardlie; and that there was a sayinge not so comon as trew, who so cow-ardlie as a Portingaill; and that after the first bravado was past they were verie cowardes, as he in former tymes had found them by experience; did therefore perswad everie man to be of good courage, and shew ourselves trew Englishmen, famousse over all the world for trew valour; and that God, in whom we trusted, would bee our helpe: to trust in God and not to feare death, although for death we were ordayned, and in a better action we could not die then in the behalfe of so worthy a countrey as we have the Comonwealth of our land, the estate of our m^rs. For death, sayth he, is the passage to heaven: He shewed a sayinge of David in his '16 Psalme, towards the latter end, I will set God alwaies before me, for He is on my right hand, therfore I shall not fall. My hart is glad, my glorie rejoiced, my flesh allso shall rest in hope. Thou shalt shewe me the path of liefe; in Thy presence is the fullnesse of joie, and at Thy right hand there is pleasure for evermore. In this manner haveing encouraged our men, furder tould them that if yt should please God that any of our men in feight were dismembred or laymed, he faithfullie promised, upon his credit and reputacon, in the hearinge of the company, that he would be a meanes unto the Wor^ll, whom we serve in ther behalfe, for reasonable mayntenance to keep them as long as yt should please God they lyve, and himselfe to be the petetioner upon his knees till his request were graunted; but that we should not need to feare, for that we served a religious and worthy company of m^rs that would never see a man go to decay or want by any harme sustayned in ther service. Haveing ended his speech he tooke a cup of wyne and drounk to the m^r (master) and all the company, and desired God to give us His blessinge, and so retourned abord his owne shipp to sermon."

"We went to prayer, Mr Canneinge being speaker: we all joyned with him that God would assist us against our aproaching enemies. After prayer we went to dynner, drunk one to another. Thinking tyme long till they were come up, we had weid apike, and was redie when the Dragon weyd, and kept of her wither bowe. We had the wynd of them, which we aymed to keep, stood right with them with flags, ancientes, and our pendants at everie yardarme. Ther Vice Admirall was the headmost shipp, the Dragon steered directlie with her, and haveing hailled her with a noise of trumpets, gave her a sallutinge peece under her sterne. She answered her agayne, then the Dragon came up with her, and gave her a holle broadside for a welcome, which we did see to raik her throw and throw. We heerd ther people make a great crie, for that yt could not otherwise bee, but that they had received great spoille and harme from the Dragon. She shot at the Dragon, but shot over and did her no harme, save onelie the sinkinge of her long boat, which that night she freed and maid fit agayne. The Dragon did so plague the Vice Admirall, that the Admirall and the rest rune away afore the wynd. We were reedy to second the Dragon, but could not, for that they rune away. The Dragon had a shot in the mainemast, which ther stuck fast: another shot she had upon the sterbord bowe, but no harme, the Lordes name be praised. The Vice Admirall bore upp with her consortes, the Dragon and we came to an anker halfe a league of them to windward. This night we see the Vice Admirall upon the carrene with all the frigotes about her, thinking she had received some shot under water."

"This feight was in the sight of the shoare, wher both our English and the country people did behold us, allthough this afternoone worke were but a preparitive to that ensewed."

"30 November. This daie being St. Andrewes daie we weied earlie in the morneing, keeping the wynd of them, bore right up with them, the Dragon being ahead, steered with the Ammerall, and gave her such a breakfast as Nuno de Cuno little expected, and sent him such tokens as maid the shipes side crack where he was. All of them this morneinge, more or lesse, hard from the Dragon. We were not far from hir, to second hir in the best manner we could; we sent them tokens, to let them tast of our curtesey; we came so neere that we never shot, but prevailed, being amongst them where they all did shot at us. We had a hot conflict this morneinge, but no harm receved, the Lordes name be praised. For the space of 3 or 4 houres our feight endured. We stood of into the channell for deepe water, and ankered in 7 fadn: water, about a league from the enemie. They spoilled us some tacklinge, but no more harme as yet. At afternone, with flod, we weid, and the Dragon weid likewise, and went up with thre of them, where she plaid hir part couragiouslie all this afternone. One being from the rest a good distance, and as we did think aground, we came upp close upon hir sterbord sid, within halfe a stone's cast, and lesse of hir: with this ship we spent all this afternone in feight; we maid 100 great shot this day, langrill, round, and crosse bar, besides our small shot: they maid many shot at us, but shot many over. We lost our boatson, Richard Barker, this day slayne by a great shot upon the forecastle: our tackleing and sailles turne, but no more harme this day, the Lordes name be praised. Our boatson had one of his armes taiken away, with other towe mortall woundes, one in his bodie, the other in the arme. I did my best endevour to give him cumfort, but being broken clene in sunder, and the wound in his body more daungerous, there was but small hop of his life, so that yt pleased God to call him within two houres he had received his hurtes. Our m^r and cape merchant, after the feight was ended, went abord the Dragon to see our Generall, and to know if all ther men were well: the Generall tould them that all his company was well, except one man slayne right out with a shot in his bodie, wherupon he died intstantly; another with the same shot lost one of his armes. This was all ye harme the Dragon received this daie, save his tackleing and sailles something torne. This night, in the begineing of the first watch, our men espied a frigot verie neere the shipp, which had rune to and agayne dyveres tymes about our shipp: the watch gave our m^r notice of her, and she being verie neare, our m^r caused the gunner to maik a shot at hir: the ordinance being reedy primed he maid a shot at hir, which, to our judgment, was verie faire over hir: he maid another, and after that the third. She presentlie put furth tow lightes, for the other frigotes to come to hir, but we did think she sunk before the frigotes came to hir, as afterwards, when we came to Swally, we did certaynelie understand, as the countrey people likewise did afirme, for that they had found a great number of Christians drove upon the shoare to the number of 30 or 40. We did think that this frigote was by the General sent to do some mischiefe against us, eyther by burneing of us or cutting of our cable; but they maid a pit for us and fell into yt themselves. They knew they had no hoppe to taik us by feighting with us, as they had reasonable well tried, and therfore they meant by treacherey to betray us; but the Lord, who was our chiefe Captayne, both by daie and night, would not suffer ther trecherous pretence to taike effect."

"1 December. This day we rested and did not feight."

"2 December. We weid and stood more to the southward to seek deep water, they keeping in sight of us. This night we ankered in 10 fadum neere unto Daman."

"3 December. We weid and stood towardes Swally Road, agayne thinking to meet with them, because that the last night we had lost sight of them. Our companyes both was sorie, for they had great desire to trie yt out with them. Our Generall was fullie resolved to have fought with them if they had followed him wher he might have bene bold to have banged yt out with them in deep water, they being lesser ships then wee and light withall, that they drew but little water. The Generall, seing all the company so willing, yt did much move him to mayntayne feight with them, allthough he was deswaded from yt by the chief in his ship, and withall to leave them and put to sea, to see if we could take any Ormus men bound for Goa, which, if the Generall had consented unto, he never had nor could have had, any trade at Suratt. The Generall, upon ther perswasion, put to sea and left them."

"6 December. We had sight of Dua.[4] Saboath daie we went to sermon."[5]

9 December. The vessels anchored off Madefraband, where the people readily supplied fresh provisions.

"This Madefraband[6] hath bene a great huge citie, but much ruinated and decayed, the walls overgrowne with wood. Yt hath a good ryver for small shippes. The Mallabars and Portingailles, sometymes with ther frigotes, put into this river, and then the people and the inhabitantes therof doth flie away upp into the countrey, for that they have bene many tymes ransacked and robbed by them, which is the reason that makes them so poore, but verie harmles people to them that offereth unto them no violence."

A few days later Captain Best, having called together on board the Dragon his own crew and the greater part of that of the Hoseander, addressed them, asking whether they thought better for the general welfare to return to Swally, and if the Portugals were there to fight them, or to lie at anchor doing nothing for the benefit of the Worshipful Company. Both crews, with one accord, voted for a return to Swally, which greatly pleased the General.

The combined crews then entreated Captain Best to spare the lives of four of the crew, who a few days previously had deserted, but had been captured and brought back by the country people. After much entreaty, he pardoned all four, whereupon the crews thanked him for his kindness. "So this being done, the cooper was called to fill some beare, and haveing drunk, we of the Hoseander repaired abord our owne shipp."

Having changed the anchorage from Madofraband to "Mea, alias Mocha",[7] the General, at the latter place, learned that the forces of the Mogul were then besieging a castle; distant some three leagues from the anchorage, held by a force of Malabars, but that the progress made by the besiegers was small, their guns being incapable of battering the walls.

Upon hearing of the arrival of the fleet, the Governor of the Army despatched two messengers to bid Captain Best welcome to those parts, and to treat with him for the purchase and sale of the various articles. The General having learned that the Governor of the Army was a friend of the Governor of Amedevar, dismissed the messengers after kind entertainment, and in their company he sent Mr Canninge and Mr Oliver to the camp.

---

4 Diu.

5 December 6th was Sunday in 1612. It was leap year.

6 Possibly Mandwa Bunder, near Diu (?) or Mowah.

7 Perhaps Miani Bunder.

"18 December. Our Generall sent his boat with a doss. shott and Capt. Hermon to examyne a boat was heere come into a kreek laden with meale and rice. I was spectator in the performance of this mes. of Mr Hermon's; which was done with too much severitie; for although they said they came from Dua, yet they did affirme yt they were Benians, and that permission they had was for the Army; but Capt. Hermon, giveinge but little credit to what was spoken, caused them to be hanged up upon a tree by ther handes, fingeres, and heades, to make them confesse themselves to be Port., but could not, because they were not so, nor could not speak a word of Portingaille. His deallinge was verie extreame, in my opinion, they being such harmles creatures."

Mr Canninge and Mr Oliver, on their return from the camp, where they had been very courteously entertained, informed the General that the Governor particularly wished to meet him. Also, on one occasion, while conversing with the Governor, a soldier came up to him, saying that the Malabars were ready to yield, provided the lives of the captain of the fort and of some of his chiefs were spared, and for the rest that they should be slaves. To this message the Governor sent answer, that the Malabars should fight for their lives; further, that the English were his friends, and that if with his own forces he could not take the castle, he had interest enough to hope for the assistance of the English, who, for their pains, should have the castle and all the goods therein. The Governor then said to Mr Canninge and the rest, that the kingdom was theirs for trade, or for any other purpose, and that as soon as he had taken the castle he would present it to the General, if it would please the latter to come up with his ships to countenance him, and that the Malabars might see he had a friend in the English, and so be induced to yield. The Governor further added, that whatever commodities that part of the country, or Amedevar[8] or Cambaia, might yield for trade, he would be a means that the General should have the same at a reasonable price with ready conveyance to the ships. He also said that he had heard of the General's fight with the Portugals, who had suffered a heavy loss. Previous to their departure from the camp, the Governor again urged Mr Canninge and the others to induce the General to anchor off the castle, and upon their promising to do so, he provided pilots to navigate the ships.

The General, as soon as he had heard the result of Mr Canninge's mission, gave orders to the master to get the ships under weigh at flood tide to move in towards the castle, which order was duly carried out.

21st December. The Governor having sent off to the ships four of his chiefs as hostages, the General, attended by forty armed men, landed and repaired to the trenches, where, with much courtesy, he was received by the Governor, who said that the country was his for trade, and then expressed a wish to have four of the best guns carried ashore from the ships to breach the walls of the castle. Cap-

---

[8] Ahmedabad.

tain Best replied, that it was contrary to his commission to land any of his guns, but in any other way he would do his best to please the Governor, and offered the assistance of one of his men with his gunner to regulate the gun platforms, which offer was thankfully accepted. From the trenches, Captain Best proceeded to the camp, where he was royally entertained, and from whence he returned to the Governor, who again attempted to persuade him to land some guns, but seeing he would not, desisted. The General, previous to returning to the ships, requested the Governor to spare the lives of the commander of the castle and of his son and daughter. This request the Governor promised to grant, although absolutely refusing to give a written promise to that effect.

Two of the smiths were left on shore to assist in making shot, and two other men to superintend the making of a platform for the guns.

22^d December. The four Portuguese galleons having been reported within sight, the General had his ships prepared for action, and sent Mr Canninge ashore to bring off his men. The Governors of the Army and of Cambaia urged Mr Canninge to persuade the General not to fight, pointing out the inequality between two merchants' vessels far from their country, and men-of-war fighting at their own doors, and thus able to obtain fresh stores. "Mr Caneing retourned them this answer, 'That there was a God in heaven would feight with us and for us. He was our Captayne, and under his banner we did feight, and those that constantlie and faithfullie trusted in him, he would deliver them in the day of battell.' Which speech they liked very well, and tould Mr Canninge that if our Generall wanted eyther powther, shot, or vittualle, or any thing else whatsoever, we should have yt from abord his frigates." For this offer Mr Canninge returned many thanks.

"23 December. In the morneinge we weid both, and steered right with the galleons, they being at anker, the Dragon with the Ammerall, and we with the Vice-Ammerall. We did maik them such a breakfast, as I do verielie think was neyther in the way of courtesy or unkindnesse, was well accepted. The Dragon being ahead steered from one to another, and gave them such banges as maid ther verie sides crack; for we neyther of us never shot, but were so neere we could not misse. We still steered after the Dragon, and when she was with one we were with another, and the truth is, we did so teare them that some of them were glad to cut cables and be gone. This morneinge's feight was in the sight of all the army, who stood so thick upon the hills beholdinge of us, that the number of them being so many they covered the ground. We lost no tyme, nor spared neyther powther nor shot, as our spectatores ashoare can well witnesse, how this day we paid them and maid them rune away about 2 leagues off into the sea, wither we followed them receiving and payinge them, to the great honor of our Generall, and the credit of our nation to have 2 merchant shippes to beat 4 men of warr. We ankered in the wynde of them. Being comed to anker, our Generall sent Capt. Hermon abord of us to know if we were well. We tould him all was well, saveing one or tow lightlie hurt in the head. Capt. Hermon tould us they had one man slayne and some lightlie hurt. This was all the harme that both our shippes receved this daie, the Lorde's name be praised, that did so wounderfullie preserve us, for some of our men escaped this daie verie narowlie from a culverin shot that came in under our half deeck."

"24 December. This morneinge, verie earlie with daie, we weid and set saille towardes the enemie, we being in the wynd of them and not alltogether without the sight of the army. This morneinge they weid too, and comeing upp with them, we did so let yt flie at the Vice-Admerall, the Dragon being with the Ammerall, as we maid her beare upp helme and go from us; and in the self same fashion we served the Admerall, the Dragon haveinge geven hir the first Bonjour. We gave her the *Besa los manōs;* but she, unwilling to complement any longer with us, did *Anda por atras.* Our men this daie did shew great vallour, everie man in his place. One of our men threw a ball of fire into ther Admirall, that busied them all to put yt out agayne; and if they had not seene yt when they did, yt had fired ther shipp. This day we tried them most cruellie; we see swiming by our shipp sides peeces of tymber, boordes, and ould hattes and clothes: ther sailles were allmost torne from yardes, some of them and ther tackling cut in peeces. Mr Canninge did much encourage our men, and verie redy himself to do what service he might. We spent thes 2 daies in feight furth of our shipp 250 great shot."

After the conclusion of this engagement the Hoseander's company petitioned the General, regard being had to the great expenditure of ammunition, either to undertake some exploit whereby the Portugals' shipping might be destroyed, or else whilst any stores were left to be gone forth from that place. Captain Best, too, had determined on this course, and according gave orders to sail for the Road of Swally.

In these engagements the Hoseander expended 27 barrels of powder, and 300 great shot, cross bar, langrel and round.

The General, having boarded the Hoseander, thanked the company for their exertions and promised to use his interest to obtain from the Worshipful Company fitting rewards for them. He further added that he was much pleased with their petition, and should occasion require it, he would not fail to make some attempt to destroy the galleons.

Twenty-seventh December. The vessel anchored off Swally, when the General learned that the Firman had not arrived, though the Governor of the Army had told him it was at Amedevar.[9] When Medeiopher, who offered a supply of powder and shot, visited the General, the latter enquired after the Firman, and received a promise of its speedy arrival.

---

[9] Ahmedabad.

On the thirty-first, a boat's crew, sent ashore for water and provisions, returned empty-handed, in consequence of Medeiopher, who was displeased with the General, having forbidden the Macadam[10] to furnish such. Mr Canninge, on his return from Surat, said that the cause of offence was the General's refusal to let Medeiopher have certain cloths, previously promised to him, without payment, but that he had been partially appeased.

Fifth January, 1612(3). Mr Complain, the preacher, and divers of the merchants, went up to Surat to despatch business and to speak with the chiefs about the Firman; further, if there was no hope of its arrival to persuade Mr Aldsworth to return to the ships. Next day the General returned Medeiopher his signet, as he had proved so inconstant. The same day a letter was received from Mr Aldsworth, saying that whether the Firman came or not, he would not leave Surat.

Seventh January. The news of the arrival of the Firman was received, which made Mr Aldsworth, who had refused to leave the country, very joyful at the prospect of remaining there; but the General doubted that it was the Firman, for it had been brought down in no state or fashion, while he had expected that Medeiopher and the chief men would have accompanied it, and to that effect he sent them a message.

Eleventh January. The chiefs having come down, the General, attended by thirty men, landed, and having met Medeiopher, went to the Macadam's house, where "the Cavellero that brought the Firman from the Court was, in verie rich apparell, reedy with the Firman in his hand covered with read silke, and maid up in cloth of gould, and did, in the presence of all the chiefs, deliver yt unto our Generall, where he demanded to know the contents, yf they were corespondent to the Articles concluded upon with the Governor of Amedevar or no. The chief affirmed it to be the same, and so our Generall, in all reverence and curtesy, received yt, our trumpetes afterwardes soundinge and a value or towe of small shot: and for the unkindnesse betwixt our Generall and Medeiopher, yt was tourned to great kindnesse and love againe, and there all discontentes was ended betwixt them. Our Generall tould them that presentlie he would apoint a merchaunt that within 6 or 7 daies should be reedy to take his journey towardes Agra with our kinge's present, which before tyme they had seene, and also our king's letter."

They then offered the General great courtesies and privileges for trade throughout the country, as well in Amedevar and Cambaia, as elsewhere, and promised to care (as for their own people) for all such persons whom the General should leave at Surat; and should all such happen to die, then they would have inventories made (as had been already done for the Dutch) of all goods, cash, and debts, and the same should be paid over to their successors.

---

10 Makaddam, a chief or head man.

"The General then yielded them many thankes, and for awhile took leave of the chief, gave them 2 valley of shot and threw amongst the souldiers tow handfulls of money, and with the sound of the trumpettes repaired downe to the waterside."

The Portuguese ships having appeared in sight, Captain Best hastened to make preparations for departure. Mr Canninge, attended by Richard Temple and Edward Hunt, was appointed to convey the presents and letters to Agra, and Anthony Starkie was selected to return overland to England with letters.

All business arrangements having been completed, the General sailed from Swally on the seventeenth January, and the day following passed close to the galleons, which, in bravado, weighed and followed the two ships for a short time, and then again anchored. "Thus we parted from these valient champions, that had vowed to do such famous actes, but yet content to give us over with great shame and infamy redounding unto themselves, but this was the Lordes doinges, and God graunt us to give him the glorie."

Nineteenth January. Four junks were captured; they were from Cananoer, bound for Surat. The General, after they had been pillaged, allowed them to continue their voyage to Surat. "I praie God our people at Surat susteyne not revenge at the handes of thes people for this daie's worke."

Between that date and the end of the month many junks were captured, all were pillaged, but some were released, whilst others were destroyed.

On one occasion, Captain Best visited the Hoseander, and addressing the crew said, that in consideration of their courage and to reward them for their services, he had allowed pillaging, but since they and the crew of the Dragon could not agree about the plunder, to put an end to the scandal caused by such quarrels, he withdrew his permission, and should any ships be captured he would take means to satisfy both crews. Afterwards, six of the Hoseander's officers went on board the Dragon to draw up an agreement on that subject.

On board one of the prizes a letter, written at Goa, was found, in which it was stated that Nuno da Cunho had captured two English ships at Surat.

Thirtieth January. The fleet anchored off Bringa, a little village some 30 leagues northwards of Cape Comorin. The General received a visit from the Ambassador of the king of that country, who offered him great kindness and trade.

Fourth February. The ships set sail from Bringa,[11] than "which place as yet we have not found in the Indies a place of better refreshing," but owing to contrary winds, which forced them to anchor, did not double Cape Comorin until the twenty-sixth, and on the following day were within sight of the Island of Ceylon. An attempt to obtain supplies from the inhabitants of that island was

---

[11] There is no port with a name resembling this on the coasts of Malabar or Travancore.

unsuccessful, as the natives, who were friendly disposed towards the Portugals, refused to hold any communications with the vessels.

While off the Island of Ceylon two vessels were sighted, which were found to be a Fleming, and her prize. The captain of the former, before the vessels separated, presented one black boy to the General and another to the preacher.

Twelfth April, 1613. The vessels entered the Road of Achin, and upon their anchoring the Shabender, according to custom, boarded the Dragon to learn what the vessels were. He told the General that he had authority from the King to bid him welcome, adding that the King was well disposed towards the English, and promised on the day following to conduct some of the company into the King's presence. Accordingly, next day some of the merchants were sent ashore and were received by one of the chief nobles, the King being absent on a hunting excursion, who promised them permission to trade, and said that the King greatly desired to have commerce with the English. He also assigned the merchants a house.

On that day the merchants were entertained by the Flemings at their house.

Fifteenth April. In compliance with a message from the King, who desired to speak with him, the General, "with 50 or 60 of his chiefest men to attend him, went ashore to the King with the Sabender and the Capt. of the Fleming. The people of the cittee received him with all joie and mirth that might bee, but the king was absent ahunting of wild ellofantes, in which sport he taikes great delight: but by some of his chiefes the General was entertayned."

Seventeenth April. "This day great disorderes abord our shipp, both with our owne men and the Dragon's men: first, by drinking drunk, and then by fighting with fistes, in the sight of the Guzurat junkes, to all our great shames and disgrace to our country and nation."

Eighteenth. "This daie our Kinge's letter was sent for by the King of Achin with an ellofant and a chaire of state in the form of a castle upon his back. After went the General to the Court, where he presented the Kinge with a rich present from our kinge; and the King likewise did give unto our General a vest, with Mr Moore and Mr Oliver. He entertayned us with the fightinge of ellofantes, buffeloes, and great rames; and afterwardes was provided a great banquet with many dishes and great store of arack. The banquet was served in dishes of pure gold and silver, brought in towe chestes of gould, which they do use to keep ther betel in, they use to eat of verie much. Great curtesy by the King was offered, and that the country was at our comaund. But our General, as yet not alltogether satisfied, for that he hopeth of furder commerce with the King and at large to deliver his mynd unto him."

Twenty-seventh April. "Our General went to the Embassador of Siam, with whom he did converse of such comodities as in ther countrey were vendible, and likewise of the qualitie of such comodities as were ther to be retourned for England. The Embassador did afirme that the quantitie of 2000 clothes would vent ther in the space of 2 monthes, with diveres other comodities highlie esteemed of. Rials of eight to be worth ther 7s. the riall: raw silk there is great store and cheapp, and likewise benjamyn, better then that of Achin: and the weight ther greater, for that 4 bahars of Achin makes but 3 at Siam; callicoes of Surat sell well there: black and read hattes: lookinge glasses: birding peeces of the smallest sort being well damaskt. All this the Embassador for certayne did afirme unto our General, and offered to affirme yt with the Kinge's sealle, seameing verie desirous to have comerce with the English. This day he had a child circumcized with great seremonyes after ther fashion."

A few days afterwards "the Embassador of Siam dyned with our General, but sent his owne cookes to dresse his vittualles, and brought his drink with him, being water in great flagons of sillver."

"First May. The King went to recreat himselfe, accompanyd with our General and the Dutch merchants, when they went to a river about 6 or 7 milles from the towne, the King riding upon an ellofant in a chaire of state upon his back. They came to a place wher they washed themselves, the King sitting upon a seat in the midst of the river, with our General and the Dutch merchantes and all his nobles about him in the water, with aboundaunce of people that were spectators on the shoare, his nephew poureing water upon him as he sat, with a golden buckit, for the space of 5 or 6 houres. Then afterwardes they had a great banquet, with aboundaunce of vittuall and arack, dressed after ther maner. Haveing ended the banquet they retourned to the Kinge's pallace with our English trumpettes sounding before them, and women playing and singing before the Kinge; and thus they came to the pallace, wher at that tyme our Generall took leave of his Majestie."

Fourteenth May. The General obtained the King's licence to cut wood upon one of the islands. On the same day, too, he heard of the arrival of a Portugal junk, and that some of the Portugals had gone to the King to inform him of their arrival with the Embassador whom he had sent to the King of Joar.[12] Next day, the Hoseander, with the Dragon's pinnace, anchored close to the junk. Previously, the Guzerats had offered for a certain sum to land the Portugals and their goods in safety; but all the latter, with the exception of one man, were ashore. He, with some goods, went on board the Guzerat, upon which the Hoseander's boat was sent after him, and he and the goods were brought back to the junk. The junk had on board certain chests and bales, which were said to be for the King. Thomas Hounsel was placed in charge of her. Upon this action, the King sent a messenger to Captain Best, to ask what had the latter done, and whether he intended to act the part of friend or foe. Captain Best satisfied the messenger that his intentions were friendly; and on the following day, in com-

---

[12] Johore.

pany with the King's Ambassador, he landed, and at an interview with his Majesty, presented him with the junk, everything on board her being intact. The King did kindly accept the gift.

On that day the General bought from the King 40 bahars of benjamin at 25 tael the bahar.

Seventeenth May. An old man, who for his knowledge of cookery and language was employed about the house, was, through the malice of the Shabender, cruelly murdered, the only cause being the "denial of the Kinge's work, because he was then employed by us."

Nineteenth May. The Hoseander, to obtain a supply of wood, crossed over to an island where "we found a great many people with ther armes and leges cut of for offences, which is the Kinge's lawe, haveing one chief apointed governor over them, in regard they should not bee idle, but be imploied in the Kinge's service for the making of brimston."

"And in the tyme of our wooding we found certayne spideres whose weebes were perfect silk, the which our chirurgion hath one to showe."

The Hoseander, having parted her cable, was near drifting ashore on this island; but the master, who was on shore, hastened aboard, and having got her under sail worked her off the shore. "But it was more Gode's providence then our men's carefullnes" to which her escape was due.

At Achin the bahar was found to weigh 395lbs., English weight.

Nathaniel Fenn was tried by a jury and condemned to death for having drawn his sword on the General, who, at the urgent request of the Ambassador of Siam, pardoned the culprit, and made him over to that dignitary.

Twenty-sixth May. A letter was received from Mr Canninge, who mentioned that on his way to Agra he had been attacked by thieves; that Hunt and Temple had deserted, carrying with them much money; and that he had heard that Nuno da Cunho was by the Viceroy imprisoned at Goa for returning without commission; also that Chaoul and other places held by the Portugals were besieged by the forces of the Mogul.

Second June. "The Generall, with all our chiefe, went to the court, where before the King we see an ollephant and a tiger maik a cruell feight, his Majestie siting upon an ollephant beholding the sport; which, being ended, the Generall accompanied his Majesty to his pallace, and so took leave."

Fifth June. The General went to Court in hopes of procuring the Kinge's letter of permission to trade at Priaman, and again on the tenth he visited the Court for that purpose, when it was promised to him.

On that day, the tenth, "at the Court, we understood how that about 3 or 4 daies past a nobleman, for lookinge at one of the Kinge's concubynes, was judged by the King to have one of his eyes puled out; another, for wearing a turband extraordinary, had a peece of his skull cut awaie."

Fourteenth June. The General went to Court, when he presented "4 murderes, 4 tergetes, 6 lances" to the King, who in great courtesy received the gift, and told the General that on his return to England he would send a present to the King.

"At our comeinge awaie from the Court, without the gait we see a man lyinge slayne, and was to lie there till the dogges had eaten his flesh, for comittinge adultery with another man's wiffe."

Seventeenth June. Captain Best presented the King with a model of an English ship, "in which ship he took great pleasure, and did accept of yt and esteeme yt more then a matter of greater worth. The letter was promised within a daie or towe, and many promises of honor and credit to our General for the fame of our nation."

The same day news of the Globe, and of the death of Captain Anthony Hippon[13] was received.

Twentieth June. The General received the King's letter. It was to the effect that the General might at pleasure found a factory at Priaman or Tecoe; all his merchants and people were to be courteously received: a bargain once made to be irrevocable: and to have the same weight in all things as the weight of Achin.

That day, too, the King by water proceeded to the castle, partly for purposes of recreation, and partly to inspect a junk of Surat, which he had confiscated (making slaves of her crew) for having touched at Perak, with which place he was at enmity.

Twenty-first June. The General took the King's letter back to the Rassedor, with reference to the remission of tributes and customs, in conformity with the Articles made between the King's uncle and Sir James Lancaster, in which it was agreed that the English should be privileged to trade in any part or port of the island without paying tribute or customs on goods sold. The Governor of Priaman and Tecoe having ignored this agreement and levied these dues, Captain Best craved redress for these wrongs. The King afterwards promised to grant this remission at Priaman and Tecoe, and at the same time offered to dispose to Captain Best of the cargo of the confiscated junk; but, owing to the conduct of the native officials, the latter was unable to take advantage of that offer.

Twenty-fourth June. The General attended at Court for despatch of business, when he sold the King 168 bahars of iron at 5 tael the bahar.

The same day, the King's letter and present were brought "to our house by a nobleman riding upon an ollephant, accompanied with other towe of the Kinge's chiefe nobles, with musick plaieing before them alongst the streetes, as ther customes is in such affaires which concernes the Kinge. The present was a rich creast of pure gold, set with pretious stones, 8 campher dishes, 4 peeces of

---

[13] Second in command, under Captain Floris, in the seventeenth voyage, 1611–1615.

121

fine stuffe, a launce enameld with gould. At the receipt of this present and letter for our King, our Generall did present the 3 nobles with some fyne calico."

"Twenty-sixth June. Our General went to the Court according to the Kinge's desire unto him the daie before, where we see the Kinge in most royall estait comeinge unto his church in most rich array, accompanied with his nobles and chief of his kingdome: from the church retourned unto a grene before his pallace gait, wher he did sit in a rich chaire of state of pure gold: his nobles standinge before him was called one by one in ther degrees to take ther places, which was done by great obeysance in bowing downe ther bodies to the grownd and holdinge upp of ther handes above ther heades. In the midest of the nobles our General was called; and all the rest of the forraine and strange ambassadores, as the honor of ther Kinge and countrey did deserve. After all the nobles were seatted, inferioures took ther places. The Kinge's guard was 200 great ollephantes compassing the place where he sat, a multitude of people expecting the fighting of ollephantes, which are the greatest and strongest beastes in the world, haveing teeth a yard and a half longe. The feight of the tame ollephantes were both fierce and furious, but the wild ones did far exceed them, for before they could be gotten together they rane amongst the houses, and (with) vehement force of there teeth and trounke did pull them downe, but being once met they maid a most furious feight, and did gore and wound one another with ther teeth most cruellie; growinge weak, the King caused them to be parted. After them came in great rames, which allso maid a good feight. Ther was much sport to be seene; but growing lait, the Kinge did pretermit the rest. The sportes being ended, all the nobles in ther degree rose upp and came before the Kinge, kissed his handes, and so with low obeysaunce going backwardes from his presence; the King sat still till they all had done in forme aforesaid, and then he himself rose upp and took ollephant and repaired to his pallace in great pomp."

Twenty-eighth June. The General proceeded to Court, when the King told him that on that day he could hold no conference, as his army had returned from Joar,[14] bringing back the King of that place as a prisoner, and that many of his nobles were assembled to confer upon matters of state. Thereupon, the General withdrew. The victory was celebrated with great solemnity in both country and city. The fleet consisted of 100 frigates and galleys, some with ordnance, some without, and the army of 20,000 soldiers. A Flemish ship, which had been at Joar, on the approach of the army had put to sea, but her captain, with some twenty of the merchants and mariners, who had been on shoare, were taken prisoners, and others of her crew were slain. Captain Best called on the Fleming to encourage him, and heard from him of Sir Henry Middleton having been at Bantam, and of the death of most of his merchants and men; further, he heard of the Salomon, that the Hector and Thomas were bound for England, and Cap-

---

[14] Johore.

tain Saris in the Clove for Japan, but no tidings could he obtain of the James, which made him uneasy about that vessel's safety.

Second July. The General being sent for by the King, "we met his Majesty in most roiall state in the waie to the church with great solemnitie. He had for his guard, (who) went before him, 200 great ollephantes, 2000 small shot, 2000 pikes, 200 launces, 100 bowmen, 20 naked swordes of pure gould carried before him; 20 fencers went before him, plaiinge with swordes and tergettes; a horse leed before him, covered with beaten gould, the bridle set with stones; at his sadle-crutch a shafte of arrowes, the quiver of beaten gould set with pretious stones. Before him went his towe sons, of 8 or 9 ould, arayed with jewelles and rich stones. His Majestie rode upon an ollephant, his sadle of pure gold, his slave behynd him in rich arraye, with his betel boxe, and a fan of pure gold in his hand to keepe the flies from the Kinge. The Kinge's robes were so rich that I cannot well describe them; he had a turband upon his head set with jewelles and pretious stones invalluable; creast and sword of pure gold, the skaberd set with stones. Before him went an ollephant, with a chaire of state covered all with beaten silver, that, if yt should chaunce to rayne, he might change ollephantes. This ollephant had casses made of pure gold to put upon his teeth. From the church he retourned to a place of pleasure prepared for his entertaynement, where his Majestie beinge seated, all his nobles, according to their custome, was called; and all forreyn embassadores, as the fame of ther countrey did deserve, were seated amongst the nobles. Which being done, we see the feighting of wild and tame ollephantes, buffolos, and rames. Thes pleasures being past, all the nobles, in great obedience, saluted his Majestie at his rising up, and did accompany him to his pallace, where we left him to his concubynes."

On this day, too, the Siamese Ambassador departed from Achin, leaving behind him Fen, whose pardon he had obtained. This Fen, shortly before the vessels sailed, entreated the General to grant him a passage to England, which request Captain Best promised to accede to if Fen would agree to work the passage home. The latter promised to do so, and then asked for money to pay his debts. The General declined to make any such advance, but added that if Fen could find his way on board, the conditions would still be open for his acceptance.

Fifth July. "At our retourne from the Court, we see a man executed for some offence in the warres. He was first laid upon the ground upon his back, and both his eyes pulled out, and after a stake was drove in at his fundement, through all his bodie, and out at the crowne of his head, and being dead his corpes were burned. Another souldier, the daie before, had his eyes puld out, his bodie cloven in tow peeces, and then burned with a doge in his bellie. Another was boyled in oille this daie, which was as cruell a tortuer as the other. These men had comitted some offence in the wars wherby some prejudice had happened."

"The Generall of the Army, for his welcome, because he did not bring the ould King of Joar, who was an ould decreped man, and had assigned his kingdome to his son, was by the King forced to eat a platter of turdes, and afterwardes to wash his bodie in them, to the Kinge's great infamie and dishonour, for so base a thing to be published amongst forreyners and strangers. Allthough this seeme strange, yett yt is trew, as God is in heaven."

Seventh July. The General at last received the Kinge's letter for Priaman and Tecoe, but the King did not keep his promise to remit the customs.

Three days later, a seaman, who had run away, was found at "the Portingailles house," and brought back to the Dragon.

At an interview with the King, the General offered him a fair piece of ordnance, if he would release four of the Guzerats, vizt., the master and his son and the two pilots. As the King would only do so upon payment of a large sum, Captain Best took his leave, "haveinge found him allwaies reedie to promise much, and, in the end, to performe litle. But his basenes hath not onelie bene evident to his owne subjectes, but allso unto us in not performeinge what formerlie he had promised unto our General. He diverse tymes shewed us his glorie, but never his loialltie, nor fidellitie, and therefore we will leave him to that infidellitie he doth professe."

Eleventh July. "Our General, hasteninge busines, sent abord 4 or 5 slaves, bought here at 4 or 5 taille."

Fourteenth July. The General having finished all his business, "we sett saille furth of the Rood of Achin, haveinge bene here 3 mounthes and 2 daies, in which tyme we have lost furth of both shipes 25 men. Our General bought and entertayned here about 25, or thereabout, Indeans for to suplie the want of our men deceased, and of Nathaniell Fen left behind at Achin."

"THE QUALITIE OF MONEY AND WEIGHT AT ACHIN."

"Yowe have a great weight called a bahar, which doth conteyne 385[lbs.] English: yowe have allso a small weight called a cattee, which maikes 2[bs.] English.[15] Yowe have gould: ther coynes called masses, at 9d. the peece: and 5 goes for a peece of 8: yowe have also lead money, of which 1000 maikes a masse, called casse: ther also doth harres go currant at 9ds. the peece, and 5 to a peece of 8; sometimes they go at a higher rate. This money is curant all the Indes over, and much profit gotten by the exchange of them."

"This Island of Sumatra, alliis called Ophir, from whence Sallomon had his gould, as the Scriptures in divers places maikes mention. They do professe Mahamat's Lawe, as for the most part of Asia and Africa doth. They have no church nor churchyard, but buries ther dead in the corner of streetes. This Citie

---

15 A bahar at Achin is equal to 200 *cattis,* or 423 lbs. 8 oz.

of Achin lieth within 6 degrees of the Equanoctiall lyne, which maikes yt so exceedinge hot, yet the people countynually goeth bare-headed and bare-footed, and so doth the Kinge and all his nobles and chief of the land. Thes people are great swimmers and divers in generall, women as well as men: they teach ther children thes arts in ther infancie, so they become verie exquisite in ther perfect aige: this swimming they hould to be a great preservaçon of ther health, for which cause they dailie exercise yt as the custome of eatinge and drinking. This island (is) verie rich, and plentie of fruit, yet the comon sort of people lives upon an erbe called Beetle, by which they fynd great sustenance, so that this aforesaid herbe and tobacco is ther ordinarie food both to men and women. The Kinge hath one loyall wife, whose child doth posesse the crowne: he hath also threskore concubynes; for where he heres of a proper woman, eyther in citie or countree, he sendeth for hir to the Court; allthoughe she bee maried she must come, and if hir husband seeme unwillinge or loath to part from hir, then he presentlie comaundes hir husbande's member to be cutt of, and oftentymes worse punishments. If the Kinge have more sones then one, when he dies they are all put to death, save the eldest, or conveyed furth of the kingdome into some other countree, because they shall not contend for the crowne after the Kinge's death. If a subject die without heire male, his goodes and landes falles to the Kinge, and the wife with hir daughters go begge. Many nations have trade for this island, more for the comoditties yt affordes then the affabillitie of the people, for they are both inhumayne and base, and much unworthie to inhabite so sweet a countree."

From the twenty-fifth of July to the end of the month, the weather was very bad, with much wind, rain, and lightning. "Divers of the Dragon's men and ours fell sick by intemperat and corupted aire."

The master of the Hoseander shaped his course for Tecoe, by the "directions of Capt. Keelinge and Daves, ther jourualles," and anchored in the road of that island on the Seventh of August.

The Governor of the Island sent off two officers to enquire whether the General had their King's letter, which was then shown to them. They then spake of the death of Sir Henry Middleton at Bantam. On the following day, Captain Best, upon landing, was received by the chiefs, to whom he presented the letter. Having read the letter, the chiefs assured the General that he was free to trade where he pleased at reasonable prices; and that they would inform the Governor of Priaman of the letter, as it concerned him. Captain Best thereupon offered to convey their messengers to that island in his smaller ship. At the close of the interview, the General was invited to visit the city, but declined on the ground of the great heat.

At Tecoe the merchants found, upon landing, that the price of pepper was 16 to 18 rials the bahar, but no price fixed as a certainty.

Twelfth August. The Hoseander was despatched by the General to Priaman, where she arrived on the following day. The Governor of that Island was "much discontented" that the vessels had not touched there, being the chief port of those parts, previous to going to Tecoe, and because the King's letter was directed to him. When Mr Oliver, merchant of the Hoseander, had presented the royal letter, the Governor assured him that he was privileged to trade there. Mr Oliver having enquired if the people of Priaman would carry their pepper to Tecoe, the Governor replied that in former times the people of Tecoe had brought pepper to Priaman, but that his people had never carried any to Tecoe, and never would do so; and if the General wished to send a ship to Priaman, they would within two months have their pepper, about 2000 bahars, ready either to sell for rialls, or to truck for calico. The price of such pepper to be the same as that purchased at Tecoe, and the pepper to be delivered at the seaside in the place where Captain Keeling and others had received their purchases.

This business being concluded, the Hoseander returned to Tecoe.

Having at Tecoe received some stores from the Dragon, and exchanged some of her lading, the Hoseander was on the twenty-first of August despatched by the General on a voyage to Bantam.

"Twenty-sixth August. Being in 3 degrees or theraboutes to the southward of Priaman, in our vaige to Bantam, we had most cruell and fearfull wether by thunderinge, lightninge, and raine for many daies together, but especiallie one night and a daie. I maie truelie saie that the greatest cannon in all the world, when it was fired, did never roare as the thunder heere did, with lightning and raine in such aboundance as I never in my life heard the like: and I do furder think that in England yt never rayned so much in 6 daies as here yt did in 24 houres. It was both wonderfull and miraculous to behold, and did justlie verifie the sayinge of that worthie Profit David in his 107 Psalme, where yt is said, that they that go downe to the sea in shipes and occupie by great waters, those men doth see the wounders of the Lord. And God of his mercie graunt that we all that heard and see thes wounders and workes of the Lord maie to his glorie maik use of the 31 verse of the same Psalme."

Twenty-ninth August, 1613. "This daie by extremitie of wether, we splitt our maine topesaile, and this night sunk our skiffe at the shipp sterne." [Here the journal concludes abruptly.][16]

---

[16] The original manuscript consists of 67 ¼ folio pages. At the Reverse of the Journal the Wills of Robert Heal, Oliver Judson, and Robert Portman, are entered. Also there are entries, each of a few lines on a page, of various debts to be paid by different members of the crew upon the return of the vessel to England. These entries, and the Index to them, are scattered over sixty-one pages.

EUROPE AND THE WIDER WORLD, 1500–1750: THE MILITARY BALANCE*

Geoffrey Parker

In the Victoria and Albert Museum in London, there is an ivory chess set, made for Tippu Sultan of Mysore during the late eighteenth century. One set of chessmen represents an Indian princely army, whose soldiers wield swords and hold shields; their adversaries, however, are the European officers and native infantry of the British East India Company—all in uniform, and all impressively equipped with firearms.[1] This contrast neatly symbolizes a central feature of European overseas expansion since the Middle Ages: namely, the absolute or relative superiority of Western weaponry and Western military organization over all others. Amid the wealth of statistics on Europe's import of Asian spices, on the silver production of colonial America, or on the export of African slaves, it is easy to forget that each of these lucrative economic enterprises rested in the last analysis upon force. Although other chapters in this volume stress lower transaction costs as a key explanation of Europe's commercial expansion, it was often a minor consideration overseas, where even the sharpest and most sophisticated business methods would scarcely have been competitive without the sanction of superior force on the part of the Western merchants. As Irfan Habib put it in his perceptive contribution to *The Rise of Merchant Empires*:

> 'Could it be that the European triumph over Indian (and Asian) merchants was not, then, one of size and techniques, of companies over peddlars, of

---

* This paper draws heavily on G. Parker, *The Military Revolution. Military Innovation and the Rise of the West, 1500–1800* (2nd edn., Cambridge, 1990). I am grateful for important corrections and additional material to Jean Aubin, David W. Baeckelandt, William J. Hamblin, Teresa A. Hiener, Sanjay Subrahmanyam, and Ronald P. Toby.

[1] Victoria and Albert Museum (London), Catalogue no. I. M. 42-1910. See the reproduction in Parker, *Military Revolution*, 116.

joint-stock over atomized capital, of seamen over landsmen? Might it not have been more a matter of men-of-war and gun and shot?'

Indeed, Frederick C. Lane and Niels Steensgaard have gone even further, and suggest that the principal export of preindustrial Europe to the rest of the world was violence, and that the *fidalgos,* the *conquistadores,* the *vrijburghers,* and the *nabobs* were (in effect) warrior nomads who differed little from the Mongols or the Mughals.[2] Even the contrasting styles of conquest, with the Europeans commanding from the quarterdeck while the Asians rode on horseback, were more apparent than real, for the major gains of both were all made on land; and to acquire and preserve a territorial base overseas required fortifications and armies as well as ships.

It follows that, if the dynamics of European overseas expansion are to be fully comprehended, a study of the changing military balance between the West and the rest is essential. But, almost immediately, a major paradox appears. In Central and South America, small groups of Westerners in the first half of the sixteenth century caused the collapse of the mighty Inca and Aztec empires, which (between them) had ruled over nearly one-tenth of the world's population; yet in India, until the mid-eighteenth century, the Europeans made virtually no impact on even the minor states of the subcontinent. Indeed, the sudden progress of Western military methods there after the 1740s was so rapid that it left many Europeans bewildered. When, for example, Edmund Burke spoke in December 1783 in a debate in the English House of Commons on Fox's India Bill, he interrupted his tirade on the injustices and humiliations inflicted upon the Mughal emperor by officers of the Honorable East India Company to observe:

> *It is impossible, Mr. Speaker, not to pause here for a moment to reflect on the inconsistency of human greatness and the stupendous revolutions that have happened in our age of wonders. Could it be believed, when I entered into existence or when you, a younger man, were born, that on this day, in this House, we should be employed in discussing the conduct of those British subjects who had disposed of the power and person of the Grand Mogul?[3]*

No, indeed: in 1727, the year of Burke's birth, it *had* been unimaginable, for the Europeans in India were still confined to a handful of fortresses and factories huddled around the coasts of the subcontinent.

---

[2] I. Habib, 'Merchant communities in precolonial India' in J. Tracy, ed., *The Rise of Merchant Empires.* (Cambridge, 1990), 371–99, at p. 399; F. C. Lane, *Venice and History* (Baltimore, 1966), chaps. 23 and 24; N. Steensgaard, "Violence and the Rise of Capitalism: F. C. Lane's Theory of Protection and Tribute," *Review* 5 (1981): 247–73. See also the perceptive sociohistorical analysis of G. B. Ness and W. Stahl, "Western Imperialist Armies in Asia," *Comparative Studies in Society and History* 19 (1977): 2–29.

[3] P. J. Marshall, ed., *The Writings and Speeches of Edmund Burke,* V (Oxford, 1981), 392.

It used to be fashionable to attribute the rapid transformation of this situation either to the innate moral superiority of the white man, or to the added strength afforded him by the Industrial Revolution. But unfortunately there is little evidence that Britons were more virtuous in 1800 (when they held much of India in their power) than in 1700 (when they held very little) or in 1600 (when they held none at all); and proof that the factory system played a major role in conquering the non-Western world before the nineteenth century is either ambiguous or absent. Although the Machine Age helps to explain how the Europeans extended their control over the total land area of the globe from 35 percent in 1800 to 84 percent in 1914, it cannot explain how they managed to acquire that initial 35 percent.[4] By 1800 white colonists ruled all of Siberia, large parts of America and India, several enclaves in Southeast Asia, and a few outposts along the coasts of Africa; but in East Asia, by contrast, they had still scarcely made any impact. These striking differences can only be understood if the "rise of the West" is broken down into a number of distinct geographical and chronological components.

I

By 1650 the West had already achieved military mastery in four separate areas: central and northeast America; Siberia; some coastal areas of sub-Saharan Africa; and in some parts of the Indonesian and Philippine archipelagoes. Different as these regions, and their inhabitants, undoubtedly were, their experience of the European invaders was, in one crucial respect, identical: the white men, they found, fought dirty and (what was worse) fought to kill. Thus the Narragansett Indians of New England strongly disapproved of the colonists' way of making war. "It was too furious," one brave told an English captain in 1638, "and [it] slays too many men." The captain did not deny it. The Indians, he speculated, "might fight seven years and not kill seven men." Roger Williams, a colonial governor, likewise admitted that the Indians' fighting "was farre lesse bloudy and devouring than the cruell warres of Europe."[5] Meanwhile, on the other side of the world, the peoples of Indonesia were equally appalled by the all-destructive

---

[4] D. R. Headrick, *The Tools of Empire: Technology and European Imperialism in the Nineteenth Century* (Oxford, 1981), passim.

[5] Quotations from J. L. Axtell, *The European and the Indian: Essays in the Ethnohistory of Colonial North America* (Oxford, 1981), 140; and F. Jennings, *The Invasion of America* (New York, 1976), 150. Admittedly in some Mesoamerican societies those spared in battle were later slaughtered in religious rituals. The "Flower Wars" of the later Aztec Empire, for example, involved few deaths precisely because all those captured were required for sacrifice. See C. M. Maclachlan and J. E. Rodríquez O, *Forging of the Cosmic Race: A Reinterpretation of Colonial Mexico* (Berkeley, 1980), 38 ff.; and I. Clendinnen, "The Cost of Courage in Aztec Society," *Past and Present* 107 (1985): 44–89.

fury of European warfare. The men of Java, for example, were "very loth to fight if they can choose." According to Edmund Scott, who lived among them between 1603 and 1606, the reason was simple: "They say . . . their wealth lyeth altogether in slaves; so that, if their slaves be killed, they are beggared."[6]

Scott had noted a vital and unusual feature of military organization in Southeast Asia that was shared (though he probably did not know it) with America and sub-Saharan Africa: native wars in these areas were almost always fought to enslave enemies rather than to exterminate them, to control labor rather than land, to gain men rather than territory. Of course, there were exceptions. Some Amerindian tribes, such as the Algonquin, tortured their defeated enemies to death in a prolonged and painful ritual; the Zulus in the nineteenth century killed their enemies indiscriminately; and the Igorots of central Luzon in the Philippines remained, until modern times, more interested in collecting heads than slaves.[7] Conversely, the European, for their part, sometimes enslaved defeated enemies. Thus, in the 1650s, the survivors of the Scottish armies captured by the English were condemned to permanent servitude (usually in Barbados, though sometimes at home: the members of a parliamentary delegation sent to congratulate Oliver Cromwell on his victory at Worcester were each given a horse and two Scotsmen by the Lord General "for a present" to do with as they pleased.[8] But the Scots were regarded as rebels and were treated accordingly; and, even in the case of this and other civil conflicts, the *aim* of making war in Europe was never to secure slaves, as it was in the non-European areas under consideration.

---

6 Edmund Scott, "An Exact Discourse of the Subtilties of the East Indies," in W. Foster, ed., *The Voyage of Sir Henry Middleton to the Moluccas, 1604–1606* (London, 1943; Hakluyt Society, 2d ser., LXXXVIII), 142. Of course, all testimony by Europeans on the *motives* of people from different cultures must be treated with some caution: The Europeans' view of the "savages" was often insensitive and not infrequently confused. Take, for example, the assertion of the French missionary in seventeenth-century Canada, Louis Hennepin, who claimed that when the Indians went to war "'tis commonly to recover satisfaction for some injury that they pretend has been done to them. Sometimes they engage in it upon arrival of a dream; and often as Fancy takes 'em." (quoted in C. J. Jaenen, *Friend and Foe: Aspects of Franco-Amerindian Cultural Contact in the Sixteenth and Seventeenth Centuries* (Ottawa, 1976), 129.)

7 Jaenen, *Friend and Foe*, 138–41; D. R. Morris, *The Washing of the Spears. The Rise and Fall of the Great Zulu Nation* (London, 1966), 47, 108, 389; W. H. Scott, *The Discovery of the Igorots: Spanish Contacts with the Pagans of Northern Luzon* (Quezon City, 1974), 48–50, 52. A. Reid, *Europe and South-East Asia: The Military Balance* (James Cook University of North Queensland, South-East Asian Studies Committee: occasional paper XVI [1982]), 1–2, notes that some Indonesian battles ended with a suicidal charge by a few of the defeated, but this practice, known as "running amok," was merely a token of the mettle of the vanquished before the rest became slaves. It did not herald a mass slaughter.

8 Whitelocke, *Memorials of the English Affairs*, III (Oxford, 1853), 351. The author claimed to have set his Scotsmen free at once.

Another distinctive common feature of these regions lay in their settlement patterns. In America, although the Aztec and Inca empires possessed some walled cities, the less civilized peoples to the north and south of them did not. This dearth, of course, facilitated the initial conquest because the natives lacked defensible bases to fall back on, but it complicated consolidation. As Increase Mather, of New England, complained in 1675: "Every swamp is a castle to them, knowing where to find us; but we know not where to find them!" And there are innumerable examples of colonial soldiers marching out with drums beating and colors unfurled in order to destroy an Indian "town"— only to find it gone. The logic of Western superiority in fixed encounters had been thoroughly digested by the Indians: after their costly initial defeats, they were scrupulously careful to avoid pitched battles—much to the fury of the Europeans—because they always lost them. "They doe acts of hostility without proclaiming war; they don't appear openly in the field to bid us battle," was the lament of another irate New England preacher.[9] Only gradually did the Europeans recognize that the only way to beat the Indians was to adopt those same guerrilla methods. The serious native rising of 1675 in New England, known as King Philip's War, was only suppressed when the colonists followed the advice of Captain Benjamin Church and fought in small units, armed with hatchets, dogs, and knives as well as firearms, which operated in open formation rather than in lines or columns.[10]

But the Indians of New England were also learning fast. From the 1640s they managed to acquire an adequate supply of guns from the French, the English and (until the collapse of New Netherland in 1664) the Dutch; and they used them to deadly effect—soon realizing that a musket ball traveled with more force, and faster, than an arrow, and was less likely to be deflected by leaves or undergrowth. Furthermore, the Narragansetts in King Philip's War took refuge in "the Great Swamp" behind the walls and bastions of a European-style fortress that claimed the lives of seventy colonists before it was taken. In the end the "Red Indians" lost ground not so much through any technical inferiority as because their numbers dwindled throughout the seventeenth century (largely

---

[9] Quotations from Axtell, *The European and the Indian*, 145, 142. For the Indians' guerrilla tactics, see K. F. Otterbein, "Why the Iroquois Won: An Analysis of Iroquois Military Tactics," *Ethnohistory* 11 (1964): 56–63; and F. R. Secoy, *Changing Military Patterns on the Great Plains (17th through early 19th century)* (New York, 1953: Monographs of the American Ethnological Society, XXI), 52ff.

[10] For Benjamin Church, see Axtell, *The European and the Indian*, 146f.; and R. Slotkin and J. K. Flosom, eds., *So Dreadfull a Judgment: Puritan Responses to King Philip's War 1676–7* (Middletown, 1978), 370–470, which provides a critical edition of Church's *Entertaining Passages Relating to Philip's War*.

thanks to the inroads of European diseases), while those of the Westerners (largely thanks to immigration) relentlessly increased.[11]

The situation in Siberia was not dissimilar. The Cossacks who crossed the Urals into Siberia in the 1580s made excellent use of both firearms and forts to expand eastward, reaching the Pacific by the 1630s in their headlong search for furs. But their rapid progress was due also to the relative absence of concerted opposition: the native population of Siberia at the time was, after all, probably less than 200,000.[12]

Black Africa, however, was a complete contrast. In the first place the Europeans remained, until the nineteenth century, largely confined to their necklace of forts around the coast. The African interior remained inhospitable, if not impenetrable, and many of its states possessed armies that were both numerous and well disciplined. Until the mass manufacture of quinine, the Europeans possessed little defense against the malaria that raged throughout the "dark continent"; and, until the invention of the machine gun, their armament may have been enough to win battles, but it was seldom sufficient to win wars. Indeed, several African rulers, from the mid-sixteenth century onward, could match Western firepower with guns of their own—especially after the 1650s, when the Dutch began a direct exchange of guns for slaves. Some 8,000 muskets were sent to the Gold Coast for trade in the three years following July 1658, for example, exchanged at the rate of twelve per slave; a century later, the total number of firearms exported every year was around 400,000, exchanged at the rate of 4, 5, or 6 per slave. And yet, in most areas, this inflow of Western technology scarcely

---

[11] Details from Secoy, *Changing Military Patterns*, 68 ff.; P. M. Malone, "Changing Military Technology among the Indians of Southern New England 1600–77," *The American Quarterly* 25 (1973): 48–63; H. Lamar and L. Thompson, eds., *The Frontier in History: North America and Southern Africa Compared* (New Haven, 1981), chaps. 5 and 7; and F. Jennings, *The Ambiguous Iroquois Empire: The Covenant Chain Confederation of Indian Tribes with English Colonies from its Beginning to the Lancaster Treaty of 1744* (New York, 1984), 80ff. Much the same sequence of events had already taken place farther south. See the accounts offered by P. W. Powell, *Soldiers, Indians, and Silver: The Northward Advance of New Spain, 1550–1600* (2d ed., Berkeley, 1969); I. Clendinnen, *Ambivalent Conquests. Maya and Spaniard in Yucatan, 1517–1570* (Cambridge, 1987); A. Jara, *Guerre et société au Chili: essai de sociologie coloniale* (Paris, 1961); and E. Cabral de Mello, *Olinda restaurada. Guerra e açúcar no Nordeste 1630–1954* (Rio de Janeiro, 1975)—especially chapter 7.

[12] Details from D. W. Treadgold, *The Great Siberian Migration* (Princeton, 1957); and G. V. Lantzeff and R. A. Pierce, *Eastward to Empire: Exploration and Conquest on the Russian Open Frontier to 1750* (London, 1973).

affected most African military techniques.[13] As late as 1861 an English officer in Nigeria who observed the Yoruba at war noted that the native troops in battle still "spread themselves out anyhow into open order, and skirmish away until their ammunition is exhausted, upon which they return to replenish." He added that "though thousands of rounds be fired, the killed may be counted by units and the wounded by tens."[14] Tactics like these would clearly prove ineffective against highly trained European forces. But Black Africa did not import guns for this purpose: wars continued to be fought for slaves, not territories, and the irrelevance of musketry salvoes to operations aimed at securing fit and healthy slaves is obvious. Smoothbore weapons were far too inaccurate to be used with precision to wound rather than to kill; and, in any case, the injuries inflicted by lead shot, however slight, often smashed bones and created wounds that turned gangrenous and caused death. In the eighteenth century, the use of pellets rather than bullets overcame this problem in part—which perhaps explains the dramatic increase in musket imports—but this did nothing to facilitate the adoption of Western methods of musketry in warfare, for guns simply did not fit into most African military traditions at all.[15]

---

[13] However, the possession of firearms certainly influenced the rise and fall of such west African states as the Asante, whose expansion from the late seventeenth century onward seems to have been based on the gun. See I. Wilks, *The Asante in the Nineteenth Century* (Cambridge, 1975), 20, 110ff. But this is a highly controversial subject, for which much conflicting evidence has been unearthed. See R. Kea, *Settlements, Trade, and Politics in the Seventeenth-Century Gold Coast* (Baltimore, 1982), 158f.; idem, "Firearms and Warfare on the Gold and Slave Coasts from the Sixteenth to the Nineteenth Centuries," *Journal of African History* 12 (1971): 185–213; K. Y. Daaku, *Trade and Politics on the Gold Coast, 1600–1720* (Oxford, 1970), 149–53; J. E. Inikori, "The Import of Firearms into West Africa, 1750–1807: A Quantitative Analysis," *Journal of African History* 18 (1977), 339–68; and W. Richards, "The Import of Firearms into West Africa in the Eighteenth Century," ibid., 21 (1980): 43–59.

[14] J. F. Ade Ajayi and R. Smith, *Yoruba Warfare in the Nineteenth Century* (Cambridge, 1964), 31, 50. In east Africa, it has been suggested, wars in the immediate precolonial period became largely ritualized for lack of manpower: see J. de V. Allen, "Traditional History and African Literature: The Swahili Case," *Journal of African History* 23 (1982): 227–36, at p. 234.

[15] On the muted impact of the gun, which was repeatedly introduced into African societies only to fall out of use again, see (apart from the sources quoted above): H. J. Fisher and V. Rowland, "Firearms in the Central Sudan," *"Journal of African History* 12 (1971: 215–39; G. White, "Firearms in Africa: An Introduction," ibid., 173–84; R. Oliver, ed., *The Cambridge History of Africa*, III (Cambridge, 1977), 305–12; H. A. Gemery and J. S. Hogendorn, "Technological Change, Slavery, and the Slave Trade," in C. Dewey and A. G. Hopkins, eds., *The Imperial Impact: Studies in the Economic History of Africa and India* (London, 1978), 243–58; and above all, J. K. Thornton, 'The art of war in Angola, 1575–1680,' *Comparative Studies in Society and History*, XXX (1988), 360–78; and R. Elphick, *Kraal and Castle: Khoikhoi and the Founding of White South Africa* (New Haven, 1977), 53ff.

It was much the same story in the Indonesian archipelago. Sultan Iskandar Muda, of Aceh, for example, had by 1620 accumulated some 2,000 artillery pieces from various Ottoman and European sources. But it led nowhere: the guns proved inferior in action against the Portuguese and almost all were lost at the unsuccessful siege of Melaka in 1629. In reality, firearms never fully replaced Aceh's 900 war elephants as the front line of defense; and such cannon as remained after 1629 were reserved for ceremonial purposes.[16] In part this victory of tradition over innovation is explained, as in America, by the relative infrequency of walled towns. Indeed, in some cases, the boundary between town and country could be hard to find. A French visitor to the capital of Aceh in the 1620s claimed that it was despised by most Europeans "because it is a town undefended by any wall, resembling more an open village in Normandy than a city."[17]

In these areas, naturally, siege warfare was a new experience. Because wars had previously been fought to secure slaves or tribute, rather than to annexe more territory or acquire new specific strategic bases, the best defense against attack was either immediate surrender (when the enemy appeared in overwhelming strength) or temporary flight (at all other times). Thus, the last Muslim ruler of the thriving port city of Melaka was not unduly alarmed by the arrival of a small Portuguese squadron in 1511. After some resistance, he and his men withdrew inland "a day's journey" thinking (according to the *Commentaries* of Bras de Albuquerque) that the Portuguese "simply meant to rob the city and then leave it and sail away with the spoil." But, instead, they built the powerful fort known as *A Famosa*, constructed (typically) on the ruins of the Great

---

[16] See D. Lombard, *Le Sultanat d'Atjeh au temps d'Iskandar Muda* (1607–1636) (Paris, 1967), 83–100; and C. R. Boxer, "The Achinese Attack on Malacca in 1629," in J. Bastin and R. Roolvink, eds., *Malayan and Indonesian Studies* (Oxford, 1964), reprinted in Boxer, *Portuguese Conquest and Commerce in Southern Asia* (London, 1985), chap. 4; D. K. Bassett, "Changes in the Pattern of Malay Politics, 1629–c. 1655," *Journal of South-East Asian History* 10, no. 3 (1969): 429–52; and A. R. Reid, "Sixteenth-Century Turkish Influence in Western Indonesia," ibid., 395–414. For similar evidence of poor use of Western guns and military techniques by another Malayan native state, see I. A. Macgregor, "Johore Lama in the 16th century," *Journal of the Malayan Branch of the Royal Asiatic Society* 28, no. 2 (1955): 48–125.

[17] On the typology of towns in Southeast Asia, see the excellent studies of A. R. Reid; "The Structure of Cities in South-East Asia, 15th–17th centuries," *Journal of South-East Asian Studies* 10 (1980): 235–50; idem, "Southeast Asian Cities before Colonialism," *Hemisphere* 28, no. 3 (1983): 144–9; and R. Reed, *Colonial Manila: The Context of Hispanic Urbanism and Process of Morphogenesis* (Berkeley, 1978), 1–3. The Philippines on the eve of Spanish conquest in the 1560s possessed no towns at all. Beaulieu's contempt for Aceh is quoted by Lombard, *Sultanat*, 45n2.

Mosque with stones gathered from the sacred hill where the sultan's ancestors lay buried. Eventually the walls of Portuguese Melaka stretched for two kilometers and withstood some ten sieges.[18] One of these, in 1629, was undertaken on a heroic scale: Iskandar Muda, of Aceh, led in person a besieging force of 20,000, supported by 236 boats and artillery. They erected siegeworks around Melaka so well that, according to a Portuguese account, "not even the Romans could have made such works stronger or more quickly." But it was not enough to secure victory—on the contrary, the sultan eventually lost 19,000 men and his two senior commanders, as well as most of the ships and guns. In the same year, an equally formidable siege was begun by the ruler of Mataram against the Dutch fortified port of Batavia, which the sultan correctly identified as a "thorn in the foot of Java" that had to be "plucked out, for fear the whole body should be endangered." The sultan's forces, like the troops of Aceh, managed to dig trenches in the European fashion; but they made no impression against the massive moat, wall, and bastions of the new Dutch settlement.[19]

The Europeans erected many other fortifications in Southeast Asia: numerous small citadels in the "Spice Islands" (as at Ternate, Tidore, or Amboina) and the Philippines; Fort Zeelandia on Taiwan; the Monte fortress in

---

[18] Bras de Albuquerque, *The Commentaries of the Great Alfonso Dalboquerque,* III (London, 1880; Hakluyt Society, LXII), 129. See also G. Irwin, "Malacca Fort," *Journal of South-East Asian History* 3, no. 2 (1962): 19–44. The article is reprinted, with some additional material, in K. S. Sandhu and P. Wheatley, eds., *Melaka: The Transformation of a Malay Capital c. 1400–1980,* I (Oxford, 1983), 782–805. This admirable two-volume work contains much else on the subject, though unfortunately there is no chapter on Portuguese Melaka. Today only one gate (the so-called Porto de Santiago, which is in fact Dutch) and some rubble remain on the site of "A Famosa."

[19] See the sources quoted in note 16 and C. R. Boxer, "Asian Potentates and European Artillery in the 16th–18th Centuries," *Journal of the Malayan Branch of the Royal Asiatic Society* 27, no. 2 (1965); 156–72 (reprinted in Boxer, *Portuguese Conquest and Commerce,* chap. 7). There is a fine painting of the siege of 1629 in the Museum "Old Batavia" in Jakarta. See also the description in H. J. de Graff, *De Regering van Sultan Agung, Vorst van Mataram 1613–1645* (The Hague, 1958), 144–63; and the similar conclusion of R. Maclagen, "On Early Asiatic Fire-Weapons," *Journal of the Asiatic Society (Bengal)* 45, no. 1 (1876): 30–71.

Macao; and defensible factories in other places—Ayutthia, Bantam, Pegu.[20] But there was only one other fully fortified city to compare with Batavia and Melaka: Manila in the Philippines. Shortly before the arrival of the Spaniards in the 1560s, Muslims from Borneo and the Moluccas had introduced the art of fortification to the islands, but only in wood: a small fort near Puerta Galera (on Mindoro island) was the only stone building known to have existed in the pre-Hispanic Philippines. And neither that, nor the larger wooden stockade at Manila, could resist Spanish artillery and attack. But on the site of that Muslim stockade the Spaniards built massive defenses that defied all assaults for over two centuries. The citadel of Santiago itself was not much bigger than other forts (such as St. Pedro at Cebu), but it was connected to the vast stone wall, eight-feet thick and studded with bastions, which surrounded the Spanish city (known as Intramuros) and it dominated the finest natural harbor in East Asia.[21]

Impressed—or intimidated—by these developments, a few local rulers began to follow the European example: Bantam, Pati, Japura, and Surabaya all acquired brick or stone walls in the sixteenth century; the sultans of Makassar (in

---

[20] Excavations of the fort at Cebu and the factory at Ayutthia reveal a great deal about sixteenth-century European construction techniques in the tropics: see M. Maceda, "Prelimi-nary Report on the Excavation at Fort San Pedro, in Cebu City, Philippines," *Fu-Jen Studies* (Taipei, 1973), 45–59; and *The Portuguese and Ayutthaya* (exhibition catalogue, Bangkok, Portuguese embassy, 1985). It seems clear that the Iberians intended to create a fourth forti-fied port city, at Nagasaki, but the Japanese government refused to allow bastions to be built: see D. Pacheco, "The Founding of the Port of Nagasaki and Its Cession to the Society of Jesus," *Monumenta Nipponica* 25 (1970): 303–23; and G. Elison, *Deus Destroyed: The Image of Christianity in Early Modern Japan* (Cambridge, 1973: Harvard East Asian Series, LXXII), 133f. The Dutch, for their part, created a "colonial city" at Zeelandia after 1624, with its own town hall, weighhouse, hospital, orphanage, and even a house of correction for fallen women, but they only fortified the citadel and one outlying redoubt. The city itself was not provided with walls, and so it was captured in 1662 (after a lengthy siege) by the Ming loyalist forces commanded by Coxinga (Cheng Ch'eng-Kung). See R. G. Knapp, *China's Island Frontier: Studies in the Historical Geography of Taiwan* (Honolulu, 1980), 3–29; and J. L. Oosterhoff, "Zeelandia: A Dutch Colonial City on Formosa (1624–62)" in R. Ross and G. Telkamp, eds., *Colonial Cities: Essays on Urbanism in a Colonial Context* (Leiden, 1985: Comparative Studies in Overseas History, V), 52–63.

[21] Details from Reed, *Colonial Manila*, chap. 3 ("Intramuros: A City for Spaniards"); and C. Quirino, *Maps and Views of Old Maynila* (Manila, 1971). But not everyone was impressed by Intramuros. One Spanish official in Manila told the king in 1588 that the fortifications then being built were "a disgrace" and "a waste of time and money, because . . . they are made with round bulwarks in the old fashion;" and the military commandant three years later regretted that because the Spanish architect who designed them had remained in Europe, the defenses were "somewhat out of proportion, being made without architect, advice or plan." (Quotations from the excellent study of M. L. Díaz-Trechuelo Spínola, *Arquitectura española en Filipinas (1565–1800)* [Seville, 1959], 43f. See all of chaps. 2, 3, 6, 7, 12, 13.) The walls built in the 1650s, however, were more formidable.

south Sulawesi) built a brick wall and three redoubts around their capital in the mid-seventeenth century.[22] But in vain: the keys to the long-distance trade of East Asia remained in European hands: Manila for the trans-Pacific link with America; Melaka and Batavia for commerce with India and beyond. All three quickly acquired large populations of both natives and Chinese, but they remained in Western hands (albeit not always in the same Western hands) until 1942; and, with the wealth conferred by their possession, the Europeans could exercise a maritime hegemony over all other major ports in the region and prevent any rival state from mounting an effective challenge. They were also ideally placed to use the resources extracted from the area to extend that hegemony wherever an opportunity presented itself. Increasingly, their gaze was directed toward the territories, and the riches, of the Muslim rulers of India, Persia, and the Levant.

II

Slaves also played an important role in determining the Muslim response to Europe's military challenge, for they were likewise central to Islamic warfare. In the early ninth century, the Muslim states of North Africa, Spain, and Egypt began to use slave soldiers to defend themselves; by the middle of the century, the caliphs of Baghdad had followed suit; and the practice soon spread further. But the slave soldiers were not kidnapped and conscripted as adults: instead, they were recruited while still children (often as a form of tribute paid by non-Muslims to their conquerors) and brought up in the ruler's house-hold with his own children, so that they learned the ways of Islam as well as the art of war. The Mamluks of Egypt, mostly recruited in the Crimea, and the Ottoman Janissaries, mainly recruited in the Balkans, are merely the best known examples of these elite slave warriors. They were part of a military system that was unique to the world of Islam. Even the Muslim states of Indonesia had them: in the early seventeenth century the sultans of Aceh were served by 500 royal slaves born abroad and trained in warfare since their

---

[22] See the important studies of C. R. Boxer, *Francisco Vieira de Figureidó. A Portuguese Merchant-Adventurer in South-East Asia, 1624–1667* (The Hague, 1967); A. Reid, *Southeast Asia in the Age of Commerce. I: The 'Lands below the Winds'* (New Haven, 1988), 121–9; A. Reid, "The Rise of Makassar," *Review of Indonesian and Malaysian Affairs* XVII (1983): 117–80; L. Andaya, *The Heritage of Arung Palakka: a History of South Sulawei (Celebes) in the Seventeenth Century* (The Hague, 1981), chap. 3; J. A. J. Villiers, "Makassar and the Portuguese Connexion, 1540–1670" (paper presented at the *Symposium on South-East Asian Responses to European Intrusions* [Singapore, 1981]); and D. de Iongh, *Het Krijgswezen onder de Oostindische Compagnie* (The Hague, 1950), 36f. and 102–13.

youth.[23] And, although the Islamic states of India placed less reliance on slave soldiers, in compensation the sultans of the Deccan made extensive use in the fifteenth and sixteenth centuries of foreign mercenaries, particularly those from the Ottoman empire and Persia (referred to in the Portuguese records as *a gente branca* [white men] because they looked pale in comparison with the native Indians).[24] The character of Islamic warfare was thus consistent and clear: the core of every major army was composed of men lacking any local ties, devoted entirely to fulfilling their government's wishes, and fighting in the traditional manner. As a historian of Islamic institutions has written: "Mamluks were not supposed to think, but to ride horses; they were designed to be not a military elite, but military automata." The Mamluk aristocracy, like several other elites elsewhere, strongly opposed the proliferation of new weapons that threatened to erode the basis of their military predominance—thus although they eventually tolerated the use of firearms for sieges they refused to deploy them in battle.[25] And so in 1517 the imperious Mamluk knights were overthrown by the soldiers of the Ottoman Turks, whose commanders lacked such high principles.[26]

---

[23] See P. Crone, *Slaves on Horses: The Evolution of the Islamic Polity* (Cambridge, 1980); D. Pipes, *Slave Soldiers and Islam: The Genesis of a Military System* (New Haven, 1981); and R. Irwin, *The Middle East in the Middle Ages: The Early Mamluk Sultanate, 1250–1382* (London, 1986). On the slave soldiers of Aceh, see Reid, *Europe and Southeast Asia*, 7.

[24] See details in J. Aubin, "Le royaume d'Ormuz au début du XVIe siècle" in *Mare Luso-Indicum*, II (Paris, 1972), 77–179, at 175–9. For the pre-European period, see S. Digby, *War-Horse and Elephant in the Delhi Sultanate: A Study of Military Supplies* (Oxford, 1971); and M. Habib, *Politics and Society during the Early Medieval Period*, II (New Delhi, 1981), 144–8 ("Heritage of the Slave Kings") with the chronicle of Alauudin Khalji that follows (149–270).

[25] Crone, *Slaves on Horses*, 79. European elites had also opposed the use of gunpowder, but with rather less unanimity: see J. R. Hale, 'Gunpowder and the Renaissance: an Essay in the History of Ideas' in Hale, *Renaissance War Studies* (London, 1983), 389–420.

[26] See the classic account of D. Ayalon, *Gunpowder and Firearms in the Mamluk Kingdom: A Challenge to Medieval Society* (London, 1956). See also the similar situation in North Africa described by A. C. Hess, "Firearms and the Decline of Ibn Khaldun's Military Elite," *Archivum Ottomanicum* 4 (1972): 173–99. Ayalon argued that Safavid Iran was defeated by the Turks at Chaldiran because her forces were unfamiliar with firearms, but it has recently been shown that this was not so. Rather, as with the Mamluks, the Persian army sometimes used guns—but only with reluctance, and (even then) only in siege warfare: see R. N. Savory, *Iran under the Safavids* (Cambridge, 1980), 42–4; and the observations (made in the 1620s) that the Persians long continued to "detest the trouble of the cannon, and such field peeces as require carriage," in T. Herbert, *Some Yeares' Travels into Divers Parts of Asia and Afrique* (4th ed., London, 1677), 232, 298ff. Conversely, parts of the Ottoman army—the *sipahis*—refused to use the gun, or else used it unwillingly: see R. C. Jennings, "Firearms, Bandits and Gun-Control: Some Evidence on Ottoman Policy towards Firearms in the Possession of Reâya, from Judicial Records of Kayseri 1600–27," *Archivum Ottomanicum* 6 (1980): 339–80, at 340f.

At first sight, the Ottoman army appears to have adopted and mastered Western military technology with remarkable speed and thoroughness. Handguns, field guns and siege guns were all rapidly imitated by the Turks after their appearance in the West; advanced siege techniques of both offense and defense were evident from the 1520s; and, for a century and a half following this, the Turks were clearly equal to all but the largest forces that the West could throw against them.[27] And yet there were important respects in which the military revolution was imperfectly practiced by Europe's most dangerous neighbor. First, and best known, was the Ottoman decision to build their artillery big, whereas the Western powers concentrated on increasing the mobility and numbers of their guns. In part this may have been because the Ottoman Empire (not unlike the "socialist" countries of Eastern Europe today) experienced difficulty in mass producing and stockpiling manufactured items in order to build up a surplus. It must have seemed easier to produce a handful of big guns that delivered a few decisive shots than a multitude of quickfiring small ones. But, whatever the reason, it proved to be a mistake. The great Christian victory over the Ottoman army outside Vienna in 1683 came about partly because the Turks had directed all their heavy guns against the city, and could not maneuver them round in time when a large relief army, its field artillery at the ready, charged unexpectedly out of the Vienna Woods.[28] But the Turkish defeat before Vienna was the product of other factors, the chief of which was the failure to fortify their siege camp. It had become standard military practice in the West to build two sets of siege works: one against the beleaguered town, the second around the siege works to guard against any attempt at relief. That the Turks did not trouble with this elementary precaution in 1683 may have been mere carelessness by their commander on that occasion, the ill-fated Grand Vizier "Black Mustafa," but it fits in with other evidence that Ottoman troops embraced the gunpowder revolution with less enthusiasm than their Christian adversaries. Some contemporaries observed that, although Turkish craftsmen could copy any new western weapon that they found on a battlefield or that a renegade brought to them, it usually took them a long time; and that, even then, gunpowder weapons remained largely confined to the

---

[27] See on all this the important articles of G. Káldy-Nagy, "The First Centuries of the Ottoman Military Organization," *Acta Orientalia Academiae Scientiarum Hungaricae* 31, no. 2 (1977): 147–83; and D. Petrovič, "Firearms in the Balkans on the Eve of and After the Ottoman Conquests," in V. J. Parry and M. E. Yapp, eds., *War, Technology, and Society in the Middle East* (Oxford, 1975), 164–94. Sultan Mohammed the Conqueror brought 62 guns against Constantinople in 1453, but almost 200 against Belgrade three years later.

[28] On the general issue, see C. M. Cipolla, *Guns and Sails in the Early Phase of European Expansion, 1400–1700* (London, 1965), 90–9. On the siege of Vienna, see P. Broucek, *Historischer Atlas zur zweiten Turkenbelagerung Wien* (Vienna, 1983)—in which all the prints and maps show the Turkish camp undefended against attack by a relief army; and J. Stoye, *The Siege of Vienna* (London, 1964), 157–9, 255–7.

infantry.[29] But this merely reflected differences in military traditions: cavalry in Europe had not normally used missile weapons, so that adopting the gun represented a threat to which it was imperative to respond; but Muslim armies still relied heavily upon the mounted archer, whose military effectiveness would in fact have been reduced by using single-shot firearms. Given its enormous size, and its proven success, the early modern Ottoman army had no real incentive to abandon its traditional military methods. It should be remembered that the great siege of 1683 saw the Turks beneath the walls of Vienna and not the Christians beneath the walls of Istanbul.

So the Turks continued to fight, even in the eighteenth century, exactly 'as in the days of Suleiman the Magnificent,' two hundred years before. The Maréchal de Saxe in 1732 offered the following explanation:[30]

> 'It is hard for one nation to learn from another, either from pride, idleness or stupidity. Inventions take a long time to be accepted (and sometimes, even though everyone accepts their usefulness, in spite of everything they are abandoned in favour of tradition and routine) . . . The Turks today are in this situation. It is not valour, numbers or wealth that they lack; it is order, discipline and technique.'

Nevertheless, the more the Europeans improved these qualities, the greater became their superiority over the forces of Islam, until the spectacular victory of Napoleon Bonaparte at the battle of the Pyramids in 1799 heralded the opening of the entire Levant to western exploitation.

By this stage, however, industrial power had transformed the quality as well as the quantity of European gunpowder weapons. Even in the sixteenth century, contemporary sources almost invariably claimed that arms and armour taken from Islamic forces were of no use to westerners. Thus, after the Christian naval victory at Lepanto in 1571, some 225 bronze guns were captured by the Venetians alone, but almost all were melted down and recast (with reinforcement) because, according to the Council of Ten, "the metal is of such poor quality.' That is, Ottoman naval artillery was found to be too brittle for safe and

---

[29] *Encyclopaedia of Islam*, I (2d ed., Leiden and London, 1960), 1055–69 (article on "barūd"—gunpowder—by D. Ayalon, V. J. Parry, and R. N. Savory), notes *inter alia,* that the Turks still had no pistols by the 1590s, were slow to adopt new siege techniques, and, even in the 1600s, had no 'good powder but that whyche they gett from overthrone Christians, or els is broughte them out of Englande." See also some similar observations that the Turks used their handguns inefficiently in H. Inalcik, "The Socio-Political Effects of the Diffusion of Firearms in the Middle East" in Parry and Yapp, *War, Technology and Society,* 195–217.

[30] Saxe, *Rêveries,* (written 1732, published 1757), quoted by V. J. Parry, "La manière de combattre" in Parry and Yapp, *War, Technology, and Society,* 218–56 at 256.

effective use.[31] This may have been mere chauvinism, but it is indirectly supported by a recent chemical analysis of the composition of some other Muslim weapons and armor from the Middle East which showed that Western iron and steel was indeed notably stronger than the Islamic equivalents. Admittedly the sample submitted to analysis was somewhat small—because few museums will consent to the mutilation of their exhibits in the cause of science—but the results were both consistent and convincing.[32]

Much the same technological inferiority was reported from India. Artillery had been in use in the north of the subcontinent from about 1440 and in the Deccan from about 1470 and yet, in the late eighteenth century, the Europeans still considered all "country" artillery (as they called it) to be unserviceable for their needs.[33] Although the native rulers had plenty of guns, these were found to be poorly cast (even in the eighteenth century, some Indian guns were still made of iron strips held together with metal bands), poorly maintained, and too heavy to move. According to an Indian writer in the 1780s, the native artillery was as

---

[31] Order of the Council of Ten, 28 November 1572, quoted in M. E. Mallett and J. R. Hale, *The Military Organization of a Renaissance State: Venice c. 1400–1617* (Cambridge, 1984), 400; and Luis Collado, *Manual de artillería* (Milan, 1592), fo. 8v. (guns "founded by the Turks are usually poor and flawed, even though the alloy is good"). Of course, a slight technical inferiority did not normally matter to the Turks: the Ottoman fleet dominated the Mediterranean neither by virtue of superior commanders (most of their admirals were relatively inexperienced graduates of the palace school) nor through superior organization. They won thanks to greater resources. Their empire had more men, more ships, and more equipment at its disposal than any enemy, and all were directed by a unified supreme command. Minor defects in individual items scarcely mattered when the Turks could send 250 galleys against Christian adversaries who possessed only 100.

[32] See A. Williams, *The Metallurgy of Muslim Armour* (Manchester, 1978: Seminar on Early Islamic Science, monograph III), 4, 5, 11.

[33] On the introduction of ordnance to India, see B. Rathgen, "Die Pulverwaffe in Indien," *Ostasiatische Zeitschrift* 12 (1925): 11–30, 196–217; I. A. Khan, "Early Use of Cannon and Musket in India, AD 1442–1526, "*Journal of the Economic and Social History of the Orient* 24 (1981): 146–64; and idem, "Origin and Development of Gunpowder Technology in India, AD 1250–1500," *Indian Historical Review* 4, no. 1 (1977): 20–29. But the quality was often poor. When, for example, in 1525 the government of Portuguese India was computing the total quantity of ordnance available for defense, they noted: "We make little mention of moorish guns, because they are no good on our ships; however if the metal is melted down, better guns can be cast." See R. J. de Lima Felner, ed., *Subsídios para a história da Índia portuguesa* (Lisbon, 1868), part III, 12. Matters do not seem to have improved in the seventeenth century. The European traveller Jean de Thevenot noted in 1666–7 that 'The swords made by the Indians are very brittle,' and that 'They have cannon also in their towns, but since they melt the metal in diverse furnaces, so that some of it must needs be better melted than others when they mingle all together, their cannon commonly is good for nothing.' (See S. Sen, ed., *Indian Travels of Thevenot and Careri* [New Delhi, 1949], 61–2. Careri, who visited India in 1695, made much the same comments—see *ibid.*, 242–5.)

"cumbrous, ill-mounted and ill-served as was the artillery of Europe three hundred years ago." Many European sources bear him out. A report on the copious brass ordnance of the pro-British nawab of Oudh in 1777, for example, ruled 90 percent of the guns to be unfit for service, due either to metal fatigue or to rotten carriages; and the artillery captured from Tippu Sultan, of Mysore, in the 1790s was likewise reckoned by Sir Arthur Wellesley, later Duke of Wellington, to be suitable only for scrap. It was much the same with "country" handguns, which were normally of limited usefulness, either because they wore out quickly and could not easily be replaced; or because they did not conform to a single size, so that the shot often failed to fit the barrel; or because they had a shorter range than European muskets.[34]

Before the eighteenth century, however, the Europeans were not always so contemptuous. As the Portuguese in India never tired of pointing out, Asia was not like America: adversaries there were armed with firearms and steel swords, not with wooden clubs and obsidian knives. It was simply not possible for 168 men with 67 horses to destroy the Mughal empire, as Pizarro and his Spanish companions had brought down the Incas in the 1530s, for the Mughal army had almost limitless military resources. The total manpower available for the army of the emperor Akbar in the 1590s was estimated by one expert at 342,696 cavalry and 4,039,097 infantry—many of them armed with muskets.[35] Moreover the principal Indian rulers (including the Mughals) became increasingly reliant on the advice of foreign military experts, at first by the Turks (particularly in Muslim states) but later also by the Europeans. As early as 1499 two Portuguese deserted from Vasco da Gama's fleet in order to serve native rulers for higher wages. They were soon joined by others—two Milanese gunfounders to Calicut in 1503; four Venetian technicians to Malabar in 1505—until by the year 1565 there may have been as many as 2000

---

[34] Details from W. Irvine, *The Army of the Indian Moghuls: Its Organization and Administration* (London, 1903), 114–7; B. P. Lenman, "The Weapons of War in Eighteenth-Century India," *Journal of the Society for Army Historical Research* 46 (1968): 33–43; and S. N. Sen, *The Military System of the Marathas* (2d ed., Calcutta, 1979), 103.

[35] See references in Boxer, "Asian potentates," 161. On the difficulty of estimating accurately the size of Indian armies, see D. H. A. Kolff, 'An armed peasantry and its allies. Rajput tradition and state formation in Hindustan, 1450–1850' (Leiden University Ph.D. thesis, 1983), 11–17; and R. K. Phul, *Armies of the Great Mughals (1526–1707)* (New Delhi, 1978), 125–34. Phul estimates Akbar's campaign army in the later sixteenth century at some 50,000 men, and Prince Dara's in 1653 at 90,000. But there were also provincial armies, garrisons and feudal levies. In addition almost all peasants, carters and camel-drivers bore arms (and knew how to use them), raising the number of men capable of serving in the Mughals' armies to the huge figure, derived from Abū'l Fazl's *Ā'in-i Akbarī*, quoted in the text (Kolff, *op. cit.*, 13ff).

European renegades serving the various native rulers of South and East Asia. By the early seventeenth century the total may have risen to 5000.[36]

And yet the impact of the 'foreign experts' was often far from decisive. Thus Prince Dara, one of the contenders for the Mughal throne in the 1650s, employed perhaps 200 Europeans and Turks, yet still lost every battle that he fought and was at length captured and executed by his rival, Aurangzeb, who eventually became emperor and took most of the Europeans into his service.[37] But Aurangzeb, too, seems to have derived little direct benefit from their presence, for field artillery and musketry volleys simply did not fit easily into local traditions of warfare. As one of the "experts," Niccolo Manucci, perceptively observed of a battle between Dara and Aurangzeb in 1658:

> Be it known to the reader that these two armies were not ordered in the disposition obtaining in Europe. But one division was close to another, as the trees of a pinewood . . . I saw in this action, as in so many others where I was afterwards present, that the only soldiers who fought were those well to the front. Of those more to the rear, although holding their bared swords in their hands, the Moguls did nothing but shout Bakush, bakush and the

---

[36] Details from Irvine, *Army*, 152ff.; Boxer, "Asian potentates," 158; M. A. Lima Cruz, 'Exiles and renegades in early sixteenth-century Portuguese Asia,' *Indian Economic and Social History Review*, XXIII (1986): 249–62; and S. Subrahmanyam 'The *Kagemusha* effect: the Portuguese, firearms, and the state in early modern South Asia,' *Môyen Orient et Océan Indien*, IV (1987), 97–123. See also the admirable general discussion of J. N. Sarkar, *The Art of War in Medieval India* (New Delhi, 1984), 76–89. There was, of course, nothing new in Christian military personnel taking service with Muslim rulers: El Cid and many others in Spain, like numerous Franks in north Africa and the Near East, had done so in the Middle, Ages (see J. Richard, *Orient et occident au moyen âge: contacts et relations (XIIe-XVe siècles)* [London, 1976], chap. 13).

[37] We know a great deal about two of Prince Dara's European military experts: see P. H. Pott, "Willem Verstegen, een extra-ordinaris Raad van Indië, als avonturier in India in 1659," *Bijdragen tot de Taal-, Land- en Volkenkunde* 112 (1956): 355–82; and N. Manucci, *Storia do Mogor, or Mogul India 1653–1708* (4 vols., ed. W. Irvine, London, 1906–8). There are also numerous references to European military experts in Mughal service in F. Bernier, *Travels in the Mogul empire, AD 1656–1668* (London, 1891), e.g., 31, 47–56, 93. On 55 Bernier, writing in the 1660s, ventured the opinion that "I could never see these [Mughal] soldiers, destitute of order, and marching with the irregularity of a herd of animals, without reflecting upon the ease with which 25,000 of our veterans from the [French] Army of Flanders, commanded by the Prince of Condé or Marshal Turenne, would overcome these armies, however numerous." The problem, however, was to get so many Europeans (to say nothing of Condé or Turenne) to India at the same time.

Indians Mar, mar—*that is to say "Kill, kill." If those in front advanced, those behind followed the example; and if the former retired, the others fled—a custom of Hindustan quite contrary to that of Europe.*[38]

Manucci was right: Indian armies may have been huge, but they remained, essentially, aggregations of individual heroic warriors. Their principal ambition was to close with as many enemies as possible in single combat and, unless they achieved this quickly, their overall strength soon disintegrated. The drill, tactics, and disciplined volley fire of Europe were, to them, irrelevant.

It is more surprising to find that the Mughals, like other South Asian rulers, never attempted to imitate European techniques of fortification, with the bastions, ravelins and defenses in depth that had proved highly effective both in Europe and overseas. But it must be remembered that many of the larger Indian fortresses were already so huge that even the heaviest early modern artillery bombardment could make little impression on them: thus, the fourteenth-century walls of Gulbarga in the Deccan were seventeen meters thick, and those of the Purana Qila at Delhi, built between 1530 and 1545, were the same; the walls of Agra, rebuilt between 1564 and 1574, consisted of two revetments of dressed red sandstone blocks ten meters apart, filled in with sand and rubble. They lacked bastions because, on such a scale, they scarcely needed them: sieges in early modern India were decided by blockade and mines rather than by cannonade. Even in the late eighteenth century, the Europeans could not take any of these strongholds by bombardment.[39]

But, until the late eighteenth century, the Europeans—for the most part—did not even try. Recent research has stressed how anachronistic it is to see the West as bent upon world domination from the voyage of Vasco da Gama onward.[40] In fact, the Europeans originally came to Asia to trade, not to conquer,

---

[38] Manucci, *Storia do Mogor,* I, 276, 278. For the introduction of regular European military practice to Portuguese India see, for example, clause 53 of the royal Instructions to Viceroy Redondo, going to India in 1617: "We have tried many times to reorganize our troops in India according to the European manner, since experience has shown that without it we have suffered several important losses, and now that we are at war with the Dutch, who are disciplined soldiers, it is more important than ever" (R. A. Bulhão Pato, ed., *Documentos remetidos da India ou Livros das Monções;* IV, [Lisbon, 1893], 168–9). See also 287–8 (royal letter of 1618) and others in later years on the same subject. An interesting insight into Portuguese military practice in India in the early seventeenth century is offered by G. D. Winius, *The Black Legend of Portuguese India: Diogo de Couto, His Contemporaries and the 'Soldado Prático* (New Delhi, 1985).

[39] For details, see the description of sites such as Golconda, Gulbarga, and Delhi Fort in S. Toy, *The Strongholds of India* (London, 1957); idem, *The Fortified Cities of India* (London, 1965); V. Fass, *The Forts of India* (London, 1986); and Sarkar, *Art of War,* 126–74.

[40] See, in particular, P. J. Marshall, "Western Arms in Maritime Asia in the Early Phases of Expansion," *Modern Asian Studies* 1 (1980): 13–28. The following part of my argument owes much to discussions with Professor Marshall, whose generous aid I gratefully acknowledge.

and most of them only undertook military expenditure either to coerce reluctant buyers or in order to safeguard themselves against attack from their European rivals; the cost of defense would otherwise have eaten up all trading profits. The Dutch were, however, an exception to this rule: They were already fighting a bitter war in Europe and they aimed straight for the overseas bases of their Spanish and Portuguese enemies, trying to destroy them, as well as usurping their trade. Heavy military spending was therefore, for them, essential and (according to an official investigation in 1613) even the "voorcompagniëen" (the rival associations of Dutch merchants who traded in Asia before the foundation of the United East India Company) spent over 30 percent of the running costs of each voyage on war-related items. After the formation of the United Company in 1602, the annual figure rose to 50, 60, and even 70 percent. Indeed, the total cost of building Dutch forts on the principal islands of the Moluccas between 1605 and 1612 amounted to no less than 1.72 million florins, almost one-third of the company's initial capital.[41] This was because most Dutchmen in the East were utterly convinced that no profit was to be had without power, and no trade without war. In the terse (and oft-quoted) letter of Governor-General Jan Pieterszoon Coen to his directors in 1614: "You gentlemen ought to know from experience that trade in Asia should be conducted and maintained under the protection and with the aid of your own weapons, and that those weapons must be wielded with the profits gained by the trade. So trade cannot be maintained without war, nor war without trade."[42]

Some of the British in the Far East during the seventeenth century thought that their East India Company should follow the Dutch model. Dr. John Fryer, for example, a company surgeon in Surat during the 1670s, observed that the Dutch were "as powerful for men, riches and shipping in Batavia, as in Europe"; and continued:

---

[41] Figures from P. J. N. Willman, "The Dutch in Asia, 1595–1610" (St. Andrews University M.A. thesis, 1986), 21–2, 26: based on private calculations made by Grotius from the companies' own papers, and preserved in the Rijksarchief Van Zuid Holland, The Hague, *Collectie Hugo de Groot.*

[42] Coen to Heren XVII, 27 December 1614 (from Bantam in Java), quoted by H. T. Colenbrander, *Jan Pieterszoon Coen. Levenbeschrijving* (The Hague, 1934), 64. It should be noted, however, that Coen's advice was not always followed. In 1622 he was rebuked by the directors for fighting too much. Violence, they told him, should be used only in the service of profit: "One must avoid and eschew war if it is at all compatible with the preservation and safety of our state . . . No great attention should be paid to questions of 'reputation' . . . for we are mere merchants." Quoted by Steensgaard, "The Dutch East India Company As an Institutional Innovation," in M. Aymard, ed., *Dutch Capitalism and World Capitalism* (Cambridge, 1982), 235–57 at 255. The directors had good reason for concern: many of their forts and factories in the Orient were returning a loss! See M. A. P. Meilink-Roelofsz, *Asian trade and European influence in the Indonesian Archipelago between 1500 and about 1630* (The Hague, 1962), 386.

[Their strategy] is grounded on a different principle from our East India Company, who are for the present profit, not future emolument. These [the Dutch], as they gain ground, secure it by vast expences, raising forts and maintaining souldiers: ours are for raising auctions and retrenching charges, bidding the next age grow rich as they have done, but not affording them the means.[43]

But the comparison was unjust. The British, after some initial failures, preferred to concentrate their trade in areas where the native Indian states were relatively small and weak, and European competitors were not already entrenched: Golconda, the Carnatic, Bengal.[44] The directors of the company could therefore take pride in their ability to avoid hefty military expenditure. "All war is so contrary to our constitution as well as [to] our interest," they informed their officials in 1681, "that we cannot too often inculcate to you an aversion thereto." Or, in a rather more succinct message sent in 1677: "Our business is trade, not war."

As late as 1750, the directors still reproached their officials in the field for seeming "to look upon yourselves rather as a military colony than [as] the factors and agents of a body of merchants;" and in 1759 they dismissed the strategic designs of the governor of Madras on the grounds that "Were we to adopt your several plans for fortifying, half our capital would be buried in stone walls."[45] But, by then, the directors were seriously out of date. The arrival of the French on their doorsteps—at Pondichéry, close to Madras, in 1674; at Chandernagore, upstream from Calcutta, in 1686—was bad enough. But after the reorganization of the *Compagnie des Indes* in 1719 these modest toeholds on the subcontinent suddenly became threatening bridgeheads from which French territorial influence in India might be extended. It became inevitable that, whenever Britain and France went to war in Europe, the conflict would now spread to their colonies. But still the directors of the East India Company failed to see the need for change. As late as 1740, when the War of the Austrian Succession broke out, British forces in India totaled less than 2,000 men, widely distributed over the subcontinent in decrepit, poorly defended fortresses. And so, when the French in the Carnatic launched an attack on Madras in 1746, the 200 guns of Fort St.

---

[43] John Fryer, *A New Account of East India and Persia, Being Nine Years Travels, 1672–1681*, I (London, 1909: Hakluyt Society, 2d ser., XX), 124.

[44] There were some company officials who agreed with the Dutch view, and in the 1680s some of the directors supported them. Several apposite quotations will be found in I. B. Watson, "Fortifications and the 'Idea' of Force in Early English East India Company Relations with India," *Past and Present* 88 (1980): 70–87.

[45] Quotations from East India Company records in G. J. Bryant, "The East India Company and Its Army, 1600–1778" (London University Ph.D. thesis, 1975), 10, 31, 74, 138. There was a brief period of belligerence in the 1680s, under the leadership of Josiah Child, but it failed (see Bryant, 32–3; interestingly, it coincided with a similar assertiveness by England in its American colonies—S. S. Webb, *The Governors-General: The English Army and the Definition of the Empire. 1569–1681* [Chapel Hill, 1979], 447–55).

George still had only 100 men to serve them and the chief gunner, a man named Smith, died of a heart attack when he saw the French approaching. The fortress fell. Then, later that same year, the victorious French went on to defeat a superior army of Britain's Indian allies at the Battle of Adyar River with the classic European technique of the musketry salvo: 300 Europeans and 700 native troops, drawn up in three ranks, moved forward against their 10,000 adversaries firing successive volleys of shot. Almost immediately, they were masters of the field.[46]

The Battle of Adyar River was a turning point in Indian history. Admittedly, the combination of a core of European soldiers with a larger number of European-trained Indian troops was not new. All the Western powers in the Orient, from the Portuguese in the sixteenth century onward, had tried to compensate for their great numerical weakness by recruiting members of the "martial races" of Asia, such as the Ambonese in Indonesia or the Pampangas in the Philippines. They had also made use of native converts to Christianity (often descended from a European father), such as the "topazes" in British India and the "mardijkers" in Dutch Java.[47] But these various recruits served as auxiliaries, not regulars: they fought in their traditional fashion, with their traditional weapons, and in their traditional formations. The French, however, trained native troops to fight in the European fashion with European weapons and European uniforms; and after 1751 they supplied them with European officers and noncommisioned officers too.[48] In that same year, the French governor in Pondichéry informed his superiors in Europe that: "All my efforts are directed towards attaining for you vast revenues from this part of India, and consequently placing

---

[46] The Battle of the Adyar River (7 November 1746) was well described by the Tamil factor of Dupleix at Pondichéry: J. F. Price, ed., *The Private Diary of Ananda Ranga Pillai*, III (Madras, 1914), 94–5 and 444–52.

[47] See the interesting remarks on this theme by J. A. de Moor, "Militaire Interdependentie tussen Europa en de Derde Wereld. De Geschiedenis van 'Johnny Gurkha,'" *Internationale Spectator* 37 (1983): 356–64; de Iongh, *Het Krijgswezen*, chap. 4; and Marshall, "Western Arms in Maritime Asia," 25f.

[48] Exactly how this happened is something of a mystery. A. Martineau, *Dupleix et l'Inde française*, III (Paris, 1927), devoted a few pages to the sepoys (62–72), but filled them with a sustained diatribe about the shortcomings and vices of all Asian races! E. W. C. Sandes, *The Military Engineer in India*, I (Chatham, 1933), 64–5, claimed that the French trained some 5,000 Muslims as regular troops in 1741 in order to oppose an invasion of the Carnatic by the Marathas, but Dupleix himself later stated that sepoys were first used by the French only in 1746. This contradiction is resolved by the records at Pondichéry, which reveal that two companies of "cypahes" were raised by the French in January 1742 and were drilled, armed, and paid in the European manner. But they were disbanded at the end of the year, and so Dupleix in 1746 had to start all over again. See H. H. Dodwell, *Sepoy Recruitment in the Old Madras Army* (Calcutta, 1922); Studies in Indian Records, I), 3–7; and S. C. Hill, "The Old Sepoy Officer," *English Historical Review* 28 (1913): 260–91, 496–514.

the Nation in a position to maintain itself here even when it may lack support from Europe."[49]

His British rival was well aware of the threat. "Since the French have put themselves in possession of extensive domains," Governor Saunders wrote to his superiors in February 1751, "and have raised their flag at the bounds of our territory and have striven to constrain our settlements to such an extent that they can neither receive supplies nor goods, it has been judged essential to thwart their designs, lest their success render our situation worse during peace than in time of war . . . We shall therefore oppose them to the greatest extent of which we are capable." In this, the British held one decisive advantage: their superior financial resources in the subcontinent. It was not merely that the volume of British trade in Asia by 1750 was roughly four times that of France; there was also the fact that, from the 1680s onward, the company's agents in Madras accepted substantial deposits in cash from both Indian and European merchants and officials. In normal times, most of this was remitted back to London in bills of exchange, but when war threatened, or erupted, these deposits provided a useful capital fund from which to finance military expenditures. And, as the trade and population of Madras grew, so the capital on deposit increased.[50] By the 1740s, it was sufficient to allow the company to follow the French example and raise their own companies, battalions, and eventually regiments of "sepoys" (as these troops were known, from *sipahi*, the Persian word for soldier). There were two sepoy battalions in the company's service by 1758, five by 1759, and ten—some 9,000 men—by 1765. With numerical strength such as this, enhanced by the new, more reliable flintlock muskets and the quick-firing field artillery exported from Europe, it was now possible for the company to challenge not only its French rivals, but also the smaller native states of India with some chance of success.[51]

The first major opportunity occurred in Bengal in 1757. The Mughal empire in its prime had been able to mobilize perhaps a million warriors, but, after the death of Aurangzeb in 1707, a number of satraps on the imperial fron-

---

[49] Dupleix to the Directors of the Compagnie des Indes, 15 February 1751, quoted by H. Furber, *Rival Empires of Trade in the Orient, 1600–1800* (Oxford, 1976), 156.

[50] Details from Furber, ibid., 147–69 (Saunders quoted at 156); idem, *John Company at Work: A Study of European Expansion in India in the Late Eighteenth Century* (Cambridge, Mass. 1948), 204f; and A. das Gupta and M. N. Pearson, eds., *India and the Indian Ocean, 1500–1800* (Calcutta, 1987), 311ff. I am most grateful to Professor Blair B. Kling for these references and for invaluable help in formulating the argument of this paragraph.

[51] Figures from Bryant, "The East India Company and its Army," 299f.; P. Mason, *A Matter of Honour: An Account of the Indian Army, Its Officers and Men* (2nd ed., London, 1976), 62f. I am grateful to Dr. Bryant for sending me further material and additional references on this matter. See also the new insights on the social world of the sepoys in M. P. Singh, *Indian Army under the East India Company* (New Delhi, 1976); and Kolff, 'An armed peasantry,' 123–56.

tier had broken away and created their own separate states.[52] Nevertheless, the military strength of these rulers remained formidable, compared with the Europeans. The decision to send an army of sepoys and British troops to Bengal in 1757, under the command of Robert Clive, was something of a wild gesture. Admittedly the new nawab of Bengal had given provocation by taking Calcutta, and demanding increased payments from the Company in return for trade, but his army was ten times the size of Clive's 2,000 sepoys and 900 Europeans, and was assisted by French military advisers.

But, at the Battle of Plassey, Clive won. The nawab, Siraj-ud-Daulah, was executed and a replacement more acceptable to the British set up in his place. After some years of further hostilities and negotiation, in 1765 the Mughal emperor and the new nawab finally recognized the right of the British company to collect all state revenues in the provinces of Bihar, Orissa, and Bengal. It was wealth beyond the dreams of avarice: the "Net amount of territorial revenues and customs, clear of charges of collection" received officially by the company leapt from nothing before 1757 to almost £2 million in 1761–4, and to almost £7.5 million in 1766–9. With the aid of these funds (all paid in silver), it proved possible to build impregnable fortresses and to raise armies large enough to intervene effectively in the Deccan, in Mysore—indeed, anywhere in the subcontinent.[53] By 1782 the British were able to maintain 115,000 men in India (90 percent of them sepoys) and reduce the odds against them in battle from the 10 to 1 of Plassey to only 2 to 1 against states such as Mysore. The prospect of the European domination of India, to match the European domination of Amer-

---

[52] The Mughal army was probably the same size—around a million men—in circa 1700 as in circa 1600: see Kolff, 'An armed peasantry', 13. There is a tendency to write off the military strength of the native states of India in the early eighteenth century, perhaps because of the evident collapse of native seaborne trade at the same time. But this is wrong: see A. das Gupta, *Indian Merchants and the Decline of Surat, c. 1700–1750* (Wiesbaden, 1979), introduction. See also das Gupta's perceptive further thoughts in 'Asian merchants and the western Indian ocean: the early seventeenth century,' *Modern Asian Studies*, XIX (1985), 481–99; and in T. Raychaudhuri and I. Habib, eds., *The Cambridge Economic History of India*, I (Cambridge, 1982), 425–33.

[53] *Reports from Committees of the House of Commons*, IV (1804), 60–1. My thanks go to Professor P. J. Marshall for this reference. The figures are all the more striking when it is remembered that the company *lost* £2.5 million between 1753 and 1760. The massive new Fort William at Calcutta, built between 1765 and 1771 at a cost of £1 million, is just one example of how the Bengal settlement allowed the Europeans to change the art of defensive warfare in India. See P. J. Marshall, "Eighteenth-Century Calcutta," in Ross and Telkamp, *Colonial Cities*, 90.

ica, had become a real possibility.[54] And the military resources of India, once under European control, were to prove decisive for the further rise of the West. As early as 1762, a detachment of 650 sepoys was sent to assist the British to capture Manila; and, during the nineteenth century, such foreign service became commonplace—in Burma, in East Africa, above all in East Asia. For the Europeans now possessed the means to challenge even their most powerful opponents. The Western armies that invaded China in 1839–42, 1859–60, and 1900 all included important Indian contingents. Immediately after the Boxer Rising, even the traffic of Peking was directed by Sikhs. In the words of the distinguished Sinologist Louis Dermigny: "It was as if the British had subjugated the Indian peninsula simply in order to use its resources against China."[55]

III

If, therefore, the native peoples of America, Siberia, Black Africa and the Philippines lost their independence to the Europeans because they had no time to *adopt* western military technology, those of the Muslim world apparently succumbed because they saw no need to integrate it into their existing military system. But the peoples of East Asia, by contrast, were able to keep the West at bay throughout the early modern period because, as it were, they already knew the rules of the game. Firearms, fortresses, standing armies, and warships had long been part of the military tradition of China, Korea, and Japan. Indeed, both bronze and iron artillery were fully developed in China before they spread westward to Europe around 1300. However, after the mid-fourteenth century, contact between the Far East and the Far West diminished, and the subsequent

---

54 See Ness and Stahl, "Western Imperialist Armies in Asia;" J. P. Lawford, *Britain's Army in India from Its Origin to the Conquest of Bengal* (London, 1978), 72–81; Bryant. "The East India Company and its army," chaps. 3–5; and R. Callahan, *The East India Company and Army Reform, 1783–98* (Cambridge, Mass., 1972), 6. The Dutch East India Company also began to train its Asian troops to fight like Europeans in the 1740s, under Governor-General van Imhoff: see de Iongh, *Het Krijgswezen*, 165–8. In the first years of the nineteenth century, the Maratha Confederation secured sufficient European advisers and European-designed field guns to launch attacks on the British in India that came within an ace of success, but they came too late. See J. Pemble, "Resources and Techniques in the Second Maratha war," *Historical Journal* 19 (1976): 375–404; and D. H. A. Kolff, 'The end of the Ancien Régime: colonial war in India, 1798–1818' in J. A. de Moor and H. L. Wesseling, eds., *Imperialism and War. Essays on Colonial Wars in Asia and Africa* (Leiden, 1989: Comparative studies in overseas history, VIII), 22–49.

55 On the sepoys in the Philippines, see Mason, *A Matter of Honour*, 68, 242. On China, see L. Dermigny, *La Chine et l'Occident. Le commerce à Canton au XVIII- siècle, 1719–1833*, II (Paris, 1964), 781. Later, in the nineteenth century, sepoys were sent to conquer both Java (1811–15) and East Africa for Britain. See also the general remarks of A. J. Qaisar, *The Indian Response to European Technology and Culture, AD 1498–1707* (Oxford, 1982), 46–57, 144–6.

evolution of firearms in the two areas took a somewhat different course. By 1500 the iron and bronze guns of Western manufacture—whether made by Turkish or Christian founders—proved to be both more powerful and more mobile than those of the East, so that when they were brought to the Orient in the sixteenth century they attracted both attention and imitation. They may have arrived in China as early as the 1520s, perhaps with one of the numerous Ottoman diplomatic missions to the Ming Court, but, if so, knowledge of them seems to have remained confined to government circles. For most Chinese, Western-style firearms were first encountered in the hands of pirates operating from Japan against Fukien in the late 1540s.[56]

Although guns were not widely employed by Ming forces against the *wakō* pirates, they were introduced shortly afterward on China's northern frontier for use against the nomads of the steppe. In 1564, for example, the Peking garrison replaced their clay-cased cannonballs with lead; and in 1568 these too were abandoned in favor of iron. Then, in the 1570s, under the direction of Ch'i Chikuang (who had masterminded the defeat of the pirates), the Great Wall was rebuilt with pillboxes to shelter musketeers, and the reserve units of the northern army were strengthened with small carts (known as "battle wagons"), each carrying breech-loading light artillery and served by twenty men.[57]

A remarkable source that illustrates the degree to which European weaponry had been adopted on China's northern frontier under the late Ming is the illustrated *Veritable Records of the Great Ancestor (T'ai-tsu Shih-lu)*, compiled in 1635 to record the deeds of Nurhaci, founder of the Ch'ing dynasty. It is significant that in the pictures of the "Great Ancestor's" early victories all the guns are on the side of the Ming: the imperial armies are shown deploying field guns, mounted either on trestles or on two-wheeled "battle wagons," while the northern warriors seem to rely on their horsearchers.[58] But in 1629, the Ch'ing attacked and annexed four Chinese cities south of the Great Wall: in one of them, Yung-p'ing, a Chinese artillery crew "familiar with the techniques of cast-

---

[56] The suggestion that the Turks introduced Western firearms to China before the Europeans was first made by P. Pelliot, "Le Hoja et le Sayid Hussain de l'Histoire des Ming," *T'oung Pao* 38 (1948): 81–292, at 199–207. See also J. Needham, Ho Ping-Yü, Lu Gwei-Djen, and Wang Ling, *Science and Civilization in China*. Volume V part vii: *Military Technology—The Gunpowder Epic* (Cambridge, 1986), 440–9.

[57] Details from R. Huang, "Military Expenditures in Sixteenth-Century Ming China," *Oriens Extremus* 17 (1970): 39–62; idem, *1587: A Year of No Significance: The Ming Dynasty in Decline* (New Haven, 1981), chap. 6; A. Chan, *The Glory and Fall of the Ming Dynasty* (Norman, 1982), 51–63; and the important new study of A. Waldron, *The Great Wall of China. From History to Myth* (Cambridge, 1990).

[58] *T'ai-tsu shih-lu* (facsimile edition, Mukden, 1931: reproduced from an edition of 1740 that seems to be based, in turn, on an illustrated chronicle compiled in 1635—that is, by and for those who might themselves have seen the events they described).

ing Portuguese artillery" was also captured. By 1631 some forty of the new European-style artillery pieces had been made by the captives and, directed by men who had received either first- or second-hand training from Portuguese gunners, they were soon in action against Ming positions. Gradually, as shown in later illustrations from the *T'ai-tsu shih-lu*, they appeared on the Ch'ing side.

But firearms remained only a minor part of the armament of Chinese armies. After all, the Ming supported (in theory at least) some 500,000 men and 100,000 horses on the northern frontier, and the Ch'ing army that entered Peking in 1644 probably numbered 280,000 warriors: It would have been almost impossible to equip all these troops with Western-style firearms.[59] So the soldiers of the new dynasty continued to fight in the traditional manner until the nineteenth century. It is true that, in 1675, the Chinese imperial army was supported by 150 heavy guns and numerous batteries of field artillery, cast under the direction of Jesuit missionaries in Peking, but this was a specific campaign against dangerous domestic enemies (the "Three Feudatories" and their supporters). At other times, the main strength of the Ch'ing lay in the overwhelming numbers of their armed forces.[60]

The Japanese, however, whose armies in the mid-sixteenth century were considerably smaller than those of their great continental neighbour (even though much larger as a percentage of the total population), made far more use of Western firearms. It is generally accepted that they were first introduced by some Portuguese castaways in 1543 on the island of Tanegashima, south of

---

[59] The exact size of the Ch'ing army was an official secret, but it would seem that a campaign army in the later seventeenth century might number 150,000 men, with up to 40,000 men directly involved in battles. See C. Fang, "A Technique for Estimating the Numerical Strength of the Early Manchu Military Forces," *Harvard Journal of Asiatic Studies* 13 (1950): 192–215.

[60] Although the efforts of the Jesuits and other Europeans in Macao and Peking to supply first the Ming and then the Manchu with guns usually monopolize the limelight, this is just another case of Eurocentrism. The bulk of Chinese artillery was produced by Chinese craftsmen: see Needham, *The Gunpowder Epic*, 392–414; and Chan, *Glory and Fall*, 57–63. The same was definitely true in Japan, where production by local workshops far surpassed European imports: see K. Itakura, "The First Ballistic Laws by a Japanese Mathematician, and its Origin," *Japanese Studies in the History of Science* 2 (1963): 136–45. The only East Asian country that seems to have been heavily dependent on weapons imported from the West was Vietnam: the Nguyen of the north relied heavily after the 1620s on bronze guns either cast by Westerners living in Hué, or else imported from Macao, in their wars against the Tring of the south, who received (in their turn) supplies from the Dutch in Batavia. But even in Vietnam, local production continued: a French visitor to Hué in 1749 saw 800 bronze and 400 iron guns, by no means all of which were of European manufacture. See P. Y. Manguin, *Les Portugais sur les côtes de Viêtnam et du Campa* (Paris, 1972), 206–8; L. Cadière, "Le quartier des Arènes. I. Jean de la Croix et les premiers Jésuites," *Bulletin des amis du Vieux Hué* 11 (1924): 307–32 (La Croix resided in Hué and cast guns for the Nguyen from the 1650s to 1682); and C. R. Boxer, "Macao as a Religious and Commercial Entrepôt in the Sixteenth and Seventeenth Centuries," *Acta Astatica* 31 (1974): 64–90.

Kyushu, and that they were quickly copied by Japanese metalsmiths (which is why they were commonly known as *Tanegashima*).[61] Muskets were used effectively in battle by the army of Takeda Shingen in 1555, but a more spectacular demonstration of the power of Japanese musketry occurred on 21 May 1575 at the battle of Nagashino. The warlord Oda Nobunaga deployed his musketeers in 23 ranks in this action, having trained them to fire in volleys so as to maintain a constant barrage—1,000 rounds every 20 seconds according to one source. The opposing cavalry—ironically of the same Takeda clan that had pioneered the use of the gun—was annihilated. The battle scene in Kurosawa's film *Kagemusha (The Shadow Warrior)* offers a credible reconstruction, for the action is intended to represent Nagashino.[62]

The originality of Japan's rapid adoption of the gun has perhaps not always been fully appreciated. In the first place, whereas Europe concentrated on increasing the speed of reloading, the Japanese were more interested in improving accuracy. So Western military manuals explained primarily how a soldier could recharge his weapon more rapidly, and Japanese treatises—from the 1550s onward—gave instruction on how he could take better aim. The *Tanegashima* were, for their day, remarkably accurate. But this in fact accentuated the crucial defect of the muzzle-loading musket: the length of time required to recharge it. Now the only way to overcome this disadvantage was to draw up the musketeers in ranks, firing in sequence, so that the front file could reload while the others behind fired. This solution was not even suggested in Europe until 1594, and it did not pass into general use there until the 1630s. Yet Oda Nobunaga had experimented with musketry salvoes in the 1560s, and he achieved his first major

---

[61] For the precise manner in which Western guns were introduced into Japan, see the definitive account, together with a German translation of Japanese sources, in G. Schurhammer, *Gesammelte Studien, II. Orientalia* (Rome, 1963: Biblioteca Instituti Historici Societatis Iesu, XXI), 485–579. There is an English translation of one source—the *Teppō-ki* of Nampō Bunshi (1606)—in Tsunoda Ryusaku et al., eds., *Sources of Japanese Tradition*, I (New York, 1964) 308–12. It should be noted that the island of Tanegashima, where the first Portuguese guns arrived, was an ideal spot for copying them. It was, in 1543, not only an established center of trade but a major center of sword production; it was relatively easy for the sword-smiths to turn out musket barrels instead, ready for the merchants to distribute.

[62] In 1549 Oda Nobunaga was apparently asked to provide "500 musketeers and bowmen," which does not necessarily mean—as many scholars have said—500 men with muskets (Hora Tomio, *Tanegashima-jū. Denrai to sono eikyō* [Tokyo, 1958], 157). But in 1555 Takeda Shingen definitely deployed 300 musketeers at the Battle of Shinano Asahiyamajō (Nagahara Keiji, *Sengoko no dōran. Nihon no rekishi*, XIV [Tokyo, 1975], 947; and Hora, *op. cit.*, 144–54). Nagashino is depicted in a marvelous series of screen paintings, reproduced in *Sengoku kassen-e Byōbu Shūsei. I.i Kawanakajima kassen-zu Nagashino kassen-zu* (Tokyo, 1980). However, because the screens were all painted several decades after the battle, they may depict later Japanese military practice rather than the actual techniques employed by Nobunaga at Nagashino.

victory with the technique in 1575, twenty years before the Europeans— starting with Maurice of Nassau and the army of the Dutch Republic—invented it themselves.[63]

By the time Nobunaga was assassinated, in 1582, he had conquered about half of the provinces of Japan; after a brief hiatus of disorder, the work was continued by two of his most brilliant generals, first Toyotomi Hideyoshi and then Tokugawa Ieyasu. As further provinces were brought under central authority, the size of the main army was swollen by contingents from Hideyoshi's new vassals and allies. In 1587, when he decided to invade the island of Kyushu, almost 300,000 troops were mobilized. The island was conquered in a matter of weeks. The reunification of Japan might perhaps have been achieved without the gun, but the ability to turn large numbers of men into effective musketeers certainly accelerated the process. By 1610 Tokugawa Ieyasu could write: "Guns and powder . . . are what I desire more than gold."[64]

Nobunaga and his successors also saw the usefulness of the heavier guns used by the Westerners, and they seem to have realized immediately that artillery would render indefensible almost every existing castle and fortress in Japan because any wall that was built high, in order to keep besiegers out, was thereby rendered vulnerable to the impact of artillery bombardment. A new sort of defensive fortification therefore emerged, situated on a ridge and encircled by

---

[63] The general account of N. Perrin, *Giving up the Gun: Japan's Reversion to the Sword, 1543–1879* (New York; 1979), though interesting and provocative, is based almost entirely on Western sources and pushes some of the evidence too far. Greater reliance may be placed on D. M. Brown, "The Impact of Firearms on Japanese Warfare, 1543–98," *The Far Eastern Quarterly 7* (1948): 236–53. Hora, *Tanegashima*, 21–3, shows that firearms, almost certainly imported from China, were used in Japan before 1543. They were, however, few in number and limited in effect. The exact nature of early Japanese guns is difficult to establish because so few survive—perhaps only ten *Tanegashima* from the sixteenth century are known today (personal communication from Dr. Yoshioka Shin'ichi of Kyoto in 1984). And much the same is true of artillery: very few early modern pieces survive—though here the culprit (at least according to Japanese sources!) was the "liberation" of most of the beautiful guns collected in the Kudan Museum in Tokyo by American forces after 1945. Only a few firearms are to be found today in the military museum attached to the Yasakuni shrine in Tokyo. There is a concise discussion of the sources and problems in Needham, *The Gunpowder Epic*, 467–72, which relies (perhaps too heavily?) on the utopian vision of Noel Perrin. Finally, on the military changes in early modern Europe, see G. Parker, *The Military Revolution* (Cambridge, 1987), chaps. 1–2.

[64] Quotation from E. M. Satow, "Notes on the Intercourse between Japan and Siam in the Seventeenth Century," *Transactions of the Asiatic Society of Japan* ser., 1 13 (1884–5). 139–210 at 145. Army size figures in G. B. Sansom, *A History of Japan, 1334–1615* (Stanford, 1961), 322. A recent consideration of the armies commanded by Hideyoshi—which reached a total strength of 280,000 for the invasion of Korea in 1593—is provided by B. Susser, "The Toyotomi Regime and the Daimyō," in J. P. Mass and W. B. Hauser, eds., *The Bakufu in Japanese History* (Stanford, 1985), 129–52, at 135ff.

stone walls, creating a solid mass of rock and soil. A prototype was built by Nobunaga himself beside Lake Biwa at Azuchi, between 1576 and 1579, using the combination of hilltop and thick stone walls to produce a virtually solid bailey, surrounding a seven-story keep of unparalleled beauty.[65] But Azuchi was almost totally destroyed after its creator's murder in 1582 (though the ruins of the outer walls and the surviving foundations of the keep are still impressive). Even less remains of another massive fortress of this period: Odawara, the stronghold of the Hojo clan, large enough to shelter 40,000 warriors and surrounded by twenty outlying forts. It required an army of over 100,000 men to starve it out in the summer of 1590 and was destroyed after its capture by Toyotomi Hideyoshi—giving rise to a popular doggerel the following year:

> So what's the use of hauling rocks and building castles? Just look at Azuchi and Odawara![66]

Rather more exists today of the even larger citadels built by Hideyoshi and his followers, who preferred to fortify isolated hills on the plain. There is a remarkable homogeneity about the sixty or so surviving castles built in Japan between 1580 and 1630 from Sendai in the north to Kagoshima in the south, even though some were bigger than others. Kato Kiyomasa's castle at Kumamoto, for example, was twelve kilometers in circumference (with forty-nine turrets and two keeps); Ikeda Terumasa's beautiful "White Heron castle" at Himeji, almost as large, was constructed with an estimated 103,000 tons of stone; and the walls of Tokugawa Hidetada's vast citadel at Osaka extended for over thirteen kilometers. Some of the individual stones used to build the defenses of Osaka weighed 120 and 130 tons each and were brought to the site from all over Japan by feudatories anxious to prove their loyalty to the regime; even today each daimyo's mark can still be seen, affixed to "their" rocks (which were also

---

[65] Kodama Kōta et al., eds. *Nihon jōkaku taike*, XI (Tokyo, 1980), 261–9 on Kannonji; ibid., 254–60 on Azuchi; plus Naitō Akira, 'Azuchi-jō no kenkyū, *Kokka*, LXXXIII (nos. 987–8; 1976), with a brief English summary. A review of Naitō is also helpful: Takayanagi Shunichi, "The glory that was Azuchi," *Monumenta Nipponica* 32 (1977): 515–24. See also G. Elison and B. L. Smith, eds., *Warlords, Artists and Commoners: Japan in the Sixteenth Century* (Honolulu, 1981), 62–6; and M. Cooper, *They Came to Japan: An Anthology of European Reports on Japan, 1543–1640* (London, 1965), 134–5.

[66] The verse is quoted by George Elison in Elison and Smith, *op. cit.*, 66. On the siege of Odawara, see Sansom, *A History of Japan, 1334–1615*, 326–7. Concentrations of troops on this scale caused severe logistical problems and placed an almost intolerable strain on the Japanese economy, weakened by over a century of civil strife. On the link between castle size, army size, and tax demands under Hideyoshi, see the richly documented article by G. Moréchand, "'Taikō kenchi: le cadastre de Hideyoshi Toyotomi," *Bulletin de l'École française de l'Extreme Orient* 53, no. 1 (1966): 7–69, esp. 12–13. For a recent biography of the remarkable *Taikō*—Japan's only commoner ruler before modern times—see M. E. Berry, *Hideyoshi* (Cambridge, Mass., 1982).

given special auspicious names). With such blocks, more appropriate to a pyramid than to a castle, walls were built that were in places nineteen meters thick.[67] Quite possibly (as Professor J. W. Hall pointed out some years ago) these Japanese castles had "no peers in terms of size and impregnability" anywhere else in the early modern world.[68]

Once again we find that, though the Japanese leaders were perfectly prepared to take over Western military innovations, they always adapted them to local conditions in a distinctive way.[69] Early modern China, however, had no need of Western examples in the art of defensive fortification: its rulers had already been living with gunpowder for centuries, and the massive fortifications erected under the Ming dynasty had been designed to resist both artillery bombardment and mining. It is true that the Chinese had no castles, preferring to fortify whole towns—indeed the Chinese use the same character (*ch'eng*) for both "walled city" and "rampart"—but these towns were surrounded by massive walls (fifteen meters thick in places) that could withstand even modern shells. Thus in 1840, during the Opium Wars, a two-hour battery from a seventy-four-gun Royal Navy warship on a fort outside Canton "produced no effect whatever," according to an eyewitness. "The principle of their construction was such as to render them almost impervious to the efforts of horizontal fire, even from the 32-pounders." Likewise, the British expeditionary force sent to China in 1860 found the walls of Peking impregnable. According to the British commander, General Knollys:

> Ancient history tells us the walls of Babylon were so broad that several chariots could be driven abreast on top of them; but I really think those of Peking must have exceeded them. They were upwards of 50 feet in breadth, very

---

[67] Kodama, *Nihon jōkaku*, XII (1981): 152–81; Okamoto Ryōichi, *Nihon jōkaku-shi kenkyū sōsho VIII: Ōsaka-jō* (Tokyo; 1982). Both works are fully illustrated. See also the plates in K. Hirai, *Feudal Architecture in Japan* (New York, 1973), chap. 4; the account of W. B. Hauser, "Osaka Castle and Tokugawa Authority in Western Japan'" in Mass and Hauser, *The Bakufu*, 153–72; and the description of the Maeda stronghold at Kanazawa in J. McClain, *Kanazawa: a Seventeenth-Century Japanese Castle Town* (New Haven, 1982), 33f.

[68] J. W. Hall, "The Castle Town and and Japan's Modern Urbanization," *Far Eastern Quarterly* 15 (1955), a classic article reprinted in J. W. Hall and M. B. Jansen, eds., *Studies in the Institutional History of Early Modern Japan* (Princeton, 1968), 169–88 quotation at 177. Possibly the Dutch fortifications at Galle, in southern Ceylon, were in fact larger: see W. A. Nelson, *The Dutch Forts of Sri Lanka: The Military Monuments of Ceylon* (Edinburgh, 1984), 48–51.

[69] Although we know from several sources that military conversation was one of Nobunaga's chief passions, the Westerners with whom he conversed were mainly regular clergy whose knowledge of military architecture would normally not have extended to the intricacies of defensive architecture. See A. Valignano, *Sumario de las Cosas de Japón* (1583; ed. J. L. Álvarez-Taladriz, Tokyo, 1954), 152. It is true that some Jesuits in the Far East became skilled in metal casting, but this did not necessarily make them into reputable military engineers.

nearly the same in height, and paved on the top where, I am sure, five coaches-and-four could with a little management have been driven abreast.[70]

Thus, the scale of fortification in East Asia in effect rendered siege guns useless. That may be why indigenous heavy artillery never really developed there: In Japan, it was only seriously deployed against Osaka in 1615 and against the Shimabara rebels in 1636–7 (and on both occasions it proved indecisive); in China, it was seldom used offensively except during the 1670s. In both empires, sieges were usually decided by mass assaults, mining, or blockades rather than by bombardment.[71] Heavy guns, both of traditional and of Western manufacture, were certainly employed to defend the massive walls, but, otherwise, the use of artillery in the land warfare of East Asia was confined to the field.

Even so, the great states of East Asia paid more attention to the military innovations of the Europeans than to any other aspect of Western culture (except, perhaps, for astronomy and the clock). But this paradox may easily be explained when it is remembered that the seaborne arrival of the Europeans in the far East coincided with a period of sustained political disintegration in both China and Japan. In the former, instability lasted roughly from the renewal of pirate attacks on Fukien in the 1540s to the suppression of the last of the Ming loyalists in the 1680s; in the latter, the era of civil war lasted from the start of the Ōnin war in 1467 to the fall of Odawara in 1590. Throughout this long period, every military innovation was naturally accorded close attention, but, once stability was restored, the value of such things as firearms diminished. In China, they were largely confined to the frontiers; in Japan, most were kept in government arsenals and throughout the century the production of guns (which could only be made under license) was steadily reduced.[72]

But Japan did not only "give up" the gun. After 1580 successive central governments carried out a series of "sword hunts" aimed at removing *all* weapons from the temples, the peasants, the townsmen—from anyone who might try to resist the administration's taxes or policies. Some of the confiscated swords were

---

[70] Quotations from J. Ouchterlony, *The Chinese War* (London, 1844), 174–5; and H. Knollys, *Incidents in the China War of 1860* (Edinburgh; 1875), 198–9. See also Headrick, *The Tools of Empire*, 90–1; S. D. Chang, "The Morphology of Walled Capitals," in G. W. Skinner, ed., *The City in Late Imperial China* (Stanford, 1977), 75–100; and H. Franke, "Siege and Defence of Towns in Medieval China," in F. A. Kierman and J. K. Fairbank, eds., *Chinese Ways in Warfare* (Cambridge, Mass., 1974), 151–201.

[71] The new study of Needham, *The Gunpowder Epic,* replaces all earlier accounts as far as China is concerned. But see also C. R. Boxer, "Early European Military Influence in Japan (1543–1853)," *Transactions of the Asiatic Society of Japan* 2d ser., 8 (1931): 67–93; idem, "Portuguese Military Expeditions in Aid of the Mings and against the Manchus, 1621–1647," *T'ien Hsia Monthly* 7, no. 1 (August 1938): 24–36; and Cipolla, *Guns and Sails,* 114–17.

[72] Perrin, *Giving up the Gun,* 64–5.

melted down to make a great metal Buddha at Kyoto, and others were kept in state arsenals for use in emergencies (for instance, during the invasions of Korea during the 1590s), until in the end wearing the sword became largely confined to the hereditary arms-bearing class (the samurai). However, although the samurai might be left with their swords, they were deprived of most of their castles: starting (again) in 1580, the central government commenced a systematic destruction of the fortifications belonging to its defeated enemies. Then, in 1615, the shogun decreed that each lord could thenceforth maintain only one castle: All the rest should be destroyed. Thus, in the western province of Bizen, for example, where there had been over 200 fortified places at the end of the fifteenth century, there were only 10 by the 1590s, and after 1615 only 1: the great "Raven Castle" at Okayama. This "demilitarization" of Japan even affected literature. For some decades after 1671, the importation of all foreign books concerning military matters (and Christianity) was forbidden; and the *Honcho Gunki-ko (On the Military Equipment of Our Country)*, completed in 1722 and published in 1737, contained only one chapter on firearms, and that was brief.[73]

But by that time the West had also largely lost interest in Japan, for the European presence in East Asia had changed substantially. The Dutch had been expelled from Taiwan in the 1660s, and their factory in Japan no longer yielded vast profits; the Iberian powers had lost much of their trading empire in the Orient; and the English East India Company still traded relatively little in the Far East. So China and Japan remained largely outside the West's sphere of influence throughout the early modern period.[74]

IV

The almost constant wars fought by the Europeans overseas during the period 1500–1800 were entirely different from those fought at home. In the first place, whereas wars in Europe normally involved limited aims and ended with the transfer of only small portions of territory and assets, those fought abroad aimed at the permanent and total subjection of the enemy population, the destruction of their political system, and the appropriation and exploitation of as many of their assets as possible. In the second, although the aims of colonial wars were

---

[73] Data taken from Itō Tasaburo, "The Book-Banning Policy of the Tokugawa Shogunate," *Acta Asiatica* 12 (1972): 36–61; B. Susser, "The Toyotomi Regime," 140–5; Fujiki Hisashi and George Elison, "The Political Posture of Oda Nobunaga," in J. W. Hall, Nagahara Keiji, and Kozo Yamamura, eds., *Japan Before Tokugawa: Political Considerations and Economic Growth, 1500–1650* (Princeton, 1981), 149–93, at 186–93; and J. W. Hall, *Government and Local Power in Japan, 500 to 1700: A Study Based on Bizen Province* (Princeton, 1966), 248, 316.

[74] See the radically new assessment of the development of East Asian history in early modern times offered by R. P. Toby, *State and Diplomacy in Early Modern Japan; Asia in the Development of the Tokugawa Bakufu* (Princeton, 1984).

unlimited, the means deployed to fight them were not. Thus, in the wars of Europe, the investment of resources became steadily more massive, while overseas the numbers of the combatants and the means for conquest at their disposal remained exiguous almost until the end of the period. Colonial wars were, as the title of the best military manual on the subject proclaimed, "small wars."[75] In the sixteenth century, Cortés conquered Mexico with perhaps 500 Spaniards; Pizarro overthrew the Inca empire with less than 200; and the entire Portuguese overseas empire, from Nagasaki in Japan to Sofala in southern Africa, was administered and defended by less than 10,000 Europeans. In the seventeenth century, when the number of Europeans in Portuguese Asia had dwindled to perhaps 1500, those involved in the Dutch enterprise in the East involved fewer than 10,000 whites; and even in the eighteenth century, the Dutch East India Company employed in Asia an average of only 20,000 Europeans.

So by the year 1800 the West had expended, in relative terms, remarkably little effort in order to gain control of more than a third of the globe. Admittedly it then proved rather more difficult to subjugate those people who had previously escaped (or successfully resisted) the European embrace. Thus it took the construction and despatch of an ironclad steamship, the *Nemesis,* to reduce the Central Kingdom to reason during the first Opium War (although the ship's two pivot-mounted 32-pounders managed to destroy, in just one day in February 1841, nine war-junks, five forts, two military stations and a shore battery in the Pearl River); and likewise, in 1863, the defeat of a belated attempt by the Tokugawa regime to exclude Western warships from Japanese waters required an attack on Kagoshima by a full flotilla of the Royal Navy during a typhoon, and the combined efforts of French, British, Dutch and American warships in order to silence the modern gun batteries in the straits of Shimonoseki.[76] Meanwhile, not until the industrial production of effective prophylactics against tropical diseases could the Europeans bring enough of their well-armed troops into the African interior to secure the subordination of the 10,000 or so political units of the continent.

Nevertheless, although in terms of the number of combatants and the scale of resources deployed in European conflicts, this dramatic overseas expansion continued to be the product of 'small wars,' it still relied critically upon the con-

[75] C. Callwell, *Small Wars: Their Principles and Practice* (3rd edn., London, 1906). See also the excellent general remarks of de Moor and Wesseling, *Imperialism and War,* 1–11.

[76] For the fascinating story of the *Nemesis* see Headrick, *The Tools of Empire,* chap. 2 (details quoted from 47 and 50); for the 1863 naval campaign, see G. A. Ballard, *The Influence of the Sea on the Political History of Japan* (London, 1921), chap. 4 On the later episodes in the military rise of the West, see L. S. Stavrianos, *The World Since 1500: A Global History* (3d. ed., Englewood Cliffs, 1966), chaps. 13–14; and W. H. McNeill, *The Pursuit of Power: Technology, Armed Force and Society since A.D. 1000* (Oxford, 1982).

stant use of force. In the nineteenth century, as before, the West's advantage in the global 'military balance' was still vital: it was thanks to their military superiority, rather than to any social, moral or natural advantage, that the white peoples of the world managed to create and control, however briefly, the first global hegemony in History.

IDENTIFICATIONS PART II

Define each of the following items with a two-sentence identification. Your definition must specifically draw on material in one of the documents in this section.

Marco Polo

_____

_____

Afonso I

_____

_____

Ralph Crosse

_____

_____

Afamosa

_____

_____

Española

_____

_____

PART III
WESTERNIZATION/MODERNITY

The documents in this segment deal with the Age of Revolutions in the West. This epoch was marked by a series of very different types of revolutions including the Scientific Revolution, the French Revolution and the Industrial Revolution. These events also gave rise to the most formidable critique ever made of capitalism—the work of Karl Marx. Both the revolutions and Marxism had profound effects on the encounters between European and non-Western societies.

What does the essay by Francis Bacon tell you about the Scientific Revolution? How did proponents of the scientific method propose to look at and study the physical world? How would this differ from the way people elsewhere in the world viewed the material universe? What were some of the complaints of the French people which contributed to the onset of the French Revolution? What are the major points of the "Declaration of the Rights of Man"? Why is this declaration so important for human history? What was the significance of the decree abolishing feudalism? How did Robespierre justify the Terror? What is the significance of the Terror for our own time? What were some of the drawbacks to the Industrial Revolution? According to Marx how does capitalism work? What benefits does capitalism have and what problems does it create? What does Marx see as the alternative to capitalism?

THE GREAT INSTAURATION

Francis Bacon

THE ARGUMENTS OF THE SEVERAL PARTS.

One point of our design is, that every thing should be set out as openly and clearly as possible. For this nakedness, as once that of the body, is the companion of innocence and simplicity. The order and method of the work, therefore, shall first be explained. We divide it into six parts. The first part exhibits a summary, or universal description of such science and learning as mankind is, up to this time, in possession of. For we have thought fit to dwell a little even on received notions, with a view the more easily to perfect the old, and approach the new; being nearly equally desirous to improve the former and to attain the latter. This is of avail also towards our obtaining credit: according to the text, "The unlearned receives not the words of knowledge, unless you first speak of what is within his own heart." We will not, therefore, neglect coasting the shores of the now received arts and sciences, and importing thither something useful on our passage.

But we also employ such a division of the sciences as will not only embrace what is already discovered and known, but what has hitherto been omitted and deficient. For there are both cultivated and desert tracts in the intellectual as in the terrestrial globe. It must not, therefore, appear extraordinary if we sometimes depart from the common divisions. For additions, whilst they vary the whole, necessarily vary the parts, and their subdivisions, but the received divisions are only adequate to the received summary of the sciences, such as it now exists.

With regard to what we shall note as omitted, we shall not content ourselves with offering the mere names and concise proofs of what is deficient: for if we refer any thing to omissions, of a high nature, and the meaning of which may be rather obscure, (so that we may have grounds to suspect that men will not understand our intention, or the nature of the matter we have embraced in

The Distribution of the Work *The Works,* ed. and trans. Basil Montague, 3 vols. (Philadelphia: Parry & MacMillan, 1854), 3: 338–42.

our conception and contemplation,) we will always take care to subjoin to an instance of the whole, some precepts for perfecting it, or perhaps a completion of a part of it by ourselves. For, we consider it to concern our own character as well as the advantage of others, that no one may imagine a mere passing idea of such matters to have crossed our mind, and that what we desire and aim at resembles a wish; whilst in reality it is in the power of all men, if they be not wanting to themselves, and *we* ourselves are actually masters of a sure and clear method. For we have not undertaken to measure out regions in our mind, like augurs for divination, but like generals to invade them for conquest.

And this is the first part of the work.

Having passed over the ancient arts, we will prepare the human understanding for pressing on beyond them. The object of the Second Part, then, is the doctrine touching a better and more perfect use of reasoning in the investigation of things, and the true helps of the understanding; that it may by this means be raised, as far as our human and mortal nature will admit, and be enlarged in its powers so as to master the arduous and obscure secrets of nature. And the art which we employ (and which we are wont to call the interpretation of nature) is a kind of logic. For common logic professes to contrive and prepare helps and guards for the understanding, and so far they agree. But ours differs from the common, chiefly in three respects, namely, in its end, the order of demonstration, and the beginning of the inquiry.

For the end of our science is not to discover arguments, but arts, nor what is agreeable to certain principles, but the principles themselves, nor probable reasons, but designations and indications of effects. Hence, from a diversity of intention follows a diversity of consequences. For, in the one an opponent is vanquished and constrained by argument, in the other, nature by effects.

And the nature and order of the demonstrations agree with this end. For in common logic almost our whole labour is spent upon the syllogism. (p.339) The logicians appear scarcely to have thought seriously of induction, passing it over with some slight notice, and hurrying on to the formulae of dispute. But we reject the syllogistic demonstration, as being too confused, and letting nature escape from our hands. For, although nobody can doubt that those things which agree with the middle term agree with each other, (which is a sort of mathematical certainty,) nevertheless, there is this source of error, namely, that a syllogism consists of propositions, propositions of words, and words are but the tokens and signs of things. If, therefore, the notions of the mind (which are as it were the soul of words, and the basis of this whole structure and fabric) are badly and hastily abstracted from things, and vague, or not sufficiently defined and limited, or, in short, faulty (as they may be) in many other respects, the whole falls to the ground. We reject, therefore, the syllogism, and that not only as regards first principles, (to which even the logicians do not apply them,) but also in intermediate propositions, which the syllogism certainly manages in some way or other to bring out and produce, but then they are barren of effects, unfit for practice, and clearly unsuited to the active branch of the sciences. Although we would leave therefore to the syllogism, and such celebrated and applauded demonstrations, their jurisdiction over popular and speculative arts, (for here we make no alteration,) yet, in every thing relating to the nature of things, we make use of induction, both for our major and minor propositions. For we consider induction to be that form of demonstration which assists the senses, closes in upon nature, and presses on, and, as it were, mixes itself with action.

Hence also the order of demonstration is naturally reversed. For at present the matter is so managed, that from the senses and particular objects they immediately fly to the greatest generalities, as the axes round which their disputes may revolve: all the rest is deduced from them intermediately, by a short way we allow, but an abrupt one, and impassable to nature, though easy and well suited to dispute. But, by our method, axioms are raised up in gradual succession, so that we only at last arrive at generalities. And that which is most generalized, is not merely national but well defined, and really acknowledged by nature as well known to her, and cleaving to the very pith of things.

By far our greatest work, however, lies in the form of induction and the judgment arising from it. For the form of which the logicians speak, which proceeds by bare enumeration, is puerile, and its conclusions precarious, is exposed to danger from one contrary example, only considers what is habitual, and leads not to any final result.

The sciences, on the contrary, require a form of induction capable of explaining and separating experiments, and coming to a certain conclusion by a proper series of rejections and exclusions. If, however, the common judgment of the logicians has been so laborious, and has exercised such great wits, how much more must we labour in this which is drawn not only from the recesses of the mind, but the very entrails of nature.

Nor is this all, for we let down to a greater depth, and render more solid the very foundations of the sciences, and we take up the beginning of our investigation from a higher part than men have yet done, by subjecting those matters to examination which common logic receives upon the credit of others. For the logicians borrow the principles of one science from another, in the next place they worship the first formed notions of their minds, and, lastly, they rest contented with the immediate information of the senses, if well directed. But we have resolved that true logic ought to enter upon the several provinces of the sciences with a greater command than is possessed by their first principles, and to force those supposed principles to an account of the grounds upon which they are clearly determined. As far as relates to the first notions of the understanding, not any of the materials which the understanding, when left to itself, has collected, is unsuspected by us, nor will we confirm them unless they themselves be put upon their trial and be judged accordingly. Again, we have many ways of sifting the information of the senses themselves: for the senses assuredly deceive, though at the same time they disclose their errors: the errors, however, are close at hand, whilst their indication must be sought at a greater distance.

There are two faults of the senses: they either desert or deceive us. For in the first place there are many things which escape the senses, however well directed and unimpeded, owing either to the subtilty of the whole body, or the minuteness of its parts, or the distance of place, or the slowness or velocity of motion, or the familiarity of the object, or to other causes. Nor are the apprehensions of the senses very firm, when they grasp the subject; for the testimony and information of the senses bears always a relation to man and not to the universe, and it is altogether a great mistake to assert that our senses are the measure of things.

To encounter these difficulties, we have everywhere sought and collected helps for the senses with laborious and faithful service, in order to supply defects and correct errors: and that not so much by means of instruments, as by experiments. For experiments are much more delicate than the senses themselves, even when aided by instruments, at least if they are skilfully and scientifically imagined and applied to the required point. We attribute but little, therefore, to the immediate and proper perception of the senses, (p.340) but reduce the matter to this, that *they* should decide on the experiment, and the experiment on the subject of it. Wherefore, we consider that we have shown ourselves most observant priests of the senses, (by which all that exists in nature must be investigated if we would be rational,) and not unskilful interpreters of their oracles: for others seem to observe and worship them in word alone, but we in deed. These then are the means which we prepare for kindling and transmitting the light of nature: which would of themselves be sufficient, if the human understanding were plain and like a smoothed surface. But since the minds of men are so wonderfully prepossessed, that a clear and polished surface for receiving the true rays of things is wholly wanting, necessity urges us to seek a remedy for this also.

The images or idols by which the mind is preoccupied are either adventitious or innate. The adventitious have crept into the minds of men either from the dogmas and sects of philosophers, or the perverted rules of demonstration. But the innate are inherent to the very nature of the understanding, which appears to be much more prone to error than the senses. For however men may be satisfied with themselves, and rush into a blind admiration and almost adoration of the human mind, one thing is most certain, namely, that as an uneven mirror changes the rays proceeding from objects according to its own figure and position, so the mind when affected by things through the senses does not act in the most trustworthy manner, but inserts and mixes her own nature into that of things, whilst clearing and recollecting her notions.

The first two species of idols are *with difficulty* eradicated, the latter can never be so. We can only point them out, and note and demonstrate that insidious faculty of the mind, lest new shoots of error should happen to spring up, from the destruction of the old, on account of the mind's defective structure; and we should then find ourselves only exchanging instead of extinguishing errors; whilst it ought on the other hand to be eternally resolved and settled, that the understanding cannot decide otherwise than by induction and by a legitimate form of it. Wherefore the doctrine of the purifying of the understanding, so as to fit it for the reception of truth, consists of three reprehensions; the reprehension of the schemes of philosophy, the reprehension of methods of demonstration, and the reprehension of natural human reason. But when these have been gone through, and it has at last been clearly seen, what results are to be expected from the nature of things and the nature of the mind, we consider that we shall have prepared and adorned a nuptial couch for the mind and the universe; the divine goodness being our bridemaid. But let the prayer of our epithalamium be this; that from this union may spring assistance to man, and a race of such discoveries as will in some measure overcome his wants and necessities.—

And this is the second part of the work.

It is our intention not only to open and prepare the way, but also to enter upon it. The third part, therefore, of our work embraces the phenomena of the universe; that is to say, experience of every kind, and such a natural history as can form the foundation of an edifice of philosophy. For there is no method of demonstration, or form of interpreting nature, so excellent as to be able to afford and supply *matter* for knowledge, as well as to defend and support the mind against error and failure. But those who resolve not to conjecture and divine, but to discover and know, not to invent buffooneries and fables about worlds, but to inspect, and, as it were, dissect the nature of this real world, must derive all from things themselves. Nor can any substitution or compensation of wit, meditation, or argument, (were the whole wit of all combined in one,) supply the place of this labour, investigation, and personal examination of the world; our method then must necessarily be pursued, or the whole forever abandoned. But men have so conducted themselves hitherto, that it is little to be wondered at if nature do not disclose herself to them.

For in the first place the defective and fallacious evidence of our senses, a system of observation slothful and unsteady, as though acting from chance, a tradition vain and depending on common report, a course of practice intent upon effects, and servile, blind, dull, vague, and abrupt experiments, and lastly our careless and meagre natural history, have collected together, for the use of the understanding, the most defective materials as regards philosophy and the sciences.

In the next place, a preposterous refinement, and, as it were, ventilation of argument, is attempted as a late remedy for a matter become clearly desperate, and neither makes any improvement, nor removes errors. There remains no hope therefore of greater advancement and progress, unless by some restoration of the sciences.

But this must commence entirely with natural history. For it is useless to clean the mirror if it have no images to reflect, and it is manifest that we must prepare proper matter for the understanding as well as steady support. But our history, like our logic, differs in many respects, from the received, in its end or office, in its very matter and compilation, in its nicety, in its selection, and in its arrangements relatively to what follows.

For, in the first place, we begin with that species of natural history which is not so much calculated to amuse by the variety of its objects, or to offer immediate results by its experiments, as to throw a light upon the discovery of causes, and to present, as it were, its bosom as the first nurse of philosophy. For, although we regard principally effects and the active division of the sciences (p. 341) yet we wait for the time of harvest, and do not go about to reap moss and a green crop: being sufficiently aware that well formed axioms draw whole crowds of effects after them, and do not manifest their effects partially, but in abundance. But we wholly condemn and banish that unreasonable and puerile desire of immediately seizing some pledges as it were of new effects, which, like the apple of Atalanta, retard our course—such then is the office of our natural history.

With regard to its compilation, we intend not to form a history of nature at liberty and in her usual course, when she proceeds willingly and acts of her own accord, (as for instance the history of the heavenly bodies, meteors, the earth and sea, minerals, plants, animals,) but much rather a history of nature constrained and perplexed, as she is seen when thrust down from her proper rank and harassed and modelled by the art and contrivance of man. We will therefore go through all the experiments of the mechanical and the operative part of the liberal arts, and all those of different practical schemes which have not yet been put together so as to form a peculiar art: as far as we have been able to investigate them and it will suit our purpose. Besides, (to speak the truth,) without paying any attention to the pride of man, or to appearances, we consider this branch of much more assistance and support than the other: since the nature of things betrays itself more by means of the operations of art than when at perfect liberty.

Nor do we present the history of bodies alone, but have thought it moreover right to exert our diligence in compiling a separate history of properties: we mean those which may be called the cardinal properties of nature, and of which its very elements are composed, namely, matter with its first accidents and appetites, such as density, rarity, heat, cold, solidity, fluidity, weight, levity, and many others.

But, with regard to the nicety of natural history, we clearly require a much more delicate and simple form of experiments than those which are obvious. For we bring out and extract from obscurity many things which no one would have thought of investigating, unless he were proceeding by a sure and steady path to the discovery of causes; since they are in themselves of no great use, and it is clear that they were not sought for on their own account, but that they bear the same relation to things and effects, that the letters of the alphabet do to discourse and words, being useless indeed in themselves, but the elements of all language.

In the selection of our reports and experiments, we consider that we have been more cautious for mankind than any of our predecessors. For we admit nothing but as an eyewitness, or at least upon approved and rigorously examined testimony; so that nothing is magnified into the miraculous, but our reports are pure and unadulterated by fables and absurdity. Nay, the commonly received and repeated falsehoods, which by some wonderful neglect have held their ground for many ages and become inveterate, are by us distinctly proscribed and branded, that they may no longer molest learning. For, as it has been well observed, that the tales, superstitions, and trash which nurses instil into children, seriously corrupt their minds, so are we careful and anxious whilst managing and watching over the infancy, as it were, of philosophy committed to the charge of natural history, that it should not from the first become habituated to any absurdity. In every new and rather delicate experiment, although to us it may appear sure and satisfactory, we yet publish the method we employed, that, by the discovery of every attendant circumstance, men may perceive the possibly latent and inherent errors, and be roused to proofs of a more certain and exact nature, if such there be. Lastly, we intersperse the whole with advice, doubts, and cautions, casting out and restraining, as it were, all phantoms by a sacred ceremony and exorcism.

Finally, since we have learned how much experience and history distract the powers of the human mind, and how difficult it is (especially for young or prejudiced intellects) to become at the first acquainted with nature, we frequently add some observations of our own, by way of showing the first tendency, as it were, and inclination or aspect of history towards philosophy; thus assuring mankind that they will not always be detained in the ocean of history, and also preparing for the time when we shall come to the work of the understanding. And by such a natural history as we are describing, we think that safe and convenient access is opened to nature, and solid and ready matter furnished to the understanding.

THE FRENCH REVOLUTION: THE TERROR (1793–1794)

"Let us," said Danton in the new National Convention, "cast down before Europe, as the gauntlet of battle, the head of a king." While all Europe looked on in horror, Louis XVI was tried, convicted "of conspiring against the liberty of the nation and of attempts against the general safety of the state," and executed (January 21, 1793). By this act, the revolutionists multiplied their enemies outside France and intensified opposition within. Recognition of the former was given by a declaration of war against England and Holland (February 1, 1793); and a series of measures was taken to deal with counterrevolutionary efforts at home. An Extraordinary Criminal Tribunal was created (March 10) to deal with "every counterrevolutionary enterprise"; another act (March 21) authorized the organization in each commune of a Revolutionary Committee to check on the doings of the populace; and, on April 6, the Convention established a Committee of Public Safety "to take, under urgent circumstances, measures of external and internal defense." Meanwhile, between the leading factions of the Convention, Jacobins and Girondins, there had developed a serious rupture. The Jacobins, now often referred to as the "Mountain" in the Convention, had grown increasingly radical since the organization of their society (now, since August, 1792, officially called The Society of Friends of Liberty and Equality; see pages 392–394. The Mountain tended to represent the urban, Parisian, propertyless sans-culotte interests; the Girondins the rural, propertied classes. The Mountain wished to carry the revolution on to further archievements; the Girondins hoped to stop it where it was. Bitter personal antipathies boiled between leaders of the two groups and when the Girondins showed hesitancy during the King's trial, the Mountain leaders charged them with promonarchical sympathies. Finally, by an appeal to force, the Mountain purged the Convention of Girondins (May 31–June 2, 1793), thereby gaining complete mastery of a "rump" Convention. Shortly afterward (July 27), the Committee of Public Safety was reorganized with Robespierre its dominating figure and, as dangers from without and within France necessitated firm, unwavering control, the Committee became all powerful, determined to put down "enemies of the revolution" wherever found. A series of extraordinary measures followed, one of the most significant of which was the decree which conscripted the entire nation for war, the *Levée en Masse*. By means of its provisions, Carnot, Minister of War, earned the glorious title "Organizer of Victory"; and the reorganized French armies, fired with revolutionary ardor, not only repelled the enemies from the borders but also overran enemy territory. Extracts from this famous decree follow.

MOBILIZATION AGAINST THE FOREIGN ENEMIES

From the *Levée en Masse* (August 23, 1793)[1]

Article I. From this moment until that in which the enemies shall have been driven from the territory of the Republic, all Frenchmen are permanently requisitioned for service in the armies.

Young men shall go forth to battle; married men shall forge weapons and transport munitions; women shall make tents and clothing, and shall serve in hospitals; children will make lint from old linen; and old men shall be brought to public places to arouse the courage of soldiers and preach the hatred of kings and the unity of the Republic.

II. Public buildings shall be converted into barracks, public squares into workshops for arms. . . .

IV. Saddle horses are requisitioned to complete the cavalry corps; draught horses, except those employed in agriculture, will haul the artillery and provisions.

V. The Committee of Public Safety is charged to take all measures necessary to set up without delay an extraordinary manufactory of arms of all kinds to correspond to the spirit and energy of the French people. It is authorized, therefore, to set up all the establishments . . . necessary for the accomplishment of this work, and to requisition throughout the Republic the craftsmen and workers that can co-operate in making this a success. . . .

VI. The representatives of the people sent to execute the present law shall have the power of enforcement in their respective districts in concert with the Committee of Public Safety. . . .

VII. No one can furnish a substitute for the place to which he has been requisitioned. . . .

VIII. The levy shall be general. Unmarried citizens and childless widowers between the ages of eighteen and thirty-five shall be called first. . . .

---

[1] Duvergier, ed., *Collection complete des lois*, VI, 107.

MOBILIZATION AGAINST THE DOMESTIC ENEMIES

Just as the *Levée en Masse* was designed against foreign enemies of the Revolution, so the Law of Suspects was directed against the counterrevolutionaries within France. And as Carnot's armies marched against the foreign foes, so the Committee of Public Safety, working through the revolutionary committees in every commune, rounded up "suspects" at home.

From the "Law of Suspects" (September 17, 1793)[2]

Article I. Immediately after publication of the present decree, all suspect people still at liberty within the territory of the Republic shall be placed under arrest.

II. Those considered to be suspect are: 1. Those who by their conduct, relations, speech, or writings have shown themselves the partisans of tyranny or federalism, and enemies of liberty. 2. Those who cannot after the manner prescribed by the law of March 21 last justify their means of existence and the performance of their civic duties. 3. Those to whom certificates of civism have been refused. . . . 5. Those of the former nobles, including husbands, wives, fathers, mothers, sons, daughters, brothers, sisters, and agents of émigrés who have not constantly manifested their attachment to the revolution. 6. Those who have emigrated during the interval between July 1, 1789, to . . . April 8, 1792, even if they have returned to France within the period fixed by law.

III. The committees of surveillance established by the decree of March 21 last, or those which have been substituted for them . . . are charged to prepare lists of suspects in their respective districts, issue warrants of arrest against them, and seal their papers.

WAGES AND PRICE CONTROL

The Mountain's responsiveness to demands of the Parisian masses is well illustrated by the Law of the Maximum. Since the outbreak of the revolution, crop failures, currency depreciation, and profiteering had led to a general advance in prices which bore heavily upon the propertyless sans-culottes. As a kind of wartime rationing and defense of the poor against speculators, the Mountain-controlled Convention passed a series of price-fixing measures of which the most inclusive was the following Law of the Maximum.

---

[2] *Ibid.*, VI, 172.

From the "Law of the Maximum" (September 29, 1793)[3]

Art. 1. The articles which the National Convention has judged to be of prime necessity and for which it has believed that it should fix the maximum, or the highest price, are: fresh meat, salt meat and bacon, butter, sweet oil, cattle, salt fish, wine, brandy, vinegar, cider, beer, firewood, charcoal, coal, candles, lamp oil, salt, soda, sugar, honey, white paper, leather, iron, brass, lead, copper, hemp, linen, wool, woolens, fabrics, the materials which serve to make fabrics, sabots, shoes, cabbages and turnips, soap, potash, and tobacco.

2. For the articles listed above, the *maximum* price for firewood of the first quality, of charcoal and of coal, are the same as in 1790, plus a twentieth of the price. . . .

The *maximum*, or the highest price, of tobacco in rolls is twenty sous per pound (of eight ounces); that of smoking tobacco is ten sous; that of salt is two sous per pound; that of soap is twenty-five sous.

3. The *maximum* price of all the other commodities and goods included in Article 1, for the whole extent of the Republic, until the month of September next, shall be the price which each of them had in 1790, such as is established by the official price lists or the market price of each department, and a third over and above this same price, deduction being made of fiscal and other duties to which they were then subject, under whatsoever denomination they may have existed. . . .

7. All persons who buy or sell the goods listed in Article 1 above the *maximum* of the price determined and posted in each department shall pay to the municipal police a fine double the value of the article sold, the fine payable to the informer; they shall be enrolled upon the list of suspected persons and treated as such. The purchaser shall not be subject to the above penalties if he denounces the offense of the seller; and each merchant shall be required to have a list in his shop bearing the *maximum* or highest prices of his goods.

8. The *maximum* or the highest price belonging to salaries, wages, and manual labor by the day in each place shall be fixed, to commence from the publication of this law until the month of September next, by the general councils of the communes at the same amount as in 1790, to which there shall be added half of that price in addition.

9. The municipalities shall put into requisition and punish, according to circumstances, with three days' imprisonment the workingmen, factory operatives, and other laboring persons who refuse without legitimate cause to engage in their usual labors. . . .

---

[3] *Ibid.*, VI, 193–95.

[Great care is exercised in Articles 9–20, Article 17 excepted, to ensure prompt and effective enforcement of the law of the maximum. Article 17 provided:]

17. During the war, all exportation of goods or merchandise of prime necessity, under whatsoever name or commission, is prohibited at all frontiers, salt excepted.

ROBESPIERRE'S AIMS FOR THE COMMITTEE OF PUBLIC SAFETY (FEBRUARY 5, 1794)

Opinion of Maximilien Robespierre (1758–1794), the provincial lawyer who came to dominate the Terror, has varied widely. He has been treated as though he had been practically insane; he has been charged with having had a particularly bloodthirsty desire for dictatorial power; and he has been considered as a fanatical idealist whose unfortunate zeal led him to adopt methods which precluded realization of his dreams. In the main, the verdict of recent students tends toward the last view, not because it is kinder, but because it best squares with the facts of Robespierre's life and the circumstances of France during the Terror. For Robespierre was certainly not mad, and while he strove for dictatorial powers, he clearly considered dictatorship as a temporary phase of the revolution, necessary but not desirable. By the end of 1793, the newly organized republican armies had driven the foreigners from the borders of France. The foreign threat, though not entirely removed, was under control. The immediate need of revolutionary France, as the Committee of Public Safety now saw it, was to establish the Republic on a firm foundation. It was with this end in view that Robespierre made the following speech on February 5, 1794, a "Report [to the Committee of Public Safety] on the Principles of Political Morality Which Ought to Guide the National Convention in the Internal Administration of the Republic." This report is probably the best single statement of Robespierre's views, and it goes far to explain the perpetuation of the Terror until his death (July 27, 1794). The "Incorruptible" set forth *virtue* as the fundamental principle of the Republic. "Virtues," said he on another occasion, "are simple, modest, poor, often ignorant, sometimes gross; they are the appanage of misfortune and the patrimony of the people. Vices are surrounded with riches, adorned by the charms of pleasure and the snares of perfidy, escorted by all the dangerous talents, by crime." Robespierre held that "the people is sublime," that the mass of Frenchmen was virtuous, that only the virtuous could be citizens in the Republic. Others, lacking virtue, were not citizens—were, indeed, enemies of the Republic who must be wiped out. Such a Republic must inevitably remain at war with a large part of its own population. And so, in the name of virtue, Robespierre employed implacable Terror against the "enemies of the Republic." The idealistic concepts which impelled his fateful actions are portrayed in the speech which follows.

From ROBESPIERRE, Speech of February 5, 1794[4]

It is time to mark clearly the aim of the Revolution and the end toward which we wish to move; it is time to take stock of ourselves, of the obstacles which we still face, and of the means which we ought to adopt to attain our objectives. . . .

What is the goal for which we strive? A peaceful enjoyment of liberty and equality, the rule of that eternal justice whose laws are engraved, not upon marble or stone, but in the hearts of all men.

We wish an order of things where all low and cruel passions are enchained by the laws, all beneficent and generous feelings aroused; where ambition is the desire to merit glory and to serve one's fatherland; where distinctions are born only of equality itself; where the citizen is subject to the magistrate, the magistrate to the people, the people to justice; where the nation safeguards the welfare of each individual, and each individual proudly enjoys the prosperity and glory of his fatherland; where all spirits are enlarged by the constant exchange of republican sentiments and by the need of earning the respect of a great people; where the arts are the adornment of liberty, which ennobles them; and where commerce is the source of public wealth, not simply of monstrous opulence for a few families.

In our country we wish to substitute morality for egotism, probity for honor, principles for conventions, duties for etiquette, the empire of reason for the tyranny of customs, contempt for vice for contempt for misfortune, pride for insolence, the love of honor for the love of money . . . that is to say, all the virtues and miracles of the Republic for all the vices and snobbishness of the monarchy.

We wish in a word to fulfill the requirements of nature, to accomplish the destiny of mankind, to make good the promises of philosophy . . . that France, hitherto illustrious among slave states, may eclipse the glory of all free peoples that have existed, become the model of all nations. . . . That is our ambition; that is our aim.

What kind of government can realize these marvels? Only a democratic government. . . . But to found and to consolidate among us this democracy, to realize the peaceable rule of constitutional laws, it is necessary to conclude the war of liberty against tyranny and to pass successfully through the storms of revolution. Such is the aim of the revolutionary system which you have set up. . . .

Now what is the fundamental principle of democratic, or popular government—that is to say, the essential mainspring upon which it depends and which makes it function? It is virtue: I mean public virtue . . . that virtue which is nothing else but love of fatherland and its laws. . . .

---

[4] P. J. B. Buchez and P. C. Roux, eds., *Histoire parlementaire de la Revolution Française*, 40 vols, Paris, 1834–38, XXXI, 268–76.

The splendor of the goal of the French Revolution is simultaneously the source of our strength and of our weakness: our strength, because it gives us an ascendancy of truth over falsehood, and of public rights over private interests; our weakness, because it rallies against us all vicious men, all those who in their hearts seek to despoil the people. . . . It is necessary to stifle the domestic and foreign enemies of the Republic or perish with them. Now in these circumstances, the first maxim of our politics ought to be to lead the people by means of reason and the enemies of the people by terror.

If the basis of popular government in time of peace is virtue, the basis of popular government in time of revolution is both virtue and terror: virtue without which terror is murderous, terror without which virtue is powerless. Terror is nothing else than swift, severe, indomitable justice; it flows, then, from virtue.

CAHIER OF 1789, THE THIRD ESTATE OF VERSAILLES

EDITOR'S INTRODUCTION

Of the grievances, complaints and remonstrances of the members of the third estate of the bailliage of Versailles.

Art. 1. The Power of making laws resides in the king and the nation.

Art. 2. The nation being too numerous for a personal exercise of this right, has confided its trust to representatives freely chosen from all classes of citizens. These representatives constitute the national assembly.

(pg. 24) Art. 3. Frenchmen should regard as laws of the kingdom those alone which have been prepared by the national assembly and sanctioned by the king.

Art. 4. Succession in the male line and primogeniture are usages as ancient as the monarchy, and ought to be maintained and consecrated by solemn and irrevocable enactment.

Art. 5. The laws prepared by the States General and sanctioned by the king shall be binding upon all classes of citizens and upon all provinces of the kingdom. They shall be registered literally and accurately in all courts of law. They shall be open for consultation at all seats of municipal and communal government; and shall be read at sermon time in all parishes.

Art. 6. That the nation may not be deprived of that portion of legislation which is its due, and that the affairs of the kingdom may not suffer neglect and delay, the States General shall be convoked at least every two or three years.

Merrick Whitcombe, ed. "Typical Cahiers of 1789" in *Translations and Reprints From The Original Sources of European History* (Philadelphia: Dept. of History, Univ. of Pennsylvania, 1898) vol. 4, no. 5, pp. 24–36.

Art. 7. No intermediate commission of the States General may ever be established, since deputies of the nation have no right to delegate the powers confirmed to them.

Art 8. Powers shall be conferred upon delegates for one year only; but they may be continued or confirmed by a single re-election.

Art. 9. The persons of deputies shall be inviolable. They may not be prosecuted in civil cases during their term of office; nor held reponsible to the executive authorities for any speech made in the assembly; but they shall be responsible to the States General alone.

Art. 10. Deputies of the Third Estate, or their president or speaker, shall preserve the same attitude and demeanor as the representatives of the two upper orders, when they address the sovereign. As regards the three orders there shall be no difference observed in the ceremonial made use of at the convocation of the estates.

Art. 11. Personal liberty, proprietary rights and the security of citizens shall be established in a clear, precise and irrevocable manner. All *lettres de cachet* shall be abolished forever, subject to certain modifications which the States General may see fit to impose.

Art. 12. And to remove forever the possibility of injury to the personal and proprietary rights of Frenchmen, the jury system shall be introduced in all criminal cases, and in civil cases for the determination of fact, in all the courts of the realm.

Art. 13. All persons accused of crimes not involving the death penalty (pg. 25) shall be released on bail within twenty-four hours. This release shall be pronounced by the judge upon the decision of the jury.

Art. 14. All persons who shall have been imprisoned upon suspicion, and afterwards proved innocent, shall be entitled to satisfaction and damages from the state, if they are able to show that their honor or property has suffered injury.

Art. 15. A wider liberty of the press shall be accorded, with this provision alone: that all manuscripts sent to the printer shall be signed by the author, who shall be obliged to disclose his identity and bear the responsibility of his work; and to prevent judges and other persons in power from taking advantage of their authority, no writing shall be held a libel until it is so determined by twelve jurors, chosen according to the forms of a law which shall be enacted upon this subject.

Art. 16. Letters shall never be opened in transit; and effectual measures shall be taken to the end that this trust shall remain inviolable.

Art. 17. All distinctions in penalties shall be abolished; and crimes committed by citizens of the different orders shall be punished irrespectively, according to the same forms of law and in the same manner. The States General shall seek to bring it about that the effects of transgression shall be confined to the individual and shall not be reflected upon the relatives of the transgressor, themselves innocent of all participation.

Art. 18. Penalties shall in all cases be moderate and proportionate to the crime. All kinds of torture, the rack and the stake, shall be abolished. Sentence of death shall be pronounced only for atrocious crimes and in rare instances, determined by the law.

Art. 19. Civil and criminal laws shall be reformed.

Art. 20. The military throughout the kingdom shall be subject to the general law and to the civil authorities, in the same manner as other citizens.

Art. 21. No tax shall be legal unless accepted by the representatives of the people and sanctioned by the king.

Art. 22. Since all Frenchmen receive the same advantage from the government, and are equally interested in its maintenance, they ought to be placed upon the same footing in the matter of taxation.

Art. 23. All taxes now in operation are contrary to these principles and for the most part vexatious, oppressive and humiliating to the people. They ought to be abolished as soon as possible, and replaced by others common to the three orders and to all classes of citizens, without exception.

(pg. 26) Art 24. In case the present taxes are provisionally retained, it should be for a short time, not longer than the session of the States General, and it shall be ordered that the proportional contribution of the two upper orders shall be due from them on the day of the promulgation of the law of the constitution.

Art. 25. After the establishment of the new taxes, which shall be paid by the three orders, the present exceptional method of collecting from the clergy shall be done away with, and their future assemblies shall deal exclusively with matters of discipline and dogma.

Art 26. All new taxes, real and personal, shall be established only for a limited time, never to exceed two or three years. At the expiration of this term, they shall be no longer collected, and collectors or other officials soliciting the same shall be proceeded against as guilty of extortion.

Art 27. The anticipation of future revenues, loans in whatsoever disguise, and all other financial expedients of the kind, of which so great abuse has been made, shall be forbidden.

Art. 28. In case of war, or other exceptional necessity, no loan shall be made without the consent of the States General, and it shall be enacted that no loan shall be effected, without provision being made by taxation for the payment of interest, and of the principal at a specified time.

Art. 29. The amount which each citizen shall be obliged to pay, in case of war, by reason of an increase in the existing taxes, at a certain rate per livre, shall be determined beforehand by the States General in conjunction with the king. The certainty of increase ought to have a marked effect in preventing useless and unjust wars, since it clearly indicates to Frenchmen the new burden they will have to bear, and to foreign nations the resources which the nation has in reserve and at hand to repulse unjust attacks.

Art. 30. The exact debt of the government shall be established by the States General, and after verification it shall be declared the national debt.

Art. 31. Perpetual and life annuities shall be capitalized at their present value and discharged.

Art. 32. The expenses of the departments shall be determined by their actual needs, and so established by a committee of the States General, in such a manner that the expenditures may never exceed the sums appropriated.

(pg. 27) Art. 33. There shall be no increase in taxation, until the receipts and expenditures have been compared with the utmost care, and a real deficit discovered; in fact, not until all possible reductions have been made in the expenses of each department.

Art. 34. The expenses of the war department call for, the special attention of the States General. These expenses amount annually to the appalling sums of 110 and 120 millions. In order to effect their reduction, the States General shall demand the accounts of this department under the recent ministries, particularly under the ministry of the Duc de Choiseul.

Art. 35. The present militia system, which is burdensome, oppressive and humiliating to the people, shall be abolished; and the States General shall devise means for its reformation.

Art. 36. A statement of pensions shall be presented to the States General; they shall be granted only in moderate amounts, and then only for services rendered. The total annual expenditure for this purpose should not exceed a fixed sum. A list of pensions should be printed and made public each year.

Art. 37. Since the nation undertakes to provide for the personal expenses of the sovereign, as well as for the crown and state, the law providing for the inalienability of the domain shall be repealed. As a result, all parcels of the domain immediately in the king's possession, as well as those already pledged, and for the forests of His Majesty as well, shall be sold, and transferred in small lots, in so far as possible, and always at public auction to the highest bidder; and the proceeds applied to the reduction of the public debt. In the meanwhile all woods and forests shall continue to be controlled and administered, whoever may be the actual proprietors, according to the provisions of the law of 1669.

Art. 38. The execution of this law shall be confided to the provincial estates, which shall prosecute violations of the law before judges in ordinary.

Art. 39. Appanages shall be abolished and replaced, in the case of princes who possess them, with cash salaries, which shall be included in the expenses of the crown.

Art. 40. The States General shall take under advisement these transfers which have not yet been verified and completed.

Art. 40. b. Ministers and all government officials shall be responsible to the States General for their conduct of affairs. They may be impeached according to fixed forms of law and punished according to the statute.

Art. 41. All general and particular statements and accounts relative to the administration shall be printed and made public each year.

Art. 42. The coinage may not be altered without the consent of the Estates; and no bank established without their approval.

Art. 43. A new subdivision shall be made of the provinces of the realm; provincial estates shall be established, members of which, not excepting their presidents, shall be elected.

Art. 44. The constitution of the provincial estates shall be uniform throughout the kingdom, and fixed by the States General. Their powers shall be limited to the interior administration of the provinces, under the supervision of His Majesty, who shall communicate to them the national laws which have received the consent of the States General and the royal sanction: to which laws all the provincial estates shall be obliged to submit without reservation.

Art. 45. All members of the municipal assemblies of towns and villages shall be elected. They may be chosen from all classes of citizens. All municipal offices now existing shall be abolished; and their redemption shall be provided for by the States General.

Art. 46. All offices and positions, civil, ecclesiastical and military, shall be open to all orders; and no humiliating and unjust exceptions (in the case of the third estate), destructive to emulation and injurious to the interests of the state, shall be perpetuated.

Art. 47. The right of *aubaine* shall be abolished with regard to all nationalities. All foreigners, after three years residence in the kingdom, shall enjoy the rights of citizenship.

Art. 48. Deputies of French colonies in America and in the Indies, which form an important part of our possessions, shall be admitted to the States General, if not at the next meeting, at least at the one following.

Art. 49. All relics of serfdom, agrarian or personal, still remaining in certain provinces, shall be abolished.

Art. 50. New laws shall be made in favor of the negroes in our colonies; and the States General shall take measures towards the abolition of slavery. Meanwhile let a law be passed, that negroes in the colonies who desire to purchase their freedom, as well as those whom their masters are willing to set free, shall no longer be compelled to pay a tax to the domain.

(29) Art. 51. The three functions, legislative, executive and judicial, shall be separated and carefully distinguished.

The communes of the bailliage of Versailles have already expressed themselves in respect to the necessity of adopting the form of deliberation *per capita* in the coming States General. The reform of the constitution will be one of their principal duties. This magnificent monument of liberty and public felicity should be the work of the three orders in common session; if they are separated, certain pretensions, anxieties and jealousies are bound to arise; the two upper orders are likely to oppose obstacles perhaps invincible, to the reform of abuses and the enactment of laws destined to suppress such abuses. It seems indispensable that in this first assembly votes should be taken *per capita* and not by order. After the renunciation by the upper two orders of their pecuniary privileges; after all distinctions before the law have been abolished; when the exclusion of the third estate from certain offices and positions has been done away with, then the reasons which today necessitate deliberation *per capita* will no longer exist.

The communes of Versailles therefore refrain from expressing a positive opinion upon the future composition of the national assemblies and upon the method of their deliberation. They defer, with all confidence, the decision of this important question to the wisdom of the States General.

Our prayer is that the methods determined upon shall be such as will assure forever, to the king and to the nation, those portions of the legislative power which respectively belong to them; that they shall maintain between them a perfect equilibrium in the employment of this power; that they shall conserve, forever, to the nation its rights and liberties; to the king his perogatives and the executive power in all its fulness. Finally that these methods should be so combined as to produce that circumspectness and lack of haste so necessary to the enactment of laws, and that they will effectually prevent all hasty counsels, dissentions amongst deputies and immature conclusions.

May all deputies to this august assembly, impressed with the sanctity and extent of their obligations, forget that they are the mandataries of some special order, and remember only that they are representatives of the people. May they never be forgetful of the fact, that they am about to fix the destinies of the foremost nation of the world!

THE EXECUTIVE

Art. 52. It shall be ordained by the constitution that the executive power be vested in the king alone.

Art. 53. The king shall dispose of all official places and positions, ecclesiastical, civil and military, to which he has at present the right of appointment.

Art. 54. All the provincial estates, or commissions representing them shall receive his immediate orders, which it shall be their duty to obey provisionally.

Art. 55. His consent shall be necessary to all bills approved by the States General in order that they may acquire the force of law throughout the realm. He may reject all bills presented to him, without being obliged to state the reasons of his disapproval.

Art. 56. He shall have the sole right of convening, prorogueing and dissolving the States General.

THE JUDICIARY

Art. 57. The sale of the judicial office shall be suppressed as soon as circumstances will permit, and provision made for the indemnification of holders.

Art. 58. There shall be established in the provinces as many superior courts as there we provincial estates. They shall be courts of final jurisdiction.

Art. 59. All exceptional and privileged seignorial courts shall be abolished, as well as other courts rendered useless by the abolition of certain taxes which caused their erection, and by the adoption of a new system of accounts under the exclusive control of the States General.

Art. 60. All rights of *committmus* or of evocation, which tend to favor certain classes of citizens to the detriment of the general public, shall be abolished.

Art. 61. There shall be only two stages of jurisdiction.

Art. 62. Since the adoption of the jury system will have a tendency to facilitate and simplify the administration of justice, all classes of judges shall be reduced to the least number possible.

Art. 63. Each judge of the lower courts and of the superior provincial courts shall be appointed by the king out of a list of three candidates, presented by the provincial estates.

Art. 64. Judges of all courts shall be obliged to adhere to the letter (31) of the law, and may never be permitted to change, modify or interpret it at their pleasure.

Art. 65. The fees received by all officers of justice shall be fixed at a moderate rate and clearly understood; and judges who extort fees in excess of the fixed rates shall be condemned to pay a fine of four times the amount they have received.

Such are the bans of a constitution founded upon the eternal principles of justice and reason, which alone ought to regulate henceforward the government of the realm. Once they are adopted, all false pretensions, all burdensome privileges, all abuses of all kinds will be seen to disappear. Aheady a considerable number of bailliages have expressed their desires concerning the reforms and abolitions to be effected in all branches of the administration; the necessity for these drastic changes has been so evident that it is sufficient merely to indicate them.

GENERAL DEMANDS

Art. 66. The deputies of the *prevolte* and *vicomte* of Paris shall be instructed to unite themselves with the deputies of other provinces, in order to join with them in securing, as soon as able, the following abolitions:

- Of the taille;
- Of the *gabelle*;
- Of the *aides*;
- Of the *corvee*;
- Of the *ferme* of tobacco;
- Of the registry-duties;
- Of the free-hold tax;

- Of the taxes on leather;
- Of the government stamp upon iron;
- Of the stamps upon gold and silver;
- Of the interprovincial customs duties;
- Of the taxes upon fairs and markets;

Finally, of all taxes that are burdensome and oppressive, whether on account of their nature or of the expense of collection, or because they have been paid almost wholly by agriculturists and by the poorer classes. They shall be replaced with other taxes, less complicated and easier of collection, which shall fall alike upon all classes and orders of the state without exception.

Art. 67. We demand also the abolition of the royal preserves (*capitaineries*);

- Of the game laws;
- Of jurisdictions of *prevotes*;
- Of *banalites*;
- Of toll;
- Of useless authorities and governments in cities and provinces.

Art. 68. We solicit the establishment of public graneries in the provinces, under the control of the provincial estates, in order that by accumulating reserves during years of plenty, famine and excessive dearness of grain, such as we have experienced in the past may be prevented.

Art. 69. We solicit also the establishment of free schools in all country parishes.

Art. 70. We demand, for the benefit of commerce, the abolition of all exclusive privileges:

- The removal of customs barriers to the frontiers;
- The most complete freedom in trade;
- The revision and reform of all laws relative to commerce;
- Encouragement for all kinds of manufacture, viz.: premiums, bounties and advances;
- Rewards to artisans and laborers for useful inventions.

The communes desire that prizes and rewards shall always be preferred to exclusive privileges, which extinguish emulation and lessen competition.

Art. 71. We demand the suppression of various hindrances, such as stamps, special taxes, inspections; and the annoyances and visitations, to which many manufacturing establishments, particularly tanneries, are subjected.

Art. 72. The States General are entreated to devise means for abolishing guild organizations, indemnifying the holders of masterships; and to fix by the law the conditions under which the arts, trades and professions may be followed without the payment of an admission tax and at the same time to provide that public security and confidence be undisturbed.

Art. 73. Deputies shall solicit the abolition of:

- Receivers of consignments;
- Pawn-brokers
- All lotteries; (33)
- The bank of Poissy;[1]
- All taxes, of whatsoever nature, on grain and flour;
- All franchises and exemptions enjoyed by post-agents, except a pecuniary indemnity which shall be accorded them;

The exclusive privilege of the transportation companies which shall be allowed to continue their public service, in competition, however, with all private companies, which shall see fit to establish public carriages; and these, moreover, shall be encouraged.

Art. 74. They shall demand complete freedom of transport for grain among the various provinces of the kingdom, without interference from any court whatsoever.

Art. 75. They shall demand also the total abolition of all writs of suspension and of safe conduct.

Art. 76. Superior courts shall be absolutely prohibited from arresting, in any manner whatsoever, by means of decrees or decisions obtained upon petitions not made public, the execution of notarial writs or the decisions of judges of original jurisdiction, when the law shall ordain their provisional execution; under penalty that the judge shall be responsible for the amount of the debt, payment of which he has caused to be arrested.

Art. 77. The abolition of all places of refuge for debtors.

Art. 78. That no merchant or trader may be admitted to any national assembly or any municipal body, who has demanded abatement from his creditors; still less if he is a fraudulent bankrupt; and he may not be re-established in his rights until he his paid the whole amount of his indebtedness.

---

[1] The Bank of Poissy, established in the seventeenth century, acted as an intermediary between the butchers of Paris and outside cattle dealers, furninshing money to the butchers for their purchases. The result, at least in the popular mind, was to raise the price of butchers' wares. This institution had been abolished by Turgot in 1776 and re-established in 1779.

Art. 79. That individuals who have issued promissory notes shall be liable to detention.

Art. 80. That the States General shall consider means of diminishing mendicancy.

Art. 81. That civil and military offices may not be held simultaneously by the same person, and that each citizen may hold only one office.

Art. 82. That all the honorary rights of nobles shall be maintained; (34) but that they shall be allowed to hunt only upon their own lands, and not upon the lands of their vassals or tenants.

Art. 83. That nobility may be acquired neither through office nor purchase.

Art. 84. That inheritances shall be divided equally among heritors of the same degree, without regard to sex or right of primogeniture, nor to the status of the co-participants, and without distinction between nobles and non-nobles.

Art. 85. That all entails shall be limited to one generation.

Art. 86. That day laborers may not be taxed to exceed the amount of one day's labor.

Art. 87. That there shall be established in all towns and country houses commissions of arbitration, composed of a certain number of citizens elected and renewed annually, to which persons may apply and secure provisional judgment, without expense, except in case of appeal to the regular courts.

Art. 88. That all state prisons shall be abolished, and that means shall be taken to put all other prisons in better sanitary condition.

Art. 89. That it may please the States General to provide means for securing a uniformity of weights and measures throughout the kingdom.

Art. 90. That the laws upon *leds* and *ventes* shall be examined and rendered uniform throughout the kingdom.

Art. 91. That parishes shall be furnished with power to redeem the tax upon the transfer of land.

Art. 92. That *dimes* shall be suppressed and converted into a money rent based upon the price of corn and of the mark of silver, rising proportionately with the combined increase in value of corn and of the mark of silver.

Art. 93. Since clergymen in general ought not to occupy themselves with worldly affairs, there ought to be provided for bishops, archbishops and all holders of benefices a decent income and one suitable to their dignity; accordingly the property of the church in each province ought to be sold under the supervision of the provincial estates, which shall assume the duty of paying to holders of benefices the sums accorded to them by the States General.

Art. 94. That in case the above change should not be made, then it shall be ordained that no clergyman may hold two benefices at the same time, and that all persons now possessing two or more benefices shall be obliged to choose and to declare, within a prescribed time, which one of them they desire to retain.

Art. 95. That all commendatory abbacies, benefices without functions and useless convents shall be suppressed, their possessions sold for the benefit of the sure, and the funds thus realized made to constitute an endowment, the income of which shall be used for the benefit of country parish priests, for the establishment of free hospitals and other charitable institutions.

Art. 96. That continuous residence of archbishops and bishops in their dioceses and of beneficiaries in their benefices shall be required; and that resignations be not permitted.

Art. 97. That no clergyman under the age of twenty-five may be promoted to a sub-diaconate.

Art. 98. That girls may not enter religious orders until after they are twenty-five years of age, nor men until after thirty.

Art. 99. That it be forbidden to go to the Roman Curia for provisions, nominations, bulls and dispenmtions of all kinds; and each bishop in his diocese shall have full powers in these matters.

Art. 100. That the right of the pope to grant livings in France be suppressed.

Art. 101. That the Concordat be revoked, and all intervention on the part of the Roman Curia be made to cease.

Art. 102. That loans, contracted by the clergy to cover their contribution to the taxes which they were bound to support, shall be paid by them, since these loans are the obligation of the order; but loans which have been contracted on the govemment's account shall be included in the royal rich; and added to the national debt.

VARIOUS MATTERS

Art. 1. Deputies of *prevote-vicomte* shall be instructed to demand increased pay for soldiers.

Art. 2. That inhabitants of towns and rural places be paid and indemnified for troops of war quartered upon them, for the transportation of troops and of military baggage.

Art. 3. That the ordinances concerning the king's guard be revised, particularly those clauses which abolish the wise provision of Louis XIV, for the safety of his person, and the regulations made by him relative to his body-guard.

Art. 4. That barbarous punishments, taken from the codes of foreign (36) nations and introduced into the new military regulations, be abolished and replaced with regulations more in conformity with the genius of the nation.

(Articles 5, 6 and 7 relate to notarial and registry fees.)

Art. 8. That it be permitted to contract loans by means of bills or short-term certificates of debt, bearing interest at the legal rate, without it being necessary to alienate the capital so pledged.

Art. 9. In case the property of the church be not sold, that leases shall be continued by the successors of the present holders; at least that they shall not suffer a reduction of more than one-third.

Art. 10. That canals be constructed in all provinces of the kingdom where they will be useful.

Art. 11. That the working of mines be encouraged.

Art. 12. That a new schedule be made of the expenses of funerals, marriages and other church functions.

Art. 13. That cemeteries be located outside of cities, towns and villages; that the same be done with places of deposit for refuse.

Art. 14. That the funds for the support of the lazarettos, formerly located in rural parishes, having been united with the endowments of hospitals, country people shall be permitted to send their sick to the city hospitals.

Art. 15. That the laws of the kingdom shall be equally the laws of the French colonies.

Art. 16. That all kinds of employment suitable for women shall be reserved for them by special enactment.

DECREE OF THE NATIONAL ASSEMBLY ABOLISHING THE FEUDAL SYSTEM, AUGUST 11, 1789

BUCHEZ ET ROUX, HISTOIRE PARLEMENTAIRE II, 259 FF.

The abolition of the Feudal System, which took place during the famous night session of August 4 and 5, 1789, was caused by the reading of a report on the misery and disturbances in the provinces, and was carried in a fervor of enthusiasm and excitement which made some later revision necessary. The decree here given was drawn up during the following days, and contains some alterations and important amplifications of the original provisions as passed in the early morning of August 5.[1] This document, as well as numbers II. and VI., are as useful, retrospectively, in clarifying the student's ideas of the *Ancien Régime* as in explaining the new system.

ARTICLE I. The National Assembly hereby completely abolishes the feudal system. It decrees that, among the existing rights and dues, both feudal and *censuel*,[2] all those originating in or representing real or personal serfdom (*mainmorte*) or personal servitude, shall be abolished without indemnification. All other dues are declared redeemable, the terms and mode of redemption to be fixed by the National Assembly. Those of the said dues which are not extinguished by this decree shall continue to be collected until indemnification shall take place.

II. The exclusive right to maintain pigeon-houses and dove-cotes is abolished. The pigeons shall be confined during the seasons fixed by the community. During such periods they shall be looked upon as game, and every one shall have the right to kill them upon his own land.

---

[1] These may be found in the Histoire Parlementaire II., 242–3.

[2] This refers to the *cens,* a perpetual due similar to the payments made by English copy-holders.

III. The exclusive right to hunt and to maintain unenclosed warrens is likewise abolished, and every land owner shall have the right to kill or to have destroyed on his own land all kinds of game, observing, however, such police regulations as may be established with a view to the safety of the public.

All hunting captainries, including the royal forests, and all hunting rights under whatever denomination, are likewise abolished. Provision shall be made, however, in a manner compatible with the regard due to property and liberty, for maintaining the personal pleasures of the king.

The president of the assembly shall be commissioned to ask of the King the recall of those sent to the galleys or exiled, simply for violations of the hunting regulations, as well as for the release of those at present imprisoned for offences of this kind, and the dismissal of such cases as are now pending.

IV. All manorial courts are hereby suppressed without indemnification. But the magistrates of these courts shall continue to perform their functions until such time as the National Assembly shall provide for the establishment of a new judicial system.

V. Tithes of every description, as well as the dues which have been substituted for them, under whatever denomination they are known or collected (even when compounded for), possessed by secular or regular congregations, by holders of benefices, members of corporations (including the Order of Malta and other religious and military orders,) as well as those devoted to the maintenance of churches, those impropriated to lay persons and those substituted for the *portion congrue*,[3] are abolished, on condition, however, that some other method be devised to provide for the expenses of divine worship, the support of the officiating clergy, for the assistance of the poor, for repairs and rebuilding of churches and parsonages, and for the maintenance of all institutions, seminaries, schools, academies, asylums, and organizations to which the present funds are devoted. Until such provision shall be made and the former possessors shall enter upon the enjoyment of an income on the new system, the National Assembly decrees that the said tithes shall continue to be collected according to law and in the customary manner.

Other tithes, of whatever nature they may be, shall be redeemable in such manner as the Assembly shall determine. Until such regulation shall be issued, the National Assembly decrees that these, too, shall continue to be collected.

VI. All perpetual ground rents, payable either in money or in kind, of whatever nature they may be, whatever their origin and to whomsoever they may be due, as to members of corporations, holders of the domain or appanages or to the Order of Malta, shall be redeemable. *Champarts*,[4] of every kind and under

---

[3] This expression refers to the minimum remuneration fixed for the priests.

[4] The *champart* was the right of the lord to a certain portion of the crops on lands subject to the *cens*.

all denominations, shall likewise be redeemable at a rate fixed by the Assembly. No due shall in the future be created which is not redeemable.

VII. The sale of judicial and municipal offices shall be suppressed forthwith. Justice shall be dispensed *gratis*. Nevertheless, the magistrates at present holding such offices shall continue to exercise their functions and to receive their emoluments until the Assembly shall have made provision for indemnifying them.

VIII. The fees of the country priests are abolished, and shall be discontinued so soon as provision shall be made for increasing the minimum salary [*portion congrue*] of the parish priests and the payment to the curates. A regulation shall be drawn up to determine the status of the priests in the towns.

IX. Pecuniary privileges, personal or real, in the payment of taxes are abolished forever. Taxes shall be collected from all the citizens, and from all property, in the same manner and in the same form. Plans shall be considered by which the taxes shall be paid proportionally by all, even for the last six months of the current year.

X. Inasmuch as a national constitution and public liberty are of more advantage to the provinces than the privileges which some of these enjoy, and inasmuch as the surrender of such privileges is essential to the intimate union of all parts of the realm [*empire*], it is decreed that all the peculiar privileges, pecuniary or otherwise, of the provinces, principalities, districts [*pays*], cantons, cities and communes, are once for all abolished and are absorbed into the law common to all Frenchmen.

XI. All citizens, without distinction of birth, are eligible to any office or dignity, whether ecclesiastical, civil or military; and no profession shall imply any derogation.

XII. Hereafter no remittances shall be made for annates or for any other purpose to the court of Rome, the vice-legation at Avignon, or to the nunciature at Lucerne. The clergy of the diocese shall apply to their bishops in regard to the filling of benefices and dispensations, the which shall be granted *gratis* without regard to reservations, expectancies and papal months, all the churches of France enjoying the same freedom.

XIII. The rights of *déport*,[5] of *cotte-morte*,[6] *dépouilles*,[6] *vacat*,[5] *droits censaux*, Peters pence, and other dues of the same kind, under whatever denomination, established in favor of bishops, archdeacons, archpresbyters, chapters, and regular congregations which formerly exercised priestly functions [*curés primitifs*], are abolished, but appropriate provision shall be made for those benefices of archdeacons and archpresbyters which are not sufficiently endowed.

---

[5] Rights of bishops to the income of benefices during vacancies.
[6] Rights of the convent to the clothes of its deceased members.

XIV. Pluralities shall not be permitted hereafter in cases where the revenue from the benefice or benefices held shall exceed the sum of three thousand livres. Nor shall any individual be allowed to enjoy several pensions from benefices, or a pension and a benefice, if the revenue which he already enjoys from such sources exceeds the same sum of three thousand livres.

XV. The National Assembly shall consider, in conjunction with the King, the report which is to be submitted to it relating to pensions, favors and salaries, with a view to suppressing all such as are not deserved and reducing those which shall prove excessive; and the amount shall be fixed which the King may in the future disburse for this purpose.

XVI. The National Assembly decrees that a medal shall be struck in memory of the recent grave and important deliberations for the welfare of France, and that a *Te Deum* shall be chanted in gratitude in all the parishes and the churches of France.

XVII. The National Assembly solemnly proclaims the King, Louis XVI., the *Restorer of French Liberty.*

XVIII. The National Assembly shall present itself in a body before the King, in order to submit to him the decrees which have just been passed, to tender to him the tokens of its most respectful gratitude and to pray him to permit the *Te Deum* to be chanted in his chapel, and to be present himself at this service.

XIX. The National Assembly shall consider, immediately after the constitution, the drawing up of the laws necessary for the development of the principles which it has laid down in the present decree. The latter shall be transmitted without delay by the deputies to all the provinces, together with the decree of the tenth of this month, in order that it may be printed, published, announced from the parish pulpits, and posted up wherever it shall be deemed necessary.

DECLARATION OF THE RIGHTS OF MAN AND OF THE CITIZEN

Translations and Reprints from the Original Sources of European History, Vol. 1

BUCHEZ ET ROUX, HISTOIRE PARLEMENTAIRE XI, PP. 404 *sqq.*

A declaration of the rights of man, which had been demanded by many of the *cahiers,* was the part of the new constitution which the Assembly decided (Aug. 4) should be first drawn up. The members recognized that they were imitating an American precedent in doing this. Our first state constitutions, several of which are preceded by elaborate bills of rights, had very early been translated into French. An interesting comparison may be made between the spirit and aim of the French declaration and of those of our own country. The first ten amendments to our constitution, which form a bill of rights, were not proposed in Congress until Sept. 25, 1789, and could, of course, have exercised no influence upon the National Assembly.

The representatives of the French people, organized as a National Assembly, believing that the ignorance, neglect or contempt of the rights of man are the sole cause of public calamities and of the corruption of governments, have determined to set forth in a solemn declaration the natural, inalienable and sacred rights of man, in order that this declaration, being constantly before all the members of the social body, shall remind them continually of their rights and duties; in order that the acts of the legislative power, as well as those of the executive power, may be compared at any moment with the ends of all political institutions and may thus be more respected; and, lastly, in order that the grievances of the citizens, based hereafter upon simple and incontestable principles, shall tend to the maintenance of the constitution and redound to the happiness of all. Therefore the National Assembly recognizes and proclaims, in the presence and under the auspices of the Supreme Being, the following rights of man and of the citizen:—

ARTICLE 1. Men are born and remain free and equal in rights. Social distinctions may only be founded upon the general good.

2. The aim of all political association is the preservation of the natural and imprescriptible rights of man. These rights are liberty, property, security and resistance to oppression.

3. The principle of all sovereignty resides essentially in the nation. No body nor individual may exercise any authority which does not proceed directly from the nation.

4. Liberty consists in the freedom to do everything which injures no one else; hence the exercise of the natural rights of each man has no limits except those which assure to the other members of the society the enjoyment of the same rights. These limits can only be determined by law.

5. Law can only prohibit such actions as are hurtful to society. Nothing may be prevented which is not forbidden by law, and no one may be forced to do anything not provided for by law.

6. Law is the expression of the general will. Every citizen has a right to participate personally or through his representative in its formation. It must be the same for all, whether it protects or punishes. All citizens, being equal in the eyes of the law, are equally eligible to all dignities and to all public positions and occupations, according to their abilities, and without distinction except that of their virtues and talents.

7. No person shall be accused, arrested or imprisoned except in the cases and according to the forms prescribed by law. Any one soliciting, transmitting, executing or causing to be executed any arbitrary order shall be punished. But any citizen summoned or arrested in virtue of the law shall submit without delay, as resistance constitutes an offence.

8. The law shall provide for such punishments only as are strictly and obviously necessary, and no one shall suffer punishment except it be legally inflicted in virtue of a law passed and promulgated before the commission of the offence.

9. As all persons are held innocent until they shall have been declared guilty, if arrest shall be deemed indispensable, all harshness not essential to the securing of the prisoner's person shall be severely repressed by law.

10. No one shall be disquieted on account of his opinions, including his religious views, provided their manifestation does not disturb the public order established by law.

11. The free communication of ideas and opinions is one of the most precious of the rights of man. Every citizen may, accordingly, speak, write and print with freedom, but shall be responsible for such abuses of this freedom as shall be defined by law.

12. The security of the rights of man and of the citizen requires public military force. These forces are, therefore, established for the good of all and not for the personal advantage of those to whom they shall be entrusted.

13. A common contribution is essential for the maintenance of the public forces and for the cost of administration. This should be equitably distributed among all the citizens in proportion to their means.

14. All the citizens have a right to decide, either personally or by their representatives, as to the necessity of the public contribution; to grant this freely; to know to what uses it is put; and to fix the proportion, the mode of assessment, and of collection, and the duration of the taxes.

15. Society has the right to require of every public agent an account of his administration.

16. A society in which the observance of the law is not assured, nor the separation of powers defined, has no constitution at all.

17. Since property is an inviolable and sacred right, no one shall be deprived thereof except where public necessity, legally determined, shall clearly demand it, and then only on condition that the owner shall have been previously and equitably indemnified.

THE LIFE OF THE INDUSTRIAL WORKER IN 19TH-CENTURY ENGLAND: EVIDENCE GIVEN BEFORE THE SADLER COMMITTEE

[The material below was reprinted in an old history textbook, *Readings in European History Since 1814,* which was edited by Jonathan F. Scott and Alexander Baltzly and was published by Appleton-Century-Crofts Inc. in 1930. The original sources of the material are listed in footnotes in the book; I've put them in brackets after each subject heading. The explanatory notes between sections are by Scott and Baltzly; the links were, of course, added by me.]

> In 1832 Michael Sadler secured a parliamentary investigation of conditions in the textile factories and he sat as chairman on the committee. The evidence printed here is taken from the large body published in the committee's report and is representative rather than exceptional. It will be observed that the questions are frequently leading; this reflects Sadler's knowledge of the sort of information that the committee were to hear and his purpose of bringing it out. This report stands out as one of three great reports on the life of the industrial class—the two others being that of the Ashley Commission on the mines and Chadwick's report on sanitary problems. The immediate effect of the investigation and the report was the passage of the Act of 1833 limiting hours of employment for women and children in textile work.

JOSHUA DRAKE, CALLED IN; AND EXAMINED

You say you would prefer moderate labour and lower wages; are you pretty comfortable upon your present wages?

—I have no wages, but two days a week at present; but when I am working at some jobs we can make a little, and at others we do very poorly.

When a child gets 3s. a week, does that go much towards its subsistence?

—*No, it will not keep it as it should do.*

When they got 6s. or 7s. when they were pieceners, if they reduced the hours of labor, would they not get less?

—*They would get a halfpenny a day less, but I would rather have less wages and less work.*

Do you receive any parish assistance?

—*No.*

Why do you allow your children to go to work at those places where they are ill-treated or overworked?

—*Necessity compels a man that has children to let them work.*

Then you would not allow your children to go to those factories under the present system, if it was not from necessity?

—*No.*

Supposing there was a law passed to limit the hours of labour to eight hours a day, or something of that sort, of course you are aware that a manufacturer could not afford to pay them the same wages?

—*No, I do not suppose that they would, but at the same time I would rather have it, and I believe that it would bring me into employ; and if I lost 5d. a day from my children's work, and I got half-a-crown myself, it would be better.*

How would it get you into employ?

—*By finding more employment at the machines, and work being more regularly spread abroad, and divided amongst the people at large. One man is now regularly turned off into the street, whilst another man is running day and night.*

You mean to say, that if the manufacturers were to limit the hours of labour, they would employ more people?

—*Yes.*

MR. MATTHEW CRABTREE, CALLED IN; AND EXAMINED

What age are you?

—*Twenty-two.*

What is your occupation?

—*A blanket manufacturer.*

Have you ever been employed in a factory?

—*Yes.*

At what age did you first go to work in one?

—*Eight.*

How long did you continue in that occupation?

—*Four years.*

Will you state the hours of labour at the period when you first went to the factory, in ordinary times?

—*From 6 in the morning to 8 at night.*

Fourteen hours?

—*Yes.*

With what intervals for refreshment and rest?

—*An hour at noon.*

When trade was brisk what were your hours?

—*From 5 in the morning to 9 in the evening.*

Sixteen hours?

—*Yes.*

With what intervals at dinner?

—*An hour.*

How far did you live from the mill?

—*About two miles.*

Was there any time allowed for you to get your breakfast in the mill?

—*No.*

Did you take it before you left your home?

—*Generally.*

During those long hours of labour could you be punctual; how did you awake?

—*I seldom did awake spontaneously; I was most generally awoke or lifted out of bed, sometimes asleep, by my parents.*

Were you always in time?

—*No.*

What was the consequence if you had been too late?

—*I was most commonly beaten.*

Severely?

—*Very severely, I thought.*

In those mills is chastisement towards the latter part of the day going on perpetually?

—*Perpetually.*

So that you can hardly be in a mill without hearing constant crying?

—*Never an hour, I believe.*

Do you think that if the overlooker were naturally a humane person it would still be found necessary for him to beat the children, in order to keep up their attention and vigilance at the termination of those extraordinary days of labour?

—*Yes; the machine turns off a regular quantity of cardings, and of course, they must keep as regularly to their work the whole of the day; they must keep with the machine, and therefore however humane the slubber may be, as he must keep up with the machine or be found fault with, he spurs the children to keep up also by various means but that which he commonly resorts to is to strap them when they become drowsy.*

At the time when you were beaten for not keeping up with your work, were you anxious to have done it if you possibly could?

—*Yes; the dread of being beaten if we could not keep up with our work was a sufficient impulse to keep us to it if we could.*

When you got home at night after this labour, did you feel much fatigued?

—*Very much so.*

Had you any time to be with your parents, and to receive instruction from them?

—*No.*

What did you do?

—*All that we did when we got home was to get the little bit of supper that was provided for us and go to bed immediately. If the supper had not been ready directly, we should have gone to sleep while it was preparing.*

Did you not, as a child, feel it a very grievous hardship to be roused so soon in the morning?

—*I did.*

Were the rest of the children similarly circumstanced?

—*Yes, all of them; but they were not all of them so far from their work as I was.*

And if you had been too late you were under the apprehension of being cruelly beaten?

—I generally was beaten when I happened to be too late; and when I got up in the morning the apprehension of that was so great, that I used to run, and cry all the way as I went to the mill.

MR. JOHN HALL, CALLED IN; AND EXAMINED.

Will you describe to the Committee the position in which the children stand to piece in a worsted mill, as it may serve to explain the number and severity of those cases of distortion which occur?

—At the top to the spindle there is a fly goes across, and the child takes hold of the fly by the ball of his left hand, and he throws the left shoulder up and the right knee inward; he has the thread to get with the right hand, and he has to stoop his head down to see what he is doing; they throw the right knee inward in that way, and all the children I have seen, that bend in the right knee. I knew a family, the whole of whom were bent outwards as a family complaint, and one of those boys was sent to a worsted-mill, and first he became straight in his right knee, and then he became crooked in it the other way.

ELIZABETH BENTLEY, CALLED IN; AND EXAMINED.

What age are you?

—Twenty-three.

Where do you live?

—At Leeds.

What time did you begin to work at a factory?

—When I was six years old.

At whose factory did you work?

—Mr. Busk's.

What kind of mill is it?

—Flax-mill.

What was your business in that mill?

—I was a little doffer.

What were your hours of labour in that mill?

—From 5 in the morning till 9 at night, when they were thronged.

For how long a time together have you worked that excessive length of time?

—*For about half a year.*

What were your usual hours when you were not so thronged?

—*From 6 in the morning till 7 at night.*

What time was allowed for your meals?

—*Forty minutes at noon.*

Had you any time to get your breakfast or drinking?

—*No, we got it as we could.*

And when your work was bad, you had hardly any time to eat it at all?

—*No; we were obliged to leave it or take it home, and when we did not take it, the overlooker took it, and gave it to his pigs.*

Do you consider doffing a laborious employment?

—*Yes.*

Explain what it is you had to do?

—*When the frames are full, they have to stop the frames, and take the flyers off, and take the full bobbins off, and carry them to the roller; and then put empty ones on, and set the frame going again.*

Does that keep you constantly on your feet?

—*Yes, there are so many frames, and they run so quick.*

Your labour is very excessive?

—*Yes; you have not time for any thing.*

Suppose you flagged a little, or were too late, what would they do?

—*Strap us.*

Are they in the habit of strapping those who are last in doffing?

—*Yes.*

Constantly?

—*Yes.*

Girls as well as boys?

—*Yes.*

Have you ever been strapped?

—*Yes.*

Severely?

—*Yes.*

Could you eat your food well in that factory?

—*No, indeed I had not much to eat, and the little I had I could not eat it, my appetite was so poor, and being covered with dust; and it was no use to take it home, I could not eat it, and the overlooker took it, and gave it to the pigs.*

You are speaking of the breakfast?

—*Yes.*

How far had you to go for dinner?

—*We could not go home to dinner.*

Where did you dine?

—*In the mill.*

Did you live far from the mill?

—*Yes, two miles.*

Had you a clock?

—*No, we had not.*

Supposing you had not been in time enough in the morning at these mills, what would have been the consequence?

—*We should have been quartered.*

What do you mean by that?

—*If we were a quarter of an hour too late, they would take off half an hour; we only got a penny an hour, and they would take a halfpenny more.*

The fine was much more considerable than the loss of time?

—*Yes.*

Were you also beaten for being too late?

—*No, I was never beaten myself, I have seen the boys beaten for being too late.*

Were you generally there in time?

—*Yes; my mother had been up at 4 o'clock in the morning, and at 2 o'clock in the morning; the colliers used to go to their work about 3 or 4 o'clock, and when she heard them stirring she has got up out of her warm bed, and gone out and asked them the time; and I have sometimes been at Hunslet Car at 2 o'clock in the morning, when it was streaming down with rain, and we have had to stay until the mill was opened.*

PETER SMART, CALLED IN; AND EXAMINED

You say you were locked up night and day?

—*Yes.*

Do the children ever attempt to run away?

—*Very often.*

Were they pursued and brought back again?

—*Yes, the overseer pursued them, and brought them back.*

Did you ever attempt to run away?

—*Yes, I ran away twice.*

And you were brought back?

—*Yes; and I was sent up to the master's loft, and thrashed with a whip for running away.*

Were you bound to this man?

—*Yes, for six years.*

By whom were you bound?

—*My mother got 15s. for the six years.*

Do you know whether the children were, in point of fact, compelled to stop during the whole time for which they were engaged?

—*Yes, they were.*

By law?

—*I cannot say by law; but they were compelled by the master; I never saw any law used there but the law of their own hands.*

To what mill did you next go?

—*To Mr. Webster's, at Battus Den, within eleven miles of Dundee.*

In what situation did you act there?

—*I acted as overseer.*

At 17 years of age?

—*Yes.*

Did you inflict the same punishment that you yourself had experienced?

—*I went as an overseer; not as a slave, but as a slave-driver.*

What were the hours of labour in that mill?

—*My master told me that I had to produce a certain quantity of yarn; the hours were at that time fourteen; I said that I was not able to produce the quantity of yarn that was required; I told him if he took the timepiece out of the mill I would produce that quantity, and after that time I found no difficulty in producing the quantity.*

How long have you worked per day in order to produce the quantity your master required?

—I have wrought nineteen hours.

Was this a water-mill?

—Yes, water and steam both.

To what time have you worked?

—I have seen the mill going till it was past 12 o'clock on the Saturday night.

So that the mill was still working on the Sabbath morning?

—Yes.

Were the workmen paid by the piece, or by the day?

—No, all had stated wages.

Did not that almost compel you to use great severity to the hands then under you?

—Yes; I was compelled often to beat them, in order to get them to attend to their work, from their being over-wrought.

Were not the children exceedingly fatigued at that time?

—Yes, exceedingly fatigued.

Were the children bound in the same way in that mill?

—No; they were bound from one year's end to another, for twelve months.

Did you keep the hands locked up in the same way in that mill?

—Yes, we locked up the mill; but we did not lock the bothy.

Did you find that the children were unable to pursue their labour properly to that extent?

—Yes; they have been brought to that condition, that I have gone and fetched up the doctor to them, to see what was the matter with them, and to know whether they were able to rise or not able to rise; they were not at all able to rise; we have had great difficulty in getting them up.

When that was the case, how long have they been in bed, generally speaking?

—Perhaps not above four or five hours in their beds.

MANIFESTO OF THE COMMUNIST PARTY

Karl Marx and Frederick Engels

A spectre is haunting Europe—the spectre of communism. All the powers of old Europe have entered into a holy alliance to exorcise this spectre: Pope and Tsar, Metternich and Guizot, French Radicals and German police-spies.

Where is the party in opposition that has not been decried as communistic by its opponents in power? Where is the opposition that has not hurled back the branding reproach of communism, against the more advanced opposition parties, as well as against its reactionary adversaries?

Two things result from this fact:

I. Communism is already acknowledged by all European powers to be itself a power.

II. It is high time that Communists should openly, in the face of the whole world, publish their views, their aims, their tendencies, and meet this nursery tale of the spectre of communism with a manifesto of the party itself.

To this end, Communists of various nationalities have assembled in London and sketched the following manifesto, to be published in the English, French, German, Italian, Flemish and Danish languages.

BOURGEOIS AND PROLETARIANS[1]

The history of all hitherto existing society[2] is the history of class struggles.

Freeman and slave, patrician and plebian, lord and serf, guild-master[3] and journeyman, in a word, oppressor and oppressed, stood in constant opposition to one another, carried on an uninterrupted, now hidden, now open fight, a fight that each time ended, either in a revolutionary reconstitution of society at large, or in the common ruin of the contending classes.

In the earlier epochs of history, we find almost everywhere a complicated arrangement of society into various orders, a manifold gradation of social rank. In ancient Rome we have patricians, knights, plebians, slaves; in the Middle Ages, feudal lords, vassals, guild-masters, journeymen, apprentices, serfs; in almost all of these classes, again, subordinate gradations.

The modern bourgeois society that has sprouted from the ruins of feudal society has not done away with class antagonisms. It has but established new classes, new conditions of oppression, new forms of struggle in place of the old ones.

Our epoch, the epoch of the bourgeoisie, possesses, however, this distinct feature: it has simplified class antagonisms. Society as a whole is more and more splitting up into two great hostile camps, into two great classes directly facing each other—bourgeoisie and proletariat.

From the serfs of the Middle Ages sprang the chartered burghers of the earliest towns. From these burgesses the first elements of the bourgeoisie were developed.

The discovery of America, the rounding of the Cape, opened up fresh ground for the rising bourgeoisie. The East-Indian and Chinese markets, the

---

1 By bourgeoisie is meant the class of modern capitalists, owners of the means of social production and employers of wage labor. By proletariat, the class of modern wage laborers who, having no means of production of their own, are reduced to selling their labor power in order to live. [Note by Engels—1888 English edition]

2 That is, all *written* history. In 1847, the pre-history of society, the social organization existing previous to recorded history, all but unknown. Since then, August von Haxthausen (1792–1866) discovered common ownership of land in Russia, Georg Ludwig von Maurer proved it to be the social foundation from which all Teutonic races started in history, and, by and by, village communities were found to be, or to have been, the primitive form of society everywhere from India to Ireland. The inner organization of this primitive communistic society was laid bare, in its typical form, by Lewis Henry Morgan's (1818–1861) crowning discovery of the true nature of the gens and its relation to the tribe. With the dissolution of the primeaval communities, society begins to be differentiated into separate and finally antagonistic classes. I have attempted to retrace this dissolution in *Der Ursprung der Familie, des Privateigenthumus und des Staats*, second edition, Stuttgart, 1886. [Engels, 1888 English edition]

3 Guild-master, that is, a full member of a guild, a master within, not a head of a guild. [Engels: 1888 English edition]

colonisation of America, trade with the colonies, the increase in the means of exchange and in commodities generally, gave to commerce, to navigation, to industry, an impulse never before known, and thereby, to the revolutionary element in the tottering feudal society, a rapid development.

The feudal system of industry, in which industrial production was monopolized by closed guilds, now no longer suffices for the growing wants of the new markets. The manufacturing system took its place. The guild-masters were pushed aside by the manufacturing middle class; division of labor between the different corporate guilds vanished in the face of division of labor in each single workshop.

Meantime, the markets kept ever growing, the demand ever rising. Even manufacturers no longer sufficed. Thereupon, steam and machinery revolutionized industrial production. The place of manufacture was taken by the giant, MODERN INDUSTRY; the place of the industrial middle class by industrial millionaires, the leaders of the whole industrial armies, the modern bourgeois.

Modern industry has established the world market, for which the discovery of America paved the way. This market has given an immense development to commerce, to navigation, to communication by land. This development has, in turn, reacted on the extension of industry; and in proportion as industry, commerce, navigation, railways extended, in the same proportion the bourgeoisie developed, increased its capital, and pushed into the background every class handed down from the Middle Ages.

We see, therefore, how the modern bourgeoisie is itself the product of a long course of development, of a series of revolutions in the modes of production and of exchange.

Each step in the development of the bourgeoisie was accompanied by a corresponding political advance in that class. An oppressed class under the sway of the feudal nobility, an armed and self-governing association of medieval commune[4]: here independent urban republic (as in Italy and Germany); there taxable "third estate" of the monarchy (as in France); afterward, in the period of manufacturing proper, serving either the semi-feudal or the absolute monarchy as a counterpoise against the nobility, and, in fact, cornerstone of the great monarchies in general—the bourgeoisie has at last, since the establishment of Modern Industry and of the world market, conquered for itself, in the modern

---

[4] This was the name given their urban communities by the townsmen of Italy and France, after they had purchased or conquered their initial rights of self-government from their feudal lords. *[Engels: 1890 German edition]*. "Commune" was the name taken in France by the nascent towns even before they had conquered from their feudal lords and masters local self-government and political rights as the "Third Estate." Generally speaking, for the economical development of the bourgeoisie, England is here taken as the typical country, for its political development, France. *[Engels: 1888 English edition]*

representative state, exclusive political sway. The executive of the modern state is but a committee for managing the common affairs of the whole bourgeoisie.

The bourgeoisie, historically, has played a most revolutionary part.

The bourgeoisie, wherever it has got the upper hand, has put an end to all feudal, patriarchal, idyllic relations. It has pitilessly torn asunder the motley feudal ties that bound man to his "natural superiors," and has left no other nexus between man and man than naked self-interest, than callous "cash payment." It has drowned out the most heavenly ecstacies of religious fervor, of chivalrous enthusiasm, of philistine sentimentalism, in the icy water of egotistical calculation. It has resolved personal worth into exchange value, and in place of the numberless indefeasible chartered freedoms, has set up that single, unconscionable freedom—Free Trade. In one word, for exploitation, veiled by religious and political illusions, it has substituted naked, shameless, direct, brutal exploitation.

The bourgeoisie has stripped of its halo every occupation hitherto honored and looked up to with reverent awe. It has converted the physician, the lawyer, the priest, the poet, the man of science, into its paid wage laborers.

The bourgeoisie has torn away from the family its sentimental veil, and has reduced the family relation into a mere money relation.

The bourgeoisie has disclosed how it came to pass that the brutal display of vigor in the Middle Ages, which reactionaries so much admire, found its fitting complement in the most slothful indolence. It has been the first to show what man's activity can bring about. It has accomplished wonders far surpassing Egyptian pyramids, Roman aqueducts, and Gothic cathedrals; it has conducted expeditions that put in the shade all former exoduses of nations and crusades.

The bourgeoisie cannot exist without constantly revolutionizing the instruments of production, and thereby the relations of production, and with them the whole relations of society. Conservation of the old modes of production in unaltered form, was, on the contrary, the first condition of existence for all earlier industrial classes. Constant revolutionizing of production, uninterrupted disturbance of all social conditions, everlasting uncertainty and agitation distinguish the bourgeois epoch from all earlier ones. All fixed, fast frozen relations, with their train of ancient and venerable prejudices and opinions, are swept away, all new-formed ones become antiquated before they can ossify. All that is solid melts into air, all that is holy is profaned, and man is at last compelled to face with sober senses his real condition of life and his relations with his kind.

The need of a constantly expanding market for its products chases the bourgeoisie over the entire surface of the globe. It must nestle everywhere, settle everywhere, establish connections everywhere.

The bourgeoisie has, through its exploitation of the world market, given a cosmopolitan character to production and consumption in every country. To the great chagrin of reactionaries, it has drawn from under the feet of industry the national ground on which it stood. All old-established national industries have been destroyed or are daily being destroyed. They are dislodged by new industries, whose introduction becomes a life and death question for all civilized nations, by industries that no longer work up indigenous raw material, but raw material drawn from the remotest zones; industries whose products are consumed, not only at home, but in every quarter of the globe. In place of the old wants, satisfied by the production of the country, we find new wants, requiring for their satisfaction the products of distant lands and climes. In place of the old local and national seclusion and self-sufficiency, we have intercourse in every direction, universal inter-dependence of nations. And as in material, so also in intellectual production. The intellectual creations of individual nations become common property. National one-sidedness and narrow-mindedness become more and more impossible, and from the numerous national and local literatures, there arises a world literature.

The bourgeoisie, by the rapid improvement of all instruments of production, by the immensely facilitated means of communication, draws all, even the most barbarian, nations into civilization. The cheap prices of commodities are the heavy artillery with which it forces the barbarians' intensely obstinate hatred of foreigners to capitulate. It compels all nations, on pain of extinction, to adopt the bourgeois mode of production; it compels them to introduce what it calls civilization into their midst, i.e., to become bourgeois themselves. In one word, it creates a world after its own image.

The bourgeoisie has subjected the country to the rule of the towns. It has created enormous cities, has greatly increased the urban population as compared with the rural, and has thus rescued a considerable part of the population from the idiocy of rural life. Just as it has made the country dependent on the towns, so it has made barbarian and semi-barbarian countries dependent on the civilized ones, nations of peasants on nations of bourgeois, the East on the West.

The bourgeoisie keeps more and more doing away with the scattered state of the population, of the means of production, and of property. It has agglomerated population, centralized the means of production, and has concentrated property in a few hands. The necessary consequence of this was political centralization. Independent, or but loosely connected provinces, with separate interests, laws, governments, and systems of taxation, became lumped together into one nation, with one government, one code of laws, one national class interest, one frontier, and one customs tariff.

The bourgeoisie, during its rule of scarce one hundred years, has created more massive and more colossal productive forces than have all preceding generations together. Subjection of nature's forces to man, machinery, application of chemistry to industry and agriculture, steam navigation, railways, electric telegraphs, clearing of whole continents for cultivation, canalization or rivers, whole populations conjured out of the ground—what earlier century had even a presentiment that such productive forces slumbered in the lap of social labor?

We see then: the means of production and of exchange, on whose foundation the bourgeoisie built itself up, were generated in feudal society. At a certain stage in the development of these means of production and of exchange, the conditions under which feudal society produced and exchanged, the feudal organization of agriculture and manufacturing industry, in one word, the feudal relations of property became no longer compatible with the already developed productive forces; they became so many fetters. They had to be burst asunder; they were burst asunder.

Into their place stepped free competition, accompanied by a social and political constitution adapted in it, and the economic and political sway of the bourgeois class.

A similar movement is going on before our own eyes. Modern bourgeois society, with its relations of production, of exchange and of property, a society that has conjured up such gigantic means of production and of exchange, is like the sorcerer who is no longer able to control the powers of the nether world whom he has called up by his spells. For many a decade past, the history of industry and commerce is but the history of the revolt of modern productive forces against modern conditions of production, against the property relations that are the conditions for the existence of the bourgeois and of its rule. It is enough to mention the commercial crises that, by their periodical return, put the existence of the entire bourgeois society on its trial, each time more threateningly. In these crises, a great part not only of the existing products, but also of the previously created productive forces, are periodically destroyed. In these crises, there breaks out an epidemic that, in all earlier epochs, would have seemed an absurdity—the epidemic of over-production. Society suddenly finds itself put back into a state of momentary barbarism; it appears as if a famine, a universal war of devastation, had cut off the supply of every means of subsistence; industry and commerce seem to be destroyed. And why? Because there is too much civilization, too much means of subsistence, too much industry, too much commerce. The productive forces at the disposal of society no longer tend to further the development of the conditions of bourgeois property; on the contrary, they have become too powerful for these conditions, by which they are fettered, and so soon as they overcome these fetters, they bring disorder into the whole of bourgeois society, endanger the existence of bourgeois property. The conditions of bourgeois society are too narrow to comprise the wealth created by them. And how does the bourgeoisie get over these crises? On the one hand, by enforced destruction of a mass of productive forces; on the other, by the conquest of new markets, and by the more thorough exploitation of the old ones. That is to say, by paving the way for more extensive and more destructive crises, and by diminishing the means whereby crises are prevented.

The weapons with which the bourgeoisie felled feudalism to the ground are now turned against the bourgeoisie itself.

But not only has the bourgeoisie forged the weapons that bring death to itself; it has also called into existence the men who are to wield those weapons—the modern working class—the proletarians.

In proportion as the bourgeoisie, i.e., capital, is developed, in the same proportion is the proletariat, the modern working class, developed—a class of laborers, who live only so long as they find work, and who find work only so long as their labor increases capital. These laborers, who must sell themselves piecemeal, are a commodity, like every other article of commerce, and are consequently exposed to all the vicissitudes of competition, to all the fluctuations of the market.

Owing to the extensive use of machinery, and to the division of labor, the work of the proletarians has lost all individual character, and, consequently, all charm for the workman. He becomes an appendage of the machine, and it is only the most simple, most monotonous, and most easily acquired knack, that is required of him. Hence, the cost of production of a workman is restricted, almost entirely, to the means of subsistence that he requires for maintenance, and for the propagation of his race. But the price of a commodity, and therefore also of labor, is equal to its cost of production. In proportion, therefore, as the repulsiveness of the work increases, the wage decreases. What is more, in proportion as the use of machinery and division of labor increases, in the same proportion the burden of toil also increases, whether by prolongation of the working hours, by the increase of the work exacted in a given time, or by increased speed of machinery, etc.

Modern Industry has converted the little workshop of the patriarchal master into the great factory of the industrial capitalist. Masses of laborers, crowded into the factory, are organized like soldiers. As privates of the industrial army, they are placed under the command of a perfect hierarchy of officers and sergeants. Not only are they slaves of the bourgeois class, and of the bourgeois state; they are daily and hourly enslaved by the machine, by the overlooker, and, above all, in the individual bourgeois manufacturer himself. The more openly this despotism proclaims gain to be its end and aim, the more petty, the more hateful and the more embittering it is.

The less the skill and exertion of strength implied in manual labor, in other words, the more modern industry becomes developed, the more is the labor of men superseded by that of women. Differences of age and sex have no longer any distinctive social validity for the working class. All are instruments of labor, more or less expensive to use, according to their age and sex.

No sooner is the exploitation of the laborer by the manufacturer, so far at an end, that he receives his wages in cash, than he is set upon by the other portion of the bourgeoisie, the landlord, the shopkeeper, the pawnbroker, etc.

The lower strata of the middle class—the small tradespeople, shopkeepers, and retired tradesmen generally, the handicraftsmen and peasants—all these sink gradually into the proletariat, partly because their diminutive capital does not suffice for the scale on which Modern Industry is carried on, and is swamped in the competition with the large capitalists, partly because their specialized skill is rendered worthless by new methods of production. Thus, the proletariat is recruited from all classes of the population.

The proletariat goes through various stages of development. With its birth begins its struggle with the bourgeoisie. At first, the contest is carried on by individual laborers, then by the work of people of a factory, then by the operative of one trade, in one locality, against the individual bourgeois who directly exploits them. They direct their attacks not against the bourgeois condition of production, but against the instruments of production themselves; they destroy imported wares that compete with their labor, they smash to pieces machinery, they set factories ablaze, they seek to restore by force the vanished status of the workman of the Middle Ages.

At this stage, the laborers still form an incoherent mass scattered over the whole country, and broken up by their mutual competition. If anywhere they unite to form more compact bodies, this is not yet the consequence of their own active union, but of the union of the bourgeoisie, which class, in order to attain its own political ends, is compelled to set the whole proletariat in motion, and is moreover yet, for a time, able to do so. At this stage, therefore, the proletarians do not fight their enemies, but the enemies of their enemies, the remnants of absolute monarchy, the landowners, the non-industrial bourgeois, the petty bourgeois. Thus, the whole historical movement is concentrated in the hands of the bourgeoisie; every victory so obtained is a victory for the bourgeoisie.

But with the development of industry, the proletariat not only increases in number; it becomes concentrated in greater masses, its strength grows, and it feels that strength more. The various interests and conditions of life within the ranks of the proletariat are more and more equalized, in proportion as machinery obliterates all distinctions of labor, and nearly everywhere reduces wages to the same low level. The growing competition among the bourgeois, and the resulting commercial crises, make the wages of the workers ever more fluctuating. The increasing improvement of machinery, ever more rapidly developing, makes their livelihood more and more precarious; the collisions between individual workmen and individual bourgeois take more and more the character of collisions between two classes. Thereupon, the workers begin to form combinations (trade unions) against the bourgeois; they club together in order to keep up the rate of wages; they found permanent associations in order to make provision beforehand for these occasional revolts. Here and there, the contest breaks out into riots.

Now and then the workers are victorious, but only for a time. The real fruit of their battles lie not in the immediate result, but in the ever expanding union of the workers. This union is helped on by the improved means of communication that are created by Modern Industry, and that place the workers of different localities in contact with one another. It was just this contact that was needed to centralize the numerous local struggles, all of the same character, into one national struggle between classes. But every class struggle is a political struggle. And that union, to attain which the burghers of the Middle Ages, with their miserable highways, required centuries, the modern proletarian, thanks to railways, achieve in a few years.

This organization of the proletarians into a class, and, consequently, into a political party, is continually being upset again by the competition between the workers themselves. But it ever rises up again, stronger, firmer, mightier. It compels legislative recognition of particular interests of the workers, by taking advantage of the divisions among the bourgeoisie itself. Thus, the Ten-Hours Bill in England was carried.

Altogether, collisions between the classes of the old society further in many ways the course of development of the proletariat. The bourgeoisie finds itself involved in a constant battle. At first with the aristocracy; later on, with those portions of the bourgeoisie itself, whose interests have become antagonistic to the progress of industry; at all time with the bourgeoisie of foreign countries. In all these battles, it sees itself compelled to appeal to the proletariat, to ask for help, and thus to drag it into the political arena. The bourgeoisie itself, therefore, supplies the proletariat with its own elements of political and general education, in other words, it furnishes the proletariat with weapons for fighting the bourgeoisie.

Further, as we have already seen, entire sections of the ruling class are, by the advance of industry, precipitated into the proletariat, or are at least threatened in their conditions of existence. These also supply the proletariat with fresh elements of enlightenment and progress.

Finally, in times when the class struggle nears the decisive hour, the progress of dissolution going on within the ruling class, in fact within the whole range of old society, assumes such a violent, glaring character, that a small section of the ruling class cuts itself adrift, and joins the revolutionary class, the class that holds the future in its hands. Just as, therefore, at an earlier period, a section of the nobility went over to the bourgeoisie, so now a portion of the bourgeoisie goes over to the proletariat, and in particular, a portion of the bourgeois ideologists, who have raised themselves to the level of comprehending theoretically the historical movement as a whole.

Of all the classes that stand face to face with the bourgeoisie today, the proletariat alone is a genuinely revolutionary class. The other classes decay and finally disappear in the face of Modern Industry; the proletariat is its special and essential product.

The lower middle class, the small manufacturer, the shopkeeper, the artisan, the peasant, all these fight against the bourgeoisie, to save from extinction their existence as fractions of the middle class. They are therefore not revolutionary, but conservative. Nay, more, they are reactionary, for they try to roll back the wheel of history. If, by chance, they are revolutionary, they are only so in view of their impending transfer into the proletariat; they thus defend not their present, but their future interests; they desert their own standpoint to place themselves at that of the proletariat.

The "dangerous class," the social scum, that passively rotting mass thrown off by the lowest layers of the old society, may, here and there, be swept into the movement by a proletarian revolution; its conditions of life, however, prepare it far more for the part of a bribed tool of reactionary intrigue.

In the condition of the proletariat, those of old society at large are already virtually swamped. The proletarian is without property; his relation to his wife and children has no longer anything in common with the bourgeois family relations; modern industry labor, modern subjection to capital, the same in England as in France, in America as in Germany, has stripped him of every trace of national character. Law, morality, religion, are to him so many bourgeois prejudices, behind which lurk in ambush just as many bourgeois interests.

All the preceding classes that got the upper hand sought to fortify their already acquired status by subjecting society at large to their conditions of appropriation. The proletarians cannot become masters of the productive forces of society, except by abolishing their own previous mode of appropriation, and thereby also every other previous mode of appropriation. They have nothing of their own to secure and to fortify; their mission is to destroy all previous securities for, and insurances of, individual property.

All previous historical movements were movements of minorities, or in the interest of minorities. The proletarian movement is the self-conscious, independent movement of the immense majority, in the interest of the immense majority. The proletariat, the lowest stratum of our present society, cannot stir, cannot raise itself up, without the whole superincumbent strata of official society being sprung into the air.

Though not in substance, yet in form, the struggle of the proletariat with the bourgeoisie is at first a national struggle. The proletariat of each country must, of course, first of all settle matters with its own bourgeoisie.

In depicting the most general phases of the development of the proletariat, we traced the more or less veiled civil war, raging within existing society, up to the point where that war breaks out into open revolution, and where the violent overthrow of the bourgeoisie lays the foundation for the sway of the proletariat.

Hitherto, every form of society has been based, as we have already seen, on the antagonism of oppressing and oppressed classes. But in order to oppress a class, certain conditions must be assured to it under which it can, at least, continue its slavish existence. The serf, in the period of serfdom, raised himself to membership in the commune, just as the petty bourgeois, under the yoke of the feudal absolutism, managed to develop into a bourgeois. The modern laborer, on the contrary, instead of rising with the process of industry, sinks deeper and deeper below the conditions of existence of his own class. He becomes a pauper, and pauperism develops more rapidly than population and wealth. And here it becomes evident that the bourgeoisie is unfit any longer to be the ruling class in society, and to impose its conditions of existence upon society as an overriding law. It is unfit to rule because it is incompetent to assure an existence to its slave within his slavery, because it cannot help letting him sink into such a state, that it has to feed him, instead of being fed by him. Society can no longer live under this bourgeoisie, in other words, its existence is no longer compatible with society.

The essential conditions for the existence and for the sway of the bourgeois class is the formation and augmentation of capital; the condition for capital is wage labor. Wage labor rests exclusively on competition between the laborers. The advance of industry, whose involuntary promoter is the bourgeoisie, replaces the isolation of the laborers, due to competition, by the revolutionary combination, due to association. The development of Modern Industry, therefore, cuts from under its feet the very foundation on which the bourgeoisie produces and appropriates products. What the bourgeoisie therefore produces, above all, are its own grave-diggers. Its fall and the victory of the proletariat are equally inevitable.

PROLETARIANS AND COMMUNISTS

In what relation do the Communists stand to the proletarians as a whole? The Communists do not form a separate party opposed to the other working-class parties.

They have no interests separate and apart from those of the proletariat as a whole.

They do not set up any sectarian principles of their own, by which to shape and mold the proletarian movement.

The Communists are distinguished from the other working-class parties by this only:

1. In the national struggles of the proletarians of the different countries, they point out and bring to the front the common interests of the entire proletariat, independently of all nationality.

2. In the various stages of development which the struggle of the working class against the bourgeoisie has to pass through, they always and everywhere represent the interests of the movement as a whole.

The Communists, therefore, are on the one hand practically, the most advanced and resolute section of the working-class parties of every country, that section which pushes forward all others; on the other hand, theoretically, they have over the great mass of the proletariat the advantage of clearly understanding the lines of march, the conditions, and the ultimate general results of the proletarian movement.

The immediate aim of the Communists is the same as that of all other proletarian parties: Formation of the proletariat into a class, overthrow of the bourgeois supremacy, conquest of political power by the proletariat.

The theoretical conclusions of the Communists are in no way based on ideas or principles that have been invented, or discovered, by this or that would-be universal reformer.

They merely express, in general terms, actual relations springing from an existing class struggle, from a historical movement going on under our very eyes. The abolition of existing property relations is not at all a distinctive feature of communism.

All property relations in the past have continually been subject to historical change consequent upon the change in historical conditions.

The French Revolution, for example, abolished feudal property in favor of bourgeois property.

The distinguishing feature of communism is not the abolition of property generally, but the abolition of bourgeois property. But modern bourgeois private property is the final and most complete expression of the system of producing and appropriating products that is based on class antagonisms, on the exploitation of the many by the few.

In this sense, the theory of the Communists may be summed up in the single sentence: Abolition of private property.

We Communists have been reproached with the desire of abolishing the right of personally acquiring property as the fruit of a man's own labor, which property is alleged to be the groundwork of all personal freedom, activity and independence.

Hard-won, self-acquired, self-earned property! Do you mean the property of petty artisan and of the small peasant, a form of property that preceded the bourgeois form? There is no need to abolish that; the development of industry has to a great extent already destroyed it, and is still destroying it daily.

Or do you mean the modern bourgeois private property?

But does wage labor create any property for the laborer? Not a bit. It creates capital, i.e., that kind of property which exploits wage labor, and which cannot increase except upon conditions of begetting a new supply of wage labor for fresh exploitation. Property, in its present form, is based on the antagonism of capital and wage labor. Let us examine both sides of this antagonism.

To be a capitalist, is to have not only a purely personal, but a social STATUS in production. Capital is a collective product, and only by the united action of many members, nay, in the last resort, only by the united action of all members of society, can it be set in motion.

Capital is therefore not only personal; it is a social power.

When, therefore, capital is converted into common property, into the property of all members of society, personal property is not thereby transformed into social property. It is only the social character of the property that is changed. It loses its class character.

Let us now take wage labor.

The average price of wage labor is the minimum wage, i.e., that quantum of the means of subsistence which is absolutely requisite to keep the laborer in bare existence as a laborer. What, therefore, the wage laborer appropriates by means of his labor merely suffices to prolong and reproduce a bare existence. We by no means intend to abolish this personal appropriation of the products of labor, an appropriation that is made for the maintenance and reproduction of human life, and that leaves no surplus wherewith to command the labor of others. All that we want to do away with is the miserable character of this appropriation, under which the laborer lives merely to increase capital, and is allowed to live only in so far as the interest of the ruling class requires it.

In bourgeois society, living labor is but a means to increase accumulated labor. In communist society, accumulated labor is but a means to widen, to enrich, to promote the existence of the laborer.

In bourgeois society, therefore, the past dominates the present; in communist society, the present dominates the past. In bourgeois society, capital is independent and has individuality, while the living person is dependent and has no individuality.

And the abolition of this state of things is called by the bourgeois, abolition of individuality and freedom! And rightly so. The abolition of bourgeois individuality, bourgeois independence, and bourgeois freedom is undoubtedly aimed at.

By freedom is meant, under the present bourgeois conditions of production, free trade, free selling and buying.

But if selling and buying disappears, free selling and buying disappears also. This talk about free selling and buying, and all the other "brave words" of our bourgeois about freedom in general, have a meaning, if any, only in contrast with restricted selling and buying, with the fettered traders of the Middle Ages, but have no meaning when opposed to the communist abolition of buying and selling, or the bourgeois conditions of production, and of the bourgeoisie itself.

You are horrified at our intending to do away with private property. But in your existing society, private property is already done away with for nine-tenths of the population; its existence for the few is solely due to its non-existence in the hands of those nine-tenths. You reproach us, therefore, with intending to do away with a form of property, the necessary condition for whose existence is the non-existence of any property for the immense majority of society.

In one word, you reproach us with intending to do away with your property. Precisely so; that is just what we intend.

From the moment when labor can no longer be converted into capital, money, or rent, into a social power capable of being monopolized, i.e., from the moment when individual property can no longer be transformed into bourgeois property, into capital, from that moment, you say, individuality vanishes.

You must, therefore, confess that by "individual" you mean no other person than the bourgeois, than the middle-class owner of property. This person must, indeed, be swept out of the way, and made impossible.

Communism deprives no man of the power to appropriate the products of society; all that it does is to deprive him of the power to subjugate the labor of others by means of such appropriations.

It has been objected that upon the abolition of private property, all work will cease, and universal laziness will overtake us.

According to this, bourgeois society ought long ago to have gone to the dogs through sheer idleness; for those who acquire anything, do not work. The whole of this objection is but another expression of the tautology: There can no longer be any wage labor when there is no longer any capital.

All objections urged against the communistic mode of producing and appropriating material products, have, in the same way, been urged against the communistic mode of producing and appropriating intellectual products. Just as to the bourgeois, the disappearance of class property is the disappearance of production itself, so the disappearance of class culture is to him identical with the disappearance of all culture.

That culture, the loss of which he laments, is, for the enormous majority, a mere training to act as a machine.

But don't wrangle with us so long as you apply, to our intended abolition of bourgeois property, the standard of your bourgeois notions of freedom, culture, law, etc. Your very ideas are but the outgrowth of the conditions of your bourgeois production and bourgeois property, just as your jurisprudence is but the will of your class made into a law for all, a will whose essential character and direction are determined by the economical conditions of existence of your class.

The selfish misconception that induces you to transform into eternal laws of nature and of reason the social forms stringing from your present mode of production and form of property—historical relations that rise and disappear in the progress of production—this misconception you share with every ruling class that has preceded you. What you see clearly in the case of ancient property, what you admit in the case of feudal property, you are of course forbidden to admit in the case of your own bourgeois form of property.

Abolition of the family! Even the most radical flare up at this infamous proposal of the Communists.

On what foundation is the present family, the bourgeois family, based? On capital, on private gain. In its completely developed form, this family exists only among the bourgeoisie. But this state of things finds its complement in the practical absence of the family among proletarians, and in public prostitution.

The bourgeois family will vanish as a matter of course when its complement vanishes, and both will vanish with the vanishing of capital.

Do you charge us with wanting to stop the exploitation of children by their parents? To this crime we plead guilty.

But, you say, we destroy the most hallowed of relations, when we replace home education by social.

And your education! Is not that also social, and determined by the social conditions under which you educate, by the intervention direct or indirect, of society, by means of schools, etc.? The Communists have not intended the intervention of society in education; they do but seek to alter the character of that intervention, and to rescue education from the influence of the ruling class.

The bourgeois claptrap about the family and education, about the hallowed correlation of parents and child, becomes all the more disgusting, the more, by the action of Modern Industry, all the family ties among the proletarians are torn asunder, and their children transformed into simple articles of commerce and instruments of labor.

But you Communists would introduce community of women, screams the bourgeoisie in chorus.

The bourgeois sees his wife a mere instrument of production. He hears that the instruments of production are to be exploited in common, and, naturally, can come to no other conclusion that the lot of being common to all will likewise fall to the women.

He has not even a suspicion that the real point aimed at is to do away with the status of women as mere instruments of production.

For the rest, nothing is more ridiculous than the virtuous indignation of our bourgeois at the community of women which, they pretend, is to be openly and officially established by the Communists. The Communists have no need to introduce free love; it has existed almost from time immemorial.

Our bourgeois, not content with having wives and daughters of their proletarians at their disposal, not to speak of common prostitutes, take the greatest pleasure in seducing each other's wives. (Ah, those were the days!)

Bourgeois marriage is, in reality, a system of wives in common and thus, at the most, what the Communists might possibly be reproached with is that they desire to introduce, in substitution for a hypocritically concealed, an openly legalized system of free love. For the rest, it is self-evident that the abolition of the present system of production must bring with it the abolition of free love springing from that system, i.e., of prostitution both public and private.

The Communists are further reproached with desiring to abolish countries and nationality.

The working men have no country. We cannot take from them what they have not got. Since the proletariat must first of all acquire political supremacy, must rise to be the leading class of the nation, must constitute itself **the** nation, it is, so far, itself national, though not in the bourgeois sense of the word.

National differences and antagonism between peoples are daily more and more vanishing, owing to the development of the bourgeoisie, to freedom of commerce, to the world market, to uniformity in the mode of production and in the conditions of life corresponding thereto.

The supremacy of the proletariat will cause them to vanish still faster. United action of the leading civilized countries at least is one of the first conditions for the emancipation of the proletariat.

In proportion as the exploitation of one individual by another will also be put an end to, the exploitation of one nation by another will also be put an end to. In proportion as the antagonism between classes within the nation vanishes, the hostility of one nation to another will come to an end.

The charges against communism made from a religious, a philosophical and, generally, from an ideological standpoint, are not deserving of serious examination.

Does it require deep intuition to comprehend that man's ideas, views, and conception, in one word, man's consciousness, changes with every change in the conditions of his material existence, in his social relations and in his social life?

What else does the history of ideas prove, than that intellectual production changes its character in proportion as material production is changed? The ruling ideas of each age have ever been the ideas of its ruling class.

When people speak of the ideas that revolutionize society, they do but express that fact that within the old society the elements of a new one have been created, and that the dissolution of the old ideas keeps even pace with the dissolution of the old conditions of existence.

When the ancient world was in its last throes, the ancient religions were overcome by Christianity. When Christian ideas succumbed in the eighteenth century to rationalist ideas, feudal society fought its death battle with the then revolutionary bourgeoisie. The ideas of religious liberty and freedom of conscience merely gave expression to the sway of free competition within the domain of knowledge.

"Undoubtedly," it will be said, "religious, moral, philosophical, and juridicial ideas have been modified in the course of historical development. But religion, morality, philosophy, political science, and law, constantly survived this change."

"There are, besides, eternal truths, such as Freedom, Justice, etc., that are common to all states of society. But communism abolishes eternal truths, it abolishes all religion, and all morality, instead of constituting them on a new basis; it therefore acts in contradiction to all past historical experience."

What does this accusation reduce itself to? The history of all past society has consisted in the development of class antagonisms, antagonisms that assumed different forms at different epochs.

But whatever form they may have taken, one fact is common to all past ages, viz., the exploitation of one part of society by the other. No wonder, then, that the social consciousness of past ages, despite all the multiplicity and variety it displays, moves within certain common forms, or general ideas, which cannot completely vanish except with the total disappearance of class antagonisms.

The communist revolution is the most radical rupture with traditional relations; no wonder that its development involved the most radical rupture with traditional ideas.

But let us have done with the bourgeois objections to communism.

We have seen above that the first step in the revolution by the working class is to raise the proletariat to the position of ruling class to win the battle of democracy.

The proletariat will use its political supremacy to wrest, by degree, all capital from the bourgeoisie, to centralize all instruments of production in the hands of the state, i.e., of the proletariat organized as the ruling class; and to increase the total productive forces as rapidly as possible.

Of course, in the beginning, this cannot be effected except by means of despotic inroads on the rights of property, and on the conditions of bourgeois production; by means of measures, therefore, which appear economically insufficient and untenable, but which, in the course of the movement, outstrip themselves, necessitate further inroads upon the old social order, and are unavoidable as a means of entirely revolutionizing the mode of production.

These measures will, of course, be different in different countries.

Nevertheless, in most advanced countries, the following will be pretty generally applicable.

1. Abolition of property in land and application of all rents of land to public purposes.

2. A heavy progressive or graduated income tax.

3. Abolition of all rights of inheritance.

4. Confiscation of the property of all emigrants and rebels.

5. Centralization of credit in the banks of the state, by means of a national bank with state capital and an exclusive monopoly.

6. Centralization of the means of communication and transport in the hands of the state.

7. Extension of factories and instruments of production owned by the state; the bringing into cultivation of waste lands, and the improvement of the soil generally in accordance with a common plan.

8. Equal obligation of all to work. Establishment of industrial armies, especially for agriculture.

9. Combination of agriculture with manufacturing industries; gradual abolition of all the distinction between town and country by a more equable distribution of the populace over the country.

10. Free education for all children in public schools. Abolition of children's factory labor in its present form. Combination of education with industrial production, etc.

When, in the course of development, class distinctions have disappeared, and all production has been concentrated in the hands of a vast association of the whole nation, the public power will lose its political character. Political power, properly so called, is merely the organized power of one class for oppressing another. If the proletariat during its contest with the bourgeoisie is compelled, by the force of circumstances, to organize itself as a class; if, by means of a revolution, it makes itself the ruling class, and, as such, sweeps away by force the old conditions of production, then it will, along with these conditions, have swept away the conditions for the existence of class antagonisms and of classes generally, and will thereby have abolished its own supremacy as a class.

In place of the old bourgeois society, with its classes and class antagonisms, we shall have an association in which the free development of each is the condition for the free development of all.

IDENTIFICATIONS PART III

Define each of the following items with a two sentence identification. Your definition must specifically draw on material in one of the documents in this section.

Declaration of the Rights of Man

_____

_____

Maximilien Robespierre

_____

_____

Levee en Masse

_____

_____

Communist Manifesto

_____

_____

Peter Smart

_____

_____

PART IV
COLONIALISM

The documents in this part offer two very different perspectives on colonialism. On the one hand there are documents in which Westerners offer justifications for the imposition of colonialism. In contrast, other items in this segment examine reactions by colonized people against Western control. What ideas, values, events justified for Westerners their imposition of colonial control? What criticisms did people in Asia, Africa and the Western Hemisphere make of colonialism and colonizers? What actions did they take against the imposition of Western control?

THE WHITE MAN'S BURDEN

Rudyard Kipling

Imperialism was often glorified both by those actively involved in it and by the public at home. Part of this glorification involved perceiving imperialism as a Christian and nationalistic venture. More broadly it involved portraying imperialism as a heroic deed carried out by idealistic leaders of Western civilization in an effort to spread the "benefits" of "true civilization" to "less advanced" peoples of the world. One of the most popular expressions of this is found in the writings of Rudyard Kipling (1865–1936), particularly in his poem "The White Man's Burden," written in 1899 to celebrate the American annexation of the Philippines.

Consider: *What Kipling means by "the White Man's burden"; how Kipling justifies imperialism; why such a justification might be so appealing.*

Take up the White Man's burden—
    Send forth the best ye breed—
Go, bind your sons to exile
    To serve your captives' need;
To wait, in heavy harness,
    On fluttered folk and wild—
Your new-caught sullen peoples,
    Half devil and half child.

Take up the White Man's burden—
    In patience to abide,
To veil the threat of terror
    And check the show of pride;
By open speech and simple,
    An hundred times made plain,
To seek another's profit
    And work another's gain.

Source: Rudyard Kipling, "The White Man's Burden," *McClure's Magazine*, vol. XII, no. 4 (February 1899), pp. 290–91.

Take up the White Man's burden—
    The savage wars of peace—
Fill full the mouth of Famine,
    And bid the sickness cease;
And when your goal is nearest
    (The end for others sought)
Watch sloth and heathen folly
    Bring all your hope to nought.

Take up the White Man's burden—
    No iron rule of kings,
But toil of serf and sweeper—
    The tale of common things.
The ports ye shall not enter,
    The roads ye shall not tread,
Go, make them with your living
    And mark them with your dead.

Take up the White Man's burden,
    And reap his old reward—
The blame of those ye better
    The hate of those ye guard—
The cry of hosts ye humour
    (Ah, slowly!) toward the light:—
"Why brought ye us from bondage,
    Our loved Egyptian night?"

Take up the White Man's burden—
    Ye dare not stoop to less—
Nor call too loud on Freedom
    To cloke your weariness.
By all ye will or whisper,
    By all ye leave or do,
The silent sullen peoples
    Shall weigh your God and you.

Take up the White Man's burden!
    Have done with childish days—
The lightly-proffered laurel,
    The easy ungrudged praise:
Comes now, to search your manhood
    Through all the thankless years,
Cold, edged with dear-bought wisdom,
    The judgment of your peers.

WHY BRITAIN ACQUIRED EGYPT IN 1882

The Earl of Cromer

This is the Earl of Cromer's (first British Viceroy of Egypt) account of why the British took over Egypt. It is also a good example of Political Imperialism—i.e., we don't really want the damned place but if we don't someone else will grab it and the whole balance of power will be mucked up. . . .

Egypt may now almost be said to form part of Europe. It is on the high road to the Far East. It can never cease to be an object of interest to all the powers of Europe, and especially to England. A numerous and intelligent body of Europeans and of non-Egyptian orientals have made Egypt their home. European capital to a large extent has been sunk in the country. The rights and privileges of Europeans are jealously guarded, and, moreover, give rise to complicated questions, which it requires no small amount of ingenuity and technical knowledge to solve. Exotic institutions have sprung up and have taken root in the country. The capitulations impair those rights of internal sovereignty which are enjoyed by the rulers or legislatures of most states. The population is heterogeneous and cosmopolitan to a degree almost unknown elsewhere. Although the prevailing faith is that of Islam, in no country in the world is a greater variety of religious creeds to be found amongst important sections of the community.

In addition to these peculiarities, which are of a normal character, it has to be borne in mind that in 1882 the [Egyptian] army was in a state of mutiny; the treasury was bankrupt; every branch of the administration had been dislocated; the ancient and arbitrary method, under which the country had for centuries been governed, had received a severe blow, whilst, at the same time, no more

Source: The Earl of Cromer, *Modern Egypt*, 2 Vols., (New York: Macmillan, 1908), Vol. I. xvii–xviii.

Scanned by: J. S. Arkenberg, Dept. of History, Cal. State Fullerton. Prof. Arkenberg has modernized the text.

orderly and law-abiding form of government had been inaugurated to take its place. Is it probable that a government composed of the rude elements described above, and led by men of such poor ability as Arabi and his coadjutors, would have been able to control a complicated machine of this nature? Were the sheikhs of the El-Azhar mosque likely to succeed where Tewfik Pasha and his ministers, who were men of comparative education and enlightenment, acting under the guidance and inspiration of a first-class European power, only met with a modified success after years of patient labor? There can be but one answer to these questions. Nor is it in the nature of things that any similar movement should, under the present conditions of Egyptian society, meet with any better success. The full and immediate execution of a policy of "Egypt for the Egyptians," as it was conceived by the Arabists in 1882, was, and still is, impossible.

History, indeed, records some very radical changes in the forms of government to which a state has been subjected without its interests being absolutely and permanently shipwrecked. But it may be doubted whether any instance can be quoted of a sudden transfer of power in any civilized or semi-civilized community to a class so ignorant as the pure Egyptians, such as they were in the year 1882. These latter have, for centuries past, been a subject race.

Persians, Greeks, Romans, Arabs from Arabia and Baghdad, Circassians, and finally, Ottoman Turks, have successively ruled over Egypt, but we have to go back to the doubtful and obscure precedents of Pharaonic times to find an epoch when, possibly, Egypt was ruled by Egyptians. Neither, for the present, do they appear to possess the qualities which would render it desirable, either in their own interests, or in those of the civilized world in general, to raise them at a bound to the category of autonomous rulers with full rights of internal sovereignty.

If, however, a foreign occupation was inevitable or nearly inevitable, it remains to be considered whether a British occupation was preferable to any other. From the purely Egyptian point of view, the answer to this question cannot be doubtful. The intervention of any European power was preferable to that of Turkey. The intervention of one European power was preferable to international intervention. The special aptitude shown by Englishmen in the government of Oriental races pointed to England as the most effective and beneficent instrument for the gradual introduction of European civilization into Egypt. An Anglo-French, or an Anglo-Italian occupation, from both of which we narrowly and also accidentally escaped, would have been detrimental to Egyptian interests and would ultimately have caused friction, if not serious dissension, between England on the one side and France or Italy on the other. The only thing to be said in favor of Turkish intervention is that it would have relieved England from the responsibility of intervening.

By the process of exhausting all other expedients, we arrive at the conclusion that armed British intervention was, under the special circumstances of the case, the only possible solution of the difficulties which existed in 1882. Probably also it was the best solution. The arguments against British intervention, indeed, were sufficiently obvious. It was easy to foresee that, with a British garrison in Egypt, it would be difficult that the relations of England either with France or Turkey should be cordial. With France, especially, there would be a danger that our relations might become seriously strained. Moreover, we lost the advantages of our insular position. The occupation of Egypt necessarily dragged England to a certain extent within the arena of Continental politics. In the event of war, the presence of a British garrison in Egypt would possibly be a source of weakness rather than of strength. Our position in Egypt placed us in a disadvantageous diplomatic position, for any power, with whom we had a difference of opinion about some non-Egyptian question, was at one time able to retaliate by opposing our Egyptian policy. The complicated rights and privileges possessed by the various powers of Europe in Egypt facilitated action of this nature.

There can be no doubt of the force of these arguments. The answer to them is that it was impossible for Great Britain to allow the troops of any other power to occupy Egypt. When it became apparent that some foreign occupation was necessary, that the Sultan would not act save under conditions which were impossible of acceptance, and that neither French nor Italian cooperation could be secured, the British government acted with promptitude and vigor. A great nation cannot throw off the responsibilities which its past history and its position in the world have imposed upon it. English history affords other examples of the government and people of England drifting by accident into doing what was not only right, but was also most in accordance with British interests.

THE DEATH OF GENERAL GORDON AT KHARTOUM, 1885

Alfred Egmont Hake

[Tappan Introduction] In 1882 there arose in the Soudan, a province of Upper Egypt, one Mohammed Ahmed, who called himself the Mahdi or Messiah, and invited all true believers to join in a holy war against the Christians. Thousands of wild tribesmen flocked to his banner, and in the following year he annihilated an army of eleven thousand English and Egyptians that had attempted to subdue the revolt. Rather than send more soldiers to die in the deserts of the Upper Nile, England decided to abandon the province. But first the thousands of Europeans who had taken refuge in Khartoum and other towns of the Soudan must be rescued from their perilous position. In this crisis the Government turned to the one man who could effect the withdrawal if it was still possible, and in January, 1884, appointed General Gordon to superintend the evacuation of the Soudan.

General Gordon arrived at Khartoum on February 18th, and spent his time between that date and the investment on March 12, in sending down women and children, two thousand of whom were sent safely through to Egypt, in addition to six hundred soldiers. It was stated by Sir Evelyn Baring (English consul-general to Egypt) that there were fifteen thousand persons in Khartoum who ought to be brought back to Egypt—Europeans, civil servants, widows and orphans, and a garrison of one thousand men, one third of whom were disaffected. To get these people out of Khartoum was General Gordon's first duty, and

Source: Eva March Tappan, ed., *The World's Story: A History of the World in Story, Song and Art*, (Boston: Houghton Mifflin, 1914), Vol. III: *Egypt, Africa, and Arabia*, pp. 240–249. Scanned by Jerome S. Arkenberg, Cal. State Fullerton. The text has been modernized by Prof. Arkenberg.

Note: Many Western sources about Islamic countries exhibit what has become known as *orientalism*. The terms used ("Mohammedan" for instance rather than "Muslim"), and the attitudes exhibited by the writers need to be questioned by modern readers.

the first condition of evacuation was the establishment of a stable government in the Soudan. The only man who could establish that government was Zebehr. Gordon demanded Zebehr with ever-increasing emphasis, and his request was decisively refused. He had then two alternatives—either to surrender absolutely to the Mahdi, or to hold on to Khartoum at all hazards. While Gordon was strengthening his position the Mahdi settled the question by suddenly assuming the offensive. The first step in this memorable siege was the daring march of four thousand Arabs to the Nile, by which, on March 12, they cut off the eight hundred men at Halfaya, a village to the north of Khartoum, from the city. A steamer was sent down to reconnoiter, and the moment she reached the front of the Arab position a volley was fired into her, wounding an officer and a soldier. The steamer returned the fire, killing five.

Thus hostilities began. "Our only justification for assuming the offensive," wrote General Gordon on March 13, "is the extrication of the Halfaya garrison." The Arabs, however, did not give him the chance. They cut off three companies of his troops who had gone out to cut wood, capturing eight of their boats, and killing or dispersing one hundred to one hundred and fifty men. They intrenched themselves along the Nile, and kept up a heavy rifle-fire. Retreat for the garrison was obviously impossible when the Arab force covered the river, the only line of retreat, with their fire. Twelve hundred men were put on board two grain-barges, towed by three steamers defended with boiler plates, and carrying mountain-guns protected by wooden mantlets; and, with the loss of only two killed, they succeeded in extricating the five hundred men left of the garrison of Halfaya, and capturing seventy camels and eighteen horses, with which they returned to Khartoum.

The Arabs, however, held Halfaya, and on March 16 Gordon tried to drive them away. Advancing from a stockaded position covering the north front of the town, two thousand troops advanced across the open square, supported by the fire of the guns of two steamers. The Arabs were retreating, when Hassan and Seid Pashas, Gordon's black generals, rode into the wood and called back the enemy. The Egyptians, betrayed by their officers, broke and fled after firing a single volley, and were pursued to within a mile of the stockade, abandoning two mountain guns with their ammunition—"sixty horsemen defeated two thousand men"—and leaving two hundred of their number on the field. After this affair he was convinced that he could not take the offensive, but must remain quiet at Khartoum, and wait till the Nile rose. Six days later, the black pashas were tried by court-martial, found guilty, and shot.

A very determined attack upon one of the steamers coming up from Berber, at the Salboka Pass, was beaten off with great slaughter, Gordon's men firing no fewer than fifteen thousand rounds of Remington ammunition. Meanwhile, his efforts to negotiate with the Mahdi failed. "I will make you Sultan of Kordofan," he had said on arrival to the Mahdi. "I am the Mahdi," replied

Mahomet Ahmet, by emissaries who were "exceedingly cheeky," keeping their hands upon their swords, and laying a filthy, patched dervish's coat before him. "Will you become a Mussulman?" Gordon flung the bundle across the room, canceled the Mahdi's sultanship, and the war was renewed. From that day to the day of the betrayal no day passed without bullets dropping into Khartoum.

Gordon now set to work in earnest to place Khartoum in a defensible position. Ten thousand of the Madhi's sympathizers left Khartoum and joined the enemy. The steamers kept up a skirmishing fight on both Niles. All the houses on the north side of Khartoum were loopholed. A sixteen-pounder Krupp was mounted on a barge, and wire was stretched across the front of the stockade. The houses on the northern bank of the Blue Nile were fortified and garrisoned by Bashi-Bazouks. Omdurman was held and fortified on the west and Buri on the east. On March 25, Gordon had to disarm and disband two hundred and fifty Bashi-Bazouks who refused to occupy stockaded houses in a village on the south bank of the Blue Nile. The rebels advanced on Hadji Ali, a village to the north of the Nile, and fired into the palace. They were shelled out of their position, but constantly returned to harass the garrison. They seemed to Gordon mere rag-tag and bob-tail, but he dared not go out to meet them, for fear of the town. Five hundred brave men could have cleared out the lot, but he had not a hundred. The fighting was confined to artillery fire on one side, and desultory rifle-shooting on the other. This went on till the end of March. The Arabs clustered more closely round the town.

On April 19, Gordon telegraphed that he had provisions for five months, and if he only had two thousand to three thousand Turkish troops he could soon settle the rebels. Unfortunately, he received not one fighting man. Shendy fell into the hands of the Mahdi. Berber followed, and then for months no word whatever reached this country from Khartoum.

On September 29, Mr. Power's telegram, dated July 31, was received by the "Times." From that we gathered a tolerably clear notion of the way in which the war went on. Anything more utterly absurd than the accusation that Gordon forced fighting on the Mahdi cannot be conceived. He acted uniformly on the defensive, merely trying to clear his road of an attacking force, and failing because he had no fighting men to take the offensive. He found himself in a trap, out of which he could not cut his way. If he had possessed a single regiment, the front of Khartoum might have been cleared with ease; but his impotence encouraged the Arabs, and they clustered round in ever-increasing numbers, until at last they crushed his resistance. After the middle of April the rebels began to attack the palace in force, having apparently established themselves on the north bank.

The loss of life was chiefly occasioned by the explosion of mines devised by General Gordon, and so placed as to explode when trodden on by the enemy. Of all his expedients these mines were the most successful and the least open to any accusation of offensive operations. The Arabs closed in all round towards the end of April, and General Gordon surrounded himself with a formidable triple barrier of land torpedoes, over which wire entanglement and a formidable *chevaux-de-frise* enabled the garrison to feel somewhat secure. On April 27, Valeh Bey surrendered at Mesalimeh, a disaster by which General Gordon lost one steamer, seventy shiploads of provisions, and two thousand rifles.

General Gordon was now entirely cut off from the outside world, and compelled to rely entirely upon his own resources. He sent out Negroes to entice the slaves of the Arabs to come over, promising them freedom and rations. This he thought would frighten the Arabs more than bullets. On April 26, he made his first issue of paper-money to the extent of 2,500 redeemable in six months. By July 30, it had risen to 26,000 besides the 50,000 borrowed from merchants. On the same day he struck decorations for the defense of Khartoum—for officers in silver, silver-gilt and pewter for the private soldiers. These medals bear a crescent and a star, with words from the Koran, and the date, with an inscription,—"Siege of Khartoum,"—and a hand-grenade in the center. "School-children and women," he wrote, "also received medals; consequently, I am very popular with the black ladies of Khartoum."

The repeated attacks of the Mahdi's forces on Khartoum cost the Arabs many lives. On May 25, Colonel Stewart was slightly wounded in the arm, when working a mitrailleuse near the palace. All through May and June his steamers made foraging expeditions up and down the Nile, shelling the rebels when they showed in force, and bringing back much cattle to the city. On Midsummer Day, Mr. Cuzzi, formerly Gordon's agent at Berber, but now a prisoner of the Mahdi's, was sent to the wells to announce the capture of Berber. It was sad news for the three Englishmen alone in the midst of a hostile Soudan. Undaunted, they continued to stand at bay, rejoicing greatly that in one, Saati Bey, they had, at least, a brave and capable officer.

Saati had charge of the steamers, and for two months he had uninterrupted success, in spite of the twisted telegraph wires which the rebels stretched across the river. Unfortunately, on July 10, Saati, with Colonel Stewart and two hundred men, after burning Kalaka and three villages, attacked Gatarnulb. Eight Arab horsemen rode at the two hundred Egyptians. The two hundred fled at once, not caring to fire their Remingtons, and poor Saati was killed. Colonel Stewart narrowly escaped a similar fate.

After July 31, there is a sudden cessation of regular communications. Power's journal breaks off then, and we are left to more or less meager references in Gordon's dispatches. On August 23, he sent a characteristic message, in which he announces that, the Nile having risen, he has sent Colonel Stewart, Mr. Power, and the French consul to take Berber, occupy it for fifteen days, burn it, and then return to Khartoum. All the late messages from Gordon, except a long dispatch of November 4, which has never been published, were written on tissue paper no bigger than a postage-stamp, and either concealed in a quill thrust into the hair, or sewn in the waistband of the natives employed. Gordon seems to have been the most active in August and September, when the Nile was high. He had eight thousand men at Khartoum and Senaar. He sent Colonel Stewart and the troops with the steamers to recapture Berber. A steamer which bore a rough effigy of Gordon at the prow was said to be particularly dreaded by the rebels. On August 26, he reported that he had provisions for five months, but in the forays made by his steamer on the Southern Niles he enormously replenished his stores. On one of these raids he took with him six thousand men in thirty-four boats towed by nine steamers.

After his defeat before Omdurman, the Mahdi is said to have made a very remarkable prophecy. He retired into a cave for three days, and on his return he told his followers that Allah had revealed that for sixty days there would be a rest, and after that blood would flow like water. The Mahdi was right. Almost exactly sixty days after that prophecy there was fought the battle of Abu Klea.

Stewart had by this time been treacherously killed on his way down from Berber to Dongola. Gordon was all alone. The old men and women who had friends in the neighboring villages left the town. The uninhabited part was destroyed, the remainder was enclosed by a wall. In the center of Khartoum he had built himself a tower, from the roof of which he kept a sharp lookout with his field-glass in the daytime. At night he went the rounds of the fortifications, cheering his men and keeping them on the alert against attacks. Treachery was always his greatest dread. Many of the townsfolk sympathized with the Mahdi; he could not depend on all his troops, and he could only rely on one of his pashas, Mehmet Ali. He rejoiced exceedingly in the news of the approach of the British relieving force. He illuminated Khartoum and fired salutes in honor of the news, and he doubled his exertions to fill his granaries with grain.

On December 14, a letter was received by one of his friends in Cairo from General Gordon, saying, "Farewell. You will never hear from me again. I fear that there will be treachery in the garrison, and all will be over by Christmas." It was this melancholy warning that led Lord Wolseley to order the dash across the Desert. On December 16 came news that the Mahdi had again failed in his attack on Omdurman. Gordon had blown up the fort which he had built over against the town, and inflicted great loss on his assailants, who, however, invested the city closely on all sides. The Mahdi had returned to Omdurman, where he had concentrated his troops. Thence he sent fourteen thousand men to Berber to recruit the forces of Osman Digma, and it was these men, probably, that fought the English relief army at Abu Klea.

After this nothing was heard beyond the rumor that Omdurman was captured and two brief messages from Gordon, sent probably to hoodwink the enemy, by whom most of his letters were captured. The first, which arrived January 1, was as follows: "Khartoum all right.—C. G. Gordon. December 14, 1884." The second was brought by the steamers which met General Stewart at

Mentemneh on January 21st: "Khartoum all right; could hold out for years.—C. G. Gordon. December 29." On January 26, Faraz Pasha opened the gates of the city to the enemy, and one of the most famous sieges in the world's history came to a close. It had lasted from March 12 to January 26—exactly three hundred and twenty days.

When Gordon awoke to find that, through the treachery of his Egyptian lieutenant, Khartoum was in the hands of the Mahdi, he set out with a few followers for the Austrian consulate. Recognized by a party of rebels, he was shot dead on the street and his head carried through the town at the end of a pike, amid the wild rejoicings of the Mahdi's followers. Two days later the English army of relief reached Khartoum.

EXCERPTS FROM THE RISE OF OUR EAST AFRICAN EMPIRE, 1893

Capt. F. D. Lugard, modernized by Jerome S. Arkenberg

It is sufficient to reiterate here that, as long as our policy is one of free trade, we are compelled to seek new markets; for old ones are being closed to us by hostile tariffs, and our great dependencies, which formerly were the consumers of our goods, are now becoming our commercial rivals. It is inherent in a great colonial and commercial empire like ours that we go forward or go backward. To allow other nations to develop new fields, and to refuse to do so ourselves, is to go backward; and this is the more deplorable, seeing that we have proved ourselves notably capable of dealing with native races and of developing new countries at a less expense than other nations. We owe to the instincts of colonial expansion of our ancestors those vast and noble dependencies which are our pride and the outlets of our trade today; and we are accountable to posterity that opportunities which now present themselves of extending the sphere of our industrial enterprise are not neglected, for the opportunities now offered will never recur again. Lord Rosebery in his speech at the Royal Colonial Institute expressed this in emphatic language: "We are engaged in 'pegging out claims' for the future. We have to consider, not what we want now, but what we shall want in the future. We have to consider what countries must be developed either by ourselves or some other nation. . . . Remember that the task of the statesman is not merely with the present, but with the future. We have to look forward beyond the chatter of platforms, and the passions of party, to the future of the race of which we are at present the trustees, and we should, in my opinion, grossly fail in the task that has been laid upon us did we shrink from responsibilities, and decline to

Source: Eva March Tappan, ed., *The World's Story: A History of the World in Story, Song, and Art.* Volume 1: *China, Japan, and the Islands of the Pacific,* (Boston: Houghton Mifflin, 1914), pp. 536–540.

Scanned by Jerome S. Arkenberg, Cal. State Fullerton. The text has been modernized by Prof. Arkenberg.

take our share in a partition of the world which we have not forced on, but which has been forced upon us."

If some initial expense is incurred, is it not justified by the ultimate gain? I have already pointed out what other nations are doing in the way of railway extension. The government is not asked to provide the capital of the railway, but only a guarantee on the subscribed capital. . . . Independently of money spent on railways, the conquest of Algeria alone cost France £150,000,000, and it is estimated that her West Coast colonies cost her half a million yearly. Italy spends on her Abyssinian protectorate a sum variously estimated at £400,000 or £600,000 per annum. Belgium, besides her heavy expenses for the Congo railway, the capital of which she has advanced without interest, guarantees £80,000 per annum to the Congo state, and is altering her constitution in order to allow her to take over that state as a colonial possession. Germany has spent over a million sterling in East Africa, besides her expenditure on the west and southwest colonies. The parallel is here complete, for the German company failed, and government stepped in to carry out the pledges and obligations incurred. Even Portugal is content to support a yearly deficit on each of her African possessions, gives heavy subsidies to the mail steamers, and £10,000 per annum to the cable. All these nations are content to incur this yearly cost in the present, confident that in the future these possessions will repay the outlay, and willing to be at a national expense to fulfill their treaty obligations under the Brussels Act.

The Zanzibar Gazette, which is in a good position to judge, since the imports and exports from German East Africa can be fairly assessed there, speaking of "the comparatively large sums from the national resources" invested in this country, says, "We think it is only a question of time for such investments, with a careful management of the territory, to show highly profitable returns." Such a view from those on the spot and possessing local knowledge, should be a strong testimony in favor of the far richer British sphere. . . .

A word as to missions in Africa. Beyond doubt I think the most useful missions are the medical and the industrial, in the initial stages of savage development. A combination of the two is, in my opinion, an ideal mission. Such is the work of the Scotch Free Church on Lake Nyasa. The medical missionary begins work with every advantage. Throughout Africa the ideas of the cure of the body and of the soul are closely allied. The "medicine man" is credited, not only with a knowledge of the simples and drugs which may avert or cure disease, but owing to the superstitions of the people, he is also supposed to have a knowledge of the charms and *dawa* which will invoke the aid of the Deity or appease His wrath, and of the witchcraft and magic (*ulu*) by which success in war, immunity from danger, or a supply of rain may be obtained. As the skill of the European in medicine asserts its superiority over the crude methods of the medicine man, so does he in proportion gain an influence in his teaching of the great truths of Christianity. He teaches the savage where knowledge and art cease, how far natural remedies produce their effects, independent of charms or supernatural agencies, and where divine power overrules all human efforts. Such demonstration from a medicine man, whose skill they cannot fail to recognize as superior to their own, has naturally more weight than any mere preaching. A mere preacher is discounted and his zeal is not understood. The medical missionary, moreover, gains an admission to the houses and homes of the natives by virtue of his art, which would not be so readily accorded to another. He becomes their adviser and referee, and his counsels are substituted for the magic and witchcraft which retard development.

The value of the industrial mission, on the other hand, depends, of course, largely on the nature of the tribes among whom it is located. Its value can hardly be overestimated among such people as the Waganda, both on account of their natural aptitude and their eager desire to learn. But even the less advanced and more primitive tribes may be equally benefited, if not only mechanical and artisan work, such as the carpenter's and blacksmith's craft, but also the simpler expedients of agriculture are taught. The sinking of wells, the system of irrigation, the introduction and planting of useful trees, the use of manure, and of domestic animals for agricultural purposes, the improvement of his implements by the introduction of the primitive Indian plough, etc.—all of these, while improving the status of the native, will render his land more productive, and hence, by increasing his surplus products, will enable him to purchase from the trader the cloth which shall add to his decency, and the implements and household utensils which shall produce greater results for his labor and greater comforts in his social life.

In my view, moreover, instruction (religious or secular) is largely wasted upon adults, who are wedded to custom and prejudice. It is the rising generation who should be educated to a higher plane, by the establishment of schools for children. They, in turn, will send their children for instruction; and so a progressive advancement is instituted, which may produce really great results. I see, in a recent letter, that Dr. Laws supports this view, and appositely quotes the parallel of the Israelites after their exodus from Egypt, who were detained for forty years in the desert, until the generation who had been slaves in Egypt had passed away. The extensive schools at his mission at Bandawi were evidence of the practical application of his views. These schools were literally thronged with thousands of children, and chiefs of neighboring tribes were eagerly offering to erect schools in their own villages at their own cost.

The Established Church of Scotland Mission at Blantyre was (if I may so call it) an administrative mission. It was started under a wholly different set of conditions. The site of the mission, instead of being in a densely populated country, like the Free Church mission stations, was in a district largely depopulated. Around the mission grew up a population chiefly consisting of fugitive slaves. This initial mistake led to serious difficulties later, and I believe the resentment of the tribes from whom these slaves had run away was eventually disarmed only by the payment of ransom money by the mission. Thus the missions became the administrators and lawgivers of the native community which grew up around them. Just as the mission houses and plantations were themselves an object lesson to the natives of Africa, so the little colony became itself a model. The spotless clothes of the children, the neatness, and order, and discipline enforced, were like nothing I have ever seen elsewhere in Africa. The children in the schools were boarders; native chiefs from surrounding tribes sent their sons to live in Blantyre, and be taught in the schools; neighboring chiefs came to the white man of Blantyre, as arbitrator in disputes; his intervention on more than one occasion prevented war.

The great coffee plantation and buildings of the missions, the Lakes Company, and Messrs. Buchanan, were the means of instituting on a large scale the experiment of free labor in Africa, and natives came from great distances, even from the warlike Angoni tribe, to engage themselves for regular wages. . . .

An administrative mission can, of course, only be founded in a country not under the aegis of any European power. Under such circumstances, a mission may be justified in undertaking to some extent administrative functions, pending the absorption of the country under European protection, especially where no central native authority exists, and there is no cohesion to repel the attacks of slavetraders, or the tyranny of the dominant tribe. This is, of course, more especially the case when the community has grown up in a previously unpopulated country, as at Blantyre. But when a secular administration is established, it appears to me that the missions should resign entirely into the hands of the authorized executive government all functions pertaining to administration. . . .

One word as regards missionaries themselves. The essential point in dealing with Africans is to establish a respect for the European. Upon this—the prestige of the white man—depends his influence, often his very existence, in Africa. If he shows by his surroundings, by his assumption of superiority, that he is far above the native, he will be respected, and his influence will be proportionate to the superiority he assumes and bears out by his higher accomplishments and mode of life. In my opinion—at any rate with reference to Africa—it is the greatest possible mistake to suppose that a European can acquire a greater influence by adopting the mode of life of the natives. In effect, it is to lower himself to their plane, instead of elevating them to his. The sacrifice involved is wholly unappreciated, and the motive would be held by the savage to be poverty and lack of social status in his own country. The whole influence of the European in Africa is gained by this assertion of a superiority which commands the respect and excites the emulation of the savage. To forego this vantage ground is to lose influence for good. I may add, that the loss of prestige consequent on what I should term the humiliation of the European affects not merely the missionary himself, but is subversive of all efforts for secular administration, and may even invite insult, which may lead to disaster and bloodshed. To maintain it a missionary must, above all things, be a gentleman; for no one is more quick to recognize a real gentleman than the African savage. He must at all times assert himself, and repel an insolent familiarity, which is a thing entirely apart from friendship born of respect and affection. His dwelling house should be as superior to those of the natives as he is himself superior to them. And this, while adding to his prestige and influence, will simultaneously promote his own health and energy, and so save money spent on invalidings to England, and replacements due to sickness or death. . . .

I am convinced that the indiscriminate application of such precepts as those contained in the words to turn the other cheek also to the smiter, and to be the servant of all men, is to wholly misunderstand and misapply the teaching of Christ. The African holds the position of a late-born child in the family of nations, and must as yet be schooled in the discipline of the nursery. He is neither the intelligent ideal crying out for instruction, and capable of appreciating the subtle beauties of Christian forbearance and self-sacrifice, which some well-meaning missionary literature would lead us to suppose, nor yet, on the other hand, is he universally a rampant cannibal, predestined by Providence to the yoke of the slave, and fitted for nothing better, as I have elsewhere seen him depicted. I hold rather with Longfellow's beautiful lines—

> In all ages
> Every human heart is human;
> There are longings, yearnings, strivings
> For the good they comprehend not.
> That the feeble hands and helpless,
> Groping blindly in the darkness,
> Touch God's right hand in that darkness.

That is to say, that there is in him, like the rest of us, both good and bad, and that the innate good is capable of being developed by culture.

A VISIT TO AGUINALDO, LEADER OF THE PHILIPPINE REBELS, 1898

Edwin Wildman

[Tappan Introduction]: The Philippines were visited by Magellan in 1521. Half a century later, the Spanish took possession of them and named them in honor of Philip II of Spain. In 1896, the natives, led by Aguinaldo, revolted against Spanish rule. After the Spanish-American War, Aguinaldo fought against the United States, into whose hands the islands had now fallen. In 1901, he was captured and American rule was established throughout the Philippines.

In November, 1898, I visited Aguinaldo at his capital at Malolos. I was laboring under the popular delusion as to Aguinaldo's greatness, and judged him largely from the documents that bore his name, although I was in possession of some information which aided me in understanding somewhat the situation at Malolos. I was well acquainted with a number of revolutionary sympathizers, and several members of Aguinaldo's cabinet who resided in Manila, and, considering their views and the positions they held, I was somewhat surprised at the open manner in which they depreciated Aguinaldo's ability and deplored the prominence accorded him, even while they themselves admitted that his name was the only one that held the natives in check and united in the aspirations for independence. It was humiliating to them that Aguinaldo, instead of one of their number, held the confidence of the people.

I shall not soon forget my pilgrimage to the Filipino Mecca. Those were the palmy days of the Republica Filipina, and Aguinaldo's name was on every lip. There was a cordon of insurgent soldiers around Manila, and to pass this line one

Source: Eva March Tappan, ed., *The World's Story: A History of the World in Story, Song, and Art*, Volume I: *China, Japan, and the Islands of the Pacific*, (Boston: Houghton Mifflin, 1914), pp. 536–540.

Scanned by Jerome S. Arkenberg, Cal. State Fullerton. The text has been modernized by Prof. Arkenberg.

must needs have a pass signed by Aguinaldo. I boarded the diminutive train on the Manila-Dagupan Railroad, and in company with twelve carloads of bare-footed natives was soon speeding along the little narrow gauge toward Malolos. In half an hour we had passed the cordon, and I and my Filipino companion were landed on the Malolos platform, which was patrolled by a half-dozen or more Filipino soldiers, who strutted up and down, and, it seemed to me, looked upon me with suspicion. I greeted their looks with an affable smile—we all did then—and they withdrew their stare and passed on.

After the little train puffed out of the station, I pushed my way through a crowd of palm-extended beggars, trading upon deformed limbs and leprous faces, and reached the opposite side of the station, where lingered beneath the shade of some scraggly palms a half-dozen *caromettas,* attached by crude hemp harnesses to ponies, long strangers to *sacati* and *pali.* Though naturally merciful to the animal kingdom, I was prevailed upon by Malolos Ahackmen, augmented by the persuasive rays of the midday sun, to take a seat in one of their crude carts, and was soon bumping and joggling over the occasionally planked road toward the pueblo.

It was tiffin time, and I knew better than to disturb any Filipino gentle-man at midday. For a siesta follows tiffin with as much regularity as a demi-tasse does dinner in America. My Filipino friend and myself therefore repaired to a public house and partook of a native meal, which was washed down by native drinks—the combination fitting one for any crime. After visiting the church, the public square, and the town pump, I presented myself at the Casa Aguinaldo. The Presidente made his headquarters in the second story of a large convent, or priest's house, as it is called, adjoining the Malolos church, which was utilized to accommodate the sessions of the Filipino Congress. Two Maxim guns protruded from the windows of the convent, and the entrance was guarded by a patrol of Filipino soldiery.

We passed this gauntlet without challenge and ascended the convent stairs. At the top extended a long, broad hall. On either side of this passageway were stationed Aguinaldo's bodyguards armed with halberds. Diminutive Filipinos, almost comical in their toy-like dignity, were ranged along the wall, giving themselves an extra brace as we passed. The halberds were cheap imitations of those customarily used in the palace of the governor-general at Manila upon state occasions.

Our cards were sent in. The Presidente would receive us. Would we wait for a brief space? The dapper but brave little insurgent general, Pio del Pinar, was pleased to greet us. The Presidente knew of my coming. Had it not been telegraphed to him when we crossed the line? Ah, Señor, the Presidente knows everything. He desires to protect Americans when they do him so much honor. But did one need special protection in Aguinaldo's country? No, Señor, but there are Spaniards who yet hope and hate. Too much caution cannot be exercised.

Would we look at the council room—and so on. I early learned that if one wished to get information from a Filipino, one must not ask it. Aguinaldo's council chamber was interesting. Down the center of the hall were parallel rows of chairs, Filipino style, facing each other. Here sat the dignitaries of state like rows of men awaiting their turns in a barber shop. The walls were hung with creditable paintings by native artists. A large Oriental rug covered the mahogany floor.

On bamboo pedestals around the rooms were miniature wood-carvings representing Filipino victims undergoing tortures of various descriptions at the hands of friars and Spanish officials for refusing to divulge the secrets of the Katipunan. One showed a native suspended on tiptoes by a cord tied around his tongue, while a Spanish hireling slashed his back with a knife. Another represented a native of the province of Nueva Ecija falsely accused of hostility to the Spanish, so I was told. A cord passed through his nose, as if he were a beast of burden. A Spaniard was cudgeling his bare shoulders with a bamboo stick. Another showed a Filipino hung up by his feet with a big stone bound to each shoulder. Still another represented a native with his back bent backward, a pole passing under his knees, a cord around his chest holding him bent over in a most painful position. And others equally terrible. All these were actual cases. I was told the history of each one. Finally Aguinaldo was ready to receive us. The red plush curtains that separated his private room from the council chamber were drawn aside by guards, and we entered the holy of holies. The little chieftain was already standing to receive us.

His spacious room was adorned with Japanese tapestries. Around the walls were handsome Japanese vases, and emblazoned high on one side of the room was a shield of ancient Japanese and Mindanao arms. On another side of the room was a huge Spanish mirror. Back of Aguinaldo's desk hung from its staff a handsome Spanish flag. I jokingly asked Aguinaldo if he would present it to me as a souvenir of my visit. "Not for twenty-five thousand pesos," he replied. "I captured it at Cavite, my native town. The Spaniards have offered thousands of pesos as a bribe for the restoration of that flag, so I keep it here." Aguinaldo is short. His skin is dark. His head is large, but well posed on a rather slight body. His hair is the shiny black of the Tagalog, and is combed pompadour, enhancing his height somewhat. On that day he was dressed in a suit of fine piña-cloth of native manufacture, and he wore no indication of his rank.

Through my Filipino friend, as interpreter, I had an extended conversation with him. He told me that he hoped to avoid a rupture with the Americans, but that his people felt that they had been wronged and slighted, and that they were becoming turbulent and difficult to control. He said that his Government was thoroughly organized; that throughout the provinces, where insurrection had been incessant for years, all was quiet, and the peaceful pursuits of labor were being carried on. "I hope these conditions will not be disturbed," he added, not without meaning. I asked him if the charges were true that the Spanish friars were maltreated, and if women, also, were imprisoned. He replied that he was not responsible to any one for the treatment of his prisoners, but that if an accredited emissary of General Otis would call upon him, he would permit him to visit the places where the Spanish prisoners were confined. As to the women, he said that they were "wives" of the priests and voluntarily shared captivity with them. As I left the room he spoke to my Filipino friend, calling him back. Being somewhat curious at this not altogether polite act, I later asked the reason. My friend smiled, and told me that Aguinaldo wished to make a purchase in Manila, and requested him to attend to it.

"But what did he want?" I said. My friend again smiled, and said: "You know he is vain. He wants me to get him another large mirror like the one in his room. He desires it to be the finest plate-glass, and the frame, also, Spanish style, to be set with mirrors. He wants, too, some other decorations and knick-knacks for his room. He is fond of finery—like the rest of us, you know."

I saw that great French plate-glass mirror several months later. It was removed from the Aguinaldo sanctum, however, and braced up against a mango tree in front of the "palace" headquarters. A big, swarthy Kansan was taking his first shave before it after the capture of Malolos, March 31, 1899.

WHAT CONCESSIONS ARE, AND WHY

North China Daily News & Herald

The tradition of Chinese superiority over all the rest of mankind is very ancient, and collateral with it there has always been a contempt for the alien and a desire to keep him at arm's length. Only when the ruling families of China have been themselves alien and, at the same time, powerful enough to over-ride native tradition, has it been possible for outsiders to travel and reside in the country even on legitimate business. Under even the most liberal regimes, however, the whole tendency was to isolate such groups of foreign traders as contrived to take up their residence in the ports or the frontier trading centres and forbid them residence in the purely Chinese communities. Under the T'ang Dynasty, which collapsed a thousand years ago, there were such isolated Arab settlements in the Southern ports. An effort has always been made in Western China to keep the Mohammedans to their own communities and to allow Tibetans access to certain quarters only of certain specified trading towns. Under the late Manchu Dynasty, as under the earlier Mongol Dynasty, the subject Chinese were only too pleased that the conquerors built themselves cities apart and confined themselves to them. A hundred years or more before "extraterritoriality" was ever heard of, the Russians were limited to specified areas in Kalgan and Peking within which they had the right to reside and trade. In almost every city in Chinese Turkestan to-day the Chinese have arranged that they shall have one community and the Moslems another.

With this policy of isolating the alien has always gone the policy of extraterritorial jurisdiction, *at the suggestion of the Chinese authorities*. The idea behind it was that the Chinese could not condescend to understand the strange customs of the "barbarian" and that it was below their dignity to interfere with them. They therefore preferred that the alien communities settle their own affairs among themselves in their own outlandish ways, their only duty to China being the appointment of some one supreme authority who would be responsible to

China for the good order of the community and for the collection and remission of taxes. Within each such community its own customs and traditions, though they might be in contravention of everything Chinese, constituted the law of the community and were no concern of the Chinese authorities. The Turki, Afghans, Indians, Kazzaks, Mongols, Persians and other non-Chinese in Chinese Turkestan actually live under such an extraterritorial system to-day, to the perfect satisfaction of the Chinese authorities. The antiquity of the system is indicated by the fact that the term used to designate the headman of each alien community is a Chinese corruption of the term in the language of the ancient Huns for chieftain. Along the Chinese Tibetan border a great variety of tribes live in Chinese territory under an extraterritorial system with headmen known in Chinese as *T'u-ssu*. In Asiatic countries this system has been assumed to be the most convenient for all concerned and the Chinese themselves enjoyed extraterritorial rights on the Russian side of the Amur river down to comparatively recent times and have still later insisted upon such rights in Mongolia and Tibet.

All the early feuds, from the beginning of the sixteenth century down to the end of the eighteenth, came of the foreign trader's resentment of Chinese impositions and outrages, the foreigner's insistence upon his right to barter on fair terms with those Chinese who wanted to buy and sell and the Chinese official contention that the foreigner had no such right. No seizure of Chinese territory nor acquisition of any other right than that of peaceful access to Chinese markets, was then contemplated. In the defence of their right of arbitrary persecution of traders the Chinese finally lost in 1842, and then for the first time the question of how foreigners who were granted the right to trade in Chinese markets were to live and be governed, came up for discussion. The most natural and acceptable solution to the problems that arose was the one to which the Chinese were accustomed in their dealings with other "barbarians" on their frontiers; namely a system under which the detested aliens were to be segregated on otherwise worthless sites and were to be responsible to their headmen (their consuls), who would in turn be responsible to the Chinese authorities for the administration of justice, the punishment of crime and the keeping of order within the "barbarian" communities, thereby relieving the Chinese of the arduous task of meddling with their affairs.

This arrangement did not redound to the foreigner's honour and was no "concession" to any recognized superiority until the Concessions themselves began to develop and to surpass in magnificence, prosperity, peace, order and the administration of justice, as well as volume of trade, the squalid communities about them. The arrangement was not uncomplimentary to the Chinese until the Concessions, developed on supposedly worthless sites, made China's best efforts look puerile and clumsy, nor until the foreigner's systems of administration and justice proved the Chinese systems barbarous by attracting all the Chinese and all the Chinese wealth that could be crowded into them for greater security. The development of these communities by the foreigner has cost China and the Chinese neither fortune nor inconvenience, but has made a trade secure which has brought incalculable wealth into the country. The wretched sites rented to the foreigners as their ghettos, less than a century ago in nearly all cases, are now the most valuable property in China, thanks to foreign enterprise and Chinese enterprise under foreign direction, protection, and control. This increase in values is due in small measure only to the growth of the foreign populations within their ghettos, but to the passionate desire of the Chinese to crowd into territory where Chinese imposition and injustice do not strangle trade and industry, where they can publicly enjoy the fruits of their labours without fear of their confiscation. There can be no more striking argument than these patent facts against the return to Chinese administration of any territory which the foreigner has rented and developed.

As a matter of abstract justice the Chinese have no legitimate claim upon the control of properties developed by the alien. She has not opened her country to free residence, purchase of land and trade, and has not yet proposed to do so. She leased us ghettos to restrict our movements and limit our trade activities, and now that the least of these ghettos is worth more than her greatest and finest city, she says that their existence is derogatory to her dignity and insists upon cancelling the leases. Suppose that a corrupt, sluggish and shabby community in England or America gave a stranger a perpetual lease on swampy land in an undesirable slum, that he developed on it great commercial emporiums and desirable residences, and ran his affairs so fairly and honestly that every enterprising and decent member of an otherwise unhealthy community desired to live and do business nowhere else, would it be thought just if the leaders in the community, which had grown still more shabby, corrupt and demoralized, were to demand the cancellation of the lease, demand control of the whole business enterprise and threaten to hound the stranger out of the community if he did not comply? This is precisely the relative position of the foreigner in his Concessions and Settlements and of the Chinese "patriots" who demand the "return" to China of all that we have contributed to their war-torn and lawless country, as well as the surrender of their prosperous and happy fellow nationals within the Concession to the mercies of an officialdom, whether southern or northern, "nationalist" or militarist, from which any Chinese will pay all that he has to escape.

THE STRUGGLE AGAINST EXCLUSION

At the time of Marco Polo's visit to China, at the end of the 13th century, overland trade between the Near and Far East met with no obstacles and few impositions, and there is increasing evidence to show that under the Mongol régime European participation in this trade was important. A century later, however, China reverted under the native Ming dynasty to a policy of jealous, rigid exclusion, while political disruption in Central Asia barred all access by land. The search for a means of access by sea then became the dream of all the mariner-adventurers of Europe, but it was not until 1516 that the Portuguese navigator Perestrello, sailing from Malacca, actually reached the Chinese coast; while the first navigator to attempt trade was Andrade, who arrived at Canton in 1517 with two ships, received permission to trade and established a post there. Andrade's men showed no disposition, however, to carry themselves as suppliant barbarians or tribute bearers, and an anti-foreign demonstration—Canton's first—was fomented against them in 1522, during which their post was destroyed. The diminutive harbour of Macao, on the tip of a rugged peninsula at the mouth of the West River, was, however, leased to the Portuguese in 1537 and remained the only genuine "concession" in China until 1842.

The history of the various endeavours of the Portuguese, Spanish, Dutch, British, French, Americans and others to establish the right to trade with China in peace, free from imposition and insult, during the next three centuries is too long and intricate to outline here. Mutual jealousies among the trading nations enhanced the difficulties which the Chinese official passion for exclusion put in the way of free access. Contempt for the foreigner subjected all who were grudgingly given the right to live in restricted trading stations to almost unbearable abuse, and resentment of such abuse often led to friction which interrupted all trade except through the little port of Macao. Official greed, satisfying itself through the Co-hong monopoly, was a heavy burden at Canton, while the exactions imposed at other ports often forced complete withdrawal. No foreign official, let alone trader, was permitted to have any direct dealings with the Chinese officials, to enter a Chinese city, nor to wander away from the congested base assigned to the "barbarians." No trader was permitted to import a wife, or indeed women of any sort.

THE FIRST TREATIES

Under these conditions, adverse as they were, trade had grown to such proportions at the opening of the 19th century that a conflict was so inevitable that anyone but a short-sighted and arrogant Chinese Viceroy would have seen it coming; and it needed a very small spark in 1842 to start it. In this war the Chinese and Manchu armies were everywhere overwhelmingly defeated by a small British force and the war ended with the treaty of Nanking, the first "unequal treaty," by virtue of which China had for the first time to pretend to acknowledge the equality of an alien state. Hongkong, then a barren rock frequented by fishermen and pirates only, was ceded to Great Britain as a trading base, while Canton, Foochow, Ningpo and Shanghai were declared open to foreign trade, and provision was made for British subjects to reside in isolated communities on leased land in these ports. It was also agreed that the Chinese Government should fix and adhere to a fair Customs tariff to replace the erratic impositions that had so frequently throttled trade altogether.

It was not until 1847 that permission was given for the erection of churches *within the foreign communities,* and it was not until 1858 that the French made provision for missionary work and the toleration of Christianity outside the ports. It was not until 40 years later that diplomatic officials were granted access to the Court at Peking as the envoys of equal nations and consular officials were permitted to deal with Chinese provincial officials on a basis of equality. The whole history of foreign relations with China up to 1901, in fact, is the story of obstinate Chinese resistance to the foreign "barbarian's" assumption of equality or of his right to any other consideration than that of contemptuous tolerance.

By no means all of the treaty ports, settlements, open marts and ports of call, to which the foreigner now has access in China and her dependencies, were made available to international trade under duress or threat of war, as seems to be commonly believed abroad. Many have been thrown open at one time or another, to invite trade, by officials of the local and central Governments. It has been said by uninformed persons like Mr. Lloyd-George and Senator Borah that the foreigner holds 49 of China's finest cities. It can be said without the slightest fear of contradiction that, with the exception of the leased territories of Kuantung (Japanese), Kuangchowan (French), and Weihaiwei (British), the last two to be returned when the Chinese will have them, *there is not a single Chinese native city in this whole land* that is under foreign control or government of any sort. The foreigner controls nothing but what he built up himself, and if there happen to be many thousands of Chinese dwelling in these communities, under foreign police control (but not subject to foreign courts), they are rather intruders into the foreign ghettos than victims of foreign oppression, who have crowded into the areas allotted to the alien because they trusted him more than they did their own officials. In only 17 out of the 49 cities, of which the agitators have so much to say, are there Concessions or Settlements under any form of foreign administration. In the others the foreigners are scattered about through the native communities, subject to consular jurisdiction, but also subject in most respects to Chinese police regulations and, indirectly, to local taxation.

The great misconception abroad seems to be that the Concessions and Settlements coincide with the Chinese cities from which, for convenience, they take their names. Nothing could be more misleading. In many cases they are at no little distance from the cities from which they take their names, though by the nature of things, as the foreign Settlement grows in importance the Chinese population edges up to it, surrounds it and all but overflows it. The best way to make this clear is to take the major foreign communities, one by one, and give some account of their creation, character and present circumstances.

HONGKONG

As we have already stated, Hongkong was in 1842 a barren island whose mountains rose precipitously from the sea, a refuge for a handful of pirates and fishermen. For a century or more the life of the trader at Canton had been so uncomfortable and precarious, thanks to systematic persecution, that Great Britain felt the need of a trading base somewhat removed from the turbulent Cantonese and their truculent officials, where she could warehouse her goods and protect her subjects. The intrinsic worth of the base was no consideration and the little island chosen was known to be of no real value to China. Nothing grew on it and, so far as then appeared, there was no room for the development of a city between the shore and the base of the mountains. By private treaty with the few inhabitants, the entire island could probably have been purchased for less than a thousand pounds.

We know from the records of the negotiations that the Chinese did not demur in the slightest degree to its cession. They considered it worthless and probably were glad to know that the British contemplated establishing their trading station on an island so far from Canton. Neither the makers of the treaty of 1842 nor the founders of this little colony could possibly have foreseen the amazing development that has come in less than a century. There are a thousand other similar rocks along the China coast, as barren as Hongkong was in 1842, but Hongkong is one of the great ports of the world. There was little room for a city on the level; so the city grew up the precipitous mountain side. It was a bleak place then and uninviting; it is now one of the most beautiful places in the world. The total trade in 1841 would not have kept a modern Chinese shopkeeper in cigarettes. In 1924 the trade amounted to £135,830,272, and the shipping to 56,731,077 tons.

The building up of this amazing little colony was due to British energy, imagination, enterprise and probity, but the benefits derived have never been jealously guarded for British subjects. The non-Chinese residents numbered, in 1924, 16,000; the Chinese residents 783,550. It is estimated that between 80 and 90 percent. of the property and commercial shares held in Hongkong are in Chinese hands. It is impossible to estimate what share of the wealth which this big Chinese population amasses in Hongkong goes into investments on the mainland, but it must be large. No Chinese has ever dreamed of developing a port like Hongkong on any other rock along the coast. They would all laugh at the thought of attempting it. Yet the acquisition and development of Hongkong is represented in all "nationalist" literature as one of the grossest of Britain's imperialistic sins against China, something which she would expiate by the return to Chinese control if she had a conscience. Though the trade of Hongkong has poured unlimited wealth into Canton and all the commercial centres of the South, and has made possible an enormous development in the export trade from Kuangtung, the "Nationalists" have been scheming for many years to wreck the colony and look forward greedily to the day when they can recover it and swagger through its desolated streets.

CANTON

The present foreign Concessions at Canton, on the little island of Shameen, were acquired by the British and French in 1861, simply to give foreigners a place adjacent to the ever-hostile city where they could at least live in peace, even when trade was disrupted by anti-foreign demonstrations. It lies in the Pearl River, some hundreds of yards from what was once the walled city, separated from a suburb by a narrow creek or canal. The total area of the island is about 53 acres, and it is not made up of land taken from the Chinese, but was *actually built up* at great cost, between stone retaining walls, on a sand bank in shallow water, by British and French enterprise. It is now a park-like residential quarter, with fine trees and gardens, such as one sees nowhere else about squalid, shabby Canton. It has no commercial value, in that no river steamer can approach within a furlong of it, and it is not near enough to the business centres of Canton to be a suitable site for a shopping district. Yet the Cantonese, with their own huge city under their untrammelled jurisdiction, resent its existence bitterly and are forever talking about how they will "improve" it when it comes under their control.

SHANGHAI

The right of foreigners to buy land in the vicinity of the city of Shanghai and reside on the mud flats on the Huangpu river front was granted the British under treaty of 1842, and to the French and Americans by their treaties of 1844. What was then the British Concession was opened in perpetuity, at a fixed land rent or tax, in 1843; the French Concession in 1849. The Americans also acquired a Concession in an area known as Hongkew. The British Concession stretched along the west bank of the Huangpu river, about a mile from the Chinese city. The French Concession was south of the British Concession, almost contiguous with the Chinese city, while the American Concession lay to the north of the British Concession, separated from it by a creek. All three plots of land were wretchedly low, swampy and unsuitable for building. Water could be struck almost anywhere three feet below the surface, drainage seemed impossible, and it promised to be an unhealthy site. Yet here again foreign courage and enterprise reared an edifice which never fails to astonish tourists on their first visit.

In 1869 the British and American Concessions were pooled. Land Regulations, which virtually consitute a charter, were agreed upon with the approval of the Chinese Government and the various foreign Powers represented in the community, and the International Settlement blossomed forth with a Municipal

Council elected by the "Ratepayers," or renters of land. The French Concession maintained its identity, but is, like the International Settlement, open to the residence of all nationalities. The Municipal Council now numbers nine members of various nationalities. The Council elects one of its own members Chairman, who functions somewhat in the capacity of a Mayor, the present Chairman being an American.

The one fact that must be clearly understood abroad is that the city of Shanghai, as it existed prior to 1843, is still as much under Chinese jurisdiction as it ever was and is subject to no foreign control whatsoever. The same is true of the vast suburbs of the foreign-controlled area that have grown up about it. Since according to Treaty, the foreigners who originally settled within their prescribed Concessions were limited to them, it was also understood that no Chinese was to own land within the bounds of the Concessions. This has always been easily evaded by the purchase of land in the name of a foreigner, so that now there are in the combined foreign areas 30,000 alien residents of all nationalities and 1,100,000 Chinese. In the immediate suburbs which crowd around the Settlement and the French Concession there are 1,200,000 Chinese, the majority of whom would be inside the foreign boundaries under foreign police regulation if they could find space or could afford the higher rentals.

The original city of Shanghai, over which foreigners have never sought jurisdiction, is a tawdry little walled town about a mile in diameter which, though it has a generous waterfront of its own, has not progressed in any degree since 1843. Its houses are hovels, its streets average ten feet in width and are filthy and ill-paved. It has no drainage system and its public water is undrinkable. A mile down the waterfront is an imposing row of marble, granite, steel and concrete buildings—on no better site than the native city or a score of other shabby Chinese communities on the river. Some of the newer communities that have grown up around the Settlement have emulated the foreigner to some degree and are more respectable, but their land values are far below those within the Settlement. Land in the heart of the old city can be bought for £300 an acre or less. The nearer the Settlement the higher the price, until, within the boundaries of the foreign controlled areas, the values per acre range from £25,000 to £200,000.

These contrasts have not inspired the "Nationalist" to preach emulation, but to demand control—in short, confiscation. The Shanghai community is visited every year by enormous numbers of Chinese from every province who make the inevitable comparisons. Under "Nationalist" tuition they are led to believe that such an astonishing display of the foreigner's capacity is not only derogatory to China's prestige but is the emblem of a menace to her independent existence. They are therefore easily persuaded to join in the cry for the retrocession of Shanghai, knowing that that would mean ruin. The worse conditions become elsewhere in China, the greater the contrast between foreign efficiency and native ineptitude, and therefore the louder the anti-foreign cry. In such situations as this any clear-headed observer will find the key to the quality of "Nationalism" and to most of the agitator's "legitimate aspirations."

HANKOW

The native town of Hankow is officially and historically the least of three cities grouped about the confluence of the Han and Yangtze Rivers, within a rifle shot of one another, Wuchang, Hanyang and Hankow. They are collectively known to the Chinese as the Wu-Han cities. Wuchang is the provincial capital of the Province of Hupeh; Hanyang was once an important county seat and is now an industrial town; Hankow was until a generation ago a mushroom growth, a market town of no official status, grown into a great commercial city because its foreshore on both the Han and Yangtze Rivers afforded the safest and best junk anchorage. The Yangtze River flows generally from west to east, but in its course through the Wu-Han cities it flows from south to north. Wuchang, then, is on the east side of the Yangtze, while Hankow and Hanyang, divided by the Han River which flows in from the west, are on the west bank, Hanyang being to the south, almost immediately opposite Wuchang, and Hankow to the north. The foreign Concessions, as they once were, extend in a narrow strip along the Yangtze river front from the city of Hankow northwards, British, Russian, French, German and Japanese, in that order. These relative positions are essential to an understanding of the vast body of news that has emanated from Hankow during the past ten months.

The Yangtze Valley was thrown open to foreign trade by virtue of the British and French treaties of 1858 ratified in 1860, after the allied forces had taken Peking. In 1861 the renowned Harry Parkes, whose name is associated with the creation of so many of the British trading settlements in China, sailed up the Yangtze, visiting the various ports and arranging single-handed for the lease of land for British commercial colonies in such centres as he thought suitable for trade. Having arrived at Hankow, he negotiated without any difficulty or friction for the lease of a narrow strip of river front, then wholly unoccupied, north of and adjacent to the ruined city of Hankow, which had been fired and totally destroyed by the Taiping rebels seven years before. The business quarter of Hankow was then at the other end of the city and Hanyang was still an important commercial centre, so that the unoccupied land that Parkes bought was not precisely in the thick of things.

Some years later the Concession was deepened by treaty, so that the total area is now 149 acres. The area was so small, in fact, that before the advantage of being near the foreign Concession had dawned upon the Chinese merchants of the port, it had been pretty well taken up by British and other foreign establishments, so that it was physically impossible for the Chinese to flow into it as they have done into Shanghai, and the Chinese population has never numbered much more than seven thousand, except in seasons of panic such as the advent of the "Nationalists" in September, when more than thirty thousand persons contrived to pack into the Concession for safety. As usual, however, all the big business of the native city has crowded up to the Concession, and the narrow street dividing the native town from the British Concession is occupied on both sides by the banks, jewellers, silk shops and others whose wares are precious. Also, as in all such foreign centres, commerce has emerged from the city and flowed around behind the Foreign Concessions, so that a very great and rich Chinese commercial quarter parallels the narrow strip of Concessions, running from south to north. Steamers of all nationalities lie off the foreign foreshore, or as near to it as they can get, while the Hankow city waterfront is patronized by nothing but junks and launches.

The situation here is the same as in all other similar communities. The foreigner took an unoccupied site, away from the centre of things, and within a few years made that site the commercial centre of a great community. There was no geographical advantage in his position, for if there had been the Chinese, who were more than two thousand years before him, would have discovered it. He made his community the centre by virtue of his own enterprise and the fact that under the jurisdiction of his own people he was able, until recently betrayed in the name of "conciliation," to live and trade in peace of mind and without fear of impositions, exactions or official tyranny. As usual, his special position enabled him to bring a great deal more wealth to his Chinese neighbours than to himself, so his Chinese neighbours crowded around to be near the source of prosperity and to share, if possible, a little of his immunity from danger and oppression.

It is to this situation that the "Nationalists" have put an end in Hankow through virulent propaganda and mob violence; and by signing the recent agreement—now notorious in the East as "the Great Betrayal"—the British Government has not only acquiesced in the humiliation and deliberately planned abuse of their nationals, but to the inevitable ruin of a trade establishment founded upon the foreigner's right to conduct his business in a state of immunity from persecution and imposition. There is no sane Chinese nor foreigner in this country who can see how the "Nationalist's" mad passion for economic destruction, nor the British Government's weak deference to this passion, can bring anything but the demoralization of trade and ensuing misery to the people of Central China. The criminal folly of the whole British *debacle* in Hankow stands out all the more clearly when it is remembered that neither the French nor the Japanese, with their similar Concessions under similar administration, have been asked by the "Nationalists," nor have expressed any intention, to make such a surrender as Britain has made. The open discrimination in Hankow against Great Britain is overwhelming proof, if any were required, that Red Chinese diplomacy is completely under the control of Red Russia, so the British surrender does not appear to any competent observer in China as satisfying China's "legitimate aspirations," but as a retreat before Moscow's conquest of the East.

KIUKIANG AND KULING

Kiukiang, strictly speaking, was never created a Concession, but simply grew to be one for the greater convenience of the Chinese authorities and the foreign residents. Like Hankow, it was leased by Harry Parkes in 1861. It is a very small bit of land, a few hundred yards either way, on the river front, remote, like most leaseholds, from the Chinese city and the Chinese waterfront. As elsewhere, the native communities have crept up upon it and surrounded it. The administration, which was of the simplest and most unpretentious sort, was evolved by the residents to relieve the Chinese of the task of policing it and attending to its public works, or rather to do what the Chinese would not do to the foreigner's satisfaction. No community in China could have been as innocent of "imperialism" nor have lived on fairer and more honest relations with the Chinese community that benefited by foreign trade.

A short distance from Kiukiang, in the Lushan range, is a mountain summer resort known as Kuling, long patronized by foreigners and, in recent years, by an increasingly large number of wealthy Chinese. The existence of this resort is said to give highly remunerative employment to 1,500 Chinese of the Kiukiang district. The "Nationalists" not only hounded the foreigners, including the British Consul out of Kiukiang, but permitted their soldiers to loot and befoul all foreign premises, while urging the mob to an antiforeign frenzy in Kiukiang which forced all foreign residents of Kuling to withdraw while escape was possible. In the face of this Russian-inspired patriotism the Concession at Kiukiang has now been turned over to the local Red administration by the British Government, and foreigners have been generally notified that Kuling will not be a safe summer residence. The cost of this to the Chinese community will be enormous, while no foreign resident of the port of Kiukiang, in the face of the continued agitation that has followed the yielding up of the Concession, presumes to believe that British or other foreign trade can amount to anything under the new conditions.

TIENTSIN

In Tientsin the foreign Concessions, closely grouped together along the windings of the Hai or Pei River, form a compact community, but were orginally even further removed from the native city and its suburbs than most such communities. Much of the land upon which Tientsin has grown up is, like Shanghai, lowlying, waterlogged, difficult to drain and subject to flood. The British and French Concessions were leased in 1861, following upon the ratification of the treaty of 1858, which opened the port to foreign trade. After the British came the Russians, Belgians, Austrians, and Italians. Even the Americans had a small leased area, later incorporated in the British Concession. As in all other ports, the land leased and developed by foreign enterprise was unoccupied and a great part of it could not even be cultivated. Like Shanghai there was ample room in the Tientsin Concessions for a Chinese invasion, commercial and other. With each collapse of Government in Peking, the Tientsin Concessions become the refuge of a host of unseated officials, fleeing from imprisonment or execution. This flight has come to be anticipated by successive groups of officials as an inevitable procedure, so that most old officials already have houses in one Concession or another, and it is now the concern of every new official who rises to eminence in Peking to build or purchase such a "funk-hole." Nearly all the handsomest residences and a great deal of the most valuable property are therefore owned by wealthy Chinese of the official class. The number of establishments of this sort, of almost palatial proportions, runs into the hundreds. The small trader and the big merchant are also present. In the British, Belgian, Japanese, Italian and French Concessions there are therefore 8,969 foreigners as against 98,544 Chinese. There are no figures available for the former Russian, German, and Austrian Concessions, which have now reverted to Chinese control, with depressing results, but the proportions are estimated to be about the same. The adjoining native city, suburbs and environs are presumed to have a population of about half a million. They are, of course, under untrammelled Chinese control.

The foreign Concessions in Tientsin, being well out of the zone of "nationalistic" endeavour and beyond the reach of organized Russian propaganda, have so far been free from molestation and are not an immediate Red objective as the International Settlement at Shanghai is, but there can be no doubt that the "nationalistic" spirit is pervading the North. It is very contagious, and the discomfiture of the foreigner, even at enormous cost to trade and the well-being of those who live under foreign jurisdiction, is sufficiently flattering to Chinese vanity to appeal in any quarter as a noble aim. It is, therefore, not surprising that while no anti-foreign demonstrations have as yet occurred in the North, the present Peking Administration, unrecognized by the Powers as it is, has given the British Legation to understand that it expects the surrender of the British Concession to Chinese control.

Persisting in its infatuation, its discredited theory that conciliation would eventually create an atmosphere in which reasonable negotiations could be conducted and normal trade resumed, the British Government responded to this demand by offering to modify the status of the Tientsin Concession so that the Chinese would not only have equal representation on the Council, but so that there would be a Chinese president of the Council also, a political appointee of whatever Government happened to be adjacent who would have power to veto any action by the Council that he considered detrimental to China's "sovereign rights." The opportunities which such a scheme offered for official meddling with the affairs of the Concession, for the introduction of all manner of corruption and knavery, was at once apparent to every Chinese resident and the value of land promptly went into a decline, real estate was thrown on the market, capital went abroad, and land values and all other investments in the Japanese Leased Territory of Liaotung rose proportionately. No more eloquent appraisement than this of the folly of Britain's policy could possibly be written.

THE MORAL

As a last word on the subject of Concessions, it must be reasserted that it has only been within the past few years that any class of Chinese looked upon them as derogatory to China's dignity or as infringements of her sovereignty. The idea of isolating the unwelcome foreigner on patches of waste land where he would not interfere with the even flow of Chinese life, and could be left to his own strange devices, was for many years a most satisfactory conception. The word "concession" is an unfortunate translation of the term which the Chinese applied to these isolation camps from the very beginning. The Chinese phrase means a "rented enclosure," and there is no implication of cession in the term, but rather the thought of fencing the alien off on a rented tract.

At a later date, when the great growth and prosperity of these "rented enclosures" overcame native prejudice, and commerce began to crowd into and around them, the foreigner in his Concession was looked upon very much as a landlord might view a tenant in a neighbouring house, whose enterprise enriched the whole neighbourhood and raised property values and whose prestige and influence gave his neighbours a feeling of importance and security.

The unreasoning, rabid resentment of the "Nationalists," who would rather wreck all China than see the foreigner prosper on Chinese soil, was instilled into the popular mind by disillusioned students from abroad and has latterly been whipped into a frenzy by Russian agitators. While the Concessions are intact and the foreigner retains control of them, China cannot be wholly ruined nor can China's foreign trade, for the commerce and industry of tortured and distracted China can take refuge in them. Once get the "Nationalist" and his mob into them, however, and the foreigner must go, leaving China to be Bolshevized, reduced to the depths of Russian wretchedness, at Moscow's discretion.

MID-CENTURY REBELS

Translated by Jeh-hang Lai

Over the centuries China witnessed thousands of violent uprisings. Yet no period suffered so many as the mid-nineteenth century, from 1850 to 1873, when the vast Taiping Rebellion brought in its wake the Nian Rebellion in the North, Moslem rebellions in the Southwest and Northwest, a Miao rebellion in the Southwest, secret society rebellions along the coast, and many more.

Rebellions varied considerably in their origins and organization. Some were started by bands of hungry peasants, others by well-organized secret societies that had elaborate ideologies incorporating elements from popular Buddhism and Daoism. The Taiping Rebellion even made use of some Christian beliefs. Nevertheless, virtually all rebellions that had any success also invoked the Confucian theory of the mandate of Heaven: the emperor had ceased to rule with virtue; therefore, he had lost his mandate and his subjects had the right to rebel.

Sources for the goals, organizing principles, and behavior of rebels are scarce. When rebellions failed, the documents they produced were destroyed as dangerous. The officials who suppressed the rebels wrote reports, but most of them lacked firsthand knowledge, objectivity, or sympathy. To overcome some of these shortcomings, the mid-century rebellions are probed here through three sources of differing origin. The first is a group of proclamations of the Small Sword Society, issued when they took over the city of Xiamen on the coast of Fujian, and preserved by British diplomats stationed there. The Small Sword Society was one of the secret societies that joined in the general initiative of the Taipings to take several cities in the early 1850s. These proclamations reveal typical rebel ideology—for instance, evoking the name of the Ming dynasty and the Han people as an anti-Manchu gesture. The second source is the "confessions" a group of rebels made after their capture. These rebels were members of bandit groups loosely related to the Taipings. The third source is a request for military aid sent in by members of the gentry of that same area. These two pieces, which were also preserved by British officials, can be used together to analyze the social milieu that gave rise to banditry and rebellion.

PROCLAMATIONS OF THE XIAMEN SMALL SWORD SOCIETY

1

The Grand Marshal Huang of the Ming dynasty and the Han people, in order to safeguard the lives of the commoners and merchants, proclaims martial law:

I have heard that Heaven and earth change their course of order: after a time of great prosperity, there must follow a period of chaos, and after a period of great turmoil, there must arise a general desire for peace.

The Qing dynasty has been governing China for more than two hundred years. Corruption of officials and oppression of the people clearly indicate that its mandate has come to an end. I now lead the Righteous and Benevolent Army to save the people and to punish those who have been cruel. I have ordered that my soldiers shall pillage neither the merchants nor the common people nor shall they rape women. The arrival of my armies will not cause the slightest disturbance to the people. If any soldier disobeys my orders I shall punish him in accordance with martial law, permitting no favoritism. You, the merchants and the people, should apply yourselves to your tasks and should not be frightened. I am strict in abiding by my words and enforcing my orders. You should obey them unerringly.

10th day of the fourth month, 1853

2

Concerning the safety of the people and normal business:

I, the grand marshal, have led my army to recover the southern provinces, to stabilize peace for the four classes of people, and to eliminate bad officials.

Since the emperor of the Qing government is young and ignorant, power has been concentrated in the hands of wicked advisors and officials of the prefectures and counties plunder the wealth of the people and use it to ingratiate themselves with their superiors. As a result the people are oppressed by greedy officials.

I, the grand marshal, have led the Righteous and Benevolent Army and have recovered Haicheng, Zhangzhou, Guankou, and Tongan. My army has advanced with irresistible power. If my subordinates have any unruly soldiers who rape women and create disturbances in the streets, you should report them to my officers immediately. I shall execute them and display their heads in public in accordance with the law.

All the people—merchants and commoners alike—should carry on with their work and trade as usual. Do not be afraid of my soldiers. After issuing an order I enforce it immediately and do not tolerate offenders. My orders must be obeyed.

3

In the name of the Grand Ming dynasty, Marshal Huang of the Han people proclaims:

It is well known that the way to good government is through benevolent policies; yet military strength is essential in governing a state. At this moment I have already conquered Xiamen and must now appoint capable persons to govern it. When employing capable individuals in the government one should pay special attention to their military ability. For this reason those who are able to pacify the world must exert care in choosing men.

Now the people of Xiamen come seeking to take the oaths and join our society. There are hundreds of millions of them. If I do not proclaim the rules of recruitment, I am afraid that the wrong persons will be selected, thereby causing an unnecessary waste of time and resources. With the proclamation of this edict, those of you who have obtained the righteous banners from me and who are willing to reconstruct the nation with me should be very careful in the recruitment of more members. Only the young and the strong and those with experience in the martial arts should be selected as our members. We must eliminate the very old, the very young, and the disabled. In other words, we must eliminate all those over sixty years of age and all those under sixteen. Only by following this method can we strengthen our forces. Do not transgress this order.

15th day of the fourth month, 1853

A STATEMENT OF VOLUNTARY SURRENDER BY MEMBERS OF THE GUANGXI ROVING BANDIT GROUP

We men from Guangdong—Da Liyu, Zhang Zhao, Zhang Guihe, Wen Xi—and we men from Guangxi—Tian Fang, Huang Shou, and Liang Fu—make this appeal.

We were born in a time of prosperity and were good people. We lived in towns and were taught to distinguish right from wrong. But because of continuous flooding in our area, we could not get a grain of rice to eat even if we worked hard in the fields, and we could not engage in business because we lacked the funds. As a result we all joined the bandits.

Not long ago we came to Guangxi to try to make a living. We met others who had come from our hometowns. We pitied each other because of our sad situation, and together we began to imitate outlaws in order to relieve our hungry stomachs. In other words, no one forced us to join the outlaws. We were driven to join them because we were desperate. Given the chance, we would have returned gladly to our normal way of life.

We thought constantly of our families, but we could not return to them. Indeed, we were drifting on a hungry, painful sea and knew not when we would reach the other side. We hope Your Excellency will forgive our past sins. We hope you will think of the great benevolence of our imperial house and give us a chance to start a new life.

We, humble people, Big-Headed Yang, Lo Da, Hou Jiu, Wang Liu, Lu Xiongjie, report our grievance and appeal to you. . . .

We hate the army runners who recently made heavy demands on us and disturbed our villages. They used the excuse of establishing a local militia to cause trouble for the good and honest people and create opportunities for the wicked ones. The words they used were virtuous-sounding; yet the deeds they actually perpetrated were most wicked. They allied themselves with government officials and formed cliques so that they could oppress our village and falsely reported that certain persons were connected with the bandits. This was due to personal grudges against the accused or to the fact that they wanted to obtain rewards. They burned down our houses and took all we had; they robbed us of our property and threatened our lives. Therefore we banded together to insure our own safety. Those who still remain in the village may run away someday while those who have left can hardly come back. Therefore, for each ordinary person who ran away, there was one more bandit, and the numbers of bandits became greater and greater. Since there are so many of us, we could not survive except by pillage, nor could we save our lives if we did not fight against the imperial troops that were sent out to exterminate us. As a consequence, we have offended the court and hurt the merchants.

We have always wanted to correct our behavior and to purge ourselves of our beastly nature. We would have liked to return to our homes to enjoy long and happy lives, but we have been left rambling around, wandering through unknown places because the officials did not have mercy on us. Usually after interrogating a bandit, they would kill him or at least expel him. Therefore those who sincerely wanted to correct their past sins were actually risking their lives. If we had surrendered to the officials, we also would have had to depend on their mercy. The thought of it tortures us day and night. Now, fortunately, Your Excellency has arrived in this area with a commission to pacify the people. You have loved the people like your own children; you have disciplined yourself strictly; you have worked diligently for the good of the nation and have relieved the suffering of the masses. We hope that you will understand our situation and judge fairly. We hope you will treat us leniently and extend your benevolence to us. We are willing to sell our weapons and buy cows for farming. We render all our respect and gratitude to you.

We respectfully report our situation to you.

MEMORIAL OF LI YUYING, JUREN DEGREE HOLDER, AND TAN DUANYUAN, SHENGYUAN DEGREE HOLDER, FROM WU PREFECTURE, GUANGXI PROVINCE

Our dynasty has followed the teachings of the ancient sages. As a result everyone in Rong county has lived in harmony for a long time. The population was increasing, and the resources were plentiful; even our dogs and chickens never had to fear disturbance. . . . However, in 1846 bandits and rebels began gathering on the east side of Liangxu and disturbed our local tranquillity. As their power grew, their influence spread. They even captured the city and took the government officials prisoner. There was no order in the city, and the rebels roamed everywhere. Gentry members were killed and captured; women were raped. Corpses were left lying all over the ground; houses were left in ashes; the farmers' fields were thick with weeds. It was sad indeed to see these things happen. . . . They pillaged property even at great distances from their base area and forced the people who were under their control to pay land taxes to them. They connived to force officials to send up false reports saying that loyalist forces had recaptured areas that had fallen to the rebels. The bandits used official seals and issued false edicts to the populace. It was intolerable to have these ruffians dominate the local government!

Last year we were lucky to have the governor and the governor-general decide to lead out their armies to destroy the bandits at Xunzhou. The governor then promised to transfer the army to Rong county where the local militia was trying to consolidate its positions pending the arrival of the government troops. The militia have been fighting for a long time and have become quite weary. I am afraid that, if the local militia collapses, the bandits will roam all over the county and prove very difficult for the government troops to control.

The local militia is capable of mustering ten thousand troops, all battle-tested veterans who hate the rebels. It is our opinion that, if only we could get a skilled commander, the militia would be quite effective against the rebels. Unfortunately, we have not been able to get an experienced officer to lead them. There have been constant arguments over battle plans, and the militia has never acted in unison. As a result we have often been defeated by the rebels. The prefect and governor-general appointed a pair of officers to supervise the local militia. They issued orders, gave out banners and seals, but did not come to take command personally. The local militia, therefore, has not been united and cannot contribute much to alleviating the critical situation.

Now that the governor of Guangxi province has dispatched his army to wipe out the bandits in Xunzhou, we hope that, after finishing with the bandits there, it will come immediately to Rong county to exterminate the rebels and save the people. If Your Excellency sympathizes with all that the people have suffered, please hasten to have the army come here to suppress the rebels. . . . We might suggest that you consolidate the militias of Teng, Pingnan, Beiliu, Chenqi, and Xinyi counties under your command so that the bandits may not escape our troops by hopping back and forth across county borders. When the government armies arrive in Rong county, have them train the local militia so that it can put up a better defense against the bandits. We would suggest also that you proclaim a general amnesty for those who were forced to join the rebels. We have confidence in the strategy of encircling bandit hideouts; we are sure they could not resist your attacks and their days would be numbered. . . .

Huang Pengfen and Feng Weireng are two leaders well respected by the local militia. If you were to appoint them commanders, they would get cooperation and would be able to help achieve the goal of ridding our area of rebels. When your armies arrive here we would personally like to join them to take your orders and give you assistance if needed. With your great talent and ability as a high civil and military official, you will certainly save our people from their hardships. . . .

With the greatest humility we present these opinions to you.

THE BOXER REBELLION, 1900

Fei Ch'i-hao

Fei Ch'i-hao was a Chinese Christian. Here he recounts the activities of the millenialist "Boxers" in the Boxer Rebellion of 1900.

THE GATHERING OF THE STORM

The people of Shansi are naturally timid and gentle, not given to making disturbances, being the most peaceable people in China. So our Shansi Christians were hopeful for themselves, even when the reports from the coast grew more alarming. But there was one thing which caused us deep apprehension, and that was the fact that the wicked, cruel Yü Hsien, the hater of foreigners, was the newly appointed Governor of Shansi. He had previously promoted the Boxer movement in Shantung, and had persuaded the Empress Dowager that the Boxers had supernatural powers and were true patriots.

Early in June my college friend K'ung Hsiang Hsi came back from T'ung-chou for his vacation, reporting that the state of affairs there and at Peking was growing worse, that the local officials were powerless against the Boxers, and that the Boxers, armed with swords, were constantly threatening Christians scattered in the country.

From this time we had no communication with Tientsin or Peking. All travellers were searched, and if discovered bearing foreign letters they were killed. So though several times messengers were started out to carry our letters to the coast, they were turned back by the Boxers before they had gone far. It was not long before the Boxers, like a pestilence, had spread all over Shansi. School had not closed yet in Fen Chou Fu, but as the feeling of alarm deepened, fathers came to take their boys home, and school was dismissed before the end of June.

Source: Luella Miner, *Two Heroes of Cathay*, (N.Y.: Fleming H. Revell, 1907), pp. 63–128, quoted in Eva Jane Price, *China Journal, 1889–1900* (N.Y.: Charles Scribner's Sons, 1989), pp. 245–247, 254–261, 268–274.

Mr. and Mrs. Lundgren and Miss Eldred of the China Inland Mission had come to Mrs. Price's about the middle of June, and after the Boxer trouble began they were unable to leave. Mr. and Mrs. Lundgren soon heard that their mission at P'ing Yao had been burned.

During the two long months that followed not a word reached us from beyond the mountains. The church in Shansi walked in darkness, not seeing the way before it.

The wicked Governor, Yü Hsien, scattered proclamations broadcast. These stated that the foreign religions overthrew morality and inflamed men to do evil, so now gods and men were stirred up against them, and Heaven's legions had been sent to exterminate the foreign devils. Moreover there were the Boxers, faithful to their sovereign, loyal to their country, determined to unite in wiping out the foreign religion. He also offered a reward to all who killed foreigners, either titles or office or money. When the highest official in the province took such a stand in favor of the Boxers, what could inferior officials do? People and officials bowed to his will, and all who enlisted as Boxers were in high favor. It was a time of license and anarchy, when not only Christians were killed, but hundreds of others against whom individual Boxers had a grudge.

Crowds of people kept passing our mission gate to see what might be happening, for the city was full of rumors. "The foreigners have all fled." "Many foreigners from other places have gathered here." "A great cannon has been mounted at the mission gate." "The foreigners have hired men to poison wells, and to smear gates with blood."

I was staying in the compound with the Prices, inside the west gate of the city, and Mr. and Mrs. Atwater, with their children, Bertha and Celia, lived near the east gate. On the 28th of June all day long a mob of one or two hundred roughs, with crowds of boys, stood at the gate of the Atwater place, shouting:

"Kill the foreigners, loot the houses."

Mr. Atwater came out once and addressed the crowd:

"Friends, don't make this disturbance; whoever would like to come in, I invite to come, and we will talk together."

When the crowd saw Mr. Atwater come out, they all retreated, but when he shut the gate they thronged back again with mad shouts. This happened several times. By six or seven in the evening the crowd had increased and gathered courage. The gate was broken down and they surged in, some shouting, some laying hands on whatever they could find to steal, some throwing stones and brickbats at the windows. As they rushed in, Mr. Atwater and his family walked through their midst and took refuge in the Yamen of the District Magistrate, which was near by. The Magistrate, not even waiting for his official chair, ran at once to the mission and arrested two men with his own hands. His attendants followed close behind him, and the mob scattered. The Magistrate then sent soldiers to stand guard at the mission gate, and the Atwaters came to live with the Prices. We expected the mob to make an attack on us that same night, but we were left in peace. . . .

Late in July a proclamation of the Governor was posted in the city in which occurred the words, "Exterminate foreigners, kill devils." Native Christians must leave the church or pay the penalty with their lives. Li Yij and I talked long and earnestly over plans for saving the lives of our beloved missionaries. "You must not stay here waiting for death," we said. Yet we realized how difficult it would be to escape. Foreigners with light hair and fair faces are not easily disguised. Then where could they go? Eastward toward the coast all was in tumult. Perhaps the provinces to the south were just as bad. Our best way would be to find a place of concealment in the mountains. Li Yo and I thought that the chances of escape would be better if the missionaries divided into two companies; they must carry food, clothing, and bedding, and the large company would surely attract attention. Moreover, if they were in two parties, and one was killed, the other might escape. So Li Yü and I went to talk the matter over with Mr. Han, the former helper, and a Deacon Wang. Both of these men had recanted, but they still loved their foreign friends. Deacon Wang, who lived in a village over ten miles from Fen Chou Fu, wished to conceal Mr. and Mrs. Price and little Florence in his home for a day or two, and then take them very secretly to a broken-down temple in the mountains. Li Yü said to me:

"If you can escape with Mr. and Mrs. Price to the mountains, I will try to take the Atwaters, Mr. and Mrs. Lundgren, and Miss Eldred to another place in the mountains."

But when I proposed this plan to Mr. and Mrs. Price, they said:

"We missionaries do not wish to be separated. We must be in one place, and if we die we want to die together."

When I spoke to them again about going, they said:

"Thank you for your love, but we do not want to desert the other missionaries."

"You will not be deserting them," I pleaded. "If you decide to flee with me, Mr. Li will do his best to escape with the others."

Then I brought forward all my arguments to persuade them. Again all consulted together, and decided to go. I think this was the last day of July—the very day of the Tai Ku tragedy. Mr. and Mrs. Price made up two bundles of baggage and gave them to Mr. Han, to be carried secretly to Deacon Wang's home. Mr. Han paid a large price for a covered cart to wait for us secretly at ten o'clock in the evening at the gate of an old temple north of the mission. We were to walk to the cart, as it would attract attention if the cart stopped near the mission. We could not leave by the front gate, for the four Yamen men were guarding it; and patrolling the streets in front by day and night were twenty soldiers, ostensibly protecting us, but, as we surmised, stationed there to prevent the escape of foreigners. I went privately to the back of the compound and unlocked an unused gate, removing also a stone which helped to keep it shut. I had already made up a bundle to carry with me, and asked Mr. Jen, a Christian inquirer, to take care of it while I was helping Mr. and Mrs. Price to get ready. After I had opened the gate I asked Mr. Jen to wait there until I went into the south court to call the Prices.

Man proposes, but God disposes. A Mr. Wang who had often come to the mission knew that we were planning to escape that night and saw me give my bundle to Mr. Jen. Thinking that it must contain some valuable things belonging to the Prices, an evil thought entered his heart. He watched when Mr. Jen laid the bundle in a small empty room close by the gate, and after he came out, Mr. Wang went into the room. Mr. Jen thought nothing of this, supposing that Mr. Wang was a friend. But in a minute he saw Mr. Wang rush out of the room, leap over the wall, and run away. Going at once into the room and not finding the bundle, he lost his head completely, and set up a loud wail. His one thought was that he had been faithless to his trust, and sitting down in the back gate which I had opened so secretly, he cried at the top of his voice, thus bringing to naught our carefully laid plans to escape. Up ran the four Yamen men and the soldiers from the street. Everyone in the compound appeared on the scene. When I heard his outcry I thought that he had received some serious injury. All gathered about him asking his trouble, but overcome with emotion he jumped up and down, slapping his legs and crying lustily. Finally he managed to say through his tears, "Mr. Fay [Fei], Mr. Wang has stolen the things which you gave me."

When I heard this I could neither laugh nor cry nor storm at him. The Yamen men and soldiers at once picked up their lanterns and began to search. When they saw that the back gate had been unlocked and the stone removed, not knowing that I had done it, they began to scold and mutter:

"These things! How contemptible they are! When did they open this gate in order to steal the foreigners' things?"

As they muttered they locked the gate and replaced the stone, then left two men to guard it.

It was after midnight when this commotion was over, and every gate was guarded. Mr. Price and I saw that it would be impossible to get out that night. Even if we could leave the compound, we could not reach Deacon Wang's before daylight. If we attempted it, the Prices would not be saved, and Deacon Wang's whole family would be endangered.

So I went alone outside the compound to tell Mr. Han to dismiss the cart. As soon as he saw me, he said quickly:

"It is indeed well that the Prices have not come. I just came across several thieves, and was mistaken for one of their company. One of them said to me, 'If you get anything, you must divide with me.' If the Prices had come out, I fear they would have been killed."

The next day we consulted again about flight. Li Yü said:

"Let us flee all together to the mountains from thirty to sixty miles away."

So we hired a large cart and loaded it with food and other necessities, and sent it ahead of us into the mountains. Two Christian inquirers went with the cart to guard it. When it had entered the mountains about seven miles from the city, suddenly a man ran up and said to the inquirers:

"Run quick for your lives! Your mission in the city is burning, and the foreigners have all been killed."

As soon as they had jumped down from the cart and run away, rascals came up and stole all that was on the cart.

When we heard this we gave up all hope of escape, especially as we were told that bad men in the city had heard of our intention, and were hiding outside the city day and night ready to kill and rob the foreigners if they should appear. So we talked no more of fleeing, but committed our lives into the hands of our Heavenly Father, to do as seemed to Him best. We had little hope that we would be saved. Still we kept guard every night, Mr. Atwater and Mr. Lundgren being on duty the first half of the night, and Mr. Price and I the last half. At that time all of the servants had left us, and Mrs. Price did all the cooking, Mrs. Lundgren and Miss Eldred helping her. It was the hottest time in summer, and Mrs. Price stood over the stove with flushed face wet with perspiration. Li Yo and I were so sorry for her, and wanted to help her, but alas! neither of us knew how to cook foreign food, so we could only wash the dishes and help to wash the clothes.

Li Yü was so helpful those days. He alone went outside the compound to see the Magistrate, to transact business, to purchase food, and every day to get the news.

August had come, and we were still alive. Could it be that God wishing to show His mighty power, would out of that whole province of Shansi save the missionaries at Fen Chou Fu and Tai Ku?

The second day of August, a little after noon, a man came into our compound with the saddest story that our ears had heard during those sad summer days. He was Mrs. Clapp's cook, and two days before, in the afternoon, he had fled from the Tai Ku compound when flame and sword and rifle were doing their murderous work. As he fled he saw Mr. Clapp, Mr. Williams, and Mr. Davis making a last vain effort to keep back the mob of hundreds of soldiers and Boxers, and saw Mrs. Clapp, Miss Partridge, Miss Bird, and Ruth taking refuge in a little court in the back of the compound. Miss Bird had said to him as he ran:

"Be quick! be quick!"

Over the compound wall, then the city wall, he had taken shelter in a field of grain, where he still heard the howling of the mob and saw the heavens gray with smoke from the burning buildings. He hid in the grain until morning broke, then started on his journey to Fen Chou Fu.

So to our little company waiting so long in the valley of the shadow of death, came the tidings that our Tai Ku missionaries had crossed the river. Several native Christians who counted not their lives dear unto themselves, had gone with the martyr band. Eagerly I asked about my sister, her husband and child. The messenger did not know whether they were living or dead—only that they had been staying in the mission buildings outside the city. Two days later full accounts of the massacre reached us, and I knew that they were among the slain.

Bitter were the tears which we shed together that afternoon. It seemed as if my heart was breaking as I thought of the cruel death of those whom I loved so much, and whom I should never again see on earth. What words can tell my grief? I could not sleep that night, nor for many nights following. I thought how lovingly Mr. and Mrs. Clapp had nursed me through my long illness. I wept for Miss Bird, who had sympathized with me and helped me. "My dear ones, my dear ones, who loved and helped me as if I were your very flesh and blood, who brought so much joy and peace to the lonely one far from his home, who worked so earnestly for God, who pitied and helped the suffering and poor, would that I could have died for you! Could my death have saved one of you, gladly would I have laid down my life."

The Tai Ku missionaries were gone, the Christians were killed or scattered, the buildings were all burned. We of Fen Chou Fu alone were left. We all thought that our day was at hand, but God still kept us for nearly two weeks. And now I want to tell you the story of those remaining days.

LAST DAYS AT FEN CHOU FU

The next day after we heard of the Tai Ku tragedy a man ran in to tell us that several hundred Boxers were coming from the east. They were those who had killed the missionaries at Tai Ku, and now they were resting in a village outside the east gate, prepared to attack our mission that afternoon. We all believed this report, for we were hourly expecting death. There was nothing the foreigners could do but to wait for the end. Mr. Price urged me to leave them at once and flee. Mr. Price, Mrs. Atwater, Mrs. Lundgren, and Miss Eldred all gave me letters to home friends. All of my foreign friends shook hands with me at parting, and Mrs. Atwater said, with tears in her eyes:

"May the Lord preserve your life, and enable you to tell our story to others."

Miss Eldred had prepared for herself a belt into which was stitched forty taels of silver. She thought that she was standing at the gate of death and would have no use for money, so she gave it to me for my travelling expenses. Mrs. Price gave me her gold watch and an envelope on which an address was written, and asked me to take the watch to Tientsin and find someone who would send it to her father. Before I went out of the gate I saw Mrs. Price holding her little daughter to her heart, kissing her through her tears, and heard her say:

"If the Boxers come today, I want my little Florence to go before I do."

My heart was pierced with grief as I saw the sad plight of my friends, but I could do nothing for them. Had I died with them it could not have helped them. So we parted with many tears.

While I was away the Magistrate had sent for Li Yü and demanded that all the firearms of the foreigners be given up to him. Li Yü replied, "I know the missionaries will use their weapons only in self-defense."

The Magistrate was very angry, and ordered that Li Yü be beaten three hundred blows, with eighty additional blows on his lips because he had used the word 'I' in speaking to the Magistrate, instead of the humble "little one" which was customary. Li Yü was then locked in the jail, and the Magistrate sent men to the mission to demand the firearms. The missionaries could not refuse to comply, so their two shotguns and two revolvers were given up.

In this time of need two Christians named Chang and Tien came to help the missionaries. They worked for Mrs. Price to the last. The sufferings of the missionaries were indeed sore. Their patience and perfect trust in God greatly moved my heart. In the summer heat Mrs. Price three times a day hung over the stove preparing food for her family of ten, yet I never heard a word of complaint. Her face was always peaceful, and often she sang as she went about her work. One evening when we were all standing in the yard together Mrs. Price said to me:

"These days my thoughts are much on 'the things above.' Sometimes when I think of the sufferings through which my loved friends passed it seems as if a voice from heaven said to me, 'Dear sister, see how happy we are now; all of earth's sufferings are over, and if our sorrows on earth are compared with our bliss in heaven, they are nothing, nothing.'"

Miss Eldred was very young, and had come from England only a year or two before, so she could speak little Chinese. The expression of her gentle face moved one to pity. When she was not helping Mrs. Price, she played outdoors with the three children, and gave Mrs. Price's little daughter music lessons.

We still patrolled the place at night, I continuing to take my turn with Mr. Price in the last half of the night. So I had an opportunity for forming a most intimate friendship with Mr. Price. He told me many things during those long hours, sometimes relating his own experiences when a soldier during the American Civil War.

Every day at sunset I played with Florence Price and Celia and Bertha Atwater. Ever since I had come to Fen Chou Fu I had played an hour with Florence. This had been good for both of us, for me because I learned English by talking with her, and for Florence because she had no children for companions and was very lonely. If there was a day when something prevented my going to her as usual, she would come or send for me. When Mr. Atwater moved to the same place his two little girls were very fond of romping with me too. I often carried the children on my shoulder, and they loved me very much. At seven o'clock, when their mothers called them to go to bed, all three would kiss me, saying: "Good-night, Mr. Fay, good-night. Pleasant dreams, pleasant dreams." So it was until the day when they left the earth.

At this time it seemed as if the Boxer trouble might be over. There were few rumors on the streets, and there had never been organized Boxer bands in Fen Chou Fu. So our hearts were more peaceful. Perhaps it was God's will after all to save our little band. Still no word reached us from the outside world. We walked on in the darkness. It was because of the friendliness of the Fen Chou Fu Magistrate that the little Christian community there was preserved so long after the floods of destruction had swept over every other mission in the province. His superior officer, the Prefect, a weak old man, died July 27. Upon the character of his successor might depend the life or death of the missionaries.

On August 12 the new Prefect appointed by the Governor arrived from Tai Yuan Fu. He was a man of great learning but little practical ability, the tool of the Governor, who had sent him expressly to murder the foreigners. So he made their extermination his first business on reaching Fen Chou Fu. It was the 13th when he took the seals of office, and that same day he went to the Magistrate and upbraided him for his remissness in the work of massacre. . . .

OUTSIDE THE CITY WALL

It was a clear, beautiful day, with a gentle wind blowing, a bright sun shining, and not a cloud within sight. As we drove out of the gate we saw the streets packed with a dense crowd of spectators. From the mission to the North Gate of the city they seemed a solid mass, while house roofs and walls swarmed with men and women eager for a sight of us. There were tens of thousands, and when we left the city gate behind, many flocked after us and stood watching until we were out of sight. So we left Fen Chou Fu on that fateful morning, August 15.

We had been imprisoned within walls for two or three months, and our hearts had all the time been burdened and anxious. Now suddenly we were outside the city in the pure, bracing air, in the midst of flowers and trees, luxuriant in summer beauty, riding through fields ripe for the harvest. It was all so beautiful and peaceful and strength-giving. So as soon as we were out in the country air our spirits rose and fresh life and joy came to us.

In the front of our cart sat Mr. Atwater with the carter, behind him were Mrs. Atwater and Mrs. Lundgren, and I sat in the back of the cart with the two little girls. On both sides, before and behind, walked the twenty soldiers, while in front of all, mounted on my white horse, with chin held high and a very self-satisfied manner, rode the leader. After ten o'clock the sun's rays grew warmer, and Mrs. Lundgren handed her umbrella to a soldier, asking him to offer it to the leader to shield him from the heat.

We talked as we rode along. Mrs. Lundgren remarked: "What a beautiful day it is!" Mrs. Atwater said, "Who would have thought that when we left Fen Chou Fu we would have such an escort?" "See the soldiers' uniforms, gay with red and green trimmings," said Mrs. Lundgren.

So the light conversation went on. Mrs. Atwater said to me, "I'm afraid they'll not give your horse back to you at P'ing Yao."

"I'm afraid not," I replied.

Then the two ladies turned and talked in English with Mr. Atwater, and I talked and laughed with the two children close beside me. We played a finger game, and they prattled ceaselessly.

"Mr. Fay, please tell us where we are going," they said.

After a while little Bertha grew sleepy, and nestled to rest in her mother's arms.

When we left Fen Chou Fu we thought that we might meet Boxers or robbers by the way, but we said, "If any danger comes, these soldiers will protect us with all their might."

Little did we dream that these very soldiers were to murder us.

We passed through several villages, and every man, woman, and child was out to stare at us. Then we came to a large village. It was nearly noon and very hot, so we stopped to rest a while, and the carters watered their mules. A man happened to be there peddling little sweet melons. We were all thirsty, so we bought some, and as Mr. Atwater had no change handy I paid for them with the cash in my bag. We passed some back to those in the other cart, and Mrs. Lundgren took out a package of nice foreign candy and passed some to us. After a few minutes we were on our way again.

As we travelled the young soldier who had taken my horse away walked close behind my cart, never taking his eyes off me. I thought that he was angry because I had objected to giving him the horse, so I gave little attention to it.

Then I noticed something strange in his way of looking at me, as if there was something he wished to say to me.

After we had gone on a little farther with the soldier walking behind the cart, still keeping his eyes on me, he heaved a great sigh, and said:

"Alas for you—so very young!"

The soldier walking at the side looked sternly at the speaker and said something to him which I could not hear, but I heard the reply:

"This is our own countryman, and not a foreigner."

When I saw the expression on their faces and heard these words, suddenly it flashed across me that they had some deep meaning, and I asked the young soldier what was up.

"I don't know," he replied.

"If anything is going to happen," I said, "please tell me."

He hung his head and said nothing, but followed still close to the cart, and after a while said to me plainly:

"You ought to escape at once, for only a short distance ahead we are to kill the foreigners."

I jumped down from the cart, but another soldier came up: saying, "Don't go away."

Then I began to think it was true that the foreigners were to be killed, and wanted to get farther away from the cart, but the soldier who had first talked with me, said:

"You can't go yet; you must first leave your money with us."

I said, "I have only a little, barely enough for my journey."

But I knew that they would not let me off without money, so I gave my watch to the soldier who had taken my horse. Another soldier demanded money, saying:

"If you have no money you may give me your boots."

So I took off my newly purchased boots and gave them to him putting on the well-worn shoes which he gave me in exchange. Another soldier took away my straw hat and the whip which I carried in my hand. It happened that at just this point a little path branched off from the main road through a field of sorghum higher than my head. I started off on the path. While I had been talking with the soldiers Mr. Atwater had conversed with the two ladies and had not noticed our words. As I left my friends I took a last look at them, saying in my heart:

"I fear that I shall never again on earth see your faces."

I had no chance to speak to them, for the village where they were to be killed was only a quarter of a mile away, the carts had not stopped, and many people were following close behind. A crowd was also coming out from the village which they were approaching.

I had walked only a short distance on the little path when I heard footsteps following, and looking back saw that it was the two soldiers hastening after me. My heart stood still, for I thought that they were coming to prevent my escape and kill me. I did not dare to run, for they had rifles in their hands. Soon they overtook me, one seizing my queue and another my arm, and saying:

"You must have some money; we'll only let you escape with your life; your money must be given to us."

Before I had time to answer, the soldier snatched from my purse all the silver which Mr. Price had given me. I made an effort to get it back, but the soldier said:

"If we kill you, nothing will be yours. If we let you escape with your life, should not your silver be given to us?"

There was some reason in their talk, so I only entreated them to leave me a little money, for I had many hundred miles to travel before I would reach my home. The soldiers had a little conscience, for dividing the silver between them they took out a small piece amounting to about a tael, and gave it to me.

The young soldier who had first talked with me said:

"Don't go far away yet. Wait until you see whether we kill the foreigners or not. If we don't do it, hunt me up and I'll give you your watch and all of your silver. If we kill them consider that we did not take your money without cause."

They then hurried back to the road.

When I had gone on a little farther I heard a loud rifle report. By that time I was almost convinced that they were indeed going to kill the foreigners. So I ran with all my might. It was about one o'clock and the sun beat down fiercely. After I had gone several miles I felt very weary, and though I was not afraid, my heart still fluttered and my flesh crept.

The sun was sinking westward, and I looked up to the sky with a sigh. The atmosphere was clear, wind and light were fair, and I asked myself:

"Can the great Lord who rules heaven and earth permit evil men under this bright heaven, in this clear light of day, to murder these innocent men and women, these little children? It cannot be. Perhaps I can still reach P'ing Yao, and look in the faces of those whom I love."

Then I thought that if the soldiers had really killed them in that village, as they said they would, they were no longer on the earth, but were happy with God. When this thought came I lifted my face toward heaven, saying:

"My beloved Mr. and Mrs. Price and other dear friends, if you are truly in heaven now, do you see my trouble and distress?"

So I walked on, my heart now in heaven, now on earth, a thousand thoughts entangling themselves in my bewildered mind.

I was weary and would walk a mile or two, then rest. I came to the bank of the Fen River, five miles from P'ing Yao, and waited some time at the ferry to hear what men were saying; for if the foreigners had not been killed they must certainly cross by this ferry, and everyone would be talking about it. But though I stood there a long time I heard no one mention the subject, and the dread that my friends had been killed took full possession of my heart. Then I crossed on the ferry with others, and strange to say the ferryman did not ask me for money.

Once across the river I reached a small inn outside the wall of P'ing Yao. I had walked twenty miles that day—the longest walk I had ever taken, and I threw myself down to sleep without eating anything. Often I awoke with a start and turned my aching body, asking myself, "Where am I? How came I here? Are my Western friends indeed killed? I must be dreaming."

But I was so tired that sleep would soon overcome me again.

The sun had risen when I opened my eyes in the morning. I forced myself to rise, washed my face, and asked for a little food, but could not get it down. Sitting down I heard loud talking and laughter among the guests. The topic of conversation was the massacre of foreigners the day before! One said:

"There were ten ocean men killed, three men, four women, and three little devils.
"Another added, "Lij Cheng San yesterday morning came ahead with twenty soldiers and waited in the village. When the foreigners with their soldier escort arrived a gun was fired for a signal, and all the soldiers set to work at once."

Then one after another added gruesome details, how the cruel swords had slashed, how the baggage had been stolen, how the very clothing had been stripped from the poor bodies, and how they had then been flung into a wayside pit.

"Are there still foreigners in Fen Chou Fu?" I asked.
"No, they were all killed yesterday."
"Where were they killed?"
"In that village ahead—less than two miles from here," he said, pointing as he spoke. "Yesterday about this time they were all killed."
"How many were there?" I asked.

He stretched out the fingers of his two hands for an answer.

"Were there none of our people?"
"No, they were all foreigners."

My heart was leaden as I rode on the cart, with my face turned toward Fen Chou Fu. It was eight when the carter drove up to an inn in the east suburb of Fen Chou Fu, and I walked on into the city. Fortunately it was growing dark, and no one saw my face plainly, as, avoiding the main street, I made my way through alleys to the home of a Mr. Shih, a Christian who lived near the mission. When I knocked and entered Mr. Shih and his brother started up in terror and amazement, saying:

"How could you get here?"

We three went in quickly, barring the gate, and when we were seated in the house I told my sad story. Sighing, Mr. Shih said:

"We knew when the foreigners left yesterday that death awaited them on the road. Not long after you had gone the Prefect and the Magistrate rode in their chairs to the gate of the mission, took a look inside without entering, and then sealed up the gate."

Mr. Shih told me also how the Prefect, as soon as he had returned to his Yamen, had ordered Li Yü brought before him, and inflicted more cruel blows on his bruised body. Then he told details of the massacre. There was one young soldier named Li who had studied several years in the mission school, and whose sword took no part in the carnage. When the leader knew this he beat him from head to foot with his great horsewhip. The poor remains of the missionaries would have been left on the village street had not the village leaders begged that they be taken away. So the soldiers dragged them to a pit outside the city, where they found a common grave.

IMPERIALISM OF DECADENCE

Francisco Garcia Calderón

Calderón was a Peruvian diplomat and writer. Here he criticizes U.S. policy, as well as U.S. businesses, for exploiting Latin Americans. He also warns of the dangers of cultural imperialism.

Interventions have become more frequent with the expansion of frontiers. The United States have recently intervened in the territory of Acre, there to found a republic of rubber gatherers; at Panama, there to develop a province and construct a canal; in Cuba, under cover of the Platt Amendment, to maintain order in the interior; in Santo Domingo, to support the civilising revolution and overthrow the tyrants; in Venezuela, and in Central America, to enforce upon these nations, torn by intestine disorders, the political and financial tutelage of the imperial democracy. In Guatemala and Honduras the loans concluded with the monarchs of North American finance have reduced the people to a new slavery. Supervision of the customs and the dispatch of pacificatory squadrons to defend the interests of the Anglo-Saxon have enforced peace and tranquility: such are the means employed. The New York American announces that Mr. Pierpont Morgan proposes to encompass the finances of Latin America by a vast network of Yankee banks. Chicago merchants and Wall Street financiers created the Meat Trust in the Argentine. The United States offer millions for the purpose of converting into Yankee loans the moneys raised in London during the last century by the Latin American States; they wish to obtain a monopoly of credit. It has even been announced, although the news hardly appears probable, that a North American syndicate wished to buy enormous belts of land in Guatemala, where the English tongue is the obligatory language. The fortification of the Panama Canal, and the possible acquisition of the Galapagos Island in the Pacific, are fresh manifestations of imperialistic progress. . . .

Source: From Francisco, Garcia Calderón: *Latin America: Its Rise and Progress* (London: T. F. Unwin, 1913), pp. 392–393.

Warnings, advice, distrust, invasion of capital, plans of financial hegemony all these justify the anxiety of the southern peoples. . . . Neither irony nor grace nor scepticism, gifts of the old civilizations, can make way against the plebeian brutality, the excessive optimism, the violent individualism of the [North American] people.

All these things contribute to the triumph of mediocrity; the multitude of primary schools, the vices of utilitarianism, the cult of the average citizen, the transatlantic M. Homais, and the tyranny of opinion noted by Tocqueville; and in this vulgarity, which is devoid of traditions and has no leading aristocracy, a return to the primitive type of the redskin, which has already been noted by close observers, is threatening the proud democracy. From the excessive tension of wills, from the elementary state of culture, from the perpetual unrest of life, from the harshness of the industrial struggle, anarchy and violence will be born in the future. In a hundred years men will seek in vain for the "American soul," the "genius of America," elsewhere than in the undisciplined force or the violence which ignores moral laws. . . .

Essential points of difference separate the two Americas. Differences of language and therefore of spirit; the difference between Spanish Catholicism and multiform Protestantism of the Anglo-Saxons; between the Yankee individualism and the omnipotence of the State natural to the nations of the South. In their origin, as in their race, we find fundamental antagonism; the evolution of the North is slow and obedient to the lessons of time, to the influences of custom; the history of the southern peoples is full of revolutions, rich with dreams of an unattainable perfection.

IDENTIFICATIONS PART IV

Define each of the following items with a two-sentence identification. Your definition must specifically draw on material in one of the documents in this section.

White Man's Burden

_____

_____

Earl of Cromer

_____

_____

Khartoum

_____

_____

Emiliano Aguialdo

_____

_____

Extraterritorial Jurisdiction

_____

_____

PART V
DOUBTS ABOUT MODERNITY

People in the West viewed the process of Modernization with great optimism, believing that humankind now had at its command the material and intellectual tools that would allow it to master the material universe and create a Utopia on earth. But by the beginning of the twentieth centuries a number of developments and events began to raise troubling concerns and doubts about modernization. The documents in this part illustrate the sources of some of those concerns. What kinds of concerns would the works of Darwin and Freud raise for people with strong religious values, and even those who were confident that humans could reshape the world with the power of their rational minds? How might the theory of relativity have caused concern even for people who accepted a scientific explanation of the physical universe? What kinds of concerns about science and modern governments were raised by World War I, the Influenza epidemic and the Holocaust?

EXCERPTS FROM THE ORIGIN OF SPECIES

Charles Darwin

When on board H.M.S. "Beagle," as naturalist, I was much struck with certain facts in the distribution of the organic beings inhabiting South America, and in the geological relations of the present to the past inhabitants of that continent. These facts, as will be seen in the latter chapters of this volume, seemed to throw some light on the origin of species—that mystery of mysteries, as it has been called by one of our greatest philosophers. On my return home, it occurred to me, in 1837, that something might perhaps be made out on this question by patiently accumulating and reflecting on all sorts of facts which could possibly have any bearing on it. After five years' work I allowed myself to speculate on the subject, and drew up some short notes; these I enlarged in 1844 into a sketch of the conclusions, which then seemed to me probable: from that period to the present day I have steadily pursued the same object. I hope that I may be excused for entering on these personal details, as I give them to show that I have not been hasty in coming to a decision.

My work is now (1859) nearly finished; but as it will take me many more years to complete it, and as my health is far from strong, I have been urged to publish this Abstract. I have more especially been induced to do this, as Mr. [Alfred Russel] Wallace, who is now studying the natural history of the Malay archipelago, has arrived at almost exactly the same general conclusions that I have on the origin of species. In 1858 he sent me a memoir on this subject, with a request that I would forward it to Sir Charles Lyell, who sent it to the Linnean Society, and it is published in the third volume of the Journal of that society. Sir C. Lyell and Dr. Hooker, who both knew of my work—the latter having read my sketch of 1844—honoured me by thinking it advisable to publish, with Mr. Wallace's excellent memoir, some brief extracts from my manuscripts.

This Abstract, which I now publish, must necessarily be imperfect. I cannot here give references and authorities for my several statements; and I must trust to the reader reposing some confidence in my accuracy. No doubt errors will have crept in, though I hope I have always been cautious in trusting to good authorities alone. I can here give only the general conclusions at which I have arrived, with a few facts in illustration, but which, I hope, in most cases will suffice. No one can feel more sensible than I do of the necessity of hereafter publishing in detail all the facts, with references, on which my conclusions have been grounded; and I hope in a future work to do this. For I am well aware that scarcely a single point is discussed in this volume on which facts cannot be adduced, often apparently leading to conclusions directly opposite to those at which I have arrived. A fair result can be obtained only by fully stating and balancing the facts and arguments on both sides of each question; and this is here impossible.

In considering the Origin of Species, it is quite conceivable that a naturalist, reflecting on the mutual affinities of organic beings, on their embryological relations, their geographical distribution, geological succession, and other such facts, might come to the conclusion that species had not been independently created, but had descended, like varieties, from other species. Nevertheless, such a conclusion, even if well founded, would be unsatisfactory, until it could be shown how the innumerable species inhabiting this world have been modified, so as to acquire that perfection of structure and coadaptation which justly excites our admiration. Naturalists continually refer to external conditions, such as climate, food, &c., as the only possible source of variation. In one limited sense, as we shall hereafter see, this may be true; but it is preposterous to attribute to mere external conditions, the structure, for instance, of the woodpecker, with its feet, tail, beak, and tongue, so admirably adapted to catch insects under the bark of trees. In the case of the mistletoe, which draws its nourishment from certain trees, which has seeds that must be transported by certain birds, and which has flowers with separate sexes absolutely requiring the agency of certain insects to bring pollen from one flower to the other, it is equally preposterous to account for the structure of this parasite, with its relations to several distinct organic beings, by the effects of external conditions, or of habit, or of the volition of the plant itself.

It is, therefore, of the highest importance to gain a clear insight into the means of modification and coadaptation. At the commencement of my observations it seemed to me probable that a careful study of domesticated animals and of cultivated plants would offer the best chance of making out this obscure problem. Nor have I been disappointed; in this and in all other perplexing cases I have invariably found that our knowledge, imperfect though it be, of variation under domestication, afforded the best and safest clue.

From these considerations, I shall devote the first chapter of this Abstract to Variation under Domestication. We shall thus see that a large amount of hereditary modification is at least possible; and, what is equally or more important, we shall see how great is the power of man in accumulating by his Selection successive slight variations. I will then pass on to the variability of species in a state of nature; but I shall, unfortunately, be compelled to treat this subject far too briefly, as it can be treated properly only by giving long catalogues of facts. We shall, however, be enabled to discuss what circumstances are most favourable to variation. In the next chapter the Struggle for Existence amongst all organic beings throughout the world, which inevitably follows from the high geometrical ratio of their increase, will be considered. This is the doctrine of Malthus, applied to the whole animal and vegetable kingdoms. As many more individuals of each species are born than can possibly survive; and as, consequently, there is a frequently recurring struggle for existence, it follows that any being, if it vary however slightly in any manner profitable to itself, under the complex and sometimes varying conditions of life, will have a better chance of surviving, and thus be *naturally selected*. From the strong principle of inheritance, any selected variety will tend to propagate its new and modified form.

This fundamental subject of Natural Selection will be treated at some length in the fourth chapter; and we shall then see how Natural Selection almost inevitably causes much Extinction of the less-improved forms of life, and leads to what I have called Divergence of Character. In the next chapter I shall discuss the complex and little known laws of variation. In the five succeeding chapters, the most apparent and gravest difficulties in accepting the theory will be given: namely, first, the difficulties of transitions, or how a simple being or a simple organ can be changed and perfected into a highly developed being or into an elaborately constructed organ; secondly, the subject of Instinct, or the mental powers of animals; thirdly, Hybridism, or the infertility of species and the fertility of varieties when intercrossed; and fourthly, the imperfection of the Geological Record. In the next chapter I shall consider the geological succession of organic beings throughout time; in the twelfth and thirteenth, their geographical distribution throughout space; in the fourteenth, their classification or mutual affinities, both when mature and in an embryonic condition. In the last chapter I shall give a brief recapitulation of the whole work, and a few concluding remarks.

No one ought to feel surprise at much remaining as yet unexplained in regard to the origin of species and varieties, if he make due allowance for our profound ignorance in regard to the mutual relations of the many beings which live around us. Who can explain why one species ranges widely and is very numerous, and why another allied species has a narrow range and is rare? Yet these relations are of the highest importance, for they determine the present welfare and, as I believe, the future success and modification of every inhabitant of this world. Still less do we know of the mutual relations of the innumerable inhabitants of the world during the many past geological epochs in its history. Although much remains obscure, and will long remain obscure, I can entertain no doubt, after the most deliberate study and dispassionate judgment of which I am capable, that the view which most naturalists until recently entertained, and which I formerly entertained—namely, that each species has been independently created—is erroneous. I am fully convinced that species are not immutable; but that those belonging to what are called the same genera are lineal descendants of some other and generally extinct species, in the same manner as the acknowledged varieties of any one species are the descendants of that species. Furthermore, I am convinced that Natural Selection has been the most important, but not the exclusive, means of modification.

I see no good reason why the views given in this volume should shock the religious feelings of any one. It is satisfactory, as showing how transient such impressions are, to remember that the greatest discovery ever made by man, namely, the law of the attraction of gravity, was also attacked by Leibnitz, "as subversive of natural, and inferentially of revealed, religion." A celebrated author and divine has written to me that "he has gradually learnt to see that it is just as noble a conception of the Deity to believe that He created a few original forms capable of self-development into other and needful forms, as to believe that He required a fresh act of creation to supply the voids caused by the action of His laws."

Why, it may be asked, until recently did nearly all the most eminent living naturalists and geologists disbelieve in the mutability of species? It cannot be asserted that organic beings in a state of nature are subject to no variation; it cannot be proved that the amount of variation in the course of long ages is a limited quality; no clear distinction has been, or can be, drawn between species and well-marked varieties. It cannot be maintained that species when intercrossed are invariably sterile, and varieties invariably fertile; or that sterility is a special endowment and sign of creation. The belief that species were immutable productions was almost unavoidable as long as the history of the world was thought to be of short duration; and now that we have acquired some idea of the lapse of time, we are too apt to assume, without proof, that the geological record is so perfect that it would have afforded us plain evidence of the mutation of species, if they had undergone mutation.

But the chief cause of our natural unwillingness to admit that one species has given birth to clear and distinct species, is that we are always slow in admitting great changes of which we do not see the steps. The difficulty is the same as that felt by so many geologists, when Lyell first insisted that long lines of inland cliffs had been formed, the great valleys excavated, by the agencies which we see still at work. The mind cannot possibly grasp the full meaning of the term of even a million years; it cannot add up and perceive the full effects of many slight variations, accumulated during an almost infinite number of generations.

Although I am fully convinced of the truth of the views given in this volume under the form of an abstract, I by no means expect to convince experienced naturalists whose minds are stocked with a multitude of facts all viewed, during a long course of years, from a point of view directly opposite to mine. It is so easy to hide our ignorance under such expressions as the "plan of creation," "unity of design," &c., and to think that we give an explanation when we only re-state a fact. Any one whose disposition leads him to attach more weight to unexplained difficulties than to the explanation of a certain number of facts will certainly reject the theory. A few naturalists, endowed with much flexibility of mind, and who have already begun to doubt the immutability of species, may be influenced by this volume; but I look with confidence to the future,—to young and rising naturalists, who will be able to view both sides of the question with impartiality. Whoever is led to believe that species are mutable will do good service by conscientiously expressing his conviction; for thus only can the load of prejudice by which this subject is overwhelmed be removed.

Authors of the highest eminence seem to be fully satisfied with the view that each species has been independently created. To my mind it accords better with what we know of the laws impressed on matter by the Creator, that the production and extinction of the past and present inhabitants of the world should have been due to secondary causes, like those determining the birth and death of the individual. When I view all beings not as special creations, but as the lineal descendants of some few beings which lived long before the first bed of the Cambrian system was deposited, they seem to me to become ennobled. Judging from the past, we may safely infer that not one living species will transmit its unaltered likeness to a distant futurity. And of the species now living very few will transmit progeny of any kind to a far distant futurity; for the manner in which all organic beings are grouped, shows that the greater number of species in each genus, and all the species in many genera, have left no descendants, but have become utterly extinct. We can so far take a prophetic glance into futurity as to foretell that it will be the common and widely-spread species, belonging to the larger and dominant groups within each class, which will ultimately prevail and procreate new and dominant species. As all the living forms of life are the lineal descendants of those which lived long before the Cambrian epoch, we may feel certain that the ordinary succession by generation has never once been broken, and that no cataclysm has desolated the whole world. Hence we may look with some confidence to a secure future of great length. And as natural selection works solely by and for the good of each being, all corporeal and mental endowments will tend to progress towards perfection.

It is interesting to contemplate a tangled bank, clothed with many plants of many kinds, with birds singing on the bushes, with various insects flitting about, and with worms crawling through the damp earth, and to reflect that these elaborately constructed forms, so different from each other, and dependent upon each other in so complex a manner, have all been produced by laws acting around us. These laws, taken in the largest sense, being Growth with Reproduction; Inheritance which is almost implied by reproduction; Variability from the indirect and direct action of the conditions of life, and from use and disuse: a

Ratio of Increase so high as to lead to a Struggle for Life, and as a consequence to Natural Selection, entailing Divergence of Character and the Extinction of less-improved forms. Thus, from the war of nature, from famine and death, the most exalted object which we are capable of conceiving, namely, the production of the higher animals, directly follows. There is grandeur in this view of life, with its several powers, having been originally breathed by the Creator into a few forms or into one; and that, whilst this planet has gone cycling on according to the fixed law of gravity, from so simple a beginning endless forms most beautiful and most wonderful have been, and are being evolved.

EXCERPT FROM PSYCHOPATHOLOGY OF EVERYDAY LIFE: THE FREUDIAN SLIP

Sigmund Freud

[Examples:]. . .

(*k*) Before calling on me a patient telephoned for an appointment, and also wished to be informed about my consultation fee. He was told that the first consultation was ten dollars; after the examination was over he again asked what he was to pay, and added: "I don't like to owe money to any one, especially to doctors; I prefer to pay right away." Instead of *pay* he said *play.* His last voluntary remarks and his mistake put me on my guard, but after a few more uncalled-for remarks he set me at ease by taking money from his pocket. He counted four paper dollars and was very chagrined and surprised because he had no more money with him, and promised to send me a check for the balance. I was sure that his mistake betrayed him, that he was only *playing* with me, but there was nothing to be done. At the end of a few weeks I sent him a bill for the balance, and the letter was returned to me by the post office authorities marked "Not found." . . .

(*q*) Dr. Stekel reports about himself that he had under treatment at the same time two patients from Trieste, each of whom he always addressed incorrectly. "Good morning, Mr. Peloni!" he would say to Askoli, and to Peloni, "Good morning, Mr. Askoli!" He was at first inclined to attribute no deeper motive to this mistake, but to explain it through a number of similarities in both persons. However, he easily convinced himself that here the interchange of names bespoke a sort of boast—that is, he was acquainting each of his Italian patients with the fact that neither was the only resident of Trieste who came to Vienna in search of his medical advice.

(*r*) Two women stopped in front of a drugstore, and one said to her companion, "If you will wait a few *moments* I'll soon be back," but she said *movements* instead. She was on her way to buy some castoria for her child.

(s) Mr. L., who is fonder of being called on than of calling, spoke to me over the telephone from a nearby summer resort. He wanted to know when I would pay him a visit. I reminded him that it was his turn to visit me, and called his attention to the fact that, as he was the happy possessor of an automobile, it would be easier for him to call on me. (We were at different summer resorts, separated by about one half-hour's railway trip.) He gladly promised to call, and asked: "How about Labor Day (September 1st), will it be convenient for you?" When I answered affirmatively, he said, "Very well, then, put me down for *Election* Day" (November). His mistake was quite plain. He likes to visit me, but it was inconvenient to travel so far. In November we would both be in the city. My analysis proved correct.

(t) A friend described to me a nervous patient, and wished to know whether I could benefit him. I remarked: "I believe that in time I can remove all his symptoms by psychoanalysis, because it is a durable case," wishing to say "curable"!

(u) I repeatedly addressed my patient as Mrs. Smith, her married daughter's name, when her real name is Mrs. James. My attention having been called to it, I soon discovered that I had another patient of the same name who refused to pay for the treatment. Mrs. Smith was also my patient and paid her bills promptly.

(v) A *lapsus linguae* sometimes stands for a particular characteristic. A young woman, who is the domineering spirit in her home, said of her ailing husband that he had consulted the doctor about a wholesome diet for himself, and then added: "The doctor said that diet has nothing to do with his ailments, and that he can eat and drink what *I* want."

(w) I cannot omit this excellent and instructive example, although, according to my authority, it is about twenty years old. A lady once expressed herself in society—the very words show that they were uttered with fervor and under the pressure of a great many secret emotions: "Yes, a woman must be pretty if she is to please the men. A man is much better off. As long as he has *five* straight limbs, he needs no more!"

This example affords us a good insight into the intimate mechanisms of a mistake in speech by means of condensation and contamination. It is quite obvious that we have here a fusion of two similar modes of expression:

"As long as he has his four *straight limbs*."
"As long as he has all his *five senses*."
Or the term "straight" may be the common element of the two intended expressions:

"As long as he has his *straight* limbs."
"All *five* should be *straight*."
It may also be assumed that both modes of expression—viz., those of the five senses and those of the straight five—have co-operated to introduce into the

sentence about the straight limbs first a number and then the mysterious five instead of the simple four. But this fusion surely would not have succeeded if it had not expressed good sense in the form resulting from the mistake; if it had not expressed a cynical truth which, naturally, could not be uttered unconcealed, coming as it did from a woman.

Finally, we shall not hesitate to call attention to the fact that the woman's saying, following its wording, could just as well be an excellent witticism as a jocose speech-blunder. It is simply a question whether she uttered these words with conscious or unconscious intention. The behavior of the speaker in this case certainly speaks against the conscious intention, and thus excludes wit.

(x) Owing to similarity of material, I add here another case of speech-blunder, the interpretation of which requires less skill. A professor of anatomy strove to explain the nostril, which, as is known, is a very difficult anatomical structure. To his question whether his audience grasped his ideas he received an affirmative reply. The professor, known for his self-esteem, thereupon remarked: "I can hardly believe this, for the number of people who understand the nostril, even in a city of millions like Vienna, can be counted on a finger—pardon me, I meant to say on the fingers of a hand."

In the psychotherapeutic procedure which I employ in the solution and removal of neurotic symptoms, I am often confronted with the task of discovering from the accidental utterances and fancies of the patient the thought contents, which, though striving for concealment, nevertheless unintentionally betray themselves. In doing this the mistakes often perform the most valuable service, as I can show through most convincing and still most singular examples.

For example, patients speak of an aunt and later, without noting the mistake, call her "my mother," or designate a husband as a "brother." In this way they attract my attention to the fact that they have "identified" these persons with each other, that they have placed them in the same category, which for their emotional life signifies the recurrence of the same type. Or, a young man of twenty years presents himself during my office hours with these words: "I am the father of N. N., whom you have treated—pardon me, I mean the brother; why, he is four years older than I." I understand through this mistake that he wishes to express that, like the brother, he too, is ill through the fault of the father; like his brother, he wishes to be cured, but that the father is the one most in need of treatment. At other times an unusual arrangement of words, or a forced expression, is sufficient to disclose in the speech of the patient the participation of a repressed thought having a different motive.

Hence, in coarse as well as in finer speech disturbances, which may, nevertheles, be subsumed as "speech-blunders," I find that it is not the contact effects of the sound, but the thoughts outside the intended speech, which determine the origin of the speech-blunder, and also suffice to explain the newly formed mistakes in speech.

PHILOSOPHICAL CONSEQUENCES OF RELATIVITY

Bertrand Russell

[The mathematician, philosopher, and social thinker Bertrand Russell was at work on his classic exposition of Einstein's theory of relativity, The A. B. C. of Relativity, when he agreed to write this piece for the Thirteenth Edition (1926) of Britannica. It makes for an unusual encyclopadia article—it is tentative, somewhat speculative—but it provides an interesting counterpoint to Einstein's own, more technical article.]

Of the consequences in philosophy which may be supposed to follow from the theory of relativity, some are fairly certain, while others are open to question. There has been a tendency, not uncommon in the case of a new scientific theory, for every philosopher to interpret the work of Einstein in accordance with his own metaphysical system, and to suggest that the outcome is a great accession of strength to the views which the philosopher in question previously held. This cannot be true in all cases; and it may be hoped that it is true in none. It would be disappointing if so fundamental a change as Einstein has introduced involved no philosophical novelty. (See SPACE-TIME.)

SPACE-TIME

For philosophy, the most important novelty was present already in the special theory of relativity; that is, the substitution of space-time for space and time. In Newtonian dynamics, two events were separated by two kinds of interval, one being distance in space, the other lapse of time. As soon as it was realised that all motion is relative (which happened long before Einstein), distance in space became ambiguous except in the case of simultaneous events, but it was still thought that there was no ambiguity about simultaneity in different places. The special theory of relativity showed, by experimental arguments which were new, and by logical arguments which could have been discovered any time after it

305

became known that light travels with a finite velocity, that simultaneity is only definite when it applies to events in the same place, and becomes more and more ambiguous as the events are more widely removed from each other in space.

This statement is not quite correct, since it still uses the notion of "space." The correct statement is this: Events have a four-dimensional order, by means of which we can say that an event A is nearer to an event B than to an event C; this is a purely ordinal matter, not involving anything quantitative. But, in addition, there is between neighbouring events a quantitative relation called "interval," which fulfils the functions both of distance in space and of lapse of time in the traditional dynamics, but fulfils them with a difference. If a body can move so as to be present at both events, the interval is time-like. If a ray of light can move so as to be present at both events, the interval is zero. If neither can happen, the interval is space-like. When we speak of a body being present "at" an event, we mean that the event occurs in the same place in space-time as one of the events which make up the history of the body; and when we say that two events occur at the same place in space-time, we mean that there is no event between them in the four-dimensional space-time order. All the events which happen to a man at a given moment (in his own time) are, in this sense, in one place; for example, if we hear a noise and see a colour simultaneously, our two perceptions are both in one place in space-time.

When one body can be present at two events which are not in one place in space-time, the time-order of the two events is not ambiguous, though the magnitude of the time-interval will be different in different systems of measurement. But whenever the interval between two events is space-like, their time-order will be different in different equally legitimate systems of measurement; in this case, therefore, the time-order does not represent a physical fact. It follows that, when two bodies are in relative motion, like the sun and a planet, there is no such physical fact as "the distance between the bodies at a given time"; this alone shows that Newton's law of gravitation is logically faulty. Fortunately, Einstein has not only pointed out the defect, but remedied it. His arguments against Newton, however, would have remained valid even if his own law of gravitation had not proved right.

TIME NOT A SINGLE COSMIC ORDER

The fact that time is private to each body, not a single cosmic order, involves changes in the notions of substance and cause, and suggests the substitution of a series of events for a substance with changing states. The controversy about the aether thus becomes rather unreal. Undoubtedly, when light-waves travel, events occur, and it used to be thought that these events must be "in" something; the something in which they were was called the aether. But there seems no reason except a logical prejudice to suppose that the events are "in" anything. Matter, also, may be reduced to a law according to which events succeed each other and spread out from centres; but here we enter upon more speculative considerations.

PHYSICAL LAWS

Prof. Eddington has emphasised an aspect of relativity theory which is of great philosophical importance, but difficult to make clear without somewhat abstruse mathematics. The aspect in question is the reduction of what used to be regarded as physical laws to the status of truisms or definitions. Prof. Eddington, in a profoundly interesting essay on "The Domain of Physical Science,"[1] states the matter as follows:

> In the present stage of science the laws of physics appear to be divisible into three classes—the identical, the statistical and the transcendental. The "identical laws" include the great field-laws which are commonly quoted as typical instances of natural law—the law of gravitation, the law of conservation of mass and energy, the laws of electric and magnetic force and the conservation of electric charge. These are seen to be identities, when we refer to the cycle so as to understand the constitution of the entities obeying them; and unless we have misunderstood this constitution, violation of these laws is inconceivable. They do not in any way limit the actual basal structure of the world, and are not laws of governance (op. cit., pp. 214–5).

It is these identical laws that form the subject-matter of relativity theory; the other laws of physics, the statistical and transcendental, lie outside its scope. Thus the net result of relativity theory is to show that the traditional laws of physics, rightly understood, tell us almost nothing about the course of nature, being rather of the nature of logical truisms.

This surprising result is an outcome of increased mathematical skill. As the same author[2] says elsewhere:

> In one sense deductive theory is the enemy of experimental physics. The latter is always striving to settle by crucial tests the nature of the fundamental things; the former strives to minimise the successes obtained by showing how wide a nature of things is compatible with all experimental results.

The suggestion is that, in almost any conceivable world, something will be conserved; mathematics gives us the means of constructing a variety of mathematical expressions having this property of conservation. It is natural to suppose that it is useful to have senses which notice these conserved entities; hence mass, energy, and so on seem to have a basis in our experience, but are in fact merely certain quantities which are conserved and which we are adapted for noticing. If

---

[1] In Science, Religion and Reality, ed. by Joseph Needham (1925).

[2] A. S. Eddington, Mathematical Theory of Relativity, p. 238 (Cambridge, 1924)

this view is correct, physics tells us much less about the real world than was formerly supposed.

FORCE AND GRAVITATION

An important aspect of relativity is the elimination of "force." This is not new in idea; indeed, it was already accepted in rational dynamics. But there remained the outstanding difficulty of gravitation, which Einstein has overcome. The sun is, so to speak, at the summit of a hill, and the planets are on the slopes. They move as they do because of the slope where they are, not because of some mysterious influence emanating from the summit. Bodies move as they do because that is the easiest possible movement in the region of space-time in which they find themselves, not because "forces" operate upon them. The apparent need of forces to account for observed motions arises from mistaken insistence upon Euclidean geometry; when once we have overcome this prejudice, we find that observed motions, instead of showing the presence of forces, show the nature of the geometry applicable to the region concerned. Bodies thus become far more independent of each other than they were in Newtonian physics: there is an increase of individualism and a diminution of central government, if one may be permitted such metaphorical language. This may, in time, considerably modify the ordinary educated man's picture of the universe, possibly with far-reaching results.

REALISM IN RELATIVITY

It is a mistake to suppose that relativity adopts an idealistic picture of the world—using "idealism" in the technical sense, in which it implies that there can be nothing which is not experience. The "observer" who is often mentioned in expositions of relativity need not be a mind, but may be a photographic plate or any kind of recording instrument. The fundamental assumption of relativity is realistic, namely, that those respects in which all observers agree when they record a given phenomenon may be regarded as objective, and not as contributed by the observers. This assumption is made by common sense. The apparent sizes and shapes of objects differ according to the point of view, but common sense discounts these differences. Relativity theory merely extends this process. By taking into account not only human observers, who all share the motion of the earth, but also possible "observers" in very rapid motion relatively to the earth, it is found that much more depends upon the point of view of the observer than was formerly thought. But there is found to be a residue which is not so dependent; this is the part which can be expressed by the method of "tensors." The importance of this method can hardly be exaggerated; it is, however, quite impossible to explain it in non-mathematical terms.

RELATIVITY PHYSICS

Relativity physics is, of course, concerned only with the quantitative aspects of the world. The picture which it suggests is somewhat as follows:—In the four-dimensional space-time frame there are events everywhere, usually many events in a single place in space-time. The abstract mathematical relations of these events proceed according to the laws of physics, but the intrinsic nature of the events is wholly and inevitably unknown except when they occur in a region where there is the sort of structure we call a brain. Then they become the familiar sights and sounds and so on of our daily life. We know what it is like to see a star, but we do not know the nature of the events which constitute the ray of light that travels from the star to our eye. And the space-time frame itself is known only in its abstract mathematical properties; there is no reason to suppose it similar in intrinsic character to the spatial and temporal relations of our perceptions as known in experience. There does not seem any possible way of overcoming this ignorance, since the very nature of physical reasoning allows only the most abstract inferences, and only the most abstract properties of our perceptions can be regarded as having objective validity. Whether any other science than physics can tell us more, does not fall within the scope of the present article.

Meanwhile, it is a curious fact that this meagre kind of knowledge is sufficient for the practical uses of physics. From a practical point of view, the physical world only matters in so far as it affects us, and the intrinsic nature of what goes on in our absence is irrelevant, provided we can predict the effects upon ourselves. This we can do, just as a person can use a telephone without understanding electricity. Only the most abstract knowledge is required for practical manipulation of matter. But there is a grave danger when this habit of manipulation based upon mathematical laws is carried over into our dealings with human beings, since they, unlike the telephone wire, are capable of happiness and misery, desire and aversion. It would therefore be unfortunate if the habits of mind which are appropriate and right in dealing with material mechanisms were allowed to dominate the administrator's attempts at social constructiveness.

A. S. Eddington, Space, Time, and Gravitation (Cambridge, 1921); Bertrand A. W. Russell, The A. B. C. of Relativity (1925).

ACROSS THE OPEN

Patrick MacGill

"The firefly lamps were lighted yet,
As we Crossed the top of the parapet,
But the East grew pale to another fire,
As our bayonets gleamed by the foeman's wire.
And the Eastern sky was gold and grey,
And under our feet the dead men lay,
As we entered Loos in the morning."

The moment had come when it was unwise to think. The country round Loos was like a sponge; the god of war had stamped with his foot on it, and thousands of men, armed, ready to kill, were squirted out on to the level, barren fields of danger. To dwell for a moment on the novel position of being standing where a thousand deaths swept by, missing you by a mere hair's breadth, would be sheer folly. There on the open field of death my life was out of my keeping, but the sensation of fear never entered my being. There was so much simplicity and so little effort in doing what I had done, in doing what eight hundred comrades had done, that I felt I could carry through the work before me with as much credit as my code of self respect required. The maxims went crackle like dry brushwood under the feet of a marching host. A bullet passed very close to my face like a sharp, sudden breath; a second hit the ground in front, flicked up a little shower of dust, and ricochetted to the left, hitting the earth many times before it found a resting place. The air was vicious with bullets; a million invisible birds flicked their wings very close to my face. Ahead the clouds of smoke, sluggish low-lying fog, and fumes of bursting shells, thick in volume, receded towards the German trenches, and formed a striking background for the soldiers who were marching up a low slope towards the enemy's parapet, which the smoke still hid from view. There was no haste in the forward move, every step was taken with regimental

The Great Push: An Episode of the Great War by Patrick MacGill. Author of "The Red Horizon," "The Rat-Pit . . . Children of the Dead End." etc. New York, George H. Doran Company, 1916 precision, and twice on the way across the Irish boys halted for a moment to correct their alignment. Only at a point on the right there was some confusion and a little irregularity. Were the men wavering? No fear! The boys on the right were dribbling the elusive football towards the German trench.

Raising the stretcher, my mate and I went forward. For the next few minutes I was conscious of many things. A slight rain was falling; the smoke and fumes I saw had drifted back, exposing a dark streak on the field of green, the enemy's trench. A little distance away from me three men hurried forward, and two of them carried a box of rifle ammunition. One of the bearers fell flat to earth, his two mates halted for a moment, looked at the stricken boy, and seemed to puzzle at something. Then they caught hold of the box hangers and rushed forward. The man on the ground raised himself on his elbow and looked after his mates; then sank down again to the wet ground. Another soldier came crawling towards us on his belly, looking for all the world like a gigantic lobster which had escaped from its basket. His lower lip was cut clean to the chin and hanging apart; blood welled through the muddy khaki trousers where they covered the hips.

I recognised the fellow.

"Much hurt, matey?" I asked.

"I'll manage to get in," he said.

"Shall I put a dressing on?" I inquired.

"I'll manage to get into our own trench," he stammered, spitting the blood from his lips. —There are others out at the wires. S—— has caught it bad. Try and get him in, Pat."

"Right, old man," I said, as he crawled off. "Good luck."

My cap was blown off my head as if by a violent gust of wind, and it dropped on the ground. I put it on again, and at that moment a shell burst near at hand and a dozen splinters sung by my ear. I walked forward with a steady step.

"What took my cap off?" I asked myself. "It went away just as if it was caught in a breeze. God!" I muttered, in a burst of realisation, "it was that shell passing." I breathed very deeply, my blood rushed down to my toes and an airy sensation filled my body. Then the stretcher dragged.

"Lift the damned thing up," I called to my mate over my shoulder. There was no reply. I looked round to find him gone, either mixed up in a whooping rush of kilted Highlanders, who had lost their objective and were now charging parallel to their own trench, or perhaps he got killed. . . . How strange that the Highlanders could not charge in silence, I thought, and then recollected that most of my boyhood friends, Donegal lads, were in Scottish regiments. . . . I placed my stretcher on my shoulder, walked forward towards a bank of smoke which seemed to be standing stationary, and came across our platoon sergeant and part of his company.

"Are we going wrong, or are the Jocks wrong?" he asked his men, then shouted, "Lie flat, boys, for a minute, until we see where we are. There's a big crucifix in Loos churchyard, and we've got to draw on that."

The men threw themselves flat; the sergeant went down on one knee and leant forward on his rifle, his hands on the bayonet standard, the fingers pointing upwards and the palms pressed close to the sword which was covered with rust. . . . How hard it would be to draw it from a dead body! . . . The sergeant seemed to be kneeling in prayer. . . . In front the cloud cleared away, and the black crucifix standing over the graves of Loos became revealed.

"Advance, boys!" said the sergeant. "Steady on to the foot of the Cross and rip the swine out of their trenches."

The Irish went forward. . . .

A boy sat on the ground bleeding at the shoulder and knee.

"You've got hit," I said.

"In a few places," he answered, in a very matter-of-fact voice. "I want to get into a shellhole."

"I'll try and get you into one," I said. "But I want someone to help me. Hi! you there! Come and give me a hand."

I spoke to a man who sat on the rim of a crater near at hand. His eyes, set close in a white, ghastly face, stared tensely at me. He sat in a crouching position, his head thrust forward, his right hand gripping tightly at a mud-stained rifle. Presumably he was a bit shaken and was afraid to advance further.

"Help me to get this fellow into a shell-hole," I called. "He can't move."

There was no answer.

"Come along," I cried, and then it was suddenly borne to me that the man was dead. I dragged the wounded boy into the crater and dressed his wounds.

A shell struck the ground in front, burrowed, and failed to explode.

"Thank Heaven!" I muttered, and hurried ahead. Men and pieces of men were lying all over the place. A leg, an arm, then again a leg, cut off at the hip. A finely formed leg, the latter, gracefully putteed. A dummy leg in a tailor's window could not be more graceful. It might be X; he was an artist in dress, a Beau Brummel in khaki. Fifty yards further along I found the rest of X. . . .

The harrowing sight was repellent, antagonistic to my mind. The tortured things lying at my feet were symbols of insecurity, ominous reminders of danger from which no discretion could save a man. My soul was barren of pity; fear went down into the innermost parts of me, fear for myself. The dead and dying lay all around me; I felt a vague obligation to the latter; they must be carried out. But why should I trouble! Where could I begin? Everything was so far apart. I was too puny to start my labours in such a derelict world. The difficulty of accommodating myself to an old task under new conditions was enormous.

A figure in grey, a massive block of Bavarian bone and muscle, came running towards me, his arms in air, and Bill Teake following him with a long bayonet.

"A prisoner!" yelled the boy on seeing me. "'Kamerad! Kamerad!' 'e shouted when I came up. Blimey! I couldn't stab 'im, so I took 'im prisoner. It's not 'arf a barney! 'Ave yer got a fag ter spare?"

The Cockney came to a halt, reached for a cigarette, and lit it.

The German stood still, panting like a dog.

"Double! Fritz, double!" shouted the boy, sending a little puff of smoke through his nose. "Over to our trench you go! Grease along if yer don't want a bayonet in your————!"

They rushed off, the German with hands in air, and Bill behind with his bayonet perilously close to the prisoner. There was something amusing in the incident, and I could not refrain from laughing. Then I got a whiff from a German gas-bomb which exploded near me, and I began spluttering and coughing. The irritation, only momentary, was succeeded by a strange humour. I felt as if walking on air, my head got light, and it was with difficulty that I kept my feet on earth. It would be so easy to rise into space and float away. The sensation was a delightful one; I felt so pleased with myself, with everything. A wounded man lay on the ground, clawing the earth with frenzied fingers. In a vague way, I remembered some ancient law which ordained me to assist a stricken man. But I could not do so now, the action would clog my buoyancy and that delightful feeling of freedom which permeated my being. Another soldier whom I recognised, even at a distance, by his pink-and-white bald pate, so often a subject for our jokes, reeled over the blood-stained earth, his eyes almost bursting from their sockets.

"You look bad," I said to him with a smile.

He stared at me drunkenly, but did not answer.

A man, mother-naked, raced round in a circle, laughing boisterously. The rags that would class him as a friend or foe were gone, and I could not tell whether he was an Englishman or a German. As I watched him an impartial bullet went through his forehead, and he fell headlong to the earth. The sight sobered me and I regained my normal self.

Up near the German wire I found our Company postman sitting in a shell-hole, a bullet in his leg below the knee, and an unlighted cigarette in his mouth.

"You're the man I want," he shouted, on seeing me. And I fumbled in my haversack for bandages.

"No dressing for me, yet," he said with a smile. "There are others needing help more than I. What I want is a match."

As I handed him my match box a big high explosive shell flew over our heads and dropped fifty yards away in a little hollow where seven or eight figures in khaki lay prostrate, faces to the ground. The shell burst and the wounded and dead rose slowly into air to a height of six or seven yards and dropped slowly again, looking for all the world like puppets worked by wires.

"This," said the postman, who had observed the incident, "is a solution of a question which diplomacy could not settle, I suppose. The last argument of kings is a damned sorry business."

By the German barbed wire entanglements were the shambles of war. Here our men were seen by the enemy for the first time that morning. Up till then the foe had fired erratically through the oncoming curtain of smoke; but when the cloud cleared away, the attackers were seen advancing, picking their way through the wires which had been cut to little pieces by our bombardment. The Irish were now met with harrying rifle fire, deadly petrol bombs and hand grenades. Here I came across dead, dying and sorely wounded; lives maimed and finished, and all the romance and roving that makes up the life of a soldier gone for ever. Here, too, I saw, bullet-riddled, against one of the spider webs known as *chevaux de frise*, a limp lump of pliable leather, the football which the boys had kicked across the field.

I came across Flannery lying close to a barbed wire support, one arm round it as if in embrace. He was a clumsily built fellow, with queer bushy eyebrows and a short, squat nose. His bearing was never soldierly, but on a march he could bear any burden and stick the job when more alert men fell out. He always bore himself however with a certain grace, due, perhaps, to a placid belief in his own strength. He never made friends; a being apart, he led a solitary life. Now he lay close to earth hugging an entanglement prop, and dying.

There was something savage in the expression of his face as he looked slowly round, like an ox under a yoke, on my approach. I knelt down beside him and cut his tunic with my scissors where a burnt hole clotted with blood showed under the kidney. A splinter of shell had torn part of the man's side away. All hope was lost for the poor soul.

"In much pain, chummy?" I asked.

"Ah, Christ! yes, Pat," he answered. "Wife and two kiddies, too. Are we getting the best of it?"

I did not know how the fight was progressing, but I had seen a line of bayonets drawing near to the second trench out by Loos.

"Winning all along," I answered.

"That's good," he said. "Is there any hope for me?"

"Of course there is, matey," I lied. "You have two of these morphia tablets and lie quiet. We'll take you in after a while, and you'll be back in England in two or three days' time."

I placed the morphia under his tongue and he closed his eyes as if going to sleep. Then, with an effort, he tried to get up and gripped the wire support with such vigour that it came clean out of the ground. His legs shot out from under him, and, muttering something about rations being fit for pigs and not for men, he fell back and died.

The fighting was not over in the front trench yet, the first two companies had gone ahead, the other two companies were taking possession here. A sturdy

Bavarian in shirt and pants was standing on a banquette with his bayonet over the parapet, and a determined look in his eyes. He had already done for two of our men as they tried to cross, but now his rifle seemed to be unloaded and he waited. Standing there amidst his dead countrymen he formed a striking figure. A bullet from one of our rifles would have ended his career speedily, but no one seemed to want to fire that shot. There was a moment of suspense, broken only when the monstrous futility of resistance became apparent to him, and he threw down his rifle and put up his hands, shouting "Kamerad! kamerad!" I don't know what became of him afterwards, other events claimed my attention.

Four boys rushed up, panting under the machine gun and ammunition belts which they carried. One got hit and fell to the ground, the maxim tripod which he carried fell on top of him. The remainder of the party came to a halt.

"Lift the tripod and come along," his mates shouted to one another.

"Who's goin' to carry it?" asked a little fellow with a box of ammunition.

"You," came the answer.

"Some other one must carry it," said the little fellow. "I've the heaviest burden."

"You've not," one answered. "Get the blurry thing on your shoulder."

"Blurry yourself!" said the little fellow. "Someone else carry the thing. Marney can carry it."

"I'm not a damned fool!" said Marney. "It can stick there 'fore I take it across."

"Not much good goin' over without it," said the little fellow.

I left them there wrangling: the extra weight would have made no appreciable difference to any of them.

It was interesting to see how the events of the morning had changed the nature of the boys. Mild-mannered youths who had spent their working hours of civil life in scratching with inky pens on white paper, and their hours of relaxation in cutting capers on roller skates and helping dainty maidens to teas and ices, became possessed of mad Berserker rage and ungovernable fury. Now that their work was war the bloodstained bayonet gave them play in which they seemed to glory.

"Here's one that I've just done in," I heard M'Crone shout, looking approvingly at a dead German. "That's five of the bloody swine now."

M'Crone's mother never sends her son any money lest he gets into the evil habit of smoking cigarettes. He is of a religious turn of mind and delights in singing hymns, his favourite being, "There is a green hill far away." I never heard him swear before, but at Loos his language would make a navvy in a Saturday night taproom green with envy. M'Crone was not lacking in courage. I have seen him wait for death with untroubled front in a shell-harried trench, and now, inflicting pain on others, he was a fiend personified; such transformations are of common occurrence on the field of honour.

The German trench had suffered severely from our fire; parapets were blown in, and at places the trench was full to the level of the ground with sandbags and earth. Wreckage was strewn all over the place, rifles, twisted distortions of shapeless metal, caught by high-velocity shells, machine guns smashed to atoms, bombproof shelters broken to pieces like houses of cards; giants had been at work of destruction in a delicately fashioned nursery.

On the reverse slope of the parapet broken tins, rusty swords, muddy equipments, wicked-looking coils of barbed wire, and discarded articles of clothing were scattered about pell-mell. I noticed an unexploded shell perched on a sandbag, cocking a perky nose in air, and beside it was a battered helmet, the brass glory of its regal eagle dimmed with trench mud and wrecked with many a bullet.

I had a clear personal impression of man's ingenuity for destruction when my eyes looked on the German front line where our dead lay in peace with their fallen enemies on the parapet. At the bottom of the trench the dead lay thick, and our boys, engaged in building a new parapet, were heaping the sandbags on the dead men and consolidating the captured position.

THE PATHOLOGY OF INFLUENZA IN FRANCE

S. W. Patterson, M.D., D.Sc.

Director of the Walter and Eliza Hall Institute of Research in Pathology and Medicine, Melbourne

INTRODUCTION, 1996

The following article was written by Dr S. W. Patterson, the Director of the very prestigious Walter and Eliza Hall Institute of Research in Pathology in Melbourne, in 1920 and is the text of an address that he gave to a meeting of the Victorian Branch of the British Medical Association. Dr Patterson had served in France as a Major in the Army during the Great Influenza pandemic.

It must be remembered that the discovery of the Influenza virus, the true cause of the influenza pandemic, was not made until 1933 and yet Dr. Patterson was able to predict this when he wrote: "The experimental results of Gibson, Bowman and Connor and of Wilson and Bashford confirming Nicolle and Lebailly point to an "invisible" or "filter passing" organism as the exciting cause." This "filter passing" organism was, of course, the virus. During the Great War, it was considered that the Bacillus Influenzae of Pfeiffer was the causative agent. Dr Patterson was able to demonstrate that this was not so and the infection by this organism was a secondary infection.

It was also found that two of the patients, who died, suffered from tuberculosis. This represented the spectrum of disease in the Great War period when tuberculosis was common. *Dr Geoffrey Miller*

From: *The Medical Journal of Australia*, Vol. I, 7th Year. Sydney: Saturday, March 6, 1920. No. 10

THE PATHOLOGY OF INFLUENZA IN FRANCE

I propose to relate our own experience in Rouen, France, and then to discuss some of the epidemiological and pathological points that have arisen as the result of work and observations during the recent epidemic.

We had read of the spread of so-called Spanish influenza in the newspapers, but our first contact with it in Rouen was the arrival, in April, 1918, of a hospital train full of "sitting" patients, the majority convalescing from malaria and sandfly fever, from Italy. Most of the Royal Army Medical Corps personnel and patients had suffered during the journey from a three to five day fever of great contagiousness. Several patients were admitted to the No. 25 Stationary Hospital on a Thursday for observation and investigation. The Laboratory staff was busy getting ready to take blood and other cultures. I was working at a neighbouring hospital and on going over on the following Sunday afternoon, I found that 26 orderlies at No. 25 Stationary Hospital, several nurses and five medical Officers, including the whole of the laboratory staff, had been taken ill on the previous days with fever up to 38.50 or 39.50 C.

Lieutenant-Colonel C. J. Martin, in his indefatigable way, was carrying on the investigation, although he was suffering from a severe attack.

The blood cultures he had prepared from the personnel of the No. 25 Stationary Hospital yielded only one pathogenic organism, a haemolytic streptococcus. As the majority of the patients had some cough, we investigated the mucus from the throat and made cultures with the sputum. In nearly every case we found small, Gram-negative rods which would not grow in sub-culture on agar unless blood was present, but would sometimes grow on ordinary agar smeared with tracheal or pharyngeal mucus. We found great difficulty in purifying the culture and even in keeping it going on citrated human blood agar. Eventually we obtained pure cultures on rabbit's blood agar. The bacillus was pleomorphic and conformed to the description of Pfeiffer's Bacillus influenzae. In three cases Lieutenant-Colonel Martin found that the fresh sputum examined daily swarmed with these bacilli, all lying in the mucus outside the leucocytes. On the 12th, 14th and 17th. days respectively from the onset of the illness the picture changed with striking suddenness. The majority of the leucocytes contained the small bacilli, often to the number of 40 to 50 in one field. This active phagocytosis continued as long as the sputum contained the bacilli. In many cells they were obviously undergoing digestion, being enclosed in minute vacuoles and having lost their power of taking up carbol-fuchsin used to stain the films. In many of these cases, coincident with the phagocytosis, improvement occurred in the condition of the patient. The sputum became more purulent, but rapidly diminished in quantity.

During the next few months we had many cases, but few deaths. The post-mortem examination of the patients showed the characteristic haemorrhagic

Broncho-pneumonia. Then the epidemic diminished, to rise again in October, November and December, with a great influx of cases of a more severe type. Clinically the most noteworthy features were the tendency to haemorrhages, including epistaxis, haematemesis, blood-stained sputum, which was usually profuse and watery, profound toxaemia and little evidence of consolidation of the lungs.

General Post-Mortem Appearances

Frothy, sanious fluid was often exuding from the mouth and nostrils. The veins of the neck were engorged and full of dark fluid blood. When the thoracic cavity was opened it was seen that the front of the turgid lungs was pushed upwards, usually full of air and crackling. Rupture of the air vesicles had taken place in many cases, leading to patches of acute emphysema beneath the pleura. There were frequently small areas of sub-pleural haemorrhages.

In a few cases there was a considerable amount of dark straw-coloured fluid in one pleural cavity. In these, the pleura affected had patches of soft, greenish yellow, thick fibrin scattered over the lower parts of the lung and between the lobes. From this exudate a pneumococcus was always grown. One half of the cases showed recent, soft fibrinous adhesions, scattered over one or both lungs. In some instances these were very dense, although recent, and in tearing through them, quantities of bloodstained fluid exuded from the mouth and nostrils, as it was expressed from the lung and bronchioles. In three instances there were old, firm fibrous adhesions of a previous pleurisy. The total recent pleural involvement was 60%.

In the remaining cases the pleurae in front were pale, at times emphysematous and containing petechial haemorrhages, as described above. Posteriorly, over the engorged or consolidated lung, the pleural surface had lost its glistening appearance and was of a dark plum colour.

The Lungs

The most striking feature was the general engorgement and water-logged condition of the lungs. Except in the grey consolidated patches, there was profuse exudation of frothy, sanious fluid from the cut surface. In extricating the lungs, especially when pleural adhesions were present, frothy bloodstained fluid was expressed from the bronchi and poured out of the mouth.

Microscopically it was seen that the capillaries of the pleura, of the alveolar walls and of the walls of the bronchi were greatly engorged and were frequently ruptured, with the result that extravasation of red corpuscles had taken place. The walls of the larger vessels appeared to be normal and contained no fibrin.

The alveoli were full of a homogeneous, coagulated, albuminous exudate, often containing red blood corpuscles, and in the more affected parts leucocytes and endothelial cells. To this primary inflammatory, slimy oedema and congestion were added the following types of broncho pneumonic involvement:

(I) THE PERI-BRONCHIAL TYPE

In the early stages this condition was revealed by small, bright red spots of consolidation, about 5 mm. in diameter, surrounding a small bronchus. On palpating the lung through the pleura and passing the finger over the cut surface, the impression was gained of small knots in the lung of firm consistency, resembling the sensation when feeling miliary tubercles. This condition frequently remained limited in extent, becoming grey and later softening, so that in the late stages the lung surface was pitted with small, discrete abscesses. The infection of the lung had apparently taken place through the wall of the bronchioles. The walls of the abscesses were composed of pulmonary alveoli. The lumen of the bronchioles was filled with corpuscular exudate, disintegrated mucous membrane and, in the late stages, some organisation of the exudate was taking place.

(II.) THE USUAL BRONCHO-PNEUMONIC TYPE

Here the cut surface of the lung amidst general engorgement and oedema showed firmer, raised, bright red areas, varying in diameter up to 2.5–4.0 cm. Later these areas became larger, dark red and confluent. In the next stages, greyish red patches were evident and in some instances the confluent, greyish red, massive areas resembled lobar pneumonia. The lobe, however, contained areas in various stages from dark red patches to patches in which softening and abscess formation were taking place. In some instances the whole alveolar part of the lung was diffluent, and abscesses up to 6 cm. in diameter were present. These abscesses were full of broken-down lung and were traversed by strings of more resistant bronchi.

(III.) PURULENT BRONCHITIS

From parts of the lung in all stages of involvement, worms of yellowish pus could be expressed from the small bronchi.

(IV.) ACUTE EMPHYSEMA

In one patient, whose bronchitic signs dated from one to two days before death, only one small area of bright red consolidation near the hilus of the left lower lobe was found in addition to a very extensive haemorrhagic engorgement of all parts of the lungs. In all other cases protean combinations of the pathological varieties outlined above were found throughout the lungs. On the whole, however, the parts dependent in the dorsal decubitus revealed the most wide-spread and furthest developed involvement. In two cases there was definite evidence of tuberculosis. In one there was an old calcified nodule in the apex of the upper lobe of the right lung. In the other there were acute miliary tubercles scattered widely throughout the lungs. Smears from the lungs in this case contained Bacillus tuberculosis, and both the smears and cultures yielded Bacillus Influenzae.

Respiratory Tract

In all cases the bronchi contained frothy, bloodstained fluid. The mucous membrane was congested. In many cases this congestion was intense and extended up to and involved the epiglottis, being accompanied at times by submucous haemorrhages. In cases of longer standing erosion and ulceration of the vocal cords had occurred.

The Heart

The cavities of the right side of the heart were always much dilated. They were distended with dark blood and frequently firm, white clot extended to the root of the pulmonary artery. The left ventricle was usually small, firm and contracted, but in 20% of the cases the muscle of the left ventricle was softened and flabby. No acute involvement of the valves was observed. Subpericardial haemorrhages were noted in one case. In no instance was there an excess of fluid in the pericardium, nor was pericarditis seen. The myocardium was pale, usually soft, and revealed early fatty changes.

The Liver

The liver was considerably engorged in all cases. A constant observation was the presence of patches of degeneration of the liver. In bodies examined even within two or three hours of death small subcapsular areas of yellowish degeneration were found, principally on the upper surface of both lobes and at the free anterior border, extending sometimes to a depth of from two to three centimetres, Microscopical examination proved that these areas were fatty degeneration of the liver cells. In some instances the degeneration was wide-spread throughout the organ, but this may have been due to early post-mortem changes. In two cases recent fibrinous adhesions of the diaphragm to the upper surface of the right lobe had occurred.

The Spleen

The spleen in one case contained a large infarct. The organ was small and firm in 22 cases, softened in 14 and large and softened in ten cases.

The Adrenals

The adrenals in 60% of the cases were observed to be friable. In one case both adrenals contained haemorrhages involving the whole gland.

The Kidneys

The kidneys were generally engorged, and there was some oedema of the cortex. The organs were usually pale. Microscopically it was seen that there was some fatty degeneration of the cells lining the tubules.

The Gastro-Intestinal Tract

In one case in which the gastric veins were distended the patient had suffered from haematemesis, and there were numerous sub-mucous haemorrhages in the stomach wall. In the remainder of the bodies examined, these organs appeared to be normal.

The Brain

In the brain and medulla of a patient who had died with signs of meningismus, no macroscopical abnormality was detected. The cerebro-spinal fluid proved on culture to have been sterile.

The Muscles

In some instances interstitial haemorrhages had occurred in the lower part of the rectus abdominis muscle. In many cases the muscle fibres showed degenerative changes.

I have gone into the details of the post-mortem appearances, because I wish to remind you of them later on. The pathological picture may be summarized as follows:

(i.) Intense inflammatory oedema of the lungs;

(ii.) Toxic degeneration of the special cells of all organs and tissues of the body;

(iii.) Haemorrhages.

Bacteriology

When our bacteriological methods of investigation became stabilized, a series of autopsies was submitted to analysis. The bacteriology was carried out by Dr. Marjorie Little and Sister F. E. Williams.

From the heart's blood from 44 patients B.

influenzae (Pfeiffer) was recovered once;

Pneumococcus was recovered 12 times;

Streptococcus was recovered once;

Staphylococcus was recovered once.

The pneumococci isolated in twelve cases gave a greenish colouration on blood agar, fermented inulin, and were dissolved in bile. The attempts to group them with type sera from the Rockefeller Institute were not satisfactory. Only one strain remained constantly agglutinable by Type II serum.

Captain P. Hartley, R.A.M.C., carried out experiments on the specific agglutinins for B. influenzae (Pfeiffer) with sera obtained from our patients.

Of 21 samples of serum from the heart's blood of patients dead of influenza:

10 agglutinated one or more strains of B. Influenzae in 1:200 dilution,

4 agglutinated one or more strains of B. Influenzae in 1:100 dilution,

1 agglutinated one or more strains of B. Influenzae in 1:50 dilution,

6 failed to agglutinate the strains against which they were tested.

Of 20 samples of serum from patients who ultimately recovered:

10 agglutinated one or more strains of B. Influenzae in 1:200 dilution,

4 agglutinated one or more strains of B. influenzae in 1:50 dilution,

6 failed to agglutinate any of the strains.

The serum of one patient agglutinated a strain of B. Influenzae on the sixth day in a dilution of 1: 200. On the tenth day the serum agglutinated the same strain in a dilution of 1:100. On the fifteenth day no agglutination occurred in a dilution of 1:50. It was found to be impossible to group the strains of Bacillus Influenzae according to agglutinable types.

During 1915 many cases of what for want of a better term had been called in the South African war "simple continued fever" were diagnosed as influenza in France. The medical authorities intervened and the term "P.U.O." (pyrexia of unknown origin) was introduced. At times this was referred to as "of the trench fever or influenza type." Purulent bronchitis was very prevalent and fatal in the spring of 1916 and 1917. The most frequent organisms found in the films and cultures made from sputum were B. Influenzae and pneumococci, as recorded at Aldershot and Etaples.

Then came the "Spanish disease" in the late spring of 1918. It was a five-day fever with severe pains and prostration and some catarrh of the respiratory passages. In the following autumn of the same year came the pandemic of inflammatory, suffocative oedema of the lungs with great toxaemia and haemorrhages.

This raises the fundamental question of the definition of influenza. Is it the clinical picture or the epidemiological characters of the outbreaks and course of spread that make influenza an entity? Is it one disease or a group of diseases? And is the disease that prevailed in the spring of earlier years the same as occurred in the autumn of 1918?

Epidemiologically the extreme contagiousness of the disease was proved to be by the "drop" method from person to person. The infecting agent had been regarded since 1892 as the organism described by Pfeiffer as the influenza bacillus.

But in this epidemic a great many observers failed to find the Pfeiffer bacillus. This fact, together with its prevalence in many respiratory infections, especially in children, apart from epidemics, caused much doubt to be thrown on the claim that Bacillus influenzae of Pfeiffer is the cause of the disease.

The case for Pfeiffer's bacillus consists in the argument that as it is haemolytic, it is a true parasite, that it is constantly found in all stages of the disease, that it leads to an early, albeit evanescent evolution of agglutinating substances in the blood and that it is ingested by phagocytes concurrently with the onset of convalescence.

Post-mortem examinations of patients dying in the early stages of the disease gave a picture of haemorrhagic oedema of the lungs, with abundance of haemorrhages in the mucous and serous membranes of the respiratory tract and in other organs. This was regarded as an indication of a damaged condition of the vascular capillary system. The haemorrhages in the lungs paved the way for secondary infections, the results of which dominated the whole field in the later stages. The whole picture was thus thought to resemble pneumonic plague anatomically (Oberndorfer).

But you will call to mind the description I gave in an earlier part of this paper which showed that the lining of the blood vessels was no more affected than the special cells of the organs of the body. The wedgeshaped areas in the affected lung can be equally due to interference with a branch of the bronchial tree. The infecting agent can cause such a spoiling of the capillary wall that increased transudation of lymph and escape of red blood corpuscles may take place into the lung, which is the primary organ attacked.

The question of haemorrhages is of great interest, because of the similarity between the lungs of animals infected with filtrates or Noguthi's cultures of filtered sputum and those of patients dying in the early stages of influenza. The experimental results of Gibson, Bowman and Connor and of Wilson and Bashford confirming Nicolle and Lebailly point to an "invisible" or "filter passing" organism as the exciting cause.

The resulting areas of haemorrhagic oedema thus caused form an excellent culture medium for the activities of the bacteria of the respiratory tract, of which B. Influenzae (Pfeiffer) is probably the first and most important invader, followed in the more prolonged cases by strepto and pneumococci.

Reference. (1) Medical Research Committee, *Special Report*, No. 36, 1919.

"Patterson, S. W. *The pathology of influenza in France*, MJA 1920; 1: 207–10

WANNSEE PROTOCOL
JANUARY 20, 1942

OFFICIAL U.S. GOVERNMENT TRANSLATION

Stamp: Top Secret

30 copies
16th copy
Minutes of discussion.

I.

The following persons took part in the discussion about the final solution of the Jewish question which took place in Berlin, am Grossen Wannsee No. 56/58 on 20 January 1942.

Gauleiter Dr. Meyer and Reichsamtleiter Dr. Leibbrandt	Reich Ministry for the Occupied Eastern territories
Secretary of State Dr. Stuckart	Reich Ministry for the Interior
Secretary of State Neumann	Plenipotentiary for the Four Year Plan
Secretary of State Dr. Freisler	Reich Ministry of Justice
Secretary of State Dr. Bühler	Office of the Government General
Under Secretary of State Dr. Luther	Foreign Office
SS-Oberführer Klopfer	Party Chancellery
Ministerialdirektor Kritzinger	Reich Chancellery
SS-Gruppenführer Hofmann	Race and Settlement Main Office
SS-Gruppenführer Müller SS-Obersturmbannführer Eichmann	Reich Main Security Office

SS-Oberführer Dr. Schöngarth   Security Police and SD
Commander of the Security Police
and the SD in the Government General

SS-Sturmbannführer Dr. Lange   Security Police and SD
Commander of the Security Police
and the SD for the General-District
Latvia, as deputy of the Commander
of the Security Police and the SD for
the Reich Commissariat "Eastland."

II.

At the beginning of the discussion Chief of the Security Police and of the SD, SS-Obergruppenführer Heydrich, reported that the Reich Marshal had appointed him delegate for the preparations for the final solution of the Jewish question in Europe and pointed out that this discussion had been called for the purpose of clarifying fundamental questions. The wish of the Reich Marshal to have a draft sent to him concerning organizational, factual and material interests in relation to the final solution of the Jewish question in Europe makes necessary an initial common action of all central offices immediately concerned with these questions in order to bring their general activities into line. The Reichsführer-SS and the Chief of the German Police (Chief of the Security Police and the SD) was entrusted with the official central handling of the final solution of the Jewish question without regard to geographic borders. The Chief of the Security Police and the SD then gave a short report of the struggle which has been carried on thus far against this enemy, the essential points being the following:

    a) the expulsion of the Jews from every sphere of life of the German people,

    b) the expulsion of the Jews from the living space of the German people.

In carrying out these efforts, an increased and planned acceleration of the emigration of the Jews from Reich territory was started, as the only possible present solution.

By order of the Reich Marshal, a Reich Central Office for Jewish Emigration was set up in January 1939 and the Chief of the Security Police and SD was entrusted with the management. Its most important tasks were

    a) to make all necessary arrangements for the preparation for an increased emigration of the Jews,

    b) to direct the flow of emigration,

    c) to speed the procedure of emigration in each individual case.

The aim of all this was to cleanse German living space of Jews in a legal manner.

All the offices realized the drawbacks of such enforced accelerated emigration. For the time being they had, however, tolerated it on account of the lack of other possible solutions of the problem.

The work concerned with emigration was, later on, not only a German problem, but also a problem with which the authorities of the countries to which the flow of emigrants was being directed would have to deal. Financial difficulties, such as the demand by various foreign governments for increasing sums of money to be presented at the time of the landing, the lack of shipping space, increasing restriction of entry permits, or the cancelling of such, increased extraordinarily the difficulties of emigration. In spite of these difficulties, 537,000 Jews were sent out of the country between the takeover of power and the deadline of 31 October 1941. Of these

approximately 360,000 were in Germany proper on 30 January 1933

approximately 147,000 were in Austria (Ostmark) on 15 March 1939

approximately 30,000 were in the Protectorate of Bohemia and Moravia on 15 March 1939.

The Jews themselves, or their Jewish political organizations, financed the emigration. In order to avoid impoverished Jews' remaining behind, the principle was followed that wealthy Jews have to finance the emigration of poor Jews; this was arranged by imposing a suitable tax, i.e., an emigration tax, which was used for financial arrangements in connection with the emigration of poor Jews and was imposed according to income.

Apart from the necessary Reichsmark exchange, foreign currency had to presented at the time of landing. In order to save foreign exchange held by Germany, the foreign Jewish financial organizations were—with the help of Jewish organizations in Germany—made responsible for arranging an adequate amount of foreign currency. Up to 30 October 1941, these foreign Jews donated a total of around 9,500,000 dollars.

In the meantime the Reichsführer-SS and Chief of the German Police had prohibited emigration of Jews due to the dangers of an emigration in wartime and due to the possibilities of the East.

III.

Another possible solution of the problem has now taken the place of emigration, i.e. the evacuation of the Jews to the East, provided that the Führer gives the appropriate approval in advance.

These actions are, however, only to be considered provisional, but practical experience is already being collected which is of the greatest importance in relation to the future final solution of the Jewish question.

Approximately 11 million Jews will be involved in the final solution of the European Jewish question, distributed as follows among the individual countries:

	Country	Number
A.	Germany proper	131,800
	Austria	43,700
	Eastern territories	420,000
	General Government	2,284,000
	Bialystok	400,000
	Protectorate Bohemia and Moravia	74,200
	Estonia - free of Jews -	
	Latvia	3,500
	Lithuania	34,000
	Belgium	43,000
	Denmark	5,600
	France / occupied territory	165,000
	unoccupied territory	700,000
	Greece	69,600
	Netherlands	160,800
	Norway	1,300
B.	Bulgaria	48,000
	England	330,000
	Finland	2,300
	Ireland	4,000
	Italy including Sardinia	58,000
	Albania	200
	Croatia	40,000
	Portugal	3,000
	Rumania including Bessarabia	342,000
	Sweden	8,000
	Switzerland	18,000
	Serbia	10,000
	Slovakia	88,000
	Spain	6,000
	Turkey (European portion)	55,500
	Hungary	742,800
	USSR	5,000,000
	Ukraine	2,994,684
	White Russia	
	excluding Bialystok	446,484
	Total over	11,000,000

The number of Jews given here for foreign countries includes, however, only those Jews who still adhere to the Jewish faith, since some countries still do not have a definition of the term "Jew" according to racial principles.

The handling of the problem in the individual countries will meet with difficulties due to the attitude and outlook of the people there, especially in Hungary and Rumania. Thus, for example, even today the Jew can buy documents in Rumania that will officially prove his foreign citizenship.

The influence of the Jews in all walks of life in the USSR is well known. Approximately five million Jews live in the European part of the USSR, in the Asian part scarcely 1/4 million.

The breakdown of Jews residing in the European part of the USSR according to trades was approximately as follows:

Agriculture	9.1%
Urban workers	14.8%
In trade	20.0%
Employed by the state	23.4%
In private occupations such as medical profession, press, theater, etc.	32.7%

Under proper guidance, in the course of the final solution the Jews are to be allocated for appropriate labor in the East. Able-bodied Jews, separated according to sex, will be taken in large work columns to these areas for work on roads, in the course of which action doubtless a large portion will be eliminated by natural causes.

The possible final remnant will, since it will undoubtedly consist of the most resistant portion, have to be treated accordingly, because it is the product of natural selection and would, if released, act as a the seed of a new Jewish revival (see the experience of history).

In the course of the practical execution of the final solution, Europe will be combed through from west to east. Germany proper, including the Protectorate of Bohemia and Moravia, will have to be handled first due to the housing problem and additional social and political necessities.

The evacuated Jews will first be sent, group by group, to so-called transit ghettos, from which they will be transported to the East.

SS-Obergruppenführer Heydrich went on to say that an important prerequisite for the evacuation as such is the exact definition of the persons involved.

It is not intended to evacuate Jews over 65 years old, but to send them to an old-age ghetto—Theresienstadt is being considered for this purpose.

In addition to these age groups—of the approximately 280,000 Jews in Germany proper and Austria on 31 October 1941, approximately 30% are over 65 years old—severely wounded veterans and Jews with war decorations (Iron Cross I) will be accepted in the old-age ghettos. With this expedient solution, in one fell swoop many interventions will be prevented.

The beginning of the individual larger evacuation actions will largely depend on military developments. Regarding the handling of the final solution in those European countries occupied and influenced by us, it was proposed that the appropriate expert of the Foreign Office discuss the matter with the responsible official of the Security Police and SD.

In Slovakia and Croatia the matter is no longer so difficult, since the most substantial problems in this respect have already been brought near a solution. In Rumania the government has in the meantime also appointed a commissioner for Jewish affairs. In order to settle the question in Hungary, it will soon be necessary to force an adviser for Jewish questions onto the Hungarian government.

With regard to taking up preparations for dealing with the problem in Italy, SS-Obergruppenführer Heydrich considers it opportune to contact the chief of police with a view to these problems.

In occupied and unoccupied France, the registration of Jews for evacuation will in all probability proceed without great difficulty.

Under Secretary of State Luther calls attention in this matter to the fact that in some countries, such as the Scandinavian states, difficulties will arise if this problem is dealt with thoroughly and that it will therefore be advisable to defer actions in these countries. Besides, in view of the small numbers of Jews affected, this deferral will not cause any substantial limitation.

The Foreign Office sees no great difficulties for southeast and western Europe.

SS-Gruppenführer Hofmann plans to send an expert to Hungary from the Race and Settlement Main Office for general orientation at the time when the Chief of the Security Police and SD takes up the matter there. It was decided to assign this expert from the Race and Settlement Main Office, who will not work actively, as an assistant to the police attaché.

IV.

In the course of the final solution plans, the Nuremberg Laws should provide a certain foundation, in which a prerequisite for the absolute solution of the problem is also the solution to the problem of mixed marriages and persons of mixed blood.

The Chief of the Security Police and the SD discusses the following points, at first theoretically, in regard to a letter from the chief of the Reich chancellery:

1) Treatment of Persons of Mixed Blood of the First Degree

Persons of mixed blood of the first degree will, as regards the final solution of the Jewish question, be treated as Jews.

From this treatment the following exceptions will be made:

a) Persons of mixed blood of the first degree married to persons of German blood if their marriage has resulted in children (persons of mixed blood of the second degree). These persons of mixed blood of the second degree are to be treated essentially as Germans.

b) Persons of mixed blood of the first degree, for whom the highest offices of the Party and State have already issued exemption permits in any sphere of life. Each individual case must be examined, and it is not ruled out that the decision may be made to the detriment of the person of mixed blood.

The prerequisite for any exemption must always be the personal merit of the person of mixed blood. (Not the merit of the parent or spouse of German blood.)

Persons of mixed blood of the first degree who are exempted from evacuation will be sterilized in order to prevent any offspring and to eliminate the problem of persons of mixed blood once and for all. Such sterilization will be voluntary. But it is required to remain in the Reich. The sterilized "person of mixed blood" is thereafter free of all restrictions to which he was previously subjected.

2) Treatment of Persons of Mixed Blood of the Second Degree

Persons of mixed blood of the second degree will be treated fundamentally as persons of German blood, with the exception of the following cases, in which the persons of mixed blood of the second degree will be considered as Jews:

a) The person of mixed blood of the second degree was born of a marriage in which both parents are persons of mixed blood.

b) The person of mixed blood of the second degree has a racially especially undesirable appearance that marks him outwardly as a Jew.

c) The person of mixed blood of the second degree has a particularly bad police and political record that shows that he feels and behaves like a Jew.

Also in these cases exemptions should not be made if the person of mixed blood of the second degree has married a person of German blood.

3) Marriages between Full Jews and Persons of German Blood.

Here it must be decided from case to case whether the Jewish partner will be evacuated or whether, with regard to the effects of such a step on the German relatives, [this mixed marriage] should be sent to an old-age ghetto.

4) Marriages between Persons of Mixed Blood of the First Degree and Persons of German Blood.

a) Without Children.

If no children have resulted from the marriage, the person of mixed blood of the first degree will be evacuated or sent to an old-age ghetto (same treatment as in the case of marriages between full Jews and persons of German blood, point 3.)

b) With Children.

If children have resulted from the marriage (persons of mixed blood of the second degree), they will, if they are to be treated as Jews, be evacuated or sent to a ghetto along with the parent of mixed blood of the first degree. If these children are to be treated as Germans (regular cases), they are exempted from evacuation as is therefore the parent of mixed blood of the first degree.

5) Marriages between Persons of Mixed Blood of the First Degree and Persons of Mixed Blood of the First Degree or Jews.

In these marriages (including the children) all members of the family will be treated as Jews and therefore be evacuated or sent to an old-age ghetto.

6) Marriages between Persons of Mixed Blood of the First Degree and Persons of Mixed Blood of the Second Degree.

In these marriages both partners will be evacuated or sent to an old-age ghetto without consideration of whether the marriage has produced children, since possible children will as a rule have stronger Jewish blood than the Jewish person of mixed blood of the second degree.

SS-Gruppenführer Hofmann advocates the opinion that sterilization will have to be widely used, since the person of mixed blood who is given the choice whether he will be evacuated or sterilized would rather undergo sterilization.

State Secretary Dr. Stuckart maintains that carrying out in practice of the just mentioned possibilities for solving the problem of mixed marriages and persons of mixed blood will create endless administrative work. In the second place, as the biological facts cannot be disregarded in any case, State Secretary Dr. Stuckart proposed proceeding to forced sterilization.

Furthermore, to simplify the problem of mixed marriages possibilities must be considered with the goal of the legislator saying something like: "These marriages have been dissolved."

With regard to the issue of the effect of the evacuation of Jews on the economy, State Secretary Neumann stated that Jews who are working in industries vital to the war effort, provided that no replacements are available, cannot be evacuated.

SS-Obergruppenführer Heydrich indicated that these Jews would not be evacuated according to the rules he had approved for carrying out the evacuations then underway.

State Secretary Dr. Bühler stated that the General Government would welcome it if the final solution of this problem could be begun in the General Government, since on the one hand transportation does not play such a large role here nor would problems of labor supply hamper this action. Jews must be removed from the territory of the General Government as quickly as possible, since it is especially here that the Jew as an epidemic carrier represents an extreme danger and on the other hand he is causing permanent chaos in the economic structure of the country through continued black market dealings. Moreover, of the approximately 2 1/2 million Jews concerned, the majority is unfit for work.

State Secretary Dr. Bühler stated further that the solution to the Jewish question in the General Government is the responsibility of the Chief of the Security Police and the SD and that his efforts would be supported by the officials of the General Government. He had only one request, to solve the Jewish question in this area as quickly as possible.

In conclusion the different types of possible solutions were discussed, during which discussion both Gauleiter Dr. Meyer and State Secretary Dr. Bühler took the position that certain preparatory activities for the final solution should be carried out immediately in the territories in question, in which process alarming the populace must be avoided.

The meeting was closed with the request of the Chief of the Security Police and the SD to the participants that they afford him appropriate support during the carrying out of the tasks involved in the solution.

IDENTIFICATIONS PART V

Define each of the following items with a two-sentence identification. Your definition must specifically draw on material in one of the documents in this section.

Freudian Slip

_____

_____

Theory of Evolution

_____

_____

Theory of Relativity

_____

_____

Wannsee Protocol

_____

_____

Influenza Epidemic

_____

_____

PART VI
REVOLUTIONS

The documents in this segment offer insight on many of the revolutionary movements that have swept human societies during the twentieth century. What do these materials tell you about the causes of the Mexican and Russian Revolutions? How would you compare these two revolutions in terms of causation and goals? Are they similar to or different from the later revolution in China? What course of action does Mahatma Gandhi propose for bringing about change? Can he be described as a revolutionary? Examining the works by Nehru, Ho Chi Minh, Jomo Kenyatta, and Nkrumah how would you compare their goals and objectives and methods with those of the earlier revolutionaries?

THE PLAN DE AYALA

Liberating Plan of the sons of the State of Morelos, affiliated with the Insurgent Army which defends the fulfillment of the Plan of San Luis, with the reforms which it has believed proper to add in benefit of the Mexican Fatherland.

We who undersign, constituted in a revolutionary junta to sustain and carry out the promises which the revolution of November 20, 1910 just past, made to the country, declare solemnly before the face of the civilized world which judges us and before the nation to which we belong and which we call [*sic, llamamos,* misprint for *amamos,* love], propositions which we have formulated to end the tyranny which oppresses us and redeem the fatherland from the dictatorships which are imposed on us, which [propositions] are determined in the following plan:

1. Taking into consideration that the Mexican people led by Don Francisco I. Madero went to shed their blood to reconquer liberties and recover their rights which had been trampled on, and not for a man to take possession of power, violating the sacred principles which he took an oath to defend under the slogan "Effective Suffrage and No Reelection," outraging thus the faith, the cause, the justice, and the liberties of the people: taking into consideration that that man to whom we refer is Don Francisco I. Madero, the same who initiated the above-cited revolution, who imposed his will and influence as a governing norm on the Provisional Government of the ex-President of the Republic Attorney Francisco L. de Barra [*sic*], causing with this deed repeated sheddings of blood and multiplicate misfortunes for the fatherland in a manner deceitful and ridiculous, having no intentions other than satisfying his personal ambitions, his boundless instincts as a tyrant, and his profound disrespect for the fulfillment of the preexisting laws emanating from the immortal code of '57, written with the revolutionary blood of Ayutla;

Taking into account that the so-called Chief of the Liberating Revolution of Mexico, Don Francisco I. Madero, through lack of integrity and the highest weakness, did not carry to a happy end the revolution which gloriously he initiated with the help of God and the people, since he left standing most of the governing powers and corrupted elements of oppression of the dictatorial government of Porfirio Díaz, which are not nor can in any way be the representation of National Sovereignty, and which, for being most bitter adversaries of ours and of the principles which even now we defend, are provoking the discomfort of the country and opening new wounds in the bosom of the fatherland, to give it its own blood to drink; taking also into account that the aforementioned Sr. Francisco I. Madero, present President of the Republic, tries to avoid the fulfillment of the promises which he made to the Nation in the Plan of San Luis Potosí, being [sic, siendo, misprint for ciñendo, restricting] the above-cited promises to the agreements of Ciudad Juárez, by means of false promises and numerous intrigues against the Nation nullifying, pursuing, jailing, or killing revolutionary elements who helped him to occupy the high post of President of the Republic;

Taking into consideration that the so-often-repeated Francisco I. Madero has tried with the brute force of bayonets to shut up and to drown in blood the pueblos who ask, solicit, or demand from him the fulfillment of the promises of the revolution, calling them bandits and rebels, condemning them to a war of extermination without conceding or granting a single one of the guarantees which reason, justice, and the law prescribe; taking equally into consideration that the President of the Republic Francisco I. Madero has made of Effective Suffrage a bloody trick on the people, already against the will of the same people imposing Attorney José M. Pino Suárez in the Vice-Presidency of the Republic, or [imposing as] Governors of the States [men] designated by him, like the so-called General Ambrosio Figueroa, scourge and tyrant of the people of Morelos, or entering into scandalous cooperation with the científico party, feudal landlords, and oppressive bosses, enemies of the revolution proclaimed by him, so as to forge new chains and follow the pattern of a new dictatorship more shameful and more terrible than that of Porfirio Díaz, for it has been clear and patent that he has outraged the sovereignty of the States, trampling on the laws without any respect for lives or interests, as has happened in the State of Morelos, and others, leading them to the most horrendous anarchy which contemporary history registers.

For these considerations we declare the aforementioned Francisco I. Madero inept at realizing the promises of the revolution of which he was the author, because he has betrayed the principles with which he tricked the will of the people and was able to get into power: incapable of governing, because he has no respect for the law and justice of the pueblos, and a traitor to the fatherland, because he is humiliating in blood and fire Mexicans who want liberties, so as to please the científicos, landlords, and bosses who enslave us, and from today on we begin to continue the revolution begun by him, until we achieve the overthrow of the dictatorial powers which exist.

2. Recognition is withdrawn from Sr. Francisco I. Madero as Chief of the Revolution and as President of the Republic, for the reasons which before were expressed, it being attempted to overthrow this official.

3. Recognized as Chief of the Liberating Revolution is the illustrious General Pascual Orozco, the second of the Leader Don Francisco I. Madero, and in case he does not accept this delicate post, recognition as Chief of the Revolution will go to General Don Emiliano Zapata.

4. The Revolutionary Junta of the State of Morelos manifests to the Nation under formal oath: that it makes its own the plan of San Luis Potosí, with the additions which are expressed below in benefit of the oppressed pueblos, and it will make itself the defender of the principles it defends until victory or death.

5. The Revolutionary Junta of the State of Morelos will admit no transactions or compromises until it achieves the overthrow of the dictatorial elements of Porfirio Díaz and Francisco I. Madero, for the nation is tired of false men and traitors who make promises like liberators and who on arriving in power forget them and constitute themselves as tyrants.

6. As an additional part of the plan we invoke, we give notice: that [regarding] the fields, timber, and water which the landlords, científicos, or bosses have usurped, the pueblos or citizens who have the titles corresponding to those properties will immediately enter into possession of that real estate of which they have been despoiled by the bad faith of our oppressors, maintaining at any cost with arms in hand the mentioned possession; and the usurpers who consider themselves with a right to them [those properties] will deduce it before the special tribunals which will be established on the triumph of the revolution.

7. In virtue of the fact that the immense majority of Mexican pueblos and citizens are owners of no more than the land they walk on, suffering the horrors of poverty without being able to improve their social condition in any way or to dedicate themselves to Industry or Agriculture, because lands, timber, and water are monopolized in a few hands, for this cause there will be expropriated the third part of those

monopolies from the powerful proprietors of them, with prior indemnization, in order that the pueblos and citizens of Mexico may obtain ejidos, colonies, and foundations for pueblos, or fields for sowing or laboring, and the Mexicans' lack of prosperity and wellbeing may improve in all and for all.

8. [Regarding] The landlords, científicos, or bosses who oppose the present plan directly or indirectly, their goods will be nationalized and the two third parts which [otherwise would] belong to them will go for indemnizations of war, pensions for widows and orphans of the victims who succumb in the struggle for the present plan.

9. In order to execute the procedures regarding the properties aforementioned, the laws of disamortization and nationalization will be applied as they fit, for serving us as norm and example can be those laws put in force by the immortal Juárez on ecclesiastical properties, which punished the despots and conservatives who in every time have tried to impose on us the ignominious yoke of oppression and backwardness.

10. The insurgent military chiefs of the Republic who rose up with arms in hand at the voice of Don Francisco I. Madero to defend the plan of San Luis Potosí, and who oppose with armed force the present plan, will be judged traitors to the cause which they defended and to the fatherland, since at present many of them, to humor the tyrants, for a fistful of coins, or for bribes or connivance, are shedding the blood of their brothers who claim the fulfillment of the promises which Don Francisco I. Madero made to the nation.

11. The expenses of war will be taken in conformity with Article II of the Plan of San Luis Potosí, and all procedures employed in the revolution we undertake will be in conformity with the same instructions which the said plan determines.

12. Once triumphant the revolution which we carry into the path of reality, a Junta of the principal revolutionary chiefs from the different States will name or designate an interim President of the Republic, who will convoke elections for the organization of the federal powers.

13. The principal revolutionary chiefs of each State will designate in Junta the Governor of the State to which they belong, and this appointed official will convoke elections for the due organization of the public powers, the object being to avoid compulsory appointments which work the misfortune of the pueblos, like the so-well-known appointment of Ambrosio Figueroa in the State of Morelos and others who drive us to the precipice of bloody conflicts, sustained by the caprice

of the dictator Madero and the circle of científicos and landlords who have influenced him.

14. If President Madero and other dictatorial elements of the present and former regime want to avoid the immense misfortunes which afflict the fatherland, and [if they] possess true sentiments of love for it, let them make immediate renunciation of the posts they occupy and with that they will with something staunch the grave wounds which they have opened in the bosom of the fatherland, since, if they do not do so, on their heads will fall the blood and the anathema of our brothers.

15. Mexicans: consider that the cunning and bad faith of one man is shedding blood in a scandalous manner, because he is incapable of governing; consider that his system of government is choking the fatherland and trampling with the brute force of bayonets on our institutions; and thus, as we raised up our weapons to elevate him to power, we again raise them up against him for defaulting on his promises to the Mexican people and for having betrayed the revolution initiated by him, we are not personalists, we are partisans of principles and not of men!

Mexican People, support this plan with arms in hand and you will make the prosperity and well-being of the fatherland.

Ayala, November 25, 1911

Liberty, Justice, and Law

Signed, General in Chief Emiliano Zapata; Generals Eufemio Zapata, Francisco Mendoza, Jesús Morales, Jesús Navarro, Otilio E. Montaño, José Trinidad Ruiz, Próculo Capistrán; Colonels Felipe Vaquero, Cesáreo Burgos, Quintín González, Pedro Salazar, Simón Rojas, Emigdio Marmolejo, José Campos, Pioquinto Galis, Felipe Tijera, Rafael Sánchez, José Pérez, Santiago Aguilar, Margarito Martínez, Feliciano Domínguez, Manuel Vergara, Cruz Salazar, Lauro Sánchez, Amador Salazar, Lorenzo Vázquez, Catarino Perdomo, Jesús Sánchez, Domingo Romero, Zacarías Torres, Bonifacio García, Daniel Andrade, Ponciano Domínguez, Jesús Capistrán; Captains Daniel Mantilla, José M. Carrillo, Francisco Alarcón, Severiano Gutiérrez; and more signatures follow. [This] is a true copy taken from the original. Camp in the Mountains of Puebla, December 11, 1911. Signed, General in Chief Emiliano Zapata.

From John Womack, Jr, *Zapata and the Mexican Revolution* (New York: Vintage Books, 1968, 400–404).

THE 1917 CONSTITUTION OF MEXICO, AS AMENDED

TITLE I

Chapter 1

INDIVIDUAL GUARANTEES

Article 1. Every person in the United Mexican States shall enjoy the guarantees granted by this Constitution, which cannot be restricted or suspended except in such cases and under such conditions as are herein provided.

Article 2. Slavery is forbidden in the United Mexican States. Slaves who enter national territory from abroad shall, by this act alone, recover their freedom and enjoy the protection afforded by the laws.

Article 3. The education imparted by the Federal State shall be designed to develop harmoniously all the faculties of the human being and shall foster in him at the same time a love of country and a consciousness of international solidarity, in independence and justice.

   I. Freedom of religious beliefs being guaranteed by Article 24, the standard which shall guide such education shall be maintained entirely apart from any religious doctrine and, based on the results of scientific progress, shall strive against ignorance and its effects, servitudes, fanaticism, and prejudices. Moreover:

      a. It shall be democratic, considering democracy not only as a legal structure and a political regimen, but as a system of life founded on a constant economic, social, and cultural betterment of the people;

      b. It shall be national insofar as—without hostility or exclusiveness—it shall achieve the understanding of our problems, the utilization of our resources, the defense of our political independence, the assurance of our economic independence, and the continuity and growth of our culture; and

c. It shall contribute to better human relationships, not only with the elements which it contributes toward strengthening and at the same time inculcating, together with respect for the dignity of the person and the integrity of the family, the conviction of the general interest of society, but also by the care which it devotes to the ideals of brotherhood and equality of rights of all men, avoiding privileges of race, creed, class, sex, or persons.

II. Private persons may engage in education of all kinds and grades. But as regards elementary, secondary, and normal education (and that of any kind or grade designed for laborers and farm workers) they must previously obtain, in every case, the express authorization of the public power. Such authorization may be refused or revoked by decisions against which there can be no judicial proceedings or recourse.

III. Private institutions devoted to education of the kinds and grades specified in the preceding section must be without exception in conformity with the provisions of sections I and II of the first paragraph of this article and must also be in harmony with official plans and programs.

IV. Religious corporations, ministers of religion, stock companies which exclusively or predominantly engage in educational activities, and associations or companies devoted to propagation of any religious creed shall not in any way participate in institutions giving elementary, secondary and normal education and education for laborers or field workers.

V. The State may in its discretion withdraw at any time the recognition of official validity of studies conducted in private institutions.

VI. Elementary education shall be compulsory.

VII. All education given by the State shall be free.

VIII. The Congress of the Union, with a view to unifying and coordinating education throughout the Republic, shall issue the necessary laws for dividing the social function of education among the Federation, the States and the Municipalities, for fixing the appropriate financial allocations for this public service and for establishing the penalties applicable to officials who do not comply with or enforce the pertinent provisions, as well as the penalties applicable to all those who infringe such provisions.

Article 4. No person can be prevented from engaging in the profession, industrial or commercial pursuit, or occupation of his choice, provided it is lawful. The exercise of this liberty shall only be forbidden by judicial order when the rights of third parties are infringed, or by administrative order, issued in the manner provided by law, when the rights of society are violated. No one may be deprived of the fruits of his labor except by judicial decision.

The law in each state shall determine the professions which may be practiced only with a degree, and set forth the requirements for obtaining it and the authorities empowered to issue it.

Article 5. No one can be compelled to render personal services without due remuneration and without his full consent, excepting labor imposed as a penalty by the judiciary, which shall be governed by the provisions of clauses I and II of Article 123.

Only the following public services shall be obligatory, subject to the conditions set forth in the respective laws: military service and jury service as well as the discharge of the office of municipal councilman and offices of direct or indirect popular election. Duties in relation to elections and the census shall be compulsory and unpaid. Professional services of a social character shall be compulsory and paid according to the provisions of law and with the exceptions fixed thereby.

The State cannot permit the execution of any contract, covenant, or agreement having for its object the restriction, loss or irrevocable sacrifice of the liberty of man, whether for work, education, or religious vows. The law, therefore, does not permit the establishment of monastic orders, whatever be their denomination or purpose.

Likewise no person can legally agree to his own proscription or exile, or to the temporary or permanent renunciation of the exercise of a given profession or industrial or commercial pursuit.

A labor contract shall be binding only to render the services agreed on for the time set by law and may never exceed one year to the detriment of the worker, and in no case may it embrace the waiver, loss, or restriction of any civil or political right.

Non-compliance with such contract by the worker shall only render him civilly liable for damages, but in no case shall it imply coercion against his person.

Article 6. The expression of ideas shall not be subject to any judicial or administrative investigation, unless it offends good morals, infringes the rights of others, incites to crime, or disturbs the public order.

Article 7. Freedom of writing and publishing writings on any subject is inviolable. No law or authority may establish censorship, require bonds from authors or printers, or restrict the freedom of printing, which shall be limited only by the respect due to private life, morals, and public peace. Under no circumstances may a printing press be sequestrated as the instrument of the offense.

The organic laws shall contain whatever provisions may be necessary to prevent the imprisonment of the vendors, newsboys, workmen, and other employees of the establishment publishing the work denounced, under pretext of a denunciation of offenses of the press, unless their guilt is previously established.

Article 8. Public officials and employees shall respect the exercise of the right of petition, provided it is made in writing and in a peaceful and respectful manner; but this right may only be exercised in political matters by citizens of the Republic.

Every petition shall be replied to in writing by the official to whom it is addressed, and said official is bound to inform the petitioner of the decision taken within a brief period.

Article 9. The right to assemble or associate peaceably for any lawful purpose cannot be restricted; but only citizens of the Republic may do so to take part in the political affairs of the country. No armed deliberative meeting is authorized.

No meeting or assembly shall be deemed unlawful which has for its object the petitioning of any authority or the presentation of a protest against any act; nor may it be dissolved, unless insults be proffered against said authority or violence is resorted to, or threats are used to intimidate or compel such authority to render a favorable decision.

Article 10. The inhabitants of the United Mexican States are entitled to have arms of any kind in their possession for their protection and legitimate defense, except such as are expressly forbidden by law, or which the nation may reserve for the exclusive use of the army, navy, or national guard; but they may not carry arms within inhabited places without complying with police regulations.

Article 11. Everyone has the right to enter and leave the Republic, to travel through its territory and to change his residence without necessity of a letter of security, passport, safe-conduct or any other similar requirement. The exercise of this right shall be subordinated to the powers of the judiciary, in cases of civil or criminal liability, and to those of the administrative authorities insofar as concerns the limitations imposed by the laws regarding emigration, immigration and public health of the country, or in regard to undesirable aliens resident in the country.

Article 12. No titles of nobility, or hereditary or prerogatives or honors shall be granted in the United Mexican States, nor shall any effect be given to those granted by other countries.

Article 13. No one may be tried by private laws or special tribunals. No person or corporate body shall have privileges or enjoy emoluments other than those given in compensation for public services and which are set by law. Military jurisdiction shall be recognized for the trial of crimes against and violation of military discipline, but the military tribunals shall in no case have jurisdiction over persons who do not belong to the army. Whenever a civilian is implicated in a military crime or violation, the respective civil authority shall deal with the case.

Article 14. No law shall be given retroactive effect to the detriment of any person whatsoever.

No person shall be deprived of life, liberty, property, possessions, or rights without a trial by a duly created court in which the essential formalities of procedure are observed and in accordance with laws issued prior to the act.

In criminal cases no penalty shall be imposed by mere analogy or by a prior evidence. The penalty must be decreed in a law in every respect applicable to the crime in question.

In civil suits the final judgment shall be according to the letter or the juridical interpretation of the law; in the absence of the latter it shall be based on the general principles of law.

Article 15. No treaty shall be authorized for the extradition of political offenders or of offenders of the common order who have been slaves in the country where the offense was committed. Nor shall any agreement or treaty be entered into which restricts or modifies the guarantees and rights which this Constitution grants to the individual and to the citizen.

Article 16. No one shall be molested in his person, family, domicile, papers, or possessions except by virtue of a written order of the competent authority stating the legal grounds and justification for the action taken. No order of arrest or detention shall be issued against any person other than by the competent judicial authority, and unless same is preceded by a charge, accusation, or complaint for a credible party or by other evidence indicating the probable guilt of the accused; in cases of *flagrante delicto,* any person may arrest the offender and his accomplices, turning them over without delay to the nearest authorities. Only in urgent cases instituted by the public attorney without previous complaint or indictment and when there is no judicial authority available, may the administrative authorities, on their strictest accountability, order the detention of an accused person, turning him over immediately to the judicial authorities. Every search warrant, which can be issued only by judicial authority and which must be in writing, shall specify the place to be searched, the person or persons to be arrested, and the objects sought, the proceedings to be limited thereto; at the conclusion of which a detailed statement shall be drawn up in the presence of two witnesses proposed by the occupant of the place searched, or by the official making the search in his absence or should he refuse to do so.

Administrative officials may enter private homes for the sole purpose of ascertaining whether the sanitary and police regulations have been complied with; and may demand to be shown the books and documents required to prove compliance with fiscal rulings, in which latter cases they must abide by the provisions of the respective laws and be subject to the formalities prescribed for cases of search.

Article 17. No one may be imprisoned for debts of a purely civil nature. No one may take the law into his own hands, or resort to violence in the enforcement of his rights. The courts shall be open for the administration of justice at such times and under such conditions as the law may establish; their services shall be gratuitous and all judicial costs are, accordingly, prohibited.

Article 18. Arrest is permissible only for offenses punishable by imprisonment. The place of detention shall be completely separate from the place used for the serving of sentences.

The federal and state governments shall organize the penal system within their respective jurisdictions on the basis of labor, training, and education as a means of social readjustment of the offender. Women shall serve their sentences in places separate from those intended for men for the same purpose.

Governors of States, subject to the provisions of the respective local laws, may conclude agreements of a general nature with the federal government, under which offenders convicted for common offenses may serve their sentence in establishments maintained by the federal executive.

The federal government and the state governments shall establish special institutions for the treatment of juvenile delinquents.

Article 19. No detention shall exceed three days without a formal order of commitment, which shall state the offense with which the accused is charged; the substance thereof; the place, time and circumstances of its commission; and the facts brought to light in the preliminary examination. These facts must be sufficient to establish the *corpus delicti* and the probable guilt of the accused. All authorities who order a detention or consent thereto, as well as all agents, subordinates, wardens, or jailers who execute it, shall be liable for any breach of this provision.

The trial shall take place only for the offense or offenses set forth in the formal order of commitment. Should it develop, during the course of the proceedings, that another offense, different from that charged, has been committed, a separate accusation must be brought. This, however, shall not prevent the joinder of both proceedings, if deemed advisable.

Any ill-treatment during arrest or confinement; any molesting without legal justification; any exaction or contribution levied in prison are abuses which shall be punishable by law and repressed by the authorities.

Article 20. In every criminal trial the accused shall enjoy the following guarantees:

    I. He shall be freed on demand and on furnishing bail which shall be fixed by the judge, according to his status and the gravity of the offense with which he is charged, provided, however, that such offense is not punishable with more than five years' imprisonment. No requisites shall be necessary other than placing the stipulated sum at the disposal of the proper authorities or giving adequate security or personal bond for acceptance of which the judge is responsible.

The security or bond shall be not more than 250,000 pesos except for offenses by which the offender profits or the victim suffers financially; for such offenses the security shall be at least three times the amount of the profit obtained or the damage suffered.

II. He may not be forced to be a witness against himself; wherefore denial of access or other means tending to this end is strictly prohibited.

III. He shall be publicly notified within forty-eight hours after being turned over to the judicial authorities of the name of his accuser and the nature of and cause for the accusation, so that he may be familiar with the offense with which he is charged, and reply thereto and make a preliminary statement.

IV. He shall be confronted with the witnesses against him, who shall testify in his presence if they are to be found in the place where the trial is held, so that he may cross-examine them in his defense.

V. All witnesses and other evidence which he may offer shall be heard in his defense, for which he shall be given the time which the law deems necessary for the purpose; he shall furthermore be assisted in securing the presence of the persons whose testimony he may request, provided they are to be found at the place where the trial is held.

VI. He shall be entitled to a public trial by a judge or jury of citizens who can read and write and are also residents of the place and district where the offense was committed, provided the penalty for such offense exceeds one year's imprisonment. The accused shall always be entitled to a trial by jury for all offenses committed by means of the press against the public peace or against the domestic or foreign safety of the nation.

VII. He shall be furnished with all information on record which he may request for his defense.

VIII. He shall be tried within four months, if charged with an offense whose maximum penalty does not exceed two years' imprisonment; and within one year, if the maximum penalty is greater.

IX. He shall be heard in his own defense, either personally or by counsel, or by both, as he may desire. Should he have no one to defend him, a list of official counsel shall be submitted to him, in order that he may choose one or more to act in his defense. If the accused does not wish to name any counsel for his defense, after being called upon to do so at the time of his preliminary examination, the court shall appoint his counsel for the defense. The accused may name his counsel immediately upon arrest, and shall be entitled to have him present at every stage of the trial; but he shall be obliged to make him appear as often as required by the court.

X. In no event may imprisonment or detention be extended through failure to pay counsel fees or for any other monetary obligation, on account of civil liability, or for other similar cause.

Nor shall detention be extended beyond the time set by law as the maximum for the offense charged.

The period of detention shall be reckoned as a part of the term of imprisonment imposed by sentence.

Article 21. The imposition of all penalties is an exclusive attribute of the judiciary. The prosecution of offenses pertains to the public prosecutor and to the judicial police, who shall be under the immediate command and authority of the public prosecutor. The punishment of violations of governmental and police regulations pertains to the administrative authorities, which punishment shall consist solely of imprisonment for a period not exceeding thirty-six hours or of a fine. Should the offender fail to pay the fine, it shall be substituted by a corresponding period of detention, which in no case may exceed fifteen days.

If the offender is a day laborer or a workman, his punishment cannot consist of a fine exceeding the amount of his wages, for one week.

Article 22. Punishment by mutilation and infamy, branding, flogging, beating with sticks, torture of any kind, excessive fines, confiscation of property and any other unusual or extreme penalties are prohibited.

Attachment proceedings covering the whole or part of the property of a person made under judicial authority to cover payment of civil liability arising out of the commission of an offense or for the payment of taxes or fines shall not be deemed a confiscation of property.

Capital punishment for political offenses is likewise prohibited; as regards other offenses, it can only be imposed for high treason committed during a foreign war, parricide, murder that is treacherous, premeditated, or committed for profit, arson, abduction, highway robbery, piracy, and grave military offenses.

Article 23. No criminal trial shall have more than three instances. No person, whether acquitted or convicted, can be tried twice for the same offense. The practice of absolving from the instance is prohibited.

Article 24. Everyone is free to embrace the religion of his choice and to practice all ceremonies, devotions, or observances of his respective faith, either in places of public worship or at home, provided they do not constitute an offense punishable by law.

Every religious act of public worship must be performed strictly inside places of public worship, which shall at all times be under governmental supervision.

Article 25. Sealed correspondence sent through the mail shall be exempt from search and its violation shall be punishable by law.

Article 26. No member of the army shall in time of peace be quartered in private dwellings without the consent of the owner, nor may he impose any obligation whatsoever. In time of war the military may demand lodging, equipment, provisions, and other assistance, in the manner laid down in the respective martial law.

Article 27. Ownership of the lands and waters within the boundaries of the national territory is vested originally in the Nation, which has had, and has, the right to transmit title thereof to private persons, thereby constituting private property.

Private property shall not be expropriated except for reasons of public use and subject to payment of indemnity.

The Nation shall at all times have the right to impose on private property such limitations as the public interest may demand, as well as the right to regulate the utilization of natural resources which are susceptible of appropriation, in order to conserve them and to ensure a more equitable distribution of public wealth. With this end in view, necessary measures shall be taken to divide up large landed estates; to develop small landed holdings in operation; to create new agricultural centers, with necessary lands and waters; to encourage agriculture in general and to prevent the destruction of natural resources, and to protect property from damage to the detriment of society. Centers of population which at present either have no lands or water or which do not possess them in sufficient quantities for the needs of their inhabitants, shall be entitled to grants thereof, which shall be taken from adjacent properties, the rights of small landed holdings in operation being respected at all times.

In the Nation is vested the direct ownership of all natural resources of the continental shelf and the submarine shelf of the islands; of all minerals or substances, which in veins, ledges, masses or ore pockets, form deposits of a nature distinct from the components of the earth itself, such as the minerals from which industrial metals and metalloids are extracted; deposits of precious stones, rocksalt and the deposits of salt formed by sea water; products derived from the decomposition of rocks, when subterranean works are required for their extraction; mineral or organic deposits of materials susceptible of utilization as fertilizers; solid mineral fuels; petroleum and all solid, liquid, and gaseous hydrocarbons; and the space above the national territory to the extent and within the terms fixed by international law.

In the Nation is likewise vested the ownership of the waters of the territorial seas, within the limits and terms fixed by international law; inland marine waters; those of lagoons and estuaries permanently or intermittently connected with the sea; those of natural, inland lakes which are directly connected with streams having a constant flow; those of rivers and their direct or indirect tributaries from the point in their source where the first permanent, intermittent, or torrential waters begin, to their mouth in the sea, or a lake, lagoon, or estuary forming a part of the public domain; those of constant or intermittent streams and their direct or indirect tributaries, whenever the bed of the stream, throughout the whole or a part of its length, serves as a boundary of the national territory or of two federal divisions, or if it flows from one federal division to another or crosses the boundary line of the Republic; those of lakes, lagoons, or estuaries whose basins, zones, or shores are crossed by the boundary lines of two or more divisions or by the boundary line of the Republic and a neighboring country or when the shoreline serves as the boundary between two federal divisions or of the Republic and a neighboring country; those of springs that issue from beaches, maritime areas, the beds, basins, or shores of lakes, lagoons, or estuaries in the national domain; and waters extracted from mines and the channels, beds, or shores of interior lakes and streams in an area fixed by law. Underground waters may be brought to the surface by artificial works and utilized by the surface owner, but if the public interest so requires or use by others is affected, the Federal Executive may regulate its extraction and utilization, and even establish prohibited areas, the same as may be done with other waters in the public domain. Any other waters not included in the foregoing enumeration shall be considered an integral part of the property through which they flow or in which they are deposited, but if they are located in two or more properties, their utilization shall be deemed a matter of public use, and shall be subject to laws enacted by the States.

In those cases to which the two preceding paragraphs refer, ownership by the Nation is inalienable and imprescriptible, and the exploitation, use, or appropriation of the resources concerned, by private persons or by companies organized according to Mexican laws, may not be undertaken except through concessions granted by the Federal Executive, in accordance with rules and conditions established by law. The legal rules relating to the working or exploitation of the minerals and substances referred to in the fourth paragraph shall govern the execution and proofs of what is carried out or should be carried out after they go into effect, independent of the date of granting the concessions, and their nonobservance will be grounds for cancellation thereof. The Federal Government has the power to establish national reserves and to abolish them. The declarations pertaining thereto shall be made by the Executive in those cases and conditions prescribed by law. In the case of petroleum, and solid, liquid, or gaseous hydrocarbons no concessions or contracts will be granted nor may those that have been granted continue, and the Nation shall carry out the exploitation of these products, in accordance with the provisions indicated in the respective regulatory law.

It is exclusively a function of the general Nation to conduct, transform, distribute, and supply electric power which is to be used for public service. No concessions for this purpose will be granted to private persons and the Nation will make use of the property and natural resources which are required for these ends. (Note: A transitory provision of the amendment adding the foregoing paragraph to Article 27 states:

"A regulatory law shall establish the rules to which concessions granted prior to the enactment of the present law (amendment) shall be subject".)

Legal capacity to acquire ownership of lands and waters of the Nation shall be governed by the following provisions:

I. Only Mexicans by birth or naturalization and Mexican companies have the right to acquire ownership of lands, waters, and their appurtenances, or to obtain concessions for the exploitation of mines or of waters. The State may grant the same right to foreigners, provided they agree before the Ministry of Foreign Relations to consider themselves as nationals in respect to such property, and bind themselves not to invoke the protection of their governments in matters relating thereto; under penalty, in case of noncompliance with this agreement, of forfeiture of the property acquired to the Nation. Under no circumstances may foreigners acquire direct ownership of lands or waters within a zone of one hundred kilometers along the frontiers and of fifty kilometers along the shores of the country.

The State, in accordance with its internal public interests and with principles of reciprocity, may in the discretion of the Secretariat of Foreign Affairs authorize foreign states to acquire, at the permanent sites of the Federal Powers, private ownership of real property necessary for the direct services of their embassies or legations.

II. Religious institutions known as churches, regardless of creed, may in no case acquire, hold, or administer real property or hold mortgages thereon; such property held at present either directly or through an intermediary shall revert to the Nation, any person whosoever being authorized to denounce any property so held. Presumptive evidence shall be sufficient to declare the denunciation well founded. Places of public worship are the property of the Nation, as represented by the Federal Government, which shall determine which of them may continue to be devoted to their present purposes. Bishoprics, rectories, seminaries, asylums, and schools belonging to religious orders, convents, or any other buildings built or intended for the administration, propagation, or teaching of a religious creed shall at once become the property of the Nation by inherent right, to be used exclusively for the public services of the Federal or State Governments, within their respective jurisdictions. All places of public worship hereafter erected shall be the property of the Nation.

III. Public or private charitable institutions for the rendering of assistance to the needy, for scientific research, the diffusion of knowledge, mutual aid to members, or for any other lawful purpose, may not acquire more real property than actually needed for their purpose and immediately and directly devoted thereto; but they may acquire, hold, or administer mortgages on real property provided the term thereof does not exceed ten years. Under no circumstances may institutions of this kind be under the patronage, direction, administration, charge, or supervision of religious orders or institutions, or of ministers of any religious sect or of their followers, even though the former or the latter may not be in active service.

IV. Commercial stock companies may not acquire, hold, or administer rural properties. Companies of this kind that are organized to operate any manufacturing, mining, or petroleum industry or for any other purpose that is not agricultural, may acquire, hold, or administer lands only of an area that is strictly necessary for their buildings or services, and this area shall be fixed in each particular case by the Federal or State Executive.

V. Banks duly authorized to operate in accordance with the laws on credit institutions may hold mortgages on urban and rural property in conformity with the provisions of such laws but they may not own or administer more real property than is actually necessary for their direct purpose.

VI. With the exception of the corporate entities referred to in clauses III, IV, and V hereof, and the centers of population which by law or in fact possess a communal status or centers that have received grants or restitutions or have been organized as centers of agricultural population, no other civil corporate entity may hold or administer real property or hold mortgages thereon, with the sole exception of the buildings intended immediately and directly for the purposes of the institution. The States, the Federal District, and the Territories, and all Municipalities in the Republic, shall have full legal capacity to acquire and hold all the real property needed to render public services.

The federal and state laws, within their respective jurisdictions, shall determine in what cases the occupation of private property shall be considered to be of public utility; and in accordance with such laws, the administrative authorities shall issue the respective declaration. The amount fixed as compensation for the expropriated property shall be based on the value recorded in assessment or tax offices for tax purposes, whether this value had been declared by the owner or tacitly accepted by him by having paid taxes on that basis. The increased or decreased value of such private property due to improvements or depreciation which occurred after such assessment is the only portion of the value that shall be subject to the decision of experts and judicial proceedings. This same procedure shall be followed in the case of property whose value is not recorded in the tax offices.

The exercise of actions pertaining to the Nation by virtue of the provisions of this article shall be made effective by judicial procedure, but during these proceedings and by order of the proper courts, which must render a decision within a maximum of one month, the administrative authorities shall proceed without delay to occupy, administer, auction, or sell the lands and waters in question and all their appurtenances, and in no case may the acts of such authorities be set aside until a final decision has been rendered.

VII. The centers of population which, by law or in fact, possess a communal status shall have legal capacity to enjoy common possession of the lands, forests, and waters belonging to them or which have been or may be restored to them.

All questions, regardless of their origin, concerning the boundaries of communal lands, which are now pending or that may arise hereafter between two or more centers of population, are matters of federal jurisdiction. The Federal Executive shall take cognizance of such controversies and propose a solution to the interested parties. If the latter agree thereto, the proposal of the Executive shall take full effect as a final decision and shall be irrevocable; should they not be in conformity, the party or parties may appeal to the Supreme Court of Justice of the Nation, without prejudice to immediate enforcement of the presidential proposal.

The law shall specify the brief procedure to which the settling of such controversies shall conform.

VIII. The following are declared null and void:

a. All transfers of the lands, waters, and forests of villages, *rancherías,* groups, or communities made by local officials (*jefes políticos*), state governors, or other local authorities in violation of the provisions of the Law of June 25, 1856, and other related laws and rulings.

b. All concessions, deals or sales of lands, waters, and forests made by the Secretariat of Development, the Secretariat of Finance, or any other federal authority from December 1, 1876 to date, which encroach upon or illegally occupy communal lands (ejidos), lands allotted in common, or lands of any other kind belonging to villages, rancherias, groups or communities, and centers of population.

c. All survey or demarcation-of-boundary proceedings, transfers, alienations, or auction sales effected during the period of time referred to in the preceding sub-clause, by companies, judges, or other federal or state authorities entailing encroachments on or illegal occupation of the lands, waters, or forests of communal holdings (ejidos), lands held in common, or other holdings belonging to centers of population.

The sole exception to the aforesaid nullification shall be the lands to which title has been granted in allotments made in conformity with the Law of June 25, 1856, held by persons in their own name for more than ten years and having an area of not more than fifty hectares.

IX. Divisions or allotments of land among the inhabitants of a given center of population which, although apparently legitimate are not so, due to a mistake or defect, may be annulled at the request of three fourths of the residents holding one fourth so divided, or one fourth of such residents holding three fourths of the lands.

X. Centers of population which lack communal lands (ejidos) or which are unable to have them restored to them due to lack of titles, impossibility of identification, or because they had been legally transferred, shall be granted sufficient lands and waters to constitute them, in accordance with the needs of the population; but in no case shall they fail to be granted the area needed, and for this purpose the land needed shall be expropriated, at the expense of the Federal Government, to be taken from lands adjoining the villages in question.

The area or individual unit of the grant shall hereafter be not less than ten hectares of moist or irrigated land, or in default of such land its equivalent in other types of land in accordance with the third paragraph of section XV of this article.

XI. For the purpose of carrying out the provisions of this article and of regulating laws that may be enacted, the following are established:

a. A direct agency of the Federal Executive entrusted with the application and enforcement of the agrarian laws;

b. An advisory board composed of five persons to be appointed by the President of the Republic and who shall perform the functions specified in the organic laws;

c. A mixed commission composed of an equal number of representatives of the Federal Government, the local governments, and a representative of the peasants, to be appointed in the manner set forth in the respective regulating law, to function in each State, Territory, and the Federal District, with the powers and duties set forth in the organic and regulatory laws;

d. Private executive committees for each of the centers of population that are concerned with agrarian cases;

e. A communal office (comisariado ejidal) for each of the centers of population that possess communal lands (ejidos).

XII. Petitions for a restitution or grant of lands or waters shall be submitted directly to the state and territorial governors.

The governors shall refer the petitions to the mixed commissions, which shall study the cases during a fixed period of time and render a report; the State governors shall approve or modify the report of the mixed commission and issue orders that immediate possession be given to areas which they deem proper. The case shall then be turned over to the Federal Executive for decision.

Whenever the governors fail to comply with the provisions of the preceding paragraph, within the peremptory period of time fixed by law, the report of the mixed commission shall be deemed rejected and the case shall be referred immediately to the Federal Executive.

Inversely, whenever a mixed commission fails to render a report during the peremptory time limit, the Governor shall be empowered to grant possession of the area of land he deems appropriate.

XIII. The agency of the Executive and the Agrarian Advisory Board shall report on the approval, rectification, or modification of the reports submitted by the mixed commissions, containing the changes made therein by the local governments, and so notify the President of the Republic, who as the supreme agrarian authority will render a decision.

XIV. Landowners affected by decisions granting or restoring communal lands and waters to villages, or who may be affected by future decisions, shall have no ordinary legal right or recourse and cannot institute *amparo* proceedings.

Persons affected by such decisions shall have solely the right to apply to the Federal Government for payment of the corresponding indemnity. This right must be exercised by the interested parties within one year counting from the date of publication of the respective resolution in the *Diario Oficial*. After this period has elapsed, no claim is admissible.

Owners or occupants of agricultural or stockraising properties in operation who have been issued or to whom there may be issued in the future certificates of non-affectability may institute amparo proceedings against any illegal deprivation or agrarian claims on their lands or water.

XV. The mixed commissions, the local governments and any other authorities charged with agrarian proceedings cannot in any case affect small agricultural or livestock properties in operation and they shall incur liability for violations of the Constitution if they make grants which affect them.

Small agricultural property is that which does not exceed one hundred hectares of first-class moist or irrigated land or its equivalent in other classes of land, under cultivation.

To determine this equivalence one hectare of irrigated land shall be computed as two hectares of seasonal land; as four of good quality pasturage (agostadero) and as eight as *monte* (scrub land) or arid pasturage.

Also to be considered as small holdings are areas not exceeding two hundred hectares of seasonal lands or pasturage susceptible of cultivation; or one hundred fifty hectares of land used for cotton growing if irrigated from fluvial canals or by pumping; or three hundred, under cultivation, when used for growing bananas, sugar cane, coffee, henequen, rubber, coconuts, grapes, olives, quinine, vanilla, cacao, or fruit trees.

Small holdings for stockraising are lands not exceeding the area necessary to maintain up to five hundred head of cattle (ganado mayor) or their equivalent in smaller animals (ganado menor—sheep, goats, pigs) under provisions of law, in accordance with the forage capacity of the lands.

Whenever, due to irrigation or drainage works or any other works executed by the owners or occupants of a small holding to whom a certificate of non-affectability has been issued, the quality of the land is improved for agricultural or stockraising operations, such holding shall not be subject to agrarian appropriation even if, by virtue of the improvements made, the maximums indicated in this section are lowered, provided that the requirements fixed by law are met.

XVI. Lands which are subject to individual adjudication must be partitioned precisely at the time the presidential order is executed, according to regulatory laws.

XVII. The Federal Congress and the State Legislature, within their respective jurisdictions, shall enact laws to fix the maximum area of rural property, and to carry out the subdivision of the excess lands, in accordance with the following bases:

  a. In each State, Territory, or the Federal District, there shall be fixed a maximum area of land of which a single individual or legally constituted society may be the owner.

  b. The excess over the fixed area shall be subdivided by the owner within the time fixed by the local law, and these parcels shall be offered for sale under terms approved by the governments, in accordance with the aforementioned laws.

  c. If the owner should oppose the subdivision, it shall be carried out by the local government, by expropriation.

  d. The value of the parcels shall be paid by annual installments which will amortize principal and interest, at an interest rate not exceeding 3% per annum.

  e. Owners shall be required to receive bonds of the local Agrarian Debt to guarantee payment for the property expropriated. For this purpose, the Federal Congress shall enact a law empowering the States to create their Agrarian Debt.

  f. No subdivision can be sanctioned which fails to satisfy the agrarian needs of neighboring settlements (poblados inmediatos). Whenever subdivision projects are to be executed, the agrarian claims must be settled within a fixed period.

  g. Local laws shall organize the family patrimony, determining what property shall constitute it, on the basis that it shall be inalienable and shall not be subject to attachment or encumbrance of any kind.

XVIII. All contracts and concessions made by former Governments since the year 1876, which have resulted in the monopolization of lands, waters, and natural resources of the Nation, by a single person or company, are declared subject to revision, and the Executive of the Union is empowered to declare them void whenever they involve serious prejudice to the public interest.

Article 28. In the United Mexican States there shall be no monopolies or estancos of any kind; nor exemption from taxes; nor prohibitions under the guise of protection to industry; excepting only those relating to the coinage of money, the mails, telegraph, and radiotelegraphy, to the issuance of paper money by a single bank to be controlled by the Federal Government, and to the privileges which for a specified time are granted to authors and artists for the reproduction of their works, and to those which, for the exclusive use of their inventions, may be granted to inventors and those who perfect some improvement.

Consequently, the law shall punish severely and the authorities shall effectively prosecute every concentration or cornering in one or a few hands of articles of prime necessity for the purpose of obtaining a rise in prices; every act or proceeding which prevents or tends to prevent free competition in production, industry or commerce, or services to the public; every agreement or combination, in whatever manner it may be made, of producers, industrialists, merchants, and common carriers, or those engaged in any other service, to prevent competition among themselves and to compel consumers to pay exaggerated prices; and in general, whatever constitutes an exclusive and undue advantage in favor of one or more specified persons and to the prejudice of the public in general or of any social class.

Associations of workers, formed to protect their own interests, do not constitute monopolies.

Nor do cooperative associations or societies of producers constitute monopolies, which in defense of their interests or of the general interest, sell directly in foreign markets the domestic or industrial products which are the main source of wealth in the region in which they are produced, and which are articles of prime necessity, provided that such associations are under the supervision and protection of the Federal or State Governments and that they were previously duly authorized for the purpose by the respective legislatures, which latter of themselves or on proposal of the Executive may, when the public need so requires, repeal the authorizations granted for the formation of the associations in question.

Article 29. In the event of invasion, serious disturbance of the public peace, or any other event which may place society in great danger or conflict, only the President of the Mexican Republic, with the consent of the Council of Ministers and with the approval of the Federal Congress, and during adjournments of the latter, of the Permanent Committee, may suspend throughout the country or in a determined place the guarantees which present an obstacle to a rapid and ready combatting of the situation; but he must do so for a limited time, by means of general preventive measures without such suspensions being limited to a specified individual. If the suspension should occur while the Congress is in session, the latter shall grant such authorizations that it deems necessary to enable the Executive to meet the situation. If the suspension occurs during a period of adjournment, the Congress shall be convoked without delay in order to grant them.

Chapter II

MEXICANS

Article 30. Mexican nationality is acquired by birth or by naturalization:
  A. Mexicans by birth are:
    I. Those born in the territory of the Republic, regardless of the nationality of their parents:
    II. Those born in a foreign country of Mexican parents; of a Mexican father and a foreign mother; or of a Mexican mother and an unknown father;
    III. Those born on Mexican vessels or airships, either war or merchant vessels.
  B. Mexicans by naturalization are:
    I. Foreigners who obtain letters of naturalization from the Secretariat of Foreign Relations;
    II. A foreign woman who marries a Mexican man and has or establishes her domicile within the national territory.

Article 31. The obligations of Mexicans are:
  I. To see that their children or wards, under fifteen years of age, attend public or private schools to obtain primary, elementary and military education during the time prescribed by the Law on Public Education in each State.
  II. To be present on the days and hours designated by the Ayuntamiento of the place in which they reside, to receive civic and military instruction which will equip them for the exercise of their rights as citizens, give them skill in the handling of arms, and acquaint them with military discipline.
  III. To enlist and serve in the National Guard, according to the respective organic law, to secure and defend the independence, the territory, the honor, the rights and interests of the homeland, as well as domestic tranquility and order.
  IV To contribute to the public expenditures of the Federation, and the State and Municipality in which they reside, in the proportional and equitable manner provided by law.

Article 32. Mexicans shall have priority over foreigners under equality of circumstances for all classes of concessions and for all employment, positions, or commissions of the Government in which the status of citizenship is not indispensable. In time of peace no foreigner can serve in the Army nor in the police or public security forces.

In order to belong to the National Navy or the Air Force, and to discharge any office or commission, it is required to be a Mexican by birth. This same status is indispensable for captains, pilots, masters, engineers, mechanics, and in general, for all personnel of the crew of any vessel or airship protected by the Mexican merchant flag or insignia. It is also necessary to be Mexican by birth to discharge the position of captain of the port and all services of pratique and airport commandant, as well as all functions of customs agent in the Republic.

Chapter III

FOREIGNERS

Article 33. Foreigners are those who do not possess the qualifications set forth in Article 30. They are entitled to the guarantees granted by Chapter I, Title I, of the present Constitution; but the Federal Executive shall have the exclusive power to compel any foreigner whose remaining he may deem inexpedient to abandon the national territory immediately and without the necessity of previous legal action.

Foreigners may not in any way participate in the political affairs of the country.

Chapter IV

MEXICAN CITIZENS

Article 34. Men and women who, having the status of Mexicans, likewise meet the following requirements are citizens of the Republic:

I. Having reached eighteen years of age, if married, or twenty-one years of age if unmarried;

II. Having an honest means of livelihood.

Article 35. The prerogatives of citizens are:

I. To vote at popular elections;

II. To be voted for, for all offices subject to popular election, and to be appointed to any other employment or commission, if they have the qualifications established by law;

III. To associate together to discuss the political affairs of the country;

IV. To bear arms in the Army or National Guard in the defense of the Republic and its institutions, under the provisions prescribed by law;

V. To exercise in all cases the right of petition.

Article 36. The obligations of citizens of the Republic are:

    I. To register on the tax lists of the municipality, declaring the property they possess, the industry, profession, or occupation by which they subsist; and also to register in the electoral poll-books, according to the provisions prescribed by law;

    II. To enlist in the National Guard;

    III. To vote in popular elections in the electoral district to which they belong;

    IV. To serve in the elective offices of the Federation or of the States, which shall in no case be gratuitous;

    V. To serve in municipal council positions where they reside, and to fulfill electoral and jury functions.

Article 37.

    A. Mexican nationality is lost:

        I.   By the voluntary acquisition of a foreign nationality;

        II. By accepting or using titles of nobility which imply submission to a foreign state;

        III. By residing, if a Mexican by naturalization, for five consecutive years in the country of origin;

        IV. By passing in any public instrument, when Mexican by naturalization, as a foreigner, or by obtaining and using a foreign passport;

    B. Mexican citizenship is lost:

        I.   By accepting or using titles of nobility which imply submission to a foreign government;

        II. By rendering voluntary services to a foreign government without permission of the Federal Congress or of its Permanent Committee;

        III. By accepting or using foreign decorations without permission of the Federal Congress or of its Permanent Committee;

        IV By accepting titles or functions from the government of another country without previous permission of the Federal Congress or its Permanent Committee, excepting literary, scientific, or humanitarian titles which may be freely accepted;

        V. By aiding a foreigner or a foreign country, against the Nation, in any diplomatic claim or before an international tribunal;

        VI. In other cases which the laws may specify.

Article 38. The rights or prerogatives of citizens are suspended:

I. Through failure to comply, without sufficient cause, with any of the obligations imposed by Article 36. This suspension shall last for one year and shall be in addition to any other penalties prescribed by law for the same offense.

II. Through being subjected to criminal prosecution for an offense punishable by imprisonment (pena corporal), the suspension to be reckoned from the date of the formal order of commitment;

III. Throughout a term of imprisonment;

IV. Through vagrancy or habitual drunkenness, affirmed in the manner prescribed by law;

V. Through being a fugitive from justice, the suspension being reckoned from the date of the order of arrest until the prescription of the criminal action;

VI. Through final sentence imposing such suspension as a penalty.

The law shall specify those cases in which civil rights may be lost or suspended and the manner of rehabilitation.

TITLE II

Chapter I

NATIONAL SOVEREIGNTY AND FORM OF GOVERNMENT

Article 39. The national sovereignty resides essentially and originally in the people. All public power originates in the people and is instituted for their benefit. The people at all times have the inalienable right to alter or modify their form of government.

Article 40. It is the will of the Mexican people to organize themselves into a federal, democratic, representative Republic composed of free and sovereign States in all that concerns their internal government, but united in a Federation established according to the principles of this fundamental law.

Article 41. The people exercise their sovereignty through the powers of the Union in those cases within its jurisdiction, and through those of the States, in all that relates to their internal affairs, under the terms established by the present Federal Constitution and the individual constitutions of the States, respectively, which latter shall in no event contravene the stipulations of the Federal Pact.

Chapter II

Integral Parts of the Federation and of the National Territory

Article 42. The national territory comprises:

I. The integral parts of the Federation;

II. The islands, including the reefs and keys in adjacent seas;

III. The islands of Guadalupe and the Revillagigedos situated in the Pacific Ocean;

IV. The continental shelf and the submarine shelf of the islands' keys, and reefs;

V. The waters of the territorial seas to the extent and under terms fixed by international law and domestic maritime law;

VI. The space located above the national territory to the extent and according to rules established by international law on the subject.

Article 43. The integral parts of the Federation are the States of Aguascalientes, Baja California, Campeche, Coahuila, Colima, Chiapas, Chihuahua, Durango, Guanajuato, Guerrero, Hidalgo, Jalisco, México, Michoacán, Morelos, Nayarit, Nuevo León, Oaxaca, Puebla, Querétaro, San Luis Potosí, Sinaloa, Sonora, Tabasco, Tamaulipas, Tlaxcala, Veracruz, Yucatán, Zacatecas, the Federal District, and the Territories of Baja California Sur, and Quintana Roo.

Article 44. The Federal District shall embrace its present territory, and in the event of the removal of the federal branches to some other place, it shall be erected into the State of Valle de México, with such boundaries and area as the General Congress shall assign to it.

Article 45. The States and Territories of the Federation shall keep their present area and boundaries as of this day, provided no difficulties arise concerning them.

Article 46. The States having pending boundary questions shall arrange or settle them as provided in this Constitution.

Article 47. The State of Nayarit shall have the territorial area and boundaries which at present comprise the Territory of Tepic.

Article 48. The islands, keys, and reefs of the adjacent seas which belong to the national territory, the continental shelf, the submarine shelf of the islands, keys, and reefs, the inland marine waters, and the space above the national territory shall depend directly on the Government of the Federation, with the exception of those islands over which the States have up to the present exercised jurisdiction.

OIL: MEXICO'S POSITION

A Statement by the Bureau of Information of the Mexican Government
February, 1940

The Standard Oil Company of New Jersey has distributed a booklet under the title of "The Mexican Oil Seizure," with the manifest purpose of conveying to the mind of its readers the impression that the government of Mexico, in expropriating the properties of the oil companies, has acted in violation of the laws of Mexico and of the principles of International Law; and also, that in the negotiations conducted with some of the oil companies for the purpose of finding a solution to the problem, the Government of Mexico, from motives which are likely to be misunderstood, has repudiated its offers formally propounded, thereby making impossible any kind of settlement.

Out of respect for public opinion we will set forth in a subsequent special publication the misrepresentations and erroneous interpretations made by the Standard Oil Company in its pamphlet as to the origin of the dispute and as to the negotiations in which the agents of the expropriated companies participated.

For the time being, reference will only be made to the chief misrepresentations which are found in the booklet:

It is stated that the oil companies had an investment in Mexico of several hundred million dollars and that the Mexican Government has admitted its financial inability to pay. The conclusion drawn in the pamphlet is that the companies had no other recourse than to request diplomatic protection from their own governments in support of their claims. These arguments are based on the contention that Mexico could not legally expropriate the properties because of

Distributed by the Consulate General of Mexico in New York, 70 Pine Street, New York, N.Y. Printed in U.S.A.

its obvious inability to pay prompt and adequate compensation to the owners. The conclusion is false, because it is based on two premises both of which are equally false:

a) It is not true that the value of the properties of the oil companies lies between 262 million dollars as a minimum and 500 million dollars as a maximum, as is alleged in the pamphlet. Such figures were taken, as therein stated, from an article published in the magazine "Hoy" of July 31, 1939, the author of which is Mr. Luis Cabrera, an attorney of Mexico City.

As an instance of the hasty manner in which the writer of that pamphlet proceeds in attempting to establish his assertions, a literal translation of what was really said by Mr. Cabrera follows:

"I shall therefore take at random 300 million dollars as representing the value of the various properties of the 17 companies, the expropriation of which has been decreed; and I shall fix the further sum of one hundred million dollars as the value of the properties that must yet be expropriated in order to complete the socialization plan of the oil industry. The total, therefore, is four hundred million dollars which Mexico must pay, theoretically, right down and in cash. If anybody was to tell me that this figure is arbitrary, I would answer to him that indeed it is, and that it is devoid of any scientific basis; but that all the other figures which are mentioned are just as arbitrary, etc. . . ."

The writer of the article published in "Hoy" simply figures the sum of 262 million dollars as within Mexico's capacity to pay.

The Mexican Government characterizes as enormously exaggerated the figures which the companies have spread abroad regarding the value of their properties. Inasmuch as there has been no appraisal up to the present time, the only basis available for valuation is the company's own figures in the company's own books. According to the consolidated balance sheets of all the expropriated companies on March 18, 1938, the value of their permanent assets in Mexican pesos, amounted to 112,899,890.44.

It seems proper to point out that in this figure the American interests represent only a very small part of the total capital investment as well as of the actual production, because those companies, bent upon amortizing their capital, limited their activities to exploiting wells already in operation, without undertaking by means of new investments to increase production, or even to maintain the level previously reached. It is a matter of public knowledge that the production of the American companies reveals a definite decrease, owing to a complete absence of exploration and exploitation works of any importance, as well as to the reduced activity of their refineries, pipe lines and other installations.

The companies have systematically refused to discuss the value of their properties. Their representative admits that he proposed during the negotiations with the Government that the question of appraisal should not be considered. Such an attitude on the part of the companies is due to the fact that since they can not deny our right to expropriate private property with, naturally, payment of just compensation, they are actually seeking to create the impression that Mexico could not lawfully carry out the expropriation because of its inability to pay the fantastic sum of millions of dollars which the companies arbitrarily and prematurely assigned to their properties.

b) It is not true that Mexico has recognized her inability to pay, but, quite to the contrary, the Mexican Government has repeatedly declared its willingness to pay to the companies the full value of their properties. The assertion of their representative that the Government of Mexico promised to pay compensation to the companies with only a part of the net proceeds from the oil operations of the expropriated properties, is likewise untrue, for the Government has declared on different occasions its willingness to place at the disposal of the companies a substantial part of all the oil products destined for export, namely, a portion of the total production, including the oil reserves which belonged to the Government of Mexico prior to the expropriation and which have a great potential and actual value.

The fact that Mexico has suspended payment of its foreign debt does not mean, as is suggested in the pamphlet, that Mexico is unable to pay for the oil properties which were expropriated, inasmuch as it actually has at its disposal, an industry obviously productive, the income from which shall be devoted preferentially to the full payment of the compensation.

Among the most important nations of the world there are many who have postponed payment of some of their obligations, and it has not yet occurred to any one to say that such countries are actually suffering a permanent incapacity to meet their obligations.

The pamphlet makes reference to the compensation to American citizens for the value of their agricultural lands. In this particular it is pertinent to point out that an agreement has been reached with the Government of the United States whereby a commission has been created and is already functioning and that the Government of Mexico is making annual payments even before the exact value of the lands has been finally determined.

In the pamphlet an incomplete and malicious narrative of the oil controversy is given, misrepresenting the facts in order to fit them to the conclusion which is sought to be reached, and which conclusion is that the Government of Mexico always entertained the avowed purpose of expropriating the oil companies, taking advantage of various events in the accomplishment of that purpose. The evidence justifies no such conclusion.

It is true, as it is stated in the Standard Oil publication, that the oil companies were always the object of spirited attacks, they being considered as the exploiters of the natural and human resources of the country. In this connection, it should be remembered that the agents of the oil companies, over the years, committed countless rapacious acts such as defrauding the national treasury, bribing officials, seeking to impair the political stability of the government, and that they even made attacks against private property and human life. In fact, they went so far as to disturb at times the friendly relations between the peoples and the governments of the United States and Mexico.

It is also true that the aim of the various Governments of Mexico in the last few years was to place under the control of the Nation, for the benefit of the Mexican people, this important industry on which the national economy depends to a large extent. The methods employed by the oil companies and their attempts to create a political and economic power stronger than the State itself, were deemed prejudicial to public policy in Mexico. Various Mexican administrations, including the present one, have had the purpose in mind of accomplishing such an aim through a slow and gradual process, by creating a national organization to undetake the exploitation of the national reserves, and then gradually increasing the production of the oil lands. This plan was already being developed and important results had already been obtained when the expropriation took place.

Why was the Government compelled to change this plan and to decree the expropriation, placing all the oil properties in Mexico in the hands of a governmental institution? An examination of the events which preceded the expropriation proves that the present Administration had no other course open to it but the one it actually followed, thus being obliged to give a different direction to its policy from that originally intended. These were the actual facts:

I.   The workers demanded from the various companies operating in Mexico a revision of their labor contracts. This was a spontaneous act on the part of the labor unions and constituted a normal request, normal not only in Mexico, but in all other countries where the workers are granted freedom and where the workers' right to organize themselves for the defense of their interests is recognized.

II. In view of the fact that the Unions and the companies could not come to an agreement concerning the conditions of the new contract, the workers chose to declare a strike. This is, also, a spontaneous act on the part of the workers and, likewise, a lawful act in any country where the right to strike is recognized.

III. Inasmuch as the strike lasted for some time and there was no indication of an early agreement between the parties to the controversy, and furthermore, as due to the lack of fuel caused by the strike, it was feared that all economic life in Mexico would be paralyzed, the Mexican Government deemed it its duty to intervene in the dispute, in order to bring about a rapid solution and to prevent a grave danger to the entire Nation. This was the first official or governmental action taken by the Mexican authorities in the controversy between the companies and their workers.

IV. After an unsuccessful attempt was made, first through the Department of Labor and afterwards by the President personally, to obtain a conciliation between the parties, the President suggested to the workers that they should return to their work immediately, and submit their case to the Board of Conciliation and Arbitration which is located in the City of Mexico.

The intervention of the Mexican Government to that end is beyond reproach, from any point of view whatsoever, and was inspired by the highest regard for the public interest.

V. The Board of Conciliation and Arbitration appointed a committee of three experts to study the different aspects of the dispute. After having heard a considerable number of expert witnesses on the questions submitted, chosen both by the companies and the workers, the committee produced a comprehensive and well-reasoned report which served the Board as the basis for its decision.

VI. It is not true that the award rendered by the Board of Conciliation and Arbitration conceded to the workers their full demands. The Board took a reasonable course between the demands of the labor organizations and the concessions the companies were willing to grant. The award, based on the reports of the experts, decrees that the companies must guarantee certain benefits to the workers, by way of increase of wages, medical attention, hygienic dwellings, vacations, payment for extra-time, extra payment for labor in unhealthy regions, etc., amounting to the sum of twenty-six million Mexican pesos, in addition to the amounts covered by the former pay schedules of the workers.

The statement made by the representatives of the companies that the net profit of all the said companies amounted to twenty-three million pesos is false. The experts showed that the companies had previously earned much higher profits and the Mexican Government, which now controls the oil industry, is in a position to declare that the assertion made by the experts is fundamentally correct.

VII. As soon as the decision of the Board of Conciliation and Arbitration was known, the companies announced both in the American and Mexican press, that they were not willing to submit themselves to the decision of the Board and that in case the Supreme Court of Justice, to which they had already appealed, did not grant the application for a review of the award rendered by the Board of Conciliation and Arbitration, they would abandon their fields, plants, and equipment.

The Supreme Court, after a careful study, held that the decision of the Board did not contain any constitutional violations and that, therefore, it could not be reversed.

VIII. Both before and after the Court rendered its decision, several efforts for conciliation were made by various high officials and even by the President himself, offering fair and concrete suggestions to both parties with a view to putting an end to the dispute. Inasmuch as the companies maintained that the decision required an expenditure of more than twenty-six million pesos, the Mexican Government offered to appoint a commission that would supervise, under the guarantee of the Federal Executive, the execution of the Board's decision, in order to insure to the Companies that they would not pay more than the aforesaid twenty-six millions. The Government also suggested that in order to clarify the meaning of some of the provisions of the award, the parties agree to a binding interpretation of those provisions which the companies feared might deprive them of the necessary freedom to manage their business economically and efficiently.

At a meeting held in the President's office the companies' representatives definitely stated that they could not accept the President's suggestion.

Under these circumstances, what alternative was there left to the Government?—Could it permit non-compliance with a decision rendered by a legitimate authority and confirmed by the Highest Tribunal of the Country?—Can anyone imagine that any foreign corporation in any other country would be permitted to look with contempt upon, and refuse to obey the decision of, the highest court of the land?—Could the Mexican Government permit the companies to carry out their threat that they would close down their plants and stop the entire production of the fuel used all over Mexico? The Mexican Government, after carefully weighing its own responsibility, resolved that the public interests demanded that the oil production should not be suspended and that, in view of the fact that the owners were not willing to continue operations, the Government was fully justified in expropriating the oil industry in order that it might be managed by the State.

The above proves conclusively that, contrary to what is stated in the pamphlet, the expropriation was accomplished as the imperative result of a state of national emergency precipitated by the companies themselves.

The Government of Mexico announced from the very beginning that it would pay compensation to the companies, and the latter were asked to cooperate in reaching a proper appraisal of their properties, but this request the companies hastened to reject. If no payment of compensation has as yet been commenced, the blame falls upon the companies which have placed every possible obstacle in the way of arriving at a fair determination of the value of their properties.

The Mexican Government, however, still being willing to reach a friendly solution of the controversy, agreed to listen to the companies' special representative. Before the latter started for Mexico, the American press published a statement of a director of one of the principal companies, containing the bases upon which the companies would be prepared to enter into an agreement. The statement in the pamphlet is not correct when it asserts that these bases were accepted by the Mexican Government, because, quite to the contrary, such tentative provisions were obviously unacceptable. The granting of the companies' proposals would have created precisely the same situation which existed prior to the expropriation, and also would have placed the companies in a privileged position in regard to taxation as well as in their relations with their workers.

What the companies demanded was that the Government should fix in advance the taxes to be paid during the life of the proposed contract and to establish therein, under the pledge of the Government, rigid rules to govern the labor relations between the companies and their workers. Obviously, neither of these conditions could be legally complied with under the Mexican Constitution.

The Mexican Government cannot guarantee to any corporation that the latter shall not be liable in the future to pay higher taxes than those provided in a contract. This would amount to a curtailment of the powers of Congress.

It is also unconstitutional to impose on the workers inflexible labor standards, as these must be fixed by means of collective bargaining processes.

Furthermore, said bases did not take into consideration the origin of the dispute, to wit, the inability of the companies to arrive at an understanding with their workers regarding labor conditions, and the companies' refusal to accept the conditions which the Courts had recognized as just and reasonable. By what right could the Government compel the workers to work for the companies under stipulations arbitrarily fixed between the Government and the companies and in direct opposition to a judicial decision?

The companies' special representative thought that it was possible to arrive at an arrangement whereby the oil industry could be operated for mutual benefit. This idea was accepted by the Mexican Government, but when the companies' representative was compelled to offer concrete proposals, he never was able to find his way out of vague formulas and declarations of a general nature.

The President of Mexico was always of the opinion that any arrangement based upon effective cooperation would require a previous appraisal of the properties involved; and, if the Government agreed to postpone the appraisal, it did so only for the purpose of determining whether there existed any possibility of a settlement along the lines above mentioned.

Not until the time when the parleys were held in Saltillo in May, 1939, was the attorney for the companies able to abandon vague formulas and present instead a definite proposal in the form of a tentative draft of a "Preliminary Agreement." It is, therefore, untrue that this latter document was drafted jointly with the Mexican Ambassador.

It was considered that in Saltillo definite progress had been made over the parleys conducted in Mexico City, because for the first time that the companies' attorney was actually presenting for discussion a definite draft of a contract. Unfortunately, the bases which had already been considered as unacceptable, were substantially unchanged in the draft; but the hope was then entertained that the companies would realize that it was legally and practically impossible for the Government to accept such conditions, particularly those relating to labor.

What has just been stated shows the meaning of the declaration of May 3, which reads:

> "The discussions have been profitable. An effective progress towards a mutual and satisfactory agreement has been attained. . . . It is anticipated that in the near future the discussions will reach a definite conclusion, and it is not necessary to hold new oral discussions between President Cardenas and Mr. Richberg."

It is inaccurately stated in the pamphlet that in Saltillo the opinion was jointly expressed by both parties, that an understanding had been reached on most of the issues involved and that experts, representing both the Government and the companies, could draw the contracts laying down the future relations which would permit a settlement of the controversies between the companies and the Government.

By merely comparing the text of the joint statement with its interpretation by the author of the booklet one can readily discern the discrepancies between the two. It is one thing to have a profitable discussion and to make progress toward a certain understanding, and a very different thing to reach a substantial agreement on most of the points discussed.

The companies' special representative led his principals into error if, as inferred from the booklet, he advised them that a substantial agreement on all vital points of the controversy had been arrived at in Saltillo.

The assertion which is made at the end of the pamphlet sponsored by the Standard Oil Company is, therefore, both untrue and impertinent in expressing that, after the Saltillo parleys, the President of Mexico changed his mind on the subjects discussed.

It is not necessary to take up the insidious speculations in which the writer engages or to try to explain the motives of a change in attitude by the President. The President is still of the same mind as he was at Saltillo.

The pamphlet concludes by stating that it has been written to aid the public in an understanding of the causes which keep the controversy alive. In reality, this is only one more chapter in the propaganda campaign which is supported mainly by the Standard Oil in order to create confusion and to disparage the truly high ideals which actuate

Mexico. The companies have not made, as they allege, any serious attempt to arrive at a satisfactory solution of the conflict which they themselves brought about, limiting their action, as a simple reading of the pamphlet demonstrates, to making proposals which they knew beforehand to be impossible of acceptance, in order that they might hold themselves out as victims of the obstinacy of the Mexican Government.

Both in the notes from the American Government to the Mexican Government signed July 31 and August 22, 1938, and in the statement made by Undersecretary Welles on August 14, 1939, to which document the pamphlet refers, there is expressed the doctrine that the expropriation of private property, for public use, is legitimate, provided that prompt, just and adequate compensation for such property is granted. This doctrine is concurred in by Mexico. The Government of Mexico, in expropriating the properties of the oil companies and in rejecting the demand for restoration made by the latter, has not declared, as it is falsely stated in the pamphlet, its inability and unwillingness to make prompt, just and adequate compensation.

Therefore, the actual solution of the controversy in accordance with the principles of law, lies in reaching a determination as to what is a just and adequate compensation, namely, in fixing the value of the expropriated properties. Mexico has continuously sought a solution along these lines, but has failed so far due entirely to the persistent refusal of the companies.

The laws of Mexico provide that when a friendly agreement in controversies of this character cannot be reached, the Courts shall be open for the ascertainment of value, after hearing the opinion of experts appointed by both sides. In the event either side fails to appoint such experts, the Courts shall appoint experts for it. The companies, following their inveterate attitude of contempt for the laws of the land in which they have operated, have refused to appoint their own experts, and so, the appraisal must be made by experts appointed by the Mexican Courts.

Without availing themselves of the remedies provided by Mexican law and without resort to the Mexican Courts, the companies are now seeking to becloud the issues for the very purpose of avoiding a settlement by the means prescribed by the laws of Mexico and sanctioned by the principles and doctrines of International Law.

RUSSIAN EMPIRE LAW CODE: PEASANTS REDUCED TO SERFDOM, 1649

Tsar Alexis

CHAPTER XI. PROCEDURE CONCERNING THE PEASANTS

1. All peasants who have fled from lands belonging to the Tsar and are now living on lands belonging to church officials, hereditary landowners, and service landowners are to be returned to the Tsar's lands according to the land cadastres of 1627–31 regardless of the fifteen-year limit. These peasants are to be returned with their wives, children, and all movable property.

2. The same applies to peasants who have fled from hereditary landowners and service landowners to other hereditary landowners and service landowners, or to the towns, to the army, or to lands belonging to the Tsar.

3. Fugitive peasants must be returned with their wives, children, and movable property, plus their standing grain and threshed grain. But the possessions which the fugitive peasants owned in the years prior to this code are not to be claimed. If a fugitive peasant gave his daughter, sister, or niece in marriage to a local peasant, do not break up the marriage. Leave the girl with the local peasant. It was not a crime in the past to receive fugitive peasants—there was only a time limit for recovering them. Therefore the lord of the local peasant should not be deprived of his labor, especially as lands have changed hands frequently so that the present lord may not have been the person who received the fugitives anyway.

4. All hereditary landowners, service landowners, and officials managing the Tsar's lands must have proper documents identifying their peasants in case of dispute. Such documents must be written by public

scribes. . . . Illiterate landholders must have their documents signed by impartial, trustworthy persons. . . .

12. If a girl flees after the promulgation of this code and marries another landholder's peasant, then her husband and children will be returned with her to her former landholder. The movable property of her husband, however, will not be returned with them.

13. When a widower marries a fugitive peasant girl, any children he had by a previous marriage will not be surrendered with him to the lord of his new wife, but will remain with the lord of his first wife. . . .

15. If a widowed peasant remarries in flight, then both she and her husband will be returned to the lord of her first husband, provided her first husband was registered with a landholder.

16. If the peasant widow's first husband was not registered with a landholder, then she must live on the premises belonging to the lord of the peasant she married.

17. If a peasant in flight marries off his daughter, then his son-in-law will be returned to the landholder of his wife. . . .

18. A peasant woman in flight who marries will be returned with her husband to her former landholder.

19. Peasant women who are permitted to marry another landholder's peasant must be given release documents in which they are precisely described.

20. When peasants arrive in a hereditary estate or in a service estate and say that they are free people and wish to live with the landholder as peasants, the landholder must ascertain the truth of their claim. Within a year such people must be brought to Moscow or another large city for certification.

21. The lord who did not check carefully whether such people were free must pay the plaintiff to whom the peasants rightfully belong ten rubles per year per fugitive to compensate the plaintiff for his lost income and the taxes he paid while the peasant was absent.

22. Peasant children who deny their parents must be tortured. . . .

33. Bondmen and peasants who flee abroad and then return to Russia cannot claim that they are free men, but must be returned to their former hereditary landowners and service landowners.

34. When fugitive peasants of different landowners marry abroad, and then return to Russia, the landholders will cast lots for the couple. The winning service landowner gets the couple and must pay five rubles to the landholder who lost because both of the peasants were in flight abroad.

RUSSIAN EMPIRE LAW CODE: WESTERNIZING BY PETER THE GREAT, 1701–1714

Tsar Peter the Great

DECREE ON WESTERN DRESS (1701)

Western dress shall be worn by all the boyars, members of our councils and of our court . . . gentry of Moscow, secretaries . . . provincial gentry, gosti, government officials, strel'tsy, members of the guilds purveying for our household, citizens of Moscow of all ranks, and residents of provincial cities . . . excepting the clergy and peasant tillers of the soil.[1] The upper dress shall be of French or Saxon cut, and the lower dress . . . —(including) waistcoat, trousers, boots, shoes, and hats—shall be of the German type. They shall also ride German saddles. Likewise the womenfolk of all ranks, including the priests', deacons', and church attendants' wives, the wives of the dragoons, the soldiers, and the strel'tsy, and their children, shall wear Western dresses, hats, jackets, and underwear—undervests and petticoats—and shoes. From now on no one of the above-mentioned is to wear Russian dress or Circassian coats, sheepskin coats, or Russian peasant coats, trousers, boots, and shoes. It is also forbidden to ride Russian saddles, and the craftsmen shall not manufacture them or sell them at the marketplaces.

DECREE ON SHAVING (1705)

A decree to be published in Moscow and in all the provincial cities: Henceforth, in accordance with this, His Majesty's decree, all court attendants . . . provincial service men, government officials of all ranks, military men, all the gosti, members of the wholesale merchants' guild, and members of the guilds purveying for

---

[1] "Boyars" were nobles; "gosti" were merchants; and "strel'tsy" were soldiers in the imperial guard.

our household must shave their beards and moustaches. But, if it happens that some of them do not wish to shave their beards and moustaches, let a yearly tax be collected from such persons; from court attendants . . . provincial service men, military men, and government officials of all ranks—60 rubles per person; from the gosti and members of the wholesale merchants' guild of the first class—100 rubles per person; from members of the wholesale merchants' guild of the middle and the lower class (and) . . . from (other) merchants and townsfolk—60 rubles per person; . . . from townsfolk (of the lower rank), boyars' servants, stagecoachmen, waggoners, church attendants (with the exception of priests and deacons), and from Moscow residents of all ranks—30 rubles per person. Special badges shall be issued to them from the Administrator of Land Affairs of Public Order . . . which they must wear. . . . As for the peasants, let a toll of two halfcopecks per beard be collected at the town gates each time they enter or leave a town; and do not let the peasants pass the town gates, into or out of town, without paying this toll.

DECREE ON COMPULSORY EDUCATION OF THE RUSSIAN NOBILITY (1714)

Send to every administrative district some persons from mathematical schools to teach the children of the nobility—except those of freeholders and government clerks—mathematics and geometry; as a penalty for evasion establish a rule that no one will be allowed to marry unless he learns these subjects. Inform all prelates to issue no marriage certificates to those who are ordered to go to schools. . . .

The Great Sovereign has decreed; in all administrative districts children between the ages of ten and fifteen of the nobility, of government clerks, and of lesser officials, except those of freeholders, must be taught mathematics and some geometry. Toward that end, students should be sent from mathematical schools as teachers, several into each administrative district to prelates and to renowned monasteries to establish schools. During their instruction these teachers should be given food and financial remuneration . . . from district revenues set aside for that purpose by personal orders of His Imperial Majesty. No fees should be collected from students. When they have mastered the material, they should then be given certificates written in their own handwriting. When the students are released they ought to pay one ruble each for their training. Without these certificates they should not be allowed to marry nor receive marriage certificates.

AN INSTRUCTION TO RUSSIAN STUDENTS ABROAD STUDYING NAVIGATION (1714)

1. Learn how to draw plans and charts and how to use the compass and other naval indicators.

2. Learn how to navigate a vessel in battle as well as in a simple maneuver, and learn how to use all appropriate tools and instruments; namely, sails, ropes, and oars, and the like matters, on row boats and other vessels.

3. Discover as much as possible how to put ships to sea during a naval battle. Those who cannot succeed in this effort must diligently ascertain what action should be taken by the vessels that do and those that do not put to sea during such a situation (naval battle). Obtain from foreign naval officers written statements, bearing their signatures and seals, of how adequately you are prepared for naval duties.

4. If, upon his return, anyone wishes to receive from the Tsar greater favors for himself, he should learn, in addition to the above enumerated instructions, how to construct those vessels abroad which he would like to demonstrate his skills.

5. Upon his return to Moscow, every foreign-trained Russian should bring with him at his own expense, for which he will later be reimbursed, at least two experienced masters of naval science. They the returnees will be assigned soldiers, one soldier per returnee, to teach them what they have learned abroad. And if they do not wish to accept soldiers they may teach their acquaintances or their own people. The treasury will pay for transportation and maintenance of soldiers. And if anyone other than soldiers learns the art of navigation the treasury will pay 100 rubles for the maintenance of every such individual.

ON THE TWO LINES IN THE REVOLUTION

V. I. Lenin, translated by Julius Katzer

In *Prizyv*[1] (No. 3), Mr. Plekhanov attempts to present the fundamental theoretical problem of the impending revolution in Russia. He quotes a passage from Marx to the effect that the 1789 Revolution in France followed an ascending line, whereas the 1848 Revolution followed a descending line. In the first instance, power passed gradually from the moderate party to the more radical—the Constitutionalists, the Girondists, the Jacobins. In the second instance, the reverse took place—the proletariat, the petty-bourgeois democrats, the bourgeois republicans, Napoleon III. "It is desirable," our author infers, "that the Russian revolution should be directed along an ascending line," i.e., that power should first pass to the Cadets and Octobrists, then to the Trudoviks, and then to the socialists. The conclusion to be drawn from this reasoning is, of course, that the Left wing in Russia is unwise in not wishing to support the Cadets and in prematurely discrediting them.

Mr. Plekhanov's "theoretical" reasoning is another example of the substitution of liberalism for Marxism. Mr. Plekhanov reduces the matter to the question of whether the "strategic conceptions" of the advanced elements were "right" or wrong. Marx's reasoning was different. He noted a fact: in each case the revolution proceeded in a different fashion; he did *not* however seek *the explanation* of this difference in "strategic conceptions." From the Marxist point of view it is ridiculous to seek it in conceptions. It should be sought in the difference in the *alignment of classes.* Marx himself wrote that in 1789 the French bourgeoisie united with the peasantry and that in 1848 petty-bourgeois democracy betrayed the proletariat. Mr. Plekhanov knows Marx's opinion on the matter, but he does not mention it, because he wants to depict Marx as looking like Struve. In the

---

Sotsial-Demokrat No. 48. November 20, 1915. Translated by Julius Katzer.

[1] *Prizyv* (The Call)—A weekly published in Paris by the Mensheviks and the Socialist-Revolutionaries, from October 1915 to March 1917. The reference is to Plekhanov's article "Two Lines in the Revolution," published in this newspaper on October 17, 1915.

France of 1789, it was a question of overthrowing absolutism and the nobility. At the then prevalent level of economic and political development, the bourgeoisie believed in a harmony of interests; it had no fears about the stability of its rule and was prepared to enter into an alliance with the peasantry. That alliance secured the complete victory of the revolution. In 1848 it was a question of the proletariat overthrowing the bourgeoisie. The proletariat was unable to win over the petty bourgeoisie, whose treachery led to the defeat of the revolution. The ascending line of 1789 was a form of revolution in which the mass of the people defeated absolutism. The descending line of 1848 was a form of revolution in which the betrayal of the proletariat by the mass of the petty bourgeoisie led to the defeat of the revolution.

Mr. Plekhanov is substituting vulgar idealism for Marxism when he reduces the question to one of "strategic conceptions," not of the alignment of classes.

The experience of the 1905 Revolution and of the subsequent counter-revolutionary period in Russia teaches us that in our country two lines of revolution could be observed, in the sense that there was a struggle between two classes—the proletariat and the liberal bourgeoisie—for leadership of the masses. The proletariat advanced in a revolutionary fashion, and was leading the democratic peasantry towards the overthrow of the monarchy and the landowners. That the peasantry revealed revolutionary tendencies in the democratic sense was proved on a *mass* scale by *all* the great political events: the peasant insurrections of 1905–06, the unrest in the army in the same years, the "Peasants' Union" of 1905, and the first two Dumas, in which the *peasant* Trudoviks stood not only "to the left of the Cadets," *but were also more revolutionary* than the intellectual *Social-Revolutionaries* and Trudoviks. Unfortunately, this is often forgotten, but still it is a fact. Both in the Third and in the Fourth Dumas, the *peasant* Trudoviks, despite their weakness, showed that the peasant masses were *opposed* to the landed proprietors.

The first line of the Russian bourgeois-democratic revolution, as deduced from the facts and not from "strategic" prattle, was marked by a resolute struggle of the proletariat, which was irresolutely followed by the peasantry. Both these classes fought against the monarchy and the landowners. The lack of strength and resolution in these classes led to their defeat (although a partial breach was made in the edifice of the autocracy).

The behaviour of the liberal bourgeoisie was the second line. We Bolsheviks have always affirmed, especially since the spring of 1906, that this line was represented by the Cadets and Octobrists as a *single* force. The 1905–15 decade has proved the correctness of our view. At the decisive moments of the struggle, the Cadets, together with the Octobrists betrayed democracy and went to the aid of the tsar and the landowners. The "liberal" line of the Russian revolution was marked by the "pacification" and the fragmentary character of the masses' struggle so as to enable the bourgeoisie to make peace with the monarchy. The international background to the Russian revolution and the strength of the Russian proletariat rendered this behaviour of the liberals inevitable.

The Bolsheviks helped the proletariat consciously to follow the first line, to fight with supreme courage and to lead the peasants. The Mensheviks were constantly slipping into the second line; they demoralised the proletariat by adapting its movement to the liberals—from the invitation to enter the Bulygin Duma (August 1905), to the Cadet Cabinet in 1906 and the bloc with the Cadets *against* democracy in 1907. (From Mr. Plekhanov's point of view, we will observe parenthetically, the "correct strategic conceptions" of the Cadets and the Mensheviks suffered a defeat at the time. Why was that? Why did the masses not pay heed to the wise counsels of Mr. Plekhanov and the Cadets, which were publicised a hundred times more extensively than the advice from the Bolsheviks?)

Only these trends—the Bolshevik and the Menshevik—manifested themselves in the politics of the *masses* in 1904–08, and later, in 1908–14. Why was that? It was because only these trends had firm class roots—the former in the proletariat, the latter in the liberal bourgeoisie.

Today we are again advancing towards a revolution Everybody sees that. *Khvostov himself* says that the mood of the peasants is reminiscent of 1905–06. And again we see the *same* two lines in the revolution, the *same* alignment of classes, only modified by a changed international situation. In 1905, the entire European bourgeoisie supported tsarism and helped it either with their thousands of millions (the French), or by training a counter-revolutionary army (the Germans). In 1914 the European war flared up. Everywhere the bourgeoisie vanquished the proletariat for a time, and swept them into the turbid spate of nationalism and chauvinism. In Russia, as hitherto, the petty-bourgeois masses of the people, primarily the peasantry, form the majority of the population. They are oppressed first and foremost by the landowners. Politically, part of the peasantry are dormant, and part vacillate between chauvinism ("the defeat of Germany," "defence of the fatherland") and revolutionary spirit. The political spokesmen of these masses—and of their vacillation—are, on the one hand, the Narodniks (the Trudoviks and Social-Revolutionaries), and on the other hand, the opportunist Social-Democrats (*Nashe Dyelo*, Plekhanov, the Chkheidze group, the Organising Committee), who, since 1910, have been determinedly following the road of liberal-labour politics, and in 1915 have achieved the social-chauvinism of Potresov, Cherevanin, Levitsky, and Maslov, or have demanded "unity" with them.

This state of affairs patently indicates the task of the proletariat. That task is the waging of a supremely courageous revolutionary struggle against the monarchy (utilising the slogans of the January Conference of 1912, the "three pillars"), a struggle that will sweep along in its wake all the democratic masses, i.e., mainly the peasantry. At the same time, the proletariat must wage a ruthless struggle against chauvinism, a struggle in alliance with the *European* proletariat for the socialist revolution in Europe. The vacillation of the petty bourgeoisie is no accident; it is inevitable, for it logically follows from their class stand. The war crisis has *strengthened* the economic and political factors that are impelling the petty bourgeoisie, including the peasantry, to the left. Herein lies the objective foundation of the full possibility of victory for the democratic revolution in Russia. There is no need here for us to prove that the objective conditions in Western Europe are ripe for a socialist revolution; this was admitted before the war by all influential socialists in all advanced countries.

To bring clarity into the alignment of classes in the impending revolution is the main task of a revolutionary party. This task is being shirked by the Organising Committee, which within Russia remains a faithful ally to *Nashe Dyelo*, and abroad utters meaningless "Left" phrases. This task is being wrongly tackled in *Nashe Slovo* by Trotsky, who is repeating his "original" 1905 theory and refuses to give some thought to the reason why, in the course of ten years, life has been bypassing this splendid theory

From the Bolsheviks, Trotsky's original theory has borrowed their call for a decisive proletarian revolutionary struggle and for the conquest of political power by the proletariat, while from the Mensheviks it has borrowed "repudiation" of the peasantry's role. The peasantry, he asserts, are divided into strata, have become differentiated; their potential revolutionary role has dwindled more and more, in Russia a "national" revolution is impossible; "we are living in the era of imperialism," says Trotsky, and "imperialism does not contrapose the bourgeois nation to the old regime, but the proletariat to the bourgeois nation."

Here we have an amusing example of playing with the word "imperialism." If, *in Russia,* the proletariat already stands contraposed to the "bourgeois nation," then Russia is facing a *socialist* revolution (!), and the slogan "Confiscate the landed *estates*" (repeated by Trotsky in 1915, following the January Conference of 1912), is incorrect, in that case we must speak, not of a "revolutionary workers'" government, but of a "workers' *socialist*" government! The length Trotsky's muddled thinking goes to is evident from his phrase that by their resoluteness the proletariat will attract the "non-proletarian [!] popular masses" as well (No. 217)! Trotsky has not realised that if the proletariat induce the non-proletarian masses to confiscate the landed estates and overthrow the monarchy, then that will be the consummation of the "national bourgeois revolution" in Russia; it will be a revolutionary-democratic dictatorship of the proletariat and the peasantry!

A whole decade—the great decade of 1905–15—has shown the existence of two and only two class lines in the Russian revolution. The differentiation of the peasantry has enhanced the class struggle within them; it has aroused very many hitherto politically dormant elements. It has drawn the rural proletariat closer to the urban proletariat (the Bolsheviks have insisted ever since 1906 that the former should be *separately* organised, and they included this demand in the resolution of the Menshevik congress in Stockholm). However, the antagonism between the peasantry, on the one hand, and the Markovs, Romanovs and Khvostovs, on the other, has become stronger and more acute. This is such an obvious truth that not *even* the thousands of phrases in scores of Trotsky's Paris articles will "refute" it. Trotsky is in fact helping the liberal-labour politicians in Russia, who by "repudiation" of the role of the peasantry understand a *refusal* to raise up the peasants for the revolution!

That is the crux of the matter today. The proletariat are fighting, and will fight valiantly, to win power, for a republic, for the confiscation of the land, *i.e.,* to win over the peasantry, make *full* use of their revolutionary powers, and get the "non-proletarian masses of the people" to take part in liberating *bourgeois* Russia from *military-feudal* "imperialism" (tsarism). The proletariat will at once utilise this ridding of bourgeois Russia of tsarism and the rule of the landowners, not to aid the rich peasants in their struggle against the rural workers, but to bring about the socialist revolution in alliance with the proletarians of Europe.

PASSIVE RESISTANCE

Mahatma Ghandi

READER: Is there any historical evidence as to the success of what you have called soul-force or truth-force? No instance seems to have happened of any nation having risen through soul-force. I still think that the evil-doers will not cease doing evil without physical punishment.

EDITOR: The poet Tulsidas has said: "Of religion, pity, or love, is the root, as egotism of the body. Therefore, we should not abandon pity so long as we are alive." This appears to me to be a scientific truth. I believe in it as much as I believe in two and two being four. The force of love is the same as the force of the soul or truth. We have evidence of its working at every step. The universe would disappear without the existence of that force. But you ask for historical evidence. It is, therefore, necessary to know what history means. The Gujarati equivalent means: "It so happened." If that is the meaning of history, it is possible to give copious evidence. But, if it means the doings of kings and emperors, there can be no evidence of soul-force or passive resistance in such history. You cannot expect silver ore in a tin mine. History, as we know it, is a record of the wars of the world, and so there is a proverb among Englishmen that a nation which has no history, that is, no wars, is a happy nation. How kings played, how they became enemies of one another, how they murdered one another, is found accurately recorded in history, and if this were all that had happened in the world, it would have been ended long ago. If the story of the universe had commenced with wars, not a man would have been found alive today. Those people who have been warred against have disappeared as, for instance, the natives of Australia of whom hardly a man was left alive by the intruders. Mark, please, that these natives did not use soul-force in self-defence, and it does not require much foresight to know that the Australians will share the same fate as their victims. "Those that take the sword shall perish by the sword." With us the proverb is that professional swimmers will find a watery grave.

The fact that there are so many men still alive in the world shows that it is based not on the force of arms but on the force of truth or love. Therefore, the greatest and most unimpeachable evidence of the success of this force is to be found in the fact that, in spite of the wars of the world, it still lives on.

Thousands, indeed tens of thousands, depend for their existence on a very active working of this force. Little quarrels of millions of families in their daily lives disappear before the exercise of this force. Hundreds of nations live in peace. History does not and cannot take note of this fact. History is really a record of every interruption of the even working of the force of love or of the soul. Two brothers quarrel; one of them repents and re-awakens the love that was lying dormant in him; the two again begin to live in peace; nobody takes note of this. But if the two brothers, through the intervention of solicitors or some other reason take up arms or go to law—which is another form of the exhibition of brute force,—their doings would be immediately noticed in the press, they would be the talk of their neighbours and would probably go down to history. And what is true of families and communities is true of nations. There is no reason to believe that there is one law for families and another for nations. History, then, is a record of an interruption of the course of nature. Soul-force, being natural, is not noted in history.

READER: According to what you say, it is plain that instances of this kind of passive resistance are not to be found in history. It is necessary to understand this passive resistance more fully. It will be better, therefore, if you enlarge upon it.

EDITOR: Passive resistance is a method of securing rights by personal suffering; it is the reverse of resistance by arms. When I refuse to do a thing that is repugnant to my conscience, I use soul-force. For instance, the Government of the day has passed a law which is applicable to me. I do not like it. If by using violence I force the Government to repeal the law, I am employing what may be termed body-force. If I do not obey the law and accept the penalty for its breach, I use soul-force. It involves sacrifice of self.

Everybody admits that sacrifice of self is infinitely superior to sacrifice of others. Moreover, if this kind of force is used in a cause that is unjust, only the person using it suffers. He does not make others suffer for his mistakes. Men have before now done many things which were subsequently found to have been wrong. No man can claim that he is absolutely in the right or that a particular thing is wrong because he thinks so, but it is wrong for him so long as that is his deliberate judgment. It is therefore meet that he should not do that which he knows to be wrong, and suffer the consequence whatever it may be. This is the key to the use of soul-force.

READER: You would then disregard laws—this is rank disloyalty. We have always been considered a law-abiding nation. You seem to be going even beyond the extremists. They say that we must obey the laws that have been passed, but that if the laws be bad, we must drive out the law-givers even by force.

EDITOR: Whether I go beyond them or whether I do not is a matter of no consequence to either of us. We simply want to find out what is right and to act accordingly. The real meaning of the statement that we are a law-abiding nation is that we are passive resisters. When we do not like certain laws, we do not break the heads of law-givers but we suffer and do not submit to the laws. That we should obey laws whether good or bad is a newfangled notion. There was no such thing in former days. The people disregarded those laws they did not like and suffered the penalties for their breach. It is contrary to our manhood if we obey laws repugnant to our conscience. Such teaching is opposed to religion and means slavery. If the Government were to ask us to go about without any clothing, should we do so? If I were a passive resister, I would say to them that I would have nothing to do with their law. But we have so forgotten ourselves and become so compliant that we do not mind any degrading law.

A man who has realized his manhood, who fears only God, will fear no one else. Man-made laws are not necessarily binding on him. Even the Government does not expect any such thing from us. They do not say: "You must do such and such a thing," but they say: "If you do not do it, we will punish you." We are sunk so low that we fancy that it is our duty and our religion to do what the law lays down. If man will only realize that it is unmanly to obey laws that are unjust, no man's tyranny will enslave him. This is the key to self-rule or home-rule.

It is a superstition and ungodly thing to believe that an act of a majority binds a minority. Many examples can be given in which acts of majorities will be found to have been wrong and those of minorities to have been right. All reforms owe their origin to the initiation of minorities in opposition to majorities. If among a band of robbers a knowledge of robbing is obligatory, is a pious man to accept the obligation? So long as the superstition that men should obey unjust laws exists, so long will their slavery exist. And a passive resister alone can remove such a superstition.

To use brute force, to use gunpowder, is contrary to passive resistance, for it means that we want our opponent to do by force that which we desire but he does not. And if such a use of force is justifiable, surely he is entitled to do likewise by us. And so we should never come to an agreement. We may simply fancy, like the blind horse moving in a circle round a mill, that we are making progress. Those who believe that they are not bound to obey laws which are repugnant to their conscience have only the remedy of passive resistance open to them. Any other must lead to disaster.

READER: From what you say I deduce that passive resistance is a splendid weapon of the weak, but that when they are strong they may take up arms.

EDITOR: This is gross ignorance. Passive resistance, that is, soul-force, is matchless. It is superior to the force of arms. How, then, can it be considered only a weapon of the weak? Physical-force men are strangers to the courage that is requisite in a passive resister. Do you believe that a coward can ever disobey a law that he dislikes? Extremists are considered to be advocates of brute force. Why do they, then, talk about obeying laws? I do not blame them. They can say nothing else. When they succeed in driving out the English and they themselves become governors, they will want you and me to obey their laws. And that is a fitting thing for their constitution. But a passive resister will say he will not obey a law that is against his conscience, even though he may be blown to pieces at the mouth of a cannon.

What do you think? Wherein is courage required—in blowing others to pieces from behind a cannon, or with a smiling face to approach a cannon and be blown to pieces? Who is the true warrior—he who keeps death always as a bosom-friend, or he who controls the death of others? Believe me that a man devoid of courage and manhood can never be a passive resister.

This however, I will admit: that even a man weak in body is capable of offering this resistance. One man can offer it just as well as millions. Both men and women can indulge in it. It does not require the training of an army; it needs no jiu-jitsu. Control over the mind is alone necessary, and when that is attained, man is free like the king of the forest and his very glance withers the enemy.

Passive resistance is an all-sided sword, it can be used anyhow; it blesses him who uses it and him against whom it is used. Without drawing a drop of blood it produces far-reaching results. It never rusts and cannot be stolen. Competition between passive resisters does not exhaust. The sword of passive resistance does not require a scabbard. It is strange indeed that you should consider such a weapon to be a weapon merely of the weak.

READER: You have said that passive resistance is a speciality of India. Have cannons never been used in India?

EDITOR: Evidently, in your opinion, India means its few princes. To me it means its teeming millions on whom depends the existence of its princes and our own.

Kings will always use their kingly weapons. To use force is bred in them. They want to command, but those who have to obey commands do not want guns: and these are in a majority throughout the world. They have to learn either body-force or soul-force. Where they learn the former, both the rulers and the ruled become like so many madmen; but but where they learn soul-force, the commands of the rulers do not go beyond the point of their swords, for true men disregard unjust commands. Peasants have never been subdued by the sword, and never will be. They do not know the use of the sword, and they are not frightened by the use of it by others. That nation is great which rests its head upon death as its pillow. Those who defy death are free from all fear. For those who are labouring under the delusive charms of brute-force, this picture is not overdrawn. The fact is that, in India, the nation at large has generally used passive resistance in all departments of life. We cease to co-operate with our rulers when they displease us. This is passive resistance.

I remember an instance when, in a small principality, the villagers were offended by some command issued by the prince. The former immediately, began vacating the village. The prince became nervous, apologized to his subjects and withdrew his command. Many such instances can be found in India. Real Home Rule is possible only where passive resistance is the guiding force of the people. Any other rule is foreign rule.

READER: Then you will say that it is not at all necessary for us to train the body?

EDITOR: I will certainly not say any such thing. It is difficult to become a passive resister unless the body is trained. As a rule, the mind, residing in a body that has become weakened by pampering, is also weak, and where there is no strength of mind there can be no strength of soul. We shall have to improve our physique by getting rid of infant marriages and luxurious living. If I were to ask a man with a shattered body to face a cannon's mouth I should make a laughing-stock of myself.

READER: From what you say, then, it would appear that it is not a small thing to become a passive resister, and, if that is so, I should like you to explain how a man may become one.

EDITOR: To become a passive resister is easy enough but it is also equally difficult. I have known a lad of fourteen years become a passive resister; I have known also sick people do likewise; and I have also known physically strong and otherwise happy people unable to take up passive resistance. After a great deal of experience it seems to me that those who want to become passive resisters for the service of the country have to observe perfect chastity, adopt poverty, follow truth, and cultivate fearlessness.

Chastity is one of the greatest disciplines without which the mind cannot attain requisite firmness. A man who is unchaste loses stamina, becomes emasculated and cowardly. He whose mind is given over to animal passions is not capable of any great effort. This can be proved by innumerable instances. What, then, is a married person to do is the question that arises naturally; and yet it need not. When a husband and wife gratify the passions, it is no less an animal indulgence on that account. Such an indulgence, except for perpetuating the race, is strictly prohibited. But a passive resister has to avoid even that very limited indulgence because he can have no desire for progeny. A married man, therefore, can observe perfect chastity. This subject is not capable of being treated at greater length. Several questions arise: How is one to carry one's wife with one, what are her rights, and other similar questions. Yet those who wish to take part in a great work are bound to solve these puzzles.

Just as there is necessity for chastity, so is there for poverty. Pecuniary ambition and passive resistance cannot well go together. Those who have money are not expected to throw it away, but they *are* expected to be indifferent about it. They must be prepared to lose every penny rather than give up passive resistance.

Passive resistance has been described in the course of our discussion as truth-force. Truth, therefore, has necessarily to be followed and that at any cost. In this connection, academic questions such as whether a man may not lie in order to save a life, etc., arise, but these questions occur only to those who wish to justify lying. Those who want to follow truth every time are not placed in such a quandary; and if they are, they are still saved from a false position.

Passive resistance cannot proceed a step without fearlessness. Those alone can follow the path of passive resistance who are free from fear, whether as to their possessions, false honour, their relatives, the government, bodily injuries or death.

These observances are not to be abandoned in the belief that they are difficult. Nature has implanted in the human breast ability to cope with any difficulty or suffering that may come to man unprovoked. These qualities are worth having, even for those who do not wish to serve the country. Let there be no mistake, as those who want to train themselves in the use of arms are also obliged to have these qualities more or less. Everybody does not become a warrior for the wish. A would-be warrior will have to observe chastity and to be satisfied with poverty as his lot. A warrior without fearlessness cannot be conceived of. It may be thought that he would not need to be exactly truthful, but that quality follows real fearlessness. When a man abandons truth, he does so owing to fear in some shape or form. The above four attributes, then, need not frighten anyone. It may be as well here to note that a physical-force man has to have many other useless qualities which a passive resister never needs. And you will find that whatever extra effort a swordsman needs is due to lack of fearlessness. If he is an embodiment of the latter, the sword will drop from his hand that very moment. He does not need its support. One who is free from hatred requires no sword. A man with a stick suddenly came face to face with a lion and instinctively raised his weapon in self-defence. The man saw that he had only prated about fearlessness when there was none in him. That moment he dropped the stick and found himself free from all fear.

MARXISM, CAPITALISM AND NON-ALIGNMENT

Jawaharlal Nehru

*Nehru, India's first Prime Minister after independence (1947), was the cre-
ator of such terms as "neutralism," "Third World," and "non-alignment."*

MARXISM, CAPITALISM AND INDIA'S FUTURE (1941)[1]

As our struggle toned down and established itself at a low level, there was little
of excitement in it, except at long intervals. My thoughts traveled more to other
countries, and I watched and studied, as far as I could in jail, the world situation
in the grip of the great depression. I read as many books as I could find on the
subject, and the more I read the more fascinated I grew. India with her problems
and struggles became just a part of this mighty world drama, of the great struggle of political and economic forces that was going on everywhere, nationally and
internationally. In that struggle my own sympathies went increasingly toward the
communist side.

I had long been drawn to socialism and communism, and Russia had
appealed to me. Much in Soviet Russia I dislike—the ruthless suppression of all
contrary opinion, the wholesale regimentation, the unnecessary violence (as I
thought) in carrying out various policies. But there was no lack of violence and
suppression in the capitalist world, and I realized more and more how the very
basis and foundation of our acquisitive society and property was violence. Without violence it could not continue for many days. A measure of political liberty
meant little indeed when the fear of starvation was always compelling the vast
majority of people everywhere to submit to the will of the few, to the greater
glory and advantage of the latter.

---

[1] from *Toward Freedom: The Autobiography of Jawaharlal Nehru* (New York: John Day Co.,
1941), pp. 228–231.

Violence was common in both places, but the violence of the capitalist order seemed inherent in it; while the violence of Russia, bad though it was aimed at a new order based on peace and co-operation and real freedom for the masses. With all her blunders, Soviet Russia had triumphed over enormous difficulties and taken great strides toward this new order. While the rest of the world was in the grip of the depression and going backward in some ways, in the Soviet country a great new world was being built up before our eyes. Russia, following the great Lenin, looked into the future and thought only of what was to be, while other countries lay numbed under the dead hand of the past and spent their energy in preserving the useless relics of a bygone age. In particular, I was impressed by the reports of the great progress made by the backward regions of Central Asia under the Soviet regime. In the balance, therefore, I was all in favor of Russia, and the presence and example of the Soviets was a bright and heartening phenomenon in a dark and dismal world.

But Soviet Russia's success or failure, vastly important as it was as a practical experiment in establishing a communist state, did not affect the soundness of the theory of communism. The Bolsheviks may blunder or even fail because of national or international reasons, and yet the communist theory may be correct. On the basis of that very theory it was absurd to copy blindly what had taken place in Russia, for its application depended on the particular conditions prevailing in the country in question and the stage of its historical development. Besides, India, or any other country, could profit by the triumphs as well as the inevitable mistakes of the Bolsheviks. Perhaps the Bolsheviks had tried to go too fast because, surrounded as they were by a world of enemies, they feared external aggression. A slower tempo might avoid much of the misery caused in the rural areas. But then the question rose if really radical results could be obtained by slowing down the rate of change. Reformism was an impossible solution of any vital problem at a critical moment when the basic structure had to be changed, and, however slow the progress might be later on, the initial step must be a complete break with the existing order, which had fulfilled its purpose and was now only a drag on future progress.

In India, only a revolutionary plan could solve the two related questions of the land and industry as well as almost every other major problem before the country. . . .

Russia apart, the theory and philosophy of Marxism lightened up many a dark corner of my mind. History came to have a new meaning for me. The Marxist interpretation threw a flood of light on it, and it became an unfolding drama with some order and purpose, howsoever unconscious, behind it. In spite of the appalling waste and misery of the past and the present, the future was bright with hope, though many dangers intervened. It was the essential freedom from dogma and the scientific outlook of Marxism that appealed to me. It was true that there was plenty of dogma in official communism in Russia and elsewhere, and frequently heresy hunts were organized. That seemed to be deplorable, though it was not difficult to understand in view of the tremendous changes taking place rapidly in the Soviet countries when effective opposition might have resulted in catastrophic failure.

The great world crisis and slump seemed to justify the Marxist analysis. While all other systems and theories were groping about in the dark, Marxism alone explained it more or less satisfactorily and offered a real solution.

As this conviction grew upon me, I was filled with a new excitement, and my depression at the nonsuccess of civil disobedience grew much less. Was not the world marching rapidly toward the desired consummation? There were grave dangers of wars and catastrophes, but at any rate we were moving. There was no stagnation. Our national struggle became a stage in the longer journey, and it was as well that repression and suffering were tempering our people for future struggles and forcing them to consider the new ideas that were stirring the world. We would be the stronger and the more disciplined and hardened by the elimination of the weaker elements. Time was in our favor.

ECONOMIC DEVELOPMENT AND NONALIGNMENT (1956)[2]

We are now engaged in a gigantic and exciting task of achieving rapid and large-scale economic development of our country. Such development, in an ancient and underdeveloped country such as India, is only possible with purposive planning. True to our democratic principles and traditions, we seek, in free discussion and consultation as well as in implementation, the enthusiasm and the willing and active cooperation of our people. We completed our first Five-Year Plan 8 months ago, and now we have begun on a more ambitious scale our second Five-Year Plan, which seeks a planned development in agriculture and industry, town and country, and between factory and small-scale and cottage production. I speak of India because it is my country and I have some right to speak for her. But many other countries in Asia tell the same story, for Asia today is resurgent, and these countries which long lay under foreign yoke have won back their independence and are fired by a new spirit and strive toward new ideals. To them, as to us, independence is as vital as the breath they take to sustain life, and colonialism, in any form, or anywhere, is abhorrent. . . .

. . . Peace and freedom have become indivisible, and the world cannot continue for long partly free and partly subject. In this atomic age peace has also become a test of human survival.

Recently we have witnessed two tragedies which have powerfully affected men and women all over the world. These are the tragedies in Egypt and Hungary.

From a speech in Washington, D.C., December 18, 1956, printed in the U.S. *Department of State Bulletin,* January 14, 1957, pp. 49–50.

Our deeply felt sympathies must go out to those who have suffered or are suffering, and all of us must do our utmost to help them and to assist in solving these problems in a peaceful and constructive way. But even these tragedies have one hopeful aspect, for they have demonstrated that the most powerful countries cannot revert to old colonial methods or impose their domination over weak countries. World opinion has shown that it can organize itself to resist such outrages. Perhaps, as an outcome of these tragedies, freedom will be enlarged and will have a more assured basis.

The preservation of peace forms the central aim of India's policy. It is in the pursuit of this policy that we have chosen the path of nonalinement [nonalignment] in any military or like pact of alliance. Nonalinement does not mean passivity of mind or action, lack of faith or conviction. It does not mean submission to what we consider evil. It is a positive and dynamic approach to such problems that confront us. We believe that each country has not only the right to freedom but also to decide its own policy and way of life. Only thus can true freedom flourish and a people grow according to their own genius.

We believe, therefore, in nonaggression and non-interference by one country in the affairs of another and the growth of tolerance between them and the capacity for peaceful coexistence. We think that by the free exchange of ideas and trade and other contacts between nations each will learn from the other and truth will prevail. We therefore endeavor to maintain friendly relations with all countries, even though we may disagree with them in their policies or structure of government. We think that by this approach we can serve not only our country but also the larger causes of peace and good; fellowship in the world.

REPORT ON AN INVESTIGATION OF THE PEASANT MOVEMENT IN HUNAN, MARCH 1927

Mao Tse-Tung

THE IMPORTANCE OF THE PEASANT PROBLEM

. . . The present upsurge of the peasant movement is a colossal event. In a very short time, in China's central, southern and northern provinces, several hundred million peasants will rise like a mighty storm, like a hurricane, a force so swift and violent that no power, however great, will be able to hold it back. They will smash all the trammels that bind them and rush forward along the road to liberation. They will sweep all the imperialists, warlords, corrupt officials, local tyrants and evil gentry into their graves. Every revolutionary party and every revolutionary comrade will be put to the test, to be accepted or rejected as they decide. There are three alternatives. To march at their head and lead them? To trail behind them, gesticulating and criticizing? Or to stand in their way and oppose them? Every Chinese is free to choose, but events will force you to make the choice quickly.

GET ORGANIZED!

The development of the peasant movement in Hunan[1] may be divided roughly into two periods. . . . The first, from January to September of last year, was one of organization. In this period . . . the membership of the peasant associations did not exceed 300,000 to 400,000, and the masses directly under their leadership numbered little more than 1 million. . . .

---

[1] Hunan Province in 1926–27 was the center of Communist organization of peasants in China, and a massive slaughter of landlords took place at that time.

The second period, from last October to January of this year, was one of revolutionary action. The membership of the associations jumped to 2 million and the masses directly under their leadership increased to 10 million. . . .

DOWN WITH THE LOCAL TYRANTS AND EVIL GENTRY! ALL POWER TO THE PEASANT ASSOCIATIONS!

The main targets of attack by the peasants are the local tyrants, the evil gentry and the lawless landlords. . . . As a result, the privileges which the feudal landlords enjoyed for thousands of years are being shattered to pieces. With the collapse of the power of the landlords, the peasant associations have now become the sole organs of authority. . . .

Even such trifles as a quarrel between husband and wife are brought to the peasant association. Nothing can be settled unless someone from the peasant association is present. Quite literally, "Whatever it says, goes." . . .

In the face of the peasant associations' power and pressure, the top local tyrants and evil gentry have fled to Shanghai, those of the second rank to Hankow, those of the third to Changsha, and those of the fourth to the country towns, while the fifth rank and the still lesser fry surrender to the peasant associations in the villages. . . .

"IT'S TERRIBLE!" OR "IT'S FINE!"

The peasants' revolt disturbed the gentry's sweet dreams. . . . From the middle social strata upward to the Kuomintang right-wingers, there was not a single person who did not sum up the whole business in the phrase, "It's terrible!" . . .

In a few months the peasants have accomplished what Dr. Sun Yat Sen wanted, but failed, to accomplish in the forty years he devoted to the national revolution. This is a marvelous feat never before achieved, not only in forty but in thousands of years. It's fine. It is not "terrible" at all. . . . What the peasants are doing is absolutely right; what they are doing is fine! . . .

THE QUESTION OF "GOING TOO FAR"

Then there is another section of the people who say, "Yes, peasant associations are necessary, but they are going rather too far." This is the opinion of the middle-of-the-roaders. But what is the actual situation? True, the peasants are in a sense "unruly" in the countryside. Supreme in authority, the peasant association allows the landlord no say and sweeps away his prestige. This amounts to striking the landlord down to the dust and keeping him there. . . .

People swarm into the houses of local tyrants and evil gentry who are against the peasant association, slaughter their pigs and consume their grain. . . .

Doing whatever they like and turning everything upside down, they have created a kind of terror in the countryside. This is what some people call "going too far," or "exceeding the proper limits in righting a wrong." Such talk may seem plausible, but in fact it is wrong.

First, the local tyrants, evil gentry and lawless landlords have themselves driven the peasants to this. For ages they have used their power to tyrannize over the peasants and trample them underfoot; that is why the peasants have reacted so strongly. . . .

Secondly, a revolution is not a dinner party, or writing an essay, or painting a picture, or doing embroidery; it cannot be so refined, so leisurely and gentle, so temperate, kind, courteous, restrained and magnanimous. A revolution is an insurrection, an act of violence by which one class overthrows another. A rural revolution is a revolution by which the peasantry overthrows the power of the feudal landlord class. . . .

To put it bluntly, it is necessary to create terror for a while in every rural area, otherwise it would be impossible to suppress the activities of the counter-revolutionaries in the countryside or overthrow the authority of the gentry. . . .

THE "MOVEMENT OF THE RIFFRAFF"

The right wing of the Kuomintang says, "The peasant movement is a movement of the riffraff, of the lazy peasants." . . . The gentry say, "It is all right to set up peasant associations, but the people now running them are no good. They ought to be replaced." . . . In short, all those whom the gentry had despised, those whom they had trodden into the dirt, people with no right to speak, have now audaciously lifted up their heads and taken power into their hands. . . . They are issuing orders and are running everything. Those who used to rank lowest now rank above everybody else; and so this is called "turning things upside down."

VANGUARDS OF THE REVOLUTION

. . . The peasants have done an important job for the national revolution. . . . But has this been performed by all the peasants? No. There are three kinds of peasants, the rich, the middle, and the poor peasants . . . who have different views about the revolution. . . .

Thus an official of the township peasant association (generally one of the "riffraff" type) would walk into the house of a rich peasant, register in hand, and say: "Will you please join the peasant association?" How would the rich peasant answer? A tolerably well-behaved one would say: "I never heard of such a thing before, yet I've managed to live all right. I advise you to give it up." A really vicious rich peasant would say: "Peasant association! Nonsense! Association for getting your head chopped off! Don't get people into trouble." . . .

How about the middle peasants? . . . They think, ". . . Can the Three People's Principles prevail?" Their conclusion is, "Afraid not!" They imagine it all depends on the will of Heaven and think, "A peasant association? Who knows if Heaven wills it or not?" . . . It is essential for the peasant associations to get the middle peasants to join and to do a good deal more explanatory work among them. . . .

The poor peasants have always been the main force in the bitter fight in the countryside. They have fought militantly through the two periods of underground work and of open activity. They are the most responsive to Communist Party leadership. . . . "We joined the peasant association long ago," they say to the rich peasants, "why are you still hesitating?" The rich peasants answer mockingly, "What is there to keep you from joining? You people have neither a tile over your heads nor a speck of land under your feet!" . . . What, indeed, is there to keep them from joining the associations? . . .

Without the poor peasants there would be no revolution. To deny their role is to deny the revolution. . . .

FOURTEEN GREAT ACHIEVEMENTS

Most critics of the peasant associations allege that they have done a great many bad things. . . . The peasants have done a great many things, and in order to answer people's criticism we must closely examine all their activities. . . . The peasants under the leadership of the peasant associations have the following fourteen great achievements to their credit.

1. Organizing the Peasants into Peasant Associations

This is the first great achievement of the peasants. . . . Roughly speaking, the counties in central Hunan, with Changsha as the center, are the most advanced, those in southern Hunan come second, and western Hunan is only just beginning to organize. According to the figures compiled by the provincial peasant association last November, organizations with a total membership of 1,367,727 have been set up in thirty-seven of the province's seventy-five counties. . . .

2. Hitting the Landlords Politically

Once the peasants have their organization, the first thing they do is to smash the political prestige and power of the landlord class. . . .

Checking the accounts. More often than not the local tyrants and evil gentry have helped themselves to public money passing through their hands, and their books are not in order. Now the peasants are using the checking of accounts as an occasion to bring down a great many of the local tyrants and evil gentry. . . .

Imposing fines. The peasants work out fines for such offenses as irregularities revealed by the checking of accounts. . . . A man who has been fined by the peasants completely loses face.

Levying contributions. The unscrupulous rich landlords are made to contribute for poor relief, for the organization of co-operatives or peasant credit societies, or for other purposes. . . .

Minor protests. When someone harms a peasant association and the offense is a minor one . . . he is usually let off after writing a pledge to "cease and desist."

Major demonstrations. A big crowd is rallied to demonstrate against a local tyrant or one of the evil gentry who is an enemy of the association. The demonstrators eat at the offender's house, slaughtering his pigs and consuming his grain as a matter of course. . . .

"Crowning" the landlords and parading them through the villages. This sort of thing is very common. A tall paper hat is stuck on the head of one of the local tyrants or evil gentry, bearing the words "Local tyrant So-and-so." He is led by a rope, brass gongs are beaten and flags are waved to attract people's attention. This form of punishment makes the local tyrants and evil gentry tremble. Anyone who has once been crowned with a tall paper hat loses face altogether and can never again hold up his head. . . .

Locking up the landlords in the county jail. This is a heavier punishment than wearing the tall paper hat. A local tyrant or one of the evil gentry is arrested and sent to the county jail; he is locked up and the county magistrate has to try him and punish him. . . .

"Banishment." The peasants have no desire to banish the most notorious criminals among the local tyrants and evil gentry, but would rather arrest or execute them. Afraid of being arrested or executed, they run away . . . and this amounts to banishment. . . .

Execution. This is confined to the worst local tyrants and evil gentry and is carried out by the peasants jointly with other sections of the people. . . . The execution of one big landlord reverberates through a whole county and is very effective in eradicating the remaining evils of feudalism. . . . The head of the defense corps in the town of Hsinkang was personally responsible for killing almost 1,000 poverty-stricken peasants, which he euphemistically described as "executing bandits." . . . Such was the cruelty in former days of the White terror in the countryside, and now that the peasants have risen and shot a few and created just a little terror in suppressing the counterrevolutionaries, is there any reason for saying they should not do so?

3. Hitting the Landlords Economically

Prohibition on sending grain out of the area, forcing up grain prices, and hoarding and cornering. . . . Since last October, the poor peasants have prevented the out-flow of the grain of the landlords and rich peasants and have banned the forcing up of grain prices and hoarding and cornering. . . .

Prohibition on increasing rents and deposits, agitation for reduced rents and deposits. Last July and August, when the peasant associations were still weak, the land-lords, following their long-established practice of maximum exploitation, served notice one after another on their tenants that rents would be increased. But by October, when the peasant associations had grown considerably in strength and had all come out against the raising of rents and deposits, the landlords dared not breathe another word on the subject. . . .

Prohibition on cancelling tenancies. In July and August of last year there were still many instances of landlords cancelling tenancies and reletting the land. But after October nobody dared cancel a tenancy. Today, the cancelling of tenancies and the reletting of land are quite out of the question. . . .

Reduction of interest. Interest has been generally reduced . . . and wherever the peasant associations are powerful, rural moneylending has virtually disappeared; the landlords fear the money will be "communized." . . . Not only is the interest on . . . old loans reduced, but the creditor is actually forbidden to press for repayment of the principal. . . .

4. Overthrowing the Feudal Rule of the Local Tyrants and Evil Gentry—Smashing the TU and TUAN

The old organs of political power in the *tu* and *tuan* (i.e., the district and the township), and especially at the *tu* level, just below the county level, used to be almost exclusively in the hands of the local tyrants and evil gentry. . . . The evil gentry who ran these organs were virtual monarchs of the countryside. . . . As a consequence of the present revolt in the countryside the authority of the landlord class has generally been struck down, and the organs of rural adminis-tration dominated by the local tyrants and evil gentry have naturally collapsed in its wake. . . .

5. Overthrowing the Armed Forces of the Landlords and Establishing Those of the Peasants

The armed forces of the landlord class were smaller in central Hunan than in the western and southern parts of the province. . . . Taking over these old armed forces is one way in which the peasants are building up their own armed forces. A new way is through the setting up of spear corps under the peasant associations. The spears have pointed, double-edged blades mounted on long shafts. . . . The revolutionary authorities in Hunan should see to it that such a corps is built up on a really extensive scale among the more than 20 million peasants in the seventy-five counties of the province; that every peasant, whether young or in his prime, possesses a spear; and that no restrictions are imposed as though a spear were something dreadful. . . .

6. Overthrowing the Political Power of the County Magistrate and His Bailiffs

. . . County government cannot be clean until the peasants rise up. . . . In a county where the peasants have risen there is clean government, whoever the magistrate. . . . In counties where the peasant power was very strong, the word of the peasant association worked miracles. If it demanded the arrest of a local tyrant in the morning, the magistrate dared not delay till noon; if it demanded arrest by noon, he dared not delay till the afternoon. . . .

In the past the villagers were afraid of the townspeople, but now the townspeople are afraid of the villagers. In particular, the vicious curs kept by the county government—the police, the armed guards and the bailiffs—are afraid to go to the villages; or if they do so, they no longer dare to practice their extortions. They tremble at the sight of the peasants' spears.

7. Overthrowing the Clan Authority of the Ancestral Temples and Clan Elders, the Religious Authority of Town and Village Gods, and the Masculine Authority of Husbands

A man in China is usually subjected to the domination of three systems of authority: (1) the state system (political authority) . . . ; (2) the clan system (clan authority) . . . ; and (3) the supernatural system (religious authority). . . . As for women, in addition to being dominated by these three systems of authority, they are also dominated by the men (the authority of the husband). These four authorities . . . are the four thick ropes binding the Chinese people. . . . The old rule barring women and poor people from banquets in the ancestral temples has also been broken. The women of Paikuo in Hengshan County gathered in force and swarmed into their ancestral temple, firmly planted their backsides on the seats and joined in the eating and drinking, while the venerable clan bigwigs had willy-nilly to let them do as they pleased. . . .

. . . Our present task is to lead the peasants to put their greatest efforts into the political struggle, so that the landlords' authority is entirely overthrown. . . . As for the clan system, superstition, and inequality between men and women, their abolition will follow as a natural consequence of victory in the political and economic struggles. . . .

While I was in the countryside, I did some propaganda against superstition among the peasants. I said:

"If you believe in the Eight Characters,[2] you hope for good luck; if you believe in geomancy,[3] you hope to benefit from the location of your ancestral graves. This year within the space of a few months the local tyrants, evil gentry and corrupt officials have all toppled from their pedestals—is it possible . . . their ancestral graves have ceased to exert a beneficial influence? The local tyrants and evil gentry jeer at your peasant association and say . . . : 'You can't even go to pass water without bumping into a committeeman.' . . . And the gods? Worship them by all means. But if you had only Lord Kuan[4] and the Goddess of Mercy and no peasant association, could you have overthrown the local tyrants and evil gentry? The gods and goddesses are indeed miserable objects. You have worshipped them for centuries, and they have not overthrown a single one of the local tyrants or evil gentry for you! Now you want to have your rent reduced. Let me ask, how will you go about it? Will you believe in the gods or in the peasant association?"

My words made the peasants roar with laughter.

8. Spreading Political Propaganda

Even if ten thousand schools of law and political science had been opened, could they have brought as much political education as the peasant associations have done in so short a time? I don't think they could. "Down with imperialism!" "Down with the warlords!" "Down with the corrupt officials!" . . . These political slogans have . . . penetrated into their minds and are on their lips. . . .

Some of the peasants can also recite Dr. Sun Yat Sen's Testament. They pick out the terms "freedom," "equality," "the Three People's Principles" and "unequal treaties," and apply them, if rather crudely, in their daily life. . . . When a policeman strikes or swears at a peasant selling vegetables, the peasant immediately answers back by invoking the Three People's Principles and that shuts the policeman up. . . .

The spread of political propaganda throughout the rural areas is entirely an achievement of the Communist Party and the peasant associations. . . . From now on, care should be taken to use every opportunity gradually to enrich the content and clarify the meaning of those simple slogans.

---

2 The "Eight Characters" was a method of fortunetelling in China based on the examination of the two cyclic characters for the year, month, day, and hour of a person's birth.

3 Mao Tse-tung is referring to the superstition that the location of one's ancestors' graves influences one's fortune. The geomancers claimed to be able to tell whether a particular site and its surroundings were auspicious, guided in part by the mystic *feng* (wind) and *shui* (water).

4 Lord Kuan (Kuan Yu, A.D. 160–219), a warrior in the epoch of the Three Kingdoms, was widely worshipped by the Chinese as the God of Loyalty and War.

9. Peasant Bans and Prohibitions

When the peasant associations, under Communist Party leadership, establish their authority in the countryside, the peasants begin to prohibit or restrict the things they dislike. Gaming, gambling and opium-smoking are the three things that are most strictly forbidden.

Gaming. Where the peasant association is powerful, mahjong, dominoes and card games are completely banned. . . .

Gambling. . . . This abuse, too, has been swept away in places where the peasant association is powerful.

Opium-smoking. The prohibition is extremely strict. . . . In Liling County one of the evil gentry who did not surrender his pipes was arrested and paraded through the villages. . . .

The flower drum. Vulgar performances are forbidden in many places.

Sedan chairs. . . . In many counties . . . there have been cases of smashing of sedan chairs. . . . But peasant associations . . . say, "If you smash the chairs, you only save the rich money and lose the carriers their jobs." Seeing the point, the peasants worked out a new tactic . . . to increase the fares charged by the chair-carriers so as to penalize the rich.

Distilling and sugar-making. The use of grain for distilling spirits and making sugar is everywhere prohibited. . . .

Pigs. The number of pigs a family can keep is limited, for pigs consume grain.

Chickens and ducks. . . . In many places the raising of chickens and ducks is prohibited; ducks not only consume grain but also ruin the rice plants and so are worse than chickens.

Feasts. Sumptuous feasts are generally forbidden. . . .

Oxen. Oxen are a treasured possession of the peasants. "Slaughter an ox in this life and you will be an ox in the next" has become almost a religious tenet; oxen must never be killed. . . .

10. Eliminating Banditry

In my opinion, no ruler in any dynasty from Yu,[5] Tang, Wen and Wu down to the Ching Emperors and the Presidents of the Republic has ever shown as much prowess in eliminating banditry as have the peasant associations today.

---

[5] Emperor Yu is recorded as the eighth ruler of China. He is held to have dealt successfully with draining off the waters of a great flood and is credited with founding the first dynasty, the Hsia, to which are ascribed the doubtful dates of 2205–1705 B.C.

. . . The reasons are: First, the members of the peasant associations are spread out over the hills and dales, spear or cudgel in hand. . . . Second, since the rise of the peasant movement the price of grain has dropped . . . and the problem of food has become less serious. . . . Third, members of secret societies . . . can now openly and legally vent their grievances. . . . Fourth, the armies are recruiting large numbers and many of the "unruly" have joined up. . . .

11. Abolishing Exorbitant Levies

As the country is not yet unified and the authority of the imperialists and warlords has not been overthrown, there is as yet no way of removing . . . the burden of expenditure for the revolutionary army. However, the exorbitant levies imposed on the peasants . . . have been abolished or reduced with the rise of the peasant movement. . . .

12. The Movement for Education

In China education has always been the exclusive preserve of the landlords, and the peasants have had no access to it. . . . In China 90 percent of the people have had no education, and of these the overwhelming majority are peasants. . . .

Now the peasants are enthusiastically establishing evening classes, which they call "peasant schools." . . . Before long, tens of thousands of schools will have sprung up in the villages throughout the province. . . .

13. The Co-operative Movement

The peasants really need co-operatives, and especially consumers' marketing and credit co-operatives. When they buy goods, the merchants exploit them; when they sell their farm produce, the merchants cheat them; . . . when they borrow money or rice, they are fleeced by the usurers; and they are eager to find a solution to these three problems. . . A major problem is the absence of detailed, standard rules of organization. . . Given proper guidance, the co-operative movement can spread everywhere along with the growth of the peasant associations.

14. Building Roads and Repairing Embankments

This, too, is one of the achievements of the peasant associations. Before there were peasant associations the roads in the countryside were terrible. . . .

The same is true of the embankments. The ruthless landlords . . . would never spend even a few coppers on embankment repairs; they would leave the ponds to dry up and the tenant-peasants to starve, caring about nothing but the rent. Now that there are peasant associations, the landlords can be bluntly ordered to repair the embankments. . . .

Curiously enough, it is reported from Nanchang[6] that Chiang Kaishek, Chang Ching-chiang,[7] and other such gentlemen do not altogether approve of the activities of the Hunan peasants. This opinion is shared by Liu Yueh-chih and other right-wing leaders in Hunan, all of whom say, "They have simply gone Red." But where would the national revolution be without this bit of Red? To talk about "arousing the masses of the people" day in and day out and then to be scared to death when the masses do rise—what difference is there between this and Lord Sheh's[8] love of dragons?

---

[6] When Nanchang (Kiangsi) was captured by the Northern Expeditionary Army in November 1926 under General Chiang Kai-shek, the Communist-dominated forces in Hankow (Hupeh), under the guidance of the Soviet Union's Michael Borodin, declared Hankow the capital of "liberated" China. A fierce battle broke out between Chiang's forces inside the walls of Nanchang and those of the Communist faction on the outside; the Communists were defeated after several days of bitter fighting. Mao denounced this as a "counter-revolutionary plot against Wuhan" (the tri-city area on the banks of the Yangtze River, of which Hankow was the principal commercial city).

[7] Chang Ching-chiang was a member of Chiang Kai-shek's planning staff.

[8] As told by Liu Hsiang (77 B.C.) in his *Hsin Hsu,* Lord Sheh was so food of dragons that he adorned his whole palace with drawings and carvings of them. But when a real dragon heard of his infatuation and paid him a visit, he was frightened out of his wits.

THE VIETNAMESE DECLARATION OF INDEPENDENCE

Ho Chi Minh

One of the many results of World War II was the stirring of independence movements in the European colonies. Many of these colonies had been conquered by Japan during the war and entertained hopes of independence after the defeat of Japan. Vietnam was one example. In any case, the Vietminh, the communist-Vietnamese nationalist movement, had fought the Japanese throughout the war. They did not expect the victorious Allies to turn the colony back over to France. No one then would have imagined that independence would have to await a nine-year war with the French followed by twenty years of war with the United States.

What seems to be Ho Chi Minh's attitude toward the United States and France in 1945? Notice the striking similarity of the form of the declaration to the American Declaration of Independence. Why do you suppose he did that?

"All men are created equal. They are endowed by their Creator with certain inalienable rights; among these are Life, Liberty, and the pursuit of Happiness."

This immortal statement was made in the Declaration of Independence of the United States of America in 1776. In a broader sense, this means: All the peoples on the earth are equal from birth, all the peoples have a right to live, to be happy and free.

The Declaration of the French Revolution made in 1791 on the Rights of Man and the Citizen also states: "All men are born free and with equal rights, and must always remain free and have equal rights."

Those are undeniable truths.

Nevertheless, for more than eighty years, the French imperialists, abusing the standard of Liberty, Equality, and Fraternity, have violated our Fatherland and oppressed our fellow-citizens. They have acted contrary to the ideals of humanity and justice.

In the field of politics, they have deprived our people of every democratic liberty.

They have enforced inhuman laws; they have set up three distinct political regimes in the North, the Center and the South of Vietnam in order to wreck our national unity and prevent our people from being united.

They have built more prisons than schools. They have mercilessly slain our patriots; they have drowned our uprisings in rivers of blood.

They have fettered public opinion; they have practised obscurantism against our people.

To weaken our race they have forced us to use opium and alcohol.

In the field of economics, they have fleeced us to the backbone, impoverished our people, and devastated our land.

They have robbed us of our rice fields, our mines, our forests, and our raw materials. They have monopolized the issuing of bank-notes and the export trade.

They have invented numerous unjustifiable taxes and reduced our people, especially our peasantry, to a state of extreme poverty.

They have hampered the prospering of our national bourgeoisie; they have mercilessly exploited our workers.

In the autumn of 1940, when the Japanese Fascists violated Indochina's territory to establish new bases in their fight against the Allies, the French imperialists went down on their bended knees and handed over our country to them.

Thus, from that date, our people were subjected to the double yoke of the French and the Japanese. Their sufferings and miseries increased. The result was that from the end of last year to the beginning of this year, from Quang Tri province to the North of Vietnam, more than two million of our fellow-citizens died from starvation. On March 9, the French troops were disarmed by the Japanese. The French colonialists either fled or surrendered, showing that not only were they incapable of "protecting" us, but that, in the span of five years, they had twice sold our country to the Japanese.

On several occasions before March 9, the Vietminh League urged the French to ally themselves with it against the Japanese. Instead of agreeing to this proposal, the French colonialists so intensified their terrorist activities against the Vietminh members that before fleeing they massacred a great number of our political prisoners detained at Yen Bay and Caobang.

Notwithstanding all this, our fellow-citizens have always manifested toward the French a tolerant and humane attitude. Even after the Japanese putsch of March 1945, the Vietminh League helped many Frenchmen to cross the frontier, rescued some of them from Japanese jails, and protected French lives and property.

From the autumn of 1940, our country had in fact ceased to be a French colony and had become a Japanese possession.

After the Japanese had surrendered to the Allies, our whole people rose to regain our national sovereignty and to found the Democratic Republic of Vietnam.

The truth is that we have wrested our independence from the Japanese and not from the French.

The French have fled, the Japanese have capitulated, Emperor Bao Dai has abdicated. Our people have broken the chains which for nearly a century have fettered them and have won independence for the Fatherland. Our people at the same time have overthrown the monarchic regime that has reigned supreme for dozens of centuries. In its place has been established the present Democratic Republic.

For these reasons, we, members of the Provisional Government, representing the whole Vietnamese people, declare that from now on we break off all relations of a colonial character with France; we repeal all the international obligation that France has so far subscribed to on behalf of Vietnam and we abolish all the special rights the French have unlawfully acquired in our Fatherland.

The whole Vietnamese people, animated by a common purpose, are determined to fight to the bitter end against any attempt by the French colonialists to reconquer their country.

We are convinced that the Allied nations which at Tehran and San Francisco have acknowledged the principles of self-determination and equality of nations, will not refuse to acknowledge the independence of Vietnam.

A people who have courageously opposed French domination for more than eight years, a people who have fought side by side with the Allies against the Fascists during these last years, such a people must be free and independent.

For these reasons, we, members of the Provisional Government of the Democratic Republic of Vietnam, solemnly declare to the world that Vietnam has the right to be a free and independent country—and in fact is so already. The entire Vietnamese people are determined to mobilize all their physical and mental strength, to sacrifice their lives and property in order to safeguard their independence and liberty.

I SPEAK OF FREEDOM

Kwame Nkrumah

Kwame Nkrumah (1909–1972) was the leader of Ghana, the former British colony of the Gold Coast and the first of the European colonies in Africa to gain independence with majority rule. Until he was deposed by a coup d'état in 1963, he was a major spokeman for modern Africa.

For centuries, Europeans dominated the African continent. The white man arrogated to himself the right to rule and to be obeyed by the non-white; his mission, he claimed, was to "civilise" Africa. Under this cloak, the Europeans robbed the continent of vast riches and inflicted unimaginable suffering on the African people.

All this makes a sad story, but now we must be prepared to bury the past with its unpleasant memories and look to the future. All we ask of the former colonial powers is their goodwill and co-operation to remedy past mistakes and injustices and to grant independence to the colonies in Africa. . . .

It is clear that we must find an African solution to our problems, and that this can only be found in African unity. Divided we are weak; united, Africa could become one of the greatest forces for good in the world.

Although most Africans are poor, our continent is potentially extremely rich. Our mineral resources, which are being exploited with foreign capital only to enrich foreign investors, range from gold and diamonds to uranium and petroleum. Our forests contain some of the finest woods to be grown anywhere. Our cash crops include cocoa, coffee, rubber, tobacco and cotton. As for power, which is an important factor in any economic development, Africa contains over 40% of the potential water power of the world, as compared with about 10% in Europe and 13% in North America. Yet so far, less than 1% has been developed. This is one of the reasons why we have in Africa the paradox of poverty in the midst of plenty, and scarcity in the midst of abundance.

From Kwame Nkrumah, *I Speak of Freedom: A Statement of African Ideology* (London: William Heinemann Ltd., 1961), pp. xi–xiv.

Never before have a people had within their grasp so great an opportunity for developing a continent endowed with so much wealth. Individually, the independent states of Africa, some of them potentially rich, others poor, can do little for their people. Together, by mutual help, they can achieve much. But the economic development of the continent must be planned and pursued as a whole. A loose confederation designed only for economic co-operation would not provide the necessary unity of purpose. Only a strong political union can bring about full and effective development of our natural resources for the benefit of our people.

The political situation in Africa today is heartening and at the same time disturbing. It is heartening to see so many new flags hoisted in place of the old; it is disturbing to see so many countries of varying sizes and at different levels of development, weak and, in some cases, almost helpless. If this terrible state of fragmentation is allowed to continue it may well be disastrous for us all.

There are at present some 28 states in Africa, excluding the Union of South Africa, and those countries not yet free. No less than nine of these states have a population of less than three million. Can we seriously believe that the colonial powers meant these countries to be independent, viable states? The example of South America, which has as much wealth, if not more than North America, and yet remains weak and dependent on outside interests, is one which every African would do well to study.

Critics of African unity often refer to the wide differences in culture, language and ideas in various parts of Africa. This is true, but the essential fact remains that we are all Africans, and have a common interest in the independence of Africa. The difficulties presented by questions of language, culture and different political systems are not insuperable. If the need for political union is agreed by us all, then the will to create it is born; and where there's a will there's a way.

The present leaders of Africa have already shown a remarkable willingness to consult and seek advice among themselves. Africans have, indeed, begun to think continentally. They realise that they have much in common, both in their past history, in their present problems and in their future hopes. To suggest that the time is not yet ripe for considering a political union of Africa is to evade the facts and ignore realities in Africa today.

The greatest contribution that Africa can make to the peace of the world is to avoid all the dangers inherent in disunity, by creating a political union which will also by its success, stand as an example to a divided world. A Union of African states will project more effectively the African personality. It will command respect from a world that has regard only for size and influence. The scant attention paid to African opposition to the French atomic tests in the Sahara, and the ignominious spectacle of the U.N. in the Congo quibbling about constitutional niceties while the Republic was tottering into anarchy, are evidence of the callous disregard of African Independence by the Great Powers.

We have to prove that greatness is not to be measured in stockpiles of atom bombs. I believe strongly and sincerely that with the deep-rooted wisdom and dignity, the innate respect for human lives, the intense humanity that is our heritage, the African race, united under one federal government, will emerge not as just another world bloc to flaunt its wealth and strength, but as a Great Power whose greatness is indestructible because it is built not on fear, envy and suspicion, nor won at the expense of others, but founded on hope, trust, friendship and directed to the good of all mankind.

The emergence of such a mighty stabilising force in this strife-worn world should be regarded not as the shadowy dream of a visionary, but as a practical proposition, which the peoples of Africa can, and should, translate into reality. There is a tide in the affairs of every people when the moment strikes for political action. Such was the moment in the history of the United States of America when the Founding Fathers saw beyond the petty wranglings of the separate states and created a Union. This is our chance. We must act now. Tomorrow may be too late and the opportunity will have passed, and with it the hope of free Africa's survival.

THE KENYA AFRICA UNION IS NOT THE MAU MAU

Jomo Kenyatta

Speech at the Kenya African Union Meeting at Nyeri, July 26, 1952

. . . I want you to know the purpose of K.A.U. It is the biggest purpose the African has. It involves every African in Kenya and it is their mouthpiece which asks for freedom. K.A.U. is you and you are the K.A.U. If we unite now, each and every one of us, and each tribe to another, we will cause the implementation in this country of that which the European calls democracy. True democracy has no colour distinction. It does not choose between black and white. We are here in this tremendous gathering under the K.A.U. flag to find which road leads us from darkness into democracy. In order to find it we Africans must first achieve the right to elect our own representatives. That is surely the first principle of democracy. We are the only race in Kenya which does not elect its own representatives in the Legislature and we are going to set about to rectify this situation. We feel we are dominated by a handful of others who refuse to be just. God said this is our land. Land in which we are to flourish as a people. We are not worried that other races are here with us in our country, but we insist that we are the leaders here, and what we want we insist we get. We want our cattle to get fat on our land so that our children grow up in prosperity; we do not want that fat removed to feed others. He who has ears should now hear that K.A.U. claims this land as its own gift from God and I wish those who are black, white or brown at this meeting to know this. K.A.U. speaks in daylight. He who calls us the *Mau Mau* is not truthful. We do not know this thing *Mau Mau*. We want to prosper as a nation, and as a nation we demand equality, that is equal pay for equal work. Whether it is a chief, headman or labourer he needs in these days increased salary. He needs a salary that compares with a salary of a European who does equal work. We will

From F. D. Cornfield, *The Origins and Growth of Mau Mau*, Sessional Paper No. 5 of 1959–1960 (Nairobi: 1960), pp. 301–308.

never get our freedom unless we succeed in this issue. We do not want equal pay for equal work tomorrow—we want it right now. Those who profess to be just must realize that this is the foundation of justice. It has never been known in history that a country prospers without equality. We despise bribery and corruption, those two words that the European repeatedly refers to. Bribery and corruption is prevalent in this country, but I am not surprised. As long as a people are held down, corruption is sure to rise and the only answer to this is a policy of equality. If we work together as one, we must succeed.

Our country today is in a bad state for its land is full of fools—and fools in a country delay the independence of its people. K.A.U. seeks to remedy this situation and I tell you now it despises thieving, robbery and murder for these practices ruin our country. I say this because if one man steals, or two men steal, there are people sitting close by lapping up information, who say the whole tribe is bad because a theft has been committed. Those people are wrecking our chances of advancement. They will prevent us getting freedom. If I have my own way, let me tell you I would butcher the criminal, and there are more criminals than one in more senses than one. The policeman must arrest an offender, a man who is purely an offender, but he must not go about picking up people with a small horn of liquor in their hands and march them in procession with his fellow policemen to Government and say he has got a *Mau Mau* amongst the Kikuyu people. The plain clothes man who hides in the hedges must, I demand, get the truth of our words before he flies to Government to present them with false information. I ask this of them who are in the meeting to take heed of my words and do their work properly and justly. . . .

. . . Do not be scared of the few policemen under those trees who are holding their rifles high in the air for you to see. Their job is to seize criminals, and we shall save them a duty today. I will never ask you to be subversive but I ask you to be united, for the day of Independence is the day of complete unity and if we unite completely tomorrow, our independence will come tomorrow. This is the day for you to work hard for your country, it is not words but deeds that count and the deeds I ask for come from your pockets. The biggest subscribers to K.A.U. are in this order. First, Thomson's Falls branch, second, Elburgon branch and third Gatundu branch. Do you, in Nyeri branch, want to beat them? Then let us see your deeds come forth.

I want to touch on a number of points, and I ask you for the hundredth time to keep quiet whilst I do this. We want self-government, but this we will never get if we drink beer. It is harming our country and making people fools and encouraging crime. It is also taking all our money. Prosperity is a prerequisite of independence and, more important, the beer we are drinking is harmful to our birthrate. You sleep with a woman for nothing if you drink beer. It causes your bones to weaken and if you want to increase the population of the Kikuyu you must stop drinking.

. . . K.A.U. is not a fighting union that uses fists and weapons. If any of you here think that force is good, I do not agree with you: remember the old saying that he who is hit with a rungu returns, but he who is bit with justice never comes back. I do not want people to accuse us falsely—that we steal and that we are *Mau Mau*. I pray to you that we join hands for freedom and freedom means abolishing criminality. Beer harms us and those who drink it do us harm and they may be the so-called *Mau Mau*. Whatever grievances we have, let us air them here in the open. The criminal does not, want freedom and land—he wants to line his own pocket. Let us therefore demand our rights justly. The British Government has discussed the land problem in Kenya and we hope to have a Royal Commission to this country to look into the land problem very shortly. When this Royal Commission comes, let us show it that we are a good peaceful people and not thieves and robbers.

SECOND DECLARATION OF HAVANA, 1962

Fidel Castro

The Cuban Revolution of 1959 was a broadly based nationalist revolution against a corrupt government. It was a revolution faciltated by the long Cuban revolutionary tradition. [There had been major disturbances in the Ten Years' War (1868–1878), a failed attempt to break with Spain; during the war of independence that began in 1895 but which resulted only depen- dence on the U.S.; and the revolution of 1933, which tried to restore consti- tutional order and democracy.] In the 1933 events Fulgencio Batista, an army sergeant, emerged and he dominated Cuba for decades. Cuban nation- alists, with some reason, blamed U.S. foreign policy for Cuba's problems.

The revolution in 1959 was led by Fidel Castros. He apparently had the support of most Cubans in his broad-based "provisional government." Cas- tro turned to the Cuban Communist Party for support in internal struggles. By 1962, after the US began to give "covert" assistance to Cuban exiles oppoing the revolution, Castro had adopted Marxism-Leninism as the ide- ology of the Cuban Revolution. This is can be seen in the Second Declara- tion of Havana, delivered on February 4, 1962.

What is Cuba's history but that of Latin America? What is the history of Latin America but the history of Asia, Africa, and Oceania? And what is the history of all these peoples but the history of the cruelest exploitation of the world by imperialism?

At the end of the last century and the beginning of the present, a handful of economically developed nations had divided the world among themselves sub- jecting two thirds of humanity to their economic and political domination.

From *Fidel Castro's Personal Revolution in Cuba: 1959–1973*, by James Nelson Goodsell (New York: Knopf, 1975), pp. 264–268.

Humanity was forced to work for the dominating classes of the group of nations which had a developed capitalist economy.

The historic circumstances which permitted certain European countries and the United States of North America to attain a high industrial development level put them in a position which enabled them to subject and exploit the rest of the world.

What motives lay behind this expansion of the industrial powers? Were they moral, "civilizing" reasons, as they claimed? No. Their motives were economic.

The discovery of America sent the European conquerors across the seas to occupy and to exploit the lands and peoples of other continents; the lust for riches was the basic motivation for their conduct. America's discovery took place in the search for shorter ways to the Orient, whose products Europe valued highly.

A new social class, the merchants and the producers of articles manufactured for commerce, arose from the feudal society of lords and serfs in the latter part of the Middle Ages.

The lust for gold promoted the efforts of the new class. The lust for profit was the incentive of their behavior throughout its history. As industry and trade developed, the social influence of the new class grew. The new productive forces maturing in the midst of the feudal society increasingly clashed with feudalism and its serfdom, its laws, its institutions, its philosophy, its morals, its art, and its political ideology. . . .

Since the end of the Second World War, the Latin American nations are becoming pauperized constantly. The value of their capita income falls. The dreadful percentages of child death rate do not decrease, the number of illiterates grows higher, the peoples lack employment, land, adequate housing, schools, hospitals, communication systems and the means of subsistence. On the other hand, North America investments exceed 10 billion dollars. Latin America, moreover, supplies cheap raw materials and pays high prices for manufactured articles. Like the first Spanish conquerors, who exchanged mirrors and trinkets with the Indians for silver and gold, so the United States trades with Latin America. To hold on to this torrent of wealth, to take greater possession of America's resources and to exploit its long-suffering peoples: this is what is hidden behind the military pacts, the military missions and Washington's diplomatic lobbying. . . .

Wherever roads are closed to the peoples, where repression of workers and peasants is fierce, where the domination of Yankee monopolies is strongest, the first and most important lesson is to understand that it is neither just nor correct to divert the peoples with the vain and fanciful illusion that the dominant classes can be uprooted by legal means which do not and will not exist. The ruling classes are entrenched in all positions of state power. They monopolize the teaching field. They dominate all means of mass communication. They have infinite financial resources. Theirs is a power which the monopolies and the ruling few will defend by blood and fire with the strength of their police and their armies.

The duty of every revolutionary is to make revolution. We know that in America and throughout the world the revolution will be victorious. But revolutionaries cannot sit in the doorways of their homes to watch the corpse of imperialism pass by. The role of Job does not behoove a revolutionary. Each year by which America's liberation may be hastened will mean millions of children rescued from death, millions of minds, freed for learning, infinitudes of sorrow spared the peoples. Even though the Yankee imperialists are preparing a bloodbath for America they will not succeed in drowning the people's struggle. They will evoke universal hatred against themselves. This will be the last act of their rapacious and cave-man system. . . .

IDENTIFICATIONS PART VI

Define each of the following items with a two-sentence identification. Your definition must specifically draw on material in one of the documents in this section.

Passive Resistance

_____

_____

Plan de Ayala

_____

_____

Serfdom

_____

_____

Lenin

_____

_____

Ho Chi Minh

_____

_____

PART VII
THE AMERICAN CENTURY

This final segment contains documents that shed light on the American Century. More specifically, these items examine the dramatic economic changes reshaping the American economy at the beginning of the century, and the subsequent efforts of the United States to spread its influence, value and ideas around the globe. How would you describe the most important changes affecting the U.S. economy at the turn of the century? What do American policies in Cuba and Nicaragua tell us about American attitudes toward people in the Third World? What do "U.S. Aid to Greece and Turkey" and NSC 68 tell us about how U.S. leaders viewed Communism and how they intended to cope with the influence of Communism? What do the segments on the debt crisis and globalization in Latin America tell us about the process of Americanization at the end of the twentieth century?

THE WEDDING OF SCIENCE TO THE USEFUL ARTS: THE RISE OF SCIENCE-BASED INDUSTRY

David F. Noble

Science and capitalism press forward by nature. When the two are combined, the pace of social production quickens into a sustained drive. With scientific investigation and discovery as the engine of competitive innovation, capitalism becomes revolutionary at the core and competitors are compelled routinely to anticipate the future in order to survive. Those who are able to harness science itself, therefore, and direct it for their own ends, have gained a considerable advantage. For them, the competitive task of anticipating the future has become easier since they now have the means for determining that future themselves. So it was with the alchemists of the late nineteenth century, and their successors of the twentieth, who undertook to transform science into gold and, in the process, gave rise to modern science-based industry.

Benjamin Franklin, at once a prominent scientist and a successful man of practical affairs, proclaimed toward the end of his life that science would serve the coming century as "handmaiden to the arts." A generation later, in a series of lectures at Harvard, the physician Jacob Bigelow introduced into general usage the word which came to signify that union: "technology." "There has probably never been an age," he observed, "in which the practical applications of science have employed so large a portion of talent and enterprise of the community, as in the present. To embody . . . the various topics which belong to such an undertaking, I have adopted the general name of Technology, a word sufficiently expressive, which is found in some of the older dictionaries, and is beginning to be revived in the literature of practical men at the present day. Under this title is attempted to include an account . . . of the principles, processes, and nomenclatures of the more conspicuous arts, particularly those which involve applications of science, and which may be considered useful, by promoting the benefit of society, together with the emolument of those who pursue them."

Both Franklin and Bigelow were ahead of their times. The small world in which science and the useful arts were first brought together, a world inhabited primarily by gentlemen like themselves who cultivated an interest in both, remained restricted throughout much of the nineteenth century. For the most part, the scientists who occupied the universities pursued what they called natural philosophy and aimed in their investigations toward the discovery of the loftier metaphysical truths about the nature of the universe and the role of the mortal within it; in general, they had nothing but disdain for the practical application of their work and its correlate, money-making. The practical men who inhabited the shop and the countinghouse, on the other hand, had little use for theories and speculation; in their all-consuming search for utility and profit, they relied exclusively upon traditional lore and the hard-won lessons of experience.

Thus, the weight of centuries of separate, isolated traditions impeded the union of science to the useful arts foreseen by Bigelow and Franklin. When this union did occur on a scale significant enough to alter the nature of both science and industry, it was only because the arts had become the spur to science rather than the other way around. The scientific community overcame its Platonic prejudices, at first haltingly and then with a rush, only after the men in the workshops and offices of industry had begun to appropriate the haphazard discoveries of science for their own practical and pecuniary ends. The locus of modern technology in America was thus the domain of "manufactures" rather than the realm of science, and modern science-informed technology was characterized from the outset by the overriding imperative of manufactures: profitable utility. From the start, modern technology was nothing more nor less than the transformation of science into a means of capital accumulation, through the application of discoveries in physics and chemistry to the processes of commodity production.

Science was introduced into the world of production through the combined efforts of innovative craftsmen in the shops who had read about the discoveries of university-based science in the popular scientific publications of the day, and prescient capitalists who had learned from the same literature, from inventive employees, or from university-based associates. Where the former saw in new scientific knowledge about the nature of the material world the basis for new or refined methods of production, the latter recognized the potential for enhancing profitability. Of course, it was often true that these two visions took shape as one in a single mind: the capitalist was frequently an inventor of sorts, while the inventive craftsman shared not a little of the entrepreneurial spirit of the capitalist. The distinction is drawn merely to emphasize the fact that, in a capitalist society, the development of modern technology presupposed both. The efforts of the inventor remained stillborn without access to or collaboration with a source of capital.

Modern science-based industry—that is, industrial enterprise in which ongoing scientific investigation and the systematic application of scientific knowledge to the process of commodity production have become routine parts of the operation—emerged very late in the nineteenth century. It was the product of significant advances in chemistry and physics and also of the growing willingness of the capitalist to embark upon the costly, time-consuming, and uncertain path of research and development. This willingness reflected both the intensifying demand to outproduce competitors at home and abroad and the unprecedented accumulation of sufficient surplus capital—the product of traditional manufactures, financial speculation, and industrial consolidation—with which to underwrite a revolution in social production. As Marx observed, at a time when such development had barely begun to unfold, science-based industry sees the light of day "only once heavy industry has reached an advanced stage, when machinery itself has yielded very considerable resources. Invention then becomes a branch of business, and the application of science to immediate production [aims] at determining the inventions at the same time it solicits them."

Of the new industries which emerged between 1880 and 1920 and transformed the nature of social production in America, only two grew out of the soil of scientific rather than traditional craft knowledge: the electrical and chemical industries. The creation of both presupposed and stimulated advances in physics and chemistry and would have been unthinkable without some basic knowledge about the behavior of atoms, molecules, gases, light, magnetism, and electricity. Of the two, the electrical industry arose first, in the 1880s; by the turn of the century it had become a major force in the world of production, dominated by a handful of large, powerful, and dynamic corporations. Although a healthy heavy-chemical and powder industry existed throughout the second half of the nineteenth century in the United States, it was not until World War I, with the seizure of German-owned patents and the establishment of a protective tariff, that a domestic dyestuff industry, and thus a chemical industry proper, was established on a par with the electrical industry.

As the first science-based industries in the country, the electrical and chemical industries set the pattern of production and management for modern industry as a whole. Moreover, they produced the people—industry-minded physicists and chemists and, especially, the electrical and chemical engineers—who would carry the scientific revolution into the older and the new industries: extractive, petroleum, steel, rubber, and, most important of all in terms of American economic development, automotive. In all of these industries the systematic introduction of science as a means of production presupposed, and in turn reinforced, industrial monopoly. This monopoly meant control not simply of markets and productive plant and equipment but of science itself as well. Initially the monopoly over science took the form of patent control—that is, control over the *products* of scientific technology. It then became control over the *process* of scientific production itself, by means of organized and regulated industrial research. Finally it came to include command over the social prerequisites of this process: the development of the institutions necessary for the production of both scientific knowledge and knowledgeable people, and the integration of these institutions within the corporate system of science-based industry. "The scientific-technical revolution," as Harry Braverman has explained, "cannot be understood in terms of specific innovations. . . ." Rather, it "must be understood in its totality as a mode of production into which science and exhaustive engineering have been integrated as part of ordinary functioning. The key innovation is not to be found in chemistry, electronics, automatic machinery . . . or any of the products of these science-technologies, but rather in the transformation of science itself into capital."

In the period between 1880 and 1920 the first and second generations of men who created and ran the modern electrical industry formed the vanguard of science-based industrial development in the United States. These were the people who first successfully combined the discoveries of physical science with the mechanical know-how of the workshop to produce the much-heralded electrical revolution in power generation, lighting, transportation, and communication; who forged the great companies which manufactured that revolution and the countless electric utilities, electric railways, and telephone companies which carried it across the nation. At the same time, it was they who introduced the now familiar features characteristic of modern science-based industry: systematic patent procedures, organized industrial-research laboratories, and extensive technical-training programs.

The source of the electrical revolution was the electrical manufacturing industry, the producer of the complex machinery and equipment which made it possible. By the turn of the century three companies had come to dominate this industry. General Electric and Westinghouse had grown out of the interrelated development of electric lighting, power, and traction. The American Telephone and Telegraph Company had arisen as both product and producer of the telephone.

Although the arc light was demonstrated as early as 1808 by Sir Humphry Davy, commercial development had to await the necessary improvements in constant-current dynamos. The early pioneers in arc lighting were therefore also pioneers in the development of better and cheaper sources of current, primarily through improvements upon Faraday's dynamo of 1831. The major breakthroughs, technically speaking, came in the 1870s. The dynamo developed by Charles F. Brush fared the best in a comparative test held by the Franklin Institute in 1877, and Brush went on to make improvements in the arc light, setting up the California Electric Light Company and the Brush Electric Company, in 1879 and 1881, respectively.

Neither the arc lamp nor the dynamo proved patentable in court tests, however, and, as a result, the manufacture of arc-lighting systems became fiercely competitive. The most successful challenger to Brush was Elihu Thomson, a

Philadelphia high-school "professor" and electrical wizard who had teamed up with a colleague, E. J. Houston, to form the American Electric Company in 1880. A few years later the New Britain, Connecticut, businessmen who had provided the initial financial support for the venture sold the company to a group from Lynn, Massachusetts, headed by Charles A. Coffin, and its name was changed to the Thomson-Houston Electric Company. Primarily because of the inventive genius of Thomson and his skill at managing his small band of researchers, the company soon developed the best arc-lighting system on the market. At the same time it patented all the improvements for which a patent could be granted—current regulator, air-blast commutator, and lightning arrester—in an effort to monopolize the infant industry. In addition to securing patents on its own inventions, the Thomson-Houston company, under the strong leadership of Coffin and with the solid financial backing of Boston financiers, initiated a policy of either buying out or merging with competitors, with the purpose of both eliminating rivals and securing control over essential patents. According to the company's annual report of February 1890, "From 1882 until 1888 active competition was experienced from numerous manufacturing companies of more or less strength, which was so severe as to seriously affect the profits of the business. . . . Since 1887, however, alliances have been made with most of the manufacturing companies controlling important patent systems." By 1890, then, through the success of its own lighting system and the aggressive merger policy made possible by ample financial support, Thomson-Houston had become the dominant firm in the arc-lighting industry.

The development of incandescent lighting also dates back to the pioneering experiments of Sir Humphry Davy, but it was only with the appearance of Herman Sprengel's mercury vacuum pump in 1865 and the improvements in the dynamo of the 1870s that incandescent lighting became commercially viable. The central figure in this work, of course, was Thomas Edison. After achieving considerable financial success in the manufacture of stock tickers for Western Union, Edison had set himself up in Menlo Park, New Jersey, with a well-equipped laboratory and a permanent staff "to spend full-time in making new inventions." By deliberately transforming invention from a haphazard phenomenon into a routine, businesslike enterprise, he expected to make "a minor invention every ten days, and a big one every six months or so." Edison's investigations and experiments were inextricably informed by economic considerations; as in all engineering work, the profit motive did not lie behind the inventive activity but was bound up with it.* In 1877 he turned his attention to the problem of incandescent lighting. As one historian of modern industry has observed, Edison "chose electric lighting over other possible areas such as the telegraph, the tele-

---

* Edison did not fit the mythical image of the humble tinkerer. As Thomas P. Hughes has made clear, Edison was familiar with the latest scientific work and conceived his projects "systematically," consciously incorporating economic factors within technical designs.

phone, and the phonograph because he felt there were bigger rewards in lighting. . . . He decided that he would have to set the price for light equivalent to the price of gas light. With the price thus fixed, the path to greatest profits was to reduce costs as much as possible. To lower costs, he made a series of inventions which were designed to economize the materials used in his incandescent lighting system."

To realize his plans for a commercially viable system, Edison required financial support beyond his own resources and formed a company, the Edison Electric Light Company, toward that end. His backers included several bankers, the president and general counsel of Western Union, and a J. P. Morgan partner, Egisto P. Fabbri, who served as director and treasurer of the company until 1883. Edison's ultimate success depended heavily upon the Morgan support; although not an official of the Edison company himself, J. P. Morgan took an active interest in Edison's work, having visited him at Menlo Park in 1879. During the 1880s the Morgan interests invested heavily in Edison lighting companies in Boston and New York, and Morgan was one of the first New York residents to have his home supplied with its own electric-lighting plant. In 1892 Morgan played a leading role in the formation of the General Electric Company and served on that corporation's executive board until his death in 1913.

By October 21, 1879, Edison had produced the first successful incandescent electric light and a scant three years later, thanks to the ample financial support he enjoyed, had begun operation of the Pearl Street central power station in New York, under the auspices of the Edison Electric Illuminating Company. In 1889 the various Edison manufacturing companies, which had been established to produce the lamps, dynamos, and street mains, were merged, together with the Sprague Electric Railway and Motor Company (a pioneer in electric traction), to form the Edison General Electric Company. At this point Edison himself withdrew from active participation in the electrical manufacturing business.

The most important impetus behind the formation of the General Electric Company, according to Thomson-Houston lawyer Frederick P. Fish, was the patent situation. (Fish was one of the country's leading patent attorneys and he was soon to become president of AT&T, largely as a result of his prowess in handling that company's patent cases.) Edison General Electric, through its acquisition of the Sprague company, controlled some vital electric railway patents in addition to the important Edison patents. Thomson-Houston, on the other hand, held some key patents needed by Edison General Electric, particularly in lighting. Because each company owned patents required by the other, neither could develop lighting, railway, or power equipment without fear of infringement suits and injunctions. To get beyond this impasse, the two companies merged in 1892, to form the General Electric Company.

The major competitor of General Electric in the electrical manufacturing field was Westinghouse. George Westinghouse had invented the air brake in

1869 and founded the Westinghouse Air Brake Company in Pittsburgh the same year. In 1881 he set up the Union Switch and Signal Company to attack the problems of automatic switching and signaling devices, and these led him into the electrical manufacturing field. He entered the incandescent-lighting market after he had secured the services of an electrical engineer, William Stanley, who held some lamp and dynamo patents. In 1885 Westinghouse and Stanley revolutionized the electrical industry with the introduction of their alternating-current system, a new method of transmitting electricity. Having purchased the key patents for the system from Nikola Tesla, Westinghouse dominated the alternating-current field for a few years, until Thomson-Houston began successfully producing its own such system.

By the 1890s two large companies, General Electric and Westinghouse, monopolized a substantial part of the American electrical manufacturing industry, and their success and expansion had been in large measure the result of patent control. In addition to the original patents upon which the companies were established, they had gained control over others, and hence over large parts of the electrical manufacturing market, through acquisition of the patent rights of individual inventors, acquisition of competing firms, mergers with competitors, and the systematic and strategic development of their own patentable inventions. As these two giants steadily eliminated smaller competitors, the competition between them intensified. By 1896 over three hundred patent suits between them were pending and the cost of litigation for each company was enormous. In that year, therefore, after a few years of preliminary negotiation, the two companies entered into a patent agreement under a joint Board of Patent Control. The immediate motivations behind the agreement were recent decisions in favor of General Electric's claims on certain railway apparatus and in favor of Westinghouse's claims on Tesla's patents on the rotating field. Now the companies agreed to pool their patents, with General Electric handling 62.5 percent of their combined business. Thus yet another means of patent and market control had been developed: corporate patent-pooling agreements. Designed to minimize the expense and uncertainties of conflict between the giants, they greatly reinforced the position of each vis-á-vis lesser competitors and new entrants into the field.

THE PLATT AMENDMENT, 1901

Whereas the Congress of the United States of America, by an Act approved March 2, 1901, provided as follows:

Provided further, That in fulfillment of the declaration contained in the joint resolution approved April twentieth, eighteen hundred and ninety-eight, entitled "For the recognition of the independence of the people of Cuba, demanding that the Government of Spain relinquish its authority and government in the island of Cuba, and withdraw its land and naval forces from Cuba and Cuban waters, and directing the President of the United States to use the land and naval forces of the United States to carry these resolutions into effect," the President is hereby authorized to "leave the government and control of the island of Cuba to its people" so soon as a government shall have been established in said island under a constitution which, either as a part thereof or in an ordinance appended thereto, shall define the future relations of the United States with Cuba, substantially as follows:

"I. That the government of Cuba shall never enter into any treaty or other compact with any foreign power or powers which will impair or tend to impair the independence of Cuba, nor in any manner authorize or permit any foreign power or powers to obtain by colonization or for military or naval purposes or otherwise, lodgement in or control over any portion of said island."

"II. That said government shall not assume or contract any public debt, to pay the interest upon which, and to make reasonable sinking fund provision for the ultimate discharge of which, the ordinary revenues of the island, after defraying the current expenses of government shall be inadequate."

"III. That the government of Cuba consents that the United States may exercise the right to intervene for the preservation of Cuban independence, the maintenance of a government adequate for the protection of life, property, and individual liberty, and for discharging the obligations with respect to Cuba

Source: "The Platt Amendment," in *Treaties and Other International Agreements of the United States of America, 1776–1949,* vol. 8, ed. C. I. Bevans (Washington, D.C.: United States Government Printing Office, 1971), pp. 1116–17.

imposed by the treaty of Paris on the United States, now to be assumed and undertaken by the government of Cuba."

"IV. That all Acts of the United States in Cuba during its military occupancy thereof are ratified and validated, and all lawful rights acquired thereunder shall be maintained and protected."

"V. That the government of Cuba will execute, and as far as necessary extend, the plans already devised or other plans to be mutually agreed upon, for the sanitation of the cities of the island, to the end that a recurrence of epidemic and infectious diseases may be prevented, thereby assuring protection to the people and commerce of Cuba, as well as to the commerce of the southern ports of the United States and the people residing therein."

"VI. That the Isle of Pines shall be omitted from the proposed constitutional boundaries of Cuba, the title thereto being left to future adjustment by treaty."

"VII. That to enable the United States to maintain the independence of Cuba, and to protect the people thereof, as well as for its own defense, the government of Cuba will sell or lease to the United States lands necessary for coaling or naval stations at certain specified points to be agreed upon with the President of the United States."

"VIII. That by way of further assurance the government of Cuba will embody the foregoing provisions in a permanent treaty with the United States."

INTERVENTION IN NICARAGUA

Calvin Coolidge

While conditions in Nicaragua and the action of this government pertaining thereto have in general been made public, I think the time has arrived for me officially to inform the Congress more in detail of the events leading up to the present disturbances and conditions which seriously threaten American lives and property, endanger the stability of all Central America, and put in jeopardy the rights granted by Nicaragua to the United States for the construction of a canal.

It is well known that in 1912 the United States intervened in Nicaragua with a large force and put down a revolution, and that from that time to 1925 a legation guard of American Marines was, with the consent of the Nicaragua government, kept in Managua to protect American lives and property. In 1923 representatives of the five Central American countries, namely, Costa Rica, Guatemala, Honduras, Nicaragua, and Salvador, at the invitation of the United States, met in Washington and entered into a series of treaties.

These treaties dealt with limitation of armament, a Central American tribunal for arbitration, and the general subject of peace and amity. The treaty last referred to specifically provides in Article II that the governments of the contracting parties will not recognize any other government which may come into power in any of the five republics through a coup d'etat, or revolution, and disqualifies the leaders of such coup d'etat, or revolution, from assuming the presidency or vice-presidency. . . .

The United States was not a party to this treaty, but it was made in Washington under the auspices of the secretary of state, and this government has felt a moral obligation to apply its principles in order to encourage the Central American states in their efforts to prevent revolution and disorder. The treaty, it may be noted in passing, was signed on behalf of Nicaragua by Emiliano Chamorro himself, who afterwards assumed the presidency in violation thereof and thereby contributed to the creation of the present difficulty.

In October 1924 an election was held in Nicaragua for president, vice-president, and members of the Congress. This resulted in the election of a

Source: *Record,* 69 Cong., 2 Sess., pp. 1324–1326.

coalition ticket embracing Conservatives and Liberals. Carlos Solorzano, a Conservative Republican, was elected president, and Juan B. Sacasa, a Liberal, was elected vice-president. This government was recognized by the other Central American countries and by the United States. It had been the intention of the United States to withdraw the Marines immediately after this election, and notice was given of the intention to withdraw them in January 1925. At the request of the president of Nicaragua, this time was extended to Sept. 1, 1925. Pursuant to this determination and notice, the Marines were withdrawn in August 1925. . . .

Notwithstanding the refusal of this government and of the other Central American governments to recognize him, General Chamorro continued to exercise the functions of president until Oct. 30, 1926. In the meantime a revolution broke out in May on the east coast in the neighborhood of Bluefields and was speedily suppressed by the troops of General Chamorro. However, it again broke out with considerable more violence. The second attempt was attended with some success, and practically all of the east coast of Nicaragua fell into the hands of the revolutionists. Throughout these events, Sacasa was at no time in the country, having remained in Mexico and Guatemala during this period.

Repeated requests were made of the United States for protection, especially on the east coast, and on Aug. 24, 1926, the secretary of state addressed to the secretary of the navy the following communication:

> *I have the honor to suggest that war vessels of the Special Service Squadron proceed as soon as possible to the Nicaraguan ports of Corinto and Bluefields for the protection of American and foreign lives and property in case that threatened emergencies materialize. The American chargé d'affaires at Managua has informed the department that he considers the presence of war vessels at these ports desirable, and the American consul at Bluefields has reported that a warship is urgently needed to protect life and property at that port. An attack on The Bluff and Bluefields is expected momentarily.*

Accordingly, the Navy Department ordered Admiral Latimer, in command of the Special Service Squadron, to proceed to Bluefields. Upon arriving there he found it necessary for the adequate protection of American lives and property to declare Bluefields a neutral zone. This was done with the consent of both factions, afterwards, on Oct. 26, 1926, reduced to a written agreement, which is still in force. In October 1926 the good offices of the United States were sought by both parties for the purpose of effecting a settlement of the conflict. Admiral Latimer, commanding the Special Service Squadron, brought about an armistice to permit of a conference being held between the delegates of the two factions. The armistice was originally for fifteen days and was later extended for fifteen days more.

At the request of both parties; Marines were landed at Corinto to establish a neutral zone in which the conference could be held. Doctor Sacasa was invited to attend this conference but refrained from doing so and remained in Guatemala City. The United States government did not participate in the conference except to provide a neutral chairman; it simply offered its good offices to make the conference possible and arranged a neutral zone at Corinto at the request of both parties during the time the conference was held. I understand that at this conference General Chamorro offered to resign and permit the Congress to elect a new designate to assume the presidency. The conference led to no result, since, just at the time when it seemed as though some compromise agreement would be reached, the representatives of Doctor Sacasa suddenly broke off negotiations. . . .

The Nicaraguan constitution provides in Article 106 that in the absence of the president and vice-president the Congress shall designate one of its members to complete the unexpired term of president. As President Solorzano had resigned and was then residing in California, and as the vice-president, Doctor Sacasa, was in Guatemala, having been out of the country since November 1925, the action of Congress in designating Señor Díaz was perfectly legal and in accordance with the constitution. Therefore, the United States government on Nov. 17 extended recognition to Señor Díaz. . . .

Immediately following the inauguration of President Díaz, and frequently since that date, he has appealed to the United States for support, has informed this government of the aid which Mexico is giving to the revolutionists, and has stated that he is unable solely because of the aid given by Mexico to the revolutionists to protect the lives and property of American citizens and other foreigners.

When negotiations leading up to the Corinto conference began, I immediately placed an embargo on the shipment of arms and ammunition to Nicaragua. The Department of State notified the other Central American states, to wit, Costa Rica, Honduras, Salvador, and Guatemala, and they assured the department that they would cooperate in this measure. So far as known, they have done so. The State Department also notified the Mexican government of this embargo and informally suggested to that government like action. The Mexican government did not adopt the suggestion to put on an embargo but informed the American ambassador at Mexico City that in the absence of manufacturing plants in Mexico for the making of arms and ammunition the matter had little practical importance.

As a matter of fact, I have the most conclusive evidence that arms and munitions in large quantities have been, on several occasions since August 1926, shipped to the revolutionists in Nicaragua. Boats carrying these munitions have been fitted out in Mexican ports, and some of the munitions bear evidence of having belonged to the Mexican government. It also appears that the ships were fitted out with the full knowledge of and, in some cases, with the encouragement of Mexican officials and were in one instance, at least, commanded by a Mexican naval reserve officer.

At the end of November, after spending some time in Mexico City, Doctor Sacasa went back to Nicaragua, landing at Puerto Cabezas, near Bragmans Bluff. He immediately placed himself at the head of the insurrection and declared himself president of Nicaragua. He has never been recognized by any of the Central American republics nor by any other government, with the exception of Mexico, which recognized him immediately. As arms and munitions in large quantities were reaching the revolutionists, I deemed it unfair to prevent the recognized government from purchasing arms abroad, and, accordingly, the secretary of state notified the Díaz government that licenses would be issued for the export of arms and munitions purchased in this country. It would be thoroughly inconsistent for this country not to support the government recognized by it while the revolutionists were receiving arms and munitions from abroad.

During the last two months the government of the United States has received repeated requests from various American citizens, both directly and through our consuls and legation, for the protection of their lives and property. The government of the United States has also received requests from the British chargé at Managua and from the Italian ambassador at Washington for the protection of their respective nationals. Pursuant to such requests, Admiral Latimer, in charge of the Special Service Squadron, has not only maintained the neutral zone at Bluefields under the agreement of both parties but has landed forces at Puerto Cabezas and Rio Grande and established neutral zones at these points where considerable numbers of Americans live and are engaged in carrying on various industries. He has also been authorized to establish such other neutral zones as are necessary for the purposes above mentioned.

For many years numerous Americans have been living in Nicaragua, developing its industries and carrying on business. At the present time there are large investments in lumbering, mining, coffee growing, banana culture, shipping, and also in general mercantile and other collateral business. All these people and these industries have been encouraged by the Nicaraguan government. That government has at all times owed them protection, but the United States has occasionally been obliged to send naval forces for their proper protection. In the present crisis such forces are requested by the Nicaraguan government, which protests to the United States its inability to protect these interests and states that any measures which the United States deems appropriate for their protection will be satisfactory to the Nicaraguan government.

In addition to these industries now in existence, the government of Nicaragua, by a treaty entered into on the 5th of August 1914, granted in perpetuity to the United States the exclusive proprietary rights necessary and convenient for the construction, operation, and maintenance of an oceanic canal. . . .

There is no question that if the revolution continues, American investments and business interests in Nicaragua will be very seriously affected, if not destroyed. The currency, which is now at par, will be inflated. American as well as foreign bondholders will undoubtedly look to the United States for the protection of their interests. It is true that the United States did not establish the financial plan by any treaty, but it nevertheless did aid through diplomatic channels and advise in the negotiation and establishment of this plan for the financial rehabilitation of Nicaragua.

Manifestly, the relation of this government to the Nicaraguan situation and its policy in the existing emergency are determined by the facts which I have described. The proprietary rights of the United States in the Nicaraguan canal route, with the necessary implications growing out of it affecting the Panama Canal, together with the obligations flowing from the investments of all classes of our citizens in Nicaragua, place us in a position of peculiar responsibility. I am sure it is not the desire of the United States to intervene in the internal affairs of Nicaragua or of any other Central American republic. Nevertheless, it must be said that we have a very definite and special interest in the maintenance of order and good government in Nicaragua at the present time, and that the stability, prosperity, and independence of all Central American countries can never be a matter of indifference to us.

The United States cannot, therefore, fail to view with deep concern any serious threat to stability and constitutional government in Nicaragua tending toward anarchy and jeopardizing American interests, especially if such state of affairs is contributed to or brought about by outside influences or by any foreign power. It has always been and remains the policy of the United States in such circumstances to take the steps that may be necessary for the preservation and protection of the lives, the property, and the interests of its citizens and of this government itself. In this respect I propose to follow the path of my predecessors.

Consequently, I have deemed it my duty to use the powers committed to me to ensure the adequate protection of all American interests in Nicaragua, whether they be endangered by internal strife or by outside interference in the affairs of that republic.

FIRST INAUGURAL ADDRESS

Franklin D. Roosevelt

The former Governor of New York rode to the Capitol with President Hoover. Pressures of the economy faced the President-elect as he took his oath of office from Chief Justice Charles Evans Hughes on the East Portico of the Capitol. He addressed the nation by radio and announced his plans for a New Deal. Throughout that day the President met with his Cabinet designees at the White House.

I am certain that my fellow Americans expect that on my induction into the Presidency I will address them with a candor and a decision which the present situation of our Nation impels. This is preeminently the time to speak the truth, the whole truth, frankly and boldly. Nor need we shrink from honestly facing conditions in our country today. This great Nation will endure as it has endured, will revive and will prosper. So, first of all, let me assert my firm belief that the only thing we have to fear is fear itself—nameless, unreasoning, unjustified terror which paralyzes needed efforts to convert retreat into advance. In every dark hour of our national life a leadership of frankness and vigor has met with that understanding and support of the people themselves which is essential to victory. I am convinced that you will again give that support to leadership in these critical days.

In such a spirit on my part and on yours we face our common difficulties. They concern, thank God, only material things. Values have shrunken to fantastic levels; taxes have risen; our ability to pay has fallen; government of all kinds is faced by serious curtailment of income; the means of exchange are frozen in the currents of trade; the withered leaves of industrial enterprise lie on every side; farmers find no markets for their produce; the savings of many years in thousands of families are gone.

More important, a host of unemployed citizens face the grim problem of existence, and an equally great number toil with little return. Only a foolish optimist can deny the dark realities of the moment.

Yet our distress comes from no failure of substance. We are stricken by no plague of locusts. Compared with the perils which our forefathers conquered because they believed and were not afraid, we have still much to be thankful for. Nature still offers her bounty and human efforts have multiplied it. Plenty is at our doorstep, but a generous use of it languishes in the very sight of the supply. Primarily this is because the rulers of the exchange of mankind's goods have failed, through their own stubbornness and their own incompetence, have admitted their failure, and abdicated. Practices of the unscrupulous money changers stand indicted in the court of public opinion, rejected by the hearts and minds of men.

True they have tried, but their efforts have been cast in the pattern of an outworn tradition. Faced by failure of credit they have proposed only the lending of more money. Stripped of the lure of profit by which to induce our people to follow their false leadership, they have resorted to exhortations, pleading tearfully for restored confidence. They know only the rules of a generation of self-seekers. They have no vision, and when there is no vision the people perish.

The money changers have fled from their high seats in the temple of our civilization. We may now restore that temple to the ancient truths. The measure of the restoration lies in the extent to which we apply social values more noble than mere monetary profit.

Happiness lies not in the mere possession of money; it lies in the joy of achievement, in the thrill of creative effort. The joy and moral stimulation of work no longer must be forgotten in the mad chase of evanescent profits. These dark days will be worth all they cost us if they teach us that our true destiny is not to be ministered unto but to minister to ourselves and to our fellow men.

Recognition of the falsity of material wealth as the standard of success goes hand in hand with the abandonment of the false belief that public office and high political position are to be valued only by the standards of pride of place and personal profit; and there must be an end to a conduct in banking and in business which too often has given to a sacred trust the likeness of callous and selfish wrongdoing. Small wonder that confidence languishes, for it thrives only on honesty, on honor, on the sacredness of obligations, on faithful protection, on unselfish performance; without them it cannot live.

Restoration calls, however, not for changes in ethics alone. This Nation asks for action, and action now.

Our greatest primary task is to put people to work. This is no unsolvable problem if we face it wisely and courageously. It can be accomplished in part by direct recruiting by the Government itself, treating the task as we would treat the emergency of a war, but at the same time, through this employment, accomplishing greatly needed projects to stimulate and reorganize the use of our natural resources.

Hand in hand with this we must frankly recognize the overbalance of population in our industrial centers and, by engaging on a national scale in a redistribution, endeavor to provide a better use of the land for those best fitted for the land. The task can be helped by definite efforts to raise the values of agricultural products and with this the power to purchase the output of our cities. It can be helped by preventing realistically the tragedy of the growing loss through foreclosure of our small homes and our farms. It can be helped by insistence that the Federal, State, and local governments act forthwith on the demand that their cost be drastically reduced. It can be helped by the unifying of relief activities which today are often scattered, uneconomical, and unequal. It can be helped by national planning for and supervision of all forms of transportation and of communications and other utilities which have a definitely public character. There are many ways in which it can be helped, but it can never be helped merely by talking about it. We must act and act quickly.

Finally, in our progress toward a resumption of work we require two safeguards against a return of the evils of the old order; there must be a strict supervision of all banking and credits and investments; there must be an end to speculation with other people's money, and there must be provision for an adequate but sound currency.

There are the lines of attack. I shall presently urge upon a new Congress in special session detailed measures for their fulfillment, and I shall seek the immediate assistance of the several States.

Through this program of action we address ourselves to putting our own national house in order and making income balance outgo. Our international trade relations, though vastly important, are in point of time and necessity secondary to the establishment of a sound national economy. I favor as a practical policy the putting of first things first. I shall spare no effort to restore world trade by international economic readjustment, but the emergency at home cannot wait on that accomplishment.

The basic thought that guides these specific means of national recovery is not narrowly nationalistic. It is the insistence, as a first consideration, upon the interdependence of the various elements in all parts of the United States—a recognition of the old and permanently important manifestation of the American spirit of the pioneer. It is the way to recovery. It is the immediate way. It is the strongest assurance that the recovery will endure.

In the field of world policy I would dedicate this Nation to the policy of the good neighbor—the neighbor who resolutely respects himself and, because he does so, respects the rights of others—the neighbor who respects his obligations and respects the sanctity of his agreements in and with a world of neighbors.

If I read the temper of our people correctly, we now realize as we have never realized before our interdependence on each other; that we can not merely take but we must give as well; that if we are to go forward, we must move as a trained and loyal army willing to sacrifice for the good of a common discipline, because without such discipline no progress is made, no leadership becomes effective. We are, I know, ready and willing to submit our lives and property to such discipline, because it makes possible a leadership which aims at a larger good. This I propose to offer, pledging that the larger purposes will bind upon us all as a sacred obligation with a unity of duty hitherto evoked only in time of armed strife.

With this pledge taken, I assume unhesitatingly the leadership of this great army of our people dedicated to a disciplined attack upon our common problems.

Action in this image and to this end is feasible under the form of government which we have inherited from our ancestors. Our Constitution is so simple and practical that it is possible always to meet extraordinary needs by changes in emphasis and arrangement without loss of essential form. That is why our constitutional system has proved itself the most superbly enduring political mechanism the modern world has produced. It has met every stress of vast expansion of territory, of foreign wars, of bitter internal strife, of world relations.

It is to be hoped that the normal balance of executive and legislative authority may be wholly adequate to meet the unprecedented task before us. But it may be that an unprecedented demand and need for undelayed action may call for temporary departure from that normal balance of public procedure.

I am prepared under my constitutional duty to recommend the measures that a stricken nation in the midst of a stricken world may require. These measures, or such other measures as the Congress may build out of its experience and wisdom, I shall seek, within my constitutional authority, to bring to speedy adoption.

But in the event that the Congress shall fail to take one of these two courses, and in the event that the national emergency is still critical, I shall not evade the clear course of duty that will then confront me. I shall ask the Congress for the one remaining instrument to meet the crisis—broad Executive power to wage a war against the emergency, as great as the power that would be given to me if we were in fact invaded by a foreign foe.

For the trust reposed in me I will return the courage and the devotion that befit the time. I can do no less.

We face the arduous days that lie before us in the warm courage of the national unity; with the clear consciousness of seeking old and precious moral values; with the clean satisfaction that comes from the stern performance of duty by old and young alike. We aim at the assurance of a rounded and permanent national life.

We do not distrust the future of essential democracy. The people of the United States have not failed. In their need they have registered a mandate that they want direct, vigorous action. They have asked for discipline and direction under leadership. They have made me the present instrument of their wishes. In the spirit of the gift I take it.

In this dedication of a Nation we humbly ask the blessing of God. May He protect each and every one of us. May He guide me in the days to come.

AID TO GREECE AND TURKEY

RECOMMENDATIONS ON GREECE AND TURKEY
Message of the President to the Congress[1]

Mr. President, Mr. Speaker, Members of the Congress of the United States:

The gravity of the situation which confronts the world today necessitates my appearance before a joint session of the Congress.

The foreign policy and the national security of this country are involved.

One aspect of the present situation, which I wish to present to you at this time for your consideration and decision, concerns Greece and Turkey.

The United States has received from the Greek Government an urgent appeal for financial and economic assistance. Preliminary reports from the American Economic Mission now in Greece and reports from the American Ambassador in Greece corroborate the statement of the Greek Government that assistance is imperative if Greece is to survive as a free nation.

I do not believe that the American people and the Congress wish to turn a deaf ear to the appeal of the Greek Government.

---

[1] Delivered by the President before a joint session of Congress on Mar. 12, 1947, and released to the press by the White House on the same date. This message has also been printed as Department of State publication 2785. The full text of the President's speech was translated into eight languages and broadcast at differing times to Europe, the Soviet Union, and the Far East. Summaries of the speech were broadcast several times in all the 25 languages of the "Voice of the United States of America."

As the President was speaking at the Capitol, a "live" broadcast of his voice was transmitted to Europe and to the Middle East through relay at Algiers. A recording of the President's voice was broadcast to Latin America at 5:30 and 9:25 P.M. on March 12; to the Far East at 5:30 P.M. on March 12 and at 5 and 8:30 A.M. on March 13; and to Europe and the Middle East at 5:30 A.M. on March 13. With the time changes around the world, the rebroadcasts carried the President's voice to all parts of the world at the most favorable listening hours during the morning, afternoon, and evening.

Since the "Voice of the United States of America" does not include the Greek and Arabic languages, the President's message was heard in Greece and Turkey only in the English language.

Greece is not a rich country. Lack of sufficient natural resources has always forced the Greek people to work hard to make both ends meet. Since 1940 this industrious and peace-loving country has suffered invasion, four years of cruel enemy occupation, and bitter internal strife.

When forces of liberation entered Greece they found that the retreating Germans had destroyed virtually all the railways, roads, port facilities, communications, and merchant marine. More than a thousand villages had been burned. Eighty-five percent of the children were tubercular. Livestock, poultry, and draft animals had almost disappeared. Inflation had wiped out practically all savings.

As a result of these tragic conditions, a militant minority, exploiting human want and misery, was able to create political chaos which, until now, has made economic recovery impossible.

Greece is today without funds to finance the importation of those goods which are essential to bare subsistence. Under these circumstances the people of Greece cannot make progress in solving their problems of reconstruction. Greece is in desperate need of financial and economic assistance to enable it to resume purchases of food, clothing, fuel, and seeds. These are indispensable for the subsistence of its people and are obtainable only from abroad. Greece must have help to import the goods necessary to restore internal order and security so essential for economic and political recovery.

The Greek Government has also asked for the assistance of experienced American administrators, economists, and technicians to insure that the financial and other aid given to Greece shall be used effectively in creating a stable and self-sustaining economy and in improving its public administration.

The very existence of the Greek state is today threatened by the terrorist activities of several thousand armed men, led by Communists, who defy the Government's authority at a number of points, particularly along the northern boundaries. A commission appointed by the United Nations Security Council is at present investigating disturbed conditions in northern Greece and alleged border violations along the frontier between Greece on the one hand and Albania, Bulgaria, and Yugoslavia on the other.[2]

Meanwhile, the Greek Government is unable to cope with the situation. The Greek Army is small and poorly equipped. It needs supplies and equipment if it is to restore authority to the Government throughout Greek territory.

Greece must have assistance if it is to become a self-supporting and self-respecting democracy.

The United States must supply that assistance. We have already extended to Greece certain types of relief and economic aid, but these are inadequate.

There is no other country to which democratic Greece can turn.

---

[2] Bulletin of Jan. 5, 1917, p. 23

No other nation is willing and able to provide the necessary support for a democratic Greek Government.

The British Government, which has been helping Greece, can give no further financial or economic aid after March 31. Great Britain finds itself under the necessity of reducing or liquidating its commitments in several parts of the world, including Greece.

We have considered how the United Nations might assist in this crisis. But the situation is an urgent one requiring immediate action, and the United Nations and its related organizations are not in a position to extend help of the kind that is required.

It is important to note that the Greek Government has asked for our aid in utilizing effectively the financial and other assistance we may give to Greece, and in improving its public administration. It is of the utmost importance that we supervise the use of any funds made available to Greece, in such a manner that each dollar spent will count toward making Greece self-supporting, and will help to build an economy in which a healthy democracy can flourish.

No government is perfect. One of the chief virtues of a democracy, however, is that its defects are always visible and under democratic processes can be pointed out and corrected. The Government of Greece is not perfect. Nevertheless it represents 85 percent of the members of the Greek Parliament who were chosen in an election last year. Foreign observers, including 692 Americans, considered this election to be a fair expression of the views of the Greek people.

The Greek Government has been operating in an atmosphere of chaos and extremism. It has made mistakes. The extension of aid by this country does not mean that the United States condones everything that the Greek Government has done or will do. We have condemned in the past, and we condemn now, extremist measures of the right or the left. We have in the past advised tolerance, and we advise tolerance now.

Greece's neighbor, Turkey, also deserves our attention.

The future of Turkey as an independent and economically sound state is clearly no less important to the freedom-loving peoples of the world than the future of Greece. The circumstances in which Turkey finds itself today are considerably different from those of Greece. Turkey has been spared the disasters that have beset Greece. And during the war the United States and Great Britain furnished Turkey with material aid.

Nevertheless, Turkey now needs our support.

Since the war Turkey has sought additional financial assistance from Great Britain and the United States for the purpose of effecting that modernization necessary for the maintenance of its national integrity.

That integrity is essential to the preservation of order in the Middle East.

The British Government has informed us that, owing to its own difficulties, it can no longer extend financial or economic aid to Turkey.

As in the case of Greece, if Turkey is to have the assistance it needs, the United States must supply it. We are the only country able to provide that help.

I am fully aware of the broad implications involved if the United States extends assistance to Greece and Turkey, and I shall discuss these implications with you at this time.

One of the primary objectives of the foreign policy of the United States is the creation of conditions in which we and other nations will be able to work out a way of life free from coercion. This was a fundamental issue in the war with Germany and Japan. Our victory was won over countries which sought to impose their will, and their way of life, upon other nations.

To insure the peaceful development of nations, free from coercion, the United States has taken a leading part in establishing the United Nations. The United Nations is designed to make possible lasting freedom and independence for all its members. We shall not realize our objectives, however, unless we are willing to help free peoples to maintain their free institutions and their national integrity against aggressive movements that seek to impose upon them totalitarian regimes. This is no more than a frank recognition that totalitarian regimes imposed upon free peoples, by direct or indirect aggression, undermine the foundations of international peace and hence the security of the United States.

The peoples of a number of countries of the world have recently had totalitarian regimes forced upon them against their will. The Government of the United States has made frequent protests against coercion and intimidation, in violation of the Yalta agreement, in Poland, Rumania, and Bulgaria. I must also state that in a number of other countries there have been similar developments.

At the present moment in world history nearly every nation must choose between alternative ways of life. The choice is too often not a free one.

One way of life is based upon the will of the majority, and is distinguished by free institutions, representative government, free elections, guaranties of individual liberty, freedom of speech and religion, and freedom from political oppression.

The second way of life is based upon the will of a minority forcibly imposed upon the majority. It relies upon terror and oppression, a controlled press and radio, fixed elections, and the suppression of personal freedoms.

I believe that it must be the policy of the United States to support free peoples who are resisting attempted subjugation by armed minorities or by outside pressures.

I believe that we must assist free peoples to work out their own destinies in their own way.

I believe that our help should be primarily through economic and financial aid which is essential to economic stability and orderly political processes.

The world is not static, and the *status quo* is not sacred. But we cannot allow changes in the *status quo* in violation of the Charter of the United Nations by such methods as coercion, or by such subterfuges as political infiltration. In helping free and independent nations to maintain their freedom, the United States will be giving effect to the principles of the Charter of the United Nations.

It is necessary only to glance at a map to realize that the survival and integrity of the Greek nation are of grave importance in a much wider situation. If Greece should fall under the control of an armed minority, the effect upon its neighbor, Turkey, would be immediate and serious. Confusion and disorder might well spread throughout the entire Middle East.

Moreover, the disappearance of Greece as an independent state would have a profound effect upon those countries in Europe whose peoples are struggling against great difficulties to maintain their freedoms and their independence while they repair the damages of war.

It would be an unspenkable tragedy if these countries, which have struggled so long against overwhelming odds, should lose that victory for which they sacrificed so much. Collapse of free institutions and loss of independence would be disastrous not only for them but for the world. Discouragement and possibly failure would quickly be the lot of neighboring peoples striving to maintain their freedom and independence.

Should we fail to aid Greece and Turkey in this fateful hour, the effect will be far-reaching to the West as well as to the East.

We must take immediate and resolute action.

I therefore ask the Congress to provide authority for assistance to Greece and Turkey in the amount of $400,000,000 for the period ending June 30, 1948. In requesting these funds, I have taken into consideration the maximum amount of relief assistance which would be furnished to Greece out of the $350,000,000 which I recently requested that the Congress authorize for the prevention of starvation and suffering in countries devastated by the war.

In addition to funds, I ask the Congress to authorize the detail of American civilian and military personnel to Greece and Turkey, at the request of those countries, to assist in the tasks of reconstruction, and for the purpose of supervising the use of such financial and material assistance as may be furnished. I recommend that authority also be provided for the instruction and training of selected Greek and Turkish personnel.

Finally, I ask that the Congress provide authority which will permit the speediest and most effective use, in terms of needed commodities, supplies, and equipment, of such funds as may be authorized.

If further funds, or further authority, should be needed for purposes indicated in this message, I shall not hesitate to bring the situation before the Congress. On this subject the Executive and Legislative branches of the Government must work together.

This is a serious course upon which we embark.

I would not recommend it except that the alternative is much more serious.

The United States contributed $341,000,000,000 toward winning World War II. This is an investment in world freedom and world peace.

The assistance that I am recommending for Greece and Turkey amount to little more than one tenth of one percent of this investment. It is only common sense that we should safeguard this investment and make sure that it was not in vain.

The seeds of totalitarian regimes are nurtured by misery and want. They spread and grow in the evil soil of poverty and strife. They reach their full growth when the hope of a people for a better life has died.

We must keep that hope alive.

The free peoples of the world look to us for support in maintaining their freedoms.

If we falter in our leadership, we may endanger the peace of the world—and we shall surely endanger the welfare of our own Nation.

Great responsibilities have been placed upon us by the swift movement of events.

I am confident that the Congress will face these responsibilities squarely.

EXCERPTS FROM NSC 68: UNITED STATES OBJECTIVES AND PROGRAMS FOR NATIONAL SECURITY

National Security Council

IV. THE UNDERLYING CONFLICT IN THE REALM OF IDEAS AND VALUES BETWEEN THE U.S. PURPOSE AND THE KREMLIN DESIGN

A. Nature of Conflict

The Kremlin regards the United States as the only major threat to the conflict between idea of slavery under the grim oligarchy of the Kremlin, which has come to a crisis with the polarization of power described in Section I, and the exclusive possession of atomic weapons by the two protagonists. The idea of freedom, moreover, is peculiarly and intolerably subversive of the idea of slavery. But the converse is not true. The implacable purpose of the slave state to eliminate the challenge of freedom has placed the two great powers at opposite poles. It is this fact which gives the present polarization of power the quality of crisis.

The free society values the individual as an end in himself, requiring of him only that measure of self-discipline and self-restraint which make the rights of each individual compatible with the rights of every other individual. The freedom of the individual has as its counterpart, therefore, the negative responsibility of the individual not to exercise his freedom in ways inconsistent with the freedom of other individuals and the positive responsibility to make constructive use of his freedom in the building of a just society.

From this idea of freedom with responsibility derives the marvelous diversity, the deep tolerance, the lawfulness of the free society. This is the explanation of the strength of free men. It constitutes the integrity and the vitality of a free and democratic system. The free society attempts to create and maintain an environment in which every individual has the opportunity to realize his creative powers. It also explains why the free society tolerates those within it who would use their freedom to destroy it. By the same token, in relations between nations, the prime reliance of the free society is on the strength and appeal of its idea, and it feels no compulsion sooner or later to bring all societies into conformity with it.

For the free society does not fear, it welcomes, diversity. It derives its strength from its hospitality even to antipathetic ideas. It is a market for free trade in ideas, secure in its faith that free men will take the best wares, and grow to a fuller and better realization of their powers in exercising their choice.

The idea of freedom is the most contagious idea in history, more contagious than the idea of submission to authority. For the breadth of freedom cannot be tolerated in a society which has come under the domination of an individual or group of individuals with a will to absolute power. Where the despot holds absolute power—the absolute power of the absolutely powerful will—all other wills must be subjugated in an act of willing submission, a degradation willed by the individual upon himself under the compulsion of a perverted faith. It is the first article of this faith that he finds and can only find the meaning of his existence in serving the ends of the system. The system becomes God, and submission to the will of God becomes submission to the will of the system. It is not enough to yield outwardly to the system—even Gandhian non-violence is not acceptable—for the spirit of resistance and the devotion to a higher authority might then remain, and the individual would not be wholly submissive.

The same compulsion which demands total power over all men within the Soviet state without a single exception, demands total power over all Communist Parties and all states under Soviet domination. Thus Stalin has said that the theory and tactics of Leninism as expounded by the Bolshevik party are mandatory for the proletarian parties of all countries. A true internationalist is defined as one who unhesitatingly upholds the position of the Soviet Union and in the satellite states true patriotism is love of the Soviet Union. By the same token the "peace policy" of the Soviet Union, described at a Party Congress as "a more advantageous form of fighting capitalism," is a device to divide and immobilize the non-Communist world, and the peace the Soviet Union seeks is the peace of total conformity to Soviet policy.

The antipathy of slavery to freedom explains the iron curtain, the isolation, the autarchy of the society whose end is absolute power. The existence and persistence of the idea of freedom is a permanent and continuous threat to the foundation of the slave society; and it therefore regards as intolerable the long continued existence of freedom in the world. What is new, what makes the continuing crisis, is the polarization of power which now inescapably confronts the slave society with the free.

The assault on free institutions is world-wide now, and in the context of the present polarization of power a defeat of free institutions anywhere is a defeat everywhere. The shock we sustained in the destruction of Czechoslovakia was not in the measure of Czechoslovakia's material importance to us. In a material sense, her capabilities were already at Soviet disposal. But when the integrity of Czechoslovak institutions was destroyed, it was in the intangible scale of values that we registered a loss more damaging than the material loss we had already suffered.

Thus unwillingly our free society finds itself mortally challenged by the Soviet system. No other value system is so wholly irreconcilable with ours, so implacable in its purpose to destroy ours, so capable of turning to its own uses the most dangerous and divisive trends in our own society, no other so skillfully and powerfully evokes the elements of irrationality in human nature everywhere, and no other has the support of a great and growing center of military power.

B. Objectives

The objectives of a free society are determined by its fundamental values and by the necessity for maintaining the material environment in which they flourish. Logically and in fact, therefore, the Kremlin's challenge to the United States is directed not only to our values but to our physical capacity to protect their environment. It is a challenge which encompasses both peace and war and our objectives in peace and war must take account of it.

1. Thus we must make ourselves strong, both in the way in which we affirm our values in the conduct of our national life, and in the development of our military and economic strength.

2. We must lead in building a successfully functioning political and economic system in the free world. It is only by practical affirmation, abroad as well as at home, of our essential values, that we can preserve our own integrity, in which lies the real frustration of the Kremlin design.

3. But beyond thus affirming our values our policy and actions must be such as to foster a fundamental change in the nature of the Soviet system, a change toward which the frustration of the design is the first and perhaps the most important step. Clearly it will not only be less costly but more effective if this change occurs to a maximum extent as a result of internal forces in Soviet society.

In a shrinking world, which now faces the threat of atomic warfare, it is not an adequate objective merely to seek to check the Kremlin design, for the absence of order among nations is becoming less and less tolerable. This fact imposes on us, in our own interests, the responsibility of world leadership. It demands that we make the attempt, and accept the risks inherent in it, to bring about order and justice by means consistent with the principles of freedom and democracy. We should limit our requirement of the Soviet Union to its participation with other nations on the basis of equality and respect for the rights of others. Subject to this requirement, we must with our allies and the former subject peoples seek to create a world society based on the principle of consent. Its framework cannot be inflexible. It will consist of many national communities of great and varying abilities and resources, and hence of war potential. The seeds of conflicts will inevitably exist or will come into being. To acknowledge this is only to acknowledge the impossibility of a final solution. Not to acknowledge it can be fatally dangerous in a world in which there are no final solutions.

All these objectives of a free society are equally valid and necessary in peace and war. But every consideration of devotion to our fundamental values and to our national security demands that we seek to achieve them by the strategy of the cold war. It is only by developing the moral and material strength of the free world that the Soviet regime will become convinced of the falsity of its assumptions and that the pre-conditions for workable agreements can be created. By practically demonstrating the integrity and vitality of our system the free world widens the area of possible agreement and thus can hope gradually to bring about a Soviet acknowledgment of realities which in sum will eventually constitute a frustration of the Soviet design. Short of this, however, it might be possible to create a situation which will induce the Soviet Union to accommodate itself, with or without the conscious abandonment of its design, to coexistence on tolerable terms with the non-Soviet world. Such a development would be a triumph for the idea of freedom and democracy. It must be an immediate objective of United States policy.

There is no reason, in the event of war, for us to alter our overall objectives. They do not include unconditional surrender, the subjugation of the Russian peoples or a Russia shorn of its economic potential. Such a course would irrevocably unite the Russian people behind the regime which enslaves them. Rather these objectives contemplate Soviet acceptance of the specific and limited conditions requisite to an international environment in which free institutions can flourish, and in which the Russian peoples will have a new chance to work out their own destiny. If we can make the Russian people our allies in the enterprise we will obviously have made our task easier and victory more certain.

The objectives outlined in NSC 20/4 (November 23, 1948) . . . are fully consistent with the objectives stated in this paper, and they remain valid. The growing intensity of the conflict which has been imposed upon us, however, requires the changes of emphasis and the additions that are apparent. Coupled with the probable fission bomb capability and possible thermonuclear bomb capability of the Soviet Union, the intensifying struggle requires us to face the fact that we can expect no lasting abatement of the crisis unless and until a change occurs in the nature of the Soviet system.

C. Means

The free society is limited in its choice of means to achieve its ends.

Compulsion is the negation of freedom, except when it is used to enforce the rights common to all. The resort to force, internally or externally, is therefore a last resort for a free society. The act is permissible only when one individual or groups of individuals within it threaten the basic rights of other individuals or when another society seeks to impose its will upon it. The free society cherishes and protects as fundamental the rights of the minority against the will of a majority, because these rights are the inalienable rights of each and every individual.

The resort to force, to compulsion, to the imposition of its will is therefore a difficult and dangerous act for a free society, which is warranted only in the face of even greater dangers. The necessity of the act must be clear and compelling; the act must commend itself to the overwhelming majority as an inescapable exception to the basic idea of freedom; or the regenerative capacity of free men after the act has been performed will be endangered.

The Kremlin is able to select whatever means are expedient in seeking to carry out its fundamental design. Thus it can make the best of several possible worlds, conducting the struggle on those levels where it considers it profitable and enjoying the benefits of a pseudo-peace on those levels where it is not ready for a contest. At the ideological or psychological level, in the struggle for men's minds, the conflict is worldwide. At the political and economic level, within states and in the relations between states, the struggle for power is being intensified. And at the military level, the Kremlin has thus far been careful not to commit a technical breach of the peace, although using its vast forces to intimidate its neighbors, and to support an aggressive foreign policy, and not hesitating through its agents to resort to arms in favorable circumstances. The attempt to carry out its fundamental design is being pressed, therefore, with all means which are believed expedient in the present situation, and the Kremlin has inextricably engaged us in the conflict between its design and our purpose.

We have no such freedom of choice, and least of all in the use of force. Resort to war is not only a last resort for a free society, but it is also an act which cannot definitively end the fundamental conflict in the realm of ideas. The idea of slavery can only be overcome by the timely and persistent demonstration of the superiority of the idea of freedom. Military victory alone would only partially and perhaps only temporarily affect the fundamental conflict, for although the ability of the Kremlin to threaten our security might be for a time destroyed, the resurgence of totalitarian forces and the reestablishment of the Soviet system or its equivalent would not be long delayed unless great progress were made in the fundamental conflict.

Practical and ideological considerations therefore both impel us to the conclusion that we have no choice but to demonstrate the superiority of the idea of freedom by its constructive application, and to attempt to change the world situation by means short of war in such a way as to frustrate the Kremlin design and hasten the decay of the Soviet system.

For us the role of military power is to serve the national purpose by deterring an attack upon us while we seek by other means to create an environment in which our free society can flourish, and by fighting, if necessary, to defend the integrity and vitality of our free society and to defeat any aggressor. The Kremlin uses Soviet military power to back up and serve the Kremlin design. It does not hesitate to use military force aggressively if that course is expedient in the achievement of its design. The differences between our fundamental purpose and the Kremlin design, therefore, are reflected in our respective attitudes toward and use of military force.

Our free society, confronted by a threat to its basic values, naturally will take such action, including the use of military force, as may be required to protect those values. The integrity of our system will not be jeopardized by any measures, covert or overt, violent or non-violent, which serve the purposes of frustrating the Kremlin design, nor does the necessity for conducting ourselves so as to affirm our values in actions as well as words forbid such measures, provided only they are appropriately calculated to that end and are not so excessive or misdirected as to make us enemies of the people instead of the evil men who have enslaved them.

But if war comes, what is the role of force? Unless we so use it that the Russian people can perceive that our effort is directed against the regime and its power for aggression, and not against their own interests, we will unite the regime and the people in the kind of last ditch fight in which no underlying problems are solved, new ones are created, and where our basic principles are obscured and compromised. If we do not in the application of force demonstrate the nature of our objectives we will, in fact, have compromised from the outset our fundamental purpose. In the words of the *Federalist* (No. 28) "The means to be employed must be proportioned to the extent of the mischief." The mischief may be a global war or it may be a Soviet campaign for limited objectives. In either case we should take no avoidable initiative which would cause it to become a war of annihilation, and if we have the forces to defeat a Soviet drive for limited objectives it may well be to our interest not to let it become a global war. Our aim in applying force must be to compel the acceptance of terms consistent with our objectives, and our capabilities for the application of force should, therefore, within the limits of what we can sustain over the long pull, be congruent to the range of tasks which we may encounter.

CONCLUSIONS

The foregoing analysis indicates that the probable fission bomb capability and possible thermonuclear bomb capability of the Soviet Union have greatly intensified the Soviet threat to the security of the United States. This threat is of the same character as that described in NSC 20/4 (approved by the President on November 24, 1948) but is more immediate than had previously been estimated. In particular, the United States now faces the contingency that within the next four or five years the Soviet Union will possess the military capability of delivering a surprise atomic attack of such weight that the United States must have substantially increased general air, ground, and sea strength, atomic capabilities, and air and civilian defenses to deter war and to provide reasonable assurance, in the event of war, that it could survive the initial blow and go on to the eventual attainment of its objectives. In return, this contingency requires the intensification of our efforts in the fields of intelligence and research and development.

Allowing for the immediacy of the danger, the following statement of Soviet threats, contained in NSC 20/4, remains valid:

14. The gravest threat to the security of the United States within the foreseeable future stems from the hostile designs and formidable power of the USSR, and from the nature of the Soviet system.

15. The political, economic, and psychological warfare which the USSR is now waging has dangerous potentialities for weakening the relative world position of the United States and disrupting its traditional institutions by means short of war, unless sufficient resistance is encountered in the policies of this and other non-communist countries.

16. The risk of war with the USSR is sufficient to warrant, in common prudence, timely and adequate preparation by the United States.

    a. Even though present estimates indicate that the Soviet leaders probably do not intend deliberate armed action involving the United States at this time, the possibility of such deliberate resort to war cannot be ruled out.

    b. Now and for the foreseeable future there is a continuing danger that war will arise either through Soviet miscalculation of the determination of the United States to use all the means at its command to safeguard its security, through Soviet misinterpretation of our intentions, or through U.S. miscalculation of Soviet reactions to measures which we might take.

17. Soviet domination of the potential power of Eurasia, whether achieved by armed aggression or by political and subversive means, would be strategically and politically unacceptable to the United States.

18. The capability of the United States either in peace or in the event of war to cope with threats to its security or to gain its objectives would be severely weakened by internal development, important among which are:

   a. Serious espionage, subversion and sabotage, particularly by concerted and well-directed communist activity.

   b. Prolonged or exaggerated economic instability.

   c. Internal political and social disunity.

   d. Inadequate or excessive armament or foreign aid expenditures.

   e. An excessive or wasteful usage of our resources in time of peace.

   f. Lessening of U.S. prestige and influence through vacillation of appeasement or lack of skill and imagination in the conduct of its foreign policy or by shirking world responsibilities.

   g. Development of a false sense of security through a deceptive change in Soviet tactics.

Although such developments as those indicated in paragraph 18 above would severely weaken the capability of the United States and its allies to cope with the Soviet threat to their security, considerable progress has been made since 1948 in laying the foundation upon which adequate strength can now be rapidly built.

The analysis also confirms that our objectives with respect to the Soviet Union, in time of peace as well as in time of war, as stated in NSC 20/4 (para. 19), are still valid, as are the aims and measures stated therein (paras. 20 and 21). Our current security programs and strategic plans are based upon these objectives, aims, and measures:

19.

   a. To reduce the power and influence of the USSR to limits which no longer constitute a threat to the peace, national independence, and stability of the world family of nations.

   b. To bring about a basic change in the conduct of international relations by the government in power in Russia, to conform with the purposes and principles set forth in the UN Charter.

In pursuing these objectives, due care must be taken to avoid permanently impairing our economy and the fundamental values and institutions inherent in our way of life.

20. We should endeavor to achieve our general objectives by methods short of war through the pursuit of the following aims:

   a. To encourage and promote the gradual retraction of undue Russian power and influence from the present perimeter areas around traditional Russian boundaries and the emergence of the satellite countries as entities independent of the USSR.

b. To encourage the development among the Russian peoples of attitudes which may help to modify current Soviet behavior and permit a revival of the national life of groups evidencing the ability and determination to achieve and maintain national independence.

c. To eradicate the myth by which people remote from Soviet military influence are held in a position of subservience to Moscow and to cause the world at large to see and understand the true nature of the USSR and the Soviet-directed world communist party, and to adopt a logical and realistic attitude toward them.

d. To create situations which will compel the Soviet Government to recognize the practical undesirability of acting on the basis of its present concepts and the necessity of behaving in accordance with precepts of international conduct, as set forth in the purposes and principles of the UN Charter.

21. Attainment of these aims requires that the United States:

a. Develop a level of military readiness which can be maintained as long as necessary as a deterrent to Soviet aggression, as indispensable support to our political attitude toward the USSR, as a source of encouragement to nations resisting Soviet political aggression, and as an adequate basis for immediate military commitments and for rapid mobilization should war prove unavoidable.

b. Assure the internal security of the United States against dangers of sabotage, subversion, and espionage.

c. Maximize our economic potential, including the strengthening of our peacetime economy and the establishment of essential reserves readily available in the event of war.

d. Strengthen the orientation toward the United States of the non-Soviet nations; and help such of those nations as are able and willing to make an important contribution to U.S. security, to increase their economic and political stability and their military capability.

e. Place the maximum strain on the Soviet structure of power and particularly on the relationships between Moscow and the satellite countries.

f. Keep the U.S. public fully informed and cognizant of the threats to our national security so that it will be prepared to support the measures which we must accordingly adopt.

In the light of present and prospective Soviet atomic capabilities, the action which can be taken under present programs and plans, however, becomes dangerously inadequate, in both timing and scope, to accomplish the rapid progress toward the attainment of the United States political, economic, and military objectives which is now imperative.

A continuation of present trends would result in a serious decline in the strength of the free world relative to the Soviet Union and its satellites. This unfavorable trend arises from the inadequacy of current programs and plans rather than from any error in our objectives and aims. These trends lead in the direction of isolation, not by deliberate decision but by lack of the necessary basis for a vigorous initiative in the conflict with the Soviet Union.

Our position as the center of power in the free world places a heavy responsibility upon the United States for leadership. We must organize and enlist the energies and resources of the free world in a positive program for peace which will frustrate the Kremlin design for world domination by creating a situation in the free world to which the Kremlin will be compelled to adjust. Without such a cooperative effort, led by the United States, we will have to make gradual withdrawals under pressure until we discover one day that we have sacrificed positions of vital interest.

It is imperative that this trend be reversed by a much more rapid and concerted build-up of the actual strength of both the United States and the other nations of the free world. The analysis shows that this will be costly and will involve significant domestic financial and economic adjustments.

The execution of such a build-up, however, requires that the United States have an affirmative program beyond the solely defensive one of countering the threat posed by the Soviet Union. This program must light the path to peace and order among nations in a system based on freedom and justice, as contemplated in the Charter of the United Nations. Further, it must envisage the political and economic measures with which and the military shield behind which the free world can work to frustrate the Kremlin design by the strategy of the cold war; for every consideration of devotion to our fundamental values and to our national security demands that we achieve our objectives by the strategy of the cold war, building up our military strength in order that it may not have to be used. The only sure victory lies in the frustration of the Kremlin design by the steady development of the moral and material strength of the free world and its projection into the Soviet world in such a way as to bring about an internal change in the Soviet system. Such a positive program—harmonious with our fundamental national purpose and our objectives—is necessary if we are to regain and retain the initiative and to win and hold the necessary popular support and cooperation in the United States and the rest of the free world.

This program should include a plan for negotiation with the Soviet Union, developed and agreed with our allies and which is consonant with our objectives. The United States and its allies, particularly the United Kingdom and France, should always be ready to negotiate with the Soviet Union on terms consistent with our objectives. The present world situation, however, is one which militates against successful negotiations with the Kremlin—for the terms of agreements on important pending issues would reflect present realities and would therefore be unacceptable, if not disastrous, to the United States and the rest of the free world. After a decision and a start on building up the strength of the free world has been made, it might then be desirable for the United States to take an initiative in seeking negotiations in the hope that it might facilitate the process of accommodation by the Kremlin to the new situation. Failing that, the unwillingness of the Kremlin to accept equitable terms or its bad faith in observing them would assist in consolidating popular opinion in the free world in support of the measures necessary to sustain the build-up.

In summary, we must, by means of a rapid and sustained build-up of the political, economic, and military strength of the free world, and by means of an affirmative program intended to wrest the initiative from the Soviet Union, confront it with convincing evidence of the determination and ability of the free world to frustrate the Kremlin design of a world dominated by its will. Such evidence is the only means short of war which eventually may force the Kremlin to abandon its present course of action and to negotiate acceptable agreements on issues of major importance.

The whole success of the proposed program hangs ultimately on recognition by this Government, the American people, and all free peoples, that the cold war is in fact a real war in which the survival of the free world is at stake. Essential prerequisites to success are consultations with Congressional leaders designed to make the program the object of non-partisan legislative support, and a presentation to the public of a full explanation of the facts and implications of the present international situation. The prosecution of the program will require of us all the ingenuity, sacrifice, and unity demanded by the vital importance of the issue and the tenacity to persevere until our national objectives have been attained.

RECOMMENDATIONS

That the President:

a. Approve the foregoing Conclusions.

b. Direct the National Security Council, under the continuing direction of the President, and with the participation of other Departments and Agencies as appropriate, to coordinate and insure the implementation of the Conclusions herein on an urgent and continuing basis for as long as necessary to achieve our objectives. For this purpose, representatives of the member Departments and Agencies, the Joint Chiefs of Staff or their deputies, and other Departments and Agencies as required should be constituted as a revised and strengthened staff organization under the National Security Council to develop coordinated programs for consideration by the National Security Council.

NOTES

1. Marshal Tito, the Communist leader of Yugoslavia, broke away from the Soviet bloc in 1948.

2. The Secretary of State listed seven areas in which the Soviet Union could modify its behavior in such a way as to permit co-existence in reasonable security. These were:

   1. Treaties of peace with Austria, Germany, Japan and relaxation of pressures in the Far East;

   2. Withdrawal of Soviet forces and influence from satellite area;

   3. Cooperation in the United Nations;

   4. Control of atomic energy and of conventional armaments;

   5. Abandonment of indirect aggression;

   6. Proper treatment of official representatives of the U.S.;

   7. Increased access to the Soviet Union of persons and ideas from other countries. [Footnote in the source text. For the text of the address delivered by Secretary Acheson at the University of California, Berkeley, on March 16, 1950, concerning United States–Soviet relations, see Department of State *Bulletin,* March 27, 1950, pp. 473–478.]

BACKGROUND TO THE CRISIS, 1940–50

SUMMARY—INDOCHINA IN U.S. WARTIME POLICY, 1941–1945

Significant misunderstanding has developed concerning U.S. policy towards Indochina in the decade of World War II and its aftermath. A number of historians have held that anti-colonialism governed U.S. policy and actions up until 1950, when containment of communism supervened. For example, Bernard Fall (e.g. in his 1967 postmortem book, *Last Reflections on a War*) categorized American policy toward Indochina in six periods: "(1) Anti-Vichy, 1940–1945; (2) Pro-Viet Minh, 1945–1946; (3) Non-involvement, 1946–June 1950; (4) Pro-French, 1950–July 1954; (5) Non-military involvement, 1954–November 1961; (6) Direct and full involvement, 1961–." Commenting that the first four periods are those "least known even to the specialist," Fall developed the thesis that President Roosevelt was determined "to eliminate the French from Indochina at all costs," and had pressured the Allies to establish an international trusteeship to administer Indochina until the nations there were ready to assume full independence. This obdurate anti-colonialism, in Fall's view, led to cold refusal of American aid for French resistance fighters, and to a policy of promoting Ho Chi Minh and the Viet Minh as the alternative to restoring the French bonds. But, the argument goes, Roosevelt died, and principle faded; by late 1946, anti-colonialism mutated into neutrality. According to Fall: "Whether this was due to a deliberate policy in Washington or, conversely, to an absence of policy, is not quite clear. . . . The United States, preoccupied in Europe, ceased to be a diplomatic factor in Indochina until the outbreak of the Korean War." In 1950, anti-communism asserted itself, and in a remarkable volte-face, the United States threw its economic and military resources behind France in its war against the Viet Minh. Other commentators, conversely—prominent among them, the historians of the Viet Minh—have described U.S. policy as consistently condoning and assisting the reimposition of French colonial power in Indochina, with a concomitant disregard for the nationalist aspirations of the Vietnamese.

473

Neither interpretation squares with the record; the United States was less concerned over Indochina, and less purposeful than either assumes. Ambivalence characterized U.S. policy during World War II, and was the root of much subsequent misunderstanding. On the one hand, the U.S. repeatedly reassured the French that its colonial possessions would be returned to it after the war. On the other hand, the U.S. broadly committed itself in the Atlantic Charter to support national self-determination, and President Roosevelt personally and vehemently advocated independence for Indochina. F.D.R. regarded Indochina as a flagrant example of onerous colonialism which should be turned over to a trusteeship rather than returned to France. The President discussed this proposal with the Allies at the Cairo, Teheran, and Yalta Conferences and received the endorsement of Chiang Kai-shek and Stalin; Prime Minister Churchill demurred. At one point, Fall reports, the President offered General de Gaulle Filipino advisers to help France establish a "more progressive policy in Indochina"—which offer the General received in "Pensive Silence."

Ultimately, U.S. Policy was governed neither by the principles of the Atlantic Charter, nor by the President's anti-colonialism but by the dictates of military strategy and by British intransigence on the colonial issue. The United States, concentrating its forces against Japan, accepted British military primacy in Southeast Asia, and divided Indochina at 16th parallel between the British and the Chinese for the purposes of occupation. U.S. commanders serving with the British and Chinese, while instructed to avoid ostensible alignment with the French, were permitted to conduct operations in Indochina which did not detract from the campaign against Japan. Consistent with F.D.R.'s guidance, U.S. did provide modest aid to French—and Viet Minh—resistance forces in Vietnam after March, 1945, but refused to provide shipping to move Free French troops there. Pressed by both the British and the French for clarification of U.S. intentions regarding the political status of Indochina, F.D.R. maintained that "it is a matter for postwar."

The President's trusteeship concept foundered as early as March 1943, when the U.S. discovered that the British, concerned over possible prejudice to Commonwealth policy, proved to be unwilling to join in any declaration on trusteeships, and indeed any statement endorsing national independence which went beyond the Atlantic Charter's vague "respect the right of all peoples to choose the form of government under which they will live." So sensitive were the British on this point that the Dumbarton Oaks Conference of 1944, at which the blueprint for the postwar international system was negotiated, skirted the colonial issue, and avoided trusteeships altogether. At each key decisional point at which the President could have influenced the course of events toward trusteeship—in relations with the U.K., in casting the United Nations Charter, in instructions to allied commanders—he declined to do so; hence, despite his lip service to trusteeship and anti-colonialism, F.D.R. in fact assigned to Indochina a status correlative to Burma, Malaya, Singapore and Indonesia: free territory to be reconquered and returned to its former owners. Non-intervention by the U.S. on behalf of the Vietnamese was tantamount to acceptance of the French return. On April 3, 1945, with President Roosevelt's approval, Secretary of State Stettinius issued a statement that, as a result of the Yalta talks, the U.S. would look to trusteeship as a postwar arrangement only for "territories taken from the enemy," and for "territories as might voluntarily be placed under trusteeship." By context, and by the Secretary of State's subsequent interpretation, Indochina fell into the latter category. Trusteeship status for Indochina became, then, a matter for French determination.

Shortly following President Truman's entry into office, the U.S. assured France that it had never questioned, "even by implication, French sovereignty over Indo-China." The U.S. policy was to press France for progressive measures in Indochina, but to expect France to decide when its peoples would be ready for independence; "such decisions would preclude the establishment of a trusteeship in Indochina except with the consent of the French Government." These guidelines, established by June, 1945—before the end of the war—remained fundamental to U.S. policy.

With British cooperation, French military forces were reestablished in South Vietnam in September, 1945. The U.S. expressed dismay at the outbreak of guerrilla warfare which followed, and pointed out that while it had no intention of opposing the reestablishment of French control, "it is not the policy of this government to assist the French to reestablish their control over Indochina by force, and the willingness of the U.S. to see French control reestablished assumes that [the] French claim to have the support of the population in Indochina is borne out by future events." Through the fall and winter of 1945–1946, the U.S. received a series of requests from Ho Chi Minh for intervention in Vietnam; these were, on the record, unanswered. However, the U.S. steadfastly refused to assist the French military effort, e.g., forbidding American flag vessels to carry troops or war materiel to Vietnam. On March 6, 1946, the French and Ho signed an Accord in which Ho acceded to French reentry into North Vietnam in return for recognition of the DRV as a "Free State," part of the French Union. As of April 1946, allied occupation of Indochina was officially terminated, and the U.S. acknowledged to France that all of Indochina had reverted to French control. Thereafter, the problems of U.S. policy toward Vietnam were dealt with in the context of the U.S. relationship with France.

U.S. NEUTRALITY IN THE FRANCO–VIET MINH WAR, 1946–1949

In late 1946, the Franco–Viet Minh War began in earnest. The U.S. during these years continued to regard the conflict as fundamentally a matter for French resolution. The U.S. in its representations to France deplored the prospect of protracted war, and urged meaningful concessions to Vietnamese nationalism. However, the U.S., deterred by the history of Ho's communist affiliation, always stopped short of endorsing Ho Chi Minh or the Viet Minh. Accordingly, U.S. policy gravitated with that of France toward the Bao Dai solution. At no point was the U.S. prepared to adopt an openly interventionist course. To have done so would have clashed with the expressed British view that Indochina was an exclusively French concern, and played into the hands of France's extremist political parties of both the Right and the Left. The U.S. was particularly apprehensive lest by intervening it strengthen the political position of French Communists. Beginning in 1946 and 1947, France and Britain were moving toward an anti-Soviet alliance in Europe and the U.S. was reluctant to press a potentially divisive policy. The U.S. [words illegible] Vietnamese nationalism relatively insignificant compared with European economic recovery and collective security from communist domination.

It is not as though the U.S. was not prepared to act in circumstances such as these. For example, in the 1945–1946 dispute over Dutch possessions in Indonesia, the U.S. actively intervened against its Dutch ally. In this case, however, the intervention was in concert with the U.K. (which steadfastly refused similar action in Indochina) and against the Netherlands, a much less significant ally in Europe than France. In wider company and at projected lower cost, the U.S. could and did show a determination to act against colonialism.

The resultant U.S. policy has most often been termed "neutrality." It was, however, also consistent with the policy of deferring to French volition announced by President Roosevelt's Secretary of State on 3 April 1945. It was a policy characterized by the same indecision that had marked U.S. wartime policy. Moreover, at the time, Indochina appeared to many to be one region in the troubled postwar world in which the U.S. might enjoy the luxury of abstention.

In February, 1947, early in the war, the U.S. Ambassador in Paris was instructed to reassure Premier Ramadier of the "very friendliest feelings" of the U.S. toward France and its interest in supporting France in recovering its economic, political and military strength:

> In spite any misunderstanding which might have arisen in minds French in regard to our position concerning Indochina they must appreciate that we have fully recognized France's sovereign position in that area and we do not wish to have it appear that we are in any way endeavoring undermine that position, and French should know it is our desire to be helpful and we stand ready assist any appropriate way we can to find solution for Indochinese problem. At same time we cannot shut our eyes to fact that there are two sides this problem and that our reports indicate both a lack French understanding of other side (more in Saigon than in Paris) and continued existence dangerously Outmoded colonial outlook and methods in area.

Furthermore, there is no escape from fact that trend of times is to effect that colonial empires in XIX Century sense are rapidly becoming thing of past. Action Brit in India and Burma and Dutch in Indonesia are outstanding examples this trend, and French themselves took cognizance of it both in new Constitution and in their agreements with Vietnam. On other hand we do not lose sight fact that Ho Chi Minh has direct Communist connections and it should be obvious that we are not interested in seeing colonial empire administrations supplanted by philosophy and political organizations emanating from and controlled by Kremlin. . . .

Frankly we have no solution of problem to suggest. It is basically matter for two parties to work out themselves and from your reports and those from Indochina we are led to feel that both parties have endeavored to keep door open to some sort of settlement. We appreciate fact that Vietnam started present fighting in Indochina on December 19 and that this action has made it more difficult for French to adopt a position of generosity and conciliation. Nevertheless we hope that French will find it possible to be more than generous in trying to find a solution.

The U.S. anxiously followed the vacillations of France's policy toward Bao Dai, exhorting the French to translate the successive "agreements" they contracted with him into an effective nationalist alternative to Ho Chi Minh and the Viet Minh. Increasingly, the U.S. sensed that French unwillingness to concede political power to Vietnamese heightened the possibility of the Franco-Viet Minh conflict being transformed into a struggle with Soviet imperialism. U.S. diplomats were instructed to "apply such persuasion and/or pressure as is best calculated [to] produce desired result [of France's] unequivocally and promptly approving the principle of Viet independence." France was notified that the U.S. was willing to extend financial aid to a Vietnamese government not a French puppet, "but could not give consideration of altering its present policy in this regard unless real progress [is] made in reaching non-Communist solution in Indochina based on cooperation of true nationalists of that country."

As of 1948, however, the U.S. remained uncertain that Ho and the Viet Minh were in league with the Kremlin. A State Department appraisal of Ho Chi Minh in July 1948, indicated that:

1. Depts info indicates that Ho Chi Minh is Communist. His long and well-known record in Comintern during twenties and thirties, continuous support by French Communist newspaper Humanite since 1945, praise given him by Radio Moscow (which for past six months has been devoting increasing attention to Indochina) and fact he has been called "leading communist" by recent Russian publications as well as Daily Worker makes any other conclusion appear to be wishful thinking.

2. Dept has no evidence of direct link between Ho and Moscow but assumes it exists, nor is it able evaluate amount pressure or guidance Moscow exerting. We have impression Ho must be given or is retaining large degree latitude. Dept considers that USSR accomplishing its immediate aims in Indochina by (a) pinning down large numbers of French troops, (b) causing steady drain upon French economy thereby tending retard recovery and dissipate ECA assistance to France, and (c) denying to world generally surpluses which Indochina normally has available thus perpetuating conditions of disorder and shortages which favorable to growth cornmunism. Furthermore, Ho seems quite capable of retaining and even strengthening his grip on Indochina with no outside assistance other than continuing procession of French puppet govts.

In the fall of 1948, the Office of Intelligence Research in the Department of State conducted a survey of communist influence in Southeast Asia. Evidence of Kremlin-directed conspiracy was found in virtually all countries except Vietnam:

Since December 19, 1946, there have been continuous conflicts between French forces and the nationalist government of Vietnam. This government is a coalition in which avowed communists hold influential positions. Although the French admit the influence of this government, they have consistently refused to deal with its leader, Ho Chi Minh, on the grounds that he is a communist.

To date the Vietnam press and radio have not adopted an anti-American position. It is rather the French colonial press that has been strongly anti-American and has freely accused the U.S. of imperialism in Indochina to the point of approximating the official Moscow position. Although the Vietnam radio has been closely watched for a new position toward the U.S., no change has appeared so far. Nor does there seem to have been any split within the coalition government of Vietnam. . . .

Evaluation. If there is a Moscow directed conspiracy in Southeast Asia, Indochina is an anomaly so far. Possible explanations are:

1. No rigid directives have been issued by Moscow.

2. The Vietnam government considers that it has no rightist elements that must be purged.

3. The Vietnam Communists are not subservient to the foreign policies pursued by Moscow.

4. A special dispensation for the Vietnam government has been arranged in Moscow.

Of these possibilities, the first and fourth seem most likely.

ORIGINS OF U.S. INVOLVEMENT IN VIETNAM

The collapse of the Chinese Nationalist government in 1949 sharpened American apprehensions over communist expansion in the Far East, and hastened U.S. measures to counter the threat posed by Mao's China. The U.S. sought to create and employ policy instruments similar to those it was bringing into play against the Soviets in Europe: collective security organizations, economic aid, and military assistance. For example, Congress, in the opening paragraphs of the law it passed in 1949 to establish the first comprehensive military assistance program, expressed itself "as favoring the creation by the free countries and the free peoples of the Far East of a joint organization, consistent with the Charter of the United Nations, to establish a program of self-help and mutual cooperation designed to develop their economic and social well-being, to safeguard basic rights and liberties, and to protect their security and independence." But, the negotiating of such an organization among the disparate powers and political entities of the Far East was inherently more complex a matter than the North Atlantic Treaty nations had successfully faced. The U.S. decided that the impetus for collective security in Asia should come from the Asians, but by late 1949, it also recognized that action was necessary in Indochina. Thus, in the closing months of 1949, the course of U.S. policy was set to block further communist expansion in Asia: by collective security if the Asians were forthcoming; by collaboration with major European allies and commonwealth nations, if possible; but bilaterally if necessary. On that policy course lay the Korean War of 1950–1953, the forming of the Southeast Asia Treaty Organization of 1954, and the progressively deepening U.S. involvement in Vietnam.

January and February, 1950, were pivotal months. The French took the first concrete steps toward transferring public administration to Bao Dai's State of Vietnam. Ho Chi Minh denied the legitimacy of the latter, proclaiming the DRV as the "only legal government of the Vietnam people," and was formally recognized by Peking and Moscow. On 29 January 1950, the French Nation, Assembly approved legislation granting autonomy to the State of Vietnam. On February 1, 1950, Secretary of State Acheson made the following public statement:

> *The recognition by the Kremlin of Ho Chi Minh's communist movement in Indochina comes as a surprise. The Soviet acknowledgment of this movement should remove any illusions as to the "nationalist" nature of Ho Chi*

Minh's aims and reveals Ho in his true colors as the mortal enemy of native independence in Indochina.

Although timed in an effort to cloud the transfer of sovereignty France to the legal Governments of Laos, Cambodia and Vietnam, we have every reason to believe that those legal governments will proceed in their development toward stable governments representing the true nationalist sentiments of more than 20 million peoples of Indochina.

French action in transferring sovereignty to Vietnam, Laos and Cambodia has been in process for some time. Following French ratification, which is expected within a few days, the way will be open for recognition of these local governments by the countries of the world whose policies support the development of genuine national independence in former colonial areas. . . .

Formal French ratification of Vietnamese independence was announced 4 February 1950; on the same date, President Truman approved U.S. recognition for Bao Dai. French requests for aid in Indochina followed within a few weeks. On May 8, 1950, the Secretary of State announced that:

The United States Government convinced that neither national independence nor democratic evolution exist in any area dominated by Soviet imperialism, considers the situation to be such as to warrant its according economic aid and military equipment to the Associated State of Indochina and to France in order to assist them in restoring stability and permitting these states to pursue their peaceful and democratic development.

The U.S. thereafter was deeply involved in the developing war. But it cannot be said that the extension of aid was a volte-face of U.S. policy precipitated solely by the events of 1950. It appears rather as the denouement of a cohesive progression of U.S. policy decisions stemming from the 1945 determination that France should decide the political future of Vietnamese nationalism. Neither the modest O.S.S. aid to the Viet Minh in 1945, nor the U.S. refusal to abet French recourse to arms the same year, signaled U.S. backing of Ho Chi Minh. To the contrary, the U.S. was very wary of Ho, apprehensive lest Paris' imperialism be succeeded by control from Moscow. Uncertainty characterized the U.S. attitude toward Ho through 1948, but the U.S. incessantly pressured France to accommodate "genuine" Vietnamese nationalism and independence. In early 1950, both the apparent fruition of the Bao Dai solution, and the patent alignment of the DRV with the USSR and Communist China, impelled the U.S. to more direct intervention in Vietnam.

AGGRESION FROM THE NORTH: STATE DEPARTMENT WHITE PAPER ON VIETNAM, FEBRUARY 27, 1965

South Vietnam is fighting for its life against a brutal campaign of terror and armed attack inspired, directed, supplied, and controlled by the Communist regime in Hanoi. This flagrant aggression has been going on for years, but recently the pace has quickened and the threat has now become acute.

The war in Vietnam is a new kind of war, a fact as yet poorly understood in most parts of the world. Much of the confusion that prevails in the thinking of many people, and even governments, stems from this basic misunderstanding. For in Vietnam a totally new brand of aggression has been loosed against an independent people who want to make their way in peace and freedom.

Vietnam is not another Greece, where indigenous guerrilla forces used friendly neighboring territory as a sanctuary.

Vietnam is not another Malaya, where Communist guerrillas were, for the most part, physically distinguishable from the peaceful majority they sought to control.

Vietnam is not another Philippines, where Communist guerrillas were physically separated from the source of their moral and physical support.

Above all, the war in Vietnam is not a spontaneous and local rebellion against the established government.

There are elements in the Communist program of conquest directed against South Vietnam common to each of the previous areas of aggression and subversion. But there is one fundamental difference. In Vietnam a Communist government has set out deliberately to conquer a sovereign people in a neighboring state. And to achieve its end, it has used every resource of its own government to carry out its carefully planned program of concealed aggression. North Vietnam's commitment to seize control of the South is no less total than

(Department of State Bulletin, March 22, 1965)

was the commitment of the regime in North Korea in 1950. But knowing the consequences of the latter's undisguised attack, the planners in Hanoi have tried desperately to conceal their hand. They have failed and their aggression is as real as that of an invading army.

This report is a summary of the massive evidence of North Vietnamese aggression obtained by the Government of South Vietnam. This evidence has been jointly analyzed by South Vietnamese and American experts.

The evidence shows that the hard core of the Communist forces attacking South Vietnam were trained in the North and ordered into the South by Hanoi. It shows that the key leadership of the Vietcong (VC), the officers and much of the cadre, many of the technicians, political organizers, and propagandists have come from the North and operate under Hanoi's direction. It shows that the training of essential military personnel and their infiltration into the South is directed by the Military High Command in Hanoi. In recent months new types of weapons have been introduced in the VC army, for which all ammunition must come from outside sources. Communist China and other Communist states have been the prime suppliers of these weapons and ammunition, and they have been channeled primarily through North Vietnam.

The directing force behind the effort to conqueror South Vietnam is the Communist Party in the North, the Lao Dong (Workers) Party. As in every Communist state, the party is an integral part of the regime itself. North Vietnamese officials have expressed their firm determination to absorb South Vietnam into the Communist world.

Through its Central Committee, which controls the Government of the North, the Lao Dong Party directs the total political and military effort of the Vietcong. The Military High Command in the North trains the military men and sends them into South Vietnam. The Central Research Agency, North Vietnam's central intelligence organization, directs the elaborate espionage and subversion effort. . . .

Under Hanoi's overall direction the Communists have established an extensive machine for carrying on the war within South Vietnam. The focal point is the Central Office for South Vietnam with its political and military subsections and other specialized agencies. A subordinate part of this Central Office is the liberation Front for South Vietnam. The front was formed at Hanoi's order in 1960. Its principle function is to influence opinion abroad and to create the false impression that the aggression in South Vietnam is an indigenous rebellion against the established Government.

For more than 10 years the people and the Government of South Vietnam, exercising the inherent right of self-defense, have fought back against these efforts to extend Communist power south across the 17th parallel. The United States has responded to the appeals of the Government of the Republic of

Vietnam for help in this defense of the freedom and independence of its land and its people.

In 1961 the Department of State issued a report called A Threat to the Peace. It described North Vietnam's program to seize South Vietnam. The evidence in that report had been presented by the Government of the Republic of Vietnam to the International Control Commission (ICC). A special report by the ICC in June 1962 upheld the validity of that evidence. The Commission held that there was "sufficient evidence to show beyond reasonable doubt" that North Vietnam had sent arms and men into South Vietnam to carry out subversion with the aim of overthrowing the legal Government there. The ICC found the authorities in Hanoi in specific violation of four provisions of the Geneva Accords of 1954.

Since then, new and even more impressive evidence of Hanoi's aggression has accumulated. The Government of the United States believes that evidence should be presented to its own citizens and to the world. It is important for free men to know what has been happening in Vietnam, and how, and why. That is the purpose of this report. . . .

The record is conclusive. It establishes beyond question that North Vietnam is carrying out a carefully conceived plan of aggression against the South. It shows that North Vietnam has intensified its efforts in the years since it was condemned by the International Control Commission. It proves that Hanoi continues to press its systematic program of armed aggression into South Vietnam. This aggression violates the United Nations Charter. It is directly contrary to the Geneva Accords of 1954 and of 1962 to which North Vietnam is a party. It is a fundamental threat to the freedom and security of South Vietnam.

The people of South Vietnam have chosen to resist this threat. At their request, the United States has taken its place beside them in their defensive struggle.

The United States seeks no territory, no military bases, no favored position. But we have learned the meaning of aggression elsewhere in the post-war world, and we have met it.

If peace can be restored in South Vietnam, the United States will be ready at once to reduce its military involvement. But it will not abandon friends who want to remain free. It will do what must be done to help them. The choice now between peace and continued and increasingly destructive conflict is one for the authorities in Hanoi to make.

EXCERPTS FROM WRISTON: WALTER WRISTON, CITIBANK, AND THE RISE AND FALL OF AMERICAN FINANCIAL SUPREMACY

The Treasury Department had fretted over Mexico for a year, and those concerns had intensified in the spring when Treasury secretary Donald Regan met with Jesús Silva Herzog, the finance minister, at a conference. According to Regan, Silva Herzog made comments that prompted Regan to ask him to give "some warning" if there was going to be trouble.

"Don't worry, Don. We'll give you plenty of warning," Silva Herzog replied, with his characteristic twinkle.

According to finance official Angel Gurria, he and Silva Herzog traveled to Washington in mid-1982 to inform Regan that "there was going to be a big problem. The money's getting out of the country, and the banks aren't rolling. They didn't want to listen. Don Regan had an obvious case of cognitive dissonance. You don't want to hear what they're telling you because you don't like it, so you block it out."

U.S. Treasury officials made the same complaint about the Mexicans. "Treasury and others had been preaching to the Mexicans: get your act in order—your economy is going to go down the tube," said a Regan aide. "There was a sense at Treasury and the Fed that these countries were following policies of folly and, particularly in the case of Mexico, that they weren't listening."

Still, the Treasury was unprepared for the debacle that was about to erupt. Between August 1982 and December 1984, about $20 billion in loans to Mexico were due to mature, and for the three months or so beginning August 23, Mexico was supposed to repay more than $8 billion. But the Fed had just executed a $700 million swap with Mexico—enough, so everyone thought, to keep Mexico afloat until September. For Donald Regan, the Latin American debt crisis began with a phone call from Jesús Silva Herzog on Thursday, August 12, just as Regan was about to leave Washington for the weekend. Silva Herzog asked him if he remembered their earlier conversation. Sensing that he was about to hear some very bad news, Regan replied, "Yeah, I remember it."

"Well, the time is here. I need money," Silva Herzog announced. In effect, Silva Herzog was informing Regan that Mexico was broke.

"How much do you need?" Regan asked.

"About a billion."

Payments of about $300 million, a sum that exceeded the country's liquid reserves, were coming due the following Monday. Though Mexico had tried to keep up interest payments, there was no way it could pay principal. Regan lit into Chucho as if Mexico's finance minister were a teenager who had squandered his allowance. "I told him I wanted to see him at Treasury in twelve hours." Silva Herzog was in no position to argue. Late that afternoon, he and his colleagues left for Washington. Right after hanging up the phone, Regan phoned Volcker. "Do you know what's going on?" Regan asked. Volcker did. While Silva Herzog was on the phone with Regan, the head of Mexico's central bank had called his counterpart in Washington. Over the following weekend, Volcker phoned the heads of the world's major central banks.

In the days before they left for Washington, Silva Herzog and Mexico's central bank chief had asked their colleagues to think about how they should break the bad news to their bankers. Day and night, they stewed over their dilemma, and whether they should bring in lawyers to draft a telegram. One morning Angel Gurria, the finance ministry aide, gave them a list of those who should be involved. It was not a list of bank chairmen, for the Mexicans had concluded this was not simply a banking problem. Instead, the list read: Ronald Reagan, Margaret Thatcher, Japanese prime minister Zenko Suzuki, and the heads of other major industrialized nations. Silva Herzog had reached the same conclusion—that this was a systemic problem, not merely a bank problem. After arriving in Washington, the Mexican officials made the rounds of the Treasury and the Fed, where they reviewed their maturing loans line by line.

Then it was the banks' turn to hear the bad news. It wasn't easy to reach the heads of the nation's top banks on a weekend in the dog days of August. Nearly all of them were playing golf, fishing, or relaxing at their summer residences. Wriston was on vacation in Sherman, Connecticut, and Tom Theobald was running the bank. Most of the bankers, Silva Herzog said later, "were taken by surprise." But Silva Herzog remembered that when he reached Wriston, he "didn't get a negative reaction. He understood the seriousness of the problem," and the two men began deliberating over how to "play it."

Regan recalled later that Wriston phoned him to emphasize "how really bad this thing is," and that "there are a lot of banks in deep trouble if we [don't] handle it correctly."

One of the reasons Wriston got "so deeply involved in the crisis was not just because Citi was at risk, but it was at my urging," Regan claimed years later. . . .

But Brazil was now the sick man of the world financial community. There, angry, hungry mobs looted supermarkets. Workers struck in protest of IMF austerity measures. Brazilians were losing all hope that their lives would ever improve and were talking seriously about debt repudiation. The country was now more than two months behind in its interest payments, and with the end of the quarter approaching, national banks, including Citibank, feared that they would have to classify their loans as "nonperforming." By June 30, Citicorp's nonperforming overseas loans had soared to $1.7 billion from $704 million the year before. In August, Bill Rhodes and other top bankers journeyed to Brazil to warn monetary officials to get their house in order.

Even central bank chief Carlos Langoni was disgusted, and in September 1983 handed in his resignation. Years later he would say only that he resigned because the government was "not able to commit itself to a serious program of adjustment." At least one other observer, however, contended that Langoni really quit because he opposed the IMF's austerity measures.

By the time the moneymen were due to gather in Washington for the annual IMF meeting, it was clear that the Brazilian package wasn't going to fly even if the banks kicked in $6.5 billion. Things came to a head in the twelfth-floor boardroom of the IMF where managing director Jacques de Larosière had convened Wriston and other top bankers. There, Volcker and de Larosière, comrades-in-arms, made it clear once again that the banks would have to pony up. The bankers, said de Larosière, thought the amounts were too large and that Brazil's balance-of-payments needs had not been well assessed. De Larosière shrugged it off later, saying, "The usual thing."

Standing at the lectern, de Larosière told the bankers, as Wriston recalled later, "It's your problem."

Wriston was the first to speak up: "Let us discuss this among ourselves."

With that, de Larosière, Volcker, and other officials left the room, allowing the bankers to caucus. For a brief moment, de Larosière's departure left a physical and spiritual void in the chairman's seat. It was up to Wriston to fill it. "I sat in the chair because nobody else was going to sit there. We had to have some leadership," Wriston recalled.

"What are we going to do about this?" Wriston asked his colleagues. Answering his own question, he said, "We're going to have to raise the money." By this time, bankers viewed Brazil and its Latin neighbors as a financial black hole. They had thought they were making the supreme sacrifice in agreeing to the earlier figure, and now they were being shaken down for even more. Manny Hanny's John McGillicuddy, whose institution was the most vulnerable to the troubles of the Latin countries, helped Wriston break the deadlock. "We've got to do it," he said regretfully.

Manny Hanny was in. One by one, the remaining bankers declared reluctantly that they were in as well. Forty minutes after John McGillicuddy stepped up, the syndicate was in place for the biggest bank loan in history, exceeding some expectations by about $1 billion. It was part of an $11.8 billion package that also included export credits and deferral of Brazil's debt to other governments. About an hour later, de Larosière and Volcker were invited back. They couldn't have been more pleased. Though some five hundred other banks would have to be persuaded to cough up their share, the logjam was broken—for the moment. In November the IMF approved the agreement.

While Wriston would never admit that cross-border lending was a flawed concept, Hans Angermueller was more contrite. He pointed out that less than a year after Mexico blew, one-third of the company's assets were in cross-border loans. In Angermueller's words, "There is no question that in our drive for the 'reward' end of the spectrum we may have lost sight of the 'risk' end."

Wriston, however, refused to bend. "The media has been watching the wrong rathole" in its concern about the possible impact of Third World lending on the banking industry, he argued at the time. Argentina, he claimed, "isn't the real problem. It's people who speak English. They live in Texas and are in the oil business."

And as Wriston's successor later discovered, they also lived in New York and were in the real estate business.

BRAZIL PAYS TO SHIELD CURRENCY, AND THE POOR SEE THE TRUE COST

Roger Cohen

Edmar Bacha, a Brazilian banker, has a new routine. Every afternoon he logs on to the Internet, reads the next day's issue of *The Korea Herald* and decides what he will tell the anxious executives from Merrill Lynch and Fidelity Investments who keep asking him where Brazil is headed.

"I get very worried on days when the Koreans don't seem as worried as I am," Mr. Bacha said. "Let's face it, if Korea or Indonesia goes and Japan is hit, then who cares about fiscal adjustments in Brazil or anywhere else? Everyone's out of here and into United States Treasury bills."

Since the Asian crisis deepened in October, Brazil has dug in for what senior Brazilian officials call "the moral equivalent of war"—a war to prevent Brazil from becoming "the next domino."

The stakes are huge. Brazil dwarfs Argentina and Mexico, constituting through its size and influence the key to a stable, prosperous Latin America. This is the world's fifth-largest country, whose population at 163 million is bigger than Russia's and whose industrial output surpasses China's. Despite its frequent bridling at American domination of the post-cold-war world, Brazil has recently opened its economy to the world. Its transformation illustrates the free-market upheaval that brought 5 percent growth to Latin America in 1997 and a record $45 billion in direct foreign investment.

But with this shift, vital to American interests, the country now seems poised on a knife edge. In stark terms, Brazil poses the question of whether global economic pressures exact too high a cost in stability in societies that are among the most unequal in the world.

The measures Brazil has taken to save its currency—steps that have thus far satisfied fast-moving global markets—are hurting the poor and the lower middle class. The Asian crisis has meant high interest rates and lost jobs. Many Brazilians who were buying cars or stoves on credit can no longer do so because efforts to attract international capital have pushed interest rates close to 40 percent a year.

Tens of thousands of state employees have been dismissed, thousands of auto workers idled. President Fernando Henrique Cardoso is paying a political price; one newspaper survey showed his popularity dropping below 50 percent for the first time.

"People are suffering," said Pedro Malan, the Finance Minister, "but they would suffer more if we did not do whatever it takes to preserve the currency. Our economic opening is irreversible."

But while opening to the world, Brazil has shunned an agreement with the International Monetary Fund; officials here equate such a deal with a loss of sovereignty, genuflection to the United States, and the failed I.M.F. programs of the 1980's debt crisis. The country is trying to bend to market forces while retaining its national identity and regional influence, in order to join the global economy on its own terms.

American companies have recently poured money into Latin America, accounting for a big share of the record $16 billion invested in Brazil last year, the record $9 billion in Argentina and the record $12 billion in Mexico. Bell South paid $2.5 billion just for the air of Sao Paulo—for which it has been granted the cellular phone license.

But international markets remain edgy about Brazil's deficits and a currency widely regarded as overvalued by about 15 percent. "Brazil looks like a ripe case for financial risk," said Jeffrey Sachs, who heads the Harvard Institute for International Development. "It has an overvalued currency and a recession looming as it moves into an election year."

Mr. Cardoso's Government, for its part, is desperate to avoid a devaluation, which it sees as a return to the hyperinflation that ended after the real, the bedrock of Mr. Cardoso's support, was introduced in 1994.

The unanswered question is whether the policies now being forced on Brazil by international markets will spread prosperity or concentrate it further. Surveys by the I.B.G.E., a Brazilian economic institute, suggest that the richest 20 percent of the Brazilian population still hold more than 60 percent of the nation's wealth, while the poorest 20 percent account for about 2 percent. In the United States, by comparison, the richest 20 percent take 42 percent of the national income, and the poorest 20 percent have 5 percent.

Brazil is thus a paramount symbol for the Latin American continent, where despite almost a decade of opening the global economy, United Nations data indicate that 40 percent of the people are poor and one in four survive on less than $1 a day.

DOMESTIC PRESSURES

Money Squeeze Turns Poor into Nomads

Out in the far west of Sao Paulo State, in an area known as the Pontal, red clouds of dust bluster across a wide and empty landscape. Cultivation is rare; the few head of cattle offer only isolated signs of life. Landless peasants camp beneath flimsy shelters, a reminder of the strains that tear at the economy even of this most advanced province.

Here in a school in the small town of Teodoro Sampaio sits Miriam Farius de Oliveira, who has just been dismissed from her $200-a-month job organizing the distribution of school lunches. She is one of the more than 30,000 state employees laid off as Brazil tries to shore up its currency against Asian buffeting.

"I was told I had not passed the requisite exam for the job," she said. "I had no warning."

Ms. Farius de Oliveira, 46 and divorced, lives with her two children in a small rented house. Even before the crisis in Asia affected her, she had had a bad year. On Feb. 23, 1997, she was shot by men apparently hired by big landowners in the area. The bullet smashed three ribs.

"I never lost consciousness," she said. "I breathed deeply, I was very sad and I prayed not to die. This is a country of violence, you see, and suffering."

She pulled down the top of her blouse to reveal the scar, a red blotch as incontrovertible as the pain in her determined eyes.

The shooting took place at a nearby estate called Sao Domingos. It had been occupied by peasants and unemployed urban poor—members of the Movimento dos Trabalhadores Rurais Sem Terra, or Landless Rural Workers Movement, known as the M.S.T. The group is the fastest-growing representative of the poor and those newly dispossessed by the global economy.

Ms. Farius de Oliveira had gone out to Sao Domingos to support the occupation. She was carrying the movement's red flag when "pistoleiros" shot her.

The shift to an open economy in Brazil had come against a backdrop of extreme poverty that leaves armies of destitute migrants drifting across the country in search of a means to survive.

During the 1970's and 80's, millions of Brazilians moved from the countryside to cities, many to the "favelas," or slums, on the outskirts of Sao Paulo, where they often found work in factories. But with many industries laying off workers in order to compete with new imports, unemployment in the Sao Paulo area has risen to 16.3 percent, from 10.2 percent in 1990. Some of these people are now drifting back to the countryside.

The rural workers movement has become the main conduit for resentment toward all the changes. It has organized 279 occupations over the last three years and now has illegal camps on 1.38 million acres of land. More than

51,000 families live in these camps, of whom 21,000—or 41 percent—arrived in 1997. Outbreaks of violence have included police killings of 17 peasants in the northern state of Para in 1996.

"Many say we are radical, but I say that we are pathetically moderate," said Gilmar Mauro, a leader of the movement. "The right to occupy an unproductive estate is not even a human right, it's practically an animal right, the right to live and eat."

Mr. Mauro, 30, sees the world as dominated by the "neo-liberal" policies of the United States—the religion of the free market. Brazil has chosen to join this global market but will remain "marginal and subjugated," he said.

Roosevelt Roque dos Santos, who heads a group that represents landowners, thinks differently. He described the workers movement as "aimed more at establishing a socialism in Brazil than land reform." Asked about the shooting of Ms. Farius de Oliveira, he said, "You think we are going to wait for these people with bouquets of flowers?"

At the Santa Clara estate, near Sao Domingos, an invasion has just begun. There are several hundred people in makeshift shacks roofed with black plastic sheeting. Red flags flutter.

The camp is well organized. Trucks arrive bringing wood. Children wearing the red caps of the group are taken to school by bus. The movement organizes daily prayers.

There is also instruction in the way neo-liberalism "produces riches but insures misery," said Celso Nespoli, a local doctor. "We tell them about Asia, we tell them how governments are stripped of power if international capital controls everything."

The movement's leaders are vague about financial support but indicate that labor unions and the Roman Catholic Church provide money. Leftist parties and unions, unable to invigorate their message or reassure people about job security, have grown weaker. But the workers movement has learned to use instant communication to advertise the actions of police officers and landowners once protected by their regions' geographical remoteness.

The landless tell their stories. A youth of 17, Wilfrido Bayer, who has a 2-year-old and a 7-month-old to support, has worked as a farmhand earning $6 a day since leaving school at 13. He now wants "a piece of land for my kids."

A 40-year-old, Walfredo Moises Nogueira da Silva, from Aracatuba, complains that authorities now demand secondary education for garbage collectors. "We never had an education," he said.

The Government tries to steer a balance, acting at times to legalize the occupations if it determines that land on estates of a minimum of 1,235 acres is unproductive. In such cases it expropriates the land, paying a fair market price. It has spent about $5 billion settling 180,000 families on expropriated land during its three years in office. Another 100,000 are supposed to be settled this year.

"The social impact of free-market reform can be very negative at first," said Milton Seligman, president of the National Institute for Land Reform in Brasilia. "But whatever the M.S.T. think, socialism is dead. We're in the international dance hall now, and we have no choice but to dance. If we can confront the challenge, provide schools, land, health, Brazil can be a major international power within 15 years."

FOREIGN DEMANDS

'Fat and Happy' U.S. Makes an Angry Brazil

"Order and Progress," proclaims the Brazilian flag, in what seems a somber rebuke to the country's tropical effervescence. But ambitious dreams, originating with the armed forces, have been a constant factor in Brazilian development since the 1930's. Then, the authoritarian President Getulio Vargas embarked on the country's remarkable industrialization program, transforming an agrarian economy into one producing steel, cars and aircraft.

Brazilian ambitions have always caused friction with Washington. They do today. The country tends to see President Clinton's push for a Free Trade Area of the Americas by 2005 as an attempt to destroy Brazilian industry. The Government prefers the consolidation of Mercosur, a regional bloc grouping Argentina, Paraguay and Uruguay whose trade has almost tripled, to $17 billion, in the last five years.

"The United States emerged after 1990 with tremendous power," said Mr. Malan, the Finance Minister. "But that should not imply that national identities do not exist or that a country like ours does not have a medium-term view of its own interests. The strengthening of Mercosur is our immediate priority."

A visit from Mr. Clinton in October almost turned into a fiasco after local officials read a United States-published "Country Commercial Guide" that described corruption as "still endemic in the culture" of Brazil. Outraged politicians said Brazil would not stand for such "humiliation." The phrase was hurriedly withdrawn, but the damage lingers.

"I don't think we've changed," one American official said. "We're still the same old fat and happy Americans. What's changed is that we are the only ones left standing and other countries have become less tolerant of us. We have to tread more carefully."

The suspicions of Brazilians—that hemisphere-wide free trade may only lead to lower wages—are of course shared by many American workers. That much was clear in President Clinton's recent failure to regain so-called "fast-track authority" to negotiate new trade accords. But in a country like Brazil, which is vulnerable to America's technological superiority, such concerns are heightened by fears of domination.

Mercosur, however, holds dangers of its own, strengthening the region but making it jointly vulnerable. About 30 percent of Argentina's exports now go to Brazil; there is anxious talk in Buenos Aires of "Brasil-dependencia." As Mr. Sachs of Harvard put it, "A major financial crisis in Brazil would take Argentina with it."

Brazil is aware of these stakes. The privatizations it is planning this year—including that of the telecommunications company Telebras—are expected to bring in a staggering $30 billion. It is also speeding the development of private pension funds similar to those in Argentina and Chile. These moves will please international investors.

The country's leaders know that a drying up of foreign investment, and a halting of private capital flows already more limited as a result of the Asian crisis, would land Brazil and Argentina in big trouble.

"The reaction to the Asian crisis has been decisive," said Daniel L. Gleizer of Banco Garantia, "and capital flows have resumed, albeit at lower volume and higher cost. But the truth is it may have come too late. The fundamental question is how adverse the international scenario will remain. Korea will be on our minds for some time."

In the north of Sao Paulo State, in an undulating landscape of intensely cultivated farms, lies the town of Ribeirao Preto, the heart of a rich region of sugar cane and orange production known as the Brazilian California.

Local notables here seem to have stepped out of an episode of "Dallas." Brazil is brash about its love of money. There is an energy in the region, however crude, that speaks of a future that international investors are hard pressed to ignore. Brazil (and it knows it) is one of the "Big Five"—along with China, Russia, India and Indonesia—whose development over the next quarter-century will be critical to the United States.

Just outside Ribeirao Preto is the town of Franca center of men's shoe production in a country that is the world's largest producer of shoes after China. The United States takes about 70 percent of Brazil's shoe exports.

When the currency plan was introduced in 1994, Franca was almost wiped out. A very strong currency—there were just 0.84 reals to a dollar for some time—suddenly made the town's exports expensive. A simultaneous opening to imports took a toll: shoe imports from China alone rose to $62.3 million in 1995, from $7.4 million in 1993.

"All we had ever known were increases in production and personnel," said Ivanio Batista, executive director of the shoe industry association. "And then, overnight, on July 4, 1994, we stopped being competitive."

More than 25 companies went bankrupt. Close to 5,000 people lost their jobs. Some factories moved to the northern state of Ceara, where monthly wages were about $160, compared to about $210 in Franca. Exports plunged.

And then Franca rolled up its sleeves. Miguel Heitor Bettarello runs Agabe, one of the largest shoe factories, exporters of the Giogrio Brutini and Le Glove brands to the United States. A plaque from J.C. Penney hangs on his wall. It's simple, Mr. Bettarello says. Agabe has to get better. It produced 4.5 shoes a day per employee in 1995; it now produces 5.2 pairs; the target is 5.8 pairs soon. Personnel is down 20 percent. Machines imported from Germany are speeding production.

In his estimate, the real—now worth about 1.11 to the dollar—is overvalued by 30 percent. "We'd need 1.66 to compete with China," he said. "O.K., forget China, we'd need 1.3 to compete with Italy."

But, he concedes, it is not going to happen unless Brazil is forced to the wall by international speculation.

In the minds of Brazilians, a major devaluation would signal a return to hyperinflation. "If we close the borders we'll go backward," Mr. Bettarello said. "If we devalue we'll go backward. So we just have to fight and prove we're a global company."

Exports have begun to rally. More shoes are being sold in Brazil. The Mercosur market is being developed. There is a new entrepreneurial spirit. Some of those laid off have set up "micro-empresas"—companies that make parts of the shoe and sell to the big manufacturers.

"We are in the middle of a revolution in people's heads," Mr. Batista said. "I never heard an entrepreneur talking about educating employees; now that is all I hear."

GLOBAL GOALS

How to Survive Till Good Times Roll

The new global culture will bring new jobs, but will Brazil educate its people in the necessary skills to hold them? Despite five years of economic growth, and a government avowedly committed to social reform, Brazil remains starkly unequal.

It is not alone in Latin America, where the United Nations Conference on Trade and Development recently estimated that since 1970, average per-capita incomes had fallen to one-quarter of first-world levels from one-third. William R. Rhodes vice chairman of Citibank, recently estimated that economic change had caused the poverty index to decline in only one state: Chile.

Of course, if growth can be maintained, this should change as per-capita income rises. That, perhaps, is the lesson of Chile, the first Latin American country to embark on free-market reform and today the least vulnerable to global financial instability.

Chile now has a high domestic savings rate: about 28 percent, compared to 18 percent in Brazil. This makes it less dependent on international capital. And the poorest 20 percent now have 4 percent of the national wealth, double that of Brazil's poorest.

But Chile began its painful reforms under a military dictatorship; today's reformers cannot simply stifle protest as Gen. Augusto Pinochet did.

In Brazil, the end of 2,000 percent annual inflation and the availability of credit that coincided with the currency plan allowed many poor families to enter the market for household appliances.

But those good times have now passed. In Sao Paulo, destitute children sleep under billboards advertising new mutual funds, imported Mitsubishis and "car rentals at Florida rates." The fences around luxury apartment buildings are electrified as the crime rate rises. When burglars are caught, the Sao Paulo police have a well-earned reputation for shooting to kill.

Mr. Clinton, on his recent trip to Latin America, tried to address a growing sense that the very reforms the United States pushes may only widen inequalities and worsen violence. He urged the private sector to help "bridge the gap between the haves and have-nots," saying it was "wrong for only a few to reap the benefits of the wonderful changes going on while many remain mired in poverty."

But the truth is that, as in Chile, it may take a generation for the benefits of "wonderful changes" to seep down.

In Ribeirao Preto, Mayor Roberto Jabali talks of many projects that are changing the town and reflect a growing prosperity; new shopping malls; new investments by Coca-Cola; new investments by Minnesota Manufacturing and Mining, which has one of its three Brazilian factories on the edge of town; an ambitious project to transform the airport into a vast regional hub for cargo.

"We're still some way from California," he said, "but we have the best quality of life in Brazil."

That quality, however, is a tenuous thing. Arriving at the airport recently, a visitor was met by an unusual sight; a pool of freshly spilled blood. A karate teacher, Edson Rogerio Goncalves, 30, had just been shot in the head. He died later at the hospital. His assailants, who stole his money, were not caught.

As Ribeirao's reputation as a California has grown, poor migrants have flocked to the town, crime and slums have spread. "People are lured by the myth," said Cintra Chagas, secretary of planning and development. "In this world, it is more and more difficult to remain an enclave."

ARGENTINE ECONOMY REBORN BUT STILL AILING

Roger Cohen

The process known awkwardly as "globalization" is many things. It is the information society. It is the erosion of national sovereignty. It is footloose corporations taking investments where labor is most productive. It is the growing premium on technical skills—and the growing plight of unskilled laborers.

It is also the daily flow across borders of more than $1.5 trillion, from investors seeking to maximize profits and minimize risk and moving, at times of crisis, with all the discernment of a herd. For them, Seoul and Sao Paulo, Bangkok and Buenos Aires are one interchangeable "funny world": developing nations that threaten the annual bonus.

"What you realize with the Asian crisis," said Ken Baxter, a Brazilian banker, "is that when there's a stampede in this postmodern world, you don't have time to say, 'Hey, look, cattle, you've got it all wrong!'"

Argentina, unlike Brazil, was supposed to have it all right. During the 1990's it adopted the International Monetary Fund program that Brazil has shunned. Ditching decades of anti-Americanism, it won the status of "major non-NATO ally" by hitching its sails to Washington's whims in a way many Brazilians consider demeaning. It tied its currency so closely to America's that the dollar is available in bank cash machines and Argentines think nothing of buying their burgers and newspapers with dollars.

The transformation was stunning, Argentina a paradigm of the newly globalized economy. The national airline, the postal service, banks—all the enterprises, it seemed, that President Carlos Saul Menem could find—were privatized or sold to international investors as the country embraced free-market capitalism with the vengeance it had once shown in nationalizing everything.

"We're a country of extremes," said Hector Sabato, director of tourism in the southern town of San Carlos de Bariloche. "The old theme of the invading Yankee has given way to the wonderful Yankee driving the global train that you'd better board immediately or you're finished!"

So the shock has been that much greater as globalization has shown its other face. Since the Asian crisis hit, plants have been idled, growth forecasts have been slashed and the Argentine stock market has plunged more than 25 percent—although from historic heights.

"What's brightening," said Jorge Bustamante of Merchant Bankers Associates, Buenos Aires representatives of Salomon Brothers, "is that however much you scream you're not a region, not the developing world, you're Argentina, you're different, it doesn't matter."

Latin American resembles Asia in its acute dependence on international capital, but in other ways it is indeed profoundly different. The region has been through two financial collapses—the debt crisis of the 1980's and the Mexican meltdown of late 1994. These battered the banking system and left sobered banks, now often in foreign hands. The scope for nasty surprises of the Korean or Indonesian variety has been curtailed.

"Hot money"—the huge short-term capital flows at the heart of the Asian crisis—has ceded its dominant place in Latin America to longer-term investment, of the kind now being made by the Ford Motor Company, RJR Nabisco Holdings Corporation, Nestle S.A. and countless others.

Yet such distinctions now appear to have only limited value. "The financial risks of globalization are a lot bigger than optimists imagined," said Paul Krugman, a professor of economics at M.I.T. "We are back to a volatile, predepression world economy of financial booms and busts quite different from the cold war years."

In Argentina, this volatility has now fueled opposition to what is widely considered neo-liberalism, or "capitalismo salvaje" (savage capitalism): the radical application of the free-market model personified by the United States. Unused to living with economic pariahs—the millions in Brazil who have never found a way to join the economy—Argentina is discovering what permanent exclusion from the job market means.

Already, a political reaction is evident. An alliance of opposition parties defeated President Menem's Peronist Party in congressional elections last October. If a new crisis enveloped the region, the reaction to neo-liberalism could be violent.

THE UNEMPLOYED POOR

When Company Profit Means Personal Loss

At the headquarters of the Roman Catholic diocese in the city of San Salvador de Jujuy, a sign on the door reads, "We regret that we cannot attend the unemployed here." Bishop Marcelo Palentini is overwhelmed. He sits behind a computer, working a cellular phone and an electronic agenda, but he does not like the modern world.

In the province of Jujuy, he estimates, 42 percent are unemployed or doing menial work. People used to ask for raises; now they ask for jobs.

Jujuy long had a bloated state payroll, a massively subsidized state-owned steel company, and labor-intensive sugar, tobacco and fruit farms. Then, in the 1990's, the free-market revolution arrived.

The provincial bank was privatized. The power utility was privitized. The postal service was privatized. The steel company was sold to Citicorp Equity Investments S.A., an Argentine group 40 percent owned by Citicorp. The phones were bought by Telecon, a private international group. Agriculture was transformed by imported American machines, each replacing 80 laborers during the cane harvest. Things began to work better, workers began losing jobs. Unemployment soared, to about 17 percent.

Last year the unemployed let their resentment show. Angry people blocked 21 provincial highways for several days. They held hunger strikes. Several people were injured.

The protests eased only after the mediation of Bishop Palentini. He helped to hammer out an accord creating six-month "work contracts" for several hundred, who agreed to do menial jobs for $200 a month.

Privatization, the bishop says, is positive, "but capital must consider a social dimension."

Still, for the Peronist Governor of Jujuy, Carlos Alfonso Ferraro, privatization is just beginning. Sitting in an office adorned with photographs of Gen. Juan Peron and his wife, Eva, he explained: "Look, it's simple. There is an Americanization of the world. We cannot go in the opposite direction. At last we are going to make America here."

And what of the photos of the Perons, the very symbols of a state-dominated, nationalist Latin American model? Peronism means revolution, said the Governor. That means nationalization in 1946 and privatization today. "The heart of Peronism is economic independence," he beamed, "and how could I be independent when my phones didn't work?"

When General Peron took power in the 1940's, he set about distributing Argentina's early-20th-century prosperity—comparable to that of leading European countries—to build a mass following. "Violence in the hands of the people isn't violence," he proclaimed, "it's justice!"

A Peronist cult grew. So, too, did the country's state industries, its rich labor unions, its debilitating militarist myths of salvation through violence and upheaval, myths that would maroon doomed soldiers in the Falkland Islands in 1982 and add the word "desaparecidos" (the disappeared) to the world's vocabulary. Elegant Buenos Aires with its gilt and statuary became an elegy for a nation plundered.

By 1990, in the words of Carlos Fedrigotti, Citicorp's chief executive in Argentina, "the place had simply collapsed beneath the waste, corruption and mismanagement of a welfare state gone wild."

Collapse took several forms. The postal service favored theft over delivery of mail. It could take a decade to get a telephone. The economy shrank by 12 percent during the 1980's.

Argentina's travails were those of a protectionist, coup-plagued continent. Because the economy had failed so completely, when the Berlin wall fell and President Menem abruptly decided to undo General Peron's legacy, the country was something close to a blank canvas. Abruptly, this faraway place "on the way to nowhere"—as despairing Argentines loved to lament—re-entered the world after a long hiatus.

With the economic reforms, growth surged, reaching 8 percent in the first nine months of this year. American investment, including that of George Soros, the New York financier, poured in. A dead dock on the banks of the Plate River was transformed into swinging Puerto Madero, where the steaks came with air conditioning and valet parking.

But if it has drawn the favors of international investors through its reforms, Argentina has also become plagued by new uncertainties.

To look into the vacant eyes of Roberto Angel Garcia, 53, is to understand something of the cruelty of the economic upheaval that competing with the world has meant for Latin America.

Mr. Garcia was dismissed in 1992 along with thousands of other workers from Citicorp Equity's Aceros Zapla steel plant in the town of Palpala. Long run by the armed forces, it was legendary for its padded contracts until privatization came. Then its work force was slashed to 709 people, from 5,000. The company now produces high-quality special steels and expects to start making a profit this year.

The change will no doubt bring benefits in the long term: postwar development shows that countries that open to trade ultimately do better. But Mr. Garcia is paying the price for the adjustment.

He was too young for a pension, too old to find other work. "They told us we were being fired because we were losing money," he said, "but nobody had ever talked about losses before."

Like other workers, Mr. Garcia received an indemnity on dismissal—about $19,000. But nobody gave the workers any guidance on how to use the money. Mr. Garcia spent most of his on a four-wheel-drive Ford. Now he has one of the temporary work contracts, moving rocks to build a dam. He knows it will not last.

Industries could once afford to be inefficient, because high inflation, repeated devaluations and scant competition from imports masked their failings. But throughout Latin America, such industries suddenly find themselves in a desperate push for productivity.

To be productive—to make more shoes or cookies per employee—generally involves using fewer people and the better machines now available from elsewhere.

The job cuts tend to fall on the old—for the purposes of Latin America's adjustment, this category begins at about 40—who then join the globally unemployable.

A garrulous union leader in Jujury, Carlos Santillan, has become the mouthpiece of the unskilled outcasts.

"Menem thinks that by putting our country at the service of the International Monetary Fund, he brought us into the first world," Mr. Santillan said. "But workers have lost in a few years rights they fought for over a century. We're a colony here. All that is missing is to have Clinton come here and plant the American flag."

As he spoke, Mr. Santillan was organizing a strike by municipal workers whose monthly salaries, about $250 each, were more than a month overdue. A lumbering state bureaucracy, in Argentina as elsewhere in Latin America, has not kept up with economic change.

So bills from privatized electricity and phone companies come on time, but services are promptly cut when bills are unpaid—even though state workers may not have received the salaries with which to pay them.

THE RICH CONSUMERS

Gliding Through Life in Shopper's Heaven

The global economy has a smell: a fresh fragrance stripped of any trace of the third world's dust and sweat. It has a sound: pipe music and floors so clean they squeak. It has a color: the very white teeth of smiling saleswomen.

These qualities are evident at the Galeria Pacifico shopping mall, a Soros property. It is in central Buenos Aires but could be anywhere. People glide past a procession of name-brand stores. Hugo Boss, Timberland, Lacoste.

"Argentina is just beginning," said Eduardo Elsztain, chairman of Irsa, the company that has been the main vehicle for turning Mr. Soros into one of the biggest landowners in Argentina.

Irsa, 25 percent owned by Mr. Soros, has bought office towers, luxury hotels, shopping malls and a large area of Puerto Madero; a sister company, Cresud, has acquired more than 850,000 acres of mainly pampa farmland and more than 180,000 cows.

Galeria Pacifico is a soothing emblem of the change that upper-class Argentines embrace. Mr. Santillan, like the Zapatistas in Mexico, may raise his voice against the United States, but most of the newly globalized Argentines, with their 50 channels of cable television and their hunger for cellular phones (1.1 million sold in the last year alone) seem to have embraced America.

Indeed the single most potent symbol of their changed country is the dollar. For decades, Argentines used to start the day by checking the dollar rate.

Inevitably the inflation-racked peso had fallen. Planning meant getting through the day.

Then, after yet another bout of hyperinflation, a currency board similar to Hong Kong's was established in 1991, and a rate of one peso to one dollar was established by law. Not a peso can be printed unless it is backed by a dollar.

Of course the dollar-peso convertibility carries a price. Argentina is expensive. Salaries—about $700 a month in a factory—are relatively high. It is hard for businesses to compete globally.

Moreover, the strong currency, in an open economy, sucks in imports. Entire industries—toys among them—have been wiped out by cheap imports from China, where a worker's wage may be no more than $40 a month. Argentina, with its exports to Brazil affected by the Asian-induced downturn there, faces a rising trade deficit in 1998.

To offset this, it is essential that international capital, already threatened by Asia, continue to flow—which it will only do if Argentina's productivity continues to rise.

"With the United States as a reference, you have to run all the time," said Mr. Bustamante, the banker. "Convertibility means you can never relax."

To run fast enough for the demands of the global market, Mr. Menem now proposes doing away with the collective bargaining still controlled by labor unions and seeking greater ease in hiring and firing. That in turn will probably mean lower wages but greater productivity.

However, this proposed labor reform is controversial. Virtually nobody—including the opposition alliance that triumphed in October—wants to undo convertibility, close the economy or return industries to state control. In this sense, as the sociologist Felipe Noguera said, "It's not an either-or political world anymore."

The symbol of the opposition victory in congressional elections last fall was not a figure of the left or right, but Graciela Fernandez Mejide, a rights advocate. The alliance she leads could block labor reform, leading markets to punish Argentina.

"A country advances not just through sound economic rules, but also by having a justice system that cannot be bought," said Domingo Cavallo, the former Economics Minister who was the architect of Argentina's transformation until he quit in 1996 in protest against corruption. "This Government seems to tolerate impunity."

The problem is widespread in Latin America, as shown by the swiftly rising crime rates in Mexico City, Sao Paulo and Buenos Aires. Because a global economy puts a high premium on technical skills and ownership of capital assets, it tends to accentuate wealth and income differentiation.

Governments, however, may plead helplessness. How, they ask, can they raise corporate and other taxes to pay for more efficient bureaucracies, education, better health services, honest police forces, stronger justice systems—things Latin America desperately needs—if global investors are generally averse to higher taxation and government spending?

Throughout Latin America, the sheer pace of global economic change appears to have left slow-moving states behind, unable to control the process of which they are a part.

American capitalism is being abruptly introduced into states that, like Argentina, Brazil or Mexico, may not have the technology, or the legal or regulatory systems, to keep up. The result can be galloping corruption and a brutal frontier capitalism.

"Increasingly we see that states need markets, but markets also need states," said Nicholas van Praag, a spokesman for the World Bank. "It's not enough to say that markets can do it all. You need security, you need an education system that works."

In some developing societies, the World Bank has recently begun linking judicial reform to loans—money that once went for railroads and is now thought to be better used for the training of judges.

THE GLOBAL COLONIZERS

Even U.S. Giants Have Ups and Downs

Wal-Mart, Buenos Aires, on a Saturday morning: an Argentine flag flutters in the store and there is a sign reading, "Proudly in Argentina." Families stroll down the wide, bright aisles, past displays of Newman's Own salad dressing.

Wal-Mart has created almost 8,000 jobs in Argentina and Brazil since it moved into the two countries three years ago. But it is impossible to say how many lost jobs—at small neighborhood stores or businesses—have stemmed from the store's arrival.

What is clear is that it is changing the Argentine way of life: families buy their bicycles here, sometimes using dollars; the corner bicycle store is no more.

Such change prompts ambivalence. A 65-year-old man, Luis Osvaldo Pazzotta, recalls the now-bankrupt textile factory that stood on this site, complains about the recent bankruptcy of his own carpentry business and mutters, "This is the new world, and I have no place in it."

Fernando Descalzo, a young telecommunications engineer working for McCaw, has other views. He is delighted with his Wal-Mart shopping, his family is about to have a hamburger at the adjacent Wendy's. "we're dollarized, we're Americanized, but frankly I don't care," he said.

Wal-Mart, attracted by the opening of Latin American economies, has already invested more than $500 million in Brazil and Argentina, opening 17 stores. The number of stores is destined to double in 1998.

"The Americas are our well-deserved first priority for now," said Bob L. Martin, chief executive of Wal-Mart International. "Even with recent difficulties stemming from Asia, especially in Brazil, we are on track to make our first profits in 1998."

But, of course, Wal-Mart is not impervious to the risks of divided societies. In the last few months, five Wal-Mart stores in Brazil have been robbed by assailants operating in large groups and armed with assault rifles.

THE TRENDY INVESTORS

Patagonian Pampas as Real Estate Craze

When Bill Clinton came to Argentina in October, he stayed at the Hotel Llao Llao near the Patagonian town of Bariloche. Long state-owned, the luxury hotel now belongs to Mr. Soros's investment vehicle, Irsa.

Mr. Soros is not alone. Patagonia is trendy; call it the nature reserve for the globally stressed. Argentina can still be bought for third-world prices, and if it becomes a first-world country the owners of property will make a lot of money.

Drive past glittering lakes, on across a steppe so flat that it induces an effect known as horizontal vertigo, and there, just four hours from the Hotel Llao Llao, lies the ghost town of Cutral-Co.

Dust blusters through the windy streets. People stare into space. The airport, once served by Aerolineas Argentinas, is closed. Aerolineas has been privatized, and it makes no economic sense to fly here.

Y.P.F., the formerly state-owned oil company that contrived to lose $6 billion between 1982 and 1990, used to employ 5,000 people here. Now there are 500; Y.P.F. made $900 million in 1996.

Mario Acosta, a Y.P.F. manager, explained that when the old system was dismantled, everyone who was not a professional was laid off. "Before," he said, "uneducated people had a certain basic security. But that's finished in the modern world."

Orlando Mendes used to work at Y.P.F. He has found a part-time job in the city administration. But he cannot support his wife and two children on $200 a month, so every few months he takes a 24-hour bus ride to Buenos Aires, and buys shoes in a factory. The shoeboxes are piled on his children's beds.

"If I'm lucky," he said, "I'll get 16 pesos here for shoes that I bought for 10 pesos. We survive. But I don't like this life. Y.P.F. was a family. Now I arrive at the train station in Buenos Aires, and there are kids everywhere stealing, and frankly I'm afraid."

Something else is troubling Mr. Mendes. There are more fences going up in Patagonia, as the internationally wealthy install themselves on newly acquired estates. "I used to go and camp or fish, but now I hear that Ted Turner is here, Rambo there, the Terminator somewhere else. And I say, no, this is not my Argentina."